W9-CBS-171

Time Out

Florence

timeout.com

Time Out Guides Ltd
Universal House
251 Tottenham Court Road
London W1T 7AB
United Kingdom
Tel: +44 (0)20 7813 3000
Fax: +44 (0)20 7813 6001
Email: guides@timeout.com
www.timeout.com

Published by Time Out Guides Ltd, a wholly owned subsidiary of Time Out Group Ltd.
Time Out and the Time Out logo are trademarks of Time Out Group Ltd.

© **Time Out Group Ltd 2011**
Previous editions 1997, 1999, 2001, 2003, 2005, 2008.

10 9 8 7 6 5 4 3 2 1

This edition first published in Great Britain in 2011 by Ebury Publishing.
A Random House Group Company
20 Vauxhall Bridge Road, London SW1V 2SA

Random House Australia Pty Ltd 20 Alfred Street, Milsons Point, Sydney, New South Wales 2061, Australia

Random House New Zealand Ltd 18 Poland Road, Glenfield, Auckland 10, New Zealand

Random House South Africa (Pty) Ltd Isle of Houghton, Corner Boundary Road & Carse O'Gowrie, Houghton 2198, South Africa

Random House UK Limited Reg. No. 954009

Distributed in the US and Latin America by Publishers Group West (1-510-809-3700)
Distributed in Canada by Publishers Group Canada (1-800-747-8147)

For further distribution details, see www.timeout.com.

ISBN: 978-1-84670-247-1

A CIP catalogue record for this book is available from the British Library.

Printed and bound in Great Britain by Butler Tanner & Dennis, Frome, Somerset.

The Random House Group Limited supports The Forest Stewardship Council (FSC®), the leading international forest certification organisation. Our books carrying the FSC label are printed on FSC® certified paper. FSC is the only forest certification scheme endorsed by the leading environmental organisations, including Greenpeace. Our paper procurement policy can be found at www.randomhouse.co.uk/environment

Time Out carbon-offsets its flights with Trees for Cities (www.treesforcities.org).

Contents

WHENEVER, WHEREVER YOU NEED MONEY...

WE GET IT THERE IN 10 MINUTES*

CHOICE IS IN YOUR HANDS

1. Arrange for the person sending the money to visit a MoneyGram agent near them. After sending the money, they will give you a reference number.

2. Find your nearest MoneyGram agent at **www.moneygram.com** or visit any Poste Italiane branch.

3. Give the reference number and your ID** to the MoneyGram agent.

4. Fill out one simple form to receive your money.

Service available anywhere you see the MoneyGram sign and in over 10.000 Poste Italiane branches

Posteitaliane

MoneyGram.
Money Transfer

Freephone: 800 088 256   www.moneygram.com

Introduction

A visitor returning to Florence after five or five hundred years might think it's barely changed. Whether it be a modern-day scholar of Vasari's architecture or Michelangelo himself, coming back to check out how that slab of marble he turned into *David* is holding up, the city, on the surface, has the appearance it has always had: a chaos of vehicles sputtering down tiny cobbled streets and across medieval bridges; elegant *palazzi* and churches filled with students studying music, art and Italian; and, everywhere you turn, a monument of staggering beauty. Brunelleschi's Duomo, Alberti's façade of Santa Maria Novella church, Masolino and Masaccio's frescoes in the Brancacci Chapel – all created by gifted craftsmen before Michelango was born, and all of them are still here. The only real difference is they're now constantly mobbed by tourists from all over the world.

What about the Florentines themselves? Well, they haven't changed much either. They're still immensely proud of their city, and still being accused of aloofness, even occasionally disdain for outsiders. But they're as welcoming to tourists as they've ever been. Even the entertainment Tuscany provides is the same: centuries-old traditions such as Siena's Palio, boat-racing on the Arno and jousting in Arezzo.

That said, Florence does get a bit of a shake-up every now and again. Under the rule of mayor Matteo Renzi, who took charge of the city in 2009, the city's politics, transport, education and social welfare are changing. Renzi is hands-on, visiting schools, working hard to reduce congestion and boost eco-friendly public transport. He's even overseeing the completion of Tramvia Line 1; no mean feat given the scheme, designed to link the city centre with the suburbs to the north-west, had started and stalled through a decade of construction. He's deservedly popular with locals, who applaud his 100-point action plan, which includes the closure of piazza del Duomo and occasional closure of piazza Pitti and via de' Tornabuoni to all vehicles, the acceleration of public internet access across the city, and free monthly admission for all Florentines to the city's museums.

As a visitor there are few downsides to Florence. You can spend your afternoons wandering the backstreets, sipping *vino della casa* or soaking up the sun on piazza della Signoria, while making the most of the fact that you're in the world's greatest living art museum.

If you've chosen to come here in peak season, then you'll want to give the city a break for a while – even if you only make it up to piazzale Michelangelo or San Miniato al Monte to take in the views. Better still, take a daycation on the Tramvia, or stay for a night or two in the ancient hilltop towns of Volterra and San Gimignano, explore the grand villas around Lucca, the wineries of Montepulciano or Chianti, or the beaches of the Maremma. If Michelangelo saw the never-ending queues that form daily at the Accademia to see his masterpiece, he'd surely also understand the need for some peace and space. *Yolanda Zappaterra, Editor*

Florence in Brief

IN CONTEXT

This series of features tells the story of Florence, and the Renaissance, through 13 centuries of war, creativity, innovation, natural disaster, and the desire on the part of Renaissance artists and scholars to expand knowledge and understanding to the benefit of humanity. From the astonishing minds of Dante, Galileo and Leonardo to the crucial role played by Lorenzo de' Medici, we explain how the city grew to become what it is today.

▶ *For more, see pp16-46.*

SIGHTS

Michelangelo's *David* and *Pietà*, Botticelli's *Venus*, Filippo Lippi's *Madonna and Child* and da Vinci's *Annunciation* are all must-sees, but make time to see quieter sights: churches such as Santa Croce and Santa Maria Novella are often packed, but at least they're packed with hushed reverie, and off the beaten track of the Oltrarno, you might even have the place to yourself at less well-known ones such as Santo Spirito and San Miniato al Monte.

▶ *For more, see pp48-96.*

CONSUME

Away from the tourist tat and gawdy jewellery on the ponte Vecchio, Florence is a delight for shoppers and browsers, from the vibrant artisan scene in Santa Croce and Oltrarno to the big designer stores on and around via de' Tornabuoni. The city's drinking and dining scene has been brought firmly into the 21st century with a stunning range of enticing *enoteche*, *gelaterie* and bars, while new restaurants give a modern twist to classic cuisine.

▶ *For more, see pp98-174.*

ARTS & ENTERTAINMENT

Pace yourself. You can't come to Florence and just do the Renaissance. Once the museums and churches have shut up for the evening, you'll need to summon up energy for a nightlife that's been revitalised by a new swathe of *enoteche*, cafés and bars in the city. And that's before you even check out what's on the bill at the local art deco cinema, or the classical concert in the piazza round the corner from your hotel.

▶ *For more, see pp176-215.*

THE BEST OF TUSCANY

If you're here for longer than a weekend, you should get out of Florence and explore the huge array of attractions that Tuscany has to offer. Head to the designer outlets and contemporary art of nearby Prato, the stunning valleys and hills of Chiantishire, the elegantly proportioned main piazza of Siena, the hundreds of antiques shops in lovely Arezzo, or the thermal spas of Pistoia, all in easy reach by train, car or tram.

▶ *For more, see pp218-301.*

Florence in 48 hours

Day 1 Grace and Fervour: the Duomo and David

8AM Start with the **Uffizi** (*see p64*). It opens at 8.15am, and as long as you're nifty and have worked out a plan of what you want to see, you can get to the *Birth of Venus* and *Annunciation* long before the tour groups do.

10AM Squeeze in a quick espresso at the piazza della Signoria, admiring the 13th-century **Palazzo Vecchio** (*see p64*) and pondering Girolamo Savonarola's fiery fate on the same spot as his venomous Bonfire of the Vanities, held here in 1497.

11AM It's time to get active before it gets too hot. Head directly north from piazza della Signoria's north-eastern corner and you'll come out at the corner of the **Baptistry** (*see p58*), with the Campanile to your right. It's 414 steps to the top, through levels by Giotto, Pisano and Francesco Talenti. Don't run, you'll need to save some puff to explore the double layers of Brunelleschi's dome, especially if you're intent on climbing the 463 steps to the lantern at its summit. (Note that the Baptistry doesn't open until noon.)

1PM Now it's off to the **Accademia** (*see p78*) for a date with dashing *David*, but not before a quick look around San Lorenzo market and sustenance at **Casa del Vino** (*see p131*).

4PM Spend the afternoon exploring the alternative shopping scene of **Santa Croce** and visiting the church that gives the area its name (*see p86*).

7PM After a change into your gladrags, head across the river for *aperitivi* and a sundowner at the city's best viewpoint, the **Terrazza Bardini** (*see p138*).

9PM Wind your way down the picturesque costa di San Giorgio to Oltrarno for supper – this is where you'll find a growing number of excellent *enoteche*; try piazza della Passera and the area immediately around it.

NAVIGATING THE CITY

Thanks to its river and diminutive centre, Florence is fairly easy to navigate, and walking is by far the best way of getting around it. The most complex thing about finding things in the city is the street-numbering system, which has two sets of numbers, in red and black. The red numbers denote a place of business, and run separately from the black, so 16r and 18r may be 100 metres away from each other, separated by a series of black numbers. Thanks to the continuing expansion of pedestrianised zones in the city, trying to use public transport to get to attractions is frustrating and often pointless: you'll often find the bus has had to take such a circuitous route that it ends up stopping a long way from your destination. Still, a variety of multi-trip tickets and passes mean you can hop on and off, and bus drivers – many of whom speak English – will do their best to help you.

Day 2 Up, Up and Away: Boboli and Beyond

9AM If you haven't done so already, cross the **ponte Vecchio**. Partly because you have to on a visit to Florence, and partly because it leads to **Palazzo Pitti** (*see p89*). This one-time home of the Medici family is huge, and hugely rewarding; topping a long list of must-dos is the Galleria Palatina, housing arguably the world's best collection of Titians and Raphaels.

11AM After the Pitti's rich rewards and sumptuous interiors, air, light and empty spaces are the order of the day. A pleasant short walk brings you to the **Boboli Gardens** (*see p90*), one of the city's best-loved open spaces and a real haven from its noise and crowds. Statues, grottoes and fountains are dotted around the splendidly formal gardens.

1PM From the currently closed Forte di Belvedere in the corner of the Boboli, it's a short but strenuous walk to the peaceful and exquisite church of **San Miniato al Monte** (*see p96*). Have lunch en route at one of the sweet restaurants around Porta San Niccolò, and time your visit to end with the Gregorian chant that's sung daily by the monks (4.30pm).

5PM Head back down to the river, stopping at **piazzale Michelangelo** for ice-cream (or an early *aperitivo*) and amazing views from the city's most famous viewpoint. Descend via the rococo staircase designed by Guiseppe Poggi, who was also behind the piazzale's layout.

7PM Browse some of the amazing jewellery, clothing, shoes and art in the narrow streets on and around via de' Bardi and San Niccolò, then meander over to **piazza Santo Spirito** for drinks or dinner. Lined with bars and restaurants, this bohemian piazza is pure laid-back Italian chic and charm, and guaranteed to make you feel you really are living *la dolce vita*.

SEEING THE SIGHTS

Don't try to cram in too much: you'll end up with sore feet and a hazy memory of lots of art and church interiors. Instead, make the most of Florence's cafés. And do enjoy the largesse of a new scheme that offers free bottled water from eight stations around town (*see p61* **Inside Track**).

PACKAGE DEALS

If you are planning to visit lots of sights, it's definitely worth investing in a €50 **Firenze Card**, which lasts 72 hours from the first time you validate it and gives you entry to 33 of the most important museums in Florence, eliminating the need to queue for tickets. The card can be used just once in each museum, and on all public transport. You can pre-order the card online at www.firenzecard.it, or buy it either at one of the tourist information offices or at the ticket offices of museums covered by the card.

Florence in Profile

DUOMO AND AROUND

Stretching from the streets just north of the Duomo to the ponte Vecchio, with via de' Tornabuoni its western boundary and via del Proconsolo its eastern, the original nucleus of Florence is a showcase for the city's historical high and low points. From the glories of the art in the Bigallo to the tragedy of the Bonfire of the Vanities in piazza della Signoria, the area that corresponds almost exactly to the ninth-century city walls is the ideal place to start your explorations.
▶ *For more, see pp51-68.*

SANTA MARIA NOVELLA

Radiating out from Santa Maria Novella church and station, separated across the wide piazza by five centuries, the area to the west of the Duomo stretches down to the river and west to the popular Parco delle Cascine. It takes in 13th-century fortified tower houses in its south-eastern tip around the Museo Ferragamo, the elegant borgo Ognissanti and the beautiful Ognissanti church and cloisters.
▶ *For more, see pp69-72.*

SAN LORENZO

The huge central market forms the hub of daily life in this area, creating a café and bar scene that is buzzing at lunchtime, but the Medicis gave the area its main tourist sites: the spectacular Cappelle Medicee mausoleum and the 15th-century Medici Palace. The plain exterior of San Lorenzo in the south of the area belies its remarkable scale and important interior, decorated with art by the likes of Filippo Lippi and Donatello.
▶ *For more, see pp73-77.*

SAN MARCO

It's a certain young man called David who draws the crowds to the otherwise unremarkable San Marco area, with queues forming daily outside the Accademia, but the university district makes for a lively café and bar scene around the beautiful porticoed piazza della Santissima Annunziata and piazza San Marco. For quiet contemplation, try the pleasures of the San Marco museum.
▶ *For more, see pp78-82.*

SANTA CROCE

If you don't have time to explore the boho chic of Oltrarno, Santa Croce makes a very good alternative. The working-class area borders the Duomo along its western edge, but is a very different beast, peopled largely by locals shopping at the wonderful *mercato* San Ambrogio, eating at some of the city's best restaurants, and enjoying free concerts and excellent ice-cream in its little piazze and bars. Art-lovers are catered for too: Santa Croce contains a wealth of incredible Renaissance art, and the Museo Horne is a treasure trove of art, architecture and eclectic *objets d'art*.
▶ *For more, see pp83-87.*

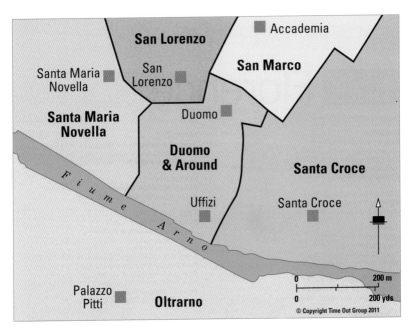

OLTRARNO

Without Oltrarno (literally, the other side of the Arno), the first-time visitor could be forgiven for thinking Florence is a large theme-park dedicated to old art and architecture. Fortunately, the areas of San Frediano and Santo Spirito in Oltrarno's western half and San Niccolò and San Miniato al Monte in its east offer something else entirely: an area of independent shops and artists' studios, contemporary jewellers' ateliers filled with work of extraordinary skill and originality, and bars, cafés and restaurants that are very hard to leave. But then you'd miss the gargantuan Palazzo Pitti, the lovely open spaces of Boboli Gardens, the delightful *coste* ('ribs') winding up the hill, spectacular views from piazzale Michelangelo, and, lording it over them all, the stunning church of San Miniato.

▶ For more, see pp88-92.

OUTSIDE THE CITY GATES

Follow the ring roads of central Florence to take in all eight of its remaining city gates and you'll realise how small the city centre is – and how easy it is to escape the throngs. To the north, roads leading to Fiesole and Settignano are dotted with charming country villas, but it's to the south that the real attactions lie: gently winding lanes immediately outside the Porta San Miniato take you within minutes into gorgeous countryside, while a 20-minute walk west of Porta Romana will bring you to the lovely hamlet of Bellosguardo (appropriately enough, meaning 'beautiful view').

▶ For more, see pp93-96.

Time Out Florence

Editorial
Editor Yolanda Zappaterra
Deputy Editor Simon Coppock
Copy Editors Holly Pick, Sarah Guy
Listings Editors Maddalena Delli
Proofreader Tamsin Shelton

Editorial Director Ruth Jarvis
Editorial Manager Holly Pick
Management Accountants Margaret Wright, Clare Turner

Design
Art Director Scott Moore
Art Editor Pinelope Kourmouzoglou
Senior Designer Kei Ishimaru
Group Commercial Designer Jodi Sher

Picture Desk
Picture Editor Jael Marschner
Picture Desk Assistant/Researcher Ben Rowe

Advertising
New Business & Commercial Director Mark Phillips
International Advertising Manager Kasimir Berger
International Sales Executive Charlie Sokol
Advertising Sales (Florence) *The Florentine*

Marketing
Senior Publishing Brand Manager Luthfa Begum
Guides Marketing Manager Colette Whitehouse
Group Commercial Art Director Anthony Huggins

Production
Group Production Manager Brendan McKeown
Production Controller Katie Mulhern

Time Out Group
Chairman & Founder Tony Elliott
Chief Executive Officer David King
Chief Operating Officer Aksel Van der Wal
Group Financial Director Paul Rakkar
Group General Manager/Director Nichola Coulthard
Time Out Communications Ltd MD David Pepper
Time Out International Ltd MD Cathy Runciman
Time Out Cultural Development Director Mark Elliott
Group IT Director Simon Chappell
Group Marketing Director Andrew Booth

Contributors
Introduction Yolanda Zappaterra. **History** Nicky Swallow. **Florence Today** Maddalena Delli. **Art** Sophia Cottier. **Architecture** Sophia Cottier (*Bland Ambition* Maddalena Delli). **Food & Wine** Adrian Smith (*New Wave Whites* Daniel Smith). **Touring Florence** Daniel Smith. **Sightseeing** Lizzie Fane, Yolanda Zappaterra (*Seeing Beyond the Façade* Sophia Cottier; *Finding your Niche* Daniel Smith; *Walk: Fictional Florence* Julia Burdet; *Hidden Depths* Maddalena Delli; *Profile: The Medicis* Anne Hanley; *Sight Spots* Julia Bardet). **Hotels** Nicky Swallow, Yolanda Zappaterra. **Restaurants & Wine Bars** Brenda Dionisi, Nicky Swallow. **Cafés, Bars & Gelaterie** Julia Burdet, Yolanda Zappaterra. **Shops & Services** Julia Burdet, Yolanda Zappaterra. **Calendar** Maddalena Delli (*Join the Literati* Jane Fortune). **Children** Maddalena Delli. **Film** James Douglas. **Galleries** Julia Burdet. **Gay & Lesbian** Bruno Casini. **Music** Nicky Swallow, Beth de Felici (*Linari Festival* Jane Fortune). **Nightlife** Julia Burdet. **Sports & Fitness** Beth de Felici **Theatre & Dance** Maddalena Delli. **Tuscany** Daniel Smith, Maddalena Delli, Paul Lay, Daniel Smith, Nicky Swallow, Christine Webb, Natasha Foges, Kate Singleton, Liv Inger. **Directory** Julia Burdet.

Maps john@jsgraphics.co.uk.

Front Cover Photography Walter Bibikow/Photolibrary.com
Back Cover Photography Gianluca Moggi

Photography Jonathan Perugia, except page 5 Timur Kulgarin/Shutterstock.com; pages 7, 8, 10 (right), 15, 25, 30, 33, 42 (right), 47, 53, 54, 55, 60, 62, 72 (left), 74, 77, 82, 84, 87, 97, 102, 106, 111, 115, 119, 123, 126 (bottom), 127, 132, 141, 144, 149, 153, 171, 175, 177, 185, 187, 193, 194, 196, 199, 201, 204, 205, 211, 213, 214, 221 (top left and middle right), 222, 223, 224, 227, 228, 231, 235, 236, 239, 244, 250, 259, 260, 273, 282, 285, 289 Gianluca Moggi; page 7 (bottom) Luciano Mortula/Shutterstock.com; pages 11 (top), 41, 176, 297 Shutterstock; pages 16, 20 Getty Images; page 24 Vittoriano Rastelli/Corbis; page 26 Pieter Stander; page 114 Giorgio Magini; page 126 (top) Keith Levit/Shutterstock.com; pages 145, 151, 155, 158, 182 Michelle Grant; page 161 Majlend Bramo/Massimo Sestini; page 178 Adriano Castelli/Shutterstock.com; page 179 APT Firenze; page 217 Lucarelli Temistocle/Shutterstock; page 301 Luciano Mortula/Shutterstock.com; page 326 Rechitan Sorin/Shutterstock.com.

The following images were supplied by the featured establishments: page 139, 189, 275.

About the Guide

GETTING AROUND

The back of the book contains street maps of Florence, as well as overview maps of the city and its surroundings. The maps start on page 328; on them are marked the locations of hotels (❶), restaurants and wine bars (❶), and cafés, bars and *gelaterie* (❶). The majority of businesses listed in this guide are located in the areas we've mapped; the grid-square references in the listings refer to these maps.

THE ESSENTIALS

For practical information, including visas, disabled access, emergency numbers, lost property, useful websites and local transport, please see the Directory. It begins on page 303.

THE LISTINGS

Addresses, phone numbers, websites, transport information, hours and prices are all included in our listings. All were checked and correct at press time. However, business owners can alter their arrangements at any time, and fluctuating economic conditions can cause prices to change rapidly.

The very best venues in the city, the must-sees and must-dos in every category, have been marked with a red star (★). In the Sights chapters, we've also marked venues with free admission with a FREE symbol.

PHONE NUMBERS

The area code for Florence is 055, which must be dialled in full (including zero) at all times, whether calling from within Italy (including Florence itself) or from abroad.

From outside Italy, dial your country's international access code (00 from the UK, 011 from the US) or a plus symbol, followed by the Italy country code (39), followed by the number as listed in the guide. For more on phones, including information on calling abroad from the UK and details of local mobile-phone access, *see p314*.

FEEDBACK

We welcome feedback on this guide, both on the venues we've included and on any other locations that you'd like to see featured in future editions. Please email us at guides@timeout.com.

Time Out Guides

Founded in 1968, Time Out has grown from humble beginnings into the leading resource for anyone wanting to know what's happening in the world's greatest cities. Alongside our influential weeklies in London, New York and Chicago, we publish more than 20 magazines in cities as varied as Beijing and Beirut; a range of travel books, with the City Guides now joined by the newer Shortlist series; and an information-packed website. The company remains proudly independent, still owned by Tony Elliott four decades after he launched *Time Out London*.

Written by local experts and illustrated with original photography, our books also retain their independence. No business has been featured because it has advertised, and all restaurants and bars are visited and reviewed anonymously.

ABOUT THE EDITOR

Based in London, **Yolanda Zappaterra** has edited a variety of books about travel and lifestyle for Time Out, and has also written articles and books on travel, arts and design for publishers Laurence King and Rotovision, and magazines including *Etapes* and *Living Spain*.

A full list of the book's contributors can be found opposite. However, we've also included details of our writers in selected chapters through the guide.

In Context

Palazzo Davanzati. *See p68.*

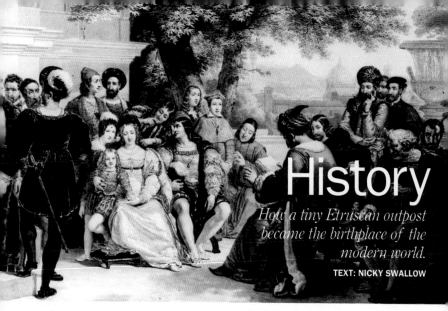

History

Practically the whole of Florence's reputation rests on its history – a tale that stretches back to an almost forgotten European civilisation and takes in some of the most monumental cultural shifts of the last 500 years. From around the eighth century BC, much of central Italy was controlled by the Etruscans, who may have been natives or may have drifted in from Asia Minor. Whatever their origins, they settled in Veio and Cerveteri, close to Rome, and further north – in what is now Tuscany – around Volterra, Populonia, Arezzo, Chiusi and Cortona. They entirely overlooked the site that we now know as Florence, making hilltop Fiesole their northernmost stronghold. Tantalisingly little evidence remains of Etruscan civilisation – the culture that was clobbered out of existence by the Romans. One of the main reasons for this is that the Etruscans made everything from wood – everything, that is, except their tombs; their graves, and the objects recovered from them, constitute most of the evidence used to piece together their history. With so little to go on, mythologisers have had a field day. The enchanting frescoes of feasts, dancing and hunting that adorn many of the tombs led DH Lawrence to conclude that 'death to the Etruscan was a pleasant continuance of life'. Others believe that the Etruscans were terrified of mortality, that the seemingly carefree paintings were a desperate plea for the gods to show mercy on the other side. Whatever the truth, their religious beliefs, extraordinary craftsmanship, trade skills and fierce protective pride founded a region that bears all those hallmarks today – not just in the archeological remains, but in its people too.

THE EARLY YEARS

Despite the scarcity of evidence, historians have come to understand the Etruscan civilisation pretty well. The Etruscans were certainly a religious people, but they were also partial to a good war, against other tribes or rival Etruscan cities. Their civilisation reached its peak in the seventh and sixth centuries BC, when their loose federation of cities dominated much of what is now southern Tuscany and northern Lazio. Their cities grew wealthy on the proceeds of mining and trading copper and iron. Their art and superbly worked gold jewellery display distinctive oriental influences, adding credence to the theory that the Etruscans migrated to Italy from the East, though such influences could have been due to their extensive trading in the eastern Mediterranean. At the end of the seventh century BC, the Etruscans captured the small town of Rome and ruled it for a century before being expelled. The next few hundred years witnessed city fighting city and tribe battling tribe until the emerging Roman republic overwhelmed all by the third century BC.

THE EMERGENCE OF TUSCANY

In 59 BC, Julius Caesar established a colony for army veterans along the narrowest stretch of the Arno, and Florentia was born. Strategically located at the heart of Italian territory, it grew into a flourishing commercial centre, becoming the capital of a Roman province in the third century AD. In the fifth century, the Roman Empire in the West finally crumbled before the pagan hordes. Italian unity collapsed as Ostrogoths, Visigoths, Huns and Lombards rampaged through the peninsula.

The Goths who swept into central Italy in the fifth century were dislodged by the Byzantine forces of the Eastern emperor in conflicts that left the area badly battle-scarred. The Goth king Totila seized Florence again in 552, only to be ejected two decades later when the Lombards stormed across the Alps and established a regional HQ at Lucca.

In the eighth century, Charlemagne and his Frankish forces crushed the last of the Lombard kings of Italy. To thank him for his intervention and ensure his future support (a move that backfired badly, leading to centuries of conflict between pontiff and emperors), Pope Leo III crowned Charlemagne Holy Roman Emperor. Much of the country then came under the (at least nominal) control of the emperor. In practice, local warlords carved out feudal fiefs for themselves and threw their weight around.

The imperial margravate of Tuscany began to emerge as a region of some promise during the tenth and 11th centuries. As a prosperous merchant class developed in cities all over Tuscany, the region sought to throw off the constraints and demands of its feudal overlords. By 1200, the majority had succeeded (Florence, Siena and Lucca had been established as independent city-states, or *comuni*, by the redoubtable Matilde di Canossa on her death in 1115). Tuscany became a patchwork of tiny but increasingly self-confident and ambitious independent entities. The potential for conflict was huge, and by the 13th century it had crystallised into the intractable, seemingly interminable struggle of Guelphs and Ghibellines.

GUELPH VERSUS GHIBELLINE

The names Guelph and Ghibelline came from the Italian forms of Welf (the family name of the German emperor Otto IV) and Waiblingen (a castle belonging to the Welfs' rivals for the role of Holy Roman Emperor, the Hohenstaufen), but by the time the appellations crossed the Alps into Italy (probably in the 12th century), their significance had changed.

'Guelph' was attached primarily to the increasingly influential merchant classes. In their continuing desire to be free from imperial control, they looked around for a powerful backer and found one in the emperor's enemy, the pope. Anyone keen to uphold imperial power and opposed to papal designs and rising commercial interests – mainly the old nobility – became known as a 'Ghibelline'.

IN CONTEXT

'Florence turned to a fire-and-brimstone-preaching monk who claimed paintings made the Virgin Mary 'look like a harlot'.'

Although bad feeling had been simmering for decades, the murder of Florentine nobleman Buondelmonte dei Buondelmonti is seen as the spark that ignited flames across Tuscany. On his wedding day in 1215, Buondelmonte was stabbed to death by a member of the Amidei family for having previously jilted an Amidei maiden. The subsequent trial dissolved into a test of wills (and soon of arms) between the pro-empire Amidei and the pro-*comune* faction mourning the demise of the groom. The Ghibelline Amidei prevailed with help from Emperor Frederick II in 1248, but were ousted with Guelph aid two years later, when a semi-democratic government by the merchant class, the *piccolo popolo*, was established.

Into and throughout the 14th century, power ebbed and flowed between the two (loosely knit) parties across Tuscany and from city to city, but antagonism flourished within the parties too. In around 1300, open conflict broke out between the virulently anti-imperial 'Blacks' and the more conciliatory 'Whites', with the Blacks eventually booting out the Whites for good. Among those sent into exile was Dante Alighieri.

Eventually, the Guelph/Ghibelline conflict ran out of steam. It says much for the energy, innovation, graft and skill of the Tuscans (or for the relative harmlessness of much medieval warfare in Italy) that throughout this stormy period, the region was booming economically.

MEDIEVAL MIGHT

By the beginning of the 14th century, Florence was one of the five biggest cities in Europe, with a population of almost 100,000. Despite a plague epidemic that carried off an estimated half of the city's population, the city prospered, due in no small part to its woollen cloth industry, whose *ciompi* (wool carders) formed guilds and gained representation in city government. By the mid 1380s, the three guilds formed in the wake of the uprising began to lose ground to the *popolo grasso*, a small group of the wealthiest merchant families, who had united with the Guelphs to form an oligarchy in 1382. The *popolo grasso* held sway in the *signoria* for 40 years, during which time intellectuals and artists were becoming increasingly involved in political life.

Not all of Florence's business community backed the *popolo grasso*. Banker Cosimo de' Medici's stance against the extremes of the *signoria* gained him the support both of other dissenting merchants and of the *popolo minuto* of the less-influential guilds. Cosimo's mounting popularity alarmed the *signoria*, and the dominant Albizzi family had him exiled on trumped-up charges in 1433. A year later he returned to Florence by popular consent and, with handy military backing from his allies in Milan, was immediately made first citizen, becoming 'king in all but name'. For most of the next 300 years, the dynasty remained more or less firmly in Florence's driving seat.

A FAMILY AFFAIR

Cosimo's habit of giving large sums to charity and endowing religious institutions with art helped make Florence a centre of artistic production. And by persuading representatives of the Eastern and Western Churches to try to mend their schism at a conference in Florence in 1439, he hosted Greek scholars who could sate his hunger for classical literature. This artistic and intellectual fervour gathered steam through the long 'reign' of his grandson Lorenzo il Magnifico, which saw Florence become, for a

The Renaissance

When Florence became the envy of Western Europe.

The Renaissance is a massive source of pride for Florence. For centuries the city has basked in its afterglow, and the world has basked with it.

The guiding doctrine of the Renaissance (Rinascimento; literally 'rebirth') was Humanism – the revival of the language, learning and art of the ancient Greeks and Romans, and the reconciliation of this pagan heritage with Christianity. Although the most visible manifestation of the Renaissance in Florence was the astonishing outpouring of art in the 15th century, it was classical studies that sparked the new age.

The groundwork had been done by a handful of men: Dante (1265-1321), Petrarch (1304-74) and Boccaccio (1313-75) all collected Latin manuscripts, which shaped their approach to writing. But it was mounting Florentine wealth that paid for dedicated manuscript detectives such as Poggio Bracciolini (1380-1459) to dig through neglected monastery libraries across Europe.

A few classical works had never been lost, but those that were known were usually corrupt. The volume of unknown works unearthed during this period was incredible. First came the discovery of Quintilian's *The Training of an Orator*, which detailed Roman education; Columella's *De Re Rustica* on agriculture; key texts on Roman architecture by Vitruvius and Frontinus; and Cicero's *Brutus* (a justification of republicanism). Whereas very few Greek works had been known in Western Europe, suddenly – almost simultaneously – most of Plato, Homer, Sophocles and many other classics were rediscovered.

The Renaissance focus on a pre-Christian age didn't mean that God was under threat. Just as the Renaissance artists had no compunction about enhancing the beauty of their forms and compositions with classical features and allusions, so Renaissance Humanists sought explanations beyond the Scriptures that were complementary to accepted religion rather than a challenge to it. Much effort was made to present the wisdom of the ancients as a precursor to the ultimate wisdom of God.

Nor did the Renaissance fascination with things semi-scientific – Leonardo's anatomical drawings, for example, or the widespread obsession with the mathematics of Pythagoras – necessarily mean that this was a scientific age. The 15th century was an era when ideas were still paramount; science, as a process of deduction based on observation and experimentation, didn't really get going until the 17th century. In medicine, the theory of the four humours still held sway. Astronomy and astrology were all but synonymous. Mathematics was an almost mystical art, while alchemy – the attempt to transform base metals into gold – flourished.

It was magnificent while it lasted, but Florence's pre-eminence in art and ideas was abruptly snuffed out on the death of Lorenzo 'il Magnifico' in 1492: the invasion by Charles VIII of France in the 1490s and Savonarola's 'Bonfire of the Vanities' (*see p20* **Twisted Firestarter**) saw to that. In the early 16th century, the cutting-edge was Rome, where Michelangelo, Bramante and Raphael were in the process of creating their finest works. Thence, after Emperor Charles V sacked Rome in 1527, to Venice, where masters such as Palladio and Titian practised. But the period left Florence with some of the most important masterpieces and artefacts in the world – many of them still in existence, and enjoyed by millions of visitors each year.

IN CONTEXT

Twisted Firestarter

The monk who came to a brutally ironic end.

Everyone knows that Florence has a higher concentration of art than anywhere else in the world, but an untold number of lost Florentine masterpieces will never be appreciated. We can lay the blame for many of these losses at the feet of Girolamo Savonarola.

With a beak-like nose and burning eyes, Savonarola was a fanatical Dominican monk who was famous for his fiery sermons. On 7 February 1497, he called on the people of Florence to cleanse the city of its sins by throwing material objects on to a 'Bonfire of the Vanities'. The bonfire, held in piazza della Signoria, was huge: 18 metres (60 feet) high and 12 metres (40 feet) wide.

Priceless works of art by Botticelli and Michelangelo are known to have been lost into its flames – rumour has it that the artists threw the paintings on the fire themselves. Other burnt items included gambling tables, pornography, mirrors, cosmetics, women's hats, chess pieces, musical instruments and 'immoral' books.

Savonarola himself met a sticky end on 23 May 1498. He was publicly hanged and burned – in piazza della Signoria, the exact spot on which he'd held his bonfire.

'Napoleon's triumphant romp down the peninsula brought him into possession of Tuscany in 1799'.

while, the intellectual and artistic centre of the Renaissance that was about to transform Christendom. Under his de facto leadership, Florence enjoyed a long period of relative peace, aided to some extent by Lorenzo's diplomatic skills in minimising squabbles between Italian states.

By the end of the 15th century, Lorenzo had handed Florence to the French king Charles VIII as he passed through on his way to Naples and there was a violent backlash against the splendour of his rule. Florence turned for inspiration and guidance to a fire-and-brimstone-preaching monk who railed against paintings that made the Blessed Virgin Mary 'look like a harlot' and against Humanist thought, which he said would prompt the wrath of the one true and very vengeful God. Girolamo Savonarola (1452-98) perfectly captured the end-of-century spirit, winning the fanatical devotion not only of the poor and uneducated, but also of the leading minds of Lorenzo's magnificent court. Artists and art patrons willingly threw their works and finery on to the monk's 'Bonfire of the Vanities' in piazza della Signoria in 1497 (*see left* **Twisted Firestarter**).

Savonarola set up a semi-democratic government, firmly allied to Charles VIII, then allowed his extremist tendencies to get the better of him, alienating the Borgia pope Alexander VI and getting excommunicated. Florence's desperate economic state saw the region devastated by pestilence and starvation, and resentment turned on Savonarola, who was summarily tried and burned at the stake in piazza della Signoria in May 1498.

The republic created after his death was surprisingly democratic but increasingly ineffective, making stronger leadership look enticing to disaffected Florentines. In 1502, Piero Soderini, from an old noble family, was elected *gonfalonier*-for-life ('banner bearer'), along the model of the Venetian doge. His pro-French policies brought him into conflict with the pro-Spanish pope Julius II, who had Cardinal Giovanni de' Medici whispering policy suggestions in his ear. In 1512, Soderini went into exile. Giuliano de' Medici, Duke of Nemours, was installed as Florence's most prominent citizen, succeeded by his nephew Lorenzo, Duke of Urbino. The family's already considerable clout was reinforced in 1513 when Giovanni became Pope Leo X. The Medici clan got a second crack at the papacy in 1524, when Giulio, Lorenzo's illegitimate nephew, became Clement VII, only to enrage the Habsburg emperor Charles V, who humiliated him in Rome. Back in Florence, the local populace exploited the Medici ignominy in Rome to reinstall a short-lived republic; the city was back in Medici hands by 1530.

When Clement brought Alessandro, his son, to power in Florence in 1530 and Charles V made him hereditary Duke of Florence, the city entered one of its most desperate periods. Buoyed by support from Charles, whose daughter he had married, the authoritarian Alessandro trampled on Florentines' traditional rights and privileges, while indulging in some shocking sexual antics.

His successor, Cosimo I, had different, though no less unpleasant, defects; nor was he much cop at reversing Tuscany's gentle slide into the economic doldrums. Still, this dark horse – whom the pope made the first Grand Duke of Tuscany in 1569 – at least gave the city a patina of action, extending the writ of the *granducato* to all of Tuscany except Lucca, and adorning the city with vast new *palazzi*, including the Uffizi and Palazzo Pitti.

IN CONTEXT

A SQUALID END

Cosimo's descendants continued to rule for 150 years: they were fittingly poor rulers for what was a very minor statelet in the chessboard of Europe. The *granducato*'s farming methods were backward; the European fulcrum of its core industry, wool-making (like that of its main service industry, banking), had shifted definitively to Northern Europe, leaving Florence to descend inexorably into depression. Its glory – and a very dusty glory it was – hung on its walls and adorned its palaces, with only the occasional spark of intellectual fervour (such as Cosimo II's spirited defence of Galileo Galilei when the astronomer was accused of heresy) to recall what the city had once represented.

The male Medici line came to a squalid end in the shape of Gian Gastone, who died in 1737. His pious sister Anna Maria couldn't wait to offload the *granducato*, handing it over to the House of Lorraine, cousins of the Austrian Habsburgs. Grand Duke Francis I and his successors spruced up the city, knocked its administration into shape, introduced new farming methods and generally shook the place out of its torpor.

Napoleon's triumphant romp down the peninsula at the end of the 18th century brought him into possession of Tuscany in 1799, to the joy of liberals and the horror of local peasantry, who drove the French out in the Viva Maria uprising, during which they also wreaked their revenge on unlucky Jews and anyone suspected of Jacobin leanings.

It wasn't long before the French returned, installing Louis de Bourbon of Parma as head of the Kingdom of Etruria in 1801. Napoleon's sister, Elisa Baciocchi, was made Princess of Piombino and Lucca in 1805, and Grand Duchess of Tuscany from 1809 to 1814.

UNIFICATION ACROSS THE NATION

By the 1820s and 1830s, under the laid-back if not overly bright Grand Duke Leopold II, Tuscany enjoyed a climate of tolerance that attracted intellectuals, dissidents, artists and writers from all over Italy and Europe.

For a time, Leopold and his ministers kept the influence of the Grand Duke's uncle, Emperor Francis II of Austria, at arm's length, while also playing down the growing populist cry for Italian unification. But by the 1840s, it was clear that the nationalist movement posed a serious threat to the status quo. Even relaxed Florence was swept up in nationalist enthusiasm, causing Leopold to clamp down on reformers and impose some censorship. In 1848 – a tumultuous year of revolutions – insurrections in Livorno and Pisa forced Leopold to grant concessions to the reformers, and they included a Tuscan constitution.

When news reached Florence that the Milanese had driven the Austrians out of their city, and that Carlo Alberto, King of Sardinia-Piedmont, was determined to push them out of Italy altogether, thousands of Tuscans joined the cause. In 1849, the pendulum seemed to be swinging back in favour of the better-trained Austrians. A turbulent decade followed and, in April 1859, Piedmont's Count Camillo Cavour was finally able to expel the Austrians, with the help of France's Napoleon III. The French and Piedmontese swept the Austrian armies before them, while in Florence nationalist demonstrations forced the government to resign. On 27 April, Leopold left Florence and his family for the last time. The following year the Tuscan people voted in favour of unification with the Kingdom of Piedmont.

TRUMPING TURIN

Five years later, with Rome holding out against the forces of unification, Florence was declared capital of Italy, much to the annoyance of the Piedmontese capital of Turin – 200 people died in riots there when the shift was announced. The Florentines greeted their new king with enthusiasm when he arrived in February 1865 to take up residence in Palazzo Pitti, but the influx of northerners was met with mixed feelings: business boomed, but the Florentines didn't take to Piedmontese flashiness.

'American bombers swooped in to destroy Campo di Marte station: 218 civilians died; the station remained in perfect working order.'

Huge changes were wrought to the city. Ring roads encircled the old centre, avenues, squares (such as piazza della Repubblica) and suburbs were built, and parks were laid out. Intellectuals and socialites crowded the salons and cafés.

When war with Prussia forced the French (who had swapped sides) to withdraw their troops from Italy in 1870, Rome finally fell to Vittorio Emanuele's troops and Italy was united for the first time since the fall of the Roman Empire. Florence's brief reign as capital ended.

FASCISM AND WAR

Florence began the 20th century pretty much as it ended it – as a thriving tourist centre. In the early 1900s, it drew an exclusive coterie of writers, artists, aesthetes and the upper-middle classes. An English-speaking industry sprang up to cater for the needs of these wealthy foreigners.

The city was neither occupied nor attacked in World War I, though it suffered. Post-war hardship inspired a fierce middle-class rage for order that found expression in the black shirt of Fascism. Groups of *squadristi* were already forming in 1919, organising parades and demonstrations in the streets of Florence.

When Mussolini was elected in 1923, there began in Florence a campaign to expunge the city of foreign elements and influences. Hotels and shops with English names were put under pressure to sever their Anglo-Saxon affiliations. The Florence that had been described as a *ville toute anglaise* by the French social-historian Goncourt brothers was under threat.

Italy entered the war on Germany's side on 10 June 1940. The Florentines were confident that their city would never be attacked from the air: Florence was a museum, a testament to artistic evolution, and its monuments were surely its best protection. Nevertheless, the Fascist regime, perhaps for propaganda reasons, began protecting the city's art. Photos of the period show statuary disappearing inside comically inefficient wooden sheds, while the Baptistery doors were bricked up and many treasures from the Uffizi and Palazzo Pitti were taken for safe-keeping to the Castello di Montegufoni – owned by the British Sitwell family – away in the Tuscan countryside.

The Germans occupied Florence on 11 September 1943, just weeks after Mussolini's arrest and the armistice was signed. Only when it became necessary to hinder the Nazis' communication lines to Rome were aesthetic scruples set aside. In September 1943, a formation of American bombers swooped in to destroy Florence's Campo di Marte station: the operation was bungled, leaving 218 civilians dead, while the station remained in perfect working order. Further air raids were banned by orders from the highest levels.

At the beginning of the war Florence had a Jewish population of more than 2,000. The chief rabbi saved the lives of many Jews in the city by advising them to hide in convents or little villages under false names. Three raids were carried out by Nazis and Fascists on the night of 27 November 1943. The largest of them was on the Franciscan Sisters of Mary in piazza del Carmine, where dozens of Jews were concealed. The second train to leave Italy bound for the gas chambers set out from Florence, carrying at least 400 Jews from Florence, Siena and Bologna; not one of them is known to have returned.

IN CONTEXT

The floods of November 1966.

By 1944, allied commanding officers had extracted permission from their leaders to attack Florence using only the most experienced squadrons, in ideal weather conditions. On 11 March, the Americans began unleashing their bombs on the city, causing casualties but leaving the *centro storico* and its art intact. On 1 August 1944, fighting broke out in various parts of the city, but poorly armed Florentine patriots couldn't prevent the Germans from destroying all the Arno bridges except the ponte Vecchio. Along with the bridges, the old quarter around the ponte Vecchio was razed to the ground.

The Val d'Orcia and Monte Amiata areas in southern Tuscany were key theatres for partisans, who held out with considerable loss of life until British and US infantry reinforced their lines on the Arno on 1 September 1944. The German army abandoned Fiesole a week later. When the Allies eventually reached Florence, they discovered a functioning government formed by the partisan Comitati di Liberazione Nazionale (CLN). Within hours of the Germans' departure, work started to put the bridges back into place. The ponte Santa Trinità was rebuilt, stone by stone, in exactly the same location.

ORDEAL BY FIRE AND WATER

Two decades later, the Florentine skill at restoration was required again, this time for a calamity of an altogether different nature: in the early hours of the morning of 4 November 1966, citizens awoke to find their homes flooded by the Arno, which had broken its banks; soon all the main *piazze* were under water. An estimated 15,000 cars were destroyed, 6,000 shops put out of business and almost 14,000 families left homeless. Many artworks, books and archives were damaged, treasures in the refectory of Santa Croce were blackened by mud, and in the church's nave Donatello's *Cavalcanti Annunciation* was soaked with oil up to the Virgin's knees. As word of the disaster spread around the world, public and private funds were pumped into restoration.

The city's cultural heritage took another direct hit in May 1993, when a bomb planted by the Mafia exploded in the city centre, killing five people. It caused structural damage to the Uffizi, destroying the Georgofili library and damaging the Vasari Corridor. Not that you'd know it now: in a restoration job carried out in record time, one of the world's most-visited art repositories was returned to its pristine state and tourists began queuing outside again, confirming the modern city's vocation for living off its past.

Florence solemnly commemorated the tenth anniversary of the Uffizi bomb in 2003, and seems to have moved on. After lean years post-9/11, post-SARS and post-recession, tourist numbers seem to be up again. However, while the queues to get into the city's most popular museums are as long as ever, restaurateurs and shopkeepers in particular grumble that people are less willing to part with their money. Tourists don't seem much happier, faced with rising prices and the appalling euro/dollar exchange rate, but while they tuck into their *ribollita* as usual, the Florentines are facing major structural changes to their city.

The new traffic system around Porta al Prato more or less functions and has alleviated congestion in the area to a certain extent. However, the ongoing (and seemingly never-ending) work on the Tramvia – the new tram system – is now causing traffic chaos in large sections of the city, leaving many seriously disgruntled citizens in its wake. Most Florentines are hugely cynical about the project, doubting that the end result will be worth all the disruption and expense, and unhappy about possible repercussions to their beautiful city. Despite the successful unveiling of Tramvia Line 1 in 2010, which linked the city with Scandicci only 52 years after the last tram departed Florence, and its soaring passenger numbers (from 25 in February 2010 to 40,000 eight months later), the debate about city transport continues to rage (for more details, *see pp26-29* **Florence Today**). For visitors, at least, there are signs that this city in flux will eventually settle into one that's a total delight to navigate.

IN CONTEXT

The site of the Mafia bomb explosion in 1993.

Florence Today

Despite rising rents and an increase in vandalism in the city, locals remain as loyal to Florence as ever.

TEXT: MADDALENA DELLI

It may seem a platitude, but it is not easy to be Florence, and it is possibly even harder to be a Florentine. Like a movie star, both the city and her inhabitants must on a daily basis put up with a huge amount of pressure, living up to sometimes fanciful expectations or even downright misconceptions. The Japanese come to Florence looking for the fine detail and unparalleled elegance of Botticelli. Americans cannot leave without seeing the *David*, Renaissance forefather of their Statue of Liberty. Northern Europeans seek the comfort of sun-kissed rolling hills, fine wine and olive oil. All are there, but no single one of them is the essence of Florence, nor what Florentines think is representative of themselves.

Maddalena Delli is a freelance journalist who lives and works in Florence.

WHOSE FLORENCE IS IT ANYWAY?

Florentines love their city sincerely and wholeheartedly: *campanilismo* (unmitigated civic pride) is worn like a badge of honour here, and anywhere in the world – when asked where they come from – Florentines always answer 'Florence' rather than 'Italy'. While true-blood Florentines are thinning in numbers as globalisation spreads, they remain attached to their home town by an invisible umbilical cord. Since piazza del Duomo was pedestrianised in 2009, some Florentines sorely miss seeing their beloved 'Bel San Giovanni' – Dante Alighieri's affectionate nickname for the Baptistery – which greeted them every morning on their way to work. But if Florentines would not be the same without their city, the reverse is also true: their character should be carefully preserved for posterity just like any statue, or painting, or *loggia* in the city. Does UNESCO not list intangible as well as artistic and natural heritage?

Instead, alas, the locals are pushed further and further outside the city gates by impossible rents and traffic restrictions – known as ZTL (Zona a Traffico Limitato) – that make it impossible for a non-ZTL-resident young man to drive his ZTL-resident girlfriend home, for instance. As historic shops are put out of business by chains and offices are relocated to more suitable quarters, Florentines have less and less reason to go into town, and the city centre is increasingly the realm of old people, poor immigrants and wealthy expats. This process began as an unwelcome by-product of the catastrophic 1966 flood of the Arno, when most families and shop owners lost all their belongings and chose to start a new life in more modern surroundings.

The latest available figures published by the Tourist Board refer to the business year 2010, and they show nearly 7.5 million visitors to the city (rising to 11 million for the province). When you consider that the resident population is a little over 370,000, you can imagine the thought every Florentine instinctively has when trying to cross a jam-packed piazza del Duomo, or when looking at an exorbitant rubbish-collection bill: whose Florence is it anyway? Is this a living city or a Renaissance theme park? So next time you have to pay a few extra euros on top of your hotel bill because of the newly levied *tassa di soggiorno*, take a moment to step into the locals' shoes, and consider it a long overdue contribution to the daily effort they have been making for centuries.

Mind you, Florentines are a mercantile lot. They know how much their economy relies on tourism and the art treasures they have been lucky enough to inherit from their crafty forefathers. Not by chance, they revere the memory of Anna Maria Luisa (1667-1743), the last of the Medici dynasty, an enlightened lady who bequeathed all her family's art treasures to the city. In summer 2010, a dispute arose between the City of Florence and the Italian government over the ownership of Michelangelo's *David*. Idle talk? Hardly: between rights and admission tickets to the Accademia, it's a matter of €10 million a year.

THE FIFTH ELEMENT

Let us eradicate a myth: *la dolce vita* does not belong in Florence. As our very own Roberto Benigni would say, here life is beautiful – not sweet. Florence is a city of stone, and Florentines are not mellow. Genius is a lonely business, and Florentines are far from sociable, by Italian standards at least. They have a sense of eternity that is much unlike the Roman, a sense of humour that could not be further from the Neapolitan, a sense of duty that is not even a distant relation of the Milanese. They are an element of their own, as a much-paraphrased remark by Pope Boniface VIII (1235-1303) goes. Like the British, the Florentine sense of humour is subtle and outrageous, sparing nothing – not sex, politics, nor religion. Self-mockery is fierce, and there is a vein of irony running straight from Dante's *Divina Commedia* to Benigni's *La vita è bella*, via Carlo Collodi's *Pinocchio*.

As author Mary McCarthy observed in her classic 1959 essay 'The Stones of Florence', 'Florentine history, in its great period, is a history of innovations.' When he was president of the Florence provincial administration a few years ago, the present mayor Matteo Renzi organised a month-long festival called 'Genio Fiorentino', celebrating past

IN CONTEXT

and present Florentine excellence in every possible field of human activity. The motto for the 2006 programme came from the *Divine Comedy*, where Ulysses exclaims: 'You were not born to live like brutes, but to follow virtue and knowledge.'

The tongue-in-cheek question was: could genius be written in the DNA, and run particularly thick in the blood of a Florentine? In the case of Florence, genius is probably a combination of an uncommon sense of measure and an irresistible instinct for thinking outside the box. It's the kind of combination that produced visionary solutions such as Brunelleschi's dome, Michelangelo's *David*, Leonardo's flying machines, Buontalenti's early version of *gelato*, Ferragamo's jewel shoes and Pucci's print patterns.

Let us call it a what-if frame of mind: the unwritten law is, there's always an alternative approach to the matter. Stand by your opinion, but don't rule out any others. This makes Florentines uncommonly tolerant, and certainly works very well whenever trial and error is an option. Yet it becomes deadly on a larger scale, where city-wide issues are at stake. Be it building a tramway or deciding if charging a *tassa di soggiorno* is good for the city coffers, the habit of discussing endless possibilities is at the heart of most of the city's present woes. From the outside, this is often mistaken for conservatism or NIMBYism. Instead, it is much like a city-wide exercise in rhetoric: the possibilities are endless.

TALES OF TRAMS, SNOW AND OTHER TYPES OF ORDINARY MADNESS

The debate about whether one of the tram lines should pass by the Duomo had been raging for some years when, in September 2009, the newly elected mayor Matteo Renzi ruled it out by announcing that, within a month, the Duomo and a considerable chunk of its immediate surroundings would be declared off limits to all sorts of motor traffic, private and public. There being no other roads wide enough for buses, all routes that formerly ran through the centre were diverted to the *viali*, so from the station they now go back to skirt the Fortezza da Basso and San Marco, resulting in heavier traffic around the already overloaded Fortezza and considerably longer transit times: if you need proof, the validity of a bus ticket has been nonchalantly extended from 70 to 90 minutes. More recently, in June 2011, the Pitti and via de'Tornabuoni areas have become pedestrian areas, and San Niccolò in the Oltrarno is rumoured to be next. This is all very well for aesthetic and environmental purposes, but takes a heavy logistical toll. Most cities with similarly sized pedestrian areas have an underground system: Florence does not.

Since the times of Giorgio Vasari (1511-74) and Bernardo Buontalenti (1536-1608), the only major redesign in the city layout dates from 1865 to 1871, when Florence was temporarily the 'reluctant' capital of Italy and architect Giuseppe Poggi (1811-1901) pulled down most of the old city walls and replaced them with a ring of Parisian-style, tree-lined boulevards. Yet these were obviously planned for horses and carriages, certainly not for modern traffic. While the ring of hills that crowns the city has protected her from outgrowing her man-centric character, it also chokes her with traffic, pollution and extreme temperatures, with icy cold winter days and steaming hot summers, often reaching the very bottom and very top temperatures in Italy. Climate is hardly one of Florence's charms, yet visitors hardly ever bring back a memory true to such facts. It's obvious that, in this case, beauty really is in the eye of the beholder.

For lack of a modern ring road, the motorway effectively serves as a bypass, and traffic is usually heavier than elsewhere. It has taken Florence about ten years to complete a 7.4-kilometre (4.6-mile), 14-stop tramway, and although the service has been comparatively successful, with seven million passengers (about 50 per cent less than expected, but you won't find that in the official reports) in its first ten months of operation, it has proved more beneficial to the satellite town of Scandicci and its residents, than to the Florentines who suffered much of the expense and discomfort.

On 10 December 2010, 28 centimetres of snowfall brought chaos to Florence and its surroundings. Public and private traffic, the airport, railway system and motorways were all paralysed. Emergency services were powerless. While chaos reigned, mayor

Matteo Renzi was sitting in his office in Palazzo Vecchio, doing what he considered to be his duty: updating his Facebook account with the latest news from the apocalypse, and blaming the weather forecasters for not issuing a warning. People were enraged. Many had to park their car as best as the circumstances allowed and take a long walk home; others were even less lucky, finding themselves stuck overnight in their vehicles. For lack of a better plan, staff at the airport had to drive to a nearby furniture store and stock up on chairs to accommodate passengers whose flights had been cancelled.

Luckily, snow melts soon: over the weekend the situation was back to normal. But everybody feels the warning signs were not taken seriously enough, nor lessons learned. There are so few alternative routes that whenever a minor accident – even a heavy rainstorm – happens, the traffic tightens like a knot that takes hours to disentangle. In true Florentine style, the inevitable what-if question is: what if the next major emergency isn't snow – a rare occurrence in Florence, despite freezing winter temperatures – but a terrorist attack or another major flood?

Round, Round, Get Around

Florence's bus routes make a great way to see the sights.

In Florence, the phrase 'within walking distance' has an ever-expanding meaning, since recent additions to the pedestrian area have been pushing both private and public transport out of the city centre. The pedestrianisation also dealt a huge blow to the appeal of the city sightseeing buses, the routes of which now run further away from most of the major landmarks.

Until the Duomo and its surroundings became the exclusive realm of strollers in October 2009, as many as 19 bus lines (between 1,850 and 2,200 buses daily) passed the cathedral. The aesthetic and environmental benefits of the move are undeniable, but the flipside is that buses are now next to useless within the city walls.

Thankfully, the most scenic bus routes – Lines 7, 12 and 13 – are unscathed; if you're in Florence for longer than a few hours, you shouldn't miss them. Line 7's terminus is now in San Marco, and it reaches the quaint hilltop village of Fiesole (*see p96* **Outside the City Gates**) in little less than 30 minutes. Lines 12 and 13 are circular routes, climbing to piazzale Michelangelo (*see p96* **Outside the City Gates**) from opposite sides.

C1 and C2, the only lines that still cut through the heart of the city

(north–south and west–east respectively), run for the most part through narrow medieval streets and are operated with dwarfish buses that are usually crammed to capacity. So while they are priceless for getting places, they hold little sightseeing appeal.

On the other hand, the D minibuses are both convenient and attractive, covering chunks of the Lungarni and much of the Oltrarno, including Santo Spirito. Additionally, they are among the very few vehicles still allowed in piazza Pitti and by the ponte Vecchio. Catch one outside the train station and run the length of the line to piazza Ferrucci, where you can switch to Line 13 (*see above*) for the *piazzale*.

A few tips. Fines are steep, so always have a valid ticket ready for inspection. Grab a bus map from the ATAF information office, off the main ticket hall inside the train station. And, much like a maze, bus routes often run in a counter-intuitive direction to circumvent off-limit areas: check the display on the front of the bus to make sure you are heading where you mean to go.

For a map of electric bus routes and timetables, see www.ataf.net or www.muoversiafirenze.it. For more on getting around, see pp304-306.

IN CONTEXT

Art

The cradle of the Italian Renaissance is unrivalled in the breadth of its artistic treasures.

TEXT: SOPHIA COTTIER

UNESCO estimates that Italy contains up to 60 per cent of the world's most important works of art, over half of which are located in Florence. Considered the spiritual home of the Renaissance, Florence and its environs spawned a huge number of great artists: Michelangelo, Botticelli, Leonardo and Fra Angelico among them. Wealthy Florentine families entrusted these artists to decorate their palaces, chapels and city with sumptuous images that would never be forgotten. This kept Florence at the forefront of the artistic and intellectual world during the 15th and 16th centuries, as poets, artists and philosophers mingled in the city, vying for patronage and fame.

MEDIEVAL MONEY

To find art, you need to follow the money. In the case of Florence, the trail takes you back to the medieval cloth and banking businesses that were the foundations of the city's wealth. In the 1320s, the Bardi, a powerful banking family, commissioned **Giotto** (1267-1337) to decorate their chapel in the church of Santa Croce (*see p86*). Here, Giotto demonstrates the stylistic shift between medieval and early Renaissance painting. Although obscured by tombs and damaged by the 1966 flood, the figures in the *Funeral of St Francis* are set in a believable environment with an outpouring of human emotion. As seen in his design for the Duomo's bell tower, Giotto's style is characterised by clarity and simplicity, rendering his works legible and accessible.

Also in the church of Santa Croce is a painted *Crucifix* by Giotto's predecessor, **Cimabue** (1240-1302). With its ties to the previous Byzantine tradition, this work brings Giotto's naturalism into focus. The Uffizi (*see p64*) provides direct comparisons between the two artists, with Cimabue's *Maestà* (1285-6) beside Giotto's *Ognissanti Madonna* (1300-10).

Ignoring the new naturalism of Giotto, **Andrea Orcagna** (1308-68) fashioned his tabernacle in the church of Orsanmichele (1359; *see p63*) in the more popular Gothic style. This highly decorative structure protected the miracle-working image of the Virgin and is inlaid with marble, lapis lazuli, gold and glass.

THE 'REBIRTH'

The Renaissance refers to a literary, intellectual and artistic movement that flourished in Florence between the 14th and 16th centuries (*see also p19* **The Renaissance**). Artists, writers and scholars reinterpreted the classical heritage of the Roman Empire, rediscovering its philosophy, art, architecture and literature. Prior to the 14th century, the Catholic Church had been the primary commissioner of works of art, but this was set to change: bankers, merchants and princes were becoming richer, so the demand for secular art grew.

The 1401 competition for the east doors of the Baptistery saw **Filippo Brunelleschi** (1377-1446) lose out to **Lorenzo Ghiberti** (1378-1455). In a huff, Brunelleschi left for Rome to study the art of the ancients. But he had the last laugh: on his return to Florence, he built the majestic cupola for the Duomo (1420-36; *see also p56* **Seeing Beyond the Façade**).

As the demand for art grew, so did the number of workshops; here, apprentices learned to paint and sculpt alongside the masters. The workshop of **Luca della Robbia** (1400-82), for example, generated signature glazed terracotta reliefs that grace prominent structures across Florence, such as Orsanmichele, Brunelleschi's Spedale degli Innocenti (*see p82*) and the interior of the Duomo (*see p52*).

As a young apprentice in the workshop of Ghiberti, **Donatello** (1386-1466) worked on the Baptistery doors. Like Brunelleschi, he had studied in Rome, and his Orsanmichele statues of *St Mark* (1411) and *St George* (1416), now in the Bargello (*see p84*), demonstrate his ability to create naturalistic drapery over believable bodies.

Commissioned by Cosimo I de' Medici, Donatello's *David* (1430), now also in the Bargello, was the first free-standing life-size nude bronze since antiquity. It was originally designed to stand on the buttress of Florence cathedral, but in 1416, the Priory of the Republic decided that the statue should become a symbol of the Florentine Republic, so *David* was placed in a more prominent position in Palazzo dei Priori.

Andrea del Verrocchio (1435-88) eventually replaced Donatello as the leading sculptor in Florence, and his *Christ and Doubting Thomas* (1476-83) takes on a new dimension as its figures step out of a niche in the exterior of the Orsanmichele (*see p63*). This skilled composition shows an acute awareness of anatomy. Verrocchio, like Donatello, worked for the Medici (*see p75* **The Medicis**), creating the tomb of Piero and Giovanni in the Old Sacristy of San Lorenzo (1469-72), as well as the charming *Putto with Dolphin* fountain (1470) in Palazzo Vecchio.

IN CONTEXT

Early Renaissance painting took its cue from sculpture, attempting to create the same sense of naturalism on a two-dimensional scale. Brunelleschi's theory of linear perspective became a tool for the realistic representation of distance and depth. Perspective was first applied to painting by artists such as **Masaccio** (1401-28), particularly in his *Trinità* fresco in Santa Maria Novella (1427; *see p71*) and, with the help of **Masolino** (1400-47), the fresco cycle in the Cappella Brancacci (1425; *see p92*). Similarly, **Paolo Uccello** (1396-1475) experimented with foreshortening and a sense of perspective in works such as *The Battle of San Romano* (1435) in the Uffizi, and the fresco of *John Hawkwood* (1436) in the Duomo.

Piero della Francesca (1416-92) was active in Florence in the 1430s, both as a painter and as an author of treatises on perspective and mathematics. His *Legend of the True Cross* fresco cycle (c1453-65), in Arezzo, reveals his adherence to mathematical order by his treatment of natural and architectural elements, which recede into the distance.

The Dominican **Fra Angelico** (1400-55) also used perspective when creating his sublime frescoes in the monastery (now museum) of San Marco (*see p80*), using them as an extension of reality. His *Annunciation* (1440-41) mirrors the architecture of the monks' cells, adding a new sense of immediacy. The stark style of Fra Angelico reflects the humility of his religious order and the function of the monastery as a place of meditation.

Placing a biblical event in a contemporary Florentine context became acceptable during the Renaissance, providing a new way for lay people to understand and connect with the story. It also became commonplace to depict one's patron in a prominent position. In his painting of the *Cappella dei Magi* (1459-60) in Palazzo Medici Riccardi (*see p76*), **Benozzo Gozzoli** (1420-97) depicts Lorenzo de' Medici as one of the participants in this lavish procession. Gozzoli also painted himself among the crowd, reflecting the growing self-awareness of 'the artist' of this period; another example is **Domenico Ghirlandaio** (1449-94), who looks out from his Cappella Sassetti frescoes in Santa Trinità (1483-85; *see p68*).

Filippo Lippi (1406-69), a Carmelite friar, had little interest in creating an illusion of the real world. In his *Madonna with Child and Angels* (1465) in the Uffizi, he depicts a fantastic background scene behind his pearl-adorned Madonna that disregards the laws of perspective and human anatomy.

Filippo passed his linear style on to his pupil, **Sandro Botticelli** (1445-1510). The figures in both *Primavera* ('Allegory of Spring'; c1482) and *The Birth of Venus* (1476-87), commissioned by the Medici and now in the Uffizi, are infused with grace and idealised beauty, seeming to float just above the ground.

PINNACLE OF ACHIEVEMENT

The artists of the 15th century developed the tools and methods that would characterise the artistic activity in the century that followed. These artists surpassed their own masters in their quest for ideal beauty, balanced proportions and structured compositions.

Leonardo da Vinci (1452-1519) emerged from the workshop of Verrocchio when he helped his master paint the *Baptism of Christ* (1469-80), now in the Uffizi. A true 'Renaissance man', Leonardo was not only a skilled painter but also a sculptor, architect, engineer and scientist. His exploration of the natural world as a scientist manifested itself in his art, which reflects his sensitive observation of nature. Da Vinci experimented extensively with oils, developing the *sfumato* technique, which creates atmospheric and subtle shading. This can clearly be seen in the carefully structured *Annunciation* (1472) in the Uffizi.

Another quintessential Florentine Renaissance artist was **Michelangelo Buonarroti**, better known as Michelangelo (1475-1564). He was catapulted to fame with his idealised male nude statue, *David* (1501-04), quickly lauded as the greatest work of sculpture ever created. Though a copy remains in piazza della Signoria (*see p59*), the original is now in the Accademia, along with the *Slaves* (1527-28) – half-finished sculptures that reveal Michelangelo's method of removing excess stone to reveal the 'pre-existing spirit' of the statue. For more about Leonardo and Michelangelo, *see p55* **Hidden Depths**.

MIND YOUR MANNERISM

The prevailing style of the late period of the High Renaissance, from 1520 until 1600, is known as Mannerism. The term originates from the Italian *maniera*, meaning 'style' or 'manner', and it is characterised by complicated compositions, garish colours, exaggerated forms and a heightened sense of drama. To a certain extent this art

Amazing Art...

...and where to find it.

PERFECT PAINTINGS, FAB FRESCOES

Botticelli *Birth of Venus* and *Primavera*, Uffizi (*see p64*).
Della Francesca *Legend of the True Cross* fresco cycle, Arezzo (*see p282*).
Fra Angelico *Annunciation*, Museo di San Marco (*see p80*).
Giotto frescoes depicting the life of St Francis, Cappella Bardi di Vernio, Santa Croce (*see p86*).
Leonardo (with Verrocchio) *Baptism of Christ*, Uffizi (*see p64*).

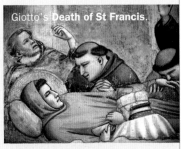
Giotto's **Death of St Francis**.

STUPENDOUS STATUES

Cellini *Perseus*, Loggia dei Lanzi (*see p60*).
Donatello *St George*, Bargello (*see p84*).
Giambologna *The Rape of the Sabine Women*, Loggia dei Lanzi (*see p60*).
Michelangelo *David*, Galleria dell'Accademia (*see p78*).
Verrocchio *Putto with Dolphin* fountain, Palazzo Vecchio (*see p64*).

Giambologna's **The Rape of the Sabine Women**.

LESSER-KNOWN TREASURES

Del Sarto *Last Supper*, Museo del Cenacolo di Andrea del Sarto (*see p94*).
Ghirlandaio Cappella Sassetti, church of Santa Trinità (*see p68*).
Gozzoli frescoes in the Cappella dei Magi, Palazzo Medici Riccardi (*see p76*).
Martini *Annunciation*, Uffizi (*see p64*).
Orcagna tabernacle, Orsanmichele (*see p63*).

IN CONTEXT

movement symbolised the anxiety and confusion that was widely felt in Italy as a result of the Protestant Reformation and the weakening power of the Catholic Church. Mannerism is also considered to be a violent reaction against the order and harmony of Renaissance art.

One of the leading artists of this style was **Andrea del Sarto** (1486-1530). A contemporary of Michelangelo and Raphael, del Sarto was an equally graceful painter and skilled draughtsman. His *Madonna of the Harpies* altarpiece (1517) in the Uffizi is a fine example of Mannerist painting, as is his *Last Supper* (1526-27), in the refectory of the monastery of San Salvi.

Giorgio Vasari (1511-74) also belonged to the Mannerist circle. In 1571, he began the fresco that decorates the interior of the Duomo's cupola, although it was completed later by the Roman **Federico Zuccari**. Vasari is the architect responsible for the Uffizi, but is perhaps best remembered for his book *The Lives of the Artists*, a collection of biographies.

Florence is also home to a number of pieces of outstanding Mannerist sculpture – some on public display in the piazza della Signoria and the Loggia dei Lanzi within it – reflecting the military strength of the Medici administration under the Grand Duke of Tuscany, Cosimo I de' Medici. **Benvenuto Cellini's** (1500-71) life-size *Perseus* (1545-54) is a chilling reminder of the Duke's authority, combining his appreciation for Renaissance sculptors with the elegance of Mannerism. **Giambologna** (or Giovanni da Bologna; 1524-1608) created the statue of Cosimo I on horseback (1598), as well as *Hercules and Centaur* (1599) and *The Rape of the Sabine Women* (1582), both also to be found in the Loggia dei Lanzi.

MODERN MASTERS

Apart from a few Florentines, such as **Ludovico Cardi** ('Cigoli'; 1559-1613), **Cristoforo Allori** (1577-1621) and **Carlo Dolci** (1616-87), the most important artists were working in Rome in the 17th century. The Medici family, however, invited several artists to their court. **Pietro da Cortona** (1596-1669), for instance, decorated the state apartments in Palazzo Pitti in the 1630s. During this time the Florentine *pietra dura* technique of decorating with inlaid marble was developed.

By the 18th century, Florence was an essential stop on the Grand Tour. The Accademia delle Belle Arti (1784) became the centre of artistic activity during the 18th and 19th centuries, when Romantic and Naturalist styles prevailed.

Throughout the Napoleonic occupation of the city (1799-1814), Florence followed the French neoclassicists, but a group of artists known as the Macchiaioli and united by social, political and artistic discontent, frequented Florence's Caffè Michelangelo. Their name, 'stain-makers', or 'splatterers', refers to their style, comprising patches of colour and inspired by French Impressionism and the Barbizon school. Leading Macchiaioli include **Giovanni Fattori** (1825-1908), **Telemaco Signorini** (1835-1901) and **Silvestro Lega** (1826-95), and their works are in the Galleria d'Arte Moderna at Palazzo Pitti (*see p89*).

Perhaps the most renowned Florentine artist of the 20th century is **Marino Marini** (1901-80), whose museum is in the former church of San Pancrazio (*see p70*). Marini devoted himself to sculpture around the 1920s, experimenting with terracotta, bronze and plaster.

A number of artists still work in the Florence area. Among them is the painter **Roberto Barni** (born 1939), known for large monochrome canvases; **Paolo Staccioli** (born 1943), whose ceramic sculpture focuses on human figures and animals on the move; and Tuscan sculptor **Enzo Pazzagli**, who specialises in outdoor sculptures with multiple layers, superimposed on each other. Much of Pazzagli's work can be seen at his Art Park on via Sant'Andrea a Rovezzano.

Contemporary art fans might not be able to sate their hunger in Florence, but can visit Prato's **Centro per l'Arte Contemporanea Luigi Pecci** (*see p222*).

Architecture

The Renaissance blueprint laid bare.

TEXT: SOPHIA COTTIER

The history of Florentine architecture begins in 900 BC, around the time the Etruscans dominated large parts of central Italy, but it was only when the Romans began to absorb Etruscan civilisation that Roman Florence was built, probably on a razed Etruscan village. Founded by Julius Caesar in 59 BC, Florentia, as it was then called, was laid out on a grid pattern typical of the Roman cities. Not much of Roman Florence remains above ground, but historians know that the theatre was located just behind Palazzo Vecchio, while the amphitheatre's shape can still be seen in the layout of the streets and buildings of piazza Santa Croce. From one of the main axes of Roman Florence grew medieval Florence, and the city we know today.

'No longer just skilled labourers, the architects became artists.'

A FLORENTINE STYLE EMERGES

Florence flourished in the tenth and 11th centuries, when a large amount of money was spent on constructing religious buildings, generating an indigenous architectural style. Piazza del Duomo's **Battistero di San Giovanni**, believed to be the oldest building in the city, was completed around the middle of the 11th century, although its foundations are thought to date back to the fourth or fifth century. Famous for Ghiberti's bronze door on the east side, the Baptistery exemplifies what can only be termed the 'Florentine style', characterised by a simple, balanced, sharp-edged design and a wide roof. A number of prominent Florentine and Tuscan architects worked and developed this style over the centuries. The most important were, chronologically: **Arnolfo di Cambio** (c1245-1302), **Giotto** (1266/7-1337), **Filippo Brunelleschi** (1377-1446), **Michelozzo di Bartolomeo Michelozzi** (1396-1472), **Leon Battista Alberti** (1404-72), **Giuliano da Sangallo** (c1445-1535), **Il Cronaca** (1454-1508), **Michelangelo Buonarroti** (1475-1564), **Giorgio Vasari** (1511-74), **Bartolomeo Ammannati** (1511-92), **Bernardo Buontalenti** (1531-1608), and later **Giuseppe Poggi** (1811-1901) and **Giovanni Michelucci** (1891-1991).

ROMANESQUE AND GOTHIC

San Miniato al Monte (*see p96*), constructed in 1018 on the site of a fourth-century chapel, is one of the most beautiful Romanesque structures in Florence. With its wonderful green and white façade, the church is actually rather simple in design, and its 15th-century campanile remains unfinished. During the Siege of Florence (1529-30), this important religious site was surrounded with fortified walls, hastily constructed by Michelangelo.

The 11th-century church of **Santissimi Apostoli** (*see p68*), in piazza del Limbo, is considered one of the most elegant examples of Romanesque architecture in the city, and is believed to have heavily influenced Brunelleschi in his designs for the church of San Lorenzo. Santissimi Apostoli was reworked during the 15th century and only restored to its original Romanesque appearance in the 1930s.

Gothic style dominated new architectural works from the 13th century, with builders using pointed arches to make higher and wider structures. The lower portion of **Santa Maria Novella** (*see p71*) was constructed between 1278 and 1360, and is perhaps the most beautiful structure commissioned by the Dominican monks. It was adorned with three open portals, each surrounded by an arch, and three blind portals located just above these, also with arches.

The **Duomo** (*see p52* and *p56* **The Duomo**) – or Santa Maria del Fiore, to give it its proper name – was designed by Arnolfo di Cambio in 1297. However, its design was altered several times, and after Arnolfo's death in 1302 the project was overseen by a number of other architects, including Francesco Talenti and Giovanni di Lapo Ghini.

Santa Croce (*see p86*) is another major Gothic church in the city; begun in 1298, it has also been attributed to Arnolfo. A timbered roof combines with seven bays with pointed arches to give the illusion of loftiness, at the same time drawing the eye down to the altar.

The **Campanile** of Santa Maria del Fiore in piazza del Duomo (*see p54*), designed by Giotto (c1330) and built with white and green marble, was only completed after his death. As the storeys rise, the windows multiply – a traditional feature of medieval Florentine architecture (*see also p56* **The Duomo**).

EARLY RENAISSANCE

Florence is a shrine to Renaissance architecture – its centre filled with palaces, monuments and churches constructed with an artistic and cultural intelligence that was unsurpassed at the time. A pilgrimage to Rome to study the ancient structures was seen as a vital part of an architect's training, and as the architects absorbed the styles of these classical structures, a new architectural vocabulary developed encompassing columns, pilasters, entablatures, arches and pediments.

The treatise of the first-century BC Roman architect Vitruvius also formed an important part of Renaissance education, helping to define Renaissance ideals concerning architectural beauty. These ideals subsequently raised the status of the profession – no longer just skilled labourers, the architects became artists (*see also p19* **The Renaissance**). Renaissance architecture is defined by strict mathematical proportions, measurements based on the human body and balanced form. In Florence, the period was dominated by three great architects: Brunelleschi, Michelozzo and Alberti.

Brunelleschi, who gave the Duomo its cupola (the largest such construction since ancient Roman times), went on to design two of the city's finest churches: **San Lorenzo** (1422-69; *see p76*), with its independent Old Sacristy (1422-29), and **Santo Spirito** (1444-81; *see p89*). Less heralded, but equally notable, is his **Capella dei Pazzi** (begun 1422; *see p86*), a small private family building in the garden of Santa Croce, based on perfect proportions. The Duomo's cupola, a symbol of the Renaissance, influenced many High Renaissance and Baroque architects: even Michelangelo's cupola for St Peter's in Rome, designed more than 100 years later, has roughly the same interior diameter at 42 metres (138 feet).

Brunelleschi's signature style can clearly be seen in piazza della SS Annunziata's **Ospedale degli Innocenti**, begun in 1419. Through a series of arcades with Corinthian columns, friezes, pedimented windows and matching loggias, Brunelleschi created the most unified square in Florence.

It's the architect Michelozzo, however, who is widely credited with developing the form of the Florentine *palazzo* (or mansion), considered among the most important architectural products of the Renaissance. Michelozzo often worked for Cosimo de' Medici (Cosimo il Vecchio), the founder of the Medici family's fortunes (*see p75* **Profile**). His most notable construction was Cosimo's town residence, Palazzo Medici,

IN CONTEXT

Piazza Santa Maria Novella.

now called **Palazzo Medici Riccardi** (1444; *see p76*). The regularity of the building, its two façades and its strongly rusticated orders heralded a new era in *palazzo* construction.

Completing the trio is Leon Battista Alberti, a Florentine who mostly worked outside the city. In Florence itself he completed the façade of **Santa Maria Novella** (1470; *see p71*), and designed the highly original **Palazzo Rucellai** (c1446-51; *see p70*) in via della Vigna Nuova, on which he first introduced to Florence his innovative system of pilasters and capitals of the three classical orders, which ascend in importance on each storey, and are separated by ornate friezes. In 1450, Alberti published his *Ten Books on Architecture* – the text became an indispensable guide for all those designing buildings during the Renaissance and beyond.

Bland Ambition

Maddalena Delli asks: has the city lost its architectural mojo?

IN CONTEXT

Long gone are the days when an architect could envisage a self-supporting cupola and convince his fellow citizens the fanciful project might be worth the investment of Florentine gold and reputation. Even in Brunelleschi's time, Florentines were distrusting and quarrelsome; yet dragging out idle debate for decades now seems to have become the institutional method for letting innovative sparks die out. Architectural gurus like Santiago Calatrava, Arata Isozaki and – more recently – Jean Nouvel seem to routinely walk out on their Florentine engagements in various degrees of indignation.

Several major projects that started with high hopes of producing architecture of a standard worthy of this city of culture, among them the renovation of the **Museo dell'Opera del Duomo** (*see p58*), eventually ended up in the hands of local architect Adolfo Natalini – a solid professional, but certainly not a visionary in the Calatrava league. Take his **university campus** in the ex-Fiat area in Novoli: the additional buildings are no duller than the surrounding buildings, but they don't even blend in – the originals are 1970s constructs, the new one mock 1930s.

A few hundred metres down the viale Guidoni from the campus, the **Palazzo di Giustizia** law courts building (watch out for its skyward spikes on your way to or from Amerigo Vespucci Airport) is easily Florence's most futuristic edifice. Yet it was designed by Leonardo Ricci almost 30 years ago (Ricci himself died in 1994), and is already obsolete by today's architectural standards: there's too much concrete, too little natural light and not enough concern for the environment.

On a happier note, over the years some enlightened renovation solutions have turned a number of historic Florentine buildings to new use: the former church of San Pancrazio became the (sadly underrated) **Marino Marini museum** (*see p70*); what was once the **Leopolda train station** is now an exhibition and events venue; and the **Oblate convent** was converted into a state-of-the-art library. Even better, the 21st century has got off to a hopeful start. Formerly a nunnery and more recently a prison, the **Murate complex** was reopened in 2011 as a stylish mix of residential and commercial units, following guidelines by Renzo Piano. The **Tramvia** finally arrived – just one of the proposed tram lines connecting the city with its suburbs, but already reducing traffic into the city significantly – and a full 80 years after Giovanni Michelucci designed the modernist temple that is the Santa Maria Novella train terminal (*see p71*), Sir Norman Foster's innovative glass-roofed underground station for the new high-speed TAV train link may finally break the curse.

LATER RENAISSANCE

The Brunelleschian and Albertian principles continued to be used by architects into the 16th century, with one of the main exponents being Il Cronaca (or Simone del Pallaiolo), whose work was extremely sober in style. Il Cronaca built the **Santo Spirito** vestibule and sacristy (1489-94) and the **Museo Horne** (formerly Palazzo Horne, 1495-1502; *see p86*), an elegant palace with an internal courtyard.

Giuliano da Sangallo, the preferred architect of Lorenzo il Magnifico, was greatly concerned with instilling in his designs a refined classicism that he'd learnt in Rome. The best example of his work is at the beautiful **Medici villa** (*see p96*) at Poggio a Caiano (begun 1480). It's a simple rectangular block, with a temple portico, plain walls and sharp eaves that project out in a horizontal design enhanced by the use of mouldings that extend outwards from the pediment.

Michelangelo was one of the most important High Renaissance architects, although he came to architecture rather late in his career, at the age of 40. He took the bold, classicising style that da Sangallo and Il Cronaca had inherited from Alberti, and gave it a sense of uncertainty, but also great energy and rhythm. Rather than making the exteriors of his buildings imitate those of ancient Rome, Michelangelo gave his creations a pagan grounding oriented towards man's emotional state.

Michelangelo undertook two key projects in Florence for Pope Leo X (formerly Giovanni de' Medici): the **New Sacristy** (*see p74*) and the **Biblioteca Mediceo-Laurenziana** (Laurentian Library; *see p77*), both in the church of San Lorenzo, which had become an important symbol of dynastic power for the Medici. A third important project designed by Michelangelo is the **Cappelle Medicee** (1519-34; *see p73*), adjacent to San Lorenzo. Although it was never entirely completed, it's arguably the best example in existence of Michelangelo's architectural-sculptural designs, where the boundaries between the walls, floors and artwork become blurred.

Both the **Fortezza da Basso** (1534; *see p94*), the strongest side of which faces the city, and the **Forte di Belvedere** (1590; *see p89*), which dominates from just above the ponte Vecchio, were commissioned by the Medici family and are symbolic of the great control that the family exercised over the city and its inhabitants. The vast **Palazzo Pitti** (1457; *see p89*), where the Medici lived in the mid 16th century, pays further tribute to the family's strength: designed by Brunelleschi and Fancelli, it was built with massive blocks of stone, some of which measure six metres in length.

The main court architects at this time were Vasari, Ammannati and Buontalenti. However, all ended up following Michelangelo to Rome. While in Florence, Vasari, assisted by Buontalenti, designed the **Uffizi Palace** (1560; *see p64*), which was filled with offices and workshops, leaving the top floor for the gallery. He also constructed the corridor that bears his name, running from the Uffizi, across the ponte Vecchio to Palazzo Pitti; it was used by the Medici family to avoid the throngs on the street.

In 1557, Ammannati designed the **ponte Santa Trinità** over the Arno to replace a bridge that had collapsed in 1557. He also began the 300-year expansion of Palazzo Pitti. Meanwhile, Buontalenti extended Palazzo Vecchio to its present eastern limits and built the palaces for the Medici at Petraia (1587) and Pratolino (1568, later demolished).

THE FALL AND RISE OF MODERN FLORENCE

From 1600 to the death of the last Medici ruler in 1737, not much new building work was commissioned in Florence and, although many of the Renaissance palaces were enlarged and gardens added, the city fell into a state of decline. Garden design, however, did come to be seen as another form of art: at Palazzo Pitti, an extra 45,000 square metres (484,000 square feet) were added to the **Boboli Gardens** (*see p90*). Between 1865 and 1870, large parts of the city underwent significant redevelopment as Florence became the capital of the unified Kingdom of Italy. Giuseppe Poggi (1811-1901) had been named the principal town planner and architect by the Florentine

IN CONTEXT

authorities in 1864, and his ambitious redevelopment project included constructing wide boulevards to accommodate carriages, as well as several elegant *piazze*: **piazza Beccaria** and **piazza della Libertà** are superb examples of these new city-centre squares, both designed in the neoclassical and neo-Renaissance styles – and both unfortunately now submerged in daily traffic.

One of Poggi's most impressive projects was constructing **piazzale Michelangelo** (1875; *see p96*) on the south side of the river. This large open space offers an excellent view over Florence. He also enlarged a number of boulevards around the *piazzale*, which continued along the side of the hills facing Florence and the Forte di Belvedere, and then came back down again to the Porta Romana. The existence of this wonderful drive of roughly six kilometres, one of Italy's prettiest, is also due in great part to Poggi's vision.

As Poggi was busy creating beauty, town planners were busy changing the architectural face of Florence through wholesale destruction of its medieval centre around piazza della Repubblica; the central government in Rome demolished further stretches of the city, in Santa Maria Novella and Santa Croce, in the early 20th century. In 1944, only 50 years after the centre of Florence had been gutted, scores more irreplaceable ancient buildings were destroyed by the Germans, who blew up almost all the bridges over the Arno (only the ponte Vecchio was spared), along with all the buildings to the immediate north and south of the ponte Vecchio.

Today, as a result of these periods of destruction, you can walk all the way from the Duomo, down via Roma, across piazza Repubblica, through via Calimala and via Santa Maria, and all the way down the ponte Vecchio without passing more than two or three buildings that are more than a century old. And the newer buildings are, on the whole, banal at best and ugly at worst (*see p38* **Bland Ambition**).

There are a few notable 20th-century buildings in the city, however, including the 1932 **Stadio Artemio Franchi** (*see p198*) designed by Pier Luigi Nervi (1891-1979) and widely considered to be one of the most impressive contemporary structures in Florence; the **Palazzina Reale**, a reception building attached to the Santa Maria Novella station that was built for the Italian royal family but is now home to the University of Florence department of science; the **Instituto Aeronautica Militare** building in the Cascine Park; and the **Cinema Puccini** in piazza Puccini. Other interesting buildings include the 1936 **Santa Maria Novella station** (*see p71*) and the church of **San Giovanni Battista**, built with vision and sensitivity by Michelucci in 1960, at the crossing of the Autostrade del Sole and del Mare.

BEST FOOT FORWARD

Florence is currently undergoing some major structural renovations, undertaken by some of the world's foremost architects and engineering companies. Sir Norman Foster has designed the enormous underground terminal of the high-speed Milano–Roma train link, due to be completed in 2016. This huge complex will be topped with an arched glazed roof that will hark back to the railway stations of the 19th century. The planned extension to the **Museo dell'Opera del Duomo** (*see p58*), headed by architects Adolfo Natalini and Guicciardini & Magni, also due for completion in 2016, will double the size of the museum to 5,250 square metres (56,500 square feet), in part by expanding exhibition space into the adjacent Teatro degli Intrepidi (Teatro Nuovo), one of Florence's oldest theatres. But controversial designs for the new Uffizi exit by Japanese architect Arata Isozaki, given the green light in 2007, are still a long way from being realised, with the ultra-modern steel and stone *loggia* only partially built as we went to press. It's possible that thrusting mayor Matteo Renzi will help realise some of these projects in the next few years, but given that he has the Italian minister of culture Sandro Bondi publicly attacking projects such as Isozaki's, it remains to be seen whether Florence will ever again crest the wave of architectural innovation.

Food & Wine in Tuscany

Be seduced by fresh, local specialities and some of the best wine in Italy.

TEXT: ADRIAN SMITH

Each Italian region thinks their cuisine is the best in the country, but Tuscany would definitely be in the running for such an accolade – and that's before you begin to look at the traditional and Super Tuscan wines of Chianti. Meat forms a large part of the cuisine, with *cinta senese* pork, wild rabbit and boar featuring on most menus, but vegetarians will be in heaven too with fine preparations of fresh produce. Grab a fork and select a glass…

IN CONTEXT

Food

THE BASICS

The three main staples of the Tuscan diet are bread, olive oil and wine. Wines are famously substantial and the olive oil peppery, but bread is deliberately bland. Made without salt, it's a neutral canvas for accompanying food.

Tuscany claims to have Italy's best olive oil. Even within Tuscany, each region claims superiority, though the consensus is that the finest oil comes from groves located slightly inland, away from the varying temperatures and high moisture levels of the coast. While you're making your way round Tuscany, be sure to seek out oil from small producers, in particular extra virgin oils that have been cold pressed from estate-grown olives.

L'ANTIPASTO

Meals generally start with the *antipasto*: literally, 'before the meal'. In Tuscany the most common *antipasto* is *crostini*, often chicken liver pâté on toast. Cured meats are a speciality – usually pork and wild boar. *Prosciutto crudo* comes from a pig haunch buried under salt for three weeks, then swabbed with spicy vinegar, covered with black pepper and hung to dry for a further five months. *Capocollo* is a neck cut, cured the same way for three days, covered with pepper and fennel seed, rolled in yellow butcher's paper and then tied up with string. It's ready to eat a few months later. The most typical Tuscan salami is *finocchiona* (pork with fennel seeds and peppercorns). *Salamini di cinghiale*, or small wild boar salamis, include chilli pepper and a little fatty pork. Look out for *milza*, a pungent pâté made from spleen, herbs, spices and wine. *Antipasti* sometimes include *prosciutto* or *salame* from the distinctively striped and highly prized *cinta senese* pig.

IL PRIMO

The *primo* (first course) is carbohydrate-based. In most parts of Italy this is pasta or rice, but in Tuscany it's as likely to be a bread-based salad or soup. Old bread is never thrown away, but is mixed with Tuscan staples such as tomatoes, garlic, cabbage and *fagioli* (white beans). These form dishes such as *panzanella* (stale bread soaked in water, squeezed, mixed with raw onion, fresh tomato and basil and dressed with oil, salt and pepper), *ribollita* (rich bean and cabbage soup with bread, made using the local *cavolo nero* or black cabbage), *acqua cotta* (toasted bread rubbed with garlic and covered with crinkly dark green cabbage, then topped with olive oil, and covered with broth – sometimes with an egg broken into it), and *pappa al pomodoro* (an exquisite thick soup with onion, garlic, tomatoes, bread, basil and chilli pepper). The ultimate winter ritual is *bruschetta* or *fettunta* (toasted bread rubbed with garlic and soaked in freshly pressed olive oil).

Fresh pasta in Tuscany usually takes the form of *tagliatelle* (flat egg-based ribbons), *pappardelle* (wide flat ribbons), *ravioli* (parcels containing ricotta and spinach) and *tordelli* (from around Lucca, stuffed with chard, meat and ricotta). South you'll find *pici* (flour and water extruded into fattish strings) and, in the Mugello, *tortelli* (stuffed with a potato mixture).

IL SECONDO

Cacciagione (game), *salsicce* (sausages) and *bistecca* (beef steak) are the main regional meats, though there is good lamb about (look out for *agnellino nostrale*, meaning young, locally raised lamb). Also common are *coniglio* (rabbit, usually roasted, sometimes with pine nuts, sometimes rolled around a filling such as egg and bacon) and *pollo* (chicken; go for *ruspante*, free-range). During the winter you'll find plenty of slowly stewed and highly spiced *cinghiale* pork. Other common game includes *lepre* (hare) and *fagiano* (pheasant). The famous *bistecca fiorentina* is a vast T-bone steak, usually served very rare.

IL CONTORNO

To accompany your meat course, you're normally offered a side plate of vegetables or a salad. *Bietole* (Swiss chard) is available almost throughout the year. It's scalded in salted water and tossed in the pan with olive oil, garlic and chilli pepper. *Fagiolini* (green beans) are likely to be boiled and dressed with oil and lemon or vinegar. The sublime white Tuscan *fagioli* are served lukewarm with olive oil and a sprinkle of black pepper. *Patatine fritte* (French fries) are available almost everywhere, though boiled potatoes dressed with oil, pepper and capers are often much tastier. *Pomodori* (tomatoes) and *cipolle* (onions) sliced, spiced and baked *al forno* (in the oven) are recommended. In early summer, artichokes are eaten raw, stripped of their tough outer leaves and dipped into olive oil and salt.

IL FORMAGGIO

The one true Tuscan cheese is pecorino, made with ewe's milk. The sheep grazing on the hillsides are more often than not there for their milk rather than meat or wool. It can be eaten *fresco* (up to a month old), *semi-stagionato* (with about a month of ripening) or up to six months later, when the cheese is fully *stagionato*, and thus drier, sharper and tastier. Fresh ricotta, which is made from whey and thus not strictly speaking a cheese, is soft, mild and wet. It should be eaten with black pepper and a few drops of olive oil on top.

IL DOLCE

The Tuscans are only recently coming round to the way of desserts. Christmas classics such as *panforte* are now available year-round, but these days you'll find *tiramisù*, *torta della nonna* and basic fruit or jam tarts almost everywhere. The Tuscans like to conclude festive meals with a glass of a dry raisin wine called *vin santo*, into which they dunk *cantucci*, little dry biscuits packed with almonds. *Vin santo* is made with a special white grape variety that's dried out in bunches for a month and then

IN CONTEXT

crushed to obtain a sweet juice, which is aged for at least five years. You could get five bottles of wine from the grapes you need for one bottle of *vin santo*.

LA FRUTTA

Cherries, then apricots and peaches, are readily available in summer, grapes in late summer, and apples and pears in early autumn. Although citrus fruits imported from the south now take pride of place in the winter months, the main indigenous fruits are quinces (*mele cotogne*, excellent baked, stewed or jellied) and persimmons (*cachi*).

Wine

The renown of Tuscan winemaking has traditionally derived almost exclusively from one grape variety: the sangiovese. More recently other grape varieties, local and international, have begun to emerge as blends and varietals, with interesting results. On the red wine shelves, merlots, syrahs and cabernet sauvignons are as popular as ever, but there are now some fine wines being made with the local ciliegiolo and alicante varieties. Vermentino, meanwhile, is at last lifting a number of Tuscan whites above mediocrity (*see also below* **New Wave Whites**).

In terms of quality of recent wines, most of the wines produced in the last decade have been excellent, with 2005 to 2007 vintages being good ones to keep for at least another few years (though most 2006 vintages will probably be on their last legs by 2012), whereas 2008 bucked the trend with a vintage that was probably best drunk before now; 2009 saw a mixed picture (the cooler growing areas with good drainage such as Chianti Classico, Chianti Rufina and Valdarno producing the best vintages), with 2010 by contrast delivering a more reliable vintage, its acidity levels high enough to predict a good ageing process.

WHAT'S UP, DOC?

With the help of oeneologists (wine technicians), winemakers have grown more aware of what their own particular vineyards should produce. Such territorial specificity ensures *tipicità*: a distinct character pertaining to a given place.

To some extent, *tipicità* is defined by the various DOCs (Denominazione di Origine Controllata, which regulate wines from a specific, controlled area); the ultra-select category of DOCGs (Denominazione di Origine Controllata e Garantita); and IGTs (Indicazione Geografica Tipica – table wines from a well-defined area). Each sets out rules and regulations to which producers must adhere. Tuscany has ten DOCGs

---

New Wave Whites

Fancy a different type of tipple? It's all white now.

Think Tuscany and you normally think Chianti, Vino Nobile di Montepulciano, Brunello di Montalcino... a rich red swirling in the bottom of your glass, the perfect accompaniment to *bistecca fiorentina*. But there are now plenty of options if you're determined to try a Tuscan white. Late-ripening **vermentino** from Poggio al Tesoro in Bolgheri presents subtle floral perfumes, while Panizzi's **vernaccia di San Gimignano** stands out from its contemporaries as brighter, fresher and more aromatic. But our favourite is **L'Anima**, from Livernano in Chianti: based on chardonnay and sauvignon blanc, but also including viognier and gewürztraminer, it's one of the most interesting Tuscan whites from the new mould.

'The wine press came up with the name Super Tuscan – and the epithet stuck.'

and almost four times as many DOCs, of which the most famous are **Chianti Classico**, **Brunello di Montalcino** and **Vino Nobile di Montepulciano**.

This trio's reputation tends to overshadow some fine younger siblings: **Bolgheri Rosso** DOC, for example, made in the coastal area north of Grosseto; **Montescudaio** DOC, a little further south; and, yet further, the **Morellino di Scansano** DOC. A little further inland is the **Montecucco** DOC, while two other newer southern Tuscan DOCs are **Capalbio**, on the coast, and **Sovana**, between the southern slopes of Monte Amiata and the coast. Due east and slightly north of here is the fairly extensive and variegated area devoted to **Orcia** DOC, whose flagship in its early years has been Donatella Cinelli Colombini at the Fattoria del Colle, near Trequanda.

The well-established Tuscan whites are the **Vernaccia di San Gimignano** DOC and the **Bianco di Pitigliano** DOC. However, a number of the newer DOCs also embrace white wines, though so far not many can stand up to comparisons with the few Tuscan whites of excellence: **Batàr** pinot bianco, made by Agricola Querciabella at Greve in Chianti, and the **Cabreo La Pietra** chardonnay, made by Ruffino at Pontassieve. For more on Tuscany's white wines, *see left* **New Wave Whites**. Small, quality producers whose names you're likely to see in restaurants and bars include **Fontodi**, **Isole e Olena** and **Castello di Ama** (all from Chianti); **Poliziano** and **Avignionesi** (Montepulciano growers); **Casanova di Neri**, **Argiano**, **Cupano** and **Colle Mattoni** (from Montalcino).

BEST OF THE BUNCH

The development from the mid 1980s of the so-called Super Tuscans has been inspired, doing much to raise the reputation of Tuscany's wines. The idea behind them was to open up the way for wines that could satisfy changing tastes, especially abroad: at the time, Tuscan table wines were seen as poor, and the production of DOC wines was stultified by excessive strictures and regulations. The far-sighted few who felt there was room for wines that didn't conform to established Tuscan models began experimenting with the grape varieties that had contributed to the renown of French viticulture: cabernet, merlot, chardonnay and sauvignon.

Alongside these enterprising producers came a new generation of highly trained wine technicians, whose wines were beautifully made, highly priced and, for consumers abroad, initially somewhat perplexing. Why should an 'ordinary' wine cost more than certain DOCs? The British and American wine press decreed that reds such as **Tignanello** and **Solaia** made by Marchesi Antinori in Chianti deserved the epithet Super Tuscan, and the name stuck.

Similar enthusiasm greeted Nicolò Incisa della Rocchetta's **Sassicaia** and Lodovico Antinori's **Ornellaia**; both are made at Bolgheri near the northern Maremma coast, an area hitherto devoted entirely to sangiovese and trebbiano. Names to have joined the top ranks in recent years include **Tenuta di Trinoro**, **Siepi**, **Il Blu** and **Solengo**.

The new wines soon spread in range, reaching areas as distant from the original Chianti region as the western foothills of Monte Amiata and Montalcino. Several of the Super Tuscans have joined the IGT category, some have continued to call themselves *vini da tavola*, and others still have achieved a more specific geographical identity by associating with the newly created DOCs.

ONES TO WATCH

Tuscan wines are currently more varied and interesting than ever before, at least partly thanks to a generation of younger winemakers who are opening up new vistas

IN CONTEXT

'Enoteche *are happy to give you a "horizontal" tasting – no reference to your final posture.'*

by fine-tuning a particular feature within a given DOC. These youngsters, better educated and travelled than their fathers, are keen to experiment with new clones, grape varieties, vinification methods and ageing techniques.

At Bolgheri, Eugenio Campolmi's winery (**Le Macchiole**) has made a name for itself with Paleo, Messorio and Scrio, all excellent reds. At Suvereto Rita Tua's winery (called **Tua Rita**) produces Redigaffi and Giusto di Notri. Around Montalcino, the number of *contadini* ('peasant farmers', but the term has no negative connotations) who have become prestigious Brunello producers has grown: Giancarlo Pacenti at the winery that bears his father's name (Pelagrilli di Pacenti Siro), Paolo Bartolommei at Caprili, Vincenzo Abbruzzese at Val di Cava, Giacomo Neri at Casanova di Neri, and the Fattoi family and winery. Outsiders too are making their mark: foremost is Irish winemaker Sèan O'Callaghan at the **Riecine** winery, outside Gaiole in Chianti; others include Martin Frölich, a former lawyer from Germany, at the **Castagnoli** winery near Castellina in Chianti, and Frenchman Lionel Cousin, who in 2003 bottled his first Brunello at **Cupano**, a small organic winery near Montalcino.

GETTING STARTED

The wine map of Tuscany is far more varied than a visit to a UK or US wine shop would ever lead you to believe. It's so rich, in fact, that Tuscany is at the forefront of *il turismo enogastronomico*, whereby tourists devote part of their holiday to visiting wineries and sampling local foods: over 90 per cent of Italy's wine and food tourism focuses on Tuscany. Such tourism is seen as sustainable, as good for the visitor as it is for the local economy. To lure discerning palates to the lesser-known reaches of Tuscan viticulture, the **Movimento del Turismo del Vino** (www.movimentoturismovino.it) has helped set up offices in most of the wine-producing areas. These **Strade del Vino** organise tasting tours, visits to cellars, meals based on local produce and other events. Another notable event is **Cantine Aperte**, on the last weekend of May, when wineries all over the country open their doors (and bottles) to visitors.

Visiting wineries under your own steam can be both interesting and frustrating, so a little research goes a long way. For our picks of wineries open to the public, *see p261* **Fine Vines**, but well-run local *enoteche* will be in a position to advise, both providing tastings on their own premises and phoning their contacts in other selected wineries. These shops are usually run by *appassionati* who will happily provide you with a number of glasses for a 'vertical' tasting of different vintages of the same wine, or a 'horizontal' tasting (no reference to your final posture) of wines of the same variety and/or year by different producers. *Enoteche* also sell wine, by the bottle or the case.

DRINKING OUT

The **Strade del Vino di Toscana** organisation is gradually working with restaurateurs to improve the level of wine expertise of their staff. In an expensive gourmet restaurant you're bound to find a waiter who really knows about the listed wines, though this isn't the case in simpler eateries. Where suggestions are not forthcoming, you have a few choices. You could arm yourself with the annually updated English edition of the generally reliable *Italian Wines Guide*, published by Slow Food and Gambero Rosso, and pick something from the wine list. You could choose a bottle made by one of the old, established wine estates, or one of the more impressive new ones (*see p45*). Or you could do some research into the local DOC and opt for a medium-priced bottle – an approach that often leads the intrepid taster to a gratifying discovery.

Sights

Campanile. *See p54.*

Touring Florence

The fine art of planning ahead.

Every part of Florence, from the top of Brunelleschi's stunning dome to the waters of the Arno, is packed with works of great finesse. Aesthetic pleasures are everywhere – Botticelli's *Birth of Venus* and Michelangelo's *David*, the incomparable Baptistery doors and the gold shops lining the ponte Vecchio – and if you've chosen to visit the city, there's a high chance you're a lover of the more refined things in life. While there's a lot to be said for just wandering the streets and soaking up the atmosphere – taking in gorgeous, art-studded churches, fascinating museums and *gelaterie* as you find them – for a truly enjoyable experience it pays to be organised.

Florence's virtually unrivalled wealth of artistic highlights – this small 'Renaissance City' has more works per square metre than anywhere else on the planet – attracts something like seven million visitors annually. If you have an itinerary planned, already know which sights need pre-booking, and quickly gain a basic knowledge of the city centre, you're a step ahead of the rest.

SIGHTS

ORIENTATION AND GEOGRAPHY

With a historic centre roughly a fifth the size of Rome's, Florence is easily navigable. Most major sights are in walking distance of any other central point and, with the dome of the Duomo and the River Arno's four central bridges as reference points, it's practically impossible to get lost. The majority of the main sights cluster north of the two central bridges (ponte Vecchio and ponte Santa Trinità), around the Duomo. Most other important sites are in the areas around this rectangle: Santa Maria Novella, San Lorenzo, San Marco, Santa Croce and Oltrarno. We use these neighbourhood designations throughout the guide, with the rest of the city's attractions in the chapter Outside the City Gates.

The main central area of Florence sits in the river valley and so is virtually flat, but the surrounding hills rise steeply on both sides, creating challenging walks and rewarding views that are easily accessible on foot or by bus. For a self-guided walk within the Boboli Gardens, *see p90* **Up the Garden Path**; for a literary and filmic walk, *see p80* **Walk Fictional Florence**.

MUSEUMS AND GALLERIES

During the summer, around Easter and on public holidays, Florence spills over with visitors: the sights are crowded and huge queues can form at the main museums. The best times to visit are from January to March (avoiding Easter), and from October to mid December.

Many of Florence's unrivalled museums have private collections at their core, whether that of a mega-family such as the Medici (Uffizi, Palazzo Pitti) or of a lone connoisseur (the Bardini, **Horne** and **Stibbert** museums). Other major museums were founded to preserve treasures too precious to expose to the elements (the Accademia, Bargello and **Museo dell'Opera del Duomo**). The main city-run museums are the **Cappella Brancacci**, **Cenacolo di Santo Spirito**, **Museo di Firenze com'era**, **Palazzo Vecchio** and **Museo Bardini**.

INSIDE TRACK
PASSPORT TO THE PAST

During 2012, you can take a self-guided Risorgimento tour courtesy of Palazzo Strozzi (*see p68*). You pick up a map and passport detailing the city's key Risorgimento locations; get your passport stamped at five of them to gain free entry to one of Florence's museums.

For general information on the state museums and for booking, call Firenze Musei on 055 294883. The state museums are the Pitti museums, Uffizi, Accademia, **Bargello**, **Museo di San Marco**, **Opificio delle Pietre Dure**, **Cappelle Medicee** and **Museo Archeologico**.

Firenze Musei strongly recommends booking for the **Uffizi** and the **Accademia**, as well as, at busy times of year, the **Pitti** museums; this could save you a two-hour wait. At more popular times of the year there are long waits (weeks, even months) for slots on pre-booked Uffizi tickets, so reserve as soon as you can. Booking costs €3 and tickets are collected from a window beside the normal ticket office or, at Palazzo Pitti, an office in the right-hand wing before you reach the main entrance. Pay when you pick up the tickets. Don't expect to be able to book tickets there directly: you will be told to phone the central number. Last issuing times for tickets vary (we give closing times, not last admission, in our listings), but try to get to the ticket office an hour before the museum closes. Alternatively, for €50 a **Firenze card** (www.firenzecard.it) gives instant access to 33 museums, including all the key ones, and free public transport for 72 hours from activation.

Art lovers should be aware that works of art are often loaned to other museums, and restoration can be carried out with little or no notice, so it's always wise to call first if you want to view a specific piece.

Temporary exhibitions are regularly held at a few locations in Florence, among them the **Palazzo Vecchio**, **Palazzo Medici Riccardi**, **Fortezza da Basso** and **Palazzo Strozzi**. For details, see *Firenze Spettacolo* magazine, *The Florentine*, *Florence & Tuscany News* (for both, see *p310*) or local newspapers.

THEY DON'T LIKE MONDAYS

For non-Italians it can be a shock to find out that some of Florence's major museums close on Monday. These include the Uffizi, Accademia and Galleria Palatina in the Palazzo Pitti. If it's the first, third or fifth Monday of the month, you could go to the Bargello or Museo di San Marco; on the second or fourth, try the Cappelle Medicee or certain Palazzo Pitti museums.

TOURIST INFORMATION

Apart from the tourist offices (*see p315*), the city police have information points in piazza della Repubblica, on via de' Calzaiuoli and borgo San Lorenzo, and at the southern end of the ponte Vecchio, from which they give directions and basic information about the main sights in various languages. Many of the city's minor sights – churches, *palazzi*, monuments – also have signs posted beside them detailing their history and distinguishing features, making a

---

INSIDE TRACK
SOCIABLE CLIMBERS

Given the large-scale pedestrianisation of Florence (*see p29*), the best way to see the city is on foot, but if you want a cheap bus tour accompanied by Florentine commuters, routes 12 and 13 make hour-long circuits, wheezing up to San Miniato for glorious views.

DIY tour that much easier. In addition, you'll see big plaques with useful maps in many squares and other strategic positions.

GUIDED TOURS

All Florence's tour companies offer a range of itineraries, with English-language options, covering the main monuments and museums on foot or by bus. The highly reputable **AGT Firenze – Florence Associated Tourist Guides** (055 2654753, www.florencetourist guides.com), **Florence Guides** (055 4220901, www.florenceguides.it) and **ACG Florence & Tuscany** (055 7877744, www.firenze-guide.com) have a big selection of standard tours. **Walking Tours of Florence** (055 2645033, mobile 329 6132730, www.italy.artviva.com; *see also p306*) and **CAF** (06 97625204, www.caftours. com) offer more unusual options. There are also interesting tours with **Florencetown** (055 0123994, www.florencetown.com), which specialises in American tourism, and **Accord Solutions** (055 282825, www.accordsolutions. it), the latter ranging from guided walking tours to rafting on the Arno. If you're after the personal touch and something that goes beyond Brunelleschi, **Context Florence** (06 97625204, www.contextflorence.com) uses expert scholars rather than tour guides, and limits groups to six. Given fiendishly complex traffic restrictions, buses can be a complicated way of navigating the city, but **Tuscany Bike Tours** (055 3860253, www.tuscany-bike tours.com) provides leisurely and more energetic explorations of Florence.

If you prefer to do it yourself, the best ways to see the city are by hiring a bike or moped (*see p306*), or taking the **busini** – electric buses that cover the centre of the city. Another bus option is an official tour: **City Sightseeing Firenze** (piazza Stazione 1, 055 290451, www. firenze.city-sightseeing.it, 9.30am-6pm daily; €15/1 day, €22/2 days; €7.50/1 day, €11/2 days reductions; no credit cards for tickets bought on board) runs two lines: Line A takes an hour, departing from Santa Maria Novella train station; Line B departs from Porta San Frediano and takes two hours.

SIGHTS

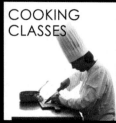

Duomo & Around

Dome is where the art is.

A creative confluence of business, religion and civic duty, the centre of Florence showcases the various forces at work on the city at its most crucial moments in history. This area takes in both the religious heartland around the magnificent cathedral, and the former administrative hub surrounding Palazzo Vecchio. Stretching from the streets just north of the Duomo to the ponte Vecchio, the district corresponds almost exactly to the city walls of the ninth century, now bordered on the east by via del Proconsolo, which follows the line of the even more ancient Roman walls (still visible on the corner of this street and via Dante Alighieri), and on the

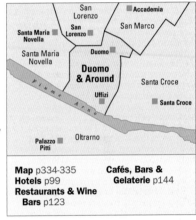

Map p334-335	Cafés, Bars &
Hotels p99	Gelaterie p144
Restaurants & Wine	
Bars p123	

west by via de' Tornabuoni, well known for its designer shops. As the original nucleus of Florence, it's the ideal place to start your explorations.

AROUND PIAZZA DEL DUOMO

The trio of stunning religious buildings at the heart of piazza del Duomo form an obvious landmark: the spacing and uniformity of their surroundings were carefully dictated in order to preserve their dignity. The glorious **Duomo** (*see p52*) is one of the most recognisable landmarks in Europe, but never fails to astound: nestled in the piazza at the heart of Florence's historic centre, the cathedral is so enormous that there's no spot nearby from which you can see the whole thing, though a walk through the surrounding streets will be punctuated by glimpses of its red-tiled dome.

In piazza del Duomo, visitors in awe of the cathedral's magnitude gape up at the patterned marble, delicate carvings and the mammoth dome, even more impressive seen in the close proximity forced by the narrowness of the road on its northern flank. The areas outside the entrance and around the south of the Duomo are pedestrianised, while mopeds and buses roar around the north and east sides. Inside the cathedral is the **Crypt of Santa Reparata** (*see p54*), the original church built on this site in the fifth century, while on the south side of the Duomo is the entrance to the dome itself, the

spectacular **Cupola** (*see p54*). The **Campanile** (*see p54*), Giotto's elegant bell tower, is also south of the Duomo, level with its façade.

In piazza San Giovanni (named after John the Baptist), the octagonal **Baptistery** (*see p58*) faces the main doors of the Duomo. This large square, always thronged with tourists, also houses the tiny **Museo di Bigallo** (*see p59*). South from the façade of the Duomo is via de' Calzaiuoli, a heaving, pedestrianised shopping street flanked by self-service restaurants, shops and *gelaterie*, while to the west of the Baptistery is via de' Cerretani, a busy shopping street and traffic thoroughfare that's home to **Santa Maria Maggiore**, an 11th-century church. Following the curve of the piazza on the north side of the Duomo, the **Museo dell'Opera del Duomo** (*see p58*), which houses many of the Duomo's treasures, is on the north-east of the square.

Near the Museo dell'Opera del Duomo is a round marble slab embedded in the pavement with no inscription to identify it. It marks the exact spot where the gilt copper ball and cross (made by Verrocchio in 1469 and containing holy relics) fell from the top of the Duomo's lantern after being struck by lightning on 17 July 1600. (It was replaced by an even larger bronze ball two years later.) Slightly further around the piazza in a clockwise direction, at the base of a flat column belonging to 54 piazza del Duomo, a plaque indicates the 'Sasso di Dante' (Dante's Stone). Now a shopfront, this is where the poet was said to sit in summer.

Situated on the same side of the piazza are Luigi Pampaloni's huge 19th-century sculptures of Filippo Brunelleschi, the creator of the great dome, and Arnolfo di Cambio, the first architect of the cathedral. Each artist is shown holding their plans and tools, and looking directly at the parts of the Duomo they worked on.

Running down from the south-west corner of the Baptistery is the more upmarket via Roma, which opens into the pompous **piazza della Repubblica**. This ungainly square was built in 1882, when the so-called Mercato Vecchio ('old market', part of the Jewish ghetto) was demolished and rebuilt in a massive clean-up after a cholera outbreak. The only remnant from before that time is the huge **Colonna dell'Abbondanza**, a column that used to mark the spot where two principal Roman roads crossed, and which was reinstated to its original position after World War II.

Vasari's delightful **Loggia del Pesce**, with its ceramic marine creature *tondi*, was once the central meeting place of the square, but has been moved to piazza de' Ciompi in Santa Croce (*see p83*). In the medieval period, the area covered by the whole of piazza della Repubblica

was given over to a huge market where you could change money, buy a hawk or falcon, pay over the odds for a quack remedy, or pick up a prostitute (distinguished by the bells on their hats and gloves). Further back, the ancient Roman Forum once occupied a quarter of the piazza, with the Campidoglio and Temple of Jupiter covering the rest. The sun-trap square is now flanked by pavement cafés, and dominated at night by street artists and strollers.

★ Duomo (Santa Maria del Fiore)

055 2302885, *www.operaduomo.firenze.it*. **Open** 10am-5pm Mon-Wed, Fri; 10am-4pm Thur; 10am-4.45pm Sat (10am-3.30pm 1st Sat of mth); 1.30-4.45pm Sun. **Admission** free. **Map** p335 B4.
Florence's most important religious building is a truly awe-inspiring sight. The result of work spanning more than six centuries, the Duomo not only dominates the skyline but also represents the geographical, cultural and historical centre of the city. A hugely successful and expanding wool industry gave the Florentine population such a boost in the 13th century that several new churches had to be built: Santa Croce (*see p86*) and Santa Maria Novella (*see p71*) were among them, but the most important was Santa Maria del Fiore, or the Duomo, which replaced the small church of Santa Reparata (*see p54*). The project marked the first time that a guild of laymen had been entrusted with financing the city's development – traditionally, this responsibility had fallen to

---

Finding Your Niche

Shrines worth your time.

The Italian tradition of creating shrines to the Madonna, Jesus or the saints on street corners is particularly strong in Florence.

This high concentration of conventicles is partly due to the early 14th-century episodes of armed conflict in the city between the orthodox followers of the Church and the so-called 'Patarine heretics', a Ghibelline-supported reform movement advocating action against corruption in the clergy, named after the street in Milan from where their most active members hailed.

To prove their devotion (and avoid the nasty repercussions of being branded heretics), many individuals, trades, confraternities and guilds built tabernacles in conspicuous positions, often on the corner of their home. The tabernacle was usually built as an *edicola*, a frame for an icon, normally of stone. It often came with a 'roof' to protect the artwork, and a mantle on which to place offerings. The icon itself could be a fresco, painting,

relief, tile or sculpture; sometimes famous artists were hired to create the venerable image and boost the cachet of the sponsor in the eyes of the Church. The result is an art heritage of sometimes astonishing value. The shrines listed below are among the most noteworthy:

Via Arte della Lana *corner with via di Orsanmichele*. **Map** p334 C3.
Via Ricasoli *corner with via de' Pucci*. **Map** p335 A4.
Via de' Tornabuoni *corner with via della Vigna Nuova*. **Map** p334 B2.

In other parts of Florence, look out for:

Piazza dell'Unità Italiana *corner with via Sant'Antonio, San Lorenzo*. **Map** p334 A2.
Via degli Alfani *corner with borgo Pinti, Santa Croce*. **Map** p335 B5.
Via della Spada *near San Pancrazio, Santa Maria Novella*. **Map** p334 B2.

Duomo

monks and priests. It thus marks the point at which religious architecture became a civic duty.

The building was commissioned by the Florentine Republic as an opportunity to show this was the most important Tuscan city. The competition to find an architect was won by Arnolfo di Cambio, a sculptor from Pisa, who had trained with Nicola Pisano. The first stones were duly laid on 8 September 1296 around the exterior of Santa Reparata. Building continued for the next 170 years – despite the attack of bubonic plague in 1348 that killed half the population of Florence – with guidance and revision from three further architects, though the church was consecrated 30 years before its completion in 1436 (at which time it was the largest cathedral in Europe).

The rich exterior, in white Carrara, green Prato and red Maremma marbles, reflects the variety of time periods that work on the building covered, with a huge variation in the styles of the inlaid patterns. The visionary Francesco Talenti had sufficient confidence to enlarge the cathedral and prepare the building for Brunelleschi's inspired dome, which wasn't completed until 1436 – 140 years after construction first started on the cathedral.

Remarkably, when this dome was conceived (at the time, the highest ever built), Brunelleschi – the man who would work out how to pull off the feat – hadn't even been born. The last significant change came in the 19th century, when Emilio de Fabris designed a neo-Gothic façade (*see p56* **Profile**). After Emilio's death, Luigi del Moro was left to crown the façade.

After the splendid exterior, the interior looks somewhat dull, though decorating one of the world's largest cathedrals was never going to be easy. It is full of fascinating peculiarities, however: notably, the clock on the Paolo Uccello inner façade, which marks 24 hours, operates anti-clockwise and starts its days at sunset (it's between four and six hours fast). The clock is surrounded by the so-called Heads of the Prophets, peering out from four roundels and showing the distinct influences of Ghiberti and Donatello.

Also by Uccello is a monument to Sir John Hawkwood, painted in 1436 as a tribute to the English soldier who led Florentine troops to victory in the Battle of Cascina of 1364. The fresco has given rise to debate about whether its perspective and the movement of the horse's right legs are wrong, or an original treatment of perspective construction, learned from Masaccio and considered by some to be visionary – even a forerunner to Cubism. Beyond Andrea del Castagno's 1456 monument to Niccolò da Tolentino, illustrating the heroic characteristics of a Renaissance man, is Domenico di Michelino's *Dante Explaining the Divine Comedy*, featuring the pink-clad poet and the new Duomo vying for prominence with the Mountain of Purgatory.

A couple of strides put you directly underneath the dome, the size of which is even more breathtaking inside than out. The lantern in the centre is 90m (295ft) above you and the diameter of the inner dome is 43m (141ft) across, housing within it one of the largest frescoed surfaces in the world. Brunelleschi had intended for the inner cupola to be mosaic, to mirror the Baptistery ceiling. However, interior work only began some 125 years after his death in 1572, when Cosimo de' Medici commissioned Giorgio Vasari to carry out the work; together with Don Vincenzo Borghini, who chose the iconographic subjects, they decided to fresco the surface instead.

The concentric rows of images were started by Vasari, whose subtle treatment of colour and form drew inspiration from Michelangelo's Sistine Chapel, but he died two years later, before completing the project. Vasari was succeeded by Federico Zuccari, who worked for a further five years until its completion. Zuccari had a much more flamboyant (and cruder) dry-painting style, believing that the distance from which the visitor would view the cupola wasted the delicacy of Vasari's wet fresco technique, especially as featured faces included some of the best-known personalities of the time. Zuccari's most crucial contribution to the cycle is the rendering of

SIGHTS

Campanile.

Dante's vision of Hell, which was inspired by Signorelli's frescoes in Orvieto Cathedral.

Crypt of Santa Reparata
Open 10am-5pm Mon-Wed, Fri; 10am-3.30pm Thur; 10am-4.45pm Sat (10am-3.30pm 1st Sat of mth); 1.30-4.45pm Sun. **Admission** €3.
No credit cards. **Map** p335 B4.

By the 13th century, Santa Reparata had served as the city's main church for some 900 years and desperately needed to be replaced, especially as, after a period of rapid population expansion, it had become too small to serve the needs of the community. It was decided in 1293 that a new cathedral would be built over the top of the original church (the original date of which is unknown, but between the fifth and seventh centuries). The entrance to this is inside the Duomo itself. The intricate mosaic floor of the church was built only 30cm above the Roman remains of houses and shops, some of which are on display in the crypt. Also here is the tomb of Brunelleschi, although no trace has been found of those of Arnolfo di Cambio and Giotto, both also supposedly buried here. Local legend has it that some of the land needed for the

building of the much bigger Duomo was occupied by the Florentine Bischeri family, who, when they continued to refuse the ever-bigger sums of money they were offered to relocate, were unceremoniously kicked out of their *palazzo* without compensation. This led to the Florentine term *bischero* (a gullible fool).

Excavations of the building between the mid 1960s and 1970s unearthed the original crypt and medieval ruins, which are now on view for visitors.

Cupola/Dome
Open 8.30am-6.20pm Mon-Fri; 8.30am-5pm Sat (8.30am-3.20pm 1st Sat of mth). **Admission** €8.
No credit cards. **Map** p335 B4.

The cathedral's spectacular 37,000-tonne dome (it uses more than four million bricks) is, as Alberti put it, 'a structure so immense, rising above the skies [that it is] broad enough to cover with its shadow all the peoples of Tuscany'. The dome isn't just visually stunning: as the first octagonal dome built without a wooden supporting frame, it is also an incredible feat of engineering. Brunelleschi had dreamed of completing the cupola ever since his childhood. He won the commission with the more experienced Lorenzo Ghiberti, riding on the back of his success with the Baptistery doors, but soon found that while he was doing the crucial work, Ghiberti was taking all the glory. So Brunelleschi pulled a sickie, halting the work, and got the recognition he deserved.

Brunelleschi first considered designing a classic semi-spherical dome like those in existing churches around Italy, but the sheer size of the structure precluded the traditional method of laying tree trunks across the diameter in order to build around them. In the end he made the dome support itself by building two shells, one on top of the other, and by laying the bricks in herringbone-pattern rings to integrate successive layers that could support themselves. The design risked becoming a victim of its own success: the ribs around the dome were in danger of 'springing' open at the top, so a heavier lantern than normal was designed to hold them in place.

Just as innovative as the design were the tools used and the organisation of the work. Brunelleschi devised pulley systems to winch materials and workers up to the dome. Between the two shells of the dome, he installed a canteen so the workforce wouldn't waste time going to ground level to eat, bringing construction time down to a mere 16 years (1420-36). A separate side entrance gives access to the top of the dome (463 steps, about 20mins up and down) with fantastic views, though the climb is not for the faint-hearted or those with limited mobility.

Campanile
055 2302885. **Open** 8.30am-6.50pm daily.
Admission €6. **No credit cards**. **Map** p335 B4.

The cathedral's three-floor, 414-step bell tower was designed by Giotto in 1334, though his plans weren't followed faithfully (the original drawing is in Siena's Museo dell'Opera del Duomo; *see p253*). Andrea

Hidden Depths

A wiped-out Leonardo is causing controversy centuries after its creation.

It is a widespread misconception that all of Florence's Renaissance masterpieces are the fruit of enlightened Medici patronage. In fact, the city's most representative individual work, Michelangelo's *David*, was commissioned by the Republic of Florence in 1501 as an anti-tyranny icon, at a time (1494-1512) when the Medici dynasty had been temporarily overthrown and exiled after the death of Lorenzo il Magnifico.

A couple of years later, the same patron, and the same theme, were behind a project that might have proved the zenith of Renaissance art: two mural paintings for the Council Hall (now Salone dei Cinquecento) in Palazzo Vecchio (*see p64*). The plan would have had Leonardo da Vinci and Michelangelo Buonarroti working back to back in the great hall, each busy on a battle scene: the Battle of Anghiari for Leonardo, the Battle of Cascina for Michelangelo. Given the fierce mutual dislike of the two prima donnas, there is little doubt that they would have gone out of their way to outdo each other.

Regrettably, Michelangelo's progress stopped at the preparatory cartoon stage when he was summoned to Rome in 1505 to create the tomb for Pope Julius II. Yet Leonardo – who had about a year's head start with the commission – began his mural in summer 1505 and worked on it for several months, probably completing 15 to 20 square metres (160 to 200 square feet) of the centrepiece, *The Fight for the Standard*. However, parts of the experimental oil-based paint dripped, and the painting was left unaccomplished when da Vinci relocated to Milan in 1506.

In 1563, the reinstated Medici asked Giorgio Vasari to remodel the hall, wipe out anything celebrating the Republic – including, we must assume, Leonardo's work. Alas, Vasari complied, and we are left with just a few drawings and copies, showing how powerfully the two titans had tackled their given topics.

Or maybe not. Maurizio Seracini, a biomedical engineer who for several decades has been repurposing non-invasive medical and military technology for art diagnostics, believes Vasari was too fine a connoisseur to destroy a masterpiece. After all, he saved at least one other masterwork by screening it with a wall during

Michelangelo's **David**.

renovations: Masaccio's ground-breaking fresco of the Holy Trinity in the left nave of Santa Maria Novella (*see p71*) was covered with a modern altar, and only accidentally rediscovered in the 19th century.

The only real-life contemporary character mentioned in *the Da Vinci Code*, Seracini has been looking for evidence of the survival of Leonardo's mural since 1975, when he first noticed that a green flag in Vasari's *Battle of Marciano* bore two tiny words in white paint: *Cerca trova* ('Seek, and Thou Shall Find'). Examination confirmed the words were of the same age as the rest of the painting; could they be a clue? Almost 30 years later, pulse laser beams and a thermo-scanner detected a 2.5-centimetre gap behind Vasari's *Cerca trova* mural. Maybe he built his new wall a small distance from the original in this particular spot to protect Leonardo's work?

At an astrophysics congress, Professor Raymond DuVarney suggested that neutron-activation analysis might reveal traces of chemicals in the hidden paint – if they exist – by measuring the gamma rays emitted by chemical compounds used to make 16th-century paint. A device was built, but Seracini estimates that €2 million are needed to complete the search, which is conducted in waves when funds are available.

Even if Seracini's theory proves correct, Leonardo's experimental technique might not have lasted as well as Masaccio's fresco in Santa Maria Novella. And what would Florence's art guardians do if faced with one masterpiece hidden by another?

The Duomo

How to read the extraordinary details of an extraordinary building.

THE SCULPTURES AND RELIEFS ON THE FAÇADE

This façade was added to the Duomo between 1871 and 1887. Dedicated to the Virgin Mary, it is distinctly patriotic. Over the middle door is a relief of Mary holding a flowered sceptre – a symbol of royalty and deity. According to 15th-century religious documents, the flowered sceptre symbolises Christ, who grew on the stalk (Mary) that flourished from the root (the House of David). On this relief, Mary is flanked by John the Baptist, who had become the patron saint of Florence after the city had converted to Christianity.

Above this level, between the tympanum and the ornate rose window, is a gallery of niches containing busts of Florentine artists, Humanists and rich merchants. Primarily a way for these important personalities to pay their respects to the Virgin, an appearance on the façade was also a vital status symbol, ensuring they would be remembered and venerated for their generosity and charity. Above them, the 12 Apostles are represented.

THE DOME

Containing four million bricks and weighing 37,000 tonnes, Brunelleschi's dome is a feat of Renaissance engineering – its octagonal design with a double wall was unprecedented. The dome was built without the support of any scaffolding – which naturally worried the Florentine authorities – and during construction Brunelleschi installed a canteen to cut workers' travel time up and down (as well as regulating the wine they consumed).

The dome is topped by a lantern with a gilt copper ball and a cross containing holy relics. These were hoisted up using machinery designed by Leonardo da Vinci. The original copper ball was hit by lightning in 1600 and replaced.

THE BRONZE DOORS

The Duomo's doors (1899-1903) are decorated with scenes from the life of the Virgin. Though these sober and slightly lifeless bronze doors are no match for Ghiberti's stunning Gates of Paradise, their figures are beautiful and sinuous, exuding an air of translucency. Each door is complemented by a mosaic lunette, by Barbarino. These represent (right to left): local artists, merchants and Humanists honouring Christ; Christ with Mary and John the Baptist; and Charity among the Florentine noblemen who had established the city's charitable foundations. Florentine civic duty thus became inextricably linked with the construction of the cathedral.

THE CAMPANILE STATUES

Between 1334 and 1435, 16 statues of
Old Testament prophets were placed in
niches above the lozenges. The statues were
to be viewed from afar, so their depictions
and attributes were dramatic and deliberately
ugly. The postures and stern expressions
of the prophets mirror the fiery messages
God had given them to relate on earth.

Arguably the most impressive is the so-
called *Zuccone*, by Donatello, who stands
drawing in his chin, implicitly condemning
human inadequacy. Zuccone (actually called
Habakkuk) lived in the seventh century BC
and is best known for providing Daniel
with food in the lion's den. *Jeremiah*,
also by Donatello, is equally frightening,
symbolising the continued conflict between
morality and sin.

THE CAMPANILE'S SECOND-STOREY LOZENGES

The second storey of the Campanile
is decorated with a series of lozenges
(rhombus-shaped panels) containing
allegorical images relating to the liberal
arts and theology. These images thematically
support the sculptural reliefs on the
storey below.

The images decorating
the southern side are
particularly impressive –
marble figures on blue
ceramic backgrounds
that represent the virtues.
Look out for the planets,
the moon and the sun
on the west side.

The Seven Sacraments, as
decreed by the Church, are illustrated on
the north side. Although these are presented
realistically rather than allegorically, they
symbolise the journey every faithful Florentine
must go on to achieve divine life and
forgiveness of sin.

Illustration by Simon Foster

THE RELIEFS ON THE BASE OF THE CAMPANILE

On this level is a series of hexagonal panels
designed by the Pisano studio, depicting the
history of mankind. This history begins with
the creation of man, with Noah portrayed on
the west side as the first farmer. The south
side is dedicated to the arts and sciences,
with panels on medicine, hunting, legislation
and wool-making. The west side details the
liberal arts, the north side the creative arts.
These figurative narratives are located on the
Campanile's base in order to illustrate to the
Florentine public the disciplines necessary
for an efficient, peaceful and happy society.

SIGHTS

Pisano, who continued the work three years after Giotto's death, took the precaution of doubling the thickness of the walls, while Francesco Talenti, who saw the building to completion in 1359, inserted the large windows high up the tower. Inlaid, like the Duomo, with pretty pink, white and green marble, the Campanile is decorated with 16 sculptures of prophets, patriarchs and pagans (the originals are in Florence's Museo dell'Opera del Duomo; *see below*), and bas-reliefs designed by Giotto and artfully executed by Pisano that recount the *Creation and Fall of Man* and *Redemption through Industry*; you can make out Eve emerging from Adam's side and a drunken Noah. The steps to the top are steep and narrow, but great views await. *Photos p54.*

Baptistery
Open *Mid Sept-May* 12.15-6.30pm Mon-Sat; 8.30am-1pm Sun. *June-mid Sept* 12.15-10.30pm Mon-Sat; 8.30am-1pm Sun. **Admission** €4. **No credit cards. Map** p334 B3.
The pan-European overhaul of intellectual endeavour we now call the Renaissance started on this spot when, in the winter of 1400, the Calimala guild of cloth importers held a competition to find an artist to create a pair of bronze doors for the north entrance. Judging works by seven artists, Brunelleschi among them (you can compare two of the finalists' entries in the Bargello; *see p84*), they gave the commission to the 20-year-old Ghiberti; Brunelleschi later got revenge with superior work on the cupola, but never sculpted again. The 28 relief panels on the three-tonne, 6m-high (20ft) doors tell the story of Christ from the Annunciation to the Crucifixion; the eight lower panels show the four evangelists and four doctors of the Church. The deep pictorial space and emphasis on figures have led many scholars to consider these doors to be the very first signs of Renaissance art.
No sooner had the north doors been installed than the Calimala commissioned Ghiberti to make another pair: the even more remarkable east doors – described by Vasari as 'undeniably perfect in every way'. These took the artist and his workshop (including Michelozzo and Benozzo Gozzoli) 27 years to complete. They're known, since Michelangelo coined the phrase, as the 'Gates of Paradise' (although 'paradise' is, in fact, what the area between a baptistery and its church is called). The doors you see are copies (the originals are in the Museo dell'Opera del Duomo; *see below*), but the casts are good enough that it's not difficult to appreciate Ghiberti's amazing work, especially his fine use of the recently discovered principles of perspective.
The very first set of Baptistery doors were those on the south side, completed by Andrea Pisano in 1336, after only six years of work. Their 28 Gothic quatrefoil-framed panels show stories from the life of St John the Baptist and the eight theological and cardinal virtues. The Latin inscription on top of the door translates as 'Andrea Pisano made me in 1330'.

SIGHT SPOT ARCHITECT AND BIOGRAPHER, NOT ARTIST

Giorgio Vasari's prowess as a painter and sculptor pales into insignificance compared to his achievements as architect of the **Uffizi** (*see p64*) and **Corridoio Vasariano** (*see p61*), and his fame as the most important chronicler of artists' lives. He studied Mannerism in Florence, hopeful of surpassing his idol Michelangelo but failing miserably. Still, his major architectural projects for Cosimo are testament to his skill, as is his redecoration of the Salone dei Cinquecento in **Palazzo Vecchio** (*see p64*).

For centuries, the likes of Brunelleschi and Alberti believed the Baptistery was converted from a Roman temple dedicated to Mars. Other scholars reckoned that the Roman site on which the octagonal church was built was the Praetorium, while others thought its origins were as a bakery. In fact, the Baptistery of St John the Baptist, patron saint of Florence, was built to an octagonal design between 1059 and 1128 as a remodelling of a sixth- or seventh-century version. In between, it functioned for a period as the cathedral for Florence (then Florentia) in place of Santa Reparata, the church on whose site the Duomo now stands (*see p52*). The octagon reappears in the shape of the cathedral dome, but also on the buttresses of the Campanile, which constitute its corners. It's also the shape of the remains of the original font where children, including many of the Medici family and Dante, were brought for a double baptism: as both Christian and Florentine. The font you can see near the exit was installed in 1658, and its relief decorations are attributed to Andrea Pisano or his school.
Today, the striped octagon is best known for its doors, but the interior is even more worth visiting for the dazzling *Last Judgement* mosaic that lines the vault ceiling: an 8m-high (26ft) mosaic figure of *Christ in Judgement* dominates the apse (1225), and the mosaics of Hell are thought to have inspired Dante's *Inferno*. The geometrically patterned marble mosaic floor showing oriental zodiac motifs was begun in 1209, around the same time as the western side of the Baptistery was enlarged. Squeezed between two columns, the tomb of Antipope John XXIII (Baldassare Coscia) was designed by Donatello and his student Michelozzo in the 1420s.

Museo dell'Opera del Duomo
Piazza del Duomo 9 (055 2302885, www.opera duomo.firenze.it). **Open** 9am-7.30pm Mon-Sat; 9am-1.40pm Sun. **Admission** €6. **No credit cards. Map** p335 B4.
Built on the site of the 15th-century cathedral workshop, where Michelangelo carved his famous *David*,

SIGHTS

the Museum of the Cathedral Works still contains the tools and machinery used to build the Duomo, the original wooden models of the cathedral and its cupola in various stages of development, as well as sculptures and artwork from the Duomo complex deemed too precious and vulnerable to be left to the mercy of the elements. It is one of the city's most interesting museums, though the explanatory panels can sometimes make for hard reading.

In the first rooms are Gothic sculptures from the exteriors of the Baptistery and the original but never-finished Duomo façade, including a classical *Madonna* with unsettling glass eyes by Arnolfo di Cambio, the cathedral's first architect. There are also pieces from Santa Reparata and a collection of relics. Halfway up the stairs, the *Pietà Bandini* is a heart-rending late Michelangelo that shows Christ slithering from the grasp of Nicodemus. The sculpture was intended as Michelangelo's tombstone; he sculpted his own features on the face of Nicodemus, showing how his obsession with the story had become too much to bear. In true tortured-artist style, frustrated with the piece, he smashed Christ's left arm.

The originals of Donatello's *Prophets* from the exterior of the Campanile are upstairs in the main chamber, notably *Habakkuk* (affectionately called *Lo Zuccone* by Florentines, meaning 'marrow head'), a work of such realism that Donatello himself is said to have gripped it and screamed, 'Speak, damn you, speak!' This room also houses two enormous and joyful *cantorie* (choir lofts). One is by Donatello, with cavorting *putti* (small, angelic boys); the other, by Luca della Robbia, is full of angel musicians. Beyond are bas-reliefs from the Campanile, most carved by Pisano to Giotto's designs.

Donatello was the first artist to free sculpture from its Gothic limitations. In the room leading off to the right of the main chamber is an extreme example of the artist's unprecedented use of naturalism: an emotive wood sculpture of Mary Magdalene, dishevelled and ugly, with coarse, dirty hair so realistic you can almost smell it. At the back of this room there is usually a stunning dossal (altar-frontal) made from 400kg (180lb) of silver and worked on by Michelozzo, Verrocchio, Antonio del Pollaiolo and Bernardo Cennini, among others; on previous visits it has been removed for restoration.

Going straight back through the main chamber is a new corridor displaying the pulleys and ropes used to winch building materials (and workers) up inside the dome. There is also Brunelleschi's death mask and an 18th-century sedan chair cleverly built in a curved form so that two servants were able to carry Grand Duke Cosimo III de' Medici up the spiral steps to the top of the Dome without getting stuck. Back on the ground floor, under the glass roof of the court-yard, are the ten original bronze panels from the east door of the Baptistery, the so-called *Porta del Paradiso* ('Gates of Paradise') sculpted by Lorenzo Ghiberti over the 27 years between 1425 and 1452; see also p31.

Museo di Bigallo

Piazza San Giovanni 1 (055 27180304, www. bigallo.net). **Open** 10am-2pm, 3-7pm Wed-Sun. **Admission** €5. **No credit cards. Map** p334 B3.
The city's smallest museum is housed in a beautiful Gothic *loggia* built in 1358 for the Misericordia, a charitable organisation that cared for unwanted children and plague victims. The *loggia* was later renovated for another fraternity, the Bigallo, and the Misericordia moved to piazza del Duomo (no.19), from where it still works as a voluntary medical service. The main room has frescoes depicting the two fraternities at work, though the two scenes on the left wall as you enter were damaged in the 18th century. The *Madonna della Misericordia*, a fresco of 1342 from the workshop of Bernardo Daddi, a pupil of Giotto, has the Virgin suspended above the earliest known depiction of Florence, showing the Baptistery, the original Arnolfo façade to the dome-less Duomo, the original Santa Reparata with its two bell towers, and an incomplete Campanile.

AROUND PIAZZA DELLA SIGNORIA

Frequently packed with perspiring tour groups, the piazza della Signoria is nonetheless the place to go to discover Florence's alternative central square, a public gathering point and former administrative district. Despite being lined with tourist-trap restaurants and cafés, Florence's civic showpiece square is delightful, especially in the early morning before the groups arrive or by the *loggia* late in the evening, where talented buskers perform.

The piazza is dominated by **Palazzo Vecchio** (*see p64*). The crenellated and corbelled building, completed at the end of the 13th century as the seat of the Signoria (top tier of the city's government), looms over the piazza and is visible from almost any point in the city. The *palazzo* still houses the main local government offices, but is also home to the **Associazione Musei dei Ragazzi** (*see p61*) and the **Quartieri Monumentali** (*see p64*), once the main quarters of the Medici.

The piazza itself started life in 1268, when the Guelphs regained control of the area from

SIGHTS

SIGHTS

the Ghibellines. They demolished their rivals' 36 houses, but left the neighbouring houses intact, hence the unusual asymmetrical shape of the square. Over the next few centuries, the piazza remained the focus of civic – though not necessarily civilised – activity. It didn't take much to ignite a crowd: on one occasion, in the 14th century, a scrap in the piazza led to a man being eaten by the mob.

It was here that the religious and political reformer Girolamo Savonarola lit his 'Bonfire of the Vanities' in 1497. Savonarola ended up burned at the stake on 23 May 1498, on the exact spot of his prophetic bonfire (marked by a plaque in front of the Neptune fountain). However, the piazza has also been the seat of civic defence. Whenever Florence was threatened by an external enemy, the bell of Palazzo della Signoria (known as the *vacca*, or cow, after its mooing tone) was tolled to summon the citizens' militia. Part of their training included playing *calcio storico* on the piazza, a version of rugby that's still played in piazza Santa Croce every June (*see p179*).

When, in the mid 1980s, it was decided that the piazza's ancient paving stones should be taken up and restored, the Sovrintendenza dei Beni Archeologici, which oversees the city's archaeological works, took the opportunity to carry out excavations. Ruins from 12th-century Florence were discovered, built over the thermal baths of Roman Florentia and parts of the Etruscans' outpost. The authorities ordered further excavation, and there was even talk of an underground museum. Local government, however, objected, fearing their showpiece piazza would become a building site.

The project ultimately resulted in an utter shambles. The company engaged to restore the paving stones apparently catalogued the position of the stones using chalk, which was washed away on the first rainy day. It also managed to 'lose' some of the slabs, now rumoured to grace the courtyards of various Tuscan villas. The decision to replace the paving with artificially aged stones and reseal the Roman site was deplorable but predictable.

Dominating the piazza are a copy of Michelangelo's **David** (the original is in the Galleria dell'Accademia; *see p78*) and an equestrian bronze of **Cosimo I** by Giambologna, notable mainly for the horse, which was cast as a single piece. Giambologna also created sexy nymphs and satyrs for Ammannati's Neptune fountain (nicknamed *il Biancone* or 'big whitey'), a Mannerist monstrosity of which Michelangelo is reputed to have wailed, 'Ammannati, what beautiful marble you have ruined.' Even Ammannati admitted it was a failure, in part because the block of marble used for Neptune lacked width, forcing him to give the god narrow

shoulders and keep his right arm close to his body. The statue has suffered a lot of damage over the years, the last time being in 2005 when a man from Empoli drunkenly climbed the statue and fell. In 32 seconds of action captured on CCTV, he pulled off the right hand, broke the trident, and landed painfully on a marble shell in the fountain, necessitating almost an entire year of restoration work.

Beyond the fountain are copies of Donatello's *Marzocco* (the original of this heraldic lion, one of Florence's oldest emblems, is in the Bargello; *see p84*) and *Judith and Holofernes* (the original is in Palazzo Vecchio; *see p64*). Like David, Judith was a symbol of the power of the people over tyrannical rulers: a Jewish widow who inveigled her way into the camp of Holofernes, Israel's enemy, she got him drunk and cut off his head. Beyond *David* is *Hercules and Cacus* by Bandinelli, much ridiculed by the exacting Florentines and described by rival sculptor Benvenuto Cellini as a 'sack of melons'. On one of the cornerstones at the edge of Palazzo Vecchio nearest the *loggia* is the etched graffiti profile of a hawk-nosed man – this is reputed to be a portrait of a prisoner by Michelangelo.

Cellini himself is represented by another monster-killer: his fabulous *Perseus*, holding the snaky head of Medusa, stands victorious in the adjacent **Loggia dei Lanzi**. It's testament to the artist's pig-headed determination: most considered it impossible to cast, but after several failed attempts, Cellini finally succeeded by burning his family furniture to fan the furnace. Also in

Cellini's **Perseus**.

the *loggia* is Giambologna's spiralling marble *Rape of the Sabine Women* (1582), a virtuoso attempt to outdo Cellini.

The *loggia* itself, the name of which derives from the *lanzichenecchi* (a private army of Cosimo I), was built in the late 1300s to shelter civic bigwigs during ceremonies. By the mid 15th century, it had become a favourite spot for old men to gossip and shelter from the sun.

Leading down to the river from piazza della Signoria, the daunting piazzale degli Uffizi is home to the world-renowned Galleria degli Uffizi (the **Uffizi**; *see p64*). Also here is the separate entrance to the **Corridoio Vasariano** ('Vasari Corridor'). Halfway down the *piazzale* on the right, in via Lambertesca, is the entrance to the **Collezione Contini-Bonacossi** (*see p62*) and the Georgofili library, where a Mafia bomb exploded in 1993.

Turning left from the riverbank leads you to the **Museo di Storia della Scienza** (*see p62*). Via Castellani heads north from the museum to piazza San Firenze and its imposing law courts; just north of the piazza, in via del Proconsolo, is the entrance to the **Badia Fiorentina** (*see below*), its elegant stone tower visible for the first time in years after a painfully drawn-out restoration. Opposite, on the corner with via Ghibellina, is the foreboding National Museum, the sculpture-laden **Bargello** (*see p84*). We're now in Danteland; just behind the Badia is the **Museo Casa di Dante** (*see p62*), while opposite the house is the **Chiesa di Dante**, the delightful church where Dante's beloved Beatrice is buried.

Back at the river end of the Uffizi and on the right is the landmark **ponte Vecchio**, north of which is the mainly modern architecture of via Por Santa Maria, much of which had to be rebuilt after German bombing in World War II. In a piazza just off the east side of the street is the **Museo Diocesano di Santo Stefano al Ponte** (*see p62*), a tiny church museum.

At the top of via Por Santa Maria, a busy shopping street, is the **Mercato Nuovo** ('new market'), a fine stone *loggia* erected between 1547 and 1551 on a site where there had been a market since the 11th century. Often referred to as the Mercato della Paglia ('straw market'), its stalls now sell leather and straw goods and cheap souvenirs, but in the 16th century it was full of silk and gold merchants. The market is also popularly known as the *Porcellino* ('piglet'), after the bronze statue of a boar, a copy of a Pietro Tacca bronze that was, in turn, a copy of an ancient marble now in the Uffizi. It's thought to be good luck to rub the boar's nose and put a coin in its mouth: proceeds go to charity, and legend says the donor is assured a return trip.

A block further up via Calimala (after the Greek for 'beautiful fleece') on the right is the

portico-and-ramparts grandeur of **Palazzo dell'Arte della Lana**, the Renaissance home to the filthy-rich guild of clothmakers. This fairytale castle is connected by an arched overpass to the church of **Orsanmichele** (*see p63*), the main entrance to which is on via de' Calzaiuoli, the pedestrian thoroughfare between piazza della Signoria and the Duomo.

On the corner of the *palazzo* facing Orsanmichele is the stunning Gothic **Madonna of the Trumpet** tabernacle, complete with spiral columns, a pointed arch, family crest decorations, and a long and complex history. The tabernacle started life in the 13th century on the corner of the Old Market and Calimala, housing the miracle-working *Madonna* painting (later destroyed by fire). The painting was replaced in 1335 by *Enthroned Madonna and Child, Saints John the Baptist and John the Evangelist and Angels* by Jacopo di Casentino; *Coronation of the Virgin and Saints* by Niccolò di Pietro Gerini was added in 1380.

Associazione Musei dei Ragazzi

Palazzo Vecchio, piazza della Signoria (entrance from via de'Gondi) (055 2768224, www.musei ragazzifirenze.it). **Open** 9am-5pm Mon-Wed, Fri, Sat; 9am-2pm Thur; 9am-7pm Sun. **Admission** €6. **No credit cards. Map** p335 C4.

One for the kids, this is more educational activity-running establishment than museum. For children aged three to seven, there's a playroom with a puppet theatre, a dressing-up corner and building blocks, all with a Renaissance theme; for older children (eight to 88 years old) there are workshops, expert talks, meetings with historical characters such as Eleonora di Toledo and Cosimo I, 'secret routes', and multimedia activities in museums around town.

Badia Fiorentina

Via Dante Alighieri (055 264402). **Open** *Cloister* 3-6pm Mon. *Church* 3-6pm Mon; 7am-6pm Tue-Sat. **Admission** donation to Eucharist. **Map** p335 C4.

A Benedictine abbey founded in the tenth century by Willa, the mother of Ugo, Margrave of Tuscany, the Badia Fiorentia was the richest religious institution in medieval Florence. Willa had been deeply influenced by Romuald, a monk who travelled

SIGHTS

around Tuscany denouncing the wickedness of the clergy, flagellating himself and urging the rich to build monasteries; it was Romuald who persuaded Willa to found the Badia in 978.

When Ugo was a child, his exiled father returned to Florence and invented a novel paternity test: asking the boy to recognise the father he'd never seen in a room of men. Happily for his mother, Ugo succeeded. The people decided he must have had divine guidance, and he was considered a visionary leader. Ugo lavished money and land on what was then known as the Badia Florentia, and was eventually buried there in a Roman sarcophagus (later replaced by a tomb made by Renaissance sculptor Mino da Fiesole) that's still housed in the abbey.

It was here in 1274, just across the street from his probable birthplace, that the eight-year-old Dante fell in love at first sight with Beatrice Portinari. He was devastated when her family arranged her marriage, at the tender age of 17, to Simone de' Bardi, and absolutely crushed when she died seven years later. Poor Dante attempted to forget his pain and anguish by throwing himself into war.

The Badia has been rebuilt many times since then, but retains a graceful Romanesque campanile and exquisite carved ceiling. The Chiostro degli Aranci dates from 1430 and is frescoed with scenes from the life of San Bernardo. Inside the church, Bernardo is celebrated once again, in a Filippino Lippi painting. The Cappella dei Pandolfini is where Boccaccio held the first public reading of the works of Dante.

FREE Collezione Contini-Bonacossi

Uffizi, entrance on via Lambertesca (055 294883, www.polomuseale.firenze.it). **Open** guided group visits by appointment only. **Admission** free. **Map** p334 C3.

Orsanmichele.

An impressive collection donated to the state by the Contini-Bonacossi family in 1974. Exhibits include renderings of the *Madonna and Child* by Duccio, Cimabue and Andrea del Castagno, and a roomful of artistic VIPs such as Bernini and Tintoretto. El Greco, Velázquez and Goya are among the foreigners considered prestigious enough for the collection.

Museo Casa di Dante

Via Santa Margherita 1 (055 219416, www.museocasadidante.it). **Open** Oct-Mar 10am-5pm Tue-Sun. *Apr-Sept* 10am-6pm daily. **Admission** €4. **No credit cards. Map** p335 B4.

Housed in the building where Dante is thought to have lived, this museum, dedicated to the father of the Italian language, reopened after three years of renovation in 2005. If you go expecting to see the poet's belongings, original works or in fact anything original at all, you'll be disappointed. What the museum offers is extensive information about the political, economic and cultural environment of Dante's time, mostly in the form of brightly coloured factual posters lining the walls on all three floors. There are miniature-model reconstructions of battles and of ancient Florence, an example of a medieval bedroom, costumed mannequins and clear illustrations of Heaven, Hell and Purgatory taken from *The Divine Comedy*.

FREE Museo Diocesano di Santo Stefano al Ponte

Piazza Santo Stefano 5 (055 2710732). **Open** *Summer* 4-7pm Fri. *Winter* 3.30-6.30pm Fri; also by appointment. Closed mid July-Sept. **Admission** free. **Map** p334 C3.

A tiny, little-known museum hidden from the tourist trail in a square north of the ponte Vecchio. Among the religious icons and church relics are a few big surprises: a *Maestà* by Giotto, *San Giuliano* by Masolino and the *Quarate Predella* by Paolo Uccello.

Museo Galileo

Piazza dei Giudici 1 (055 265311, www.museogalileo.it). **Open** 9.30am-6pm Mon, Wed-Sun; 9.30am-1pm Tue. **Admission** €8. **No credit cards. Map** p335 C4.

Galileo Galilei's scientific instruments are the big draw here, but even without them, the former Museo di Storia della Scienza would be one of the most interesting museums in Florence. Galileo's fascinatingly crafted compass and singularly unimpressive leather-bound telescope are in the two rooms dedicated to the heretical stargazer. A morbid reliquary in the shape of his middle right finger is also on display, offering unintentionally ironic echoes to the honour more usually bestowed on saints.

In the next rooms are a collection of prisms and optical games. Art continues to mingle with science in Room 7, devoted to armillary spheres and dominated by a model commissioned by Federico II in 1593. Most of the spheres have the earth placed at

The Unfinished Masterwork

Will anyone pay for a 'new' Michelangelo façade?

In 1516, Michelangelo won a competition called by Pope Leo X (a son of Lorenzo il Magnifico) to erect a monumental marble façade for the basilica of San Lorenzo (*see p76*), the Medici family church in Florence, beating Andrea and Jacopo Sansovino, Raphael, Baccio d'Agnolo and Giuliano da Sangallo. A wooden model in the Casa Buonarroti museum (*see p84*) shows how grand Michelangelo's design was. The commission was signed in 1518, and vast extant documents attest to Michelangelo having personally supervised every detail of the project until, to his great frustration, two years later the pope shifted his funds instead to the New Sacristy (*see p74*) and the Laurentian Library (*see p77*). The façade was left unfinished, its architectural elements were dispersed, and the marble already quarried was relocated elsewhere.

In recent years, interest in the project was prompted by the discovery in a marble warehouse near Pietrasanta of three columns that might be the set quarried by Michelangelo for his façade: the height, size and marble type match perfectly. In 2007, the Teseco Foundation for Art Pisa, which had purchased the three columns, sent one of them to Florence to be displayed by the church, with a 'virtual façade' projected on San Lorenzo's bare brick front.

The projections were meant to attract sponsors for an even grander display, now set to materialise in 2012: a life-size reconstruction of the façade, in plastic, to be put up in front of the church for a few months, then relocated to the airport. Meanwhile, in July 2011, mayor Matteo Renzi came up with the kind of coup de théâtre typical of his style: why not build Michelangelo's façade the way the Master meant it, in solid marble? Sponsors would flock, he believes. Is it needed? The debate is raging.

the centre of the universe, surrounded by seven spheres of the planets. The second floor has a mix of machines, mechanisms and models, including a 19th-century clock (*pianola*) that writes a sentence with a mechanical hand, and a selection of electromagnetic and electrostatic instruments (Room 14). The display of amputation implements and models of foetuses adorning the walls are rather grisly.

FREE Orsanmichele & Museo di Orsanmichele

Via dell'Arte della Lana (055 210305 church, 055 284944 museum). **Open** *Church* 10am-5pm daily. *Museum* 10am-5pm Mon. **Admission** free. **Map** p334 C3.

Most famous for the statues in the 14 niches that surround the building, Orsanmichele has become a relic of the extreme dedication and pride of Florentine trades, and a reminder that a competitive climate often heralds the greatest art. There's no spire and no overt religious symbols: Orsanmichele may not look much like a church, but it is – although one with a difference, melding as it does the relationship between art, religion and commerce.

In 1290, a *loggia* intended as a grain store was built to a design by Arnolfo di Cambio, the original architect of the Duomo, in the garden (*orto*) of the Monastery of San Michele (hence, 'Orsanmichele'). The *loggia* burned down in 1304, along with a painting of the Madonna that, from 1292, had been said to perform miracles. Such was the effect of her miracles that people flocked from across Tuscany to worship her. When the building was reconstructed in the mid 1300s by Talenti and Fioravante, the painting was replaced and honoured by the creation of a marvellously elaborate glass and marble tabernacle by Andrea Orcagna. This was replaced in 1347 by Bernardo Daddi's *Coronation of the Madonna with Eight Angels*, which is still here today.

During reconstruction of the building, two upper floors were added for religious services. From the outset, the council intended the building to be a magnificent advertisement for the wealth of the city's guilds, and in 1339 each guild was instructed to fill one of the *loggia*'s 14 niches with a statue of its patron saint. Only the wool guild obliged, so in 1406, after the building's conversion into a church, the council handed the guilds a ten-year deadline.

Six years later, the Calimala cloth importers, the wealthiest of all the guilds, commissioned Ghiberti to create a life-sized bronze of John the Baptist. It was the largest statue ever cast in Florence, and its arrival spurred the other major guilds into action. The guild of armourers was represented by a tense *St George* by Donatello (now in the Bargello; *see p84*), one of the first psychologically realistic sculptures of the Renaissance, while the Parte Guelfa guild had Donatello gild their bronze, a *St Louis of Toulouse* (later removed by the Medici in their drive to expunge all memory of the Guelphs).

All the statues in the external niches today are copies. However, the originals can be found on the first floor of the museum, displayed on a platform in their original order. And on the second floor is a

SIGHTS

collection of statues of 14th-century saints and prophets in arenaria stone. They were on the external façade of the church until the 1950s.

The church and museum do not always stick to the opening hours posted, so it's advisable to phone to check the hours before making a special trip.

★ Palazzo Vecchio
Quartieri Monumentali

Piazza della Signoria (055 2768325, www.musei civicifiorentini.it). **Open** 9am-7pm Mon-Wed, Fri, Sat; 9am-2pm Thur; 9am-7pm Sun. **Admission** €6. **Map** p335 C4.

The most important civic square in Florence is dominated by Florence's town hall; the imposing power of Palazzo Vecchio's austere and commanding walls were built to Arnolfo di Cambio's late 13th-century plans as the seat of the Signoria – the city's ruling body. The building represented the immense strength of the city at this time.

The Medici enjoyed their nine-year stay (1540-49) and instigated a Mannerist makeover of the interior from 1555 to 1574. However, the rustic stone exterior of the building and Arnolfo's tower, the highest in the city at 94m (308ft), remained largely intact. The tower, set just off-centre in order to incorporate a previous tower and to fit in with the irregularity of the square, and topped by two of the main symbols of Florence (a lion holding a lily), saw the imprisonment of Savonarola and Cosimo il Vecchio in a room euphemistically called the Albergaccio ('bad hotel'). From 1565, Palazzo Vecchio lost some of its administrative exclusivity to the Pitti Palace and the Uffizi. However, it became the seat of the Italian government's House of Deputies from 1865 to 1871, when Florence was the first capital of the Kingdom of Italy. You might recognise one balcony from a gruesome scene in the film *Hannibal* (*see p80* **Walk**).

The Salone dei Cinquecento (Hall of the Five Hundred), where members of the Great Council met, should have been decorated by Michelangelo and Leonardo, not the zestless scenes of victory over Siena and Pisa by Vasari that cover the walls. Leonardo abandoned the project; Michelangelo had only finished the cartoon for the Battle of Cascine when he was summoned to Rome by Pope Julius II. Many people believe da Vinci's sketches lie beneath the Vasari mural. One of Michaelangelo's commissions did end up here, however: the *Genius of Victory*, a statue thought to have been carved, along with the better-known *Slaves*, for the pope's never-finished tomb.

Off the Salone is the Studiolo di Francesco I, the office where Francesco hid away to practise alchemy. Also decorated by Vasari, it includes a scene from the alchemist's laboratory and illustrations of the four elements. From the vaulted ceiling, Bronzino's portraits of Francesco's parents, Cosimo I and Eleonora di Toledo, look down. The Quartiere di Eleonora, the apartments of the wife of Cosimo I, has two entirely frescoed chapels; the first was

---

SIGHT SPOT
EXALTED DOORMAN

Lorenzo Ghiberti's innovations of style and subject-matter provided a basis for many of the ideals and practices of the High Renaissance. He studied as a goldsmith, but his big break came when he beat Filippo Brunelleschi to the commission for the second (north) doors of the **Baptistery** (*see p58*). See also his *Sacrificio di Isacco* at the **Bargello** (*see p84*), and *John the Baptist, St Matthew* and *St Stephen* at **Orsanmichele** (*see p63*).

---

partly decorated by Bronzino, who used intense pastel hues to depict a surreal *Crossing the Red Sea*, while the Cappella dei Priori is decorated with fake mosaics and an idealised *Annunciation*.

Beyond here is the garish Sala d'Udienza, with a carved ceiling dripping in gold; more subtle is the Sala dei Gigli, so named because of the gilded lilies that cover the walls. Decorated in the 15th century, it has a ceiling by Giuliano and Benedetto da Maiano, and some sublime frescoes of Roman statesmen by Ghirlandaio opposite the door. Donatello's original *Judith and Holofernes*, rich in political significance, is also here. Finally, go through into the Map Room for the gigantic 16th-century globe by Egnazio Danti and, from the same period, 53 hand-decorated maps of countries and continents.

For an insight into Palazzo Vecchio's workings, book yourself on to the Visita ai Percorsi Segreti ('Secret Passageways Tour') to see private rooms not usually open to the public and climb on to the roof, where the lifts and pulleys that hold up the wooden panelled ceiling of the Sala dei Cinquecento are hidden. Other tours include An Invitation to Cosimo's Court (good for children) and the Tour of the Quartieri Monumentali, which finishes in Bianca Cappello's special chamber, a room cunningly designed so the Duchess could see the goings-on in the Salone dei Cinquecento without being seen herself. Ask at the ticket office for more information.

★ Uffizi

Piazzale degli Uffizi 6 (055 2388651, www. uffizi.firenze.it). **Open** 8.15am-6.50pm Tue-Sun. **Admission** €6.50; €3.25 reductions. Small extra charge for special exhibitions. *Advance booking* via Firenze Musei (055 294883); booking charge €3. **No credit cards. Map** p335 C4.

Statues outside the Uffizi commemorate many of the most interesting artists and scholars in Florence's history but these pale into insignificance when you enter this stunning temple of Renaissance art. The quantity and quality of the paintings on display make this without a doubt the greatest treasure trove of Renaissance art in the world. Plans to double the gallery's display space, allowing long-hidden works to come out of storage, have been long under way, with designs by Japanese architect Arata Isozaki for a new exit wing approved back in August 2007.

In the meantime the queues remain, and even booking in advance isn't foolproof: during peak times you need to reserve up to a couple of months ahead. Whether you book in advance or not, aim to arrive when the museum opens or at lunchtime, when tour groups are less prevalent. To see the whole collection takes a lot of time: it's best to jump to the rooms that most interest you or, better still, plan a return visit. Allow three hours for the unmissables. Several groups run guided tours; there are also audio tours in six languages for €4.65 (single headset) or €6.20 (double headset) from the ticket office.

The building was designed by Vasari in the mid 16th century as a public administration centre for Cosimo I ('Uffizi' means 'offices'). To make way for the *pietra serena* and white plaster building, inspired by Michelangelo's Laurentian Library (*see p77*), most of the 11th-century church of San Piero Scheraggio was demolished. By 1581, Francesco I had already begun turning the top floor into a new home for his art collection; a succession of Medici added to the collection, culminating in the bequest of most of the family's artworks by the last important member of the family, Anna Maria, in 1743.

The chronological collection begins gloriously in **Room 2**, with three *Maestàs* by Giotto, Cimabue and Duccio; all were painted in the 13th and early 14th centuries, and all are still part of the Byzantine tradition. **Room 3** is 14th-century Siena, evoked most exquisitely by Simone Martini's lavish gilt altarpiece *Annunciation*. Such delight in detail reached its zenith in the international Gothic movement (**Rooms 5** and **6**) and, in particular, the work of Gentile da Fabriano (1370-1427), whose ornate *Adoration of the Magi*, known as the Strozzi Altarpiece because it was commissioned by Palla di Noferi Strozzi for the sacristy of Santa Trinità, has been restored to its original sumptuous grandeur.

It comes as something of a surprise, then, to find a strikingly contemporary *Virgin and Child with St Anne* by Masolino and Masaccio (1401-28) in **Room 7**. Masaccio painted the Virgin, whose severe expression and statuesque pose make her an indubitable descendant of Giotto's *Maestà*. In the same room is the *Santa Lucia dei Magnoli* altarpiece by Domenico Veneziano (1400-61), a Venetian artist who had a remarkable skill for rendering the way light affects colour. His influence on pupil Piero della Francesca's work is clear in the younger artist's portraits of the Duke and Duchess of Urbino. Paolo Uccello (1396-1475) is represented by the *Battle of San Romano*: a work of tremendous energy and power, it's part of a triptych; the other thirds are in London's National Gallery and the Louvre in Paris.

Rooms 8 and **9** are dominated by Filippo Lippi and the Pollaiolo brothers. The Madonna in Lippi's *Madonna with Child and Angels* is a portrait of the

beautiful Lucrezia Buti, painted with their son Filippino. Antonio Pollaiolo's small panels of the *Labours of Hercules* demonstrate his familiarity with the skeletal form and musculature.

The two most famous paintings in the Uffizi and in Italy are in **Room 10**. Botticelli's *Birth of Venus*, the epitome of Renaissance romance, depicts the birth of the goddess from a sea impregnated by the castration of Uranus. It's an allegory of the birth of beauty from the mingling of the physical world (the sea) and the spiritual (Uranus). Scholars have been squabbling about the true meaning of Botticelli's *Primavera* ('Allegory of Spring'), since it was painted in 1482. Many now agree it was intended to represent the onset of spring and signify the triumph of Venus (centre) as true love, with the Three Graces representing her beauty and Zephyr (on the right) as lust, pursuing the nymph Chloris, who is transformed into Flora, Venus's fecundity. If you look closely at Botticelli's *Portrait of a Young Man with Medal* (1475-76), you'll see that the golden disc is not, in fact, painted but inlaid, making the portrait the only collage in the entire gallery.

In **Room 15** are several paintings by Leonardo da Vinci, including a collaboration with his master Verrocchio, *The Baptism of Christ*. Da Vinci painted the angel in profile, and parts of the landscape in this composition, and it's said that Verrocchio never painted again because his work couldn't match up to Leonardo's. The octagonal **Room 18**, known as La Tribuna, was designed to display some of the greatest masterpieces in the Medici collection. It's dominated by portraits by Agnolo Bronzino, most strikingly that of Eleonora di Toledo; assured, beautiful and very Spanish in an opulent gold and black brocade gown. The oval **Room 24**, which was originally a treasure chamber, is home to the world's biggest collection of miniatures.

In **Room 25**, the gallery makes its transition to Mannerism, led by Michelangelo's *Doni Tondo* ('Holy Family'), which shows the sculptural bodies, virtuoso composition and luscious palette that characterised the new wave. Florentine works include Mariotto Albertinelli's *Visitation*, with Elizabeth's saffron-coloured shawl glowing in what was the artist's only masterpiece. Next you'll come to the Pontormo- and Rosso Fiorentino-dominated **Room 27**; again, Michelangelo's legacy is visible, notably in *Moses Defends the Daughters of Jethro* by Rosso Fiorentino. By the same artist is the *Portrait of a Young Woman*, with the ubiquitous musical angel detail. The works by Titian in **Room 28** include his masterpiece *Venus of Urbino*, whose questionably chaste gaze has disarmed viewers for centuries. For more Venetian works, skip to **Rooms 31-35**, but don't miss the challenging *Madonna with the Long Neck* by Parmigianino en route in **Room 29**.

At this point it's very easy to become confused by the room numbers. Rooms 36-37 and 39-40 don't actually exist, 'room' 38 is a statue-lined area at the top of the stairwell and Room 41 is a restoration laboratory.

SIGHTS

SIGHTS

INSIDE TRACK ANCIENT ALMS

The 750-year-old **Misericordia museum** (piazza del Duomo 20) offers free tours in English every Monday at 3pm – a great opportunity to learn the fascinating history of this 13th-century almshouse, infirmary and poor house.

Room 42, also known as the Sala delle Niobe, is lined with four monumental canvases by Rubens and displays recently restored statues from the Villa Medici gardens in Rome. It's difficult to believe these Roman copies of Greek originals are 2,000 years old, as their dramatic poses depicting the myth of Niobe are reminiscent of 17th-century Baroque theatricality.

Downstairs, most of the first floor is reserved for the Uffizi's temporary exhibitions, but in the middle you'll find Rooms 47-51. **Room 47** is home to a particularly grisly *Judith and Holofernes* by the 17th-century Caravaggio-esque female artist Artemisia Gentileschi. Caravaggio himself is represented by his famous *Medusa* (more shocked than horror-inspiring), a *Bacchus* and a *Sacrifice of Isaac*, all demonstrating his masterly treatment of light. More Caravaggio-esque artists such as Manfredi and Gherardo delle Notti employ his use of *chiaroscuro* (dramatic light contrasts) to the paintings in the final four rooms of the corridor. It's this final collection that suffered most from the last terrorist attack. At 5am on 27 May 1993 a Mafia-related car bomb exploded outside the west wing of the Uffizi (a gnarled olive tree has been placed in the exact spot to remember the five people who were killed). In all, 32 paintings were damaged and three destroyed in the blast, which also severely hit the Sala delle Niobe. Ironically, most of the damage done to the paintings was from the shattering of their protective glass screens, which ripped the canvases to shreds. The restoration of Gherardo delle Notti's *Adoration of the Magi* is still taking place.

Note that paintings may be moved or go on loan at any time, so if you've set your heart on seeing a particular masterpiece, phone first to check it's here.

AROUND VIA DE' TORNABUONI

The Strozzi family were banking rivals of the more famous Medici; it's the gargantuan stones of fortified **Palazzo Strozzi** (*see p68*) that dominate the elegant shopping mecca of via de' Tornabuoni. The walls of the building (up to and around the main entrance in piazza Strozzi) are set with horse-tethering rings and torch holders and embellished with the three crescent-moon motifs of the family crest. The main street itself sweeps down from piazza Antinori to piazza Santa Trinità and the Santa Trinità bridge. It's crowned by **Palazzo Antinori**, an austere mid 15th-century palace of neat stone

blocks that's been inhabited by the Antinori winemaking family since 1506. The rather garish **San Gaetano** opposite is one of the only completely Baroque churches in Florence.

Heading south towards the river, passing all manner of designer names, you'll come to piazza Santa Trinità. Just before the square is via Porta Rossa, with the Renaissance house museum **Palazzo Davanzati** (*see p68*). At the far end of via Porta Rossa, on the right, the road widens into a square. The ramparts and Gothic leaded windows of the **Palagio di Parte Guelfa** date back to the 13th century, and have been modified by, among others, Brunelleschi and Vasari. The imposing building, once the headquarters of the Guelphs, is now used as a library and meeting rooms. Running parallel to via Porta Rossa is borgo Santissimi Apostoli, a narrow street in the middle of which is piazza del Limbo, so-called because it occupies the site of a graveyard for unbaptised babies. The tiny church is **Santissimi Apostoli** (*see p68*).

Piazza Santa Trinità is little more than a bulge dominated by the curved ramparts of **Palazzo Spini Feroni**, home to the shoetastic **Museo Ferragamo** (*see below*), and by an ancient column from the Baths of Caracalla in Rome, given to Cosimo I by Pope Pius I in 1560. The statue of Justice on top is by Francesco del Tadda. The first *palazzo* after via de' Tornabuoni is **Palazzo Bartolini-Salimbeni** by Baccio d'Agnolo. Opposite Palazzo Spini Feroni, on the west side of via de' Tornabuoni, is **Santa Trinità** church (*see p68*).

The ponte Santa Trinità, an elegant bridge with an elliptical arch, links piazza Santa Trinità with **Oltrarno** (*see p88*). Built in 1252 on the initiative of the Frescobaldi family, it was rebuilt in 1346 and again in 1567. It's this version, by Ammannati (but perhaps to a design by Michelangelo) that stands today; it's considered by many to be the most beautiful bridge in the world. The statues at either end represent the four seasons, and were placed there in 1608 to celebrate Cosimo II's marriage to Maria of Austria. Having been bombed on the night of 3 August 1944 by retreating Germans, the bridge was rebuilt in 1955 in the same position and to the same design. The head of the most famous statue, *Spring*, by Pietro Francavilla, on the north-east side of the bridge, remained lost until 1961, when a council employee dredged it up during a routine clean-up and claimed the reward offered by a US newspaper for its return.

Museo Ferragamo

Piazza Santa Trinità 5r (055 3360456/455, www.museoferragamo.it). **Open** 10am-6pm Mon, Wed-Sun. **Admission** €5. **Map** p334 C2.

Profile Ponte Vecchio

Up close, the oldest bridge in Florence isn't the most beautiful.

Many visitors find their first sight of the ponte Vecchio, well, a bit disappointing; even Italians have been overheard declaiming its cluster of jewellery shops as looking like a rather ropey old tenement block that should probably be replaced with some nice modern houses. There's no denying that the 14th-century bridge, Florence's oldest, lacks the medieval charm of Venice's *ponte vecchio*, the elegant and pretty Bridge of Sighs – but it is as much a symbol of the city as the Duomo or the Uffizi.

A series of bridges has occupied this spot, the narrowest on the river, for more than 1,000 years (it was famously the city's only bridge spared from destruction during the German army's retreat in 1944, supposedly on Hitler's orders), but the builders of the current one remain unknown. What is known is that bridges with shops on them were common in medieval Italy, but by 1593 the original tenants of this one, a lively mix of butchers, tanners and blacksmiths, were deemed too smelly and loud to stay, and were evicted on the orders of Ferdinando I. The quaint shops and workshops

were given over to the goldsmiths whose descendants still occupy them – though not without a sharp intervening rise in rents, which led to many of the 17th-century shopkeepers adding the back shops (*retrobotteghe*) that still hang precariously over the bridge's sides. The bust in the centre of the bridge is of goldsmith Benvenuto Cellini, sternly glaring out as if in grim disapproval of the dubious tourist tat sold in many of the old shops, and the hordes of hawkers and gawpers there. Far better to head for one of the ponte Vecchio's two neighbouring bridges, the ponte Santa Trinità or ponte alle Grazie, and take pictures of it from there – with the right light and empty of tourists, it's as pretty as they come.

SIGHTS

Down some steps from the eponymous shop and into the medieval basement (where it was moved in 2006) this museum is as elegant and stylish as the shoes on display. In the first chamber you can see order forms signed by famous actors and actresses, including John Wayne, and wooden 'lasts' (foot shapes) for Ava Gardner and Drew Barrymore. The rest of the museum is filled with a choice selection of the company's 10,000 shoes. There are pairs created for Marilyn Monroe, Judy Garland and Audrey Hepburn, affording an opportunity for shoe fetishists to drool over some of the world's most beautiful footwear.

Palazzo Davanzati/Museo dell'Antica Casa Fiorentina

Via Porta Rossa 13 (055 2388610, www.polo museale.firenze.it). **Open** 8.15am-1.50pm daily. Closed 1st, 3rd & 5th Mon, 2nd & 4th Sun of mth. **Admission** €2. **Map** p334 C3.

After years of renovation, the Ancient Florentine House Museum is open again. On the first floor are the painted Sala dei Pappagalli, the Salone Madornale and the Studiolo, displaying carved Renaissance furniture, paintings, tapestries, an incredible 16th-century strongbox and a permanent exhibition about spinning, weaving, embroidery and lace. The building itself is a wonderful example of a 14th-century *palazzo* for well-to-do Florentines; the little *cortile* with a view up to all the levels has a stone staircase leading to the first floor (as high as the noble guests would be visiting) and wooden stairs thereafter. There is a well beneath the building accessed by buckets that were lowered down a hollow column (like a dumb-waiter) from the kitchens; the kitchens themselves were hidden high up on the (inaccessible) third floor to keep smoke and smells out of the way. Access to the second and third floors is only by guided group, by request at 10am, 11pm and noon when the museum is open.

★ Palazzo Strozzi

Piazza Strozzi (055 2645155 Institute Gabinetto Vieusseux, www.palazzostrozzi.org). **Open** *Library* 9am-1.30pm, 3-6pm Mon, Wed, Fri; 9am-6pm Tue, Thur. *Exhibitions* 9am-8pm Mon-Wed, Fri-Sun; 9am-11pm Thur. **Admission** *Courtyard* free. *Exhibitions* around €10. **Map** p334 B3.

Flanked by Florence's most stylish shopping streets, Palazzo Strozzi is one of the most magnificent of the hundred or so palaces built in the city during the 15th century. Behind the imposing rusticated stone walls lies the Humanist Institute's Renaissance book and manuscript collection and the CCCS – the Centro di Cultura Contemporanea Strozzina – hosting contemporary art in the *palazzo*'s cellar. Given the auspicious setting, this is one of the most exciting new openings in Florence for years.

In 1489, work began on the construction of the *palazzo* by order of Filippo Strozzi, whose family had been exiled from Florence in 1434 for opposing the Medici. However, they'd made good use of the time,

moving south and becoming bankers to the King of Naples; by the time they returned to Florence in 1466, they'd amassed a fortune. Filippo began buying up property in the centre of Florence eight years later, until he had acquired enough real estate to build the biggest palace in the city.

An astrologer was asked to choose an auspicious day to lay the foundation stone; 6 August 1489 tied in nicely with a new law that tax-exempted anyone who built a house on an empty site. When Filippo died in 1491, he left his heirs to complete the project, which eventually bankrupted them, but the palace remained in the family up until 1937, when it became the seat of an insurance company. It was finally handed over to the state in 1999.

FREE Santa Trinità

Piazza Santa Trinità (055 216912). **Open** 8am-noon, 4-6pm Mon-Sat; 4-6pm Sun. **Admission** free. **Map** p334 C2.

This plain church was built in the 13th century over the ruins of two earlier churches belonging to the Vallombrosans. The order was founded in 1038 by San Giovanni Gualberto Visdomini, who spent much of his life attempting to persuade pious aristocrats to surrender their wealth and live a life of austerity. The order became extremely wealthy and powerful, reaching a peak in the 16th and 17th centuries, when its huge fortress abbey at Vallombrosa, in the Casentino countryside north of Arezzo, was built. Santa Trinità's façade was made at the end of the 16th century by Bernardo Buontalenti (who created the Boboli Gardens' Grotta Grande; *see p90* **Walk**), but the church is well worth a visit for the Cappella Sassetti alone. This chapel was luminously frescoed in 1486 by Ghirlandaio with scenes from the life of St Francis: one, set in the piazza della Signoria, features Lorenzo il Magnifico and his children.

FREE Santissimi: La chiesa dei Santissimi Apostoli

Piazza del Limbo 1 (055 290642). **Open** 10.15am-noon, 4-7pm Mon-Sat; 10.15am-noon Sun. **Admission** free. **Map** p334 C3.

The design of Santissimi Apostoli, like that of the early Christian churches of Rome, is based on a Roman basilica. It's one of the oldest churches in Florence, retaining much of its 11th-century façade. The third chapel on the right holds an *Immaculate Conception* by Vasari; in the left aisle is an odd glazed terracotta tabernacle by Giovanni della Robbia. The church holds pieces of flint reputed to have come from Jerusalem's Holy Sepulchre, awarded to Pazzino de' Pazzi for his bravery during the Crusades: he was the first to scale the walls of Jerusalem, though his nickname, 'Little Mad Man of the Mad Men', suggests his actions may have been more foolish than brave. These flints were used on Easter Day to light the 'dove' that set off the fireworks display at the Scoppio del Carro (*see p176*). Note that the church has a tendency to close in the afternoon without notice.

SIGHTS

Santa Maria Novella

The old Dominican stronghold now has more visitor appeal than ever.

Santa Maria Novella was one of two buildings of any substance (the other being Santa Croce) that lay immediately outside the city walls in the 13th century. Many visitors think of Santa Maria Novella in functional terms – it is, after all, where coaches and trains arrive, and where most car-hire firms can be found. However, there's a more tranquil side to an area where artistic treasures include the church and the Alinari Photography museum, the arrival of which in 2006 did much to increase the district's cultural cachet. The area has three main streets, running parallel to each other, each different in feel.

Map p334	Cafés, Bars &
Hotels p105	Gelaterie p146
Restaurants &	
Wine Bars p129	

Workaday via Palazzuolo – home to the Oratorio dei Vanchetoni (no.17), a beautiful 1602 building that occasionally hosts free concerts – is sandwiched between elegant borgo Ognissanti and traffic-heavy via della Scala, home to the famous **Farmacia Santa Maria Novella** (*see p173*).

Santa Maria Novella station (*see p71* **Profile**) has a bold form that's not to everyone's taste, but the building is regarded as a masterpiece of modernism. A short walk south, Leon Battista Alberti's exquisite, precision-built façade for the church of **Santa Maria Novella** (*see p71*) looks out on to the grassy, but scruffy, piazza of the same name, which held annual chariot races on the feast day of Florence's patron saint, John the Baptist, from 1563 to 1852. The course was marked by two obelisks for the chariots to lap, which are still in the piazza, resting on turtles sculpted by Giambologna. Opposite the church, on the southern side of the square, is the restored **Loggia di San Paolo**, a late 15th-century arcade modelled on Brunelleschi's Loggiato degli Innocenti in San Marco (*see p78*). Here you'll find the **Museo Nazionale Alinari della Fotografia** (*see p70*).

Piazza Santa Maria Novella has been the subject of long-running disputes between local residents, hotel owners and the city police, whose opinions over the degree of safety and civic care are, to say the least, at odds with one another. By day the square is a bustling and pretty tourist mecca, but nights can be dodgier. The opening of smart hotels such as JK Place (*see p106*) spruced up the eastern side of the square, but problems remain with drug dealers after dark, despite an ongoing overhaul that is brightening the place up with flowerbeds and has created a larger pedestrianised zone.

In stark contrast, walk a little south of the piazza, where the triangle formed by via de' Fossi, via della Spada and via della Vigna Nuova is not just a friendly, lively area during the day, but also generally safe for night-time window-shopping. The area is cluttered with antiques emporia, designer clothes shops,

Ognissanti.

FREE Cappella Rucellai

Via della Spada (055 216912). **Open** 10am-noon
Mon-Sat. **Admission** free. **Map** p334 B2.
It's not so much a case of blink and you'll miss this
tiny chapel; more that if you oversleep or linger over
breakfast, you'll find it's already closed for the day.
Once part of the church of San Pancrazio (now the
Museo Marino Marini, *see below*), the chapel retains
the church's charming bell tower and contains the
tombs of many members of the extended family of
15th-century wool magnate Giovanni Rucellai,
including that of his wife Iacopa Strozzi. It's worth
a visit to see Alberti's Temple of the Santo Sepolcro:
commissioned in 1467 by Giovanni, it was built to
the same proportions as the Holy Sepulchre of
Jerusalem in an attempt to ensure his salvation.

FREE Cenacolo di Ognissanti

*Borgo Ognissanti 42 (055 2398700, www.polo
museale.firenze.it).* **Open** *Last Supper* 9am-noon
Mon, Tue, Sat. **Admission** free. **Map** p334 B1.
The Ognissanti's (*see right*) lovely cloister, accessed
via a separate entrance on borgo Ognissanti, is
painted with frescoes illustrating the life of St
Francis. The cloister's main point of interest, however, is Ghirlandaio's most famous *Last Supper*,
dated 1480, housed in the refectory. There's also a
museum of Franciscan bits and bobs.

Museo Marino Marini

*Piazza San Pancrazio (055 219432, www.museo
marinomarini.it).* **Open** 10am-5pm Mon, Wed-Sat.
Closed Aug. **Admission** €4. **No credit cards**.
Map p334 B2.
The original Albertian church on this site, San
Pancrazio, was redesigned to accommodate the
works of prolific sculptor and painter Marino Marini
(1901-80). It's now a huge, bright and modern space
filled predominantly with sculptures on the theme
of horse and rider; the central exhibit is the 6m (20ft)
Composizione Equestre. The second floor has a
series of other bronze and polychrome plaster pieces,
including the hypnotic *Nuotatore* ('Swimmer'), and
some fabulous colourful paintings and sculptures of
dancers and jugglers created during the early 1950s.

★ Museo Nazionale Alinari della Fotografia

*Piazza Santa Maria Novella 14a (055 216310,
www.mnaf.it).* **Open** *Winter* 10am-6.30pm Mon,
Tue, Thur-Sun. *Summer* 10.30am-7.30pm Mon,
Tue, Thur-Sun. **Admission** €9; €6 Mon.
Map p334 B2.
The Alinari National Museum of Photography
opened in 2006 with more than four million pictures
in its archives, and found immediate success with
both Florentines and visitors. The first two rooms are
reserved as a temporary exhibition space; the actual
museum begins behind them with an introduction to
the history of Italian and world photography from
1839 to the present day. The displays include video

SIGHTS

cafés and *trattorie*; next to each other in the
centre of the triangle are fine Palazzo Rucellai
(not open to the public), the **Capella Rucellai**
and the adjacent modern art museum, the
Museo Marino Marini.
Alberti had already designed Palazzo
Rucellai in via della Vigna Nuova for the
Rucellai family when he created the façade
of Santa Maria Novella. The *palazzo*'s subtle
frontage was inspired by Rome's Colosseum:
the pilasters that section the bottom storey
have Doric capitals, those on the middle
level have Ionic capitals, and those on the
top storey are in the Corinthian style. There's
no rustication – Alberti considered it fit only
for tyrants, of whom there were then plenty.
The Rucellai were wool merchants who had
grown rich by importing a Mallorcan red dye
derived from lichen and known as *oricello*,
from which their surname derives. The
charming Orti Oricellari garden at the far
end of via della Scala was where the family
grew their crop.
Up past piazza Goldoni, lungarno Vespucci
and borgo Ognissanti open out into piazza
Ognissanti, flanked by swanky hotels and
topped by the church of **Ognissanti** (*see right*),
the cloister of which houses the **Cenacolo di
Ognissanti** (*see below*). Further up, elegant
residential roads lead out on to the main
avenues, Porta al Prato and the mammoth
park of **Parco delle Cascine** (*see p93*).

screens, camera obscuras, displays of photos and negatives, binoculars that turn photographs three-dimensional and a vast collection of cameras. Reconstructions of photographs using plastic and textiles, and explanatory panels in braille, make it possible for the museum to be appreciated by blind visitors.

FREE Ognissanti
Borgo Ognissanti 42 (055 2398700). **Open** 9am-12.30pm, 4-7.30pm daily. **Admission** free. **Map** p334 B1.

The church of Ognissanti ('All Saints') was founded in the 13th century by the Umiliati, a group of monks from Lombardy. The monks introduced the wool trade to Florence, bringing with them great prosperity; without them, perhaps, there would have been no Florentine Renaissance. The Umiliati were so rich by the 14th century that they commissioned Giotto to paint the *Maestà* for their high altar; 50 years later, they got Giovanni da Milano to create a flashier altarpiece. Both are now in the Uffizi (*see p64*). Ognissanti

was also the parish church of the Vespucci, a family of merchants that included 15th-century navigator Amerigo, who sailed to the Venezuelan coast in 1499 – and had two continents named after him.

The church has been rebuilt numerous times and is now visited mainly for paintings by Ghirlandaio: among them *St Jerome* and a *Madonna della Misericordia* that incorporates a portrait of Amerigo Vespucci: he's the young boy dressed in pink. To see Ghirlandaio's masterful *Last Supper* you have to go back outside and through the next door. Other frescoes include a *St Augustine* by Botticelli. In the Chapel of St Peter of Alcantara, look for Botticelli's tomb, marked with his family name of Filipepi.

★ Santa Maria Novella
Piazza Santa Maria Novella (055 219257, www.chiesasantamarianovella.it). **Open** 9.30am-5.30pm Mon-Thur, Sat; 11am-5.30pm Fri; noon-5pm Sun. **Admission** €3.50. **No credit cards**. **Map** p334 A2.

Santa Maria Novella Station

Florence's fabulous example of modernist architecture.

Florence doesn't do modern architecture terribly well. For nigh on a decade the city has been wrangling over designs for the new tram station (*see p69*), seemingly unable to reconcile the notion of forward-thinking state-of-the-art architecture with the city's Renaissance masterpieces by Brunelleschi, Buontalenti and Vasari. But in Santa Maria Novella station, the city can boast at least one glorious example of Italian modernist architecture – albeit one with unpleasant associations.

Designed in 1932 by a group of architects called the Gruppo Toscano (Tuscan Group), overseen by lead architect Giovanni Michelucci, the sleek, low lines of the building, constructed between 1932 and 1935, belie their origins. The Gruppo's plans, submitted as part of a competition to design a replacement for ageing Leopolda station, had to be approved by Benito Mussolini, who understandably was rather taken with the idea of a building that, viewed from above, was based on the *fascio littorio*, the logo of his National Fascist Party. The plans won the competition, but with hindsight, it's plain they deserved to. View it from any angle, and it looks beautiful. Not only a key piece of Italian modernism and one of the country's finest examples of the Functionalist style, Santa Maria Novella station – thanks to Mussolini's approval

of the design – also ushered in an acceptance of modernity in Italy that has had a huge impact on the country's design and architecture.

The station's influences clearly lay outside the country – in the work of Frank Lloyd Wright, and the Viennese architecture of Adolf Loos and Josef Hoffman – but it's a wholly original design whose exterior scale and brickwork respond to Leon Battista Alberti's gorgeous façade for the Santa Maria Novella church it sits opposite, and whose predominantly glass and metal interior is so light and airy that, despite its 59 million annual passengers, it always feels calm and spacious. This feeling is heightened by the horizontal planes of the concourse, making the most of the station's width and filling it with light that streams through angled skylights.

The interior, including the benches and platforms, were designed by Angiolo Mazzoni, an architect from the Ministry of Communication, but they echo the exterior's determinedly modern stance and use of materials, and in their 1930s feel can't help but draw you into pondering what horrendous, tragic scenes must have been played out here. If you're in any doubt, find the plaque near Platform 8: a moving memorial to the thousands of Jews who were deported from the station to Nazi concentration camps during World War II.

SIGHTS

INSIDE TRACK GIOTTO

Giotto, who, according to legend, was seen by Cimabue sketching sheep on stones and immediately apprenticed to his studio, was the first artist to break from Byzantine art by introducing an inkling of Humanism and space. See his *Crocifisso* in **Santa Maria Novella** (*see p71*), frescoes of St Francis in the Bardi/Peruzzi chapels in **Santa Croce** (*see p86*) and his *Maestà* at the **Uffizi** (*see p64*).

Called Novella ('New') because it was built on the site of the ninth-century Santa Maria delle Vigne, the church dominates the piazza with its huge, geometrical façade. Santa Maria Novella was the Florentine seat of the Dominicans, an order fond of leading street brawls against suspected heretics. The piazza outside was enlarged in 1244-45 to accommodate the crowds that came to hear St Peter the Martyr, one of the viler members of the saintly canon.

The pièce de résistance of the church is that magnificent Alberti façade. In 1465, the architect incorporated the Romanesque lower storey into a refined Renaissance scheme, adding the triangular tympanum and the scrolls that mask the side nave exteriors in an exercise of consummate classical harmony. The church interior, however, was designed by the order's monks and is fittingly severe.

The church also houses the *Crocifisso* by Giotto, a simple wooden crucifix. It was finally returned to the church in 2001 after a 12-year restoration and placed in the centre of the basilica where the Dominicans had originally positioned it in 1290.

Until Vasari had them whitewashed in the mid 16th century, the church walls were covered with frescoes. Fortunately, Masaccio's *Trinità* of 1427 remains on the left nave, a triumph of trompe l'œil, with God, Christ and two saints appearing to stand in a niche watched by the patrons Lorenzo Lenzi and his wife. The sinister inscription above the skeleton on the sarcophagus reads: 'I was what you are and what I am you shall be.'

In 1485, the Dominicans let Ghirlandaio cover the walls of the Cappella Tornabuoni, behind the altarpiece, with scenes from the life of John the Baptist, featuring lavish contemporary Florentine interiors and a supporting cast from the Tornabuoni family, all wearing beautiful clothes – effectively making the work part-advertisement, as the family were cloth merchants. Ghirlandaio also found time to train a young Michelangelo while working on the chapel. At about the same time, Filippino Lippi was at work next door in the Cappella di Filippo Strozzi, painting scenes from the life of St Philip. A wooden crucifix by Brunelleschi, the envy of Donatello, is to the left of the altarpiece.

To compare Masaccio's easeful use of perspective with the contorted struggles of Paolo Uccello, visit the Chiostro Verde (green cloister) to the left of the church (via a separate entrance). Uccello's lunettes can be considered either visionary experiments of modern art or a complete perspectival mess, depending on your tolerance of artistic licence. Off the Chiostro you'll find the Cappellone (or Cappella) degli Spagnoli, named after the Spanish wife of Cosimo I, Eleonora di Toledo, and decorated with vibrant scenes by Andrea di Bonaiuto. Look out for the odd-looking cupola on the Duomo fresco: it's the artist's own design for the dome, ultimately rejected in favour of Brunelleschi's plan.

Santa Maria Novella.

San Lorenzo

The original Medici neighbourhood is one of the city's liveliest.

Teeming with life, San Lorenzo is loved and hated in equal measure. The incongruously unfinished façade of San Lorenzo church itself and the chapel of the Medici family may be rather serious affairs, but this part of town is marked out by the frenetic activity generated by a huge central market, the high number of tourists, and the plethora of shops, delis, cafés and doughnut stands.

The market of San Lorenzo is the hub of the area, spreading its tentacles over a swathe of piazze, snaking north from the church of San Lorenzo. Its tacky street stalls all but conceal the entrance to the bustling Mercato Centrale.

Map p334	Cafés, Bars &
Hotels p109	Gelaterie p147
Restaurants & Wine	
Bars p130	

Roads lead off the *piazze* in a star shape. Head north-east from piazza San Lorenzo up via de' Ginori, alongside the gardens at the back of Palazzo Medici Riccardi, and past craft shops up to the corner of via San Gallo and via XXVII Aprile. The Benedictine refectory of **Cenacolo di Sant'Apollonia** (*see p76*) is on the left, while the **Chiostro dello Scalzo** (*see p76*) is situated north of piazza San Marco. Coming back down via Cavour, you'll pass the tacky gimmick that is the **Serial Killer & Death Penalty Museum** (no.51r, 055 210188) – it might be a good place to dump bored teenagers for an hour. In stark contrast is the nearby entrance to **Palazzo Medici Riccardi** (*see p76*); its beautiful family chapel was painted by Benozzo Gozzoli. Following the walls of the *palazzo* round to the right, you'll once more find yourself in piazza San Lorenzo.

Travelling south from this piazza will lead you past busy shoe and clothes shops in borgo San Lorenzo. If you head north-west from the **Cappelle Medicee** (*see right*) in piazza di Madonna degli Aldobrandini at the back of San Lorenzo church, you pass along via Faenza, with the **Interactive Museum of Medieval Florence** (no.13r, 055 282432, www.oscuro medioevo.com) on the corner – another naff money-spinner. Heading north-east up via Sant'Antonino takes you past tiny food stores and back towards the Mercato Centrale.

If you continue up via Faenza and cross dingy via Nazionale, you'll come to the **Cenacolo di Fuligno** (*see p74*) on the right. Heading north-east up via Nazionale, the roads widen into piazza dell'Indipendenza, where grand *palazzi* herald the beginnings of a more genteel area.

★ Cappelle Medicee

Piazza di Madonna degli Aldobrandini 6 (055 2388602, www.polomuseale.firenze.it). **Open** *Mar-Nov* 8.15am-4.50pm Tue-Sat, 1st, 3rd, 5th Mon & 2nd, 4th Sun of mth. *Dec-Feb* 8.15am-1.50pm Tue-Sat, 1st, 3rd, 5th Mon & 2nd, 4th Sun of mth. **Admission** €6. **No credit cards. Map** p334 A3. The spectacular Medici mausoleum is the most splendid and fascinating part of the basilica of San

INSIDE TRACK STRIKE A POSE

With their duckpond and flowerbeds, the public gardens surrounding the old Fortezza di Basso prison make a good spot to picnic, chill out or wait for a train. And if it's January or June, they're a fine spot from which to catch the latest style trends as Italy's fashionistas throng to the biannual Pitti Moda fashion fair, held in huge sheds within the fort's walls.

SIGHTS

Cappelle Medicee. See p73.

Lorenzo. Up the curling stairs at the back of the entrance chamber (which contains the family's reliquaries and memorial plaques) is the grand Cappella dei Principi (Chapel of the Princes), constructed from huge hunks of porphyry and ancient Roman marble hauled into the city by Turkish slaves. The chapel houses six sarcophagi of the Medici Grand Dukes. The floor plan of the Cappella dei Principi was based on that of the Baptistery and, possibly, the Holy Sepulchre in Jerusalem – it had been hoped that the tombs would be joined by that purporting to be of Christ, but the authorities in Jerusalem refused to sell it. This mausoleum was commissioned in 1602 but, amazingly, the beautifully intricate inlay of marble and precious stones wasn't completed until 1962, when workers from the Opificio delle Pietre Dure finished the last external pavement; by then, the Medici dynasty had been over for 220 years.

Although it's closed to the public, the discovery of the crypt in 1994 caused much excitement, with the sensational revelation of a stone under the chapel's altar that concealed the crypt's entrance. The exhumation of 49 Medici bodies ensued and scientists were able to determine in what manner many of them had died. It was originally thought that Francesco I de' Medici and his mistress Bianca Cappella, who died within hours of each other, had suffered from malaria: it has now been proven they had in fact undergone acute arsenic poisoning – probably at the hand of Francesco's jealous brother Ferdinando.

Out of the Cappella dei Principi, a passage to your left leads to Michelangelo's Sagrestia Nuova (New Sacristy). This chamber, begun in 1520, makes a stark contrast to the excesses of the chapel. It's dominated by the tombs of Lorenzo il Magnifico's relatives: grandson Lorenzo, Duke of Urbino, and his son Giuliano, Duke of Nemours, who grew up alongside Michelangelo. The tombs were designed by the artist with the figures of Night and Day, and, opposite, Dawn and Dusk, reclining on top; their gaze directs the visitor's eyes to a sculpture of a Madonna and child on the facing wall. Also here, under the sacristy, is the incomplete tomb of Lorenzo il Magnifico and his brother Giuliano. The chapel's coffered dome was designed to contribute to the allegory of the inevitability of death Michelangelo developed within the tomb, symbolising the 'sun' of salvation. The Sagrestia Nuova was finished by Giorgio Vasari, Michelangelo himself having been hauled off to Rome to finish the Sistine Chapel. The great man was furious at having to leave the city – 'I cannot live under pressure from patrons, let alone paint' – but he'd worked long enough on the project to leave it as one of his masterpieces.

Cenacolo del Conservatorio di Fuligno

Via Faenza 42 (055 286982, www.polomuseale.firenze.it). **Open** 9am-noon Tue, Thur, Sat, or by appointment. **Admission** free. **Map** p334 A3.

The Medicis

Florence's famous family.

The name Medici (pronounced with the stress on the first 'e') is all but synonymous with Florence and Tuscany. It suggests that the family's origins probably lie in the medical profession, though their later wealth was built on banking. The line begins back in 1360, with the birth of Giovanni di Bicci (1360-1429), who quietly amassed a fortune through his banking business – boosted immensely by the fact that it handled the papal account. This provided the basis for the Medici's later clout, but it was Giovanni's son, Cosimo il Vecchio (1389-1464) who first wielded real power in Florence, informally presiding over one of the city's most prosperous and prestigious eras from 1434. An even more astute banker than his father, Cosimo pacified opponents and his conscience by spending lavishly on charities and public building projects, introduced a progressive income tax system and balanced the interests of the volatile Florentine classes relatively successfully. Cosimo was also an intellectual, encouraging the new Humanist learning and developments in art that were sweeping Florence. He built up a public library (the first in Europe), financed scholars and artists, gave architectural commissions and founded a school along the lines of Plato's Academy – he was the epitome of the Renaissance *uomo universale*. The name 'il Vecchio' (the Elder) was a mark of respect. When he died, the Florentines inscribed on his tomb the words 'Pater Patriae' ('father of the nation').

Cosimo's grandson, Lorenzo il Magnifico (1449-92), was the big Medici, famous in his own time and legendary in later centuries. His rule marked the peak of the Florentine Renaissance, with artists such as Botticelli and Michelangelo producing superlative works. Lorenzo was himself a poet, and gathered round him a talented group of scholars and artists. The climate of intellectual freedom he fostered was a major factor in some of the greatest achievements of the Renaissance. Sadly, his sons Piero di Lorenzo (1471-1503) and Giuliano, Duke of Nemours (1478-1516), couldn't live up to their father: the former surrendered the city to the French in 1494, and the latter was little more than a puppet of his brother Giovanni, who would become Pope Leo X.

On the night of his birth, Giovanni's mother dreamed she would have not a baby but a huge lion, and Lorenzo decided early on that the child was destined for a glittering ecclesiastical career – serious papal ear-bending ensured that he became a monk at eight and a cardinal aged 16. Giovanni was a likeable, open character, but his fondness for the good life and shameless exploitation of the sale of indulgences to ease his permanent debts added fuel to the fire for critics of papal corruption.

Giovanni's illegitimate cousin Giulio (1478-1534) followed him in the papacy as Pope Clement VII in 1524, having already produced his own bastard, Alessandro (1511-37), whose penchant for debauchery, dressing in women's clothes, torturing and executing opponents, and appalling rudeness resulted in his being stabbed to death in his bed. With no heir in the direct Medici line, the Florentines chose Cosimo I (1519-74), the 18-year-old grandson of Lorenzo il Magnifico's daughter Lucrezia, to succeed him, thinking they could manipulate him. They were wrong – Cosimo was cold, secretive and cunning, and set about ruling with merciless efficiency, but also produced three sons of whom the most notable, Ferdinando I (1549-1609), reduced corruption, improved trade and farming, encouraged learning, and developed the navy and the port of Livorno. By staging lavish popular entertainments and giving dowries to poor girls, he became the most-loved Medici since Lorenzo il Magnifico. Ferdinando was also the last to be venerated by the townsfolk, since he was succeeded by a string of mediocre Medici who did little of note, preferring to hunt, eye up boys and collect bric-a-brac (Ferdinando II, 1610-70); to hang out with monks and spout anti-Semitic nonsense (Cosimo III, 1642-1723); and to whore around with stable boys in a gloomy castle near Prague, before escaping a forced marriage for a return to Florence in 1708 (Gian Gastone, 1671-1737).

There is one last Medici to whom every visitor to Florence since the mid 18th century has reason to be grateful: the strait-laced, pious Anna Maria. Gian Gastone's sister and the last surviving Medici, Anna Maria bequeathed all Medici property and treasures to the Grand Duchy in perpetuity, on the sole condition that they never leave Florence.

Chiostro dello Scalzo.

SIGHTS

The harmonious fresco on the refectory wall of the ex-convent of St Onofrio was discovered in 1845. It was at first thought to be the work of Raphael, but is, in fact, one of the best of Perugino's works: a *Last Supper* from about 1490. In the background is a representation of the Oration of the Garden set in a characteristically Umbrian landscape, giveaway evidence of the Perugian-born painter's roots.

Cenacolo di Sant'Apollonia

Via XXVII Aprile 1 (055 2388607, www. polomuseale.firenze.it). **Open** 8.15am-1.50pm Tue-Sat, 1st, 3rd, 5th Mon & 2nd, 4th Sun of mth. **Admission** free.

The works in this Benedictine refectory, such as the frescoes of the Passion of Christ, were covered over during the Baroque period and only came to light in the late 19th century. The most important is Andrea del Castagno's *Last Supper*.

Chiostro dello Scalzo

Via Cavour 69 (055 2388604). **Open** 8.15am-1.50pm Mon, Thur, Sat, or by appointment. **Admission** free. **Map** p335 A4.

The 'Cloister of the Barefoot' (so-called because the monk holding the Cross in the re-enactments of the Passion of Christ traditionally went shoeless) is frescoed with monochrome chiaroscuro episodes from the life of St John the Baptist by Andrea del Sarto. Built around a double courtyard with spindly Corinthian columns to a design by Sangallo, the cloister is a must-see epitome of delicacy and understatement.

★ Palazzo Medici Riccardi

Via Cavour 1 (055 2760340, www.palazzo-medici.it). **Open** 9am-7pm Mon, Tue, Thur-Sun. **Admission** €7. **No credit cards**. **Map** p335 B4.

In true Medici fashion, the family's 15th-century palace is strategically placed. They bought a string of adjacent houses on via Larga (now via Cavour) in the mid 14th century, when it was a fairly broad road in a peaceful residential area – but in close proximity to the Duomo and merely a few steps from their own church, San Lorenzo (*see below*). The Medici thereby made sure their home (until they moved into Palazzo Vecchio in 1540) was in a position of power, but they also ensured it would subtly intimidate any opposition with its strongbox-like appearance. Not wishing to appear too ostentatious, however, Cosimo il Vecchio rejected Brunelleschi's design as too extravagant and plumped for one by Michelozzo, who had recently proved his worth as a heavyweight architect in the rebuilding of the San Marco convent complex. Michelozzo designed a façade with a heavily rusticated lower storey (in the style of many military buildings), but a smoother and more refined first storey and a yet more restrained second storey.

The building was expanded and revamped in the 17th century by the Riccardi, its new owners, but retains Michelozzo's charming chapel. Almost entirely covered with frescoes by Benozzo Gozzoli, a student of Fra Angelico, this chapel features a vivid *Journey of the Magi* that is actually a portrait of 15th-century Medici. In another room, off the gallery, is Fra Filippo Lippi's winsome *Madonna and Child*. Don't miss the new interactive technology on the ground floor (in what was once the chamber of Lorenzo the Magnificent), where you stand under a little metal dome and point with a dramatic gesture at a large, flat screen in front of you; without touching anything, you can select parts of the chapel upstairs to find out more about them.

★ San Lorenzo

Piazza San Lorenzo (055 214042, www.opera medicealaurenziana.it). **Open** *Winter* 10am-5.30pm Mon-Sat. *Summer* 10am-5.30pm Mon-Sat; 1.30-5.30pm Sun. **Admission** €2.50. **No credit cards**. **Map** p334 A3.

Built where Florence's cathedral stood from the end of the fourth to the ninth century – and thus right on the site of Florence's oldest church – San Lorenzo's sheer size more than compensates for its very plain exterior. San Lorenzo was built between 1419 and 1469 to a design by Brunelleschi (but largely completed by Manetti, his erstwhile assistant, who made several design alterations), and was the first church to which the architect applied his theory of rational proportion. It sprawls, heavy and imposing, between piazza San Lorenzo and piazza di Madonna degli Aldobrandini, with a dome almost as prominent as that of the Duomo.

Despite the fortune spent on the place, the façade was never finished, hence the digestive biscuit-coloured bricks. In 1518, the Medici pope Leo X commissioned Michelangelo to design a façade – the models are in the Casa Buonarroti (*see p84*) – and ordained that the marble should be quarried at

Pietrasanta. Michelangelo disagreed, preferring high-quality Carrara marble. In the end, it didn't matter: the scheme was cancelled in 1520. Recently, there has been great excitement about this absent façade: a column built for the project was discovered buried in the piazza, and others that some now believe were destined for San Lorenzo were found in Pietrasanta.

A couple of artworks in the church merit a closer look. Savonarola snarled his tales of sin and doom from Donatello's bronze pulpits, but the reliefs are also powerful: you can almost hear the crowds scream in the *Deposition*. On the north wall is a *Martyrdom of St Lawrence* by Mannerist painter par excellence Bronzino. In the second chapel on the right is another Mannerist work, a *Marriage of the Virgin* by Rosso Fiorentino, while the north transept holds an *Annunciation* by Filippo Lippi with a clarity of line and a depth of perspective that make it perfect for this interior.

Opening off the north transept is the Sagrestia Vecchia (Old Sacristy): another Brunelleschi design, it has a dome segmented like a tangerine and proportions based on cubes and spheres, along with a fabulous painted *tondo* by Donatello. The doors, also by Donatello, feature martyrs, apostles and Church fathers; to the left of the entrance, an elaborate tomb made by Verrocchio out of serpentine, porphyry, marble and bronze contains the remains of Lorenzo il Magnifico's father and uncle.

Reached via the door to the left of the façade, Michelangelo's architectural classic, the Biblioteca Mediceo-Laurenziana (Laurentian Library), was built to house the Medici's large library. It still contains priceless volumes, papyri, codices and documents, though not all of them are on permanent display. The entrance corridor has a stunning red

and cream inlaid mosaic floor, while the library itself displays Michelangelo's predilection for the human form over any classical architectural norms. However, it's in the vestibule leading into the reading room that the true masterpiece of the library is found. The highly original three-sweep stairwell in *pietra serena* was a ground-breaking design, the first example ever of the expressive Mannerist style in architecture and one of the most elegant staircases ever built.

SIGHT SPOT ANDREA DEL CASTAGNO'S *LAST SUPPER*

Andrea del Castagno's masterly *Last Supper* (1445-50) is one of many works in the Benedictine refectory of Cenacolo di Sant'Apollonia (*see p76*) that were discovered only in the 1860s. The Benedictine nuns had, until this point, been a strictly closed order, and parts of the frescoes had even been whitewashed during the Baroque period. Restoration work revealed the full glory of the *cenacolo*. In this depiction, del Castagno reverts to a 14th-century seating plan: Judas is alienated on our side of the table, a dark figure breaking the pure white of the tablecloth and symbolically portrayed to resemble a satyr, a Catholic symbol of evil. The colours and enclosed space intensify the scene. Above the *Last Supper* are a *Crucifixion*, *Deposition* and *Resurrection*, also by del Castagno. Ring the bell for entry to see these masterpieces.

San Lorenzo.

San Marco

Must-see museums, and the most famous statue in the world.

The diverse museums in this visitor-friendly district contain fascinating displays of weird and wonderful things. From Egyptian mummies and flying machines to prehistoric gems and Renaissance masterpieces (not least one very famous statue), each collection vies for the attention of the visiting masses. However, it's far from just a tourist centre: head to the nigh-on perfect porticoed square of Santissima Annunziata and it's apparent that the area thrives on the crowds of students from nearby faculties – and is still an active centre of religious worship. Still, when it does come to famous attractions, San Marco has all the other outer

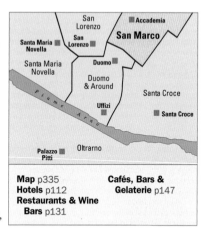

Map p335

Hotels p112

Restaurants & Wine Bars p131

Cafés, Bars & Gelaterie p147

districts of Florence trumped, since in the **Galleria dell'Accademia** (*see below*) it houses Michelangelo's *David*. Despite all the activity, there's a paucity of decent restaurants – do, however, check out **Focacceria Pugi** (*see p165*), renowned for selling the city's best *schiacciata con l'uva* (flat bread with grapes).

The **piazza della Santissima Annunziata** (abbreviated to SS Annunziata) is dominated by the powerful equestrian statue of Grand Duke Ferdinando I by Giambologna. On the eastern side is the **Spedale degli Innocenti** (*see p82*). Opened in 1445 as the first foundling hospital in Europe, it was designed by Filippo Brunelleschi and marks the advent of Renaissance town planning: Brunelleschi had designed it to fit into his greater plan for a perfectly symmetrical piazza – to be modern Europe's first – but died before realising his dream. The powder-blue medallions in the spandrels, each showing a swaddled baby, are by Andrea della Robbia.

Passing under the northernmost arch of the Spedale is via della Colonna, highlighted by the **Museo Archeologico** (*see right*). On the southernmost corner of the piazza you'll find the **Bottega dei Ragazzi** (*see right*), where children can enjoy Florence-themed creative workshops. Walking south down via de' Servi towards the Duomo will bring you to the **Museo Leonardo da Vinci** (*see p81*). On the western side of the square is upmarket hotel Loggiato dei Serviti (*see p112*); the church of **Santissima**

Annunziata (*see p82*) is to the north. West takes you to piazza San Marco, a hub for buses and site of the church of **San Marco** (*see p82*).

Beside San Marco is the **Museo di San Marco** (*see p80*). Round the corner from the queues extending from the Accademia is the **Opificio delle Pietre Dure** (*see p81*), dedicated to the art of inlaying gems in mosaics. North of the piazza is the mineral department of the city's **Museo di Storia Naturale** (*see p81*); just around the corner is the exotic **Giardino dei Semplici** (*see right*).

★ Galleria dell'Accademia

Via Ricasoli 58-60 (055 2388609, www.polo museale.firenze.it). **Open** 8.15am-6.50pm Tue-Sun. **Admission** €6.50 (€11 with special exhibitions), €10.50 with reservation (€15 with special exhibitions). **No credit cards**. **Map** p335 A4. Despite the fact that the Accademia contains a huge number of magnificent and historic works, the queue snaking around the corner is for one attraction above all: Michelangelo's monumental *David* (1501-04), still gleaming nearly a decade after its €400,000 clean-up in 2003 – it had been his first bath for 130 years.

Giardino dei Semplici.

by the University except La Specola).
No credit cards. **Map** p335 A4.
The Giardino dei Semplici, containing vegetable varieties with medicinal properties, was planted in 1545 by landscape gardener Il Tribolo for Cosimo I. His aim was to cultivate and research exotic plants, extracting essential oils, distilling perfumes, and seeking cures and antidotes for a variety of ailments and poisons.

Istituto degli Innocenti – La Bottega dei Ragazzi
Via de' Fibbiai 2 (piazza della SS Annunziata) (055 2478386, www.istitutodeglinnocenti.it). **Open** 9am-1pm, 3-7pm Mon-Sat. **Admission** (reservations recommended) €10 3 admissions; €20 6 admissions; €50 8 admissions. **Map** p335 A4.
The Children's Workshop was set up in 2006, and although it caters predominantly for Italians, four different creative workshops are available for English-speaking children aged three to 11. The sessions cover history, animals and Florentine art.

Museo Archeologico & Museo Egizio
Piazza della SS Annunziata 9b (055 23575, www.archeotoscana.beniculturali.it). **Open** 2-7pm Mon; 8.30am-7pm Tue, Thur; 8.30am-2pm Wed, Fri-Sun. **Admission** €4. **No credit cards**. **Map** p335 A5.
It's easy to come to Florence and get completely submerged in the Renaissance, but the archaeological museum, housed in Palazzo della Crocetta, explains what happened before the Golden Age. The museum has an impressive entrance hall, an enormous temporary exhibition space and a new Etruscan money display, La Mostra di Monete. Guided tours run every 45 minutes from 9am – meet at the checkpoint in Room 15 on the first floor. Elsewhere you'll find jewellery, funerary sculpture, urns and bronzes dating from the fifth century BC, as well as the fabulous

David started life as a political icon, portraying strength and resolve, designed to encourage Florentines to support their fledgling constitution. However, having carved it from a 5m-high (16ft) slab of marble, Michelangelo undoubtedly considered it a monument to his genius. He intended it to stand high up on the Duomo, giving *David* a top-heavy shape so it would look its best from the beholder's viewpoint (note the slightly oversize head and hands). However, in 1873, when the statue was moved from piazza della Signoria (where a copy still stands) following acts of vandalism, the authorities decided to keep the plinth low so visitors could witness its curves close-up.

Other Michelangelo works line the walls of the *David* salon; among them are his *Slaves*, masterly but unfinished sculptures struggling to escape from marble prisons. They were intended for Pope Julius II's tomb, a project Michelangelo was forced to abandon in order to paint the Sistine Chapel ceiling in Rome. On the right of *David* is the unfinished *Pietà Palestrina*, often attributed to Michelangelo.

The gallery also houses a mixed bag of late Gothic and Renaissance paintings on the ground floor, and a fabulous collection of musical instruments from the Conservatory of Luigi Cherubini.

Giardino dei Semplici
Via Micheli 3 (055 2757402, www.msn.unifi.it). **Open** *Winter* 10am-5pm Mon, Sat, Sun. *Summer* 10am-7pm daily. **Admission** €6 (€8 combined 3-mth ticket for all scientific museums managed

SIGHT SPOT FRA ANGELICO

Fra Angelico, described by Ruskin as 'Not an artist... but an inspired saint', carried out his most spiritual work during his redecorations at San Marco. Masaccio and Alberti influences are evident in his treatment of linear perspective, and his pioneering use of light and colour to depict movement and expression guarantee him a place in the Renaissance Hall of Fame. See his cell frescoes *Noli Me Tangere*, *Annunciazione*, *Deposizione* and *Tabernacolo dei Linaioli* at the Museo di San Marco (*see p80*), or nip into San Marco (*see p82*) next door to see his *Deposition*, San Marco altarpiece and *St Peter of Verona* triptych.

SIGHTS

Chimera, a mythical beast that's part lion, part goat and part snake. Also present is the first-century BC Etruscan bronze *Orator,* famous and historically important because the speaker in question is wearing a Roman toga. The first rooms house Egyptian artefacts (including sarcophagi complete with creepy shrivelled bodies) from prehistoric eras through to AD310. Outside, a beautiful garden lined with Etruscan tombs and monuments opens only on a Saturday.

★ Museo di San Marco

Piazza San Marco 1 (055 2388608, www.polo museale.firenze.it). **Open** 8.15am-1.50pm Tue-Fri,

1st, 3rd & 5th Mon of mth; 8.15am-4.50pm Sat, 2nd & 4th Sun of mth. **Admission** €4. **No credit cards. Map** p335 A5.

The Museo di San Marco is not only a fascinating coming-together of religion and history, but a wonderful place to rest and take in the general splendour. Housed in the monastery where he lived with his fellow monks, the museum is largely dedicated to the ethereal paintings of Fra Angelico (aka Beato Angelico), one of the most important spiritual artists of the 15th century, a man who would never lift a brush without a prayer and who wept whenever he painted a crucifixion. You're greeted on the first floor by one of the most famous images in Christendom,

Walk Fictional Florence

Step into other worlds, from Portrait of a Lady to Hannibal.

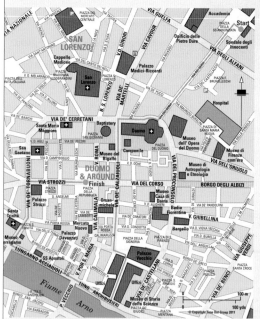

Charlotte Bartlett to see the sights in *A Room with a View.* The exquisite piazza also has a cameo role, complete with horses, carts and cabbage leaves, in Jane Campion's *Portrait of a Lady,* based on the novel by Henry James.

Follow via de' Servi down to piazza del Duomo, where in the same film Nicole Kidman's independently minded Isabel Archer rides in her carriage to a less independent destiny with John Malkovich's Gilbert Osmond. Skirt round the north of the Duomo between the Baptistery (*see p58*) and the façade steps, where Charlton Heston's Michelangelo lovingly contemplates the cathedral's carved images in *The Agony and the Ecstasy.* Continue down via de' Calzaiuoli to via de' Tavolini: in Irving Stone's source novel, Michelangelo is seconded to Ghirlandaio's studio here.

Set off from the Spedale degli Innocenti (*see p82*) in piazza della SS Annunziata. The courtyard of the foundling hospital sets the scene for Joan Plowright's Mary Wallace to rescue the illegitimate Luca from an orphanage fate in Franco Zeffirelli's *Tea with Mussolini,* while Giambologna's Grand Duke Ferdinand I statue is the starting point from which Judi Dench's Eleanor Lavish whisks Maggie Smith's

Arriving at piazza della Signoria, admire the world's most gruesome Renaissance square – in fact and fiction. This is where Savonarola made his Bonfire of the Vanities. In *A Room with a View* once again, Helena Bonham-Carter's young aristo Lucy Honeychurch swoons in the square after witnessing a murder, and, on the balcony of Palazzo Vecchio, Anthony Hopkins's Dr Hannibal Lecter brings a whole new

an other-worldly *Annunciation*, but the images Fra Angelico and his assistants frescoed on the walls of the monks' white vaulted cells are almost as impressive. Particularly outstanding are the lyrical *Noli Me Tangere*, which depicts Christ appearing to Mary Magdalene in a field of flowers, and the surreal *Mocking of Christ*, in which Christ's torturers are represented simply by relevant fragments of their anatomy (a hand holding a whip, a face spitting).

The cell that was later occupied by Fra Girolamo Savonarola is adorned with portraits of the rabid reformer by Fra Bartolomeo. You can also see his black wool cloak and his cilith, which was tied around the thigh to cause constant pain in reminder of the suffering of Christ. Near the cells reserved specially for Cosimo de' Medici is the beautiful library designed by his favourite architect, Michelozzo, in 1441.

On the ground floor, in the Ospizio dei Pellegrini (pilgrims' hospice), are more works by Fra Angelico. The *Tabernacle of the Madonna dei Linaiuoli*, his first commission from 1433 for the guild of linen makers, is here – painted on wood carved by Ghiberti, it contains some of his best-known images: the multi-coloured musical angels. You can also see a superb *Deposition* and a *Last Judgement*. The small refectory is dominated by a Ghirlandaio *Last Supper* (1479-80) in which the disciples pick at a repast of bread, wine and cherries against a symbolic background of orange trees, a peacock, a Burmese cat and flying ducks.

Museo di Storia Naturale – Sezione Mineralogia

Via la Pira 4 (055 216936, www.msn.unifi.it). **Open** 9am-1pm Mon, Tue, Thur, Fri, Sun; 9am-5pm Sat. **Admission** €6 (€8 combined 3-mth ticket for all scientific museums managed by the University except La Specola). **No credit cards. Map** p335 A4.
This clearly explained collection makes gem-lovers drool. It's packed full of strange and lovely stones, including 12 huge Brazilian quartzes.

Museo Leonardo da Vinci

Via de' Servi 66-68r (055 282966, www.mostre dileonardo.com). **Open** 10am-7pm daily. **Admission** €6. **Map** p335 A4.
The painter, sculptor, musician, engineer, inventor, scientist and all-round genius Leonardo da Vinci justly has a museum to himself. The museum offers an attractive, interactive insight into the machines that featured in da Vinci's codes. Several of his most extraordinary inventions have been built from studies taken from his drawings: flying machines, a hydraulic saw, a printing machine and even a massive tank: it measures 5.3m by 3m (17ft by 10ft) and weighs two tonnes. Most of the exhibits can be touched, moved and even dangled from, making this place immensely popular with kids.

Opificio delle Pietre Dure

Via degli Alfani 78 (055 2651357, www.opificio dellepietredure.it). **Open** 8.15am-2pm Mon-Sat. **Admission** €2. **No credit cards. Map** p335 A4.
Pietra dura is the craft of inlaying gems or semi-precious stones in intricate mosaics. You'll see fine examples in all the grandest palaces and most expensive shops of Florence. The Opificio (workshop) was founded by Grand Duke Ferdinando I in 1588; it's now an important restoration centre, but also provides a fascinating insight into this typically Florentine art, with its mezzanine exhibitions of tools and stones, and its displays of the methods used for cutting and polishing the stones, through to inlaying and mosaic techniques. *Photo p82.*

meaning to 'letting it all hang out' – at the expense of police inspector Rinaldo Pazzi's innards – in *Silence of the Lambs* sequel *Hannibal*.

Cut through piazzale degli Uffizi, where Asia Argento's detective Anna Manni was 'rescued' after suffering a bout of artistic overkill in *The Stendhal Syndrome*. When you reach the river, turn right into lungarno degli Archibusieri, where the hotel at no.4 is where James Ivory found his *Room with a View* location. (The views in the film are actually from lungarno Torrigiani, and in EM Forster's book the Pensione Bertollini was on lungarno delle Grazie.)

Carry on along the riverbank, past the ponte Vecchio, to the curved ramparts of Ferragamo's Palazzo Spini Ferroni. Turn right into via de' Tornabuoni. At no.8 is Palazzo Aldoviti Sangalletti, once home to Gran Caffè Doney and daily meeting place for I Scorpioni, the genteel group of 1930s expats remembered in *Tea with Mussolini*. Farmacia Inglese, used for a setting in the film, is now a shoe shop, but truffle parlour Procacci, shown in a scuffle with the Blackshirts, is still here.

For a final macabre touch, turn right into via Strozzi, which ends with the portico of via Pellicceria on the right, stalking ground for a hungry Hannibal Lecter in *Hannibal*; this was inspired by the real-life story of the 'Florence Monster', responsible for a series of horrific murders that gripped the city for three decades. It brings the dark underbelly of the city sharply into focus, a focus that is explored chillingly by ex-policeman and 'Florence Monster' investigator Michele Giuttari in *A Florentine Death*.

INSIDE TRACK
WHEEL OF MISFORTUNE

Once you've explored the wonders inside Brunelleschi's Spedale degli Innocenti (*see below*), take a look along its outside walls; in the far left-hand corner of the *loggia* you'll find a medieval version of the 'baby hatch', a little revolving hatch with a rotating horizontal wheel designed for people to anonymously leave their unwanted babies to be collected by the nuns inside. The system was in operation for more than 400 years, from 1445 until the hospital's closure in 1875.

★ FREE San Marco

Piazza San Marco (055 287628). **Open** 8.30am-noon, 4-6pm Mon-Sat; 4-6pm Sun. **Admission** free. **Map** p335 A4.

The amount of money lavished by the Medici family on San Lorenzo (*see p76*) is nothing compared with that spent on the church and convent of San Marco. After Cosimo il Vecchio returned from exile in 1434, he organised the transfer of the monastery of San Marco from the Silvestrine monks to the Dominicans from Fiesole. Cosimo went on to fund the renovation of the decaying church and convent by Michelozzo, and also founded a public library that greatly influenced Florentine Humanists; Florentine Humanist

Opificio delle Pietre Dure. *See p81.*

Academy meetings were held in the gardens. Ironically, later in the 15th century San Marco became the base of religious fundamentalist Fra Girolamo Savonarola, who burned countless Humanist treasures in his notorious Bonfire of the Vanities.

Inside the church you can see Giambologna's 16th-century nave with side chapels. In 1589, he completed the Cappella di Sant'Antonino, where you can now, creepily, see the whole dried body of the saint.

The altarpiece *Madonna and Child* (1440s) is by Fra Angelico, whose other more famous works can be seen next door in the Museo di San Marco (*see p80*). Two missing panels from the painting were discovered, curiously enough, in Oxford, behind the door of an elderly Englishwoman's house in 2006.

FREE Santissima Annunziata

Piazza della SS Annunziata (055 266181). **Open** 7am-12.30pm, 4-6.30pm daily. **Admission** free. **Map** p335 A4.

Despite Brunelleschi's perfectionist ambitions for the square it crowns, Santissima Annunziata – the church of the Servite order – is a place of popular worship rather than perfect proportion. Highlights include a frescoed Baroque ceiling and an opulent shrine built around a miraculous *Madonna*, purportedly painted by a monk in 1252 and, as the story goes, finished overnight by angels. Surrounding the icon are flowers, silver lamps and pewter body parts, ex votos left in the hope that the Madonna will cure the dicky heart or gammy leg of a loved one.

Michelozzo was the directing architect and built the Villani and Madonna chapels, and the oratory on the left side of the church. In 1453, after almost ten years of work and not much progress, directorship was handed to Antonio Manetti. When Manetti ran into financial difficulty, the governing priests ceded the venture to the Gonzaga family. Finally, in 1477, Leon Batisti completed the church with slight modifications. The atrium was frescoed early the following century by Pontormo, Rosso Fiorentino and, most strikingly, Andrea del Sarto, whose *Birth of the Virgin* is set within the walls of a Renaissance *palazzo* that has cherubs perched on a mantelpiece.

Spedale degli Innocenti

Piazza della SS Annunziata 12 (055 2037308, www.istitutodeglinnocenti.it). **Open** 10am-7pm daily. **Admission** €5. **No credit cards**. **Map** p335 A5.

Housed in the recreation room of Brunelleschi's foundling hospital, this collection suffered a substantial blow in 1853, when several important works were auctioned off (for a relative pittance) to raise money for the hospital. The remaining pieces include an unsurprising concentration of Madonna and Bambino pieces, including a Botticelli and a vivid Luca della Robbia. The high point, however, is Ghirlandaio's *Adoration of the Magi*, commissioned for the high altar of the hospital's church.

Santa Croce

Museums full of history and an atmosphere that's all about today.

The largest of Florence's medieval parochial areas has, like much of the centre, a heady air of history and learning – it encompasses the impressive church with which it shares its name, the city's synagogue, the national library and several fascinating museums. But it's not hard to have fun here too, with some of the best ice-cream in the city (*see p151*), a lively market, excellent shopping and two world-class restaurants, **Cibrèo** and **Enoteca Pinchiorri** (for both, *see p133*). In terms of new openings and general buzziness, Santa Croce is a close second to the Oltrarno for the title of Florence's most exciting neighbourhood.

San Lorenzo ■ Accademia
Santa Maria Novella ■ San Lorenzo ■ San Marco
Santa Maria Novella Duomo ■
Duomo & Around
■ Uffizi Arno **Santa Croce**
■ Santa Croce
Palazzo Pitti ■ Oltrarno

Map p335 **Cafés, Bars &**
Hotels p112 **Gelaterie** p148
Restaurants & Wine
Bars p131

Central **piazza Santa Croce** is a natural meeting spot where children play and adults rest their feet. It's not always so relaxing: the sui/ homicidal football game *calcio storico* is played here every June (*see p179*) and from the end of November there's a Christmas market. The **Sinagoga & Museo di Arte e Storia Ebraica** (*see p87*) lies in northern Santa Croce, just south of the piazza d'Azeglio, while the **Museo di Antropologia e Etnologia** (*see p85*) can be found at the corner of borgo degli Albizi and via del Proconsolo; south of here, piazza San Firenze houses the **Bargello** (*see p84*).

In via dell'Oriuolo, off via del Proconsolo and east of the Duomo, is the **Museo di Firenze com'era**, stuffed with the city archives, and the nearby **Museo Fiorentino di Preistoria** (for both, *see p85*). In borgo Pinti, east of the Duomo, watch out for the hard-to-find entrance to the church of **Santa Maria Maddalena dei Pazzi** (no.58). Just north of the river you return to piazza Santa Croce, with its imposing Gothic church of **Santa Croce** and attached **Museo dell'Opera di Santa Croce & Cappella dei Pazzi** (for both, *see p86*). Lining the square is a mix of shops and restaurants with outside tables. On the south side is the frescoed sepia façade of **Palazzo d'Antella**: decorated in 1620, it now houses smart rental apartments. Outside the church is Enrico Pazzi's 1865 statue of Dante.

At the head of piazza Santa Croce, via de' Benci is dotted with crafts shops and bohemian restaurants running down towards the Arno, past the **Museo Horne** (*see p86*), to the **ponte alle Grazie**. Like most of the bridges in central Florence, this one has a fascinating history: it was blown up just before the Germans' retreat at the end of World War II and only rebuilt in 1957. The bridge gets its name from a chapel, devoted to Santa Maria delle Grazie, which was popular with distraught lovers seeking solace.

Continuing east you'll come across a square dominated by the **Biblioteca Nazionale**. Built to house the three million books and two million documents that were held in the Uffizi until 1935, the national library has two towers with statues of Dante and Galileo – nicknamed by Florentines, in mock disrespect, 'the asses' ears'.

North-west of the parish square are myriad winding streets, mostly given over to leather factories and tiny souvenir shops. Until recently, the area north of Santa Croce church, stretching up past the **Casa Buonarroti** (*see p84*) in via Ghibellina to piazza de' Ciompi, was the rough-and-ready home to rival gangs of bored Florentine youths. Increasingly yuppified, it now yields trendy *trattorie* and wine bars. Piazza de' Ciompi was named after the dyers' and wool workers' revolt of 1378, and is taken over by a junk and antiques market during the week and

Bargello.

a huge day-long flea market on the last Sunday of the month (*see p164* **Market Forces**). The square is dominated by the **Loggia del Pesce**, built by Vasari in 1568 for the Mercato Vecchio, which previously occupied piazza della Repubblica. Taken apart in the 19th century, it was re-erected here.

Further east is piazza Ghiberti, home of the fruit and vegetable market of Sant'Ambrogio (*see p164* **Market Forces**), the world-famous Cibrèo restaurant and the shops, bars, *pizzerie* and restaurants of borgo La Croce. Borgo La Croce extends as far as piazza Beccaria and comes to a rest at the east city gate, Porta alla Croce, in the middle of the avenues circling the historic centre of the city.

★ Bargello

Via del Proconsolo 4 (055 2388606, www.polo museale.firenze.it). **Open** 8.15am-1.50pm Tue-Sat, 1st, 3rd & 5th Mon of mth, 2nd & 4th Sun of mth. **Admission** €4; €7.50 during special exhibitions. **No credit cards. Map** p335 C4.

This imposing, fortified structure has had so many purposes over the years that although it's now most famous for containing Florence's main set of sculptures, the building itself and its history are equally fascinating. The Bargello started life as the Palazzo del Popolo in 1250 and soon became the mainstay of the chief magistrate, or *podestà*. The bodies of executed criminals were displayed in the courtyard during the 14th century; in the 15th century, law courts, prisons and torture chambers were set up inside. The Medici made it the seat of the *bargello* (chief of police) in the 16th century.

Officially the Museo Nazionale del Bargello, the museum opened in 1865 to celebrate Florence becoming the capital of Italy. It now holds Florence's most eclectic and prestigious collection of sculpture, with treasures ranging from such famous pieces as Michelangelo's *Drunken Bacchus* and *Brutus* (the only bust he ever sculpted), and Giambologna's fleet-footed *Mercury* to Scandinavian chess sets and Egyptian ivories. The Salone Donatello contains the artist's two triumphant *Davids* and a tense *St George*, the original of which once stood outside the Orsanmichele. Also fascinating are the two bronze panels of the *Sacrifice of Isaac*, sculpted by Brunelleschi and Lorenzo Ghiberti for a competition to design the north doors of the Duomo's Baptistery. Back out on the grand *loggia* you can see Giambologna's bronze birds – they used to spout water in a Medici grotto, and include a madly exaggerated turkey. On this floor you can also find the little frescoed Magdalen Chapel, which contains the oldest confirmed portrait of Dante, painted by Giotto. The easily missed second floor has a fascinating selection of bronze statuettes and Andrea del Verrocchio's *Lady with a Posy* (1474), perhaps carved in collaboration with his student Leonardo da Vinci.

Casa Buonarroti

Via Ghibellina 70 (055 241752, www.casa buonarroti.it). **Open** 10am-5pm Mon, Wed-Sun. **Admission** €6.50. **No credit cards. Map** p335 C5.

In 1612, Michelangelo Buonarroti the Younger took the decision to create a building in order to honour the memory of his rather more famous great-uncle. Although Michelangelo (1475-1564) never actually lived here, this 17th-century house, owned by his descendants until 1858, has a collection of memorabilia that gives an insight into Florence's most famous artistic son. On the walls are scenes from the painter's life, while the pieces collected by the artist's great-nephew Filippo include a magnificent wooden model for the façade of San Lorenzo (*see p76*) and two important original works: a bas-relief *Madonna of the Stairs* breastfeeding at the foot of a flight of stairs, and an unfinished *Battle of the Centaurs*.

Cimitero degli Inglesi

Piazzale Donatello 38 (055 582608). **Open** *Summer* 9am-noon Mon-Fri. *Winter* 9am-noon Mon; 2-5pm Tue-Fri. For the English Cemetery, *see right* **Profile**.

Museo di Antropologia e Etnologia

Via del Proconsolo 12 (055 2396449, www.msn. unifi.it). **Open** 9am-1pm Mon-Fri, Sun; 9am-5pm Sat. **Admission** €6 (€8 combined 3-mth ticket for all scientific museums managed by the University except La Specola). **No credit cards**. **Map** p335 B4.

Among the mix of artefacts from all over the world on display here are a collection of Peruvian mummies, an Ostyak harp from Lapland, an engraved trumpet from the former Belgian Congo made out of an elephant tusk, Ecuadorian shrunken heads alongside a specially designed skull-beating club, and a Marini-meets-Picasso equestrian monument.

Museo Fiorentino di Preistoria

Via Sant'Egidio 21 (055 295159, www. museofiorentinopreistoria.it). **Open** 3.30-6.30pm Mon; 9.30am-12.30pm, 3.30-6.30pm Tue, Thur; 9.30am-12.30pm Wed, Fri, Sat; guided tours by appointment. **Admission** €3. **No credit cards**. **Map** p335 B4.

Florence's Museum of Prehistory traces humanity's development from the Paleolithic to the Bronze Age. The first floor contains interesting displays of illustrations following hominid physical changes, and also examines Italy's prehistoric art. The second floor includes a fascinating collection of stone implements.

The English Cemetery

Escape the hordes surrounding David for an intimate encounter with sculpture.

It may be sited in a rather unlovely roundabout in the middle of a dual carriageway on the outside perimeter of Santa Croce, but Florence's little Swiss Protestant Cemetery (*see left*), better known as the English Cemetery (Cimitero degli Inglesi), or to locals as *l'isola dei morti*, 'the island of the dead', makes a wonderful stroll – if you can get in, that is. On the day of our most recent visit, the cemetery was closed for lunch. As we strained for tantalising glimpses through the bars of extraordinary headstones, linked by cool, shady paths lined with olive trees and carefully tended pots of tumbling flowers and miniature olive trees, a kind-hearted soul inside (the caretaker, it turned out) took pity and opened the gates. He went back to his lunch, and we were free to wander through what feels like a secret garden, and one steeped in history.

The cemetery dates back to 1827, when the Swiss Evangelical Reformed Church purchased land outside the medieval wall and gate of Porta a' Pinti for an international and ecumenical cemetery. At first it was populated by Swiss, Russians, Americans and English, but by the 19th century the city's swelling English community ensured a surge in English occupants. The result is a fascinating range of elegant headstones, graves and statuary, marking the tombs of writers such as Elizabeth Barrett Browning, Walter Savage Landor, Frances Trollope and Arthur Hugh Clough, and a wealth of lesser known but equally interesting bodies: Theodore Parker, who campaigned (with Barrett Browning) against slavery; a dozen participants in the Peninsular War and the Battle of Waterloo; associates of Florence

Nightingale; and a black slave from Nubia, Nadezhda, who came to Florence aged 14 and was baptised into a Russian Orthodox family. Reflecting the prevalence of English artists in Florence in the 19th century, Lord Leighton, Roddam Spencer Stanhope and William Holman Hunt are among those who designed and sculpted these lichen-covered tombs and gravestones. We're drawn to the tomb of Beatrice Shakespeare and Edward Claude Shakespeare Clench, only later discovering them to be the last descendants of the Bard.

Thanks to the ecumenical nature of the cemetery, the tombs sport everything from full-size guardian angels to secular motifs, and range from plain headstones and unadorned crosses to designs that are totally over the top. Many were created by big artistic names: as well as Holman Hunt (who sculpted his wife Fanny's tomb), Hiram Powers, Odoardo Fantacchiotti (his *La Speranza* is one of the most beautiful sculptures here), Lorenzo Bartolini, Emilio Zocchi, Francesco Jerace, Johan Bystrom, William Wetmore Story and Pietro Bazzanti all have work here; Barrett Browning's gorgeous sarcophagus, raised on six delicate columns, was designed by Frederic, Lord Leighton.

Still owned by the small Swiss church that originally bought the land, but lovingly refurbished by a committed group of Roma, the cemetery is no longer able to accept bodies. Ashes can, however, still be buried here – and these days even Catholics are allowed a look-in. They might even wish to pay a visit, ideally outside lunchtime – and in spring, when the irises turn this gorgeous space into a sea of blue.

SIGHTS

Museo di Firenze com'era

Via dell'Oriuolo 24 (055 2616545, www.musei civicifiorentini.it). **Open** 9am-1.30pm Mon-Wed; 9am-6.30pm Sat. **Admission** €2.70. **No credit cards. Map** p335 B5.

This charmingly named museum ('Florence As It Was') traces the city's development through collections of maps, paintings and archaeological discoveries. There are rooms devoted to Giuseppe Poggi's plans from the 1860s to modernise Florence by creating Parisian-style boulevards; the famous lunettes of the Medici villas painted in 1599 by Flemish artist Giusto Utens; and the history of the region from 200 million years ago to Roman times. New exhibits include a model of 'Florentia' that shows how the city may have been in Roman times, with a Roman theatre buried below Palazzo Vecchio. Also interesting is the huge reproduction of the famous *Pianta della Catena*, a 19th-century copy of a 1470 engraving showing the first topological plan of Florence.

★ Museo Horne

Via de' Benci 6 (055 244661, www.museohorne. it). **Open** 9am-1pm Mon-Sat. **Admission** €6. **No credit cards. Map** p335 C4.

The 15th-century Palazzo Corsi-Alberti was purchased in the 1800s by English architect and art historian Herbert Percy Horne, who restored it to its Renaissance splendour. When he died in 1916, he left his *palazzo* and vast collection to the state. Objects range from ceramics and Florentine coins to a coffee grinder and a pair of spectacles. Upstairs is a damaged wooden panel from a triptych attributed to Masaccio. Also here is an *Exorcism* by the Maestro di San Severino and, the pride of the collection, a gold-black *Santo Stefano* by Giotto.

Museo dell'Opera di Santa Croce & Cappella dei Pazzi

Largo Bargellini (left side of the church) (055 2466105, www.operadisantacroce.it). **Open** 9.30am-5.30pm Mon-Sat; 1-5.30pm Sun. **Admission** €5 (incl museum & chapel). **Map** p335 C5.

Brunelleschi's geometric tour de force, the Cappella dei Pazzi was planned in the 1430s and completed almost 40 years later. The chapel is based on a central square, topped by a cupola flanked by a pair of barrel-vaulted bays. The pure lines of the interior are decorated with Luca della Robbia's painted ceramic roundels of the 12 Apostles and the four Evangelists. The chapel opens on to the cloisters of Santa Croce (*see below*), resulting in a calm, detached atmosphere.

Across the courtyard is a small museum of church treasures; the collection includes Donatello's pious *St Louis of Toulouse* from Orsanmichele (*see p63*). The backbone of the collection is in the former refectory, with Giotto's godson Taddeo Gaddi's imposing yet poetic *Tree of Life* above his *Last Supper* (unfortunately, in very bad condition). In equally poor condition is Cimabue's *Crucifixion*, which hung in the basilica until it was damaged in the flood of 1966. There's also a small permanent exhibition of the woodcuts and engravings of the modern artist Pietro Parigi. Access to the museum and chapel is through Santa Croce (*see below*).

★ Santa Croce

Largo Bargellini (left side of the church) (055 2466105, www.santacroceopera.it). **Open** 9.30am-5.30pm Mon-Sat; 1-5.30pm Sun. **Admission** €5 (incl museum & chapel). **Map** p335 C5.

The richest medieval church in the city, Santa Croce has a great deal to offer, even to visitors long tired of church-hopping. The Museo dell'Opera di Santa Croce is housed here, along with the delightful chapter house known as the Cappella dei Pazzi (for both, *see above*) and two beautiful cloistered courtyards, not to mention the church itself, which is crammed with illustrious tombs and cenotaphs. The coloured marble façade is impressive, but at first sight the interior seems big and gloomy, with overbearing marble tombs clogging the walls. Not all of them

Santa Croce.

indeed, in 1378, inspired by the Franciscans, the dyers and wool workers revolted against the guilds.

As for the Franciscans, their vow of poverty slowly eroded. By the late 13th century, the old church was felt to be inadequate and a new building was planned: intended to be one of the largest in Christendom, it was designed by Arnolfo di Cambio, architect of the Duomo and Palazzo Vecchio. The building was financed partly by confiscated Ghibelline property, and Arnolfo himself laid the first stone on 3 May 1294.

The church underwent various stages of restoration and modification, with one of Vasari's infamous remodernisations robbing it of some frescoes by Giotto's school in favour of heavy classical altars. Fortunately, he left the main chapels intact, though subsequent makeovers completely destroyed the decorations of the Cappella Tosinghi-Spinelli. Among the remaining gems are the fabulous stained-glass windows at the east end (behind the high altar) by Agnolo Gaddi, the marble tomb of Leonardo Bruni, and the Cavalcanti tabernacle (both flanking the side door on the south wall).

At the eastern end of the church, the Bardi and Peruzzi chapels, which were completely frescoed by Giotto, are masterpieces. That said, the condition of the frescoes is not brilliant – a result of Giotto painting on dry instead of wet plaster and daubing them with whitewash – and were only rediscovered in the mid 18th century. The most striking of the two chapels is the Bardi, with scenes from the life of St Francis in haunting, virtual monotone, the figures stylised just enough to make them otherworldly yet individual enough to keep them human. On the far side of the high altar is the Cappella Bardi di Vernio, frescoed by one of Giotto's most interesting followers, Maso di Banco, in vibrant colours. Don't miss the leather school behind the church (accessible from via San Giuseppe; *see p162*).

contain bodies: Dante's, for example, is simply a memorial to the poet, who is buried in Ravenna.

In the niche alongside Dante's is the tomb of Michelangelo, by Vasari. The artist had insisted on burial here when the time came, as he wanted 'a view towards the cupola of the Duomo for all eternity', and to adorn his tomb had worked obsessively on the *Pietà* (now in the Museo dell'Opera del Duomo; *see p58*). It is said that he would have disliked the finished tomb because, despite being an impressive mixture of painting, sculpture and architecture, the whole is too ostentatious and complicated for a memorial tomb (unlike his own serene Sagrestia Nuova in the Capelle Medicee; *see p73*). Further into the church are the tombs of Leonardo Bruni (by Bernardo Rossellino), Vittorio Alfieri and, best known for eating brains in the *Divine Comedy*, Ugolino della Gherardesca. Back at the top of the left aisle is Galileo's tomb, a polychrome marble confection created by Foggini more than a century after the astronomer's death, when the Church finally permitted him a Christian burial.

It's something of a paradox that, while the church is filled with the tombs of the great and the grand, it formerly belonged to the Franciscans, the least worldly of the religious orders. They founded it in 1228, ten years after arriving in the city. A recently established order, they were supposed to make their living through manual work, preaching and begging. At the time, the area was a slum, home to the city's dyers and wool workers, and Franciscan preaching, with its message that all men were equal, had a huge impact on the poor folk who lived there;

Sinagoga & Museo di Arte e Storia Ebraica

Via Farini 4 (055 2346654, www.jewishflorence. it). **Open** *Apr, May, Sept, Oct* 10am-1pm, 2-5pm Mon-Thur, Sun; 10am-1pm Fri. *June-Aug* 10am-6pm Mon-Thur, Sun; 10am-2pm Fri. *Nov-Mar* 10am-4pm Mon-Thur, Sun; 10am-2pm Fri. **Admission** €5. **No credit cards. Map** p335 B5. Built in 1870, following the demolition of the ghetto, this synagogue is an extraordinarily ornate mix of Moorish, Byzantine and Eastern influences, with its walls and ceilings covered in polychrome arabesques. The Museum of Jewish Art and History, which was extended up on to a second floor in 2007, holds a collection tracing the history of Jews in Florence, from their supposed arrival as Roman slaves to their official introduction into the city as money-lenders in 1430. Exhibits include documented stories, jewellery, ceremonial objects and furniture, photos and drawings, many of which depict the ghetto that occupied the area just north of piazza della Repubblica.

SIGHTS

Oltrarno

How the other half lives: quiet parks, lively bars and bohemian enclaves.

Spanning the width of the city centre along the southern banks of the Arno and extending down to Porta Romana in an oblique triangle is the Oltrarno (literally, 'beyond the Arno'). This part of town is a beguiling world of ornate *palazzi* with splendid gardens, church squares and tumbledown artisan workshops. To the west of Oltrarno are parishes San Frediano and Santo Spirito. At the heart of the district is the huge Palazzo Pitti (*see p89*), with its museums and Boboli Gardens (*see p90*), while to the south-east is the parish of San Niccolò and picturesque country lanes that lead uphill to the panoramic piazzale Michelangelo.

Map p334-335	Cafés, Bars &
Hotels p115	Gelaterie p148
Restaurants & Wine	
Bars p137	

Map p334-335 Hotels p115 Restaurants & Wine Bars p137 Cafés, Bars & Gelaterie p148

San Frediano parish is dominated by piazza del Carmine, a social hub by night and home to the **Santa Maria del Carmine** church and the **Brancacci Chapel** (for both, *see p92*). Despite a growing influx of long-term American students, the area still belongs to the locals.

Piazza Santo Spirito is the heart of its own bohemian neighbourhood, bustling with furniture restorers and restaurateurs. A morning market is held in the square from Monday to Saturday, with a flea market on the second Sunday of the month and an organic food market every third Sunday. In winter this is a lively but low-key space, but on summer evenings the square's bars and restaurants and the steps of **Santo Spirito** church (*see right*) are packed with concerts and events.

INSIDE TRACK TO THE BEACH!

On a raised stretch of the river at lungarno Serristori, city beach Easy Living opens from 10am to 10pm daily between June and September. Chill on a lounger under a parasol, perhaps calling over a watermelon or ice-cream vendor. Or work up a sweat with a spot of volleyball or football, before cooling off with... a shower – there's no swimming in the river.

Running south between Santo Spirito and a maze of narrow streets to the east is the grand **via Maggio** with its antiques shops and massive stone crests representing their original noble owners. At its river end is a delightful triangular house with a fountain and tiny garden room where the street joins borgo San Jacopo. Backing directly on to the river, this street mixes medieval towers, hip clothes shops and 1960s monstrosities built to replace houses bombed in the war. It leads to the southern end of the ponte Vecchio. Heading south-west down from the bridge is via Guicciardini, with expensive paper, crafts and jewellery shops (as well as purveyors of tourist tat) and little **Santa Felicità** church (*see p92*). Passing the grandeur of the Medicis' Palazzo Pitti, it ends in a square dominated by Palazzo Guidi, housing **Casa Guidi** (*see right*), where Robert Browning and Elizabeth Barrett Browning wrote some of their most famous works. Here via Maggio and via Guicciardini join to become via Romana, a long, extremely straight thoroughfare leading to Porta Romana, lined with picture framers and antiques shops, and home to the gory **La Specola** museum (*see p92*) and the second entrance to Boboli.

South-east of the ponte Vecchio are the *coste* (meaning 'ribs'). These pretty, narrow lanes snake steeply uphill towards the **Forte di Belvedere** (*see right*). Halfway up costa di San Giorgio is one of the two entrances to the

SIGHTS

spectacular **Giardino Bardini**; the other is in via de' Bardi, a quiet street, running uphill behind the riverbank, that leads into lungarno Serristori and the **Casa Museo Rodolfo Siviero** (*see below*). Behind lies **San Niccolò**, leading as far as Porta San Niccolò in piazza Poggi. This is a quiet area with a village feel until the evening, when the wine bars and *osterie* along via de' Renai open up, overlooking the riverside piazza Demidoff. Here too you'll find the recently restored **Museo Bardini** (*see p92*).

Casa Guidi

Piazza San Felice 8 (01628 825925 UK number, www.browningsociety.org/casa_guidi.html). **Open** *Apr-Nov* 3-6pm Mon, Wed, Fri. **Admission** by donation. **Map** p334 D2.
English poets Robert Browning and Elizabeth Barrett Browning came to Florence in April 1847 after a clandestine marriage, and for 14 years an apartment in this house was their home. Now owned by the Landmark Trust and partly rented out as a holiday home, key rooms of the apartment where they lived and wrote are open for visits during certain months. A few pieces in the flat are originals, including the piano used by their son Pen.

Casa Museo Rodolfo Siviero

Lungarno Serristori 1-3 (055 2345219, 055 293007 guided tours, www.museocasasiviero.it). **Open** *Sept-June* 10am-1pm Mon, Sun; 10am-6pm Sat. *July, Aug* 10am-1pm Mon, Sun; 10am-2pm, 3-7pm Sat. **Admission** free. **Map** p335 D5.
This was previously the house of government minister Rodolfo Siviero, dubbed the 'James Bond of art' for his efforts to prevent the Nazis plundering Italian masters. The pieces he saved were returned to their owners, but Siviero left his own private collection to the Regione Toscana on condition it would be open to the public. Among the 500 pieces on display are paintings and sculptures by friends of Siviero, including de Chirico, Annigoni and da Messina.

Cenacolo di Santo Spirito

Piazza Santo Spirito 29 (055 287043, www.museicivicifiorentini.it). **Open** 10am-4pm Mon, Sat, Sun. **Admission** €2.20. **No credit cards.** **Map** p334 D1.
Orcagna's 14th-century fresco *The Last Supper*, housed in a former Augustinian refectory, was butchered by an 18th-century architect commissioned to build some doors into it. Only the fringes of the fresco remain, though there's a more complete (albeit heavily restored) *Crucifixion* above it. The small Museo della Fondazione Romano here houses an eclectic collection of sculptures given to the state in 1946 on the death of sailor Salvatore Romano.

Forte di Belvedere

Via San Leonardo (055 27681). **Open** phone for details. **Admission** free. **Map** p334 D3.

This star-shaped fortress was built in 1590 by Bernardo Buontalenti to protect the city from insurgents. It was then used as a strongroom for the Medici Grand Dukes' treasures. After a painfully drawn-out restoration, the fort is open once again for temporary art exhibitions, shows and events.

Giardino Bardini

Via de' Bardi 1r, costa di San Giorgio 2 (055 290112, www.bardinipeyron.it). **Open** *Nov-Feb* 8.15am-4.30pm daily. *Mar* 8.15am-5.30pm daily. *Apr, May, Sept, Oct* 8.15am-6.30pm daily. *June-Aug* 8.15am-7.30pm daily. Closed last Mon of mth. **Admission** €9 (incl Museo degli Argenti, Museo del Costume, Museo delle Porcellane & Giardino di Boboli). **No credit cards.** **Map** p335 D4.
First created in the 1200s by the Mozzi family, this intriguing garden underwent five years of painstaking restoration recently, and is a delight. The garden is divided into three distinct areas: the Baroque steps, leading to a terrace with amazing views; the English wood, a shady haven of evergreens; and the farm park, with a dwarf orchard, rhododendrons and a 'tunnel' of wisteria and hydrangea.

★ Palazzo Pitti

Piazza Pitti 1, via Romana (055 2654321, www. polomuseale.firenze.it). **Open** 8.15am-6.50pm Tue-Sun. **Admission** €11.50. **Map** p334 D1.
The Pitti Palace was built in 1457 for Luca Pitti, a Medici rival, supposedly to a design by Brunelleschi that had been rejected by Cosimo il Vecchio as too grandiose. However, it also proved too grandiose for the Pitti, who, gallingly, were forced to sell to the Medici. Its ornate, opulent rooms now hold the vast Medici collections, as well as later additions in the various museums detailed below.

Galleria d'Arte Moderna

055 2388616. **Open** 8.15am-1.50pm (last entry 1.15pm) Tue-Sat, 2nd, 4th Mon of mth & 1st, 3rd, 5th Sun of mth. **Admission** €8.50 combined ticket with the Galleria Palatina (€13 during special exhibitions). **No credit cards.**
The 30 second-floor rooms of the Pitti were royal apartments until 1920; today they're given over to Florence's Modern Art museum. The collection covers neoclassical to early 20th-century art, with highlights including Giovanni Dupré's bronze sculptures of Cain and Abel (Room 5) and Ottone Rosai's simple *Piazza del Carmine* in Room 30. Rooms 11, 12, 18 and 19 showcase the work of the Macchiaioli school, the early Italian Impressionist group who were ridiculed for painting-by-dots (*macchie*), and house works by Giovanni Fattori and Telemaco Signorini.

Galleria Palatina & Appartamenti Reali

055 2388614. **Open** 8.15am-6.50pm Tue-Sun. **Admission** €8.50 combined ticket with the Galleria d'Arte Moderna (€13 during special exhibitions). **No credit cards.**

SIGHTS

The gallery has 28 rooms of paintings, which are hung four- or five-high on its damask walls. You'll want to linger longest in the five planet rooms, named after Venus, Mercury (Apollo), Mars, Jupiter and Saturn. The Sala di Venere (Venus), crowned by a gilded stucco ceiling, is dominated by a statue of Venus by Canova, but also contains Titian's regal *La Bella*. The Sala di Apollo houses the nine *Muses* and is crowded with works by Rosso Fiorentino and Andrea del Sarto. The Sala di Marte (Mars) is closed for restoration; Rubens's *Four Philosophers* and the other works from this room are on show in the Sala delle Nicchie. The best place to look in the Sala di Giove (Jupiter) is up, in order to admire the lofty depiction of Jupiter with his eagle and lightning. Look too for Raphael's lover, so-called 'baker girl' Margherita Luti, in his *La Velata*. Finally, the Sala di Saturno (Saturn) contains some of Raphael's best-known works: among them the *Madonna of the Grand Duke*,

which shows a distinct Leonardo influence, and his last painting, *Holy Family*, seemingly inspired by Michelangelo.

★ **Giardino di Boboli**
055 2651816/2651838. **Open** *Nov-Feb* 8.15am-4.30pm daily. *Mar, June-Aug, Oct* 8.15am-7.30pm daily. *Apr, May, Sept* 8.15am-6.30pm daily. Closed 1st & last Mon of mth. **Admission** €7 (incl Museo degli Argenti, Museo del Costume, Museo delle Porcellane & Giardino Bardini). **No credit cards**. **Map** p334 D1-D3.
Boboli is the best loved of the few green spaces and parks in the city centre, and, despite the entrance fee, is a popular oasis, particularly on hot summer days. Far to the left of the main entrance is a fountain showing Cosimo I's obese dwarf as a nude Bacchus, heralding the walkway that leads to Buontalenti's grotto with Bandinelli's statues of Ceres and Apollo, casts of Michelangelo's *Slaves*, and a second grotto

Walk Up the Garden Path

Take a peaceful stroll around the delightful Boboli Gardens.

Start at the via Romana entrance to the Boboli Gardens. Ahead of you is a small grotto sheltering statues of Adam and Eve. At the top of the hill, turn left and then right on to the viale de' Platani and continue uphill. About halfway along this covered path is the entrance to the **Botanical Gardens**, also called the **Giardino degli Ananassi** after the pineapples once grown here. Continue on the same path to the **viale de' Cipressi** ('il Viottolone'), an avenue lined with statues. Turn right here.

At the bottom of the viale de' Cipressi lies the gorgeous **Isolotto**, a small island sitting in a circular moat laid out in 1612. In the middle is the *Fountain of Oceanus*, designed by Il Tribolo for Cosimo II. Beyond the Isolotto is the English-style lawn known as the **Hemicycle**. Turn right to rejoin viale della Meridiana, passing the lovely **Orangery**. You emerge with the Meridiana wing of Palazzo Pitti on your left and a huge Roman *vasca* (basin) on your right.

Take one of the steep paths that climb the hill and get splendid views of Florence. Follow the path on the left side of the tree-lined lawn, past a bronze sculpture by Igor Mitoraj. To the right is the viale de' Cipressi. Walk straight on past the row of old houses on your right to an elegant stairway that sweeps up to the walled **Giardino del Cavaliere**. From here the views are purely rural: villas, the odd tower, olive groves and cypress trees.

Back at the bottom of the steps, the path to the right brings you to **Abundance**, an enormous statue clutching a sheaf of golden corn. Instead of going down the steps, take the path that hugs the walls of Forte di Belvedere until you come to the back gate of the fort. From here, follow the path opposite past the pale peppermint green **Kaffeehaus**, a rococo gem built in 1775 for Pietro Leopoldo, and straight on down a steep path, which brings you out above the huge **amphitheatre**. This faces the rear façade and entrance of the Pitti Palace, where you'll find the **Fontana del Carciofo**, a superb Baroque fountain, named after the bronze artichoke that once topped it.

Head around to the right, and a wide gravel path leads to a small rose garden dominated by Baccio Bandinelli's *Jupiter*. The little path to the right ends at the small **Grotticina di Madama**, dominated by bizarre statues of goats and the first of the several grottoes for which the garden is known.

Back at *Jupiter*, follow the railings to the end and descend the steps to the wonderful **Grotta Grande** or the **Grotta di Buontalenti**. It's not always possible to walk into the chambers, but you can see through the railings. The Grotta di Buontalenti was built between 1557 and 1593 by heavyweights Vasari, Ammannati and Buontalenti. The last curiosity before leaving is a statue of Pietro Barbino, Cosimo I's pot-bellied dwarf.

SIGHTS

adorned with frescoes of classical Greek and Roman myths and encrusted with shells. The ramps take you to the amphitheatre, where Jacopo Peri and Giulio Caccini's *Euridice* was staged for the Medici in 1600. At the top of the hill is the Museo delle Porcellane (*see p92*), entered through the Giardino dei Cavalieri. *See also* **Up the Garden Path**.

Museo degli Argenti

055 2388709. **Open** *Oct-May, Sept* 8.15am-6.30pm daily. *June-Aug* 8.15am-7.30pm daily. Closed 1st & last Mon of mth. **Admission** €7 (incl Museo delle Porcellane, Museo del Costume, Giardino di Boboli & Giardino Bardini). **No credit cards.**

This extravagant two-tier museum section of the Pitti Palace houses an astonishing hoard of treasures amassed by the Medici, not just silver, but everything from tapestries and rock crystal vases to breathtakingly banal miniature animals.

Museo delle Carrozze

055 2388614. **Open** by appointment only.
Plans are being made to move this fairytale collection of carriages, once belonging to the Medici, Lorraine and Savoy houses, into the former Medici stables. Until then, anyone with a Cinderella complex can visit by appointment.

Museo del Costume

055 2388713. **Open** 8.15am-6.30pm (last entry 6.15pm) Tue-Sat, 2nd, 4th Mon of mth & 1st, 3rd, 5th Sun of mth. **Admission** €7 (incl Museo degli Argenti, Museo delle Porcellane, Giardino di Boboli and Giardino Bardini). **No credit cards.**

The sumptuous Costume Museum is in the Palazzina della Meridiana, which periodically served as residence to the Lorraine family and the House of Savoy. Formal, theatrical and everyday outfits from the museum's collection of 6,000 pieces spanning five centuries are shown in rotation, changing every

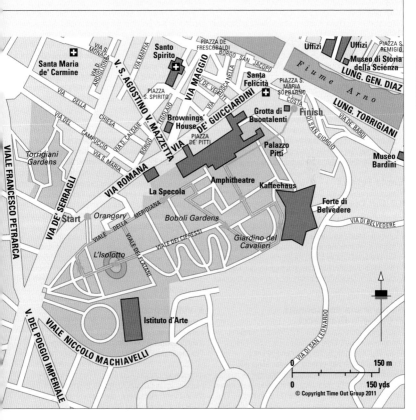

two years. Some more important get-ups are permanently on display, among them Cosimo I's and Eleonora di Toledo's clothes, including her grand velvet creation from Bronzino's portrait.

Museo delle Porcellane

055 2388709. **Open** *Nov-Feb* 8.15am-4.30pm daily. *Mar, June-Aug, Oct* 8.15am-7.30pm daily. *Apr, May, Sept* 8.15am-6.30pm daily. Closed 1st & last Mon of mth. **Admission** €7 (incl Museo degli Argenti, Museo del Costume, Giardino di Boboli & Giardino Bardini). **No credit cards**.
Built by Leopoldo de' Medici, this outhouse at the top of the Boboli Gardens was once a reception room for artists. The museum has ceramics used by the various occupants of Palazzo Pitti and includes the largest selection of Viennese china outside Vienna. Most visitors are more interested in the views.

Museo Bardini

Via de' Renai 37 (055 2342427, www.museicivici fiorentini.it/bardini). **Open** 11am-5pm Mon, Thur, Sat, Sun. **Admission** €5; €2-€4 reductions. **Map** p335 D4.
Named after its creator, antiquarian Stefano Bardini (1854-1922), this 2,000-strong collection includes sculpture, paintings and applied art from the Middle Ages and Renaissance. Brought together over decades, it was housed here by Bardini, who renovated the former church and convent of San Gregorio della Pace *palazzo* in 1881 into the elegant Renaissance-style structure it is today. Stand-out pieces include the *Madonna della Mela*, the *Madonna dei Cordai* by Donatello and *Atlas* by Guercino, as well as a gorgeous collection of oriental rugs and 15th-century chests. But the museum is as much about the collector as his collection, with the work still exhibited in a layout designed by Bardini.

Santa Felicità

Piazza Santa Felicità 3 (055 213018, www.santa felicita.it). **Open** 9.30am-noon, 3.30-5.30pm Mon-Sat. **Admission** free. **Map** p334 D2.
This church occupies the site of the first church in Florence, founded in the second century AD by Syrian Greek tradesmen. The oldest surviving part is the portico, built in 1564; the interior mainly dates to the 18th century. Most who come here do so to see Pontormo's *Deposition* altarpiece in the Cappella Barbadori-Capponi.

Santa Maria del Carmine & Cappella Brancacci

Piazza del Carmine (055 2382195, www.musei civicifiorentini.it). **Open** *Chapel* 10am-5pm Mon, Wed-Sat; 1-5pm Mon, Sun. Phone ahead to book. **Admission** €4. **No credit cards**. **Map** p334 C1.
This blowsy Baroque church is dominated by a huge single nave, with pilasters and pious sculptures overlooked by a ceiling fresco of the Ascension. This isn't what visitors queue for, however: they're here for the Brancacci Chapel. Frescoed in the 15th century by Masaccio and Masolino, it is one of the city's greatest art treasures. Masaccio, who died aged 27, reached his peak with this cycle of paintings, especially the tangibly grief-stricken Adam and Eve in the *Expulsion from Paradise*, a work that entranced Michelangelo.

★ Santo Spirito

Piazza Santo Spirito (055 210030). **Open** *Winter* 8am-noon, 4-5pm Mon, Tue, Thur, Fri; 8am-noon Wed. *Summer* 8am-noon, 4-6pm Mon, Tue, Thur, Fri; 8am-noon Wed. **Admission** free. **Map** p334 C2.
Behind the exquisitely simple 18th-century cream façade is one of Brunelleschi's most extraordinary works. In 1397, the resident Augustinian monks decided to replace the church that had been on this site from 1250, eventually commissioning Brunelleschi to design it. Work started in 1444, two years before the great master died, and the façade and exterior walls were never finished. Vasari wrote that if the church had been completed as planned, it would have been 'the most perfect temple of Christianity' and it's easy to see why. Santo Spirito's structure is a beautifully proportioned, Latin-cross church, lined with a colonnade of dove-grey *pietra serena* pilasters that shelter 38 chapels. Left of the church, the refectory houses the Cenacolo di Santo Spirito museum (*see p92*). The church is open on weekends to worshippers, but recent staffing problems mean it's worth calling ahead to make sure the official opening hours are being kept to.

★ La Specola

Via Romana 17 (055 2288251, guided visits 055 2346760, www.msn.unifi.it). **Open** *Winter* 9.30am-4.30pm Tue-Sun. *Summer* 10.30am-5.30pm Tue-Sun. **Admission** €6. **No credit cards**. **Map** p334 D1.
A dream day out for older kids with horror fixations, La Specola is the zoology department of the Natural History Museum. The first 23 rooms are crammed with stuffed and pickled animals, including many famously extinct species, and up to here the museum can also be fun for younger children. From Room 24 onwards, however, exhibits are more gruesome. A *Frankenstein*-esque laboratory is filled with wax corpses on satin beds, each a little more dissected than the last, and walls are covered with realistic body parts crafted as teaching aids in the 18th and 19th centuries.

★ Villa Bardini

Costa di San Giorgio 2 (055 2638599, www.bardinipeyron.it). **Open** 10am-6pm Tue-Sun. **Admission** €6. **No credit cards**. **Map** p335 D4.
The restored Villa Bardini is home to a permanent exhibition of the fabulously extravagant creations of couturier Roberto Capucci. The villa also contains a newer museum dedicated to the works of Italian artist Pietro Annigoni, the terrace restaurant (*see p139* **Hubba Hubba MoBa**) and a coffee shop.

Outside the City Gates

Escape the throngs.

The historic centre of Florence is home to the densest concentration of art treasures and sights in the world, but it's surprisingly small. This makes exploring beyond the area delineated by the eight surviving city gates easy even without your own means of transport, and the rewards are fabulous views, sublime countryside and fascinating cultural sights. North of the river, the old stone gates are linked by the *viali*, traffic-clogged multi-lane arteries circling the city, however the gently winding, tree-lined avenues that form an umbrella round the south of the city are more picturesque.

To the north, the roads leading to **Fiesole** and **Settignano** are dotted with charming country houses. Travelling east you'll find a mix of genteel suburbia and semi-industrial plots. **Firenze Nova**, an uninspiring satellite city and administrative centre, has been built on reclaimed land north-west of the centre. Further in this direction, dull housing and industrial development have claimed land, creating eyesores such as **Brozzi** and **Campi Bisenzio**, though there are still ancient convents and elegant villas on the hills, and the old town area of **Sesto Fiorentino** has a charm of its own.

Head south of the historic centre for the best walks, views and sights; as the hills rise, practically from the banks of the Arno, you can walk in minutes from the town into real countryside. This proximity to nature is one of the city's most unusual and attractive physical characteristics, but has its downside: situated in a basin, Florence has a climate that's hot and humid in summer, and cold and damp in winter.

The efficient ATAF bus network has good services to the suburbs.

NORTH OF THE RIVER

To the west, **Porta al Prato** and the hellish traffic of the *viali* mark the edge of the centre. Just south of the old gate, skirting the northern bank of the Arno for three kilometres (two miles) is the green oasis of the **Parco delle Cascine**, a public park backed by woods. Its name comes from *cascina*, meaning 'dairy farm', the role the area played under the Medici. It later became a hunting park and a space for theatre and public spectacles. Shelley wrote his 'Ode to the West Wind' here in 1819, while in 1870 the body of the Maharaja of Kolhapur (who died in Florence) was burned on a funeral pyre at the far end of the park, on a spot marked by an equestrian statue. The first major changes to the park for centuries have been made with the building of the new Tramvia (*see p305*), which has encroached on the eastern entrance and shifted the huge Tuesday morning market downriver.

The Cascine is the city's lung, its only large park and a popular destination for a day out, especially at weekends, with cycling children, in-line skaters, joggers, picnickers and others simply out for a stroll. There's a riding school, swimming pool, race track and tennis courts; in summer the park is used as a venue for club nights, theatre and gigs. It's safe enough when summer night-time events are held, but be aware that the area is seamy at night, with prostitutes touting for business along the park's main roads and adjoining *viali*.

Coming back towards the centre of town, five minutes' walk from Santa Maria Novella train station along viale Fratelli Rosselli, is the massive pentagonal stone **Fortezza da Basso** (*see also p73*), designed by Antonio da Sangallo. It was commissioned in 1534 by Alessandro de' Medici, who met his death within its ugly walls, and is a prototype of 16th-century military architecture; restored in the 1990s, it's now Florence's main exhibition centre. Just north of the fortress lies Florence's decorative **Russian Orthodox church** (via Leone X 12), with its five polychrome onion domes. Completed in 1904, it's a reminder that the city was once popular with wealthy Russians (Dostoevsky, Tchaikovsky and Gorky among them) as a retreat from the harsh winters back home. You can arrange for a guided tour (in English or Italian, 055 2477986/290148) or visit during mass (6pm Sat, 10.30am Sun).

Directly north is the eccentric **Museo Stibbert** (via Stibbert 26, 055 486049, www.museo stibbert.it, closed Thur, €6), a bizarre collection that belonged to Frederick Stibbert (1838-1906), a brother-in-arms to Garibaldi. Stibbert was born to an English father and Italian mother, who left him her 14th-century house. He bought the neighbouring mansion and joined the two to house his 50,000 artefacts. Crammed into the 64 rooms are Napoleon's coronation robes (Stibbert was a fan), a hand-painted harpsichord, arms and armour, shoe buckles, snuff boxes, chalices, crucifixes and even an attributed Botticelli. The rambling garden has a lily pond, stables, a neoclassical folly by Poggi, and ancient Greek- and Egyptian-inspired temples.

Piazza della Libertà, key northern access point to the city, has constant traffic jams and a massive, rather graceless triumphal arch that was built to mark the arrival in Florence of the eighth Grand Duke of Tuscany in 1744.

Heading south-east towards **piazza Beccaria** and bordering Santa Croce is the atmospheric **Cimitero degli Inglesi** (*see p85* **Profile**). Designated in 1827, it was later given its oval shape by Giuseppe Poggi (he of the harmonious *viali* south of the river and of piazzale Michelangelo). East is the **Stadio 'Comunale' Artemo Franchi** (*see p207*), Pier Luigi Nervi's football stadium near Campo di Marte station. Built in 1932 and enlarged for the 1990 World Cup, it has a capacity of 66,000. A short walk south-east is the **Museo del Cenacolo di Andrea del Sarto** (via San Salvi 16, 055 238 8603, www.polo museale.firenze.it, free). A refectory-cum-museum, it was part of the Vallombrosan monastery of San Salvi, and is notable for Andrea del Sarto's lunette-shaped Mannerist *Last Supper*.

Take a bus north-west to visit the **Villa della Petraia** (via della Petraia 40, 055 452691, www.polomuseale.firenze.it, closed 2nd & 3rd Mon of mth, free), acquired by the Medici family in 1530. Sitting on a little hill, the villa and grounds stand apart from the surrounding industrial mess. Originally a tower belonging to Brunelleschi's family, the fabulous formal terraced gardens by Il Tribolo are among the few immortalised in Giusto Utens's lunettes. Just down the hill is another Medici pad, **Villa di Castello** (via del Castello 40, 055 454791, www.polomuseale.firenze.it, closed 2nd & 3rd Mon of mth, free). The villa is known for its Il Tribolo gardens and for Ammanati's sculpture *Allegory of Winter*, as well as the extravagant Grotta degli Animali. Full of animal and bird statues and stone water features, the grotto was planned by Il Tribolo, but finished by Vasari.

FIESOLE & AROUND

Fiesole was founded centuries before Florence and it could be credited with the city's very existence – this stubborn Etruscan hill town was so difficult for the Romans to subdue they were forced to set up camp in the river valley below. When they eventually took Fiesole, it became one of the most important towns in Etruria, remaining independent until the 12th century, when Florence finally vanquished it in battle. It soon took on a new role as a refined suburb where Florentine aristocrats could escape the heat and hoi polloi; the road leading up to the town winds by beautiful villas and gardens – still highly desirable addresses. Today, around 14,000 people live in Fiesole.

Piazza Mino, the main square, is named after the 15th-century sculptor Mino da Fiesole, and is lined with cafés and restaurants, some with views over Florence. It's dominated by the honey-stone campanile of the 11th-century **Duomo** (055 599566); inside it sit columns topped with capitals dating from Fiesole's period under Roman occupation. The nearby **Museo Bandini** (via Dupré 1, 055 5961293, www.museidifiesole.it, €5 or €10 incl Teatro Romano & Museo Archeologico) houses an array of Florentine paintings dating from the 13th to 15th centuries; two newer rooms display previously unshown works, including Andrea della Robbia terracottas.

Down the hill, more relics of Roman Fiesole can be seen at the 3,000-seat **Teatro Romano** (via Portigiani 1, 055 5961293, www.musei difiesole.it, closed Tue in winter, €10 incl Museo

Walk Outside the City Gates

Leave the crowds behind you and enjoy fabulous views of the city.

From the southern end of the ponte Vecchio, with your back to the river, turn left along via de' Bardi. At piazza Santa Maria Soprarno, bear right and walk under the arch up costa de' Magnoli, which, after a short distance, merges into costa di San Giorgio just opposite the Romanian Orthodox church of San Giorgio. This is an enchanting little street, but the ascent is quite steep. A little further on to the left, a fabulous view of the Florence skyline suddenly appears in a gap between buildings. Press on, admiring the tall shuttered buildings and their oversailing rooftops as you go. Galileo's house is on the right at no.19.

Five minutes from the city centre, you'll hear the first twitters of bird song. At the top of costa di San Giorgio, pass through the city gates (Porta San Giorgio) and walk a short distance along via San Leonardo, leading straight ahead past the main entrance to Forte di Belvedere. After five

minutes, on your left, is Chi...
Leonardo in Arcetri. This medieval *pieve* (parish church) is guarded by cypress trees and contains canvases by Francesco Conti.

Retrace your steps back to the Porta and bear right, down via di Belvedere, to begin your descent. Hugging the city walls, you'll soon come to the bottom of the hill opposite Porta San Miniato. Head up via del Monte alle Croci, perhaps stopping for a slurp at the charming Fuori Porta wine bar (*see p143*). After a short walk, you'll reach the pretty, tree-lined steps of San Salvatore al Monte. Either take this, the express route to the top (past a resident feline community, about 50 metres up on the right), or follow the road on its tortuous journey past olive groves, finally arriving at the busy main road of viale Galileo Galilei. Directly opposite is splendid San Miniato al Monte (*see p95*). Now all that's left to do is admire the view.

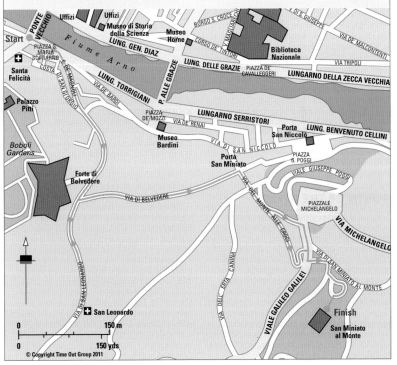

...ini & Museo Archeologico, €12 during ...ecial exhibitions). The amphitheatre, built in ...1 BC, nowadays hosts concerts and plays in summer; a complex houses the remains of two temples, partially restored Roman baths and Etruscan walls. The **Museo Archeologico** (via Dupré 1, 055 5961293, www.museidifiesole.it, €10 incl Museo Bandini & Museo Archeologico, €12 during special exhibitions) has Bronze Age, Etruscan and Roman finds, and Greek vases.

There are some lovely walks around Fiesole, the best down steep via Vecchia Fiesolana to the hamlet of San Domenico. To the left on the way down is the **Villa Medici** (via Beato Angelico 2, www.villamedicifiesole.it; €6, groups only, by arrangement, closed Sat, Sun). Built by Michelozzo for Cosimo il Vecchio, it was the childhood home of Anglo-American writer Iris Origo. At the bottom of the hill is the 15th-century church and convent where painter Fra Angelico was a monk. It now houses his delicate *Madonna and Angels* (1420), while in the chapter house of the adjacent monastery is one of his frescoes (ring the bell at no.4 for entry). Opposite the church, a lane leads down to the **Badia Fiesolana** (via Roccettini 9, 055 59155, closed Sat afternoon & Sun, free), Fiesole's cathedral until 1028. The façade incorporates the front of the older church, with its elegant green and white marble inlay. Enter via the cloister if the church doors are closed.

The village of **Settignano** lies on the hill to the east of Fiesole and has stunning views. There's no public transport from Fiesole (it is an easy ride on the no.10 bus from Santa Maria Novella station), but the long walk between the towns is picturesque. Lacking major landmarks, Settignano is an almost tourist-free trip out of town, and its history is littered with eminent names: sculptors Desiderio da Settignano and the Rossellino brothers were born here, and Michelangelo spent part of his childhood at the **Villa Michelangelo** (via della Capponcina 65); known locally as Villa Buonarotti.

SOUTH OF THE RIVER

South of the Arno, steep lanes rise sharply from the riverbank, lined with high walls and impenetrable gates that protect beautiful villas. From the city centre, the *coste* and long flights of mossy steps make short but testing walks up to fine vantage points on the hills.

The most famous viewpoint in Florence is probably from ★**piazzale Michelangelo**, on the hill directly above piazza Poggi. Considered the city's balcony, this large, open square provides vistas over the entire city. Its stone balustrade is perennially crowded with tourists. Laid out in 1869 by Giuseppe Poggi, the *piazzale* is dominated by a bronze replica of

Michelangelo's *David* and crammed all day with coaches. Buses 12 and 13 take the scenic route in opposite directions round Poggi's *viali*, but it's also a pleasant walk along via San Niccolò to Porta San Miniato, then up via del Monte alle Croci and left up the flight of stone steps winding between villas. Alternatively, take the rococo staircase Poggi designed to link piazzale Michelangelo with the piazza in his name below.

From piazzale Michelangelo it's a short walk to the exquisite ★**San Miniato al Monte** (via delle Porte Sante 34, 055 2342731, free). The church façade is delicately inlaid with white Carrara and green Verde di Prato marble, and the gold mosaic dates from the 13th century. There has been a chapel on this site since at least the fourth century; according to legend, St Miniato picked up his decapitated head and walked uphill from the banks of the Arno to here, where he finally expired. The chapel was replaced with a Benedictine monastery in the early 11th century, built on the orders of reforming Bishop Hildebrand. The church's interior is one of Tuscany's loveliest, its walls a patchwork of faded frescoes and its choir raised above a serene 11th-century crypt. One of the most remarkable features is the marble pavement in the nave, inlaid with the signs of the zodiac and stylised lions and lambs.

A 20-minute walk west of Porta Romana is a less visited but just as gorgeous viewpoint, the hamlet of ★**Bellosguardo** ('beautiful view'). A vantage point just before the piazza di Bellosguardo affords a glimpse of every important church façade in central Florence and, at the top of the hill, is a higgledy-piggledy group of old houses and grand villas around a shady square; the only sign of modern life, apart from the cars, is a postbox on a wall. The most impressive of the buildings is **Villa Bellosguardo**, down a little turning to the left. It was built in 1780 for the Marchese Orazio Pucci (ancestor of fashion designer Emilio Pucci) and bought, more than a century later, by the great tenor Enrico Caruso, who lived here for three years before his death in 1921.

About five kilometres (three miles) south-west of Porta Romana, the **Certosa del Galluzzo** (via della Certosa 1, Galluzzo, 055 2049226, www.cistercensi.info, admission by donation, closed Mon & morning Sun, bus 36 or 37) looms like a fortress above the busy Siena road. The imposing complex was founded in 1342 as a Carthusian monastery by Renaissance bigwig Niccolò Acciaiuoli and is the third of six built in Tuscany in the 14th century. It's been inhabited since 1958 by Cistercian monks, whose 12 cells surround the main cloister, each with a well, vegetable garden and study. The main entrance leads into a courtyard and San Lorenzo church, said to be by Brunelleschi.

Consume

Hemingway. *See p149.*

Hotels

From boutique to B&B, there's a budget to suit (almost) everybody.

While room rates remain among the highest in Italy, the positive side to accommodation in Florence is the sheer variety of options. Whether your bed of choice lies in a boutique hotel with a sharp design edge or a cosy B&B on the top floor of an ancient *palazzo*, chances are that you'll find something appealing. Book a bunk in a youth hostel occupying a crumbling villa, a penthouse suite with terrace views, a frescoed boudoir looking on to a private garden or an executive room with all the technical facilities necessary for a business trip; in fact, just about the only thing missing in this city (and this is a firm positive) is big chain hotels.

CONSUME

Despite the economic downturn and rising prices in Italy, the tourists have come back in force after a few years of lean pickings, leaving the city's hoteliers cautiously optimistic. In fact, there has been a steady stream of new openings since our last edition. Most significant in recent years has been the huge increase in the number of B&Bs, *afittacamere* (rooms to rent) and *residenze d'epoca* (listed buildings with no more than 12 rooms), but as these categories lie outside the star rating system (*see below*), it can be difficult to judge what you're likely to end up with. They range from spartan, gloomy rooms with threadbare towels and no breakfast (yes, B&Bs with no breakfast) to homely pads furnished with antiques where you start the day with warm brioches. The ones listed here are among our favourites, but there are plenty more on offer. Good online resources include www.bedandbreakfast.it, www.bbitalia.it and www.caffelletto.it.

There are also several new hotels in the upper price brackets, most notably Il Salviatino (*see p117*), but of more interest are the number of intimate and quirky openings since our last edition, among them the Orologio (*see p107*), Orto de' Medici (*see p111*) and the luxury Golden Tower Hotel (*see right*). The city's seen a good range of affordable boutique spaces open too – the interestingly named Black 5 Townhouse, for example (*see p114*), the gorgeous Hotel David in Oltrarno (*see p118*) and the stark white Hotel Home Florence in Santa Croce (*see p112*).

STAR RATINGS AND FACILITIES

Hotels are officially given a star rating from one to five by the tourist board (some lodgings are excluded from this system; *see above*), but the rating is an indication of the facilities on offer rather than the standards. There can be enormous disparity within any given category so it pays to do your research.

Most hotels price their rooms according to size, view, the amount of natural light they receive, the size and type of bathroom and whether rooms have balconies or terraces. Bedrooms in all the hotels listed here that fall within the star system have phones and en suite bathrooms, with the exception of some of those in the Budget category; where a Budget hotel does offer en suite facilities, we've mentioned it in the review. Many rooms also have safes and hairdryers. Facilities vary among hotels that come under the other categories, so check before you book if you require something specific. If you don't like the room you've been given, ask to see another one, and don't be put off by grumpy owners. Hotels are required by law to display official maximum room rates in each room; if you feel you've been taken for a ride, there's an office for complaints.

If you're staying in the centre of the city during the long hot summer, a private terrace or balcony – or some kind of outside space – can make a big difference. Alternatively, head for the hills, where, within a short distance of the city centre, you'll find lodgings set in wonderful rural locations. On the subject of fresh air, the Italian smoking ban means that within a hotel, you can't smoke in any public space (unless it has the legally required ventilation and special doors), and you can only smoke in officially designated smoking guestrooms (a rule not always adhered to). However, many hotels have simply banned smoking altogether. If you have strong feelings about smoking in the bedroom, one way or another, say so when you book.

Very few hotels in the centre of town have their own parking facilities; most have an arrangement with a nearby private garage, though this will be expensive (we have given rates under each hotel). A law requires hotels with three or more stars to have rooms with disabled access – but in some cases, rooms for the disabled are only accessible, absurdly, by a lift that's too narrow to take a wheelchair.

BOOKING AND PRICES

High season for Florence's hotels runs roughly from Easter (the busiest weekend of the year) until late July, and September until early November. It also covers Christmas, New Year, Italian public holidays and the Pitti fashion fairs in January and June. Hotel rooms at these times are at their most expensive and much in demand, so book well in advance. On the other hand, low season (roughly November to February and late July) offers great potential for accommodation bargains, especially among the upper-end establishments; budget hotels and B&Bs are less likely to lower their rates significantly. If you are willing to take your chances and are travelling off-season, it's worth doing the rounds to see what kind of bargain you come up with. The main tourist office at piazza Stazione (piazza Stazione 4, 055 212245, 8.30am-7pm Mon-Sat; 8.30am-2pm Sun & hols) offers a booking service and the APT booklet *Guida all'Ospitalità*, available at all tourist offices, details hotels, *affittacamere*, residences, campsites and hostels in Florence and its

province, as well as listing *case per ferie* – religious institutions that offer a number of beds. The majority are cheap, but they're often single-sex and operate curfews.

Prices given here – which are subject to change – are for double rooms with en suite bathrooms and complimentary breakfast, unless otherwise stated. The price ranges from the cost of the cheapest double in low season to the most expensive double in high season; the categories (luxury, expensive, etc) are based on the maximum price. However, given the potential for off-season discounts, these categories are fairly fluid. It's always worth haggling as rates may be lowered if occupancy is down. Most hotels will put at least one extra bed in a double room for a fee; many provide cots for which you may have to pay extra.

One sour note for both hoteliers and travellers was the council's decision in July 2011 to introduce an accomodation tax (*tassa di soggiorno*). The new tax is €1 per person per night, per hotel star, up to a maximum of five nights; so a single person staying for five nights in a four-star hotel would pay an extra €20. Children under the age of ten are exempt.

DUOMO & AROUND

Luxury

★ Gallery Hotel Art

Vicolo dell'Oro 5 (055 27263, www.lungarno hotels.com). **Rooms** 74. **Rates** €180-€418. **Map** p334 C3 ❶

Florence's original hip hotel opened in 1999, back when its East-meets-West design aesthetic was refreshingly different from the norm. Located in a tiny piazza near the ponte Vecchio, the place has a cosy library with squashy sofas, thoughtfully supplied with cashmere throws and mountains of arty books to browse. Also here is the stylish Fusion Bar, which serves *aperitivi*, brunches, light lunches and dinners, while the public rooms on the ground floor often double as show-space for contemporary artists and photographers (*see p102* **Rooms with a View**). The bedrooms are super comfortable, and the bathrooms are a dream.
Bar. Concierge. Disabled-adapted rooms. Internet (free). Parking (€32/day). Restaurant. Room service.

Golden Tower Hotel

Piazza Strozzi (via Monalda) (055 287860, www.goldentowerhotel.it). **Rooms** 27. **Rates** €264-€700. **Map** p334 C3 ❷
This boutique hotel is a vision of luxury, right in the centre of town, nestled pefectly between chic shopping street via de' Tornabuoni and the arresting piazza Strozzi. There's a wonderful spa, heavenly beds and the latest technology. The opulence

❶ Red numbers in this chapter correspond to the location of each hotel as marked on the street maps. *See pp334-335.*

CONSUME

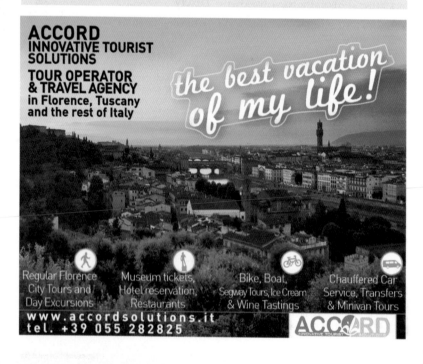

starts in the lobby, where a stunning restored fresco sets the tone, and continues through the classic rooms, where cool greys and crisp white linens are punctuated with bursts of colour provided by fresh flowers and, in the case of the tower rooms, warm exposed brickwork. The tower is where the Strozzi family lived until 1492, when they moved into Palazzo Strozzi opposite. Breakfast, as you'd expect, is lavish.

Bar. Concierge. Disabled-adapted rooms. Internet (free). Parking (€25/day). Restaurant. Spa.

Helvetia & Bristol

Via de' Pescioni 2 (055 26651, www.royal demeure.com). **Rooms** 67. **Rates** €330-€520; €26 breakfast. **Map** p334 B3 ❸

Since 2005, a new, energetic young management team has been breathing fresh life into the venerable Helvetia & Bristol, open since the late 1800s. Distinguished past guests include Igor Stravinsky and Bertrand Russell and the place is filled with antiques, fine paintings and prints, but the historic feel has a decidedly hip edge to it nowadays. Oil paintings, velvet sofas and vast *pietra serena* fireplaces characterise the beautiful salon, while background sounds are likely to be jazz or something cool and contemporary. There's an atmospheric, belle époque Winter Garden conservatory for cool-weather breakfasts (served alfresco in summer), while the restaurant, done out in vibrant oranges and reds, offers a relaxed atmosphere and an inviting new look at Florentine cooking. The sumptuous decor in the bedrooms has been updated, leaving an air of more discreet luxury, where fine fabrics and period furniture rub alongside fluffy duvets, flatscreen TVs and new 'old-fashioned' bathrooms. All things considered, this is one of central Florence's best smallish hotels.

Bar. Business centre. Concierge. Disabled-adapted rooms. Internet (€10/hr, €18/day). Parking (valet, €40-€50/day). Restaurant. Room service.

Hotel Continentale

Vicolo dell'Oro 6r (055 27262, www.lungarno hotels.com). **Rooms** 43. **Rates** €363-€451. **Map** p334 C3 ❹

Another distinguished member of the Ferragamo family's Lungarno group, the Continentale is situated across a small piazza from the Gallery Hotel Art (*see p99*), but has a different feel from its sister. Both boast a contemporary style, but the Continentale is the feminine flipside to the Gallery's more masculine image. Splashes of zingy colour are supplied by some 1960s pieces, but otherwise the design is free of fuss: blonde woods, creamy fabrics, filmy white curtains, and huge glass vases, all illuminated by soft pools of light. Bedrooms have modern four-posters and fabulous bathrooms; 'superiors' have full-on views of the river and the ponte Vecchio. There's a spectacular roof terrace and bar, but the best place to chill is the first-floor Relax Room, where

light filters through slatted blinds, and daybeds afford horizontal views of the crowds.

Bar. Concierge. Disabled-adapted rooms. Gym. Internet (free). Parking (€32/day). Room service.

Lungarno Suites

Lungarno Acciaiuoli 4 (055 27268000, www. lungarnohotels.com). **Rooms** 41. **Rates** €420-€1,089 apartment. **Map** p334 C3 ❺

Ideal for travellers who are after the comforts and levels of service typical of a four-star hotel, while maintaining a little more independence, the stylish Lungarno Suites – part of the Ferragamo hotel group, and sharing its design aesthetic – offers fully serviced self-catering apartments of various sizes, situated on the north bank of the Arno. Around half the apartments have river views; those on the top floors have terraces. Each unit has a cleverly hidden and fully equipped kitchen, but you can have your shopping done for you or order meals from the Gallery Hotel Art (*see p99*). Guests here also have free use of the gym at the Continentale (*see above*).

Bar. Concierge. Disabled-adapted rooms. Internet (free). Parking (€35/day). Room service.

Savoy

Piazza della Repubblica 7 (055 283313, www. hotelsavoy.it). **Rooms** 102. **Rates** €360-€600. **Map** p334 B3 ❻

It may occupy the shell of the 19th-century hotel of the same name, but today's Savoy doesn't bear much of a resemblance to its predecessor. Now one of the city's most popular all-rounders, big with the business, leisure and celebrity brackets, the hotel was added to the ever-expanding Rocco Forte portfolio in the late 1990s. Olga Polizzi, Sir Rocco's interior designer sister, has created a characteristically stylish and calm ambience in the period space, setting dark wood, splashes of colour and some modern art against more neutral beiges and creams. The top-of-the-range Brunelleschi and Signoria suites have their own steam rooms, and there's a rooftop gym. The L'Incontro bar and brasserie is not cheap, but it's great for people-watching.

Bar. Business centre. Concierge. Disabled-adapted rooms. Gym. Internet (€20/day). Parking (€50/day). Restaurant. Room service.

Expensive

Hotel Brunelleschi

Piazza Santa Elisabetta 3 (055 27370, www. brunelleschihotelflorence.com). **Rooms** 95. **Rates** €174-€600. **Map** p335 B4 ❼

The owners of the recently refurbished Brunelleschi, which reopened in 2011, wisely left its prime asset untouched. It's hard to believe that the hotel's Byzantine tower was once a prison – easier to credit that this is the city's oldest standing structure. The rooms are spread through the circular tower and reconstructed medieval church, retaining original

Rooms with a View

You don't need your head in the clouds to experience celestial splendour.

Florence's trademark alleyways, narrow streets and soaring *palazzi* ensure the city stays cool on the hottest of days, but it can feel a touch claustrophobic. Where better to shake the feeling than in your hotel – perhaps in the lofty heights of penthouse suites at the likes of **JK Place** (*see p106*), **Il Salviatino** (*see p117*) and **Westin Excelsior** (*see p107*)? If you can't afford that kind of luxury, there are plenty of other ways to enjoy views from your hotel. The stunning roof gardens at **Antica Torre Tornabuoni Uno** (*see p107*), **La Scaletta** (*see p116*) and **Continentale** (*see p101*) are open to all for the price of a drink, while reasonably priced rooms at **B&B Novecento** (*see p103*), **Grand Hotel Minerva** (*see p107*), **Antica Dimora Johlea** (*see p109*), **Black 5 Townhouse** (*see p114*) and **Torre Guelfa** (*see p105*) will give you access to private roof terraces offering everything from bars and breakfast to pools and gyms – Torre Guelfa even has one room, no.15, with its own private terrace. At the Belvedere apartment of the **Serristori Palace Residence** (*see p116*) or Emily Dickinson suite at **Via Santo Spirito 6** (*see p116*), you can sit and contemplate the city from your own private terrace over an espresso made in your own private kitchen.

B&B Novecento.

Thanks to the age of many of its *palazzi*, Florence also offers a different kind of view: frescoes. Ridiculously clichéd cherubs and gladiators rub shoulders with buxom maidens and plentiful fruit, but most of the scenes are totally delightful – try the **Belletini** (*see p110*), most of the rooms at the **St Regis** (*see p106*), most second-floor rooms at the **Liana** (*see p113*), room 29 at **Morandi alla Crocetta** (*see p112*), and various rooms at **Hotel Rosso 23** (*see p109*), the **Burchianti** (*see p110*) and **Palazzo Galletti** (*see p114*). Just ask for *camere con gli affreschi*.

As its name suggests, **Art Atelier** (*see p110*) takes the concept of art in hotels seriously, with a mix of wall murals and less permanent art, while **Hotel dei Macchiaioli** (*see p110*) is full of art by the 19th-century Tuscan art group of the same name.

Fans of more contemporary art will appreciate the considered approach by the owners of **Il Guelfo Bianco** (*see p110*), who started collecting in a modest way in the early 1990s in order to avoid filling the rooms with swathes of fabric and banal reproductions; the hotel houses their ample collection of mainly Italian contemporary and modern works. Some 450 works (prints, etchings and drawings), mainly dating from the early 20th century, hang in the Ferragamo-owned **Lungarno** hotel (*see p115*), a collection that was started by the previous owners in the late 1960s. The most significant pieces are on display in the suites and public areas on the ground floor, where you can ogle works by Picasso, Tuscan 'splatterer' Ottone Rosai and Jean Cocteau. Art hounds should also keep an eye on what's on offer at the **Gallery Hotel Art** (*see p99*). While it doesn't have its own permanent collection, the hotel's sleek, contemporary decor and ample public space provide an interesting backdrop for exhibitions by contemporary artists and photographers curated by the **BrancoliniGrimaldi** gallery (*see p188*).

features. Part of the restaurant is in the tower, and two penthouse suites enjoy 360° city views. An earlier reconstruction in 1980 unearthed a number of objects of archeological interest, and these are displayed in a private museum in the basement, where an original Roman *caldarium* (plunge bath) was found embedded in the foundations. Fiction fans may be interested to know this place gets a mention at the end of *The Da Vinci Code*.

Bar. Business centre. Concierge. Disabled-adapted rooms. Gym. Internet (€18/day). Parking (€35-€37/day). Restaurants (2). Room service.

Hermitage

Vicolo Marzio 1, piazza del Pesce (055 287216, www.hermitagehotel.com). **Rooms** 28. **Rates** €163-€245. **Map** p334 C3 ❽

This charming and perennially popular little three-star hotel boasts a superb location practically on top of the ponte Vecchio. It's a bit like an upside-down doll's house; the reception and public rooms are on the top floors, with the bedrooms (all 28 comfortable, some rather small) located on the lower four floors. All the rooms have jacuzzi baths or showers. Those at the front have amazing views, but they can be quite noisy.

Bar. Concierge. Internet (paid). Parking (paid). Room service.

★ NH Porta Rossa

Via Porta Rossa 19 (055 2710911, www. nh-hotels.com). **Rooms** 72. **Rates** €230. **Map** p334 C3 ❾

This stunning 12th-century *palazzo* has supposedly been a hotel since 1386, but amenities are firmly up to date: 2010 saw a complete overhaul that kept the spacious rooms and lofty-ceilinged public spaces, but added stylish bathrooms and some dubious modern sculpture. Staff are helpful and friendly, the breakfast is excellent, upgrades are occasionally offered and, best of all, the spiral staircase winding its way up the Monalda Tower leads to spectacular views over the city. There are two other NHs in Florence: the NH Anglo American (via Garibaldi 9) and NH Firenze (piazza Vittorio Veneto 4a).

Bar. Business centre. Disabled-adapted rooms. Internet (€6/hr, €10.80/day; in lobby: wireless, up to 30min/day). Room service. Parking (valet, €25/day).

Residenza d'Epoca in Piazza della Signoria

Via de' Magazzini 2 (055 2399546, www.in piazzadellasignoria.com). **Rooms** 12. **Rates** (incl breakfast) €200-€280. **Map** p334 C4 ❿

Located just a few steps from piazza della Signoria, this is a hotel for visitors who want to be right in the heart of the cultural action. Most of the rooms have views of the piazza, the best of which can be found in Leonardo and Michaelangelo: rooms are named after famous Florentine residents (with nice touches – the Dante and Beatrice rooms are adjacent). Up the absolutely tiny lift (or the more spacious stairs), rooms are furnished in a fairly traditional, unfussy style, with antiques, canopied beds, oriental rugs, wood floors and pastel walls. Imaginatively fitted bathrooms give a sense of the opulence of a much bigger hotel. Meet your neighbours over a hearty breakfast at the huge oval table on the third floor, or have it delivered to your room.

Bar. Business centre. Internet (free). Parking (€25-€32/day). Room service.

Moderate

★ B&B Novecento

Via Ricasoli 10, San Marco (055 214138, www.bbnovecentofirenze.it). **Rooms** 4. **Rates** (incl breakfast) €80-€150. **Map** p335 B4 ⓫

Franco and Sawako have been running their cosy four-room B&B with commitment and enthusiasm since 2003 and have an excellent record of return guests. The space occupies the third floor of a building between the Duomo and piazza della SS Annunziata and has the advantage of a small roof terrace where you can enjoy a glass of wine to the spectacular backdrop of Florence's skyline. There's no lift, but your luggage will be hauled up by an ingenious pulley system. The pretty rooms are mostly on the small side, but have been carefully furnished with nice touches such as colourful cushions, padded bedheads and firm, orthopaedic mattresses; they all have new, tiled bathrooms. An above-average breakfast is served at your table in the homely breakfast room. Prices are a little over the odds, but it's a charming spot.

Concierge. Internet (free). Parking (€30/day). Room service.

★ Dei Mori

Via Dante Alighieri 12 (055 211438, www. deimori.it). **Rooms** 5. **Rates** (incl breakfast) €90-€150; reduced rates for longer stays. **Map** p335 B4 ⓬

This friendly guesthouse in the heart of the medieval city was one of Florence's first B&Bs, and it's still one of the best. The rooms are keenly priced and comfortable: the ones on the first floor are more traditional (and some don't have bathrooms), while those upstairs are smarter and all en suite. The welcome is exceptionally warm: fresh flowers, bright rugs, cheerful paintings and a comfy sitting room complete with a TV, a stereo and lots of books and magazines. There's a terrace from which you can just see the top of the Duomo.

Internet (free). Parking (€25-€30/day). Room service.

La Dimora degli Angeli

Via Brunelleschi 4 (055 288478, www.ladimora degliangeli.com). **Rooms** 6. **Rates** (incl breakfast) €80-€165. **Map** p334 B3 ⓭

CONSUME

The smart way of giving

Give the perfect getaway

Browse the full range of gift boxes from Time Out
timeout.com/smartbox

Opened in 2009 by the Cherubini family (who also own the three-room Dimora del Centro in the nearby piazza della Repubblica), this sweet B&B has gone to great pains to imbue each of its rooms with individual personality. So the 'romantic' Agnesa is all lavender and purple tones, Bianca is calm whites and dark wood, Beatrice is old-style colonial elegance jazzed up with modern wallpaper, and Letizia is sweet and cosy. Most of the rooms have great views over the Duomo square, and a 24-hour tea room means you can get an early-morning espresso to sip while you take in the view. Breakfast is by tokens, redeemed at either of two nearby pâtisseries. *Internet (free). Parking (€24/day).*

Perseo

Via de' Cerretani 1 (055 212504, www.hotel perseo.it). **Rooms** 20. **Rates** €90-€165. **Map** p334 B3 ⑭

Occupying the shell of its rather down-at-heel predecessor, the new-look Perseo opened in 2006, offering 20 stylish rooms, good prices and a super-central location. The owners have gone for a clean, contemporary look so expect modern wood furniture, a palette of earthy colours, flat-screen TVs, sharp light fittings and sparkling new bathrooms. The sitting room is well supplied with books and magazines while a complimentary *aperitivo*, along with nibbles, is offered to guests each evening.
Bar. Concierge. Disabled-adapted rooms. Internet (free). Parking (€26/daily). Room service.

Relais degli Uffizi

Chiasso del Buco 16, off chiasso de' Baroncelli (055 2676239, www.relaisuffizi.it). **Rooms** 12. **Rates** €120-€220. **Map** p334 C3 ⑮

Perhaps the best-positioned hotel for the Uffizi and Palazzo Vecchio, this attractive, smart hotel is nevertheless a little tricky to locate, down a tiny alley off the south side of piazza della Signoria. Once you're upstairs, either settle down in the sitting room and enjoy its fab views, or relax in the great comfort of your own room. The ten rooms vary in shape and size but all are spacious; iron beds and parquet floors set the aesthetic tone, which is consolidated by an assortment of well-chosen antiques and paintings. Adjacent to the hotel is Uffizi House, an equally tasteful guesthouse with rates from €80 to €170.
Bar. Concierge. Disabled-adapted rooms. Internet (free). Parking (€28/day). Room service.

B&B Il Salotto di Firenze

Via Roma 6 (055 218347, www.ilsalottodifirenze. it). **Rooms** 6. **Rates** (incl breakfast) €70-€140. **Map** p334 B3 ⑯

There are plenty of good-quality B&Bs in central Florence, but Il Salotto stands out for its friendly staff and decor celebrating the Macchiaioli artists, whose Impressionistic style of painting, using natural light and outdoor settings, was revolutionary in mid 19th-century Tuscany. As you'd expect, work by the Macchiaioli painters brightens the rooms and public areas, a nicely old-fashioned counterpoint to modern, white rooms. The location is superb.
Internet (free). Parking (€25/day).

★ Torre Guelfa

Borgo SS Apostoli 8 (055 2396338, www.hotel torreguelfa.com). **Rooms** 31. **Rates** €120-€180. **Map** p334 C3 ⑰

This popular hotel literally started at the top and worked its way down; the original rooms were all on the top floor, but the hotel now occupies the whole of the 14th-century *palazzo*, which incorporates the tallest privately owned tower in Florence. Evening drinks come with stunning views at the tower-top bar. Breakfast is served in a sunny, glassed-in *loggia* on the third floor, where there's also an elegant sitting room (with Wi-Fi access) with a painted box ceiling. Bedrooms are decorated in pastel colours with wrought-iron beds (including several four-posters); some are huge. Number 15 is a romantic little den with its own roof garden – you'll need to book at least six months in advance for this. The 12 rooms on the first floor are cheaper and simpler; those facing the street are quite dark.
Bar. Concierge. Disabled-adapted rooms. Internet (free wireless internet in public areas). Parking (€24/day). Room service.

Budget

Cestelli

Borgo SS Apostoli 25 (055 214213, www.hotel cestelli.com). **Rooms** 8. **Rates** €65-€120. **Map** p334 C2 ⑱

The Cestelli is a thoughtful conversion of an old one-star hotel: super-friendly owners Alessio and Asumi Lotti have done a wonderful job in maintaining an old-fashioned feel while updating what was once something of a shabby property. At these rates it's one of the best deals in Florence for simple, pristine, generously sized rooms (even the singles are ample). The building's antique parquet floors have been scrubbed up to great effect, and a complimentary mix of antique and new furniture presides within. All but three of the rooms have a private bathroom.
Concierge. Parking (€25/day).

SANTA MARIA NOVELLA

Luxury

Hotel Santa Maria Novella

Piazza Santa Maria Novella 1 (055 271840, www.hotelsantamarianovella.it). **Rooms** 71. **Rates** €178-€375 double; €520 suite. **Map** p334 B2 ⑲

Owned by clothing manufacturer Rifle, this 45-room hotel has opened another two dozen rooms in an adjacent building. The property is done out in fairly elaborate Empire style, with rich colours, painted

CONSUME

Residenza del Moro.

wood panelling and fancy marquetry, but contemporary decorative touches mean it never feels too oppressive. Two sitting rooms on the ground floor have open fires, velvet sofas and armchairs, plus original oil paintings on the walls. The bedrooms, kitted out in bright colours with modern, country fabrics, come with canopied beds, silk curtains and plasma-screen TVs; the grand marble bathrooms are equipped with Santa Maria Novella goodies. The breakfast room is all mirrors, but there's also an intimate wood-panelled bar on the ground floor and a panoramic roof-terrace bar.

Bar. Business centre. Concierge. Disabled-adapted rooms. Gym. Internet (free). Parking (€30-€45/day). Room service.

JK Place

Piazza Santa Maria Novella 7 (055 2645181, www.jkplace.com). **Rooms** 20. **Rates** €350-€550. **Map** p334 B2 ⍟

One of the best small hotels in Florence, the ultra-sophisticated, 20-room JK Place occupies an attractive old townhouse on piazza Santa Maria Novella. Architect/designer Michele Bonan is responsible for the style, a contemporary take on a neoclassical look, where muted colours beautifully offset fine antiques, old prints, black and white photos and artful flower arrangements. The flicker of candlelight provides a soft glow. No two bedrooms are alike, though all are luxurious and lack nothing in the way of facilities: several of the larger ones overlook the piazza while others are smaller and don't have views. If you're lucky enough to stay in the top-floor penthouse suite, you'll have a 360° sweep of the city from the bathroom. Drinks, snacks and light meals are on offer in the sleek lounge, while a fire burns in the adjacent living room in winter; there's also a roof terrace.

Bar. Concierge. Disabled-adapted rooms. Internet (free). Parking (€35/day). Restaurant. Room service.

Residenza del Moro

Via del Moro 15 (055 290884, www.residenza delmoro.com). **Rooms** 11. **Rates** €265-€700. **Map** p334 B2 ⍟

The splendid *piano nobile* of 16th-century Palazzo Niccolini-Bourbon has been exquisitely restored and now houses this luxurious *residenza* with its 11 rooms and suites. You'll find eleborate stucco work, impressive frescoes and lofty, painted ceilings. The bedrooms vary enormously in shape and size (and price) from the almost affordable Biblioteca to the palatial, super-priced Marchese Suite, but all feature precious antiques, rich fabrics and canopied beds made up with fine linens and cashmere blankets. The lovely marble bathrooms are everything you'd expect from such a place. One thing you would not necessarily anticipate is the beautiful hanging garden where breakfast is served when the weather permits. Another surprise is the fine collection of art in the bedrooms and public spaces.

Bar. Business centre. Concierge. Disabled-adapted rooms. Gym. Internet (free). Parking (€15-€25/day). Room service.

St Regis Florence

Piazza Ognissanti 1 (055 27161, www.stregis florence.com). **Rooms** 100. **Rates** €920-€1,250; breakfast extra. **Map** p334 B1 ⍟

Change of ownership has meant the former Grand Hotel is undergoing major refurbishment. When it emerges, expect butler service and jazzed-up 'personal' spa rooms. Roughly half of the bedrooms and suites are done up in faux Renaissance Florentine style, complete with frescoes, painted ceilings and heavy traditional fabrics. For a river view, you'll have to pay the top rates.

Bar. Business centre. Concierge. Disabled-adapted rooms. Gym. Internet (€16/day). Parking (valet, €30-€40/day). Restaurant. Room service.

CONSUME

Westin Excelsior

Piazza Ognissanti 3 (055 27151, www.westin florence.com). **Rooms** 171. **Rates** €820-€1,095; breakfast €39. **Map** p334 B1 ㉓

While it still offers an element of old-world luxury, the Westin Excelsior has recently introduced some contemporary touches. There's now a fitness area, plus two 'Westin Workout' rooms that have been equipped for the health-conscious guest (yoghurt drinks, tisanes, a massage chair and New Age music on the sound system, for example). In addition, the restaurant now offers a special menu of low-calorie dishes. All this, however, exists within a very traditional framework: the doormen are dressed in maroon and grey livery, and the grand public rooms have polished marble floors, neoclassical columns, painted wooden ceilings and stained glass. The 171 rooms and suites are sumptuously appointed; some boast terraces with views over the river to the rooftops of the Oltrarno – for these, you'll pay the maximum rates, of course.

Bar. Business centre. Concierge. Disabled-adapted rooms. Gym. Internet (€16/day). Parking (valet, €30-€40/day). Restaurant. Room service.

Expensive

★ Antica Torre Tornabuoni Uno

Via de' Tornabuoni 1 (055 2658161, www. tornabuoni1.com). **Rooms** 12. **Rates** €180-€280. **Map** p334 C2 ㉔

The roof terrace of this 12-room hotel, which occupies the upper storeys of an ancient tower overlooking piazza Santa Trinità, has arguably the most spectacular view of any hotel in Florence. Breakfast and drinks are served here in summer to a backdrop of just about every monument in the city. In cooler weather, the glassed-in *loggia* is almost as good. While undeniably comfortable, the bedrooms (several of which have private terraces) are not terribly inspiring; however, the views that they enjoy certainly are. Aside from the terrace, though, there are no public spaces.

Bar. Business centre. Concierge. Disabled-adapted rooms. Internet (free). Parking (€20-€30/day). Room service.

THE BEST OUTDOOR SPOTS

For a rooftop *aperitivo*
Torre Guelfa. *See p105.*

For a well-earned spot of R&R
The rooftop garden and pool at the
Grand Hotel Minerva. *See above.*

For re-enacting *Butch Cassidy*
or *The Bicycle Thieves*
The vintage bikes at **Riva Lofts**. *See p118.*

Casa Howard

Via della Scala 18 (06 69924555, www.casa howard.com). **Rooms** 13. **Rates** €115-€270; €12 breakfast. **Map** p334 B2 ㉕

The owner of this stylish pied-à-terre has set out to offer comfortable, upmarket accommodation at reasonable rates in the discreet atmosphere of a private home. The 12 rooms here are classy and vaguely eccentric, decorated with strong colours and a mix of antique and custom-made furniture. Visit the website to choose the one you like best: the large, dramatic Drawing Room, perhaps, or maybe the sexy Hidden Room with its sunken bath and deep-red walls hung with Japanese erotic prints. There's even a room for those travelling with a canine companion; the Game Room has a terrace and dog beds. There's a Turkish bath to ease those museum-weary muscles and each floor is supplied with an 'honesty fridge'.

Bar. Concierge. Disabled-adapted rooms. Internet (free). No-smoking room. Parking (paid). Room service. Spa (Turkish bath, paid).

Grand Hotel Minerva

Piazza Santa Maria Novella 16 (055 27230, www.grandhotelminerva.com). **Rooms** 102. **Rates** €155-€440. **Map** p334 B2 ㉖

Once an annex hosting guests to the adjacent convent, the Minerva has been a hotel since the mid 19th century, but is determinedly 21st-century, with bright, modern colours and a young, dynamic team of staff, and it's one of the nicest hotels in this category; it's also close to the train station. Many of the appealing rooms have sunny views over piazza Santa Maria Novella (it can get noisy in summer), while extras include in-room electric kettles, a kids' package of videos and games and a shiatsu masseuse on request. Pet owners get a special deal (a room with a terrace and a wood floor, cat litter and pet food) as do women travelling alone (room upgrades, special bath goodies, magazines, free room service). There's a small pool and a bar on the panoramic roof garden.

Bar. Business centre. Concierge. Disabled-adapted rooms. Internet (free). Parking (€28/day). Pool (outdoor). Restaurant. Room service.

★ Hotel L'Orologio

Piazza Santa Maria Novella 24 (055 277380, www.hotelorologioflorence.com). **Rooms** 54. **Rates** €180-€450. **Map** p334 B2 ㉗

If you like timepieces, you'll love this rather mad hotel – as the name implies, it's dedicated to great watches. Each of the five floors is themed around one brand – Patek Philippe, Rolex, but oddly no Timex – and each bedroom is themed around one vintage model; the public spaces (a grand foyer and pleasantly intimate drawing room off it) are full of related art, antiques and furniture. A smart corridor leading to the plush and comfortable bar features a

CONSUME

modern sundial on the floor. Breakfast is served on the fourth floor, which provides wonderful views across the city.

Bar. Business centre. Concierge. Disabled-adapted rooms. Gym. Internet (free). Parking (€30-€45/ day). Room service.

Moderate

★ Hotel Rosso 23

Piazza Santa Maria Novella 23 (055 277 300, www.hotelrosso23.com). **Rooms** 42. **Rates** €110-€140. **Map** p334 B2 ❷

This intimate new hotel, billing itself a 'City Riad' thanks to the very pretty skylit inner courtyard, is in an elegant four-storey townhouse. Red and grey are the dominant tones in a determinedly modern interior, but it's nicely balanced by warm wooden floors and frescoed ceilings. Superior rooms offer great views of Santa Maria Novella church through full-length picture windows, which flood the interiors with light. Amenities in the standard rooms are the same as the superior, but sizes vary widely. Top-notch breakfasts are continental buffet style, and served in the covered courtyard. Service is efficient rather than warm, but the central staircase will make you feel like a 1950s Hollywood diva, such is its sweep and scale – don't look down, though, unless you want a decidedly Hitchcockian moment.
Concierge. Disabled-adapted rooms. Internet (€5 for unlimited use). Parking (€30/day).

Residenza Fiorentina

Via de' Fossi 12 (055 282980, www.laresidenza fiorentina.it). **Rooms** 22. **Rates** €90-€125. **Map** p334 B2 ❷

On the first and second floors of a 16th-century townhouse that was completely renovated in 2010, the Fiorentina's bright, modern rooms are great for those in search of creature comforts in a good location. Few original features remain in the rooms, but the entrance hall and grand stone staircase bear some fascinating 17th-century touches. The façade is gorgeous – look for the family crest of the house's 18th-century owners, the Bourbon del Monte di Santa Maria family, in nearby via de' Fossi and via della Spada.
Bar. Concierge. Disabled-adapted rooms. Internet (dataport, free). Parking (€24/day).

Budget

Abaco

Via de' Banchi 1 (055 2381919, www.hotel abaco.it). **Rooms** 7. **Rates** €45-€85; €5 breakfast. **Map** p334 B3 ❸

There's a bit of a climb up to the second floor of this 550-year-old building; once you've made it, you'll find a modest shell housing a handsome hotel. The friendly owner has painstakingly decorated the less-than-grand place in grand style: the seven bedrooms,

each named after a Renaissance artist, are decorated in sumptuous fabrics with reproductions of works by the relevant painter on the walls. Gilding adorns the picture and mirror frames, and most of the beds are canopied. Three rooms have their own full bathrooms, while others have only a shower. Breakfast is free if you pay in cash (and there's a further 10% discount in November and December).
Bar. Concierge. Disabled-adapted rooms. Internet (free). Parking (€24/day).

Ferretti

Via delle Belle Donne 17 (055 2381328, www. hotelferretti.com). **Rooms** 16. **Rates** €85-€115; €5 breakfast. **Map** p334 B2 ❸

This friendly, spotlessly clean little one-star hotel enjoys a great location in a network of quiet, medieval streets between the station and via de' Tornabuoni. All 16 rooms are pleasant (and all have ceiling fans), but the best are at the top of the old building; bright and sunny, they have crisp cotton covers on iron bedsteads and lovely old marble floors. There's a wood-panelled breakfast room with a free internet point. Only about half the rooms have a private bathroom, so check when you book.
Bar. Concierge. Disabled-adapted rooms. Internet (free). Parking (€25-€30/day).

Scoti

Via de' Tornabuoni 7 (055 292128, www. hotelscoti.com). **Rooms** 11. **Rates** €85-€125; €5 breakfast. **Map** p334 B2 ❸

If you want to secure a room in the wonderful Scoti, housed on the second floor of a 15th-century *palazzo*, book well ahead: it's popular with visitors worldwide. After extensive renovation a couple of years back, the lofty bedrooms are simple but bright and sunny and all are en suite; the frescoed salon has retained its air of faded glory. Breakfast is served around a big communal table or in the rooms.
Concierge. Disabled-adapted rooms. Internet (free). Parking (€30/day).

SAN LORENZO

Moderate

Antica Dimora Johlea

Via San Gallo 80 (055 4633292, www.johanna.it). **Rooms** 6. **Rates** (incl breakfast) €100-€170 double. **No credit cards.**

Lea Gulmanelli and Johanan Vitta opened the first of their mini-chain of five *residenze* back in 1994. Their latest project is the Antica Dimora Johlea (formerly the Johlea Uno), situated a ten-minute walk north of the central market and now the most upmarket of the group. Classical music and a warm glow set the scene when you enter. The bedrooms, all with four posters, are done out in a riot of strong colours with bright kilims on marble or parquet floors, Indian print covers on the beds and swathes of raw

Thai silk. Defying the low rates, all have flat-screen TVs, DVD players, digital radios and electric kettles. Breakfast is served at the top of the house where there's also a sitting room with an honesty bar; from here a wooden staircase leads up to a flower-filled roof terrace with 360° views. If there's no room at this inn, check out the other – cheaper – hotels in the group's portfolio (on the same website): all small, charming and great value.

Bar. Disabled-adapted rooms. Internet (free). Parking (€10/day).

Art Atelier

Via dell'Amorino 20r (055 283777, www.hotel artatelier.com). **Rooms** 16. **Rates** €120-€130. **Map** p334 A3 ❸

Modern by Florentine standards, this 19th-century building exudes good taste and refinement. The rooms, many of them with vaulted ceilings and original features, use an intriguing mix of materials and decorating techniques – Carrara marble, stone, ceramics, frescoes and wall paintings – to create unusual spaces that are on the austere side, but not without charm, and there's an 'Art Atelier' space where exhibitions are held. Breakfast and service are very good, and the location is excellent – Medici chapels are within 100 yards, and the key sites in easy reach.

Bar. Concierge. Disabled-adapted rooms. Internet (wireless, free). Room service.

Casci

Via Cavour 13 (055 211686, www.hotelcasci.com). **Rooms** 24. **Rates** (incl breakfast) €80-€150. Closed 3wks Jan. **Map** p335 A4 ❸

The super-helpful Lombardi family runs this friendly *pensione*, which occupies a 15th-century *palazzo* just north of the Duomo, where opera composer Giacomo Rossini lived from 1851 to 1855. The open-plan bar and breakfast area has frescoed ceilings and shelves stocked with guidebooks; the 24 bedrooms are comfortable and come with up-to-date bathrooms. Rooms at the back look on to a beautiful garden; two sizeable family rooms sleep up to five.

Bar. Concierge. Disabled-adapted rooms. Internet (free). Parking (€25/day). Room service.

Il Guelfo Bianco

Via Cavour 29 (055 288330, www.ilguelfo bianco.it). **Rooms** 40. **Rates** €99-€250. **Map** p335 A4 ❸

Inhabiting two adjacent 15th-century townhouses, this pleasant, efficiently run hotel lies just north of the Duomo. The 40 bedrooms and one self-catering apartment (sleeping four) have been thoughtfully decorated in traditional style; the more capacious rooms allow for an additional two beds, making them a good choice for families. The walls throughout are hung with the owner's impressive contemporary art collection (*see p102* **Rooms with a View**). The rooms that front on to via Cavour have

been soundproofed, but those at the back are still noticeably quieter. Two attractive courtyards offer respite from the city noise; one is used for breakfast in warm weather.

Bar. Concierge. Disabled-adapted rooms. Internet (free). Parking (valet, €26-€30/day). Restaurant. Room service.

Hotel Bellettini

Via de' Conti 7 (055 213561, www.hotel bellettini.com). **Rooms** 28. **Rates** €100-€140. **Map** p334 A3 ❸

This bustling hotel near the Medici chapels and San Lorenzo is great value for money. Dating from the 15th century, it holds one of the oldest hotel licences in the city, and has rooms that couple lovely frescoes with good amenities. The rooms in the main building will appeal to those who like faded charm, but those in the annex are better value, with a decor of elegant fabrics with marble, vibrant colours and soft lighting. There's even a gym downstairs.

Bar. Concierge. Internet (free). Parking (€24/day). Room service.

Hotel Burchianti

Via del Giglio 8 (055 212796, www.hotel burchianti.it). **Rooms** 11. **Rates** €120-€180. **Map** p334 A3 ❸

The Burchianti sisters opened their *pensione* back in 1936 on the first floor of the 17th-century Palazzo Castiglioni, filling it with Italian fabrics and antiques in keeping with the architecture of the wonderfully proportioned rooms, and the lovely frescoes that decorate most of them. Little has changed since their decorating days, though amenities are modern and spotlessly clean. The foyer looks like a throwback to pre-war years, with its wooden French windows and spindly furniture, and the rooms give a distinct sense of another era too. Still a family concern, Burchianti aims to make guests feel at home and comfortable – and Mario, with his son Niccolo, does a great job of doing just that. You'll find more chic places in the area, but you'll be hard-pressed to find anything as whimsical and charming.

Disabled-adapted rooms. Internet (wireless, free).

Hotel dei Macchiaioli

Via Cavour 21 (055 213154, www.hoteldei macchiaioli.com). **Rooms** 14. **Rates** €90-€240. **Map** p335 A4 ❸

Opened in 2010, this intriguing, well-placed boutique hotel is another that will appeal to fans of the little-known Tuscan group of avant-garde artists 'I Macchiaioli'. This was their base for more than two decades in the mid-19th century. Palazzo Morrocchi, as it was then known, was filled with unusual frescoes by the group of artists, and many of them are still visible (*see p102* **Rooms with a View**). The outstanding work is by Annibale Gatti – it covers the entire wooden ceiling of the main hall that looks out on to via Cavour. The rooms, all of them on the first floor, are old-fashioned and comfortable, and as charming as the staff.

Bar. Concierge. Internet (free). Parking (€24/day).

★ Locanda degli Artisti

Via Faenza 56 (055 213806, www.hotelazzi.it). **Rooms** 15. **Rates** (incl breakfast) €75-€130. **Map** p334 A2 ⓰

Housed on the first two floors of a rambling old *palazzo* near the station, the Locanda degli Artisti is an interesting and comfortable little hotel with good prices and a lovely terrace. The big reception area has a retro vibe and you'll probably be greeted by classical music or jazz on the sound system. Eco-friendly materials and natural colours have been used in the 29 bright, sunny bedrooms, and organic produce is served at breakfast. If you're prepared to pay a little over the odds for a touch of luxury, the Suite Blu has a big jacuzzi bath.

Bar. Disabled-adapted rooms. Internet (free). Parking (€18/day).

★ Orto de' Medici

Via Santa Gallo 30 (055 483427, www.ortodei medici.it). **Rooms** 42. **Rates** €90-€190.

It's rare to find an affordable hotel in Florence with lots of outdoor space, but Orto de' Medici has not just one but two such spaces, in the shape of a well-laid-out formal garden and an extensive terrace overlooking it, as well as first-floor rooms with their own private terrace or balcony. The name of the hotel, a 19th-century residence, is taken from the Medici gardens that once existed on the site, and the whole space has been beautifully converted by the Bufalini family, who've taken as much care with the interiors as they have with the exteriors. The terrace is used for breakfast but is also an all-day bar, and indoor public spaces are airy and cool, while the rooms are all a good size and retain some degree of character and colour despite their contemporary styling. A lovely find in the heart of town.

Bar. Business centre. Concierge. Disabled-adapted rooms. Internet (free). Parking (€26-€30/day).

Relais Grand Tour & Grand Tour Suites

Via Santa Reparata 21 (055 283955, www. florencegrandtour.com). **Rooms** 9. **Rates** €85-€145. **No credit cards**.

Any 17th-century folk sufficiently well heeled to undertake the Grand Tour would have been delighted to rest their overexcited heads at one of the luxurious suites of this hotel, named in the journey's honour. A former 16th-century house, the imaginatively restored B&B is run by welcoming couple Cristina and Giuseppe. The Mirrors Suite (use your imagination) is much loved by honeymooners, while the extraordinary Theatre Suite occupies an authentic private playhouse – the bed is on the stage, faced by several rows of seats (fashion shows are sometimes put on here). An assortment of croissants is left in a basket outside the room each morning on request. The first-floor rooms are less extravagant, but thoroughly presentable and correspondingly cheaper. The room rate includes a coupon for breakfast.

Internet (free).

CONSUME

Casa Rovai. *See p113.*

SAN MARCO
Expensive

★ Loggiato dei Serviti
*Piazza della SS Annunziata 3 (055 289592,
www.loggiatodeiservitihotel.it)*. **Rooms** 38. **Rates**
€150-€240. **No credit cards. Map** p335 A5 ⓴
This is one of the most beautiful three-star hotels in
Florence, housed in a 16th-century former convent
that looks over lovely piazza della SS Annunziata
to Brunelleschi's famous portico. Inside is a tasteful
and stylish combination of original architectural
features, wonderful antique furniture and the
modern comforts of an upmarket hotel. The 38 bedrooms, five of which are housed in an annex in via
de' Servi, vary in size and style; the four suites are
ideal for families. Breakfast is served in a bright,
elegant room with vaulted ceilings, while drinks can
be ordered in the bar area. Be aware of the live
music events plus bar and restaurant set up in the
square in summer: one man's entertainment is
another's lost sleep.
*Bar. Concierge. Disabled-adapted rooms. Internet
(free). Parking (valet, €20/day). Room service.*

Residence Hilda
*Via de' Servi 40 (055 288021, www.residence
hilda.com)*. **Rooms** 12. **Rates** €120-€280.
Map p335 A5 ㊶
With a prime location just five minutes' walk north
of the Duomo, Hilda offers stylish self-catering
accommodation ranging from small units for two
people to larger apartments for five. All of the cool,
super-modern apartments come with well-equipped
kitchen units that can be hidden away behind sliding
doors when not required. The furnishings are stylishly spare, with Philippe Starck chairs and other
modern classics on blonde-wood floors. Staff will
even collect your shopping.
*Concierge. Disabled-adapted rooms. Internet (free).
Parking (€30/day). Room service.*

Moderate

Hotel Morandi alla Crocetta
*Via Laura 50 (055 234 4747, www.hotel
morandi.it)*. **Rooms** 10. **Rates** €100-€180.
Map p335 A5 ㊷
From the minute you enter the beautifully tiled
entrance hall, this hotel is like a step back in time,
with lovely Persian rugs on warm parquet floors,
old-fashioned bedspreads in red and gold, and a
sense of peace and calm that permeates the entire
space – no wonder: the hotel is located in the former
16th-century convent of the Crocetta. Traces of the
convent can be found in many of the rooms, with
fresco fragments, vaulted ceilings and brick arches
adding real individuality. Some rooms have terraces.
*Bar. Concierge. Internet (€8/day). Parking
(€22/day). Room service.*

SANTA CROCE
Luxury

Four Seasons Hotel
*Borgo Pinti 99 (055 26261, www.fourseasons.
com/florence)*. **Rooms** 116. **Rates** €295-€595.
Map p335 A6 ㊸
In Palazzo della Gherardesca, which commands
one of the largest privately owned gardens in
Florence, this fabulous hotel is the result of a multi-
million-euro restoration project. As well as the luxurious rooms, there are all the five-star facilities
you'd anticipate, from the big spa to an outdoor
pool. The rooms and suites are located in two buildings – the original *palazzo* and the Conventino –
across four acres of garden, surrounded by winding
paths, fountains and outdoor seating. If the hotel is
out of your price range, the gardens are now open to
the public, so you can come for a coffee or cocktail
and a gawp at how the other half live; you won't
have access to the original frescoes, friezes and hand-
painted reliefs that decorate the suites, mind you.
*Bar. Business centre. Concierge. Disabled-
adapted rooms. Gym. Internet (€22/day).
Parking (€50). Pool (outdoor). Restaurants (2).
Room service. Spa.*

Relais Santa Croce
*Via Ghibellina 87 (055 2342230, www.relaisanta
croce.com)*. **Rooms** 24. **Rates** €300-€3,500.
Map p335 C5 ㊹
This hotel offers contemporary style and person-
alised service in the shell of grand, 18th-century
Palazzo Ciofi-Jacometti. The public rooms on the
first floor are suitably grandiose – especially the vast
music room, with its frescoed ceilings, old parquet
floor and stucco panels. The bedrooms, meanwhile,
have clean, modern lines with quirky design details
(including amazing light fittings). Two Royal Suites
offer the full VIP treatment; past incumbents of the
spectacular Verazzano Suite include Kate Moss,
Dave Gilmore and Marilyn Manson. Rear-facing
rooms on the upper floors have views over a jumble
of red-tiled rooftops to the façade of the Santa Croce
church. The Relais shares its entrance with one of
Italy's most celebrated restaurants, the Enoteca
Pinchiorri (*see p133*), but a more reasonably priced
alternative is the hotel's own restaurant.
*Bar. Business centre. Concierge. Disabled-adapted
rooms. Internet (€14/day). Parking (€40/day).
Restaurants. Room service.*

Expensive

Hotel Home Florence
Piazza Piave 3 (055 243668, www.hhflorence.it).
Rooms 39. **Rates** (incl breakfast) €210-€290.
There's a 'concept' behind the stark white edifice
that is Hotel Home, just on the eastern borders of
Santa Croce – phrases like 'reinterpreting design'

CONSUME

Lap of Luxury

Il Salviatino has gone from derelict villa to divine hotel.

Florence's latest luxury hotel is the real deal. **Il Salviatino** (*see p117*) is a 15th-century villa perched on a Fiesole hilltop that does away with mundane things such as lobbies and check-in desks and replaces them with chichi personal service, in the form of a 'service ambassador' who sees to your every need. There are no formal dining areas either: you eat in whichever of the gorgeous public areas takes your fancy. Once inside your room, the delights continue; where's the TV, you wonder? In James Bond style, it's the mirror, obviously (don't panic, there are more mirrors). If you're planning to visit with a wealthy Russian oligarch, make them book the Ojetti suite (named for a previous owner: art critic, journalist and writer Ugo Ojetti) in the tower – its conservatory sitting room and whole-floor jacuzzi have incredible country views.

When owner Marcello FM Pigozzo saw this derelict villa, he knew it was the perfect location, and set about carefully (and expensively, at a cost of £13 million) restoring it to its former glory, discovering unexpected delights along the way. 'Extraordinary 400-year-old frescoes were hidden underneath a false ceiling, and a 13th-century Venetian sarcophagus, which

we were able to integrate into a suite as a spectacular bath,' he recalls. Artisans carefully removed, washed and replaced centuries-old mosaics throughout the villa and its five-hectare garden, refurbished and repanelled the glorious library in its original 18th-century chestnut wood, washed and cleaned marble statuary and original paths, and restored a stunning 11th-century stone bath, all the while adding beautiful new materials and architectural features, such as Italian oak, rainwater showers and Frau furniture.

Overseen by Italian architect Luciano Colombo, Pigozzo sourced locally where he could, so local manufacturers designed and created the hand-embroidered linen and cotton bedding and towels, while skilled local artisans and builders undertook the bulk of the restoration.

Sold? Then all you need to know is which room to book. The top-floor suites, Ojetti and Marcello, have roof terraces with sweeping views of the Florentine skyline; Affresco has the aforementioned stone sarcophogus bathtub. Don't miss a relax in the 14 deluxe rooms of the Thai Devarana spa, the only one outside Asia, and arrive at night for the best effect: the villa and its gardens are lit by lanterns and candelabra.

and 'understated style' are put to dismal use in their marketing material, but a visit here does more than all the words can; it really is quite a stunning hotel, where layers of white pile up in different materials, from sleek curvy tables to delicate filigreed crockery and swathes of organza, all accentuated by gold finishing, Perspex and blonde wood. A stay here will feel like you've suddenly wandered onto the set of *2001: A Space Odyssey* as reimagined by *Wallpaper** magazine, but it will most likely be the most memorable hotel experience of your life. Have at least one drink on the panoramic terrace, where there's a jacuzzi and views over the city and the river that are out of this world.

Bar. Business centre. Concierge. Disabled-adapted rooms. Gym (mini fitness room). Internet (free). Parking (€30/day). Room service.

Moderate

★ Casa Rovai

Via Fiesolana 1 (055 2001647, www.casarovai. com). **Rooms** 6. **Rates** (incl breakfast) €70-€120 double; €110-€180 family. **Map** p335 B5 ④⑤

This reasonably priced, retro-stylish little guesthouse occupies the first floor of a 16th-century building not far from the lively Sant'Ambrogio market. Expect 19th-century *terrazzo* floors, traditional cream and dove-grey paintwork, the odd fresco, and a mix of late 19th- and early 20th-century furniture picked up at flea markets and auction houses, plus stylish, modern leather sofas and chairs. The six bedrooms (a couple of which have painted ceilings) vary in shape and size, but all are comfortable and have contemporary bathrooms. Continental breakfast is included in the rate, but for an extra €5 you can order eggs, prosciutto and cheeses. *Photo p111. Concierge. Internet (free). Parking (€5/day).*

Liana

Via Alfieri 18 (055 245303, www.hotelliana.com). **Rooms** 24. **Rates** €90-€250. **Map** p335 A6 ④⑥

Once the British Embassy, this 19th-century building is worth considering if you're travelling by car and want to be within reach of the sights but not in the crowded centre. Director Marie Therese Blot has lavished love and care on the property, renovating with a deft touch that has created a warm and

CONSUME

intimate hotel. There's a distinctly residential feel to the place, heightened by warm *terrazzo* floors in the lobby and corridors, fresh flowers and art everywhere, and a lush, lovely English garden (a few of the rooms look out on it). All the rooms are comfortable and elegant, with handsome antique furniture, soft white linens and stylish fabrics; many have gorgeous frescoes. Classical music is played in the first-floor breakfast room.

Bar. Concierge. Disabled-adapted rooms. Internet (free). Parking (€18/day). Room service.

Palazzo Galletti

Via Sant'Egidio 12 (055 3905750, www.palazzo galletti.it). **Rooms** 11. **Rates** (incl breakfast) €100-€240. **Map** p335 B5 ⑰

Offering excellent value and situated on a busy street just a few minutes' walk east of the Duomo, Palazzo Galletti occupies the first floor of an 18th-century mansion built around an internal courtyard. All the elements of a grand *palazzo* are here (weathered old *cotto* floors, lofty arched ceilings, elegant paintwork in soothing pastels, frescoes, the odd chandelier), but the overall effect is not at all pompous thanks to the addition of some carefully chosen ethnic and contemporary design details. All but two of the nine lovely bedrooms face on to the quiet *cortile* (yard) and have a tiny terrace. Even the smallest rooms are a good size, while the two entirely frescoed suites are vast. Hotel guests get special rates at the ground-floor Soul Space spa (*see p171*).

Bar. Concierge. Disabled-adapted rooms. Internet (€5/day; free wireless in the lobby). Parking (€30/day). Spa.

Le Stanze di Santa Croce

Via delle Pinzochere 6 (347 2593010 mobile, www.lestanzedisantacroce.com). **Rooms** 4.

Rates (incl breakfast) €140-€160. **No credit cards**. **Map** p335 C5 ⑱

The diminutive, three-floor townhouse that houses this little B&B has a great location, just off piazza Santa Croce, and you'll receive a genuinely friendly welcome from the owner, Mariangela. The four comfortable double bedrooms at Le Stanze have been individually furnished with pretty fabrics, lively colours and a well considered mix of old and new furniture; one has a romantic wrought-iron four-poster. Breakfast is served on a lovely flower-filled terrace where guests can hang out all day and help themselves from a well-stocked 'honesty fridge'. Mariangela is a relaxed host and a great cook; she bakes fresh cakes daily for breakfast and offers cooking courses.

Internet (free). Parking (€22-€29/day).

Budget

★ Black 5 Townhouse

Via Giuseppe Verdi 5 (055 0515147, www.black 5florencesuite.it). **Rooms** 10. **Rates** €35-€90. **Map** p335 C5 ⑲

From the outside the curiously named Black 5 Townhouse looks like any other unprepossessing Florentine block, so much so that it's easy to walk past without realising it's there, above the Teatro Verdi. But once inside, the snazzy black and mirrored elevator gives a hint of things to come: animal skins on the floor, Pollock-esque art on the walls, and muted greys punctuated by bold splashes of colour. It's young, fresh and engaging, with each of the ten rooms spanning myriad gorgeous colours and styles – some have Pop Art wall coverings, others gloriously rich fabric headboards against lime green walls, and all come with wooden caisson ceilings, period brickwork and a whirlpool bath. Views are either over a central courtyard or the main road.

Palazzo Guadagni. *See p116.*

Casa Pucci. See p117.

The attic breakfast room opens on to a sweet little terrace with great views across the rooftops to Palazzo Vecchio and the Duomo.
Internet (free).

Dalì

Via dell'Oriuolo 17 (055 2340706, www.hoteldali. com). **Rooms** 10. **Rates** €45-€85. **Map** p335 B5 ⑩
Run with genuine care by an enthusiastic young couple, Samanta and Marco, this little gem just east of the Duomo offers spotless, bright and homely rooms at budget prices and – a miracle in central Florence – free car parking. Only four of the ten rooms have private bathrooms, but all are thoughtfully decorated and furnished with hand stencilling, pretty bedcovers and old bedheads; all have ceiling fans. Those fronting on to the busy street can be a bit noisy, but double glazing helps; rooms at the back overlooking the courtyard are sunny and quiet. Breakfast is not provided, but there are electric kettles and fridges in all the rooms.
Concierge. Disabled-adapted rooms. Internet (free). Parking (free). Room service.

OLTRARNO
Luxury

Lungarno

Borgo San Jacopo 14 (055 27261, www.lungarno hotels.com). **Rooms** 73. **Rates** €230-€410. **Map** p334 C2 ⑤
The most coveted rooms in this stylish hotel, housed in a 1960s building incorporating a medieval tower, have terraces overlooking the Arno. However, even if you can't secure a river view, you can enjoy the

waterside setting from the breakfast room and lounge/bar, or the outside seating area on the river. More classic in feel than other Ferragamo-owned hotels such as the Gallery Hotel Art (*see p99*) and the Continentale (*see p101*), the Lungarno has been decorated in a cream and navy-blue colour scheme, but some lovely mahogany and cherrywood antique furniture, plus a collection of fine prints and drawings (*see p102* **Rooms with a View**), lends a reassuringly traditional touch. Bedrooms are stylish and comfy but, with the exception of a couple of spacious suites, not that big. The Borgo San Jacopo restaurant (*see p137*) a few doors down serves excellent food in a calm, elegant setting.
Bar. Concierge. Gym. Internet (free). Restaurant. Room service.

Palazzo Magnani Feroni

Borgo San Frediano 5 (055 2399544, www. palazzomagnaniferoni.com). **Rooms** 10. **Rates** €280-€800. **Map** p334 C1 ⑫
Expect top-class service and facilities with prices to match at this grand *palazzo* just south of the river. All but one of the ten big suites have separate sitting rooms elegantly furnished with squashy sofas, armchairs and antiques. The most charming room of all is actually the smallest: a romantic junior suite with floor-to-ceiling frescoes and a little private garden. The bathrooms are super-smart and equipped with slippers, robes and heated towel rails: you can even choose the smell of your soap. The fabulous roof terrace – complete with a bar serving light meals – offers views of the whole city.
Bar. Concierge. Disabled-adapted rooms. Gym. Internet (€10/day; free in Feroni Deluxe Suites). Parking (€40-€48/day). Room service.

CONSUME

Expensive

Serristori Palace Residence
*Lungarno Serristori 13 (055 2001623, www.
serristoripalace.com).* **Rooms** 12 suites. **Rates**
€150-€340 (€820-€1,815/wk). **Map** p335 D5
From the balconies of most of the suites here, you
really get to appreciate the sense of being in an
extraordinary city. The great location, between the
Pitti Palace and the ponte Vecchio, and a stone's
throw from the beach, ensure that you feel right at
the heart of things, but with the benefit of a kitchen
retreat when it all gets too much. The 12 apartments,
many of them interconnecting for larger groups, are
well-equipped, airy spaces furnished in a tasteful,
inoffensive style, and nearby supermarkets and corner shops make it easy to make a meal or your own
breakfast to enjoy on the terrace. Opt for the lovely
Belvedere, with its terrace, or the pretty San Niccolò,
and you won't want to leave.
Internet (free). Parking (€25/day).

Moderate

Annalena
*Via Romana 34 (055 222402, www.annalena
hotel.com).* **Rooms** 20. **Rates** (incl breakfast)
€100-€150. **Map** p334 D1 ⬢
The Annalena is housed in a 15th-century building
located just opposite the back entrance to the Boboli
Gardens. At various times it has been used as a
refuge for young widows and lodgings for refugees
from Mussolini's Fascist police. Today, it has a
pleasantly old-fashioned atmosphere and, after a
period of decline, has just been taken over by
enthusiastic, helpful new management, which is
determined to bring the place up to scratch. It's
brightened up the huge, atmospheric salon that
serves as lounge, bar and breakfast room, while the
pleasant, oft-spacious bedrooms have been given a
lick of paint; future plans include updating the bathrooms. The best rooms are at the back overlooking
the gorgeous gardens; they have terraces scented
with jasmine.
*Bar. Internet (free). Parking (€15-€25/day).
Room service.*

La Scaletta
*Via de' Guicciardini 13 (055 283028/214255,
www.hotellascaletta.it).* **Rooms** 11. **Rates** (incl
breakfast) €75-€140. **Map** p334 D3 ⬢
A change of management in 2005 swept away the
figurative cobwebs of the old-style Scaletta, housed
in a grand 15th-century *palazzo* between the ponte
Vecchio and Palazzo Pitti, in favour of cleaner – even
stylish – lines. The 11 buttermilk-painted bedrooms
have elegant matching curtains and bedspreads,
modern wrought-iron bedheads and nice old
wardrobes. Most are quiet; three rooms overlook
the Boboli Gardens, while those on noisy via
Guicciardini have effective double glazing. All

Una Hotel Vittoria.

rooms now have bathrooms. There are no fewer than
three roof gardens/terraces that offer breathtaking
views of Boboli and the city skyline; one has a bar
that's open in the evenings.
Bar. Internet (free). Restaurant.

Palazzo Guadagni
*Piazza Santo Spirito 9 (055 2658376, www.
palazzoguadagni.com).* **Rooms** 15. **Rates** €130-
€150. **Map** p334 D1 ⬢
In the 500 years since it was built for a silk merchant,
this glorious 16th-century *palazzo* has housed the
German Institute for Art History, Florence's first
library, and the pretty but slightly down-at-heel
Pensione Sorelle Bandini. 2011 saw a major refurb
of the latter, transforming it into a refined three-star
hotel, notable for the rooftop garden bar and terrace
in the elegant *loggia*. Centred around a courtyard,
the hotel is full of old-world charm; antiques and
chesterfields with well-stuffed leather cushions in
the comfy lounge areas hark back to a more genteel
time, while many of the variously sized rooms – in
pleasing pastel colours with lovely warm red-tiled
floors – feature fireplaces and frescoes, and great
views over the city. The location, bang on the happening piazza Santo Spirito, is ace. *Photo p114.*
*Bar. Concierge. Internet (free). Parking (from
€22/day). Room service.*

★ Via Santo Spirito 6
*Via Santo Spirito 6 (055 288082, www.
residenzadepoca-viasantospirito6.it).* **Rooms** 7;
2 apartments. **Rates** €80-€165 double; €150-
€215 apartment. **Map** p334 C2 ⬢

Sitting on the tiny rooftop terrace outside the Emily Dickinson suite, sipping your coffee (made, of course, using a proper Italian cafetière), it's easy to imagine yourself a long-term resident of Florence. But any of the lovely apartments in this charismatic *palazzo* induce the same feeling: rich warm colours of the wooden floors, woollen rugs and chaise-longue upholstery give it a home-from-home atmosphere. The envious looks you get when people see you ducking into the building help you feel there's definitely something rather magical about the place. Staff are helpful and charming, there's a little courtyard garden, and the kitchen is so well stocked and ingeniously designed that cooking your own meals, using the excellent local produce that's right on your doorstep, is a rare pleasure.

Business centre. Internet (free). Parking (€25-€30/day).

Budget

Casa Pucci

Via Santa Monaca 8 (055 216560, www.casapucci.it). **Rooms** 5. **Rates** €70-€120. **Map** p334 C1 ⑤⑧

Signora Pucci's ground-floor apartment, not far from buzzy piazza Santo Spirito, occupies part of an ex-convent dating from the 15th century. Three of the five rooms lead off a cool, plant-filled courtyard garden where a huge rustic table is laid in the mornings for summer breakfasts. The whole place has a nice, lived-in feel, from the big kitchen (which guests are free to use) to the spacious, homely rooms furnished with family antiques and paintings. Romantics should go for room no.5 with its four-poster bed and stone fireplace. A faithful clientele of return guests – plus amazingly low prices – means that you need to book well ahead. *Photo p115.*

Internet (free).

★ Foresteria Valdese

Via de' Serragli 49 (055 212576, www.istituto gould.it/foresteria/). **Open** *Office* 8.45am-1pm, 3-7.30pm Mon-Fri; 9am-1.30pm, 2.30-6pm Sat. **Rooms** 39. **Rates** €56-€68; €5.50 breakfast (booking required). **Map** p334 D1 ⑤⑨

Run by the Valdese Church, Istituto Gould runs this excellent budget accommodation in a well-kept 17th-century *palazzo*. There's a serene courtyard, stone staircases, terracotta floors, a tantalisingly lovely garden (unfortunately, not accessible to guests) and lots of atmosphere. Of the almost 40 rooms, two-thirds are doubles, while the others accommodate a maximum of four. All rooms but two (a triple and a quad) now have private bathrooms. If you want to avoid noisy via de' Serragli, ask for a room at the back; some have access to a terrace. You need to check in during office hours, but once that's done, you get your own key. And there's no maid service during your stay.

Internet (free).

OUTSIDE THE CITY GATES
Luxury

Una Hotel Vittoria

Via Pisana 9 (055 22771, www.unahotels.it). **Rooms** 84. **Rates** €99-€507.

Milan-based architect/designer Fabio Novembre's exuberant Una Hotel Vittoria (housed in the shell of a 19th-century warehouse just outside Porta San Frediano) is geared towards an upmarket business clientele, but will appeal to anyone looking for something completely different decor-wise. The building is filled with Novembre's idiosyncratic designs; the huge swooping mosaic that greets you in the entrance hall is based on a 19th-century floral brocade while the long, curving wooden table in the restaurant (designed for communal eating) was influenced by the refectory tables found in Tuscan monasteries. The spacious bedrooms are equipped with a plethora of gadgetry. They lead off black-painted corridors where each door is framed in gold leaf and sports an 'old master' portrait; effectively, you walk through the painting to enter the room. Once inside, the beds are tucked into alcoves and backed by oversized bedheads studded with star-like fibre optic lights that change colour. Anyone with a modest disposition should book elsewhere; only glass separates the mosaic bathrooms from the rest of the room.

Bar. Concierge. Disabled-adapted rooms. Internet (€3/30min). Parking (€20/day). Restaurant. Room service.

Il Salviatino

Via del Salviatino 21 (055 9041111, www.salviatino.com). **Rooms** 40. **Rates** €600-€2,790. *See p113* **Lap of Luxury**.

Bar. Business centre. Concierge. Disabled-adapted rooms. Gym. Internet (free). Parking (free). Pool. Restaurant. Room service. Spa.

Villa San Michele

Via Doccia 4, Fiesole (055 5678200, www.villa sanmichele.com). Bus 7. **Rooms** 48. **Rates** €860-€1,070. Closed late Nov-late Mar.

The rooms in this fabulous yet understated hotel, much beloved on the celebrity circuit, are among the most expensive in Italy. Housed in a 15th-century monastery, Villa San Michele enjoys a superb location, nestled in a beautiful terraced garden on the hillside just below Fiesole. Understated elegance and good taste, combined with subtle nods to the past, inform the style, which is always luxurious but never ostentatious. The views down to the city are splendid: dinner under the *loggia* at sunset is an unforgettable experience, though the bill will be too. Service throughout the property is immaculate.

Bar. Concierge. Disabled-adapted rooms. Gym. Internet (free). Parking (free). Pool (outdoor). Restaurant. Room service.

CONSUME

CONSUME

INSIDE TRACK
IN BED WITH THE BROWNINGS

To stay somewhere truly poetic in Florence, rent the first-floor apartment at Palazzo Guidi in piazza San Felice through the Landmark Trust (www.landmarktrust.org.uk); it was here that the Barrett Brownings lived after their secret marriage in 1847, up until Elizabeth's death in 1861.

Expensive

Relais Marignolle
Via di San Quirichino a Marignolle 16 (055 2286910, www.marignolle.com). No bus. **Rooms** 6. **Rates** €130-€235.
Set in rambling grounds on a south-facing hillside at Marignolle (a few kilometres south of Porta Romana), the Bulleri family's classily converted farmhouse is a great base from which to make the most of elegant country living while still keeping the sights of the city within easy reach. Sun pours into the large, bright living room, where comfortable armchairs and sofas, an open fire and an honesty bar encourage lingering. Breakfast is served on a veranda, open in summer and glassed in over the colder months. The nine bedrooms vary in shape and size, but all are decorated along the same tasteful lines, with stylish country fabrics, padded bedheads, pristine white paintwork and dark parquet floors. Signora Bulleri serves light meals on request and holds cooking classes. The attractive pool is another nice perk.
Bar. Concierge. Internet (free). Parking (free). Pool (outdoor). Room service.

★ Riva Lofts
Via Baccio Bandinelli 98 (055 7130272, www.rivalofts.com). **Rooms** 8. **Rates** €210-€550.
A welcome jolt was given to Florence's predominantly traditional hotel scene with the opening of Riva Lofts, the project of renowned local architect Claudio Nardi. It occupies a small complex of 19th-century artisan workshops on the Arno a 20-minute walk west of the ponte Vecchio. The heart of Riva is the big, open-plan living room with high vaulted ceiling and exposed brick where guests can help themselves from the honesty bar, and relax and chat in front of the huge fire. The use of natural elements (wood, stone) throughout warms the clean lines and spare design, and furniture is a mix of modern classics and vintage pieces. The suites (all but one with kitchen) range in size from 30sq m to 100sq m (320-1,080sq ft); top of the pile are the two spectacular lofts, huge spaces infused with light from tall, arched windows. All rooms have super-contemporary bathrooms and electronic gadgetry; thoughtful extras

include an exercise mat and weights. For recreation, there's a garden with a heated pool made of pale sandstone, walks along the river, and bikes (vintage, of course) to get you into town.
Business centre. Bar (24hr honesty bar). Concierge (8am-8pm). Disabled-adapted rooms. Internet (free). Parking (free, max 3 cars; otherwise, €20/day). Room service (€10/guest).

Moderate

Classic Hotel
Viale Niccolò Machiavelli 25 (055 229351, www.classichotel.it). Bus 11, 36, 37 to Porta Romana. **Rooms** 20. **Rates** €110-€160; €8 breakfast.
If you want the convenience of being able to walk into town (or catch a bus), but also like the idea of staying amid a little bit of greenery, then try the very civilised Classic Hotel. Set in a lush garden just five minutes' walk south-west of the old city gate at Porta Romana, this attractive villa has been tastefully refurbished. Breakfast is served either in a basement room or, more pleasantly, in a conservatory leading to a garden full of mature trees and shrubs. Romantics should consider booking the annex suite with its own terrace.
Bar. Concierge. Internet (free). Parking (free). Room service.

Hotel David
Viale Michelangiolo 1 (055 6811695, www.davidhotel.com). Bus D, 12, 23. **Rooms** 24. **Rates** €120-€160.
This family-run guesthouse housed in a garden villa overlooking the river is a delight, not least for its pretty and pretty unusual garden terrace – you're provided with tableware so that you can order and eat from a range of good discounted takeaway menus – and a bunch of excellent freebies that go way beyond wireless internet and breakfast, including ten minutes of free international calls every day, free parking, ten free soft drinks and a range of free snacks in your minibar and a free happy hour. All that, plus light-filled, airy and characterful rooms with parquet flooring and, in some cases, french windows leading to the terrace.
Bar. Concierge. Internet (free). Parking (free).

Pensione Bencistà
Via Benedetto da Maiano 4, Fiesole (055 59163, www.bencista.com). Bus 7. **Rooms** 41. **Rates** €100-€160.
The characterful old Bencistà has taken a few halting steps towards the 21st century (a website, credit cards, a lift) in recent years, but not so many as to destroy the delightful old-world atmosphere of the place. Housed in a former convent and run as a *pensione* by the Simoni family since 1925, it has a fabulous setting on the hillside just below Fiesole. Public rooms are furnished with antiques; one has a

fireplace and shelves stuffed with old books. Bedrooms are off a warren of passageways and staircases. No two are alike – those at the front enjoy unrivalled city views as does the flower-filled terrace. The restaurant overlooks the city and serves homely, traditional food; half-board rates are available but no longer obligatory.

Bar. Concierge. Disabled-adapted rooms. Internet (free). Parking (free). Restaurant. Room service.

Podere La Valle

Via Piero Dazzi 12 (055 4250116, www.podere lavalle.it). **Rooms** 6 apartments. **Rates** €130-€160 (min stay 3 nights).

If you're in a car and want to be close to the city but in a decidedly rural setting just north of it, Podere La Valle won't disappoint. Just a few minutes from the city walls, this well-kept farm with six self-contained apartments sits in the Florentine hills with lovely views over the city, the Arno valley, the Apennines and far-reaching expanses of fields. A pool will cool you off on hot days, and the apartments are wonderfully cosy, with lovely heavy cotton bedspreads, warm red terracotta tiles and exposed wooden beams giving a sense of rustic wellbeing that's just what you need when you get back from a day's hard art graft in the city.

Disabled-adapted rooms. Internet (free). Parking (free). Pool.

Budget

★ Casa Schlatter

Viale dei Mille 14 (347 1180215, www.casa schlatter-florence.com). Bus 10, 17. **Rooms** 3. **Rates** €85-€100; €6 breakfast.

This characterful three-roomed B&B just outside the city walls in Campo di Marte has only been opened since 2009, when restoration work that had turned it from the home and studio of idiosyncratic Swiss painter and sculptor C Adolfo Schlatter was completed. The conversion has been a wonderfully sympathetic one; the artist's work fills every available space and surface in the house, turning it into a strange but fascinating 19th-century museum that will ensure you get an eyeful of genuine weirdness at every turn, from bronze giant squids and gravestones to elegant canvases set on brilliant rose-coloured walls and unusual antique objects in the rooms. Schlatter's great-granddaughter Alessandra cooks amazing made-to-order savoury dishes and cakes for breakfast (which isn't included, but is great value at €6), serving them in a lovely garden.

Internet (free).

HOSTELS

Hostel Archi Rossi

Via Faenza 94r, Santa Maria Novella (055 290804, www.hostelarchirossi.com). **Open** 6.30am-2am daily. **Rooms** 30. **Rates** (incl

Riva Lofts.

CONSUME

breakfast) €21-€29/person in dormitory; €40-€60/person single; €30-€40/person double; €25-€35/person triple.
The reception of this hostel is covered with garish renditions of famous frescoes, done by guests. The maximum number of beds in the spacious, light rooms is nine, but many are smaller and some have private bathrooms. Just ten minutes' walk from the station, it's a good choice for early departures or late arrivals. There are now 147 beds in total, including four doubles in an annex, which have private bathrooms, TV, minibar and internet access. The management allows mixed-sex rooms as long as everyone knows each other. Facilities for the disabled are unusually good, and there's a lovely garden. Guided tours of the city in English are offered free of charge. *Bar. Disabled-adapted rooms. Internet (free). Restaurant.*

Plus Florence

Via Santa Caterina d'Alessandria 15/17, San Lorenzo (055 6286347, www.plushostels.com/plusflorence). **Rooms** 100; 420 beds. **Rates** €20-€34.50.
Pools, Duomo views and a rooftop terrace are no longer the exclusive preserve of the rich traveller in Florence thanks to the arrival of the Plus chain, which began in Venice in 2004 and opened a site here in Florence in 2009, offering both pool and view from €16 a night in youthful, university dorm-style accomodation in either Plus or Plus Girls, a women-only space with big bathrooms, cosmetic tables, personal fluffy towels and a cosmetics goodie bag. Choose from bright, colourful double rooms up to eight-person dorms, all with TV, en suite bathrooms and personal storage lockers, and back it all up with a wealth of useful extras, including a gym, Turkish steam room, a terrace bar with loungers, basement disco and café, and laundry facilities. *Bar. Disabled-adapted rooms. Concierge. Gym. Internet (free). Parking (€15/day). Pool. Restaurant.*

Youth Residence Firenze 2000

Via Raffaello Sanzio 16, Outside the City Gates (055 2335558, www.cheap-hotel-florence.com). Bus 12. **Rooms** 32; 90 beds. **Rates** €24-€45.
A decent location on the Oltrarno side of the river opposite Santa Maria Novella, plus lots of double and triple rooms and no curfew make this a good hostel choice in the city, though those who don't like walking might find the 15 minutes or so it takes to get to the sights a bit of a slog. Rooms are clean, bright white spaces with colourful artworks and bedding, and there's a pleasant breakfast room. *Internet (€1/day). Parking (€10-€15/day).*

CAMPSITES

Camping facilities in Italy are generally reliable. Bear in mind that most campsites become packed in summer, and can be very noisy.

Camping Michelangelo

Viale Michelangelo 80, Outside the City Gates (055 6811977, www.ecvacanze.it). Bus 12, 13. **Open** *Office* 7am-midnight daily. **Pitches** 240. **Rates** €9.50-€11.40 person, €5.80-€6.60 under-12s; €11.40-€13.80 tent; €12.50-€14.90 caravan, camper van or trailer.
This campsite just below piazzale Michelangelo has spectacular views of the city, yet is only a short walk from the centre. There's room on site for 240 tents and caravans, allowing for a maximum capacity of about 950 people. There are also 150 'house tents' for two people, with proper beds. Facilities are good (with a bar, a restaurant, a supermarket, an internet point, a kids' playground, a disco). *Bar. Internet (free). Restaurant.*

Camping Panoramico

Via Peramonda 1, Fiesole, Outside the City Gates (055 599069, www.florencecamping.com). Bus 7. **Open** *Office* 8am-10pm daily. **Pitches** 110. **Rates** €9-€10 person, €4-€5 3-12s; €6-€7.50 tent; €12-€15 tent with car, caravan with car or camper van.
These 110 pitches make up the most picturesque site within easy reach of Florence (it's about five miles north of the city centre). In addition to the pitches, 21 self-catering bungalows accommodate up to four people, and there are also some caravans to rent. Facilities include a bar, a restaurant, a supermarket and a pool. The campsite also puts on a free, twice-daily shuttle service to and from Fiesole. *Bar. Disabled-adapted bathrooms. Internet (€2/1hr, €5/3hrs). Pool (outdoor). Restaurant.*

LONG-TERM ACCOMMODATION

Renting a flat through an agency inevitably involves commission charges, and the minimum stay is usually a week. To avoid these charges, search through the hundreds of websites advertising holiday lets, or look in the holiday sections of UK newspapers; it's worth doing a bit of research to compare prices. The following firms employ English-speaking staff.

Florence & Abroad

Via San Zanobi 58, San Lorenzo (055 487004, www.florenceandabroad.com). **Open** 10am-5pm Mon-Fri. **No credit cards.**
This well-established agency offers long- and short-term accommodation for students and visitors to Florence. It also handles properties in Tuscany.

Your Agency In Florence (YAIF)

Via della Vigna Nuova 9, Santa Maria Novella (055 274871, www.yaif.it). Bus 6. **Open** 10am-6pm Mon-Fri. **Map** p334 B2 ⑥⓪
YAIF specialises in student accommodation and short-term holiday rentals (by the day, week and month). Expect to pay from around €900 per month for a *monolocale* (one-room flat) in low season.

Restaurants & Wine Bars

Florence's trattorie and enoteche are updated for a new generation.

According to local lore, the eating scene in Florence has always been *difficile*. In a city geared towards tourists, standards have often been low and the Florentines themselves have suffered for it. Luckily, among the faux straw wine flasks and the red-checked tablecloths, there are still some wonderfully unreconstructed *trattorie* and *osterie* where the mamma figure (maybe together with her son or daughter) continues to prepare the sort of rustic recipes that have been handed down through the generations and that make up Florentine *cucina tradizionale*. You have to look hard, but the locals know where these places are and so do we: our favourites are listed below.

A new generation of *trattorie* is emerging in Florence, places that are based on the unfussy principles of the traditional family-run eaterie, but where the chefs are adding a contemporary element to their cooking. They are also paying more attention to sourcing ingredients properly and the overall result is very successful, and often reasonably priced. These types of place, along with the old-style joints, are very popular these days as Florentines continue to rail against the rising cost of eating out.

While a meal at a good, convivial *trattoria* can be a richly rewarding experience, you may want to splash out and try something a bit different. In this case, go for one of the restaurants where chefs are experimenting with today's fashion for *cucina rivisitata* (literally 'revisited') bringing a fresh approach and new emphasis to traditional recipes. This is the kind of cooking that needs to be executed with intelligence and a sense of restraint, but done properly, it's an interesting alternative (albeit expensive) to *ribollita*.

These days, the coolest areas in town to hang out (and with the highest concentration of bars, *enoteche* and restaurants) are around Santo Spirito in the Oltrarno and in Santa Croce, and it's therefore no surprise that quite a high proportion of the places listed in this chapter fall into these two locations. There's

also a fair number of listings outside the centre of town, restaurants that involve a bus or taxi ride. But the extra effort (and expense) will be rewarded by a virtually tourist-free experience.

THE RESTAURANT

Be warned: Florence is, above all else, a tourist city, and at too many restaurants, sloppy cooking and high prices are the norm. This guide aims to list the very best eateries in and around town, but it's also worth looking out for windows displaying the recommendation stickers of respected Italian restaurant guides, such as Gambero Rosso's *Ristoranti d'Italia*, *Veronelli*, *L'Espresso*, or Slow Food's *Osterie d'Italia*. Failing that, try to pick places where there are plenty of locals, and avoid anywhere that advertises a fixed-price *menù turistico* written in several languages.

Eating out is a very social affair in Florence, especially in the evenings, and restaurants tend to be informal and quite lively. You can wear casual dress in all but the very smartest

> ❶ Blue numbers in this chapter correspond to the location of each restaurant or wine bar as marked on the street maps. *See pp334-335.*

CONSUME

CONSUME

establishments, and children are almost always welcome. The majority of restaurants are happy to produce a plate of *pasta al pomodoro* to satisfy unadventurous taste buds, and you can also ask for a half portion (*una mezza porzione*). Quite a few restaurants carry high chairs (*una seggiolona*). Booking is advisable, especially at weekends or if you want to dine at an outdoor table during the summer months.

THE MENU

An increasing number of more upmarket restaurants now offer some kind of fixed menu (and we're not talking about the ubiquitous *menù turistico* here). Usually called *menù degustazione*, it consists of a series of courses that allows diners to try the house specialities. Such menus tend to represent good value. For help with sorting through the menu, *see p126* **What's on the Menu**.

THE WINE LIST

The price of your meal will be heavily influenced by what goes into your glass and even many *trattorie* nowadays have more choice than just the house plonk. However, most budget and moderately priced restaurants do offer *vino della casa* (house wine) in quarter-litre, half-litre or litre flasks, which is invariably cheaper than buying by the bottle. It might be anything from ghastly gut-rot to quaffable country wine. If in doubt, order a *quartino* to try; if it's undrinkable, ask for the wine list.

While the *liste dei vini* in Tuscany are unsurprisingly dominated by *vini toscani*, other regional wines – and even the odd non-Italian label – are now being given more cellar space. For guidelines on choosing wines, *see p44*.

PIZZA

While pizza isn't a typically Florentine dish, pizzerias are very popular among the locals (especially young people) – firstly because they make for a cheap, casual meal out and secondly because they tend to stay open late. Most pizzerias don't serve exclusively pizza either; there's nearly always a wide selection of *primi* and various salads on the menu and some places serve complete meals too. A Florentine pizza traditionally has a thin, crisp base but, these days, most of the pizzas to be found in the city are of the Neapolitan variety with (ideally) light, puffy bases. Either way, make sure it's baked in a wood oven (*forno a legna*) rather than in the gas or electric equivalent. Pizza is an evening meal in Florence; very few pizzerias worth their *mozzarella di bufala* serve at lunchtimes.

VEGETARIANS

The days are (almost) gone when waiters would look aghast at the words *sono vegetariano* ('I'm vegetarian'). While there are few strictly vegetarian restaurants in Florence, non meat-eaters, particularly those who eat fish, are better off here than in many parts of, say, France or Germany. Indeed, reflecting a general trend in Italy towards more healthy eating habits, a number of new fish restaurants have opened in Florence since the last edition of this guide. Most restaurants offer vegetable-based pasta and rice dishes, as well as plenty of salads and vegetable side dishes (*contorni*), while an increasing number of more upmarket places serve a specifically vegetarian option.

SMOKING

Smoking was banned in public places in Italy in early 2005, and it's now no longer possible to smoke in a restaurant unless it has a separate room with the legally required ventilation system. Few do, so you'll have to go and join the other puffers on the street. Having said that, lots of restaurants have outdoor seating so it's easy enough to grab a table at which you can smoke – something non-smokers should consider when choosing places with closely set tables.

THE BILL

For restaurants and wine bars, we give the average price per person for a three-course meal (*antipasto* or *primo*, *secondo*, *contorno* and *dolce*) excluding drinks or extras. The price in a pizzeria covers an average pizza plus a *birra media*. Most pizzerias also serve more substantial fare and prices will rise accordingly. In wine bars where only snacks are on offer, we have not given an average; prices might range from 50¢ for a *crostino* to €12 for a plate of French cheeses.

Bills usually include a cover charge (*pane e coperto*) per person of anything from €1.50 to an outrageous €5; the average is about €2.50. This covers bread and, increasingly, a selection of snacks – olives, bruschetta, nuts and the like – and should reflect the standard of service and table settings. There's also a service charge, which must by law be included in the bill (though it's sometimes listed separately). Some places now include cover and service in the price of the meal. One consolation is that you're not expected to leave a hefty tip. You can leave ten per cent if you're truly happy with your service, or, in a modest place, perhaps round up the bill by a euro or so.

Although prices have risen horribly since the arrival of the euro, eating out in Florence is still cheaper than in London or New York. The restaurants here have been chosen either for their value for money or simply because the food is great. Some are out of the centre of town, but the food makes them worth the journey.

WINE BARS AND ALTERNATIVE EATS

There are various types of wine bar in Florence. Tiny street booths (known as *fiaschetteria*, *vineria* or *mescita*) with virtually no seating, serving basic Tuscan wines and rustic snacks, sit alongside comfortable, traditional drinking holes, which compete with new, upmarket *enoteche* that offer a huge range of labels from all over Italy and beyond and something more sophisticated in the way of food.

Wine bars offer one of several alternatives to full restaurant dining in Florence. *Rosticcerie* (rotisseries) serve everything from *antipasti* and roasted meats to desserts; those listed here give the option of eating in or taking away. You can also find traditional tripe stands (*tripperie*) in various parts of the city (*see p132* **If You Can Stomach It…**) – stand-up affairs where you can fill up for a few euro. In addition, many bars now offer a limited choice of hot and cold dishes for lunch. The quality isn't always the highest, and there may or may not be seating, but it's a cheap and speedy alternative to a restaurant.

DUOMO & AROUND
Restaurants

Fusion Bar
Gallery Hotel Art, vicolo dell'Oro 2 (055 27266987, www.lungarnohotels.com). **Open** noon-midnight Mon-Sat; 7-10pm Sun. **Average** €50-€60. **Map** p334 C3 ❶
This stylish-bordering-on-snobby locale is a good option for a quiet, light lunch, or an evening cocktail accompanied by nibbles or dinner. Fitting in beautifully with the East-meets-West design ethos of the hotel that hosts it, this bar/restaurant offers a set price (€28) help-yourself weekend brunch, featuring dishes with a fusion element. In the evening, there's a full menu of fusion dishes inspired by the Japanese, French and Italian cuisines, some of which, however, are more convincing than others. Go for one of two set menus (€35 and €50) that change with the seasons, or order à la carte.

Oliviero
Via delle Terme 51r (055 212421, www.ristorante-oliviero.it). **Open** 7.30-11pm Mon-Sat. Closed 1st 3wks Aug. **Average** €50. **Map** p334 C3 ❷

CONSUME

Ora d'Aria. *See p125.*

Known to be the once-favoured haunt of icons such as Sophia Loren and Maria Callas, Francesco Altomare's restaurant still has a curious retro vibe in spite of a recent refit: the revolving door, the wood-panelled bar, the silent grand piano and the rather formal service all hark back to *la dolce vita*. The food, however, is not only great but very much in keeping with today's fashion for reinterpreting traditional recipes. Menus (one traditional, the other offering contemporary cuisine) are strictly seasonal and range from fish and meat options to some vegetarian choices. In winter try the pasta with *guanciale di cinta senese* (meat of the cheek of a *cinta senese* pig) with hot pepper and in summer sample the tuna *all'erba cipollina*. A fine wine list weighted towards Tuscany is sure to please.

★ Ora d'Aria

Via de' Georgofili 11r (055 2001699, www.ora dariaristorante.com). **Open** 7.30-11.30pm Mon; 12.30-2.30pm, 7.30-11.30pm Tue-Sat. **Average** €50. **Map** p334 C3 ❸

The young Tuscan chef in charge of the kitchen at this stylishly minimalist eaterie, Marco Stabile, has impeccable credentials and his dishes are executed with skill. His seasonal menus – fish, seafood and meat options with Mediterranean flavours – are based on fresh, locally sourced ingredients. The seasonal tasting menus (one is offered at lunch for €23) range from 'traditions' to 'innovations', so alongside wild asparagus risotto with clams from Viareggio and beef tartar, you'll find Sardinian tuna with watermelon, pine nut oil from San Rossore and salad, and, when the *cavolo nero* season is over, seaweed *ribollita*. For dessert, there's a sinful dark chocolate flan with a molten liquid centre. Everything is beautifully presented, and there's an excellent and fairly priced wine list, which includes heavyweight vintages from Tuscany, Piemonte and France. Arguably the best-value gourmet dining in Florence. *Photo p123.*

La Posta

Via de' Lamberti 20 (055 212701). **Open** 12.30-11pm daily. Closed Dec, Feb, Tue lunchtime in winter. **Average** €35. **Map** p334 C3 ❹

A few blocks from the Duomo, La Posta is a traditional *trattoria* in front of the main post office. A little overpriced, it serves toothsome Florentine classics as well as fish-based dishes. Although the service can be sloppy, all in all the food is good. Try the spaghetti with truffle, the lamb chops or the *bistecca alla fiorentina*. Expect to dine among tourists and the odd Florentine. Meals in summer can be enjoyed in a cosy outdoor terrace, just around the corner from one of the city's liveliest squares, piazza della Repubblica.

Wine bars

Canova di Gustavino

Via Canova 29 (055 2399806, www.gustavino.it). **Open** noon-11.30pm daily. **Map** p335 C4 ❺

Serving light fare and great wines by the glass near the Duomo, this colourful, brick-vaulted *enoteca* is the property of the Lanciola wine estate near Impruneta and an offshoot of the fancier restaurant next door; both venues share an 800+ wine list. You can accompany your selections with a good range of salads, *crostini*, cheeses and cured meats.

Cantinetta di Verrazzano

Via de' Tavolini 18r (055 268590, www. verrazzano.com). **Open** Sept-June 8am-9pm Mon-Sat. **Average** €20. **Map** p335 B4 ❻

The wood-panelled rooms of this *cantinetta* are continually crowded with smartly dressed Florentines and discerning tourists. Owned and run by the Castello di Verrazzano, one of the major wine estates in Chianti, this locale features a bakery with a wood oven and coffee shop (serving the excellent Piansa coffee blend) on one side, and a wine bar serving (very good) estate-produced wines by the glass or bottle on the other. Snacks include focaccia straight from the wood oven (the one with creamy pecorino cheese and balsamic vinegar from Verrazzano is recommended) and an unusual selection of *crostini*.

Coquinarius

Via delle Oche 15r (055 2302153, www. coquinarius.com). **Open** 9am-11pm Mon-Sat; 9am-4pm Sun. Food served from noon Mon-Sat. Closed Aug. **Map** p335 B4 ❼

Tucked away behind the Duomo, this cosy little wine bar and café is great for a quiet lunch or an informal evening meal: unusually, the full menu is available between noon and 11pm. Bare brick walls and soft jazz provide the background for good pastas (such as pecorino and pear tortellini), carpaccio, imaginative salads and platters of cheeses and meats. For those with a sweet tooth, the own-made cakes are truly divine, but you could also pop across the road to Grom (*see p152*) for some of the best ice-cream in town.

I Due Fratellini

Via de' Cimatori 38r (055 2396096, www.idue fratellini.com). **Open** 10am-8pm daily. Closed Sat & Sun in July & Aug. Closed 3wks Aug. **No credit cards. Map** p335 C4 ❽

Florence was once brimming with these hole-in-the-wall *vinai* (wine merchants) but today I Due Fratellini, founded in 1875, is one of very few left in the city. There's nowhere to sit down: join the locals standing in the road (there's not much traffic) or squatting on the pavement for a glass of cheap and cheerful plonk or something a bit more special. Help it down with a Collonnata lard-topped *crostino* or a great slab of *finocchiona* (Tuscan salami seasoned with fennel) on bread.

Dei Frescobaldi Ristorante & Wine Bar

Vicolo de' Gondi, off via della Condotta (055 284724, www.deifrescobaldi.it/ristorante-wine-bar-

CONSUME

What's on the Menu?

Decoding the dishes.

COOKING TECHNIQUES & DESCRIPTIONS

affumicato smoked; **al forno** cooked in an oven; **arrosto** roast; **brasato** braised; **fatto in casa** home-made; **griglia** grilled; **fritto** fried; **nostrale** locally grown/raised; **ripieno** stuffed; **ruspante** free-range; **vapore** steamed.

BASICS

aceto vinegar; **burro** butter; **bottiglia** bottle; **focaccia** bread made with olive oil; **ghiaccio** ice; **miele** honey; **olio** oil; **pane** bread; **panino** sandwich; **panna** cream; **pepe** pepper; **sale** salt; **salsa** sauce; **senape** mustard; **uovo** egg.

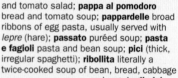

ANTIPASTI

antipasto misto mixed hors d'œuvres; **bruschetta** bread toasted and rubbed with garlic, sometimes drizzled with olive oil and often topped with tomatoes or white Tuscan beans; **crostini** small slices of toasted bread; **crostini toscani** are smeared with chicken liver pâté; **crostoni** big *crostini*; **fettunta** the Tuscan name for *bruschetta*; **prosciutto crudo** cured ham, either *dolce* (sweet, similar to parma ham) or *salato* (salty).

PRIMI

acquacotta cabbage soup usually served with a *bruschetta*, sometimes with an egg broken into it; **agnolotti** stuffed triangular pasta; **brodo** broth; **cacciucco** thick, chilli-spiked fish soup (Livorno's main contribution to Tuscan cuisine); **cecina** flat, crispy bread made of chickpea flour; **fettuccine** long, narrow ribbons of egg pasta; **frittata** type of substantial omelette; **gnocchi** small potato and flour dumplings; **minestra** soup, usually vegetable; **panzanella** Tuscan bread

and tomato salad; **pappa al pomodoro** bread and tomato soup; **pappardelle** broad ribbons of egg pasta, usually served with *lepre* (hare); **passato** puréed soup; **pasta e fagioli** pasta and bean soup; **pici** (thick, irregular spaghetti); **ribollita** literally a twice-cooked soup of bean, bread, cabbage and veg; **taglierini** thin ribbons of pasta; **tordelli/tortelli** stuffed pasta; **zuppa** soup; **zuppa frantoiana** literally, olive press soup – another bean and cabbage soup, distinguished as it's served with the very best young olive oil.

FISH & SEAFOOD

acciughe/alici anchovies; **anguilla** eel; **aragosta** lobster; **aringa** herring; **baccalà** salt cod; **bianchetti** little fish, like whitebait; **bonito** small tuna; **branzino** sea bass; **calamari** squid; **capesante** scallops; **coda di rospo** monkfish tails; **cozze** mussels; **fritto misto** mixed fried fish; **gamberetti** shrimps; **gamberi** prawns; **gefalo** grey mullet; **granchio** crab; **insalata di mare** seafood salad; **merluzzo** cod; **nasello** hake; **ostriche** oyster; **pesce** fish; **pesce spada** swordfish; **polpo** octopus; **ricci** sea urchins; **rombo** turbot; **San Pietro** John Dory; **sarde** sardines; **scampi** langoustines; **scoglio** shell- and rockfish; **seppia** cuttlefish or squid; **sgombro** mackerel; **sogliola** sole; **spigola** sea bass; **stoccafisso** stockfish; **tonno** tuna; **triglia** red mullet; **trota** trout; **trota salmonata** salmon trout; **vongole** clams.

MEAT, POULTRY & GAME

agnellino young lamb; **agnello** lamb; **anatra** duck; **animelle** sweetbreads; **arrosto misto** mixed roast meats; **beccacce** woodcock; **bistecca** beef steak; **bresaola** cured, dried

CONSUME

beef, served in thin slices; **caccia** general term for game; **capretto** kid; **carpaccio** raw beef, served in thin slices; **cervo** venison; **cinghiale** wild boar; **coniglio** rabbit; **cotoletta/costoletta** chop; **fagiano** pheasant; **fegato** liver; **lepre** hare; **lardo** pork fat; **maiale** pork; **manzo** beef; **ocio/oca** goose; **ossobuco** veal shank stew; **pancetta** like bacon; **piccione** pigeon; **pollo** chicken; **porchetta** roast pork; **rognone** kidney; **salsicce** sausages; **tacchino** turkey; **trippa** tripe; **vitello** veal.

HERBS, PULSES & VEGETABLES

aglio garlic; **asparagi** asparagus; **basilico** basil; **bietola** Swiss chard; **capperi** capers; **carciofi** artichokes; **carote** carrots; **castagne** chestnuts; **cavolfiore** cauliflower; **cavolo nero** black cabbage; **ceci** chickpeas; **cetriolo** cucumber; **cipolla** onion; **dragoncello** tarragon; **erbe** herbs; **fagioli** white Tuscan beans; **fagiolini** green, string or French beans; **farro** spelt (a hard wheat), a popular soup ingredient around Lucca and the Garfagnana; **fave** or **baccelli** broad beans (although *fava* in Tuscany also means the male 'organ', so use *baccelli*); **finocchio** fennel; **fiori di zucca** courgette flowers; **funghi** mushrooms; **funghi porcini** ceps; **funghi selvatici** wild mushrooms; **lattuga** lettuce; **lenticchie** lentils; **mandorle** almonds; **melanzane** aubergine (UK), eggplant (US); **menta** mint; **patate** potatoes; **peperoncino** chilli pepper; **peperoni** peppers; **pinoli** pine nuts; **pinzimonio** selection of raw vegetables to be dipped in olive oil; **piselli** peas; **pomodoro** tomato; **porri** leeks; **prezzemolo** parsley; **radice/ravanelli** radish; **ramerino/rosmarino** rosemary;

rapa turnip; **rucola/rughetta** rocket (UK), arugula (US); **salvia** sage; **sedano** celery; **spinaci** spinach; **tartufato** cut thin like a truffle; **tartufo** truffles; **zucchini** courgette.

FRUIT

albicocche apricots; **ananas** pineapple; **arance** oranges; **banane** bananas; **ciliegie** cherries; **cocomero** watermelon; **datteri** dates; **fichi** figs; **fragole** strawberries; **lamponi** raspberries; **limone** lemon; **macedonia di frutta** fruit salad; **mele** apples; **melone** melon; **more** blackberries; **pere** pears; **pesche** peaches; **pompelmo** grapefruit; **uva** grapes.

DESSERTS & CHEESE

cantuccini almond biscuits; **castagnaccio** chestnut flour cake, made nr Lucca; **cavallucci** spiced biscuits from Siena; **gelato** ice-cream; **granita** flavoured ice; **mandorlata** almond brittle; **panforte** cake of dried fruit from Siena; **pecorino** sheep's milk cheese; **ricciarelli** almond biscuits from Siena; **torrone** nougat; **torta** tart, cake; **zabaglione** egg custard mixed with Marsala; **zuppa inglese** trifle.

DRINKS

acqua water, *gassata* (fizzy) or *liscia/naturale* (still); **birra** beer; **caffè** coffee; **cioccolata** hot chocolate; **latte** milk; **succo di frutta** fruit juice; **tè** tea; **vino rosso/bianco/rosato** red/white/rosé wine; **vin santo** dessert wine.

GENERAL

Posso vedere il menù? May I see the menu? **Mi fa il conto, per favore?** The bill, please.

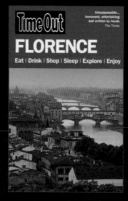

firenze). **Open** 7pm-midnight Mon; noon-midnight Tue-Sat. Closed 3wks Aug. **Map** p335 C4 ❾

Located on a side street off piazza della Signoria, this wine bar offers top-quality wines from the formidable Frescobaldi estates of Tuscany, Umbria, Friuli and even as far afield as Chile and California, where they collaborate with wine producer Robert Mondavi; unusually, all of the wine stocked here can be ordered by the glass as well as the bottle. Snacks at the wine bar, which also has an outdoor terrace, include terrines, pâtés, cheeses and salamis, but you can also choose from the full menu offered in its adjoining restaurant (average €45).

Snacks & quick meals

★ 'Ino
Via de' Georgofili 3r-7r (055 219208, www.ino-firenze.com). **Open** 11am-5pm daily. **Map** p334 C3 ❿

A stone's throw from the Uffizi, 'Ino is great for a quick midday meal. This classy, contemporary sandwich bar and deli has an impressive following, counting among its customers the mayor of Florence, Matteo Renzi. Located near to where the Mafia placed its bomb in 1993, it offers *panini* and other goodies made with top-quality ingredients, sourced from all over the country by owner Alessandro Frassica. Sandwiches (to eat in, perched at the counter, or to take away) are made to order and filled according to seasonal availability; the price of each (from €4) includes a glass of wine. The deli/shop (*see p166*) is stocked with cured meats, local cheeses, olive oils, vinegars, wines and other tempting goodies, and there's a range of sweets that make excellent gifts.

SANTA MARIA NOVELLA
Restaurants

Cantinetta Antinori
Piazza degli Antinori 3 (055 292234, www. cantinetta-antinori.com). **Open** noon-2.30pm, 7-10.30pm Mon-Fri. Closed 3wks Aug. **Average** €40. **Map** p334 B2 ⓫

Continuing to attract well-dressed tourists and classy locals since its opening in 1965, this classic restaurant/wine bar occupies an elegantly vaulted ground-floor room of the 15th-century Palazzo Antinori, the historic home of one of Tuscany's foremost wine-producing families. Expect a wide variety of wines and textbook versions of Florentine classics, such as *pappa al pomodoro* and home-made pasta with wild boar meat sauce, along with a few worthwhile desserts (try the chestnut-flour cake with ricotta cheese). Rather upscale, slightly on the expensive side.

Garga
Via del Moro 48r (055 2398898, www.garga.it). **Open** 7.30-10.30pm Tue-Sun. **Average** €55. **Map** p334 B2 ⓬

This *trattoria* with a bohemian feel continues to attract foodies from across the city and world. Ebullient owner Giuliano Gargani (known for alternately bellowing out opera arias and orders from the kitchen) presides over his colourful kingdom with its quirky decor (with whimsical frescoes painted by himself, his wife and their artist-friends, and an eccentric clutter of objects) while chatty staff serve up well-executed pastas, meats and fish dishes. The menu focuses on traditional Tuscan dishes with a twist: try the veal escalope with artichokes or the rocket, tomato and avocado salad with pine nuts. The top-quality food comes at a high price, however, so budget travellers might want to check out the online menu before booking. Co-owner and executive chef Sharon Oddson also runs popular cooking classes.

Il Latini
Via de' Palchetti 6r (055 210916, www.illatini. com). **Open** 12.30-2.30pm, 7.30-10.30pm Tue-Sun. Closed last wk Dec & 1st wk Jan. **Average** €40. **Map** p334 B2 ⓭

Run by the Latini family since 1950, this rustic eaterie has become something of a Florence classic. Overrun by tourists and the odd Florentine, what keeps people coming back to Latini is the *ciccia* (meat) – and great hunks of it too. Queues are inevitable after 8pm when reservations are no longer taken and, once inside, it'll be noisy and you'll probably be sharing a table with other customers, but that's all part of the fun. Skip the mediocre *primi*, and dive into the hefty *secondi*: this is a good place to order Florentine steak. Il Latini also produces a fine, sludgy-green olive oil, and some decent wines: the house red is very drinkable.

★ Trattoria Coco Lezzone
Via del Parioncino 26r (055 287178, www. cocolezzone.it). **Open** noon-2.30pm, 7-10.30pm Mon-Sat. Closed 3wks Aug. **Average** €40. **No credit cards**. **Map** p334 B2 ⓮

Respect for tradition, hand-selected prime ingredients and a centuries-old wood-burning stove mark out this authentic *trattoria*, in one of Florence's few medieval towers still standing. Open since the 1800s, current owner Gianfranco Paoli has brought this temple of Tuscan tastes back to the limelight, today counting among its customers the likes of Anthony Hopkins and John Malkovich. Dishes on the menu are Tuscan classics, including traditional soups, home-made pastas and a range of wild game cooked (often for hours on end) in the early

---

THE BEST LUNCH AND BRUNCH

Fusion Bar. *See p123*.
Olio e Convivium. *See p138*.
Ricchi. *See p139*.

CONSUME

20th-century oven. Daily specials are seasonal and if you want to try Coco's Florentine steak, you'll have to order it in advance.

Pizzerie & rosticcerie

Rosticceria della Spada

Via della Spada 62r (055 218757, www.laspada italia.com). **Open** noon-3pm, 6-10.30pm daily. **Average** €18. **Map** p334 B2 ⑮

A low-cost option for lunch or a snack, this centrally located *rosticceria* has been selling delicious dishes to go for a good many years, but now you can also eat in, and plenty do, especially at lunchtime. The menu is more or less the same whether you choose to sit in or take away, but you'll pay about 50 per cent less if you do the latter. There are good pastas (try the lasagne or *linguine ai porcini*), roast meats and grilled vegetables and a truly delicious *melanzane alla parmigiana*.

Snacks & fast food

★ Amon

Via Palazzuolo 28r (055 293146). **Open** noon-3pm, 6-11pm Tue-Sat. **No credit cards**. **Map** p334 B2 ⑯

One of Florence's first ethnic food eateries, Amon has been churning out authentic Egyptian fare since 1987. Amazingly, the place has only changed hands once since then and is still going strong in spite of plenty of new competition from doner kebab joints. Everything is still made in-house, from pitta breads to the veal kebab, and it's all both delicious and cheap. Try the tasty falafel or a plate of couscous or rice topped with meat and vegetables (doner kebabs cost €3.50, falafel €3).

Bar Galli

Via de' Banchi 14r (055 213776). **Open** noon-3.30pm Mon-Sat. Japanese food served 7-10pm Tue-Fri; 12.30-2.30pm, 7-10pm Sat. **Map** p334 B2 ⑰

Alongside the usual pastries, *panini* and selection of (above-average) hot and cold dishes, this busy bar offers a menu of delicious Japanese fare at dinner and on Saturday afternoons. The setting in the bar's back room is spartan (Formica-topped tables and ugly strip lighting) and the choice is limited to such homely dishes as ramen noodles and soups as well as rice dishes, but it's very good and it's cheap. A steaming bowl of noodles costs from €7, the set evening menus from €15 and a bottle of cold Asahi is €5.

SAN LORENZO

Restaurants

Amor di Vino

Piazza del Mercato Centrale 46r (055 2670119, www.amordivinoflorence.com). **Open** *Summer*

11.30am-11pm daily. *Winter* 11.30am-3.30pm, 6-10.30pm Mon-Sat. Closed 3wks Aug. **Average** €18 (at lunch). **Map** p334 A3 ⑱

The most recent addition to piazza del Mercato Centrale, Amor di Vino has made a good name for itself in little time. Its proximity to the San Lorenzo market ensures fresh, seasonal ingredients and top-quality meats cooked on a fire grill. The lunch menu features affordable pizzas, salads and starters, while the full dinner menu includes traditional first courses such as *ribollita* and *papa al pomodoro*, or choose any of the grilled meats among the *secondi*. Good value at the right price, this *trattoria* also offers a decent wine list and a charming terrace.

Antica Sosta degli Aldobrandini

Pizza Madonna 5/6r (055 2399199, www. florence.ala.it/anticasosta/def4.htm). **Open** 8.30am-10pm Mon-Sat. **Average** €10. **Map** p334 A3 ⑲

It's easy to overlook this neighbourhood watering-hole in the hustle and bustle of the San Lorenzo market, but once inside you'll be glad you gave it a chance. The walls are lined with bottles and wood panelling and grey and white checkered marble flooring will take you back to Florence's good old days. Named after the important Aldobrandini family that used to live in the piazza, and in the shadow of the majestic Medicean chapels, this traditional *enoteca* has an impressive list of Tuscan and Italian première wines, which are sold by the bottle or the glass. Attracting an eclectic mix of locals, foreign students and tourists, the Antica Sosta also offers a range of salami and cheese platters, hot and cold panini and delectable sweets.

Trattoria Mario

Via Rosina 2r (055 218550). **Open** noon-3.30pm Mon-Sat. Closed 3wks Aug. **Average** €20. **No credit cards**. **Map** p334 A3 ⑳

Reservations are not taken and the long queue for a table may not seem worth the wait, but you'll be glad you stuck it out. Run by four generations of the Colsi family, you'll be eating elbow-to-elbow with your fellow lunchers on long bare-wood tables inside this chaotic and cramped eaterie, which draws an egalitarian mix of people who are all interested in the simple yet excellent Florentine home cooking: try the earthy *ribollita*, a terrific *bollito misto* (mixed boiled meats) served with a biting garlic and parsley *salsa verde* and, for a supplement, the tasty *bistecca* or mouth-watering *lombattina*. It doesn't get much better for the price.

★ Sergio Gozzi
Piazza San Lorenzo 8r (055 281941). **Open** noon-3pm Mon-Sat. Closed Aug. **Average** €20. **Map** p334 A3 ㉑
An authentic, old-fashioned Florentine *trattoria*, this family-run eaterie hidden behind the stalls of the San Lorenzo market makes a less exciting alternative to Trattoria Mario (*see above*) as a place to sample simple and genuine home cooking. Two airy rooms house marble-top wooden tables (you may find yourselves sharing here, as well) with crisp white tablecloths. Perhaps begin with *minestrone di verdura*, *ribollita* or *minestra di farro* (spelt soup), before moving on to a roast or *bistecca alla fiorentina*. There's tripe on Mondays and Thursdays and fresh fish (including superb *seppie in inzimino* – sweet tender squid stewed with Swiss chard) on Tuesdays and Fridays.

Wine bars

★ Casa del Vino
Via dell'Ariento 16r (055 215609, www.casadel vino.it). **Open** 9.30am-5pm Mon-Sat. Closed Aug & Sat in June, July, Sept. **Map** p334 A3 ㉒
Hidden behind the stalls of the San Lorenzo market, the very limited seating in this wine bar is on a few benches and stools backed up against the wine cabinets. No matter: punters continue to pile in for a glass of good plonk and some delicious *panini, crostini* and salads to accompany it. Bottles for all budgets sit on lovely old carved wood shelves that line the room; you'll find fairly priced wines from all over Italy, plus labels from further afield and plenty of choice by the glass. In addition to the vast selection of wines, you can purchase Tuscan extra virgin olive oil, balsamic vinegar and Prato's famed Mattei *biscotti*.

Snacks & fast food

★ Nerbone
Mercato Centrale (055 219949). **Open** 7am-2pm Mon-Sat. Closed Aug. **Average** €10. **No credit cards. Map** p334 A3 ㉓
Opened way back in 1872, this food stall/*trattoria* has a strategic location on the ground floor of the covered central market in San Lorenzo. A great place to find local colour, it's packed from breakfast time with market workers: even if you can't face a *lampredotto* (cow's intestine) sarnie and a glass of rough red plonk at 7am, the locals can, and it only

costs them €3.50. Plates of simple pasta and soups (from €4) offer alternatives at lunchtime; seating is available.

SAN MARCO
Restaurants

Ristorante Accademia
Piazza San Marco 7r (055 217343, www. ristoranteaccademia.it). **Open** noon-3pm, 7-11pm daily. **Average** €30. **Pizza** €15. **Map** p335 A4 ㉔
Attracting a mix of local Florentines, resident foreigners and tourists, Ristorante Accademia is a useful spot in an area where there aren't many good eating choices. With a few exceptions (fillet steak cooked in an intense brachetto wine sauce with glazed shallots, for example), the more ambitious options on the menu are the least successful, so it's best to go for more reliable staples such as traditional pastas (try the home-made pasta with lamb meat sauce and roasted almonds). The pizzas are a decent choice too. The wine list is surprisingly comprehensive, prices are reasonable, the staff polite and the Iacovitti brothers are cheerful hosts.

Il Vegetariano
Via delle Ruote 30r (055 475030, www.il-vegetariano.it). **Open** 12.30-2.30pm, 7.30-10.30pm Tue-Fri; 7.30-10.30pm Sat, Sun. Closed 3wks Aug. **Average** €25. **No credit cards**.
Il Vegetariano was one of the first vegetarian restaurants in Florence, although they are now growing in number. The menu offers plenty of variety, including a choice of ethnic dishes, and generous portions for excellent prices. There's a fabulous salad bar and the wines are all organic.

SANTA CROCE
Restaurants

Acqua al 2
Via della Vigna Vecchia 40r (055 284170, www. acquaal2.it/Firenze.html). **Open** 7.30pm-1am daily. **Average** €30. **Map** p335 C4 ㉕
The cosmopolitan feel of this Florence eaterie (which also has outposts in Washington DC and San Diego) attracts big crowds. Its barrel-vaulted ceiling and quirky interior (the walls are lined with autographed plates of the famous who have eaten there) make it a favourite with students, travellers and garrulous Florentines, sat elbow-to-elbow at tightly lined tables in a series of small rooms. Since its opening 35 years ago, Acqua al 2 has made a name for itself thanks to its delicious pasta, cheeses, salads and desserts. If you've still space after one of these, try the veal fillet cooked with balsamic vinegar or with wild berries. Packed most evenings, the place can get noisy and chaotic, but the quality of the food and ambience are worth it.

CONSUME

If You Can Stomach It...

Traditional dishes that will test your resolve.

In an era when food is becoming more standardised and the ever more stringent Italian health and hygiene laws are strangling individual gastronomic endeavour, Florence's *trippai* (tripe vendors) are standing firm. Once a dying breed, these vendors are nowadays increasingly a new generation of 'offalophiles', proud to be carrying on an ancient Florentine culinary tradition.

When faced with a tripe stand, you would be forgiven for not knowing what was brewing. The mobile stalls are laden with bubbling cauldrons and heated trays, the contents of which are not for the faint-hearted. *Lampredotto* is probably the scariest item: the lining of the last stomach of the cow is simmered for hours in stock and served either in a *panino* with salt, pepper and maybe a lick of garlicky green salsa verde or with its broth in a little dish to be eaten with a plastic fork. Tripe (*trippa*) is served in these parts *alla fiorentina* – in rich tomato sauce topped with a sprinkling of parmesan. It's also eaten cold mixed with pickles and dressed with olive oil, salt and pepper. Other offerings vary from stall to stall, but watch out for such delights as boiled *nervetti* (tendons), stewed *budelline* (intestines) and *lingua* (tongue).

This Florentine-style fast food is cheap (a *panino con lampredotto* and a plastic cup of plonk will only set you back a few euros), healthy and has a fan base that transcends all social boundaries. You're likely to be munching your cow tummy sarnie in the company of factory workers,

builders, Senegalese street vendors, shop assistants and slick-suited business types; it's a great way to sample Florentine street life.

Trippai normally open from around 8.30am to 7pm Monday to Friday; some also open on Saturdays. You'll find city-centre stalls under the Loggia del Porcellino; on the corner of via de' Macci and borgo La Croce; on via Maso Finiguerra near the corner of via Palazzuolo; and at piazza de' Cimatori.

CONSUME

★ Baldovino

Via San Giuseppe 22r (055 241773, www.
baldovino.com). **Open** *Apr-Oct* 11.30am-2.30pm,
7-11.30pm daily. *Nov-Mar* 11.30am-2.30pm, 7-
11.30pm Tue-Sun. **Average** €30. **Pizza** €15.
Map p335 C5 ㉖

One of the most popular eateries in the Santa Croce
area, Baldovino wins points for its colourful decor
and flexible menus (you can have a full meal, snack
or a pizza or salad; try the black squid ink infused
spaghetti). The food is good and so is the service.
Prices are reasonable, there's plenty of choice and
the wine list is full and varied. Across the road, the
same owners run the smaller, quieter Baldoria,
which serves casual, snacky-type food, plus pizzas
and pastas. More recently, they opened Baldobar, a
French bistro and tapas bar, next door (*see p135*).

Boccadama

Piazza Santa Croce 25-26r (055 243640, www.
boccadama.com). **Open** 11am-10.30pm daily.
Average €30. **Map** p335 C5 ㉗

This restaurant and wine bar offers light fare at
lunchtime (salads, pastas, *bruschetta* and so on) and
full dinners featuring traditional Tuscan dishes (like
home-made *pappardelle al cinghiale* and *salsiccia e
fagioli all'uccelleto*). Wine by the glass is rather
limited for a place that stocks over 400 labels.
Nevertheless, thanks to its location, Boccadama,
which is under the same management as Finisterrae
across the square, is swamped with tourists (particularly for lunch) during the summer, when the terrace comes into its own.

★ Cibreino

Via de' Macci 122r (055 2341100, www.edizioni
teatrodelsalecibreofirenze.it). **Open** 12.50-2.30pm,
7-11.15pm Tue-Sat. Closed Aug. **Average** €30.
No credit cards. Map p335 C6 ㉘

The reasonably priced sister of Cibrèo (*see below*),
this *trattoria* doesn't take reservations (prepare to
queue or arrive early). Typical of most home-grown
trattorie in Florence, the atmosphere is rustic, the
place is often overcrowded and the menu has little
choice, but the food is excellent. Much easier on the
wallet than its more famous sibling, you'll get the
added extra of witnessing weak-stomached experi-
ence-hunters blanch when a chicken's head arrives
on their plate.

★ Cibrèo

Via Andrea del Verrocchio 8r (055 2341100,
www.edizioniteatrodelsalecibreofirenze.it). **Open**
1-2.30pm, 7-11.15pm Tue-Sat. Closed Aug.
Average €75. **Map** p335 C6 ㉙

Cibrèo is a must-stop on any Florence foodie's hit
list. The dishes at the flagship of chef/patron Fabio
Picchi's little gastronomic empire (which also
includes a bar, a *trattoria*, a theatre with buffet-style
food, a cookbook and a clothing and accessories line)
are a modern interpretation of Florence's traditional

cucina povera (peasant's food), with fresh prime
ingredients and heavy use of fresh herbs and spices
to create intense flavours. Located in the heart of the
Sant'Ambrogio market area, there's no menu (and
no pasta or coffee), but a chummy waiter will sit at
your table in the elegant, wood-panelled room to take
you through the options. A series of delicious
antipasti arrives automatically with a glass of wine
to be followed by *primi* such as a remarkable yellow
pepper soup and soft polenta dressed with intensely
herby melted butter. *Secondi* are divided between
meat and fish. Desserts are fabulous (the flourless
chocolate cake has become a classic), and the wine
list is everything you might expect. Cibrèo provokes
extreme opinions: some think it's the best restaurant
in Florence, while others claim that it's overrated,
overpriced and overcrowded with tourists. *See also
left* **Cibreino,** *p135* **Teatro del Sale** and *p148*
Caffè Cibrèo.

★ Enoteca Pinchiorri

Via Ghibellina 87 (055 242757, www.enoteca
pinchiorri.com). **Open** 7.30-10pm Tue-Sat.
Map p335 C5 ㉚

One of the most expensive restaurants in Florence
(and Italy), Enoteca Pinchiorri is considered one of
Italy's great temples to gastronomic excellence.
Although chef Annie Féolde no longer does any cooking, she oversees the kitchen and runs front-of-house
where the atmosphere is of the formal, luxuriously
old-fashioned kind. You can opt for à la carte or choose
from two tasting menus (which represent the best
value), each featuring six or nine tiny but superbly
executed courses (like the home-made tagliolini with
baby squid, sage and pumpkin flowers). Then there's
the stellar cellar: Giorgio Pinchiorri has amassed a collection of wines that's second to none and offers one
of the world's great wine lists. Wherever you eat –
inside the *palazzo* or in the gorgeous, jasmine-scented
courtyard – it all looks fabulous; service is elegant and
prices are sky high. This place is so classy that men
are now required to wear jackets.

Del Fagioli

Corso de' Tintori 47r (055 244285). **Open**
noon-2pm, 7-10.30pm Mon-Sat. **Average** €22.
Map p335 C5 ㉛

This is one of those unpretentious time-worn places
where little has changed over the years. Opened by
Luigi ('Gigi') Zucchini just after the flood in 1966, it
offers traditional Florentine cooking and such standards as *ribollita*, *pappa al pomodoro* and *bollito
misto con salsa verde* (mixed boiled meats served
with a bright green parsley sauce). Gigi is still cooking and his *involtini* (thin rolls of beef stuffed with
cheese, ham and artichokes) are delicious. There's
warm apple cake to finish.

Ganzo

Via de' Macci 85r (055 241067, www.ganzo
florence.it). **Open** noon-midnight Mon-Sat;

CONSUME

CONSUME

brunch on Sun. Closed Sat & Sun in Aug.
Average €20. **Map** p335 C6 ㉜

A cultural and culinary association established by the Florence University of Arts and the culinary school Apicius, Ganzo is not only a restaurant but also an events space for temporary art exhibitions, book presentations and artistic performances. Experimental and seasonal dishes inspired by the Tuscan culinary tradition are offered (try the *panzanella* bread salad with calamari or the spaghetti with saffron) in a modern environment. Wednesday evenings (6-10pm, drinks €5) are reserved for the ApriGanzo, offering aperitifs and an abundant buffet (dinner not served), and each Thursday the chef serves up a thematic, four-course menu that ranges from Arabic foods to vegetarian delights. An American brunch costing €15 is served on Saturday afternoons (12-3pm) and features an American breakfast classic: bacon and eggs. Remember that you must become a member of the cultural association to dine here; memberships cost €9.

La Giostra

Borgo Pinti 12r (055 241341, www.ristorantela giostra.com). **Open** 1-2.30pm, 7.30pm-midnight Mon-Fri; 7.30pm-midnight Sat, Sun. **Average** €70. **Map** p335 B5 ㉝

La Giostra's walls are covered with pictures of visiting celebs and its ceiling is draped with fairy lights. Run by elderly chef and proprietor Prince Dimitri Kunz d'Asburgo Loreno and his twin sons, this eaterie is always full of tourists, and prices are high – but the food is very good, verging on excellent. The restaurant is well known for its *primi*, which include *taglierini* with white Umbrian truffles and divine ravioli stuffed with brie and served with sautéed artichokes. If you have room for dessert, however, try the rich, gooey Sachertorte made from an old Habsburg family recipe. The wine list features big names with big prices. Jacket and tie recommended.

★ Kome

Via de' Benci 41r (055 2008009, www.kome firenze.it). **Open** *Kaiten* noon-3pm Mon, Tue; noon-3pm, 7-11pm Wed; noon-3pm, 7pm-midnight Thur-Sat; 7-11pm Sun. *BBQ* 7.30-11pm Mon-Sat. *Izakaya* 7.30pm-midnight Mon-Sat. **Average** €40 (less in Kaiten). **Map** p335 C5 ㉞

Kome is the brainchild of architect Carlo Caldini, an epochal figure on Florence's nightlife scene, who has created such a warm ambience that this eaterie is one of the nicest and best designed contemporary

---

THE BEST
FAVOURITE WINE BARS

Casa del Vino. *See p131.*
Fuori Porta. *See p143.*
Vivanda. *See p141.*

---

spaces in Florence. Downstairs in Kaiten, diners perch on avocado-green bar stools under a swooping gold ceiling to select good sushi, sashimi, nighiri and other Japanese classics from the belt, while excellent light tempura, miso soup and various 'fries' are made to order. On the more functional upper floor is BBQ, where a gas barbecue is set into each table. If you choose one of the set menus, a series of hors d'oeuvres and a soup arrive, followed by a plate of raw fish, chicken or beef fillet that you cook yourself and then eat, with sauces, folded into a lettuce leaf. In the basement is Izakaya, a wine and sake bar where smokers can light up.

Libreria Brac

Via de' Vagellai 18r (055 0944877, www.libreria brac.net). **Open** 11am-midnight Mon-Sat; noon-9pm Sun. Closed 1wk Aug; Sun in June-Sept. **Average** €15. **Map** p335 C4 ㉟

This contemporary art bookshop opened in 2009 with one important novelty: a kitchen. Its minimalist, stark white interior with exciting splashes of colour gives a nice ambience, while the charming outdoor courtyard makes it a great place to read the morning news over a soya cappuccino or enjoy one of the rich pastas or salads on its vegetarian- and vegan-inspired menu. Try the linguine with lemon and fennel or courgette, or the tagliatelle in a seitan tomato sauce. Libreria Brac also serves as a contemporary art space featuring temporary art exhibitions and installations, book launches, film screenings and more (see the website for upcoming events). Sundays are dedicated to the Brac Brunch, which features pancakes, french toasts and fresh yoghurt with fruit and home-made sweets.

Osteria de' Benci

Via de' Benci 13r (055 2344923, www.osteria deibenci.it). **Open** 12.30-3.30pm, 7.30-11pm daily. **Average** €30. **Map** p335 C4 ㊱

Small and unpretentious, there's both great atmosphere and great value for your buck at this lively *trattoria*. You'll pay about €32 a kilo for a Chianina steak, a nice price for a big chunk of meat cooked over an open fire and served *al sangue* (rare). The bean and garlic soup is disappointingly bland, but if seasonal local specialities such as *ribollita* and *trippa alla fiorentina* are available, you won't be disappointed. Pasta dishes are interesting (spaghetti cooked in red wine with garlic and hot pepper) and side dishes are extremely tasty – try the baked potatoes with onions and olives. A lunch menu is also available.

★ Ruth's

Via Farini 2a (055 2480888, www.kosheruth. com). **Open** 12.30-2.30pm, 7.30-10pm Mon-Thur; 12.30-2.30pm Fri. **Average** €15-€25. **Map** p335 B6 ㊲

With the preparation of kosher foods overlooked by Rabbi Rav Joseph Levi, Ruth's is located next to

Florence's monumental synagogue, one of the biggest in Europe. Serving kosher vegetarian food as well as fish dishes, the dining area is a pleasant, modern and bright room with a full view of the open kitchen. The cooking has palpable Middle Eastern and North African influences, resulting in dishes such as falafel and other typical meze, fish or vegetable couscous, and fish brik (deep-fried flaky pastry parcels) served with a Tunisian salad, along with a range of pastas and salads.

★ Teatro del Sale
Via de' Macci 111r (055 2001492, www.edizioni teatrodelsalecibreofirenze.it). Closed Aug. **Average** €30 (dinner, incl theatre show). **Map** p335 B6 ⓸
A sister of the Cibrèo restaurants (*see p133*), Teatro del Sale is the latest initiative from the eccentric Florentine chef Fabio Picchi. The Teatro sets itself apart on the Florentine culinary scene as a top-notch eaterie that also has entertainment, giving its members a theatrical or musical bonus après dinner. At lunch and dinner the kitchen offers Tuscan-centred yet internationally inspired seasonal buffets that change daily (here you can go back for seconds and thirds). Open all hours, from breakfast to dinner, the Teatro operates like a well-oiled machine thanks to its dedicated staff who make almost everything on the menu in-house. At the entrance, a big area sells quirky, prettily packaged homeware and food products, which would make great gifts. €10 membership required.

Il Pizzaiuolo. See p136.

La Vie en Rose
Borgo Allegri 68r (055 2346943, www.lver.it). **Open** 7-11pm Mon-Sat. **Map** p335 B6 ⓸
There's only room for a handful of tables in this small eaterie next to Florence's flea market, but the latest management has introduced several novelties in this space, among them card and board games, tastings, cooking lessons, art exhibitions and more. Choose any of the Italian-French inspired dishes on the seasonal menu (if you go in summer, try the tuna marinated in raspberries and ginger with fresh watermelon and the home-made pasta with duck sauce and prunes). Note that this is officially a *circolo* or club, so you have to register (free) for membership the first time you go.

Wine bars

All'Antico Vinaio
Via de' Neri 65r (055 2382723). **Open** 8am-8pm Tue-Sat; 8am-1pm Sun. Closed Aug. **Map** p335 C4 ⓸
Pop by the Vinaino if you're looking for some local flare. This small, and often overcrowded, no-frills neighbourhood *vineria* behind the Uffizi is often packed with locals chit-chatting over a *gottino* (a stubby glass of wine). Wash the wine down with a delicious liver pâté *crostino* or a *panino* on fresh focaccia filled with sliced prosciutto or mortadella. Benches outside provide a great opportunity for people-watching.

★ Baldobar
Via San Giuseppe 20r (055 2260107, www. cafebaldobar.com). **Open** 8am-6pm Mon-Fri; 8.30am-6pm Sat, Sun. **Average** €10. **Map** p335 C6 ⓸
The latest endeavour from the owners of Baldovino (*see p133*), the adjacent Baldobar opened in 2010 as a French-style *bistrot-café* serving fashionable French breakfasts of baguettes, butter and artisanal marmalade and pressed coffee to early-morning and weekend crowds of well-heeled locals and students.

CONSUME

CONSUME

Borgo San Jacopo.

Also a French bistro and tapas bar at lunch, the menu features interesting seasonal Mediterranean dishes, *panini* (try the *panino* with fried aubergine and *mozzarella di bufala* with a pine nut and grape sauce and marinated anchovies), salads, French and Italian cheeses, as well as a range of artisanal beers and French, Spanish and Italian wines, all of them available by the glass.

La Botte

Via San Giuseppe 18r (055 2476420, www. enotecaintelligente.com). **Open** 6pm-midnight Tue-Sun. **Map** p335 C6 ㊷

A self-service wine bar and restaurant, La Botte is a great way to try local and Italian wines while nibbling on delicious complimentary snacks. Put money on a card to taste over 60 different wines; a sampling of the nectar emerges from an automatic dispenser after a swipe of the card. Friendly staff are there to provide additional information. Stay for lunch or dinner to sample local specialities such as *lampredotto* and Florentine tripe or locally produced cheeses and cured meat platters, as well as a range of small plates.

Pizzerie & rosticcerie

★ Caffè Italiano

Via Isola delle Stinche 13r (055 289080, www. caffeitaliano.it). **Open** 12.30-2.30pm, 7.30pm-11am Tue-Sun. Closed 3wks Aug. **Average** €15. **Map** p335 C5 ㊸

This tiny venue with a wood-burning oven and just four bare tables has very little choice – marinara, margherita or Napoli – but the pizzas are authentic and delicious, their light and puffy bases topped with San Marzano tomatoes and proper *mozzarella di bufala* shipped fresh from Naples. After 10.30pm, the overflow is seated at the adjacent restaurant, Osteria del Caffè Italiano.

Il Pizzaiuolo

Via de' Macci 113r (055 241171, www.ilpizzaiuolo. it). **Open** 12.30-3pm, 7.30pm-12.30am Mon-Sat. Closed Aug. **Average** €15. **Map** p335 C6 ㊹

If you're looking to sink your teeth into a delicious Neapolitan-style pizza, then Il Pizzaiuolo is the place to get it. Long considered the go-to place for the best pizza in Florence, it also serves Neapolitan pasta dishes, which include spaghetti with tomato, olives and capers from Gaeta, or *trofie* (a kind of pasta) with pesto and cherry tomatoes. Finish the meal off with a *babà al rhum* (a rum-flavoured Neopolitan dessert). The small, white-tiled room is always packed (and often very noisy), so booking is a must here, and be prepared to find yourself sharing a table with strangers. *Photo p135.*

Trattoria I Fratellini

Via Ghibellina 27r (055 2347389). **Open** 8am-5pm Mon-Fri. **Average** €15. **No credit cards**. **Map** p335 C6 ㊺

This old-fashioned wine bar, *rosticceria* and grocer's shop has been run by the Bisazzi family since the

1950s and it's still one of the best bargains in town. Walk through the long, wood-panelled shop to the food counter and real fire, choose whatever takes your fancy, and either take it away or eat at one of the wooden tables at the back. The prices are what draw the big crowds: the home-cooked selection of *primi* (cannelloni with tomato sauce and *melanzane alla parmigiana*) and *secondi* (including spit-roasted chicken) cost around €5. Make sure you sample Simona's superbly creamy *tiramisù* to finish.

Snacks & fast food

Da Rocco

Inside Sant'Ambrogio market, piazza Ghiberti (no phone). **Open** noon-2pm, 7-10.30pm Mon-Sat. **Map** p335 C6 ⑮

Located at the edge of Florence's centre, the Sant'Ambrogio market is a smaller food haven than its larger counterpart in the San Lorenzo area. At the centre of the market, you'll find Rocco's food kiosk serving up Florentine specialities at very favourable prices. *Primi* cost from €3 to €4 while *secondi* are €5. Choose from a selection of rustic local classics such as *pappa al pomodoro*, *spezzatino* (a kind of beef stew), pasta with *ragù* and tripe salad. You'll have to queue up to order and you can take away or eat in at one of the tables. The wine is cheap too: order a flask of house wine and you only pay for what you drink.

OLTRARNO
Restaurants

5 e Cinque

Piazza della Passera 1 (055 2741583). **Open** noon-10pm Tue-Sun. **Average** €15. **No credit cards**.

Serving vegetarian-oriented dishes and organic foods and wines, 5 e Cinque gets points for quality as well as ambience. The latest eaterie to open in the charming piazza della Passera, choose between one of the cheese-filled *focaccia*, *frittata* and vegetable quiche, and the strictly seasonal soups and salads. Try the *cecina* (chickpea *focaccia*), a Tuscan speciality that you'll be hard pressed to find on other restaurant menus in the city. Although the selection is not vast, you'll be lured by the prices and friendly service.

La Beppa Fioraia

Via dell'Erta Canina 6r (055 2347681, www.la beppafioraia.it). **Open** 12.30-2.30pm, 7.30pm-midnight daily. **Average** €25.

Located between piazzale Michelangelo and the Arno, this colourful and fun new-age *trattoria* serves Florentine favourites to younger, informal crowds. It is best known for its vast and varied platters serving cured meats, grilled vegetables and cheeses as well as grilled fillets and steaks. Pizzas are also a

popular request. Close to the city centre and with ample parking, Beppa Fioraia is far off the tourist trail. It can get crowded on weekends so make sure to book ahead.

Borgo San Jacopo

Borgo San Jacopo 62r (055 281661, www. lungarnohotels.com). **Open** 7.30-10.30pm Mon-Fri; noon-3pm, 7.30-10.30pm Sat, Sun. **Average** €50. **Map** p334 C2 ⑰

This posh eaterie on the Arno wins the Oscar for the best two tables in Florence: seating eight on a mini-terrace facing the ponte Vecchio are so dramatic they could be the stage for an opera. Serving traditional Italian dishes with a creative twist, chef Beatrice Segoni hails from the Marche on the Adriatic coast and several fish dishes from her home territory are among the regional foods on the menu: *brodetto di pesce alla marchigiana*, for example, is a typical Marchigiana fish soup. Punchy meat options include a *millefoglie* of duck breast and pigeon with artichokes. The restaurant occupies a long, narrow space with a gallery stretching from the street to the river; in addition to the award-winning terrace, a huge arched window gives great views of the ponte Vecchio.

La Casalinga

Via de' Michelozzi 9r (055 218624, www. trattorialacasalinga.it). **Open** noon-2.30pm, 7-9.30pm Mon-Sat. Closed 3wks Aug. **Average** €20. **Map** p334 D2 ⑱

Expect to queue at this Oltrarno favourite. After decades of serving up wholesome Florentine home cooking at affordable prices, La Casalinga today boasts an impressive following among both tourists and locals. Still, some dishes are better than others: avoid anything made with table cream (such as the *tortellini al panna e prosciutto*) in favour of such local specialities as *minestrone di riso e cavolo* (warming soup with black cabbage and rice), roast guinea fowl and apple cake.

Cavolo Nero

Via dell'Ardiglione 22 (055 294744). **Open** 7.30-10.30pm Mon-Sat. **Average** €40. **Map** p334 C1 ⑲

Nestled on the narrow Oltrarno street where Filippo Lippi was born, this intimately lit and romantic restaurant first opened its doors in 1993. Originally the food was stoically Florentine, but today chef/owner Arturo Dori's menus (divided equally between fish and meat) have evolved to offer a more modern take on Italian and Florentine cooking that's often very good. He and his wife Michela (who makes the desserts) run their outfit with charm and enthusiasm and have a firm local fan base. Dishes come from all over Italy, but Mediterranean flavours dominate; try creamy goat's cheese wrapped in crisp filo pastry served with tapenade, the polenta with truffles and *baccalà*, lamb cutlets with spicy fig compote and a

CONSUME

triumphant soft chocolate torte to finish. The wine list is long and reasonably priced. Reserve a table in the jasmine-filled garden for added romance.

Filipepe
Via di San Niccolò 39r (055 2001397, www. filipepe.com). **Open** 7.30pm-1am daily. Closed 2wks Aug. **Average** €50. **Map** p335 D5 ㊿
The unusually funky decor borders on kitsch at this restaurant in the San Niccolò area, yet the uniqueness of the dishes make them memorable. The regularly changing list of modernised Mediterranean tastes feature punchy, sunny flavours. Menus are divided into *freddo e crudo* (cold and raw) and *caldo* (hot) sections but otherwise have no formal structure, so you can mix and match as you wish. Fish-and meat-based dishes are beautifully presented, and there's always something interesting and unusual: choose from the likes of an anchovy flan with fresh pecorino cheese and olive oil seasoned with fennel seeds and roasted peppers; fresh pasta in a lamb meat sauce with veal meatballs and porcini mushrooms; monkfish with courgettes and capers with an apple and pear salad; roasted pigeon and liquorice-flavoured risotto with caramelised figs. The wine list is interesting and well priced. All pasta dishes are available in a gluten-free version.

Il Guscio
Via dell'Orto 49 (055 224421, www.il-guscio.it). **Open** noon-2pm, 7.45-11pm Mon-Fri; 7.45-11pm Sat. Closed Aug. **Average** €30.
This new-generation *trattoria* in the heart of the San Frediano area offers carefully prepared versions of dishes that hail from Tuscany's traditional rural cuisine, with the odd variation. The strictly seasonal menu (on a cheeseboard) features three types of *primi* and *secondi*, including the fillet of beef cooked in *vin santo* and topped with a slab of liver pâté, which has become a favourite. On Fridays and in summer, the menu is dedicated to fish and seafood such as the *padella* of seafood that comes served in its pan straight from the stove. The home-made desserts are good and the wine list features over 400 labels from Italy (the vast majority of which are Tuscan) and beyond, starting at just €10. Pop in for a quick *divino panino* or a bowl of soup at lunchtimes (the only choices) – the price (€5) includes a glass of wine and a coffee.

MoBa: Terrazza Bardini
Villa Bardini, costa di San Giorgio 6 (055 2008444, www.moba.fi.it). **Open** Apr-Sept

6-11pm Tue-Sun. Closed 1wk Aug. **Average** €50. **Map** p334 D3 ㊿
See right Hubba Hubba MoBa.

Napoleone
Piazza del Carmine 24 (055 281015, www. trattorianapoleone.it). **Open** 7pm-1am daily. **Average** €35 (less for pizza). **Map** p334 C1 ㊿
A fun, buzzy place to spend an evening, either on the large summer terrace with its multicoloured fairy lights or in the chic, moody interior – a large space divided into a series of intimate rooms. While the service is not great, the menu is varied, the servings are abundant and the prices are honest. Aside from the characteristic ambience, the restaurant is well known for its steak and thin-crust pizzas. After dinner you can continue your Oltrarno entertainment just across the piazza at nightlife stalwart La Dolce Vita (*see p204*).

Olio e Convivium
Via Santo Spirito 4 (055 2658198, www. conviviumfirenze.com). **Open** *Food served* noon-3pm Mon; noon-3pm, 5.30-10.30pm Tue-Sat. Closed 3wks Aug. **Average** €30. **Map** p334 C2 ㊿
Convivium has been the top caterer in Florence for the last 30 years and, at the height of its success, it opened this commercial outpost: Olio e Convivium, a gourmet grocer (*see p167*) offering delicious food to go. Also featuring two cosy restaurant rooms – with chequerboard floors, sparkling crystal, shelves stacked with wine, olive oil and other edibles, it is a fine spot in which to enjoy a quiet meal. Specials are chalked up on a board, and feature the likes of ravioli in duck sauce, pear and artichoke risotto and roast pork with prunes. Wines are expensive, which can heavily ramp up your bill; for better value go at lunchtime: the set lunch menu is €18.

Ossi di Seppia
Via San Niccolò 24r (055 2343336, www.ossidi seppia.org). **Open** 7-11.30pm daily. Closed 3wks Aug. **Average** €50. **Map** p335 D5 ㊿
When up-and-comer Gionata Rossi decided to close his successful restaurant in Viareggio to open a new one in Florence, Florentines were curious. One of the rising stars on Italy's culinary scene, Rossi opened the Ossi di Seppia restaurant and cultural association in the über-trendy San Niccolò area. With a rather harsh minimalist interior, the restaurant has been well received by critics and local foodies, yet it is quite expensive considering the minute portions. Among the highly creative fish and meat dishes are tagliolini in a duck and chestnut sauce, a hamburger made of red shrimp on a cabbage purée, and tuna tartar dusted with frozen oyster powder.

Pane e Vino
Piazza Cestello 3 (055 2476956, www.ristorante paneevino.it). **Open** 7.30pm-midnight Mon-Sat. Closed 2wks Aug. **Average** €35. **Map** p334 C1 ㊿

CONSUME

Occupying a former warehouse near the river, Pane e Vino is often full of local and foreign wine-lovers enjoying a glass of great plonk and any of the superb Tuscan-based dishes with an experimental twist. Expect the likes of chickpea and porcini soup, artichoke-stuffed ravioli and lamb morsels flavoured with tomato and lavender on a bed of aubergine and yogurt. There are two set menus: a six-course *menu degustazione* at €45 and a three-course traditional menu at €30. The honest mark-ups on the unusual wine list and the late hours are added perks. On the downside, service can be sloppy and bordering on the rude.

Ricchi

Piazza Santo Spirito 8-9r (055 ...
10.30pm Mon-Sat. **Average** €1 ...
Ricchi is an excellent place for a ...
lunch. The menu changes daily, b ...
several pasta choices (try the las ...
cheese and *radicchio rosso*), an ... such as
roast beef and roast potatoes and a selection of generous salads. It is well known for its delicious fish dishes, served at dinner. In warm weather, you can eat on the terrace to the backdrop of one of the city's most characterful *piazze*. If you want to eat on the cheap, hot dishes are served in the adjacent bar.

Hubba Hubba MoBa

A museum? A restaurant? Yes, and it's also the chicest hangout in Florence.

Toil up the 'ribs' of St George after everyone you've met has told you that you *have* to go to MoBa, and you might be in for a frustrating few minutes as you try to find the entrance. The discreet doorway gives little inkling of the pleasures behind it: MoBa (the name is a contraction of 'monuments' and 'Bardini') is a first-rate centre for art, culture and fine food, housed in a 17th-century villa, with a stunning terrace tumbling down the hillside. Following years of abandonment and lengthy restoration, MoBa opened in 2006 as, says manager Domenico Montano, a 'top-notch restaurant and state-of-the-art contemporary art space inside the larger villa complex, in a dedicated container space known as Bardini Contemporanea'.

On the ground floor of the Villa Bardini (*see p92*), MoBa and the Terrazza Bardini offer a rich cultural programme in the warmer months, ranging from live music, art installations and exhibitions to cultural debates and conferences. Many of these events are held on the splendid Terrazza Bardini, overlooking the 16th-century gardens and the city skyline, while the art is on display (free access) inside the restaurant. The outdoor terrace really is a stunner, and can be visited for eye-wateringly pricey suppers or a simple *aperitivo*. Dress up and enjoy the incredible sunset over a cocktail while you hobnob with Florence's elite and tuck into an excellent buffet, all to a live soundtrack.

While the space is awesome, it's the food that's really the star. Under the watchful eye of expert chef-proprietor Umberto Montano, the menu is as minimalist as the locale's stark white furniture and walls, offering just five

antipasti (€25 average), five *primi* (€25 average) and five *secondi* (€35 average), but each dish is delicate and refined, whether it be one of the supposedly freshest fish dishes in Florence or meat drawing on centuries-old Tuscan recipes: pigeon breast rosé and legs stuffed with liver, or the chef's original take on the *bistecca alla fiorentina* (€55). A €90 tasting menu mixes daily specials and selections from the menu, which changes seasonally. Service is impeccable, staff are friendly and the (pricey) wine list is excellent.

So, if you're in Florence for a special occasion, you shouldn't miss MoBa; even if you can't afford the à la carte, go to town with a cocktail accompanied by some of the sexiest buffet food in the city.

Brenda Dionisi is managing editor of The Florentine *(www.theflorentine.net).*

CONSUME

anto Bevitore
a Santo Spirito 64-66r (055 211264,
www.ilsantobevitore.com). **Open** 12.30-3pm,
7.30-11.30pm daily. Closed 3wks Aug.
Average €35. **Map** p334 C1 ⑤⑦

Attracting young and trendy locals and discerning
tourists, this restaurant/wine bar is one of the best
in the Oltarano. Occupying a large, vaulted room
and adjacent tower just south of the river, it's busy
at lunch and especially crowded in the evenings.
Menus change every month to stay in line with the
seasons and the prime ingredients are all top quality.
The prices are honest as is the varied and nicely
priced wine list. As well as the ever-present wooden
platters laden with selections of cheeses and cold
meats, try the fresh *garagnelli* pasta with Calabrian
hot sauce Nduja, and the tartar of *chinaina*. The
owners recently opened Il Santino next door, which
offers cured meats, cheeses and wine by the glass.

Al Tranvai
Piazza Torquato Tasso 14r (055 225197). **Open**
noon-2.30pm, 7-11pm Mon-Sat. **Average** €25.

A favourite among local artisans, Al Tranvai is
especially busy at lunch, attracting crowds for the
wholesome, down-to-earth cooking and great prices.
Dishes hail from the *cucina popolare* tradition: *ribollita* and *pappa al pomodoro* (or *panzanella* in summer), tripe and *lampredotto* (cow's intestine), *lesso
rifatto con le cipolle* (a tasty beef and onion stew) and
squid in *inzimino* (with Swiss chard). Puddings are
own-made and the house plonk is just fine.

Trattoria Camillo
Borgo San Jacopo 57r (055 212427). **Open**
7.30-10.20pm Tue-Sun. **Average** €50.
Map p334 C2 ⑤⑧

The favoured haunt of the Florentine aristocracy
since the 1940s, Trattoria Camillo serves excellent
Florentine home cooking and revisited regional
favourites. You'll likely pay over the odds for a plate
of *tagliatelle ai porcini* but the food is top notch and
always prepared with the very best, properly
sourced seasonal ingredients. Chiara Masiero's long
and varied menus feature Florentine classics
(breaded veal cutlet and fried veg), influences from
Romagna (thanks to her Bolognese father) plus the
results of her own experiments, such as *riso al curry
con gli scampi* (rice with curry and prawns), *chianina
tartar* and a booze-infused terrine of foie gras.
Friday's menu always includes lots of fish. There's
a fairly hefty mark-up on everything including the

**THE BEST
OLD-FASHIONED INSTITUTIONS**

Cibreino. *See p133.*
Sergio Gozzi. *See p131.*
Trattoria Coco Lezzone. *See p129.*

---

wine, but the table wine (from the family farm) is
good and affordable. Pasta, bread and batter are all
available in gluten-free versions.

Trattoria del Carmine
Piazza del Carmine 18r (055 218601). **Open**
noon-2.30pm, 7.30-10.30pm Mon-Sat. Closed 3wks
Aug. **Average** €22. **Map** p334 C1 ⑤⑨

The clientele at this good-value *trattoria* in piazza
del Carmine is a mix of regular locals and tourists
seeking seasonally inspired, traditional Tuscan
fare that changes daily, or guests can also opt for
the long, fixed menu. Tuscan standards (*ribollita*,
spinach and ricotta ravioli, excellent *bistecca* and
so on) are always on offer, while daily specials
might include own-made tagliatelle with porcini or
swordfish steaks.

Trattoria 4 Leoni
*Via de' Vellutini 1r (055 218562, www.4leoni.
com).* **Open** noon-2.30pm, 7-11pm Mon, Tue,
Thur-Sun; 7-11pm Wed. **Average** €35.
Map p334 D2 ⑥⓪

Set on the delightful little piazza delle Passera,
4 Leoni today has a much stronger tourist clientele
than in past years. Locals have begun to shy away
from this eaterie due to poor service and less-than-
desirable dishes, drawn to the other eateries on the
busy square – 5 e Cinque (*see p137*) and Caffè degli
Artigiani (*see right*). Regardless, the interior, with
its vibrant colours, exposed brickwork, rustic tables
and chairs, and its charming outdoor terrace, make
it a great spot if the other places are full, and the
grilled meats are excellent: opt for the *lombatina di
vitella* (small boneless steak) before trying other
Tuscan-based foods on the menu, which features
potato-stuffed *tortelli alla Mugellana*, *pepposo* (a peppery beef stew) and the classic *gran fritto dell'aia*, a
mix of deep-fried chicken, rabbit and vegetables.

Alla Vecchia Bettola
Viale Ariosto 32-34r (055 224158). **Open** noon-
2.30pm, 7.30-10.30pm Tue-Sat. Closed
3wks Aug. **Average** €25.

Still very popular among locals, this lively *trattoria*,
situated on a busy ring road, serves up some of the
city's best traditional Florentine fare. The menu of
hearty, rustic dishes includes daily specials alongside such regulars as *penne alla Bettola* (with tomato,
chilli pepper, vodka and a dash of cream) and a
superb beef carpaccio topped with artichoke hearts
and shaved parmesan, while offal fans can enjoy
tripe and *lampredotto*. The *bistecca* is succulent,
delicious and vast.

Wine bars

Bevo Vino
Via San Niccolò 59r (055 2001709). **Open**
11.30am-midnight (last orders 10pm) Tue-Sun. **No
credit cards. Average** €15. **Map** p335 D5 ⑥①

Trattoria del Carmine.

For the best bubbly and nicest staff in town, head straight to Bevo Vino, located in the bustling San Niccolò neighbourhood. The tiny locale has outside tables where you can enjoy a great light meal while soaking in the very essence of Italian life: the piazza. With a rustic and run-down feel, Bevo Vino has a short yet impressive wine selection that features local, organic wines, flanked by a hand-selected menu that favours seasonal vegetarian dishes made with locally sourced ingredients. Other reasonably priced starters offer cured meats and cheeses, while pizzas and focaccias are prepared in a wood-burning oven. Inspired by the Ligurian culinary tradition, try the *cecina* (chickpea focaccia) and the cheese-filled focaccia from Lecco.

Caffè degli Artigiani

Via dello Sprone 16r (055 287141, www.caffedegli artigiani.it). **Open** 8am-midnight daily. **Average** €15. **Map** p334 C2 ⓺

Located in piazza della Passera, Caffè degli Artigiani is easily one of the Oltrarno's most charming neighbourhood bars. Stop by for a coffee in the afternoon or have a pre-dinner drink and assorted *aperitivo* snacks. The café serves light local fare, including *crostini*, salads, *panini* and *carpacci*, and meat and cheese platters. In summer, grab one of the bright green, outdoor tables as they go fast. If you stop in for a late-evening *digestivo*, you'll likely catch a live concert being held in the square.

Pitti Gola e Cantina

Piazza Pitti 16 (055 212704). **Open** *Summer* 10am-midnight Tue-Sun. *Winter* 12.30-4pm, 7-9pm Tue-Sun. **Map** p334 D2 ⓺

One of the few eateries with a terrace in the now pedestrian piazza Pitti, this small, charming *enoteca* is often packed with tourists looking to get a full view of Palazzo Pitti. Prices are on the high side, but the atmosphere is very pleasant and there's a good choice of wines that are heavily weighted towards Tuscany. Snacks include cured meats and cheeses.

★ Vivanda

Via Santa Monica 7 (055 2381208, www.vivanda firenze.it). **Open** 10.30-3pm, 6pm-midnight daily. **Average** €35 (less for pizza).

Florence's first *enoteca* dedicated to organic wines, Vivanda opened in 2010 and already has a big local fan base. Located between piazza Santo Spirito and piazza del Carmine, Vivanda boasts an extensive wine list of over 120 organic and biodynamic labels from across Italy and the world. It also has a kitchen offering a good assortment of *antipasti*, *primi* and *secondi* including fresh pasta and a variety of vegetable choices. Wine is self-serve by the glass and all prime ingredients are locally sourced and seasonal. You can eat here and not worry about your carbon footprint: plates and cutlery are all biodegradable.

Le Volpi e l'Uva

Piazza de' Rossi 1r (055 2398132, www. levolpieluva.com). **Open** 11am-9pm Mon-Sat. **Map** p334 D3 ⓺

Attracting a diverse range of local wine-lovers, this wine bar is a great place for a glass of plonk and a snack. It can get cramped in winter with seats only at the bar, but there's more room in summer thanks to the terrace. Much of what's on offer will be unfamiliar

CONSUME

to all but the most clued-up oenophiles: owners Riccardo and Emilio search out small, little-known producers from all over Italy, with an eye on value for money. A limited but delicious selection of snacks includes Italian and French cheeses, cured meats, a range of *crostini*, *panini tartufati* (stuffed with truffle cream), fish and pork carpaccios and rich pâtés.

Pizzerie & rosticcerie

La Mangiatoia
Piazza San Felice 8-10r (055 224060). **Open** noon-3pm, 7-10pm Tue-Sun. **Average** €18.
Map p334 D2 ⑥⑤
A combination of a *rosticceria* and pizzeria, La Mangiatoia is a popular stop among local Santo Spirito residents, students and tourists, thanks to its rock-bottom prices and good, honest home cooking. Order takeaway food from the counter in the front, or go through to one of a series of rooms behind the shop, where, aside from standard *rosticceria* fare (lasagne, spit-roast chicken, roast meats), there's a long menu of Italian classics and good pizzas. There's also a nice outdoor terrace.

OUTSIDE THE CITY GATES
Restaurants

Bibe
Via delle Bagnese 1r (055 2049085). Bus 36, 37, then taxi. **Open** 7.30-10pm Mon, Tue, Thur, Fri; 12.30-2pm, 7.30-10pm Sat, Sun. Closed last wk Jan, 1st wk Feb & 1st 2wks Nov. **Average** €28.
The best way to get to this rustic country *trattoria* is by car, but it's worth the trek. Family-run Bibe is located in an old farmhouse about 3km (2 miles) south of Porta Romana, and from the menu, try deep-fried courgette flowers stuffed with ricotta, or sublime herb-infused *zuppa di porcini e ceci* (porcini soup with chickpeas). *Secondi* are classic Tuscan dishes: frog and deep-fried chicken, rabbit and brains are specialities. In summer, eat on the flower-filled terrace.

Omero
Via Pian de' Giullari 11r (055 220053). Bus 13, 38. **Open** noon-2.30pm, 7.30-10.30pm Mon, Wed-Sun. Closed Aug. **Average** €40.
In the Florentine hillside, Omero is located in the quiet, exclusive hamlet of Pian de' Giullari. The menu features traditional Florentine food; though reliable, the prices are high. The wine list has over 300 labels, favouring Tuscan wines, and the kitchen uses only the best-quality local extra virgin olive oil. Come for the old-fashioned atmosphere, respectful service and fine location.

Povero Pesce
Via Pier Fortunato Calvi 8r (055 671218, www. poveropesce.it). **Open** noon-3pm, 7-11pm daily. **Average** €35.

Zibibbo.

Simple, unpretentious and good-value fish and seafood dishes make up the backbone of the menu at this fish-only *trattoria* located near the football stadium in the Campo di Marte area. With its modern, vaguely nautical-themed interior and keen prices, it's still rather popular among locals and is often full in the evenings. The menu changes daily, as it is based on market availability, but a typical meal might feature a starter of the house *antipasto misto* (you'll get five or six little tasters), *spaghetti alle vongole* (clams) or *all' astice* (lobster) and grilled swordfish. A tart *sorbetto al limone* is a good way to finish.

Da Ruggero
Via Senese 89r (055 220542). Bus 11, 36, 37. **Open** noon-2.30pm, 7.30-10.30pm Mon, Thur-Sun. Closed mid July-mid Aug.
Average €25.
Serving excellent value food, this rustic *trattoria* outside of Porta Romana is one of Florence's best-kept secrets. Family-run by the Colsis for over 30 years, the menu of traditional dishes changes with the seasons, but always includes a hearty soup or two and an excellent spicy *spaghetti alla carattiera*. Among the roast meats, try the tasty pigeon or go for the exemplary *bollito misto* served with tangy, parsley-fresh *salsa verde*.

Salaam Bombay

*Viale Fratelli Rosselli 45r (055 357900, www.
salaambombay.it). Bus 23.* **Open** 7.30-10pm Mon-
Fri; 7.30pm-midnight Sat, Sun. **Average** €25.

One of Florence's first Indian restaurants, Salaam
Bombay is still popular among locals and foreigners
looking for a change from the classic *ribollita* or *tagli-
etelle ai funghi*. Tapestries adorn the walls of the single, galleried room; sit upstairs if you want to look
down on the buzzy action below. The menu offers
the sort of safe but decently cooked standards found
on the menus of most Indian restaurants in Italy: tan-
dooris and mughlai dishes, vegetarian options, great
naans and own-made mango chutney. It's good
value, and you can take out or eat in.

Targa

*Lungarno Cristoforo Colombo 7 (055 677377,
www.targabistrot.net). Bus 14.* **Open** 12.30-
2.30pm, 7.30-11pm Mon-Sat. Closed 1st 3wks
Aug. **Average** €45.

Located in the Bellariva area of Florence, Gabriele
Tarchiani decided to open this 'Bistrot Fiorentino'
in 1985 and it has attracted crowds ever since. The
inviting interior – with lots of wood and glass, low
lighting and plenty of greenery – and relaxed vibe,
complement the seasonal menu, featuring a number
of Tuscan classics inspired by French cuisine. Try
the rigatoni with broccoli or the quail on a bed of
lentils. On the whole, the food is very good indeed.
The cheeseboard is impressive and the vast wine list
is superb.

Zibibbo

Via di Terzollina 3r (055 433383). Bus 14.
Open 12.30-3pm, 7.30-10pm Mon-Sat. Closed
Aug. **Average** €50.

Opened by Benedetta Vitali, co-founder and former
chef at Cibrèo (*see p133*), this eaterie is a favourite
among locals. Vitali's cuisine finds roots in both
Florentine and southern traditions (*zibibbo* is a
Sicilian white grape), and the kitchen uses only
fresh, seasonal ingredients. A faithful and mostly
local clientele comes to sample staples like the soft
liver pâté with orange peel in port, tender octopus
and potato salad, spaghetti with mussels and
clams, and stuffed duck cooked in honey with a
plum sauce. The wine list is interesting with plenty
of curiosities (from all over the world) along with
the big guns. Lunchtimes are more casual and, for
a quick snack, you can have a sandwich or a plate
of pasta at the bar.

Wine bars

★ Fuori Porta

*Via Monte alle Croci 10r (055 234 2483,
www.fuoriporta.it). Bus D.* **Open** *Nov-mid Mar*
12.30-3.30pm, 7pm-12.30am daily. *Mid Mar-Oct*
12.30pm-12.30am daily. Closed 2wks Aug.
Average €25.

One of Florence's best-stocked wine bars, Fuori
Porta is situated in the lovely San Niccolò neighbourhood at Porta San Miniato and has a charming terrace overlooking the old city gate. It's a relaxed spot
for a glass and a snack at lunch; evenings are
buzzier. At any time, there are between 500 and 650
labels on the list, with about 50 available by the glass
and 250cl carafe, which rotate roughly every week.
Tuscan and Piedmontese reds dominate, but other
Italian regions are also well represented and there
are also formidable lists of *grappa* and Scotch. It is
also known for its excellent pastas, *carpacci* and salads; the classic snack here is one of the delicious *crostini*. It is recommended you make reservations before
9pm for dinner or expect to queue.

Pizzerie & rosticcerie

Santa Lucia

*Via Ponte alle Mosse 102r (055 353255, www.
pizzeriatrattoriasantalucia.com). Bus 30, 35.*
Open 7.30pm-midnight Mon, Tue, Thur-Sun.
Closed Aug. **Average** €15. **No credit cards.**

Just a ten-minute walk north-west of Porta al Prato,
many Florentines make the trek for the Neapolitan-
style pizza, considered one of the best in town. These
pizzas are just as you'd get them in Naples: they have
a light and puffy base, sweet tomatoes and milkiest
mozzarella. If you don't want pizza, terrific fish dishes
include *spaghetti alle vongole veraci* and octopus in
spicy tomato sauce; the bill will be hiked up accordingly. Book in advance or be prepared to queue.

Vico del Carmine

Via Pisana 40-42r (055 2336862). **Open** 7-11pm
Mon-Sat. **Average** €20.

Another little bit of Naples, just a stone's throw
from Porta San Frediano, this restaurant and pizzeria is done out as a typical street in old Naples (complete with washing lines strung across a balcony).
Almost always full and noisy, but it often loses
points for brusque service and higher than average
prices. Yet the quality of the food keeps pizza-
lovers piling in. Baked in an authentic wood-burning oven and with ingredients that are strictly
sourced from the Campania region (as are most of
the wines), the pizzas have light, puffy crusts and
miraculously un-soggy bases. Highly recommended is the remarkable *a chiummenzana*; the
folded-over crust is stuffed with ricotta while the
base is topped with smoked scamorza cheese and
cherry tomatoes. Less remarkable (but perfectly
decent) are the pasta and fish choices.

THE BEST MODERN MUSTS

MoBa. *See p139* **Hubba Hubba MoBa.**
Ora D'Aria. *See p125.*
Teatro del Sale. *See p135.*

CONSUME

Cafés, Bars & Gelaterie

Excellent espressos for the coffee cognoscenti.

When it comes to coffee in Florence you can forget about global branding; this city has always prided itself on its diversity and independence. It's full of simple corner places with the buzz of local workers throwing back espressos at the bar for a quick hit of caffeine; genteel, gilded affairs where the cutlery is silver and a coffee at a table with a view costs more than the barman's hourly wage; comfy bars with students sitting at the benches with piles of books and a *caffelatte*; and all the possible combinations in between.

If anything, Florentines are even more passionate about ice-cream, loving to claim that *gelato* was invented in the city. Whether this is true or not, it would be bad luck indeed to end up with even a mediocre ice-cream here.

CAFÉS & BARS

Italians take their coffee seriously, and the comparative merits of the brew itself influence the decision of where to stop for the next. But Florentine café society isn't just about coffee. Although breakfast is almost always still a simple cappuccino and brioche, the 'light lunch' can encompass all manner of buffets, gourmet menus and brunch offerings. Tea and cake is also an increasingly popular afternoon diversion, and the early-evening *aperitivo* sees true feasts of free snacks and home-made dishes offered to drinkers. Hybrids straddling bars, cafés, restaurants and bistros have been springing up like mushrooms in recent times, blurring the traditionally clear-cut descriptions and hours that were forced on many venues by the previously stringent licensing regulations.

Classic bars come in several guises, but this still depends on their licence. In café/bars you can usually sit down for a full lunch; in bar/*tabacchi* you can also buy cigarettes, bus tickets and stamps; in *latterie* you can pick up dairy products; and in *drogherie* you can stock up on groceries. In other shops, especially *pasticcerie* and *gelaterie*, there's often also a bar. In bigger bars and cafés you pay for coffee at the till before you order it from the barman with your receipt, unless you want to sit down. And bear in mind that location is everything when it comes to the bill: it usually costs far less if you stand at the bar rather than sit at a table, and you often pay more to sit outside, especially at touristy spots.

> 1 Green numbers in this chapter correspond to the location of each café, bar or *gelateria* as marked on the street maps. *See pp334-5.*

DUOMO & AROUND

★ Art Bar

Via del Moro 4r (055 287661). **Open** 7pm-1am Mon-Thur; 7pm-2am Fri, Sat. **Map** p334 B2 1

This tiny, popular student haunt (particularly during happy hour from 7pm to 9pm) near the pizza Goldoni can be rowdy, so it's better suited to hanging out with friends than an intimate tête-a-tête, but its sweet antique shop-style decor, air of easygoing bonhomie, and ridiculously cheap cocktails, make it a great place to sample one of the huge range of drinks on offer here – most of them piled high with fresh fruit and served with nibbles like popcorn.

Bar Perseo

Piazza della Signoria 16r (055 2398316).
Open 7.30am-midnight Mon-Sat. Closed 3wks
Nov. **Map** p334 C3 ❷
Even though it doesn't have the charm of the more
celebrated Rivoire (*see below*), this bar overlooks the
city's most famous Renaissance square, along with
its namesake – Cellini's *Perseus*, in the Loggia dei
Lanzi. Inside, the centrepiece is a sculptural art deco
chandelier, but most eyes are drawn to the mountains of own-made ice-cream topped with cherries,
berries and chocolate curls.

Boulangerie del Rifrullo

*Via de' Rondinelli 24r (055 281658, www.il
rifrullo.com).* **Open** 8am-5.30pm Sun-Fri;
8am-4pm Sat. **Map** p334 B3 ❸
Owned by the people behind Rifrullo (*see p150*) and
with the same combination of great food served in a
relaxed atmosphere, the Boulangerie justly describes
itself as a cross between a New York café and a Paris
bistro. In an elegant but modern space that's all clean
white walls and wood panelling, friendly staff serve
a huge range of breakfasts, as well as great baguettes,
small Mediterranean dishes and scrumptious pastries
throughout the day – perfect for an energy injection
before shopping on nearby via de' Tornabuoni.

Caffè Rivoire

*Piazza della Signoria 5r (055 214412, www.
rivoire.it).* **Open** 8am-midnight Tue-Sun. Closed
last 2wks Jan. **Map** p334 C3 ❹

THE BEST COFFEE STOPS

Dainty bits on the side.
Caffè Florian. *See p146.*

Chocolate-topped scrumptuousness.
Caffè Serafini. *See p150.*

American coffee? Yes, you get refills…
Mama's Bakery. *See p149.*

Founded in 1872 as a chocolate factory, Rivoire is
the most famous and best loved of all Florentine
cafés. Its chocolates are divine – try the puffed rice
and *gianduja* (hazlenut and almond-flavoured chocolate) – and its own-brand coffee is among the best in
the city. The outside tables have views of Palazzo
Vecchio and the Loggia dei Lanzi. One downside:
your wallet will be hit hard for the privilege.

★ Caffetteria della Biblioteca delle Oblate

*Via dell'Oriuolo 26 (055 2639685, www.
caffetteriadelleoblate.it).* **Open** 2-7pm Mon;
9am-midnight Tue-Sat. **Map** p335 B4 ❺
With great views of the Duomo and a lovely outdoor terrace, this library café would be a find anywhere, but in the overpriced tourist trap around the
Duomo it's a real gem. Opened in 2009 on the second floor of the library, the bright, light filled café,

Colle Bereto. *See p146.*

Caption

CONSUME

filled with colourful modern furniture and offering gorgeous views over the rooftops of the *centro storico*, serves everything from breakfasts through to late-night suppers, with occasional concerts, readings and performances.

Chiaroscuro

Via del Corso 36r (055 214247). **Open** 7.30am-9.30pm daily. **Map** p335 B4 ⑥

Chiaroscuro's expert barmen consider themselves coffee connoisseurs, and the risk of being served a below-par brew here is practically non-existent. Coffee is also sold freshly ground by weight and there's a range of coffee makers and machines. There's usually room to sit down, even at busy lunchtimes. The buffet *aperitivo* is a safe bet.

Colle Bereto

Piazza Strozzi 5r (055 283156, www.collebereto. com). **Open** *Summer* 8am-midnight Mon-Sat. *Winter* 8am-9pm Mon-Sat. Food from noon. **Map** p334 B3 ⑦

Colle Bereto is a smart bar with a prime location: outside is a ludicrously luxurious covered terrace with red and white sofas and armchairs overlooking the monumental Palazzo Strozzi. The menu is a standard affair, but best of all are the tiny fruit tarts with whipped yoghurt fillings. *Photo p145.*

Gilli

Piazza della Repubblica 36-39r (055 213 896). **Open** 8am-midnight Mon, Wed-Sun. **Map** p334 B3 ⑧

With the loss in recent years of many of the city centre's most beloved shops and bars to make room for international designer flagship stores, continuing murmurings abound about the future of historic Gilli. Its closure would be a blow to its loyal clientele and to impressed visitors. Gilli's belle époque interior is original, its seasonally themed sweet window displays wickedly tempting and its rich, flavoured hot chocolates legendary. Outside seating year-round.

Procacci

Via de' Tornabuoni 64r (055 211656). **Open** 10.30am-8pm Mon-Sat. Closed Aug. **Map** p334 B3 ⑨

One of the few traditional shops to survive the onslaught of designer names on this thoroughfare, the small wood-lined bar and shop is a favourite with nostalgic Florentines. In season (Oct-Dec), truffles arrive daily at around 10am, filling the room with their soft musty aroma (the speciality is melt-in-the-mouth truffle and butter brioche).

★ La Terrazza, Rinascente

Piazza della Repubblica 1 (055 219113, www. rinascente.it). **Open** 10am-9pm Mon-Sat; 10.30am-8pm Sun. **Map** p334 B3 ⑩

The rooftop terrace café at this department store affords some of the most stunning views of the city;

La Terrazza, Rinascente.

the splendour of Brunelleschi's cupola at such close quarters more than makes up for the mediocre menu and the patchy service. Come at sundown, when you can experience the city bathed in pink light.

SANTA MARIA NOVELLA

Amerini

Via della Vigna Nuova 63r (055 284941). **Open** 8.30am-8.30pm Mon-Sat. Closed 2wks Aug. **Map** p334 B2 ⑪

Smart but cosy, Amerini is such a lunchtime favourite that you're sometimes asked to endure the classic café faux pas of unknown companions being seated at your small table. Choose from sandwiches such as grilled vegetables with brie, or order a bowl of fresh pasta. Breakfast time and afternoons are more relaxing, so you can sample luscious lemon tart relatively undisturbed.

Caffè Florian

Via del Parione 28r (055 284291, www. caffeflorian.com). **Open** 9am-8pm daily. **Map** p334 C2 ⑫

The Venice icon recently opened this pretty, genteel sister café in a small backstreet off via de' Tornabuoni. Tisanes and coffees are served with dainty petits fours that look too good to eat, and the savouries are exquisite morsels with truffle or delicious cheeses.

Caffè Megara

Via della Spada 15-17r (055 211837). **Open** 8am-2am daily (lunch noon-3pm). **Map** p334 B2 ⑬

Always full at lunchtimes with tourists and loyal regulars who know the great menu has daily specials. Pasta dishes are always a safe bet and the *bruschette* are enormous. Megara gets even busier when big matches are on. Smooth jazzy sounds play out in the evenings and in summer a hatch serves *aperitivo* snacks to the tables outside.

Caffè San Carlo

Borgo Ognissanti 32-34r (055 216879, www.caffe sancarlo.com). **Open** 7.30am-midnight Mon-Sat. **Map** p334 B1 ⓮

Pre-lunch and dinner aperitifs are the big draws in this stylish and lively small bar. In good weather, the French windows are opened up, wine barrels are used as serving tables and the canopied outside area becomes a miniature socialising hub.

Giacosa Roberto Cavalli

Via della Spada 10r (055 2776328). **Open** *Summer* 7.30am-midnight Mon-Sat. *Winter* 7.30am-8.30pm Mon-Sat. Closed 2wks Aug. **Map** p334 B2 ⓯

Alongside Florentine designer Cavalli's clothing shop and club is his café, complete with leopard-skin pouffes, catwalk shows beamed on a plasma screen and plenty of attitude. The store took over the via de' Tornabuoni corner space of the much-loved Giacosa café, and in the central bar room Cavalli continues to serve hot lunches and sweet treats.

Rose's

Via del Parione 26r (055 287090, www.roses.it). **Open** 9am-1.30am Mon-Sat (brunch 12.30-3.30pm Sat); 6pm-1.30am Sun. Closed 2wks Aug. **Map** p334 C2 ⓰

This spacious restaurant-bar, with soothing cornflower-blue velvet decor, is invariably packed with a young crowd from local offices. Breakfast means fresh brownies and apple strudel. Lunch specialities are burgers and fish carpaccios, followed by carrot cake; at night, it's the hippest sushi bar in town.

SAN LORENZO

Cruise Lounge Bar

Via XXVII Aprile 16 (055 0193059, www.cruise loungebarfirenze.com). **Open** 7am-2am daily.

THE BEST SNACK SPOTS

Tuck into truffles.
Procacci. *See left.*

Sunday brunch with a punch.
Il Rifrullo. *See p150.*

Mama's cooking reigns supreme.
Zeb. *See p150.*

With a spacious wraparound terrace and bright, lofty-ceilinged interior, it's no wonder Cruise draws a regular crowd of cocktail connoisseurs – the bar even offers a two-hour cocktail class each afternoon, with stories, recipes and secrets about the art. But it's great for breakfast and modern takes on Italian favourites for lunch too – lunch includes a range of prix fixe menus starting at €8. *Aperitivi* start at 5.30pm, when veteran cocktail barman Attilio Boddi starts to shake and free high-quality nibbles, designed to complement particular drinks, are served. There's a weekend DJ on Fridays and Saturdays from 11pm.

Nannini Coffee Shop

Via Borgo 7r (055 212680). **Open** 7.30am-7.30pm Mon-Fri, Sun; 7.30am-8.30pm Sat. **Map** p334 B3 ⓱

Perennially bustling, Nannini is perfect for coffee and *panforte* (a sticky Sienese cake made with dried fruits and nuts) after a visit to the nearby central market. Sweets from Siena are the bar's speciality, including *cantuccini* (almond biscuits) and *ricciarelli* (choc-covered marzipan petits fours).

Porfirio Rubirosa

Viale Strozzi 18-20 (055 490965). **Open** 7pm-2am Mon-Sat. Closed 2wks Aug.

This chic bar is the watering-hole of choice during trade shows in the Fortezza da Basso, just across the avenue. Lunch on truffle mozzarella or smoked tuna salad, lounge on the balcony mezzanine with a slice of passion fruit cheesecake at teatime, or come back in the evening to make a night of it. *See also p206.*

★ Sieni

Via Sant'Antonino 54r (055 213830, www. pasticceriasieni.it). **Open** 7.30am-7.30pm daily. **No credit cards.** **Map** p334 A3 ⓲

With its turn-of-the-century decor, this 1909 café and *pasticceria* is the real deal, serving up a great range of sweet and savoury breakfast pastries and snacks to a very local crowd, many of them taking a coffee break from their market shopping. Try yours with a hefty slice of perfect polenta cake.

SAN MARCO

Robiglio

Via de' Servi 112r (055 214501, www.robiglio.it). **Open** 7.30am-7.30pm Mon-Sat. Closed 3wks Aug. **Map** p335 A5 ⓴

The sublime hot chocolate served here is so thick that the spoon stands up in it, and the delicious pastries are a Florentine institution. Robiglio's sister café located on via Tosinghi (no.11r, 055 215013) has outside tables in summer.

Zona 15

Via del Castellaccio 53-55r (055 211678, www.zona15wine.it). **Open** 11am-3am Mon-Fri; 6pm-3am Sat, Sun. **Map** p335 A4 ㉑

CONSUME

Looking rather like a futuristic American diner, this decidedly hip café-cum-wine bar has leather and chrome stools that hug a massive central spotlit bar area. Walls are clad in oyster mosaics and crowned by dramatic vaulted ceilings. The *aperitivo* tapas menu, based on Basque recipes, is available daily from 6pm, while the decent wine menu offers around 200 different options.

SANTA CROCE

Caffè Sant Ambrogio
Piazza Sant'Ambrogio 7r (055 2477277).
Map p335 B6
Opposite the 11th-century Sant'Ambrogio church, on a sweet little piazza that gets crowded in the evening with locals and students, this stylish bar, café, *enoteca* and restaurant serves a great range of drinks, including classic cocktails (vodka martini or margherita for €6) and more than 50 wines by the glass. Modern Italian lunch specials draw punters from the nearby market, but it's the evening *aperitivo*, starting at 6pm, that really pulls in the young and fashionable.

★ Caffè Cibrèo
Via Andrea del Verrocchio 5r (055 2345853).
Open 8am-1am Tue-Sat. Closed 2wks Aug.
No credit cards. Map p335 C6
This delightful café has exquisite carved wood ceilings, antique furniture, a candlelit mosaic and outside tables, but also a knack for making everything it presents look as beautiful as the bar itself. As you'd expect from an outpost of Cibrèo (*see p133*, the savoury dishes are both inventive and refined, but the desserts,

like the rich, dense chocolate torte and the cheesecake with bitter orange sauce, are also amazing.

Caffellatte
Via degli Alfani 39r (055 2478878). **Open** 8am-midnight Tue-Sat; 9am-midnight Sun. **No credit cards. Map** p335 B5
The lattes in this small café, done out with rustic wooden tables and chairs, are among the best in Florence. But if they're too dull for you, the *cappuccione* comes piping hot in a giant bowl with honey and Turkish cinnamon. The pastries and cakes are made in the café's organic bakery.

La Loggia degli Albizi
Borgo degli Albizi 39r (055 2479574).
Open 7.30am-8.30pm Mon-Sat. Closed Aug.
Map p335 C5
With some of the best pastries and cakes in town, La Loggia degli Albizi is the perfect stop-off after some hard shopping. Try the *torta della nonna* (crumbly pastry filled with baked pâtisserie cream).

Nuove Poste
Via Giuseppe Verdi 73r (055 2480424).
Open 7am-1pm daily. **Map** p335 B5
This corner bar would be fairly bog standard were it not for the huge outdoor canopied seating area on the pedestrian concourse. It's right on the crossroads of streets leading to Santa Croce, the Duomo and Sant'Ambrogio, so a strategically useful pit stop.

I Visacci
Borgo degli Albizi 80r (055 2001956). **Open** 10.30am-2.30am Mon-Sat. **Map** p335 B4
Cosy up in one of the padded alcove sofa seats in this cutesy bar, decked out in different-coloured stripes. The best cappuccinos in the city are served here; the mellow music may also help to lull you into a longer stay. The lunchtime menu hits the right notes: cheap hot *crostoni* (open sandwiches), salads, omelettes and cold meat plates.

OLTRARNO

Cabiria
Piazza Santo Spirito 4r (055 215732). **Open** 8.30am-1.30am Mon, Wed-Sun. **No credit cards. Map** p334 D2
A long-standing artsy haunt, popular with students. Inside, scarlet walls are punctuated with the paintings and photographs of visiting exhibitions and there's an enclosed outside terrace. Hot focaccias with rocket and sheep's cheese are served at lunchtime and the barman shakes up a mean aperitif at noon and 7pm. *See also p204.*

★ Café Circolo Aurora
Viale Vasco Pratolini 2, corner of piazza Tasso (055 224059, www.circoloaurorafirenze.it).
Open 6.30pm-midnight daily. **Map** p334 D1

I Visacci

Il Rifrullo. *See p150.*

Located in a little tower on the city walls, this sweet spot is filled with delights – second-hand furniture and architectural salvage sit next to mad modern seats (the bum ones are particularly arresting) in a space that feels more like an overstuffed antiques shop than a café. So beguiling is the interior that it's hard to choose between it and the lovely terrace – whichever you choose, you'll be served great home cooking with a focus on local (produced within 50km), seasonal produce and organic meats.

Caffè degli Artigiani
Via dello Sprone 16r (055 291882, www.oltrarno-firenze.net). **Open** *May-Sept* 8am-4pm Mon; 8am-midnight Tue-Sat. *Oct-Apr* 8.30am-10.30pm Mon-Sat. **Map** p334 C2 ③⓪
This charming, laid-back gem of a café is worth seeking out for its country cottage atmosphere (think low ceilings and beautifully carved antique chairs). Staff are friendly and multilingual and a couple of outside tables appear in warm weather.

Caffè Ricchi
Piazza Santo Spirito 9r (055 215864, www.caffericchi.com). **Open** *Summer* 7am-1.30am Mon-Sat. *Winter* 7am-10pm Mon-Sat. Closed last 2wks Aug, last 2wks Feb. **Map** p334 D2 ③①
Ricchi is on the traffic-free piazza Santo Spirito, a charming setting for alfresco drinking. The place does a good lunch menu that changes daily. If it rains, the side room is a great place to relax with a coffee and a cake.

Hemingway
Piazza Piattellina 9r (055 284781, www.hemingway.fi.it). **Open** 4.30pm-1am Mon-Thur;

4.30pm-2am Fri, Sat; 3.30pm-1am Sun (brunch noon-2.15pm). Closed mid June-mid Sept.
This charming café has a huge selection of quality teas, unusual tea cocktails and at least 20 types of coffee, but it's best known for its chocolate delectables: the owner belongs to the Chocolate Appreciation Society, and the café's *sette veli* chocolate cake once won the World Cake Championship. Hemingway's high tea (6-7.30pm) tempts with ten different sweet delights; there's also a Sunday brunch (book in advance).

Libreria Café La Cité
Borgo San Frediano 20r (055 210387, www.lacitelibreria.info). **Open** 10.30am-1am daily. **No credit cards.** **Map** p334 C1 ③②
La Cité has given this part of the Oltrarno a true Left Bank feel. The mezzanine café area of this bookshop and cultural centre is in rustic reclaimed woods with metal bolts and serves home-baked cakes, freshly made fruit and veg juices and Fairtrade coffees. Afternoon and early-evening tastings of – mostly organic – wines, oils and cheeses from local producers are organised regularly, often with live jazz in the background. *See also p154.*

Mama's Bakery
Via della Chiesa 34r (055 219214, www.mamasbakery.it). **Open** 8am-5pm Mon-Fri; 9am-3pm Sat. **Map** p334 D1 ③③
Americans Matt and Cristina provide good service and welcome home comforts for the city's many US exiles, offering everything from freshly baked bagels and huge club sandwiches to quiche, cheesecake and muffins. They even whip up a pumpkin pie on holidays, and the coffee is truly American – right down to the free refills.

★ POP Café
Piazza Santo Spirito 18a-r (055 213852, www.popcafe.it). **Open** 12.30pm-2am Mon-Sat; 12.30-3pm Sun. **Map** p334 D1 ③④

INSIDE TRACK
A CULINARY TOUR

The **Taste food festival** (www.pittimmagine.com/corporate/fairs/taste.html), held each March in Stazione Leopolda, brings together 250 Italian artisanal producers of everything from truffle pâtés, salami, cured lard and chocolate to olive oil, wine, beer and silver-leaf spumante. For a reasonable admission and wine-glass fee, you get to sample the best that Italy has to offer. What's not to like? Hmmm, perhaps that cured lard...

You'd be forgiven for thinking you'd wandered into a Brick Lane coffee shop at Point of Presence, or POP for short. A long thin space, decked out in warm wood and white-painted exposed bricks painted with caricatures of famous Florentine art, it's lively and arty, and filled with earnest bohemian Italian youth tucking into some seriously good specials and daily filled or topped *crostoni*, a lot of them vegetarian. The mixed plate of three salads, rice, grilled vegetables and a dish of your choice is great value at €8.

Il Rifrullo
Via San Niccolò 55r (055 2342621, www.il rifrullo.com). **Open** 8am-2am daily. Closed 2wks Aug. **Map** p335 D5 ⓟ
Set in peaceful San Niccolò, this long-time favourite of Florentines is decked out in pale stained woods and cool greens. The atmosphere is usually sleepy and laid-back during the day, but the mood mutates for the evening *aperitivo*, when the music comes on, the back rooms open to accommodate the crowds and plates of snacks and cocktails are served on the charming summer roof garden in warmer weather. Sunday brunch is another crowd-puller, with its full roasts and a bar groaning with miniature glasses of *tiramisù*, cheesecake and fruit salad. *Photo p149.*

★ Volume
Piazza Santo Spirito 5r (055 2381460, www.volume.fi.it). **Open** 9.30am-2am daily. **Map** p334 D2 ⓟ
A laid-back, refreshingly unusual interior in a cool space that was once the workshop of the Bini brothers, who made hat forms. Many of these are still here, along with wooden sculptures by the brothers and their tools of the trade, plus shelves of books and animal statuary, creating a fascinating space that doesn't feel too themey – a Wurlitzer plays Creedence Clearwater Revival, menus come on cut plywood boards, chairs are stuffed leather and there's a funky, genial atmosphere. Service is good, and the fresh granitas, huge crêpes and towering cocktails utterly delicious.

★ Zeb
Via San Miniato 2r (055 2342864, www.zeb gastronomia.com). **Open** 9.30am-8pm Mon, Tue, Thur-Sun. **Map** p335 D5 ⓟ

There's no outdoor seating at this new bistro and deli, but don't let that put you off; grab a stool at the central bar or in the window of the bright and pretty interior and enjoy an excellent selection of home-style small plates, among them outrageously good pasta, *carpaccio di baccalà*, *burrata* with mixed vegetables, meatballs, *bollito* and a cheese board. The service is friendly and knowledgeable – unsurprising given it's usually owner Alberto Navari serving you dishes by his mother, Giuseppina, in a space that until 2009 was the family grocery store.

OUTSIDE THE CITY GATES

Caffè Serafini
Via Gioberti 168r (055 2476214). **Open** 7am-8.30pm Mon-Sat.
This bakery, café and bar close to piazza Beccaria is a local favourite, and what most of the locals drink in it is the Fornacino, a creamy, delicious coffee with chocolate that defies description, or belief. Equally unbelievable is the *aperitivo*, which includes not just superior quality olives, *crostini*, pizzas and nibbles, but more substantial dishes such as gnocchi with prawns and various side dishes – all yours for the taking with a €6 glass of wine. It gets crowded, so get here earlier.

GELATERIE

To find the best ice-cream in Florence, look out for '*produzione proprio*', or '*artigianale*', as this means the ice-cream is home-made. In summer, many bars install ice-cream corners, with a small selection of locally made flavours. Some of the smaller places that make their own *gelato* close in winter, but it's still easy to find one open on the main thoroughfares even in the cold months, when hot fudge and chocolate sauces are often served on top.

Badiani
Viale dei Mille 20, Outside the City Gates (055 578682, www.buontalenti.it).
Located in the Campo di Marte area just outside the city gates and, whisper it, challenging for the crown of Grom (*see p152*), this hugely popular *gelateria* is most famous for its Buontalenti, named after the Renaissance architect Bernardo Buontalenti who is said to have invented the stuff, and made using a secret recipe supposedly found by the owner among some old manuscripts more than 50 years ago. It's hard to describe, but we're thinking a confection of cream and *crème anglaise* – at €2 for a *piccolo* cup, a bargain. Gorgeous cakes, coffee and, at lunchtime, a small selection of savouries complete the picture.

★ Cantina del Gelato
Via de' Bardi 31, Oltrarno (055 0501617, www. cantinadelgelato.com). **Open** 3-9pm Mon; noon-11pm Tue-Sun. **Map** p334 D3 ⓟ

CONSUME

Nice Ice, Baby

Welcome to the capital of gelato-land.

Historians (and, were he alive, the personal chef to Alexander the Great) might argue with them, but Florentines have long claimed to have created the first *gelato*: in the 16th century, Medici architect Bernardo Buontalenti is said to have served his patrons' guests frozen desserts made from fruit and *zabaglione*, with snow and ice from his specially built ice houses in the Boboli Gardens. Around the same time, Caterina de' Medici is believed to have introduced 'cream ice' to the French courts. With such lofty antecedents, it's no wonder that rivalry among the city's *gelaterie* has always been fierce. But the form of this rivalry has recently shifted from the amount and outlandishness of flavours offered to whose cold stuff is most home-made, more natural and uses the highest-quality ingredients. The signs '*produzione proprio*' and '*artigianale*' are the buzzwords, and parlours are going to ever-greater lengths to make the authenticity grade. Ploys include making the ice-cream in full view of shoppers, shipping in fresh ingredients daily and using gourmet chocolate, organic milk, seasonal fruits and exotic spices sourced from far-flung locations. For years, local institutions **Perchè No!** (*see p152*) and **Vivoli** (*see p152*) were regularly named the best *gelaterie* in the city. Their fabulous *semi-freddi*, creamier and softer than *gelato*; wickedly rich chocolate orange and divine *riso* (rice pudding); and old favourites like caramelised pear are still up there, but there are new contenders.

Vestri (*see p152*) and, out of town, **Badiani** (*see p150*) are the locals' choices. Chocolate shop Vestri has a corner serving a curated seasonal selection of flavours – like wild strawberry *gelato* only in summer – while Badiani is famous for its secret-recipe Buontalenti coffee, but also offers a terrific selection of ice-cream. The owners of **Carabé** (*see p152*) are Sicilian and bring in fresh lemons from home to make a tangy, rustic ice-cream/sorbet cross-breed. Their crunchy granita is flavoured with almond milk, while the *cremolata* is made with the pulp of seasonal soft fruits. At **Gelateria dei Neri** (*see p152*) all the ice-cream is made in the workshop behind the counter, as it is at Oltrarno newcomer's **Cantina del Gelato** (*see p150*) and **Le Parigine** (*see p152*), where ice-cream made from Madagascan chocolate and the best seasonal produce is just a stone's throw from the Duomo.

For many who've found **Grom** (*see p152*), though, the contest is over. Here, monthly specials may be delicate matcha (green tea) or refreshing milk and fresh mint in the summer, and chunky marrons glacés or zingy ginger in the winter months; the year-round speciality is the sensational Crema di Grom, made with organic egg, soft cookies and Valrhona Ecuadorian chocolate. Grom raised the bar for ice-cream in Florence, and *gelaterie* all over the city have taken up the challenge – which means we get to enjoy the fruits of their labour all year round.

CONSUME

Cantina del Gelato.

Sitting in a superb spot next to the Santa Maria Sopr'arno in Oltrarno, this sweet new *gelateria*, converted from an old wine shop, is a great place to pick up an ice-cream before crossing the road to the riverside views of the Uffizi, ponte Vecchio and the Vasari Corridor. Given the incredible selection, it could take you a while to get there; here are exotic *vin santo* and *cantuccini*, or goat's cheese and walnut, alongside seasonal flavours such as Sicilian lemon – prices start at €1 for a reasonably sized baby cone, so you can always try a few different flavours.

Carabé

Via Ricasoli 60r, San Marco (055 289476).
Open *Summer* 9am-1am daily. *Winter* 9am-8pm daily. Closed mid Dec-mid Jan. **No credit cards.**
Map p335 A4 ③

The Sicilian owners of this *gelateria* near the Accademia are third-generation ice-cream makers and proud of their heritage. They excel in the island's specialities – one crunchy granita is flavoured with almond milk, fresh lemons are brought in weekly from Sicily to make a tangy ice-cream/sorbet crossbreed and the *cremolata* is made with the pulp of seasonal soft fruits. One of the few places in the city to offer authentic *cassata* (cream *gelato* pyramid blocks with candied fruit) and *cannoli* (the round ricotta-filled snaps immortalised as weapons in *The Godfather III*).

★ Carapina

Piazza G Oberdan 2r (055 676930, http:// gelateriacarapina.simplicissimus.it). **Open** 8am-midnight Tue-Sun.

This artisanal *gelato* maker prides itself on only offering 22 flavours at any one time, a largely fruit-based selection determined by season and quality of the fruit. Of course, when you operate in a country where fruit ranges from figs, chestnuts and almonds to apricots, peaches and pine nuts, you've a pretty good selection to choose from. But just in case, the standards are also there: chocolate, stracciatella, pistaccio… all served by friendly, patient staff in a high-tech space.

Gelateria dei Neri

Via de' Neri 22r, Santa Croce (055 210034).
Open 11am-midnight daily. **No credit cards.**
Map p335 C4 ④

A gem for those who want to sample the Florentine frozen assets but have an intolerance to milk – it's one of the few parlours to serve soya ice-cream alongside the classic creamy *gelati*.

Grom

Via del Campanile (corner of via delle Oche), Duomo & Around (055 216158, www.grom.it).
Open *Summer* 10.30am-midnight daily. *Winter* 10.30am-11pm daily. **No credit cards.**
Map p335 B4 ④

Everything about this newcomer – and strong contender for best *gelateria* in Florence – is comfortingly traditional, from the limestone flagging and metal jars to the *gelataio*'s apron. Flavours of the month may be the refreshing milk and fresh mint in the summer, or zingy ginger (*zenzero*) in winter. Fortunately, the sensational Crema di Grom, made with organic eggs, soft cookies and Valrhona Ecuadorian chocolate, is served year-round.

Le Parigine

Via de' Servi 41r (055 2398470). **Open** 11am-11pm daily. **Map** p335 A4 ④

Don't be fooled by the retro styling, Le Parigine (named after those old-fashioned ice-cream and biscuit sandwiches, which are served here in three sizes) is a recent addition to Florence's *gelaterie*, and a welcome one in an area that doesn't have enough really good ones. Flavours are seasonal and unusual – pink grapefruit, anyone? – and you can sit in or outside on little benches to eat your cone. With all ice-creams made on-site and using natural ingedients, you'll be hard pressed to find a better ice-cream this close to the Duomo.

Perchè No!

Via de' Tavolini 19r, Duomo & Around (055 239 8969, www.percheno.firenze.it). **Open** *Summer* 11am-midnight daily. *Winter* noon-7.30pm Mon, Wed-Sun. **No credit cards. Map** p334 C3 ④

This is a favourite with the locals – many have been coming for generations. Not by chance, it is often cited as the best *gelateria* for the more traditional flavours – *crema* (vanilla), pistachio and chocolate.

Vestri

Borgo degli Albizi 11r, Santa Croce (055 2340374, www.vestri.it). **Open** *Summer* 10am-8pm daily. *Winter* 10am-8pm daily. Closed Aug. **Map** p335 B5 ④

Primarily a gourmet chocolate shop, in summer Vestri installs a few metal churns, from which are served up exquisite own-made ice-cream concoctions. The flavours are few but ingenious and adventurous – white chocolate with wild strawberries, chocolate and *peperoncino* (Italian chillies) and bitter chocolate with Cointreau.

★ Vivoli

Via Isola delle Stinche 7r, Santa Croce (055 292334, www.vivoli.it). **Open** *Summer* 7.30am-midnight Tue-Sun. *Winter* 7.30am-9pm Tue-Sun. Closed mid Aug. **No credit cards. Map** p335 C5 ④

Local institution Vivoli has clung on jealously to its long-standing but increasingly threatened reputation as the best *gelateria* in Florence. The wickedly rich chocolate orange and divine *riso* (rice pudding) are still up there with the best of them. So too are its famous *semi-freddi* – which are creamier and softer than ordinary *gelato*.

Shops & Services

Gorgeous food and fine fragrances, plus indie design aplenty.

The fiercely independent spirit of Florentines ensures a wonderful array of interesting shops and studios alongside the international designer togs on via de' Tornabuoni. From the little leathermakers' ateliers and alternative fashion stores in Santa Croce to the age-old authentic grocers and *salumerie* around San Lorenzo, into the *centro storico* for ancient perfumeries and herbalists, and across the river to tiny streets studded with startlingly original pieces of jewellery, Florence is a shopper's – and browser's – dream.

OPENING HOURS AND INFORMATION

Supermarkets and larger stores in the city centre tend to stay open throughout the day (*orario continuato*), but most shops still operate standard hours, closing at lunchtime and on Monday mornings. The standard opening times are 3.30pm to 7.30pm on Monday, and 9am to 1pm then 3.30pm to 7.30pm Tuesday to Saturday, with clothes shops sometimes opening around 10am. Food shops usually open earlier in the morning, close at 1pm and reopen at 5pm, and are closed Wednesday afternoons. Many of the central stores stay open for at least part of Sunday; several more open on the last Sunday of the month.

Hours alter slightly in mid June until the end of August, when most shops close on Saturday afternoons. Small shops tend to shut completely at some point during July or August for a week to a month. The opening times listed here apply most of the year – we have noted closures of more than two weeks whenever possible – but they can vary, particularly in the case of smaller shops. Visitors from outside the EU are entitled to a VAT rebate on purchases of goods over €160. Look for the 'tax-free' signs in shop windows.

General

DEPARTMENT STORES

COIN
Via de' Calzaiuoli 56r, Duomo & Around (055 280531, www.coin.it). **Open** 10am-7.30pm daily. **Map** p334 B3.

Furnishings are the strong point of this mid-range store, with bright contemporary homeware and regular consignments of Far Eastern furnishings.

Principe
Via del Sole 2, Santa Maria Novella (055 292764, www.principedifirenze.com). **Open** 10.30am-7.30pm Mon; 9.30am-7.30pm Tue-Sat. *Sept-June* also 11am-7.30pm last Sun of mth. **Map** p334 B2.
Stuffy staff run this grande dame of a department store in Santa Maria Novella. Highlights include bedlinens in Egyptian cotton, bath and kitchen accessories and quality toiletries.

La Rinascente
Piazza della Repubblica 1, Duomo & Around (055 219113, www.rinascente.it). **Open** 9am-9pm Mon-Sat; 10.30am-8pm Sun. **Map** p334 B3.
This classic store has casual and designer clothes, the most extensive cosmetics and perfume department in the city, a decent lingerie section and smart bedding supplies. The rooftop café, reached via the top floor, has fantastic views (*see p146*).

MALLS

I Gigli
Via San Quirico 165, Campi Bisenzio (055 8974546, www.igigli.it). **Open** 9am-8pm Mon-Sat, 1st Sun of mth.
An authentic covered mall outside Florence, about 30 minutes from the centre by bus, with over 120 Italian and international chains and restaurants.

MARKETS

See p164 **Market Forces**.

Specialist

BOOKS & MAGAZINES

English-language

It's generally easy to find English-language titles in Florence, but you'll find that prices are higher than back home.

BM American British Bookstore

Borgo Ognissanti 4r, Santa Maria Novella (055 294575, www.bmbookshop.com). **Open** 9.30am-7.30pm Mon-Sat. **Map** p334 B1.
A good collection of books in English, many with Italian and Florentine themes. Some used books and a range of children's titles are stocked, as well as an odd array of gifts. *See also p182.*

BRAC

Via de' Vagellai 18r, Santa Croce (055 0944877, www.libreriabrac.net). **Open** 11am-midnight (kitchen closes at 10.30pm) Mon-Sat; noon-8pm Sun. Closed Sun for 2mths in summer. **Map** p335 C4.
Is it a bookshop? Is it a restaurant? Fortunately for hungry readers, it's both, serving up a great selection of books alongside veggie lunches, snacks and café staples. Two shop spaces are separated by a small garden, and you can pull large format art books, graphic novels, cookery books and the like off the numerous shelves to read in any of the three comfy spaces. A real gem. *See also p134.*

General

Edison

Piazza della Repubblica 27r, Duomo & Around (055 213110, www.libreriaedison.it). **Open** 9am-midnight Mon-Sat; 10am-midnight Sun. **Map** p334 B3.
This multi-storey superstore sells books, maps, magazines, calendars and CDs. The travel section includes lots of guides in English. Internet terminals, a café and a lecture area are further attractions.

Feltrinelli International

Via Cavour 12-20r, San Marco (055 219524, www.lafeltrinelli.it). **Open** 9am-7.30pm Mon-Sat. **Map** p335 A4.
This modern bookshop has strong art, photography and comic-book sections, plus a huge selection of titles in English, language-teaching books, original-language videos and a gift section.

Libreria Café La Cité

Borgo San Frediano 20r, Oltrarno (055 210387, www.lacitelibreria.info). **Open** 10.30am-1am daily. **Map** p334 C1.
As much of a cultural centre as a bookshop, La Cité organises creative writing sessions, readings,

debates and presentations, as well as promoting young and new authors. Most activities are held in Italian, but international guest writers are occasionally invited. *See also p149.*

Libreria Martelli

Via de' Martelli 22r, Duomo & Around (055 2657603, www.libreriamartelli.it). **Open** 9am-8pm Mon-Sat; 10am-8pm Sun. **Map** p335 B4.
This big, light and airy store has an excellent range of books in various languages, including English. The selection of travel guides is particularly strong.

Specialist

Alinari

Largo Alinari 15, Santa Maria Novella (055 2395232, www.alinari.it). **Open** 9am-1pm, 2-6pm Mon-Fri; 10am-1pm, 2-6pm Sat. Closed 3wks Aug. **Map** p334 A2.
One of the world's first and most famous photographic firms, established in 1852. Photography books and exhibition catalogues are stock; prints can be ordered from its archives.

Fashion Room

Via de' Palchetti 3-3a, Santa Maria Novella (055 213270, www.fashionroom.it). **Open** 9.30am-1pm, 3-7.30pm Mon-Fri; 10am-1pm, 3-6pm Sat. **Map** p334 A2.
An unrivalled collection of books, catalogues and magazines on interior design, architecture and fashion, including hard-to-find limited editions and coffee-table tomes.

Franco Maria Ricci/Babele

Via delle Belle Donne 41r, Santa Maria Novella (055 283312, www.babelefirenze.com). **Open** 3.30-7.30pm Mon; 10am-1pm, 3.30-7.30pm Tue-Sat. **Map** p334 B2.
A delightful art bookshop and arts and crafts gallery stocking mainly limited editions, numbered prints and handmade stationery.

Libreria delle Donne

Via Fiesolana 2b, Santa Croce (055 240384, http://libreriadelledonnefirenze.blogspot.com). **Open** 3.30-7.30pm Mon; 9.30am-1pm, 3.30-7.30pm Tue-Fri. Closed Aug. **Map** p335 B5.
A good reference point for women in Florence, not just for its books but also for the useful noticeboard that has details on local activities.

Used

Paperback Exchange

Via delle Oche 4r, Duomo & Around (055 293460, www.papex.it). **Open** 9am-7.30pm Mon-Fri; 10am-7.30pm Sat. Closed 2wks Aug. **Map** p335 B5.
This old favourite stocks thousands of new and used English-language fiction and non-fiction

CONSUME

Libreria Café La Cité.

titles, specialising in art, art history and Italian culture. The noticeboard has information about literary events, courses, accommodation and language lessons. Second-hand books can be traded.

CHILDREN

For children's toys, *see p182*.

Fashion

Children's clothes can be more expensive than the adult versions in Italy, so check the tags. Via Gioberti (Outside the City Gates) also has a concentration of children's clothing shops.

Anichini
Via del Parione 59r, Santa Maria Novella (055 284977, www.anichini.net). **Open** 3.30-7.30pm Mon; 9.30am-1.30pm, 3.30-7.30pm Tue-Sat. Closed 1wk Aug. **Map** p334 B2.
Ridiculously cute kids' clothing has been the mainstay of this sweet shop, housed in the 15th-century Ricasoli Palace, for 100 years, and some of the styles have barely changed. Christening and ceremonial gowns plus newborn's clothing are as traditional as they come, featuring hand-smocking, embroidery and lace, but older girls will adore the girly frocks and the little boys' suits are to die for.

Baroni
Via de' Tornabuoni 9r, Duomo & Around (055 210562, www.baroni-firenze.com). **Open** *Sept-June* 3.30-7.30pm Mon; 10am-7.30pm Tue-Sat, last Sun of mth. *July-Aug* 10am-7.30pm Mon-Fri; 10am-1pm Sat. **Map** p334 C2.

Founded by three sisters as an embroidery studio in 1912, this lovely shop, still owned by the great-granddaughter of one of the founders, offers its own brand children's knitwear, shoes, accessories and clothing, made in Florence, alongside carefully chosen international brands. There are additional branches at via Porta Rossa 56r, and at via Senese 25r.

Petit Bateau
Via della Vigna Nuova 74r, Santa Maria Novella (055 215167/290457, www.petit-bateau.it). **Open** 3.30-7.30pm Mon; 10am-7.30pm Tue-Fri; 11am-7.30pm Sun. **Map** p334 B2.
This French chain sells well-made clothes in natural fibres with simple motifs. Adult sizes are available for some of the T-shirts. Surprisingly easy on the wallet.

Sarà
Via della Spada 42r, Santa Maria Novella (055 281048). **Open** 3.30-7.30pm Mon; 10am-1pm, 3.30-7.30pm Tue-Sat. **Map** p334 B2.
Stylish maternity clothes in crinkled silks and cottons, plus baby and children's clothing and footwear.

ELECTRONICS & PHOTOGRAPHY

Bongi
Via Por Santa Maria 82r, Duomo & Around (055 2398811, www.otticabongi.com). **Open** 3-7pm Mon; 10am-7pm Tue-Sun. **Map** p334 C3.
One of the best-stocked photographic shops in the city centre, offering a wide range of new and used equipment for sale, digital photo reprographics services and print developing.

1000s of things to do…

Foto Ottica Fontani
*Viale Strozzi 18-20a, San Lorenzo (055 470981,
www.fotocamerefontani.com).* **Open** 9am-1pm,
3-7.30pm Mon-Sat. **Map** p334 B3.
Photography enthusiasts in Florence make a beeline
for this shop, where the prices for processing and
developing are the lowest in town.

FASHION
Designer

Gerard Loft
*Via de' Pecori 36r, Duomo & Around (055
282491, www.gerardloft.com).* **Open** 2.30-7.30pm
Mon; 10am-7.30pm Tue-Sat. **Map** p334 B3.
Hip clothing with men's and women's lines by the
likes of Marc Jacobs, Chloé and Helmut Lang.

Luisa Via Roma
*Via Roma 19-21r, Duomo & Around (055
217826, www.luisaviaroma.com).* **Open** 10am-
7.30pm Mon-Sat; 11am-7pm Sun. **Map** p334 B3.
Renowned for its inventive window displays, this
multi-level store features designer collections from
Issey Miyake, Roberto Cavalli and others.

Matucci
*Via del Corso 71r, Duomo & Around (055
2396420).* **Open** 3.30-8pm Mon; 10am-7.30pm
Tue-Sat. **Map** p334 B4.
Collections by Armani, Diesel, Boss and Versace.
Womenswear is just down the road at no.46r.

Michele Negri
*Via degli Agli 3r (corner of via Pescioni), Duomo
& Around (055 212781, www.michelenegri.com).*
Open 10.30am-7.30pm daily. **Map** p334 B3.
The new flagship store of one of Florence's most
famous home-grown menswear designers. Suits and
shirts are fairly staid but well made – the rarity here
is the bar within the shop. Womenswear is also sold.
Other locations Via Roma 24r, Duomo &
Around (055 216524); via Porta Rossa 54r,
Duomo & Around (055 215606).

Miu Miu
*Via Roma 8r, Duomo & Around (055 2608931,
www.miumiu.com).* **Open** 10am-7.30pm Mon-Sat;
10am-7pm Sun. **Map** p334 B3.
Miuccia Prada's concession to the younger and less
moneyed fans of her feminine style.

Patrizia Pepe
*Via Strozzi 11/19r, Duomo & Around (055
2302518, www.patriziapepe.com).* **Open**
10am-7.30pm daily. **Map** p334 B3.
This Florentine designer sells internationally and has
five stores in Florence, all of them selling her full range
of menswear, womenswear, children's and babies and
teenage range. Prices are upper end high street.

**INSIDE TRACK
INSIDE THE OUTLETS**

Florence is famous for its out-of-town
fashion outlets, but if you only have time
to do one, make it the Mall (via Europa
8, Leccio Reggello, 055 865 7775, www.
outlet-firenze.com). Just a half-hour drive
from the city, it's home to many designer
names, including Fendi, Armani, Gucci,
Stella McCartney and Valentino, all of
them offering discounts from 30% to 70%.

Raspini
*Via Roma 25-29r, Duomo & Around (055
213077, www.raspini.com).* **Open** 3.30-7.30pm
Mon; 9.30am-1.30pm, 3.30-7.30pm Tue-Fri;
9.30am-7.30pm Sat. **Map** p334 B3.
A one-stop shop for Romeo Gigli, Armani, Prada,
Miu Miu, Anna Molinari, D&G and many others. For
the Raspini Vintage store, *see p165.*
Other locations Via Por Santa Maria 72r,
Duomo & Around (055 213901); via Martelli 3-7,
Duomo & Around (055 2398336).

Space
*Via de' Tornabuoni 17r, Duomo & Around (055
216943, www.abbigliamentospace.com).* **Open**
3-7.30pm Mon; 10am-7.30pm Tue-Sat, last Sun
of mth except July-Aug. Closed 1wk Aug. **Map**
p334 C2.
The well-heeled international brand fans beat a path
to Space, where men's brands include Comme des
Garçons, Dolce & Gabbana, Martin Margiela and
Paul Smith, while women pick up the latest from
Demeulemeester, Diane Von Furstenberg, Dries van
Noten and Marni. Staff are friendly and the ambience unstuffy, making it a pleasant browse.

Discount

Il Guardaroba
*Via Giuseppe Verdi 28r, Santa Croce (055
2478250).* **Open** 3.30-7.30pm Mon; 9.30am-
7.30pm Tue-Sat. **Map** p335 C5.
Il Guardaroba deals in designer end-of-lines and past
seasons' stock with good deals to be had.
Other locations throughout the city.

General

A Piedi Nudi nel Parco
*Via del Proconsolo (corner of via Dante Alighieri),
Duomo & Around (055 218099, www.apiedinudi
nelparco.com).* **Open** noon-8pm Mon; 10am-8pm
Tue-Sat. **Map** p335 B4.
These sister shops take their name from the 1960s
film *Barefoot in the Park*, but the style is more
neo-1970s, with beautifully cut, long, fluid and

CONSUME

asymmtrical styles with a decorative twist, in understated colours and high-quality fabrics.
Other locations Via Santa Margherita 2r, Duomo & Around (055 280179).

AteSeta
Via de' Calzaiuoli 1r, Duomo & Around (055 214959). **Open** 10am-8pm daily. **Map** p334 C3.
AteSeta displays row upon row of mix 'n' match men's shirts and ties.
Other locations Via Porta Rossa 21r, Duomo & Around (055 283301); via Cerretani 33r, Duomo & Around (055 215085); via Por Santa Maria 1r, Duomo & Around (055 2382851).

BP Studio
Via della Vigna Nuova 15r, Santa Maria vella (055 213243, www.bpstudio.it). **Open** 3-7pm Mon; 10am-2pm, 3-7pm Tue-Sat. **Map** p334 B2.
Delicate knitwear, rosebud-edged chiffon skirts and mohair stoles from young designers are shown at this upmarket but youthful store.

Dixie
Via del Corso 52r, Duomo & Around (055 2670445, http://dixie.it). **Open** 10am-7.30pm Mon-Sat; 11am-7.30pm Sun. **Map** p335 B4.
This Prato-based mini-fashion chain (there are four outlets in Florence, as well as discount outlets outside town) offers affordable, young styles that tend to be interesting takes on new trends, with a Banana Republic palette that's very popular among its 20-30-something Italian and American clientele. The Santa Maria Novella store is at Galleria la Stazione 14 (055 2349533).

Eredi Chiarini
Via Roma 16r, Duomo & Around (055 284478, www.eredichiarini.com). **Open** 3.30-7.30pm Mon; 10am-7.30pm Tue-Sat; also 1st & last Sun of mth. **Map** p334 B3.
A favourite with Florentines, who love its effortlessly stylish polos, softly tailored jackets and cool wool suits. Womenswear is nearby at via Porta Rossa 39r.

(ethic)
Borgo degli Albizi 37r, Santa Croce (055 2344413, www.ethic.it). **Open** 3-8pm Mon, Sun; 10am-8pm Tue-Sat. **Map** p335 B5.
Unique clothing store with low to mid-range prices as well as a cutting-edge selection of CDs and a home section with curtains, cushions and accessories.

Flow
Via Vecchietti 22r, Duomo & Around (055 215504, www.flow-store.it). **Open** 3-7.30pm Mon; 10am-7.30pm Tue-Sat; 2.30-7.30pm Sun. **Map** p334 B3.
Exposed brick arches, large flexible space and old-fashioned vitrines make this a pleasant space in which to browse a great range of collections by up-and-coming designers and independent young brands from Italy and beyond, among them Depaertment 5, Collection Privée, and Soho de Luxe. Expect chic, affordable clothing for men and women, and a great range of accessories. There's a dedicated shoe store further down on via Vecchietti (behind Fendi).

★ Giorgia Atelier
Via de' Ginori 58r, San Lorenzo (055 280374). **Open** 10am-2pm, 3.30-7.30pm Mon-Sat. **Map** p335 A4.

Société Anonyme.

THE BEST LOCAL DESIGNERS

For quirky original fashions
Quelle Tre. See p159.

For cheap sandals with bags of style
Laudato. See p162.

For ever
Alessando Dari. See p160.

On the corner of via Guelfa just round the corner from San Lorenzo market, this studio-turned-showroom houses the designs of several local stylists, ranging from elegant hats and silk scarves to bags, clothing and winter woollies. Prices are reasonable, service helpful and friendly, and you know you'll be bagging something that will be unique when you get home.

Liu Jo

Via Calimala 14r, Duomo & Around (055 2645881, www.liujo.it). **Open** 3.30-7.30pm Mon; 10am-7.30pm Tue-Sat; 11am-1.30pm, 2.30-7pm Sun. **Map** p334 B3.
Net dresses, pretty vest tops, dressy combat gear and high wooden mules from this hip designer.

Massimo Rebecchi

Via della Vigna Nuova 26r, Santa Maria Novella (055 268053, www.massimorebecchi.it). **Open** 3.30-7.30pm Mon, last Sun of mth; 10am-1.30pm, 3-7.30pm Tue-Fri; 10am-7.30pm Sat. **Map** p334 B2.
Quality jumpers and casual suits for men and women.

Quelle Tre

Via Santo Spirito 42r, Oltrarno (055 219374, www.quelletre.it). **Open** 10am-7.30pm Mon-Sat; 10am-7pm Sun. **Map** p334 C2.
Kooky clothing and accessories in colourful combinations of different textures and prints.
Other locations Via Santo Spirito 42r, Oltrarno (055 219374); dressmaking by appointment at via de' Giandonati 15, Outside the City Gates (055 2321214).

Replay

Via de' Pecori 7-9r, Duomo & Around (055 293041). **Open** 10am-7.30pm Mon-Sat; 2.30-7.30pm Sun. **Map** p334 B3.
Men's and women's casualwear par excellence.
Other locations Via Por Santa Maria 27r, Duomo & Around (055 287950).

Sandro P.2

Via de' Tosinghi 7r, Duomo & Around (055 215063). **Open** 3-7.30pm Mon; 10am-1pm, 3.30-7.30pm Tue-Sat. **Map** p334 B3.
One of Florence's hippest men's and unisex clothing shops, with the latest from New York and London.

★ Société Anonyme

Via de' Niccolini 3f (corner of via della Mattonaia), Santa Croce (055 3860084, www.societeanonyme. it). **Open** *Winter* 3.30-7.30pm Mon; 10am-2pm, 3.30-7.30pm Tue-Sun. *Summer* 4-8pm Mon; 10am-2pm, 4-8pm Tue-Sun.
With its list of brands chalked on to a blackboard at the entrance, Société Anonyme screams 'trendy', and it is. Inside, a deftly styled space filled with art and architectural oddities houses international brands, but also men's and women's fashion and accessories by up-and-coming Italian designers. You could spend hours just poking around and trying things on, and prices are on the right side of reasonable.

Tommy Hilfiger

Piazza Antinori 3d, Duomo & Around (055 2741041). **Open** 3-7pm Mon, last Sun of mth; 10am-7pm Tue-Sat. **Map** p334 B3.
The bright king of casual for men and women; yet there's nothing casual about this new shop, with its swanky sofas, chandeliers and glass skylight.

WP Store

Via della Vigna Nuova 71/73/75r, Santa Maria Novella (055 2776399, www.wplavori.com, www. wpstore.com). **Open** 3.30-7.30pm Mon; 10am-1.30pm, 3.30-7.30pm Tue-Sat. Closed 1wk Aug. **Map** p334 B2.
Serving stylish Florentine men with clothing and accessories from labels such as BD Baggies, Barbour and Woolrich, WP's expansive and imaginative store between Santa Maria Novella and via de' Tornabuoni is a nice space in which to find the best of men's fashion in the city, some of it unique, given the store's collaborations with designers such as Daiki Suzuki, the Woolen Mills Prime Line designer for Woolrich.

FASHION ACCESSORIES & SERVICES

Cleaning & repairs

Lucy & Rita

Via de' Serragli 71r, Oltrarno (055 224536). **Open** 7am-1pm, 2.30-7pm Mon-Fri. Closed 2wks Aug. **Map** p334 D1.
A generally reliable dry-cleaners in Oltrarno, which also offers regular service washes.

Silvana e Ombretta Riparazioni

Borgo San Frediano 38r, Oltrarno (368 7571418 mobile). **Open** 9am-noon, 3.30-6.30pm Mon-Fri. Closed Aug. **No credit cards**. **Map** p334 C1.
Repairs and alterations to clothes.

Vincenzo Arezzo

Via delle Terme 8r, Duomo & Around (055 280177). **Open** 10am-12.30pm, 3-7pm Mon-Fri. **No credit cards**. **Map** p334 C3.
Shoe repairs, though usually not while you wait.

CONSUME

Walter's Silver & Gold

Borgo de' Greci 11c-r, Santa Croce (055 2396678, www.waltersilverandgold.com). **Open** 10am-6pm daily. Closed 3wks Feb & 3wks Nov. **Map** p335 C4.

English-speaking Walter is able to repair all types of jewellery. Italian-made chains, bracelets, earrings and rings are also sold.

Wash & Dry

Via Ghibellina 143r, Santa Croce (055 580480, www.washedry.it). **Open** 8am-10pm daily.
No credit cards. **Map** p334 A3.

A self-service launderette chain that has eight centrally located branches.

Gloves

Madova

Via de' Guicciardini 1r, Oltrarno (055 2396526, www.madova.com). **Open** 9.30am-7pm Mon-Sat. **Map** p334 C3.

Madova makes gloves in every imaginable style and colour in its factory, just behind this tiny shop.

Jewellery

The **ponte Vecchio** and **via Por Santa Maria** are the places to go for traditional and antique gold and silver jewellery, but all the interesting work lies in small ateliers in the Oltrarno.

★ Alessandro Dari

Via di San Niccolò 115r, Oltrarno (055 244747, 339 7457200 mobile, www.alessandrodari.com). **Open** 9.30-1.30pm, 2.30-7pm Mon-Fri; 9.30-1pm Sat. **Map** p335 D4.

Physically close to the ponte Vecchio, Alessandro Dari's stunning creations couldn't be further away from so much of the tat you find on the bridge, with the craftsman's pieces inspired by everything from the Renaissance art he is surrounded by to more obscure and arcane art from earlier periods and ancient mythology. Dari has a school and offers everything from one-day to three-month courses.

Angela Caputi

Via Santo Spirito 58r, Oltrarno (055 212 972, www.angelacaputi.com). **Open** 10am-1pm, 3.30-7.30pm Mon-Sat. **Map** p334 C3.

Colourful costume jewellery in plastics, resin and crystal. Styles are exuberant, with ethnic, art deco and psychedelic patterns.
Other locations Borgo SS Apostoli, Duomo & Around (055 292993).

Antica Orologeria Nuti

Via della Scala 10r, Santa Maria Novella (055 294594). **Open** 4-7pm Mon; 9am-12.30pm, 4-7pm Tue-Sat. Closed Aug. **Map** p334 B2.

Fabulous antique and reproduction art deco and art nouveau jewellery, plus an eclectic collection of lantern, long-case, bracket and mantel clocks.

Aprosio & Co

Via Santo Spirito 11, Oltrarno (055 290534, www.aprosio.it). **Open** 9.30am-1.30pm, 3-7pm Mon-Sat. Closed 1wk Aug. **Map** p334 C2.

An aloof dog guards the intricate necklaces, bracelets, earrings, evening bags and belts, all made from tiny glass beads, at this sleek showroom.

Frey Wille

Via de' Calzaiuoli 106r (corner via delle Oche), Duomo & Around (055 286227, www.frey-wille.com). **Open** 10am-7.30pm Mon-Sat. **Map** p334 B3.

Near the Duomo, Frey Wille's artistically inspired jewels that draw on works by the likes of Klimt, Hundertwasser and Alphonse Mucha span a range from classical and elegant to funky and futuristic. There's a nice men's collection too.

Graziella Jewels Sculptures

Lungarno degli Acciaiuoli 74r, Duomo & Around (055 211498, www.gruppograziella.it). **Open** 10am-7pm daily. **Map** p334 C3.

This shop is so stunning that it outshines even its sumptuous jewellery. The spiralling silver, silver gilt and gold chunky swirl rings and flower bracelets encrusted with tiny diamonds and semi-precious stones are shown in glass 'safes' set into black walls, while a gold resin bench inset with fibre optics ripples down the middle of the room.

Parenti

Via de' Tornabuoni 93r, Santa Maria Novella (055 214438). **Open** 3-7pm Mon; 9am-1pm, 3-7pm Tue-Sat. Closed Aug. **Map** p334 B2.

Parenti is a slightly daunting-looking emporium with Baccarat rings, art deco pieces and 1950s Tiffany jewellery.

Pomellato

Via de' Tornabuoni 89-91r, Santa Maria Novella (055 288530, www.pomellato.it). **Open** 10am-7pm Mon-Sat. **Map** p334 B2.

The gilt ceiling in this swish shop reflects a golden glow on to the cabinets. Within them are rings with gems the size and colours of fruit gums, contemporary watches and the Dodo line of animal pendants.

Vhernier

Via della Vigna Nuova 65r, Santa Maria Novella (055 218028, www.vhernier.com). **Open** 3-7pm Mon; 10am-7pm Tue-Sat. **Map** p334 B2.

Modern takes on classical styles and materials make for a nice browse in this lovely shop between Santa Maria Movella and via de' Tornabuoni. Shapes are chunky and organic rather than dainty, suggesting natural forms that are eye-catching statement pieces.

CONSUME

Profile Flo

This vintage paradise offers clothing with a conscience.

The vintage clothing boom in Florence has taken such a hold that virtually every street has a shop piled high with old Levis, army uniforms, classic sunglasses and floaty frocks, but few have a story as interesting as Flo's. Opened in 2011 on the lungarno Corsini facing the Arno, the store interior immediately made waves with two innovations; an interior design by well-known Italian visual designer Sergio Colantuoni, and stock that is billed as 'used and new clothing with a social conscience' – old clothing and fabrics turned into imaginative fashionwear and accessories designed and made by social co-operatives and disadvantaged youngsters on training schemes and apprenticeships.

It's an ambitious project with lofty aims, but it's no mere exercise in do-goodery; rather, it's the brainchild of Elisabetta Renzoni, who brought 15 years of experience in fashion retail with the likes of Gucci and Valentino to the project, and three other women on board: Maria Serena Ace and Guia Michelagnoli, who liaise with the various organisations involved in the shop, and Cinzia Guido, responsible for the creative direction of the store. And it's this creative direction that first catches the eye, in the shape of Colantuoni's lovely interiors, modelled on a deconstructed home rather than a retail space.

Walls painted in warm, lively colours are dotted with homeware pressed into service as something new; a wrought iron bedstead acts as a clothes rail, shelving is held together by old table legs, and vintage wallpaper, modernist furniture and funky lamps give the whole a homely feel with a slightly surreal take; the kind of home you'd be more likely to find in a Tim Burton movie than a fashionable Florentine street. Draped over the bedstead might be jewellery made from old ties and bags made from shirts, designed by Usato Bene; clothes sold on *conto vendito*, in which individuals can bring in old clothing to be sold by the store, which receives a cut of the sale; gorgeous, affordable organic clothing for kids; clothing made by unemployed mums' organisation Tutti per Uno; and bags by Braghetterosse, which works with women in Ethiopia; even the tags are made by disabled people via a mental health charity. The store's owners hope to eventually create a needlework school at which disadvantaged and unemployed youngsters can learn the trades of tailoring, but for now, it's putting all its efforts into attracting customers looking for something that goes beyond vintage, something that is not only unique, but has the sort of aims that truly encompass the spirit of the Renaissance.

CONSUME

WHERE IT'S AT
For shop listings, see p163.

CONSUME

Lingerie & underwear

Cocò

Via dello Studio 14r, Duomo & Around (055 0119934, www.cocoflorence.it). **Open** 10.30am-7.30pm Mon-Sat. **Map** p335 B4.

At Cocò you'll find gorgeously unusual styles and fabrics decorated with feathers and tiny jewels in this sleek store dedicated to lingerie, swimwear and accessories.

Emilio Cavallini

Via della Vigna Nuova 24r, Santa Maria Novella (055 2382789, www.emiliocavallini.com). **Open** 3-7pm Mon; 10am-7pm Tue-Sat. Closed 2wks Aug. **Map** p334 B2.

Cavallini's trademark wacky tights are stocked here, plus lines of black and white clothing, and lingerie with Warhol Marilyn and motif prints.

Intimissimi

Via de' Calzaiuoli 99r, Duomo & Around (055 2302609, www.intimissimi.it). **Open** 10.30am-8pm Mon; 9.30am-8pm Tue-Sat; 10.30am-8pm Sun. **Map** p334 B3.

Well-priced cotton lingerie is the speciality at Intimissimi, though there are also jersey vests and trousers, silk satin pyjamas and boa-trimmed tops. **Other locations** Via de' Panzani 22, Santa Maria Novella (055 2608636); piazza di Madonna degli Aldobrandini 3, San Lorenzo (055 210540).

La Perla

Via Strozzi 24r, Duomo & Around (055 215242, www.laperla.com). **Open** 3-7.30pm Mon; 10am-2pm, 3-7.30pm Tue-Sat. **Map** p334 B3.

Luxury lingerie, swimwear and boudoir apparel, in pastel silks, devoré and handmade lace.

Luggage & bags

Il Bisonte

Via del Parione 31r, Santa Maria Novella (055 215722, www.ilbisonte.com). **Open** 9.30am-7pm Mon-Sat. **Map** p334 B2.

A renowned, long-established outlet for top-tier soft leather bags and accessories and rugged cases.

Bojola

Via de' Rondinelli 25r, Duomo & Around (055 211155, www.bojola.it). **Open** 3.30-7.30pm Mon; 9.30am-7.30pm Tue-Sat. **Map** p334 B2.

Top-notch craftsmanship and high-quality hides add up to the city's best classic-style leather goods.

Coccinelle

Via de' Calzaiuoli 28r, Duomo & Around (055 295200, www.coccinelle.com). **Open** 10.30am-7.30pm daily. **Map** p334 B3.

Smart, contemporary leather bags in seasonal colours, crafted in smooth durable leather.

Scuola del Cuoio

Via San Giuseppe 5r, Santa Croce (055 244533, www.leatherschool.com). **Open** 9.30am-6pm Mon-Sat; 10am-6pm Sun. **Map** p335 C5.

At this leather school in the cloisters of Santa Croce (*see p86*), you can watch the craftsmen making bags and accessories. The prices add further appeal.

Segue...

Via degli Speziali 6r, Duomo & Around (055 288949, www.segue.it). **Open** 10am-7.30pm Mon-Sat; 1-7.30pm Sun. **Map** p334 B3.

The full Benetton range of smart bags and luggage, plus seasonal accessories, such as funky umbrellas.

Shoes

46 Santospirito

Via Santo Spirito 46r, Oltrarno (055 210659). **Open** 10.30am-1.30pm, 2.30-7.30pm Mon-Sat. **Map** p334 C2.

This funky and friendly shoe shop sells everthing from big brands (Emma Hope) through to local designers' gladiator jellies and shoes designed by architects. Prices are reasonable, and staff helpful.

Calvani

Via degli Speziali 7r, Duomo & Around (055 2654043). **Open** 2.30-7.30pm Mon; 10am-7.30pm Tue-Sat; 3-7pm Sun. **Map** p334 B3.

Men's and women's shoes in hip styles and colours from young designers such as Roberto del Carlo.

Geox

Via de' Panzani 4r, Duomo & Around (055 283606, www.geox.it). **Open** 10am-7.30pm Mon-Sat; 11am-7.30pm Sun. **Map** p334 B3.

The 'breathing' shoes that have taken the footwear market by storm; good for traipsing around the city. **Other locations** Via Calimala 11r, Duomo & Around (055 2645016).

Laudato

Via Santa Monaca 17r, Oltrarno (055 292229). **Open** *Summer* 10.30am-1pm, 4.30-7pm Mon-Sat. *Winter* 4.30-7pm Mon; 10.30am-1pm, 4.30-7pm Tue-Sat. **Map** p334 C1.

It won't win any prizes for shop design, but this great store in Oltrarno is stuffed from floor to ceiling with tantalising brown carboard boxes filled with lovely affordable sandals, in everything from funky luminous yellow to blacks and browns, all hand-made by four sibling cobblers who've been here for what looks like decades.

Marco Candido

Piazza del Duomo 5r, Duomo & Around (055 215342). **Open** 10am-7.30pm daily. Closed Sun Feb, July, Aug. **Map** p335 B4.

Sexy but stylish modern shoes and boots for women, and classic but modern shoes for men.

Otisopse

Via Porta Rossa 13r, Duomo & Around (055 2396717, www.otisopse.it). **Open** 2-8pm Mon; 10am-1pm, 2-7.30pm Tue-Sat; 11am-7.30pm Sun. **Map** p335 B4.

Wearable styles for men and women all at €59. There are mocassins, simple pumps and courts, and the odd find from Hobbs. The outlet at piazza N Sauro 17r stocks previous seasons' stock for even less. **Other locations** Via de' Neri 58r 14r, Duomo & Around (055 2645036).

Peppe Peluso

Via del Corso 5-6r, Duomo & Around (055 268283). **Open** 2-8pm Mon; 10am-8pm Tue-Sat; 11am-7.30pm Sun. **Map** p335 B4.

A pair of shoes or boots from the vast (men's and women's) ranges here may or may not last the season, but at these bargain prices, who cares? The branch opposite (no.6r) has even cheaper footwear.

Romano Shoes

Via degli Speziali 10r, Duomo & Around (055 216535, www.romanofirenze.com). **Open** 10.30am-7.30pm Mon; 10.30am-1.30pm, 2.30-7.30pm Tue-Sat; noon-1.30pm, 2.30-7.30pm Sun. **Map** p334 B3.

This small Florentine chain sells a great range of women's shoes, from delicate ballerina pumps to chunky boots, from its flagship store between via de' Calzaiuoli and via Roma.

Stefano Bemer

Via de' Camaldoli 10r, Oltrarno (055 222462, www.stefanobemer.it). **Open** 9am-1pm, 3.30-7.30pm Mon-Sat. Closed Aug.

Well-heeled Florentine men come here for handmade luxury shoes. The branch does a ready-to-wear line.

Vintage

A.N.G.E.L.O. Vintage Clothing

Via de' Cimatori 25r (corner of via de' Calzaiuoli), Duomo & Around (055 214916, www.angelo.it). **Open** 3-7.30pm Mon, Sun; 10.30am-7.30pm Tue-Sat. **Map** p334 C3.

This great two-storey store near the piazza della Signoria makes good repurposed clothing with vintage fabrics, but also has a terrific range of accessories – glasses, hats and scarves are particularly strong. The ground floor holds general menswear, womenswear and children's clothing, the first-floor rooms are dedicated to more precious items.

Boutique Nadine

Lungarno degli Acciaiuoli 22r, Duomo & Around (055 287851, www.boutiquenadine.it). **Open** 3-7.30pm Mon; 10am-7.30pm Tue-Sat, most Sun. **Map** p334 C3.

This great vintage store stocks mainly1940s and '50s clothing, including Gucci bags, Louis Vuitton

trunks, Pucci dresses and costume jewellery, as well as some old but unused stock, probably dug out from dusty storerooms and still in the original packaging. Since April 2011, Nadine has had another shop in via de' Benci 32r (055 2478274), which also stocks menswear.

Ceri Vintage

Via de' Serragli 26r, Oltrarno (055 217978, 335 8390356 mobile, www.cerivintage.it). **Open** 3.30-7pm Mon; 9.30am-12.30pm, 3.30-7pm Tue-Sat. **Map** p334 C1.

You could spend many a happy hour in here, browsing everything from 1960s prints, posters and postcards, to buttons, boas and boots, as well as stacks of chic cocktail dresses and menswear.

★ Elio Ferraro

Via del Parione 47r, Santa Maria Novella (055 290425, www.elioferraro.com). **Open** 9.30am-7.30pm Mon-Sat; by appointment Sun. **Map** p334 B2.

Elio Ferraro's shop stocks vintage designer gear and furnishings at heart-stopping prices, sourced from Ferraro's extensive worldwide contacts. Clothes may be by Chanel, Dior or Schiaparelli, or more recent design divas such as Romeo Gigli and Vivienne Westwood, while the eccentric selection of original 1950s and '60s furniture and accessories includes pieces by icons Fornasetti, Giò Ponti and Ettore Sottsass.

Flo

Lungarno Corsini 30/34r (055 5370568, www.flo-firenze.org). **Open** 3.30-7pm Mon; 10am-1pm, 3.30-7pm Tue-Sun; closed some Sun. **Map** p334 C2.

See p161 **Profile**.

Lady Jane B Vintage Boutique

Via de' Pilastri 32b, Santa Croce (055 242863, www.ladyjaneb.net). **Open** 2.30-8pm Mon, Wed-Sat. **Map** p335 B6.

Near piazza Sant'Ambrogio Lady Jane B is great for leather bags, but also stocks a good range of clothing, jewellery and accessories. If you're after a specific item, staff will happily join in the hunt.

Officina Vintage

Via del Giglio 41r, San Lorenzo (055 215828, www.officina-vintage.com). **Open** 10am-1.30pm, 2.30-7.30pm daily. **Map** p334 A3.

With several stores around the city, Officina Vintage offers a huge range of vintagewear, including some great footwear (Adidas and Converse), sunglasses spanning the last five decades, and a particularly strong menswear selection of clothing, with sports brands to the fore. The colourful via de' Giglio store spans two floors of general vintage, while the Borgo degli Albizi shop (83r, 055 243941) focuses more on formalwear.

CONSUME

Market Forces

There's plenty of treasure among the tat in Florence's many mercati.

The suckling pig gazing out from Egidio's stall looks disarmingly cheerful given that it's, well, glistening with golden fat and has an apple stuffed into its mouth. Maybe it's to do with the life it led; Egidio assures me, as he hands me samples of *cinta sinese* salami and pecorino cheese, that this was one happy piglet in life. He should know, his brother killed it. His stall at San Ambrogio market in piazza Ghiberti just north of Santa Croce (7am-2pm Mon-Sat) is one of the many occupied by stallholders who have direct contact with the producers of their goods, and it's a foodies' heaven, with the freshest and cheapest farmers' produce in the city.

Markets abound in Florence and are a shopping staple for its inhabitants, and a treasure trove for visitors after great photos, nibbles and unusual souvenirs. The annual arrival of the German Christmas market in piazza Santa Croce, the autumn farmers' market in piazza SS Annunziata and the book fair in piazza Santa Croce are greeted with as much excitement as they would have been centuries ago. More regularly, the main market of San Lorenzo (8.30am-7pm Mon-Sat) covers a cobweb of streets around San Lorenzo church, with stalls selling leather goods, clothes and souvenirs. At its centre is the 19th-century covered market in the piazza del Mercato Centrale (entrances on the piazza and on Via dell' Ariento; 7am-2pm Mon-Sat), dedicated to fruit, vegetables, meats, fish and cheeses.

Round the corner, in piazza de' Ciompi (9am-7pm Mon-Sat), the Mercato delle Pulci flea market is a great place to browse bric-a-brac in the hope of finding a tiny piece of the Renaissance to take home with you. Better still is the piazza Santo Spirito monthly antique and flea market, held on the second Sunday of the month (8am-6pm). You can usually find the odd treasure among the old photos, items of furniture, jewellery and frames. The square is also home to a small daily weekday morning market, and plays host to Fierucola on the third Sunday of the month (8am-6pm), a market whose stalls sell organic foods and wines, handmade clothing, cosmetics and natural medicines.

If it's raining, head for the Mercato Nuovo, in the covered Loggia del Mercato Nuovo just off via Calimala (9am-7pm Mon-Sat); you may not come across anything of value, but the alabaster chess sets, cheap tapestries and lace, stationery, leather goods and scarves make fine souvenirs and gifts. And rubbing the nose of the bronze boar statue that gives the market its more colloquial name of Mercato del Porcellino is de rigueur if you want a return visit to Florence.

Mercato Nuovo.

Pitti Vintage

Borgo degli Albizi 72r, Santa Croce (055 2344115, www.pittivintage.com). **Open** 3.30-7.30pm Mon; 10am-1.30pm, 3-7.30pm Tue-Sat; 3-6pm 2nd & 3rd Sun of mth. **Map** p335 B4.
Round the corner from Ceri Vintage (*see p163*), Pitti seems to have a near-monopoly on the attic and wardrobe clear-outs of classy Florentines, with regularly replenished rails of clothing dating back as far as the early 1900s. Some 'vintage' pieces, though, date from eras as recent as the 1980s.

Raspini Vintage

Via Calimaruzza 17r, Duomo & Around (055 213901, www.raspini.com/negozio_vintage_eng.html). **Open** 2.30-7.30pm Mon, Sun; 10.30am-7.30pm Tue-Sat. **Map** p334 C3.
Such is the success of Florence's retro revisit that even designer shops are jumping on the bandwagon. Raspini has big savings on previous seasons' designer stock from the main Raspini stores (*see p157*).

FOOD & DRINK

For markets, *see p164* **Market Forces**.

Bakeries

Focacceria Pugi

Piazza San Marco 10, San Marco (055 280981, www.focacceria-pugi.it). **Open** 7.45am-8pm Mon-Fri; 8.30am-8pm Sat. **Map** p335 A4.
An institution since 1924, and justly famed for its *schiacciata* – a delicious flat bread served with olive oil or grapes.
Other locations Via San Gallo 62r, San Lorenzo (055 475975); viale de Amicis 49r, Outside the City Gates (055 669666).

Il Forno di Stefano Galli

Via Faenza 39r, San Lorenzo (055 215314). **Open** 7am-8pm daily. **No credit cards.** **Map** p334 A3.
Great for early-morning pastries and brioches.
Other locations throughout the city.

Forno Top

Via della Spada 23r, Santa Maria Novella (055 212461). **Open** 7.30am-1.30pm, 5-7.30pm Mon-Sat. **No credit cards.** **Map** p334 B2.
Tasty sandwiches, hot focaccia, fabulous carrot or chocolate and pear cakes, and seasonal specialities.
Other locations Via Orsanmichele 8r, Duomo & Around (055 216564).

Sartoni

Via de' Cerchi 34r, Duomo & Around (055 212570). **Open** 7.30am-1.30pm, 5-7.30pm Mon-Sat. **Map** p335 B4.
A central pit stop stocking slices of delicious hot pizza, filled focaccia and apple pies.

Drinks

For more on wine, *see p41-46.* Most wine bars (*see p121-143*) also sell by the bottle to take away; for wineries out of town, *see p261* **Fine Vines**.

Alessi

Via delle Oche 27r, Duomo & Around (055 214966, www.enotecaalessi.it). **Open** 9am-1pm, 3.30-7.30pm Mon-Sat. **Map** p335 B4.
This fabulous *enoteca* is piled high with cakes, biscuits and chocs. Coffee is ground on the spot.

Enoteca Bonatti

Via de' Gioberti 66/68r, Outside the City Gates (055 660050, www.enotecabonatti.it). **Bus** C2, 14. **Open** 3.30-7.30pm Mon; 9.30am-1pm, 3.30-7.30pm Tue-Fri; 9.30am-1pm Sat.
Arguably the best selection of wines in town, with good prices, helpful service from a family who set up the wine and olive store in 1934, and weekly wine tasting events. French wines complement the huge Italian selection, along with a nice range of artisan beers.

Millesimi

Borgo Tegolaio 35r, Oltrarno (055 2654675). **Open** 2-8pm Mon; 11am-8pm Mon-Fri. Closed 2wks Aug. **Map** p334 D2.
Home to one of the biggest selections in town, Millesimi offers a wide range of wines from Piedmont as well as Tuscan labels, and has the best choice of wines from France (the owner is French).

Obsequium

Borgo San Jacopo 17, Oltrarno (055 216849). **Open** 3.30-7.30pm Mon; 11am-7.30pm Tue-Sat. **Map** p334 C2.
A treasure trove for wine-lovers, in a 12th-century tower. As well as an incredible cellar of fine and everyday wines, spirits and liqueurs, the place stocks all manner of drink-themed gadgets.

Zanobini

Via Sant'Antonino 47r, San Lorenzo (055 2396850, www.esercizistorici.it, www.lelame.com). **Open** 8.30am-2pm, 3.30-8pm Mon-Sat. **Map** p334 A3.

THE BEST GOURMET GIFTS

Extra-virgin olive oils
La Bottega dell'Olio. *See p168.*

Cute jars of bruschetta toppings.
Ortolano. *See p166.*

Own-label Zanobini wine.
Zanobini. *See above.*

CONSUME

Gino and Silvano Zanobini opened their wine shop here in 1944, and it's barely changed since, still selling an astonishing range of wines and liqueurs with the help of their trained sommelier sons Mario and Simon. The shop has a stand-up wine bar serving wine by the glass (including its own label), and a great range of Tuscan wines, as well as a careful selection of wines from further afield.

General

A clutch of mini-supermarkets around the city centre makes buying picnic ingredients and everyday items easy. Some of the best and most convenient include **Esselunga** (via Pisana 130-132, Outside the City Gates, 055 706556), **Pegna** (via dello Studio 8, Duomo & Around, 055 282701, www.pegnafirenze.com), **Margherita Conad** (via L Alamanni 2-8r, Santa Maria Novella, 055 211544) and **Billa** (via Pietrapiana 42-44, Santa Croce, 055 2347856, www.billa.it).

Bottega della Frutta
Via de' Federighi 31r, Santa Maria Novella (055 2398590). **Open** 8am-7.30pm Mon, Tue, Thur-Sat; 8am-1.30pm Wed. Closed Aug. **Map** p334 B4.
Alongside fruit and vegetables, this charming shop sells wines, vintage balsamic vinegars, truffle-scented oils and speciality sweets. You'll need to be prepared to queue, however.

Ortolano
Via degli Alfani 91r, San Marco (055 2396466, www.osteriafirenze.com). **Open** 10am-8pm Mon-Fri; 10am-2pm Sat. Closed Aug. **Map** p335 A4.
This excellent San Lorenzo grocery store is a great place to pick up gourmet gifts, from fruit-infused honey to a huge selection of cheeses from Tuscany and beyond; the cacio cavallo is incredible. The store produces its own range of lovely little jars of *bruschetta* toppings too, among them cream of artichoke and cream of asparagus, and the *salumi* includes *cinta sinese* prosciutto – get some made up into a *panini* and enjoy a very special lunch.

Pâtisseries

Most *pasticcerie* serve breakfast, coffee and snacks, plus takeaway cakes and savouries.

INSIDE TRACK
ARTIGIANATO E PALAZZO

Over a three-day weekend in May, the normally closed Palazzo Corsini opens its gardens to artisans from all over Tuscany (www.artigianatoepalazzi.it), offering a great chance to find gorgeous gifts while enjoying the spectacular setting.

Dolci e Dolcezze
Piazza Beccaria 8r, Santa Croce (055 2345458). **Open** 8.30am-8pm Tue-Sat; 9am-1pm, 4.30-7.30pm Sun. Closed 2wks Aug. **No credit cards.**
This pâtisserie is famous for its delectable, flourless chocolate cake, but you may also be tempted by the strawberry meringue. Savouries are just as good.

I Dolci di Patrizio Cosi
Borgo degli Albizi 11r, Santa Croce (055 2480367, www.pasticceriacosi.com). **Open** 8.30am-7.30pm Tue-Sat; 9am-1pm Sun. Closed Aug. **No credit cards. Map** p335 B5.
A huge range of sweet treats. Delicious hot doughnuts (*bomboloni caldi*) are served at 5pm.

Dolcissima Firenze
Via Maggio 61r, Oltrarno (055 2396268). **Open** 8am-1pm, 2-8pm Tue-Sat; 9am-2pm Sun. **Map** p334 D2.
A delightful shop from another age. Exquisite chocolates are displayed in gilded cabinets, and glass cake stands hold delicious-looking concoctions, including an unmissable chocolate and pear cake.

Robiglio
Via de' Servi 112r, San Marco (055 212784, www.robiglio.it). **Open** 7.30am-7.30pm Mon-Sat. Closed 3wks Aug. **Map** p335 A5.
Pietro Robiglio founded his mini *pasticceria* empire in Florence back in 1928, since which time the chain has opened five stores selling deliciously light brioches, galette biscuits, meringues, crème-filled pastries and celebration cakes.

Sugar & Spice
Via de' Servi 43r, Duomo & Around (055 290263, www.sugar-spice.it). **Open** 3.30-7.30pm Mon; 10am-2.30pm, 3.30-7.30pm Tue-Sat. Closed Aug. **No credit cards. Map** p334 A4.
Own-made, American-style sweets and cakes, including muffins. There's also a bar.
Other locations Sugar & Spice Bakery, borgo La Croce 15r (055 499503).

Specialist

Dolceforte
Via della Scala 21, Santa Maria Novella (055 219116, www.dolceforte.it). **Open** 10am-1pm, 3.30-8pm Mon-Sat. **Map** p334 B2.
Connoisseur chocolates, plus novelty-shaped treats such as chocolate Duomos. In hot months, melting stock is replaced with jams, sugared almond flowers and jars of *gianduja*, a chocolate hazelnut spread.

'Ino
For listings, *see p129.*
A gourmet's dream kitchen-cupboard store, with wines, chocolates, cured meats, cheeses and pots of pâtés, chutneys and jams in unusual flavours.

Dolci e Dolcezze.

Northern European specialities, including Dutch cheeses with cumin, mustard seeds or herbs, smoked herrings, gourmet chocs and caramel-filled wafers.

Olio e Convivium

Via Santo Spirito 4, Oltrarno (055 2658198, www.conviviumfirenze.it). **Open** 10am-2.30pm Mon; 10am-2.30pm, 5.30-10.30pm Tue-Sat. **Map** p334 C2.

A wonderful place for Tuscan olive oils and wines, sweet and savoury preserves and superlative treats, although you're likely to pay more here than at the various food markets in the city. There's also a restaurant/wine bar (*see p138*).

Peter's Tea House

Via de' Fossi 57r, Santa Maria Novella (055 215913, www.peters-teahouse.com). **Open** 3.30-7pm Mon; 10am-1pm, 3.30-7pm Tue-Sat. Closed 3wks Aug. **Map** p334 B2.

Hundreds of different types of tea from around the world, alongside biscuits to dunk in them and a range of tea-themed gift sets.

Procacci

Via de' Tornabuoni 64r, Duomo & Around (055 211656, www.procacci1885.it). **Open** 10am-8pm Mon-Sat. **Map** p334 B2/C2.

Famous for its truffle *panini*, Procacci also sells the 'white gold' and its black cousin. Other nice gifts are the chocs in Duomo-shaped boxes.

Sugar Blues

Via de' Serragli 57r, Oltrarno (055 268378). **Open** 9am-1.30pm, 4.30-8pm Mon-Fri; 9am-1.30pm Sat. *Sept-June* also 4.30-8pm Sat. **Map** p334 D1.

A great source of organic health foods and produce, eco-friendly detergents and ethical beauty products.

Vestri

Borgo degli Albizi 11r, Santa Croce (055 2340374, www.vestri.it). **Open** 10.30am-8pm Mon-Sat. Closed Aug. **Map** p335 B5.

Handmade chocolates with chilli pepper, cinnamon and more prosaic fillings, as well as a full range of pralines and bars. The upmarket shop is beautifully designed to evoke a luxurious experience all-round, and it's an excellent bet for gifts for sweet-toothed friends. Flavoured hot chocolates are served in winter, with rich ice-creams the speciality in summer. *See also p152.*

GIFTS & SOUVENIRS
Handmade marble paper

Alberto Cozzi

Via del Parione 37r, Santa Maria Novella (055 294968). **Open** 3.30-7.30pm Mon; 10am-1pm, 3.30-7.30pm Tue-Sat. **Map** p334 B2/C2.

La Bottega del Cioccolato

Via de' Macci 50, Santa Croce (055 2001609, www.andreabianchini.net). **Open** 10am-1pm, 3.30-7.30pm Mon-Sat. **Map** p335 C6.

Andrea Bianchini's chocolate shop is a delight in every sense, not least visual and olfactory. The award-winning chocolatier happily mixes up the most unexpected flavours in his beautiful products, which include *pastarelle* and *biscotti* at his dedicated *pasticceria* in 61 via de' Gioberti.

Mariano Alimentari

Via del Parione 19r, Santa Maria Novella (055 214067). **Open** 8am-3pm, 5-7.30pm Mon-Fri; 8am-3pm Sat. Closed 3wks Aug. **Map** p334 C2.

This tiny, rustic food shop-cum-sandwich bar offers focaccia filled with marinated aubergines and oil-preserved pecorino, and an array of delicacies. Have a coffee at the bar or in the vaulted wine cellar.

Migone

Via de' Calzaiuoli 85r, Duomo & Around (055 214004). **Open** 9.30am-7.30pm Mon-Sat; 10.30am-7pm Sun. **Map** p334 B3.

Lydia Migone's sweet shop is a delight to spend time in, admiring the lovely cardboard Duomos filled with chocolates or sweets, the pretty cellophane bags of candies and *biscottini* and the slabs of *torrone*. Prices aren't cheap but you can pick up a filled Battistero for €12.50, as well as dainty pieces of *panforte* for €2.60.

L'Olandese Volante

Via San Gallo 44r, San Lorenzo (055 473240). **Open** 10am-1pm, 3.30-8pm Mon-Sat. Closed 3wks Aug. **Map** p335 A4.

CONSUME

A bookbinder's workshop and showroom with a wonderful selection of books with swirled-coloured paper covers, and some bound in leather.

Giulio Giannini e Figlio

Piazza Pitti 36r, Oltrarno (055 212621, www.giuliogiannini.it). **Open** 10am-7.30pm Mon-Sat; 11am-6.30pm Sun. **Map** p334 D2.
Family-run firm stocking marbled paper, leather desk accessories and greetings cards.

Il Papiro

Via Cavour 49r, San Marco (055 215262, www.ilpapirofirenze.it). **Open** 9am-7.30pm Mon-Sat; 10am-6pm Sun. **Map** p335 A4.
A chain of olde-worlde shops with bright paper desk accessories, photo frames, playing cards and more. **Other locations** throughout the city.

Il Torchio

Via de' Bardi 17, Oltrarno (055 2342862, www. legatoriailtorchio.com). **Open** 9.30am-1.30pm, 2.30-7pm Mon-Fri; 9.30am-1.30pm Sat. **Map** p335 D4.
Watch bookbinding in action, and stock up on handmade paper boxes, stationery and albums.

General

La Bottega dell'Olio

Piazza del Limbo 2r, Duomo & Around (055 2670468). **Open** *Mar-Sept* 10am-7pm Mon-Sat. Closed 2wks Jan. *Oct-Feb* 3-7pm Mon; 10am-1pm, 2-7pm Tue-Sat. **Map** p334 C3.
La Bottega dell'Olio stocks all things olive oil, from soaps and delicacies to olive-wood breadboards and pestles and mortars.

Carte Etc

Via de' Cerchi 13r, Duomo & Around (055 268302, www.carteetc.it). **Open** 10am-7.30pm daily. **Map** p335 B4.
Exquisite glass and stationery, unusual postcards of Florence and handmade greetings cards.

Cartoleria Ecologica La Tartaruga

Borgo degli Albizi 60r, Santa Croce (055 2340845). **Open** 1.30-7.30pm Mon; 9.30am-7.30pm Tue-Sat. **Map** p335 B5.
Unusual stationery, toys and gifts made of recycled paper, wood and papier mâché.

Giuseppe Veneziano

Via de' Fossi 53r, Santa Maria Novella (055 287925). **Open** 3-7pm Mon; 9am-1pm, 3-7pm Tue-Sat. Closed Aug. **Map** p334 B2.
Giuseppe Veneziano is a friendly, upmarket place to find Venetian glass jewellery, bottle-stoppers and plates, funky printed crockery, flower-embroidered cushions and tablecloths and a quirky Barbapapa range of gifts.

THE BEST SOUVENIRS

For chocolate Duomos
Dolceforte. *See p166.*

For hand-painted plates
La Botteghina del Ceramista. *See p171.*

For gold-leaf, frankincense and myrrh
Bizzarri. *See p169.*

Lungarno Details

Lungarno degli Acciaiuoli 2P-4D, Duomo & Around (055 27264095, www.lungarno hotels.com). **Open** 10.30am-1.30pm, 3.30-7.30pm Mon-Fri; 10.30am-1.30pm Sat. **Map** p335 A4.
So many guests of the Lungarno Suites above asked where they could find items from their hotel apartments that this shop was opened below. On sale are furniture, framed photos, lighting, food gifts and beautifully packaged candles and toiletries by Sicilian company Ortigia.

Mandragora ArtStore

Piazza del Duomo 50r, Duomo & Around (055 292559, www.mandragora.it). **Open** 2.30-7.30pm Mon; 11am-1.30pm, 2.30-7.30pm Tue-Sat. **Map** p335 B4.
Decent reproductions by local artists of famous Florentine works of art, on furnishings, scarves, bags and ornaments, plus great books, cards and prints.

Moleria Locchi

Via Burchiello 10, Outside the City Gates (055 2298371, www.locchi.com). **Open** 9am-1pm, 3-6.30pm Mon-Fri.
It's worth the trek to visit this unique old-fashioned glass and lead crystal workshop. Moleria Locchi offers a restoration service and creates bespoke replacements for glass objects such as chandeliers. *Photo p171.*

Sandra Dori

Via de' Macci 103r, Santa Croce (348 3574726 mobile, www.sandradori.com). **Open** 10am-2pm, 3.30-7.30pm Mon-Sat. **Map** p335 C6.
Sandra Dori is mostly in the business of unusual lamps and candelabra, but her shop, next door to Teatro del Sale, intersperses her unusual designs with sweet paintings, handmade chunky plastic and fabric jewellery, fans and all manner of oddities. It's a pleasure to browse.

Signum

Borgo de' Greci 40r, Santa Croce (055 280621, www.signumfirenze.it). **Open** 9am-7.30pm Mon-Sat; 10am-7pm Sun. **Map** p335 C4.
This delightful shop, housed in an ancient wine cellar, stocks an appealingly wide range of gifts, among

them miniature models of shop windows and bookcases, and Murano glass inkwells and pens.
Other locations Lungarno degli Archibusieri 14r, Duomo & Around (055 289393); via de' Benci 29r, Santa Croce (055 244590).

Teatro del Sale

For listings, see p135.

Fabio Picchi's empire of Cibrèo eateries (*see p133*), clustered around piazza Sant'Ambrogio, took a step in a retail direction with Teatro del Sale (*see p135*), which not only offers imaginative dinner theatre evenings but also includes a huge foyer filled with lovely things for sale; lots of gorgeous Tuscan foodstuffs, as you'd expect, but also plenty of little personal gifts in the form of toiletries, candles and quirky homeware.

Stationery & art supplies

Le Dune

Piazza Ottaviani 9r, Santa Maria Novella (055 214377). **Open** 9am-7pm Mon-Fri; 9am-1pm Sat. Closed 2wks Aug. **Map** p334 B2.

A small stationery and gift shop with a good choice of greetings cards. The shop also offers photocopying, photo developing and faxing services.

Pineider

Piazza della Signoria 13r, Duomo & Around (055 284655, www.pineider.com). **Open** 10am-7pm daily. **Map** p335 C4.

Pineider is famous for its high-quality writing paper and accessories and top-notch office leather goods.

Romeo 1931

Via della Condotta 43r, Duomo & Around (055 210350). **Open** 10am-7.30pm Mon-Sat. **Map** p335 C4.

The interior of this lovely stationery shop is filled to the ceiling with Spalding's full range, Aurora pens and Giorgio Fedon's smart coloured leather bags.

Zecchi

Via dello Studio 19r, Duomo & Around (055 211470, www.zecchi.it). **Open** Sept-June 8.30am-12.30pm, 3.30-7.30pm Mon-Fri; 8.30am-12.30pm Sat. *July* 8.30am-12.30pm, 3.30-7.30pm Mon-Fri. Closed Aug. **Map** p335 B4.

The best shop in town for art supplies, with everything from pencils to gold leaf.

HEALTH & BEAUTY

Herbs and perfumes

Bizzarri

Via della Condotta 32r, Duomo & Around (055 211580, www.bizzarri-fi.biz). **Open** 9.30am-1pm, 4-7.30pm Mon-Fri; 9.30am-1pm Sat. Closed Aug. **Map** p335 C4.

Alessandro Bizzarri opened his first apothecary in piazza della Signoria back in 1842, but in the 20th century moved his business to this cornucopia-like premises, which still sells everything you'd expect an apothecary to sell; herbs and spices, plant extracts, tinctures, natural dyes and even pipettes and glassware for making your own fragrances.

De Herbore

Via del Proconsolo 43r, Duomo & Around (055 211706, www.deherbore.com). **Open** 9am-7.30pm Mon-Fri; 10am-7.30pm Sat. **Map** p335 C4.

This old herbal shop and perfumery is filled with all kinds of lovely skincare, smelly things and even a little organic food section. The soap range alone is enormous, with everything from delicate little packets of soap paper to gaily packaged doorstop floral bars.

Erboristeria Inglese

Via de' Tornabuoni 19, Duomo & Around (055 210628, www.officinadetornabuoni.it). **Open** 3.30-8pm Mon; 10am-8pm Tue-Sat. Closed 2wks Aug. **Map** p334 B2.

From a 15th-century *palazzo*, the very knowledgeable Donatella sells handmade gifts, perfumes and candles from Diptyque, herbal remedies and Dr Hauschka toiletries and cosmetics. She can also recommend alternative medicine practitioners. There's no main shop window so look for the raised entrance set off the street.

Farmacia del Cinghiale

Piazza del Mercato Nuovo 4r, Duomo & Around (055 212128, www.farmaciadelcinghiale.it). **Open** 9am-1pm, 3.30-7.30pm Mon-Fri; Sat according to rota. **Map** p334 C3.

Named after the famous wild boar statue in the square opposite, Cinghiale was founded in the 18th century by the herbalist Guadagni, and still makes its own herbal remedies and cosmetics.

Münstermann

Piazza Goldoni 2r, Santa Maria Novella (055 210660, www.munstermann.it). **Open** 9am-1pm, 4-8pm Mon-Fri. **Map** p334 B1.

This charming shell-shaped corner icon was opened in 1897, a stone's throw from the ponte Vecchio, and still has its original shop fittings. It stocks pharmaceutical and herbal medicines, toiletries, silver pillboxes, hair accessories and bathroom oddities. Its own-brand products (body lotions, hand creams, fragrances) use high-quality, natural ingredients.

Officina Profumo-Farmaceutica di Santa Maria Novella

Via della Scala 16, Santa Maria Novella (055 216276, www.smnovella.it). **Open** 9.30am-7.30pm daily. *Museum* 10.30am-7pm daily. **Map** p334 B2.

See p173 **Profile** *and p170* **Natural Selections**.

CONSUME

Profumeria Aline

Via de' Calzaiuoli 53, Duomo & Around (055 219073, www.profumeriaaline.com). **Open** 3.30-7.30pm Mon; 9am-7.30pm Tue-Sat. **Map** p335 B4.
A well-stocked perfumery and cosmetics shop, set in a prime location. There's also a beauty centre in an annex to the store.
Other locations Via Vaccereccia 11r, Duomo & Around (055 294976); piazza San Giovanni 26-27, Duomo & Around (055 212864).

Spezierie-Erboristerie Palazzo Vecchio

Via Vaccereccia 9r, Duomo & Around (055 2396055, www.spezieriefirenze.com, www. spezieriepalazzovecchio.it). **Open** 9.30am-7.30pm Mon-Sat. **Map** p334 C3.
A beautiful frescoed interior selling herbal products made to centuries-old recipes, and, supposedly, original Florentine perfumes commissioned by the Medici family. Whatever, when they smell this divine, we don't mind who commissioned them.

Hairdressers & barbers

All hairdressers and barbers in Florence are closed on Mondays.

Gabrio Staff Olimpo

Via de' Tornabuoni 5, Santa Maria Novella (055 214668, www.gabriostaff.it). **Open** 1-8pm Mon; 9am-8pm Tue-Sat. Closed 2wks Aug. **Map** p334 C2.
This unisex hair and beauty centre is set in an amazing atelier. Staff dish out buffet snacks to clients at lunchtime. Cuts cost from €60.

Jean Louis David

Lungarno Corsini 52r, Santa Maria Novella (055 216760, www.jldfirenze.it). **Open** 10am-7pm Mon-Sat. Closed 2wks Aug. **Map** p334 C2.
A women's wash and cut at Jean Louis David is €35; men are also welcome, and there's a student discount of 20%. If you're feeling brave and adventurous, call ahead to book a free haircut in the salon's school.

Natural Selections

An ancient devotion to lotions and potions.

Step inside many of Florence's beautiful old perfumeries (*see p169*) and you're stepping back in time; as far back as the 11th century, when Benedictine monks began making alcoholic elixirs, and peaking 500 years later, when Caterina de' Medici employed infamous 'perfumer' and herbalist Rene the Florentine as her court doctor in Paris, the city has been renowned for its knowledge of the therapeutic qualities of herbs. Its fields of lavender and herbs have helped Tuscany maintain its reputation as a centre for alternative remedies, and many locals call at an *erboristeria* rather than a chemist for most minor ailments.

Some of these stores are joys to behold even if you're not shopping, though their products double as gorgeous gifts. The Erboristeria Inglese (*see p169*), set in a frescoed 15th-century *palazzo*, sells handmade gifts, perfumes and candles from Diptyque, plus herbal remedies and goods from famed natural skincare line Dr Hauschka. The Spezieria Erboristeria Palazzo Vecchio (*see above*), a stone's throw from the piazza della Signoria's towering landmark, is an old-fashioned and quite charming frescoed apothecary that specialises in handmade perfumes and floral eaux de toilette with such evocative names as Acqua di Caterina de' Medici.

The Officina Profumo-Farmaceutica di Santa Maria Novella (*see p173* **Profile**),

the most famous of the Florentine herbalists' shops, has such power that it hushes visitors into reverent silence as they walk through its doors. Two other notable shops are Elisir (Borgo degli Albizi 70r, Santa Croce, 055 2638218, closed most Sun), a charming shop with creams, lotions and remedies all made from natural ingredients, and Bizzarri (*see p169*), a relic that has shelves of bell jars filled with substances in every conceivable colour. Its herbal concoctions are made to secret, generations-old recipes.

Homeopathy can be sold only in chemists' shops, but some Florentine chemists stock more herbal remedies than pharmaceutical concoctions. Farmacia Franchi (via de' Ginori 65r, San Lorenzo, 055 210565, closed Sun & some Sat) is housed in a stunning vaulted and frescoed room, while Farmacia del Cinghiale (*see p169*), named after the famous wild boar statue in the square opposite, was founded in the 1700s by the herbalist Guadagni and still makes its own herbal remedies and cosmetics. A newcomer by comparison, the charming Münstermann pharmacy (*see p169*) was opened in 1897 and still has its original shop fittings. As well as stocking pharmaceutical and herbal medicines, the mahogany cabinets are filled with unusual hair accessories, jewellery and toiletries.

CONSUME

Opticians

Camera and optical lenses go hand in hand in Italy: photography shops (*see p155*) sell glasses and opticians sell basic photo equipment.

Pisacchi
Via della Condotta 22-24r, Duomo & Around (055 214542, www.visionotticapisacchi.it). **Open** *July-Aug* 10am-2pm, 3.30-7.30pm Mon-Fri, Sun; 10am-2pm Sat. *Sept-June* 3.30-7.30pm Mon; 10am-2pm, 3.30-7.30pm Tue-Sun. Closed 2wks Aug. **Map** p335 C4.

Pharmacies

See also left **Natural Selections**.

Farmacia all'Insegna del Moro
Piazza San Giovanni 20r, Duomo & Around (055 211343, www.farmaciadelmoro.com). **Open** 24hrs daily. **Map** p334 B3.

Farmacia Comunale No.13
Santa Maria Novella train station, Santa Maria Novella (055 216761/289435). **Open** 24hrs daily. **Map** p334 A2.

Farmacia Molteni
Via de' Calzaiuoli 7r, Duomo & Around (055 215472/289490, www.farmacia-molteni.com). **Open** 24hrs daily. **Map** p334 C3.

Spas & salons

Freni
Via Calimala 1, Duomo & Around (055 2396647). **Open** 1-7.30pm Mon; 9am-7.30pm Tue-Fri; 9am-1pm Sat. **Map** p334 A3.
If your feet give out after tramping around all those museums, come here to revive them with a pedicure. Facials, manicures and massages are also offered.

Hito Estetica
Via de' Ginori 21, San Lorenzo (055 284424, www.centroesteticofirenze.eu). **Open** 9am-7.30pm Mon-Fri; 9am-7pm Sat. **Map** p335 A4.
A range of natural treatments and pampering for men and women, including Ayurvedic techniques. Prices start at around €40 for a facial.

International Studio
Via Porta Rossa 82r, Duomo & Around (055 293393, www.internationalstudio.com). **Open** 1-8pm Mon; 10am-8pm Tue-Sat. **Map** p334 C3.
A solarium, hair and beauty centre, box office and showcase for objets d'art, all rolled into one.

Soul Space
Via Sant'Egidio 12, Santa Croce (www.soulspace.it). **Open** 10am-8pm Mon-Sat. **Map** p334 C3.

Moleria Locchi. *See p168.*

A luxurious new spa with pool, garden, real hammam, relaxation room with a fireplace, and a range of spa treatments including hot stone therapies.

Wave
Via Santo Spirito 27, Oltrarno (055 2654650, www.waveitalia.net). **Open** 9am-7pm Mon-Fri; 9am-6pm Sat. **Map** p334 C1.
A swanky new hair and beauty centre, with Ayurvedic and other speciality treatments.

HOUSE & HOME

For antiques, head to via Maggio, via de' Serragli and via de' Fossi.

Ceramics & glass

La Bottega dei Cristalli
Via de' Benci 51r, Santa Croce (055 2344891, www.labottegadeicristalli.com). **Open** 10am-7.30pm daily. Closed mid Jan-mid Feb. **Map** p335 C5.
A lovely range of Murano and Tuscan-made glass plates, picture frames, lamps and chandeliers, and tiny glass 'sweets' and bottles.

La Botteghina del Ceramista
Via Guelfa 5r, San Lorenzo (055 287367, www.labotteghinadelceramista.it). **Open** 10am-1.30pm, 3.30-7.30pm Mon-Fri; 10am-1.30pm Sat. Closed 2wks Aug. **Map** p335 A4.
Superb hand-painted ceramics in intricate designs and vivid colours.

Sbigoli Terrecotte
Via Sant'Egidio 4r, Santa Croce (055 2479713, www.sbigoliterrecotte.it). **Open** 9am-1pm, 3-7.30pm Mon-Sat. **Map** p335 B5.
Handmade Tuscan ceramics and terracotta in traditional designs are the order of the day here.

Florists

Al Portico
Piazza San Firenze 1, Duomo & Around (055 213716, www.semialportico.it). **Open** 8.30am-7.30pm Mon-Sat; 10am-1pm Sun. **Map** p335 C5.
An extraordinary shop in the Renaissance courtyard of a magnificent *palazzo*, with trees, fountains, huge plants and flowers. The owner is happy to show customers round, even if they don't want to buy.
Other locations Piazza della Signoria 37r, Duomo & Around (055 2608658).

Il Fiorile di Ceni Sandra
Via Santo Spirito 26r, Oltrarno (055 2049032, www.fiorile.it). **Open** 9.30am-1.30pm, 3.30-7.30pm Tue-Sat. Closed Aug. **Map** p334 C2.
Italians tend to hold to the big is better school of floral arranging, but at Il Fiorile staff have a great eye and can make you up anything from a delicated posy to, yes, a very large bouquet.

La Rosa Canina
Via dell'Erta Canina 1r, Outside the City Gates (055 2342449, www.larosacaninafioristi.it). Bus 23. **Open** 9.30am-1.30pm, 4.30-9.30pm Tue-Sat; 9.30am-1.30pm Sun.
On a stroll up to piazzale Michelangelo, take time to admire the lovely displays of plants and flowers.

General

Arte sì di Paola Capecchi
Via de' Fossi 23r, Santa Maria Novella (055 264 5504). **Open** 3.30-7.30pm Mon; 10am-1pm, 3.30-7.30pm Tue-Sat. Closed 3wks Aug. **Map** p334 B2.
More gallery than shop, this mezzanine space is dotted with outlandish design objets and furniture: think silver and frosted pink leather dining chairs, or a papier mâché throne. Capecchi herself is an interior designer so opening hours can be erratic.

Bartolini
Via de' Servi 30r, San Marco (055 211895, www.dinobartolini.it). **Open** 3.30-7.30pm Mon; 10am-1pm, 3.30-7.30pm Tue-Sat. Closed 2wks Aug. **Map** p335 A4.
This charming kitchen shop has extensive selections of cutlery and crockery, plus accessories.

Frette
Via Cavour 2r, San Marco (055 211369, www.frette.com). **Open** 3-7pm Mon; 10am-7pm Tue-Sat. Closed 3wks Aug. **Map** p335 A4.
The full range of bedding, towels and robes so beloved of boutique hotels the world over.

Lisa Corti Home Textiles Emporium
Piazza Ghiberti 33r, Santa Croce (055 2001860, www.lisacorti.com). **Open** 9am-7pm Mon-Sat. **Map** p335 C6.

Brightly coloured cushions, bedspreads, quilts and curtains, in silks and cottons and with an oriental feel. Designer Lisa Corti has also created a small range of furniture and pottery.

Passamaneria Toscana
Piazza San Lorenzo 12r, San Lorenzo (055 214670, www.passamaneriatoscana.com). **Open** 9.30am-7.30pm Mon-Sat; 10am-7.30pm Sun. **Map** p334 B2.
This shop sells all kinds of soft furnishings: everything from rich brocade cushions to embroidered Florentine crests, wall hangings and tassels.

Repairs

Ferramenta Masini
Via del Sole 19-21r, 18-20r, Santa Maria Novella (055 212560). **Open** 9am-1pm, 3.30-7.30pm Mon-Fri; 9am-1pm Sat. **Map** p334 B2.
Two friendly shops, under the same management, with plugs and adaptors, hardware, a key-cutting service and door and lock repairs.
Other locations Via San Gallo 60, San Lorenzo (055 480827).

Specialist

Arredamenti Castorina
Via Santo Spirito 13-15r, Oltrarno (055 212885, www.castorina.net). **Open** 9am-1pm, 3.30-7.30pm Mon-Fri; 9am-1pm Sat. Closed Aug. **Map** p334 C1.
An extraordinary old shop in Oltrarno, full of all things baroque, including gilded mouldings, frames, cherubs, trompe l'œil tables and fake malachite and tortoiseshell obelisks.

Borgo degli Albizi 48 Rosso
Borgo degli Albizi 48r, Santa Croce (055 2347598, www.borgoalbizi.it). **Open** 3.30-7.30pm Mon; 10am-1pm, 3.30-7.30pm Tue-Sat. **Map** p335 B5.
Opulent chandeliers and glass pear-drop lamps made with antique or new crystals. You can also order items to your own design.

Casa della Cornice
Via Sant'Egidio 26r, Santa Croce (055 2480222, www.casadellacornice.com). **Open** 9am-1pm, 3-7.30pm Mon-Fri; 9.30am-1pm Sat. **No credit cards**. **Map** p335 B5.
A huge catalogue of traditional and contemporary picture frames in silver and gold leaf.

MUSIC & ENTERTAINMENT
CDs, DVDs & records

Alberti
Borgo San Lorenzo 41r-47r, San Lorenzo (055 294271, www.albertinuova.it). **Open** 3.30-7.30pm Mon; 9am-7.30pm Tue-Sat. **Map** p334 B3.

Profile Officina Profumo-Farmaceutica di Santa Maria Novella

A beautiful 13th-century frescoed chapel in Santa Maria Novella is home to one of the world's oldest herbal pharmacies – now a global brand. The Officina Profumo-Farmaceutica di Santa Maria Novella (*see p169*) was officially founded in 1612 by Fra' Angiolo Marchissi, though its origins date back as far as 1221, to the time of the Dominican friars. As you reach the entrance, the scent of the *antica farmacia*'s potpourri fills the air, a mix of locally grown flowers and herbs, macerated in terracotta jars. A domed marble passageway leads to the main hall, which was turned into the shop in 1848. It's lined with mahogany and glass cabinets, and filled with the pharmacy's signature soaps (reputed to be the best in the world), delicate glass bottles of pure oils and perfume essences, and scented paper. Through a gilded archway is the apothecary, a grand antechamber decorated with Medici portraits, where herbal concoctions are still weighed up on brass scales. A back room dotted with ancient apothecary tools is where jams, sweets and soaps are packaged in lovely cream vellum boxes. The pharmacy's serenity and beauty are in stark contrast to the bloodthirsty nature of some of its past patrons. The pharmacy must have its roots in the gentler side of Florence's torture-loving Dominican monks. Perfumes – including the original Eau de Cologne – were also created here for the notorious Caterina de' Medici. And more recently, the olfactory powers of Thomas Harris's Hannibal the cannibal led him to the Officina Profumo-Farmaceutica when it came to choosing a scent for his paramour. But it's the contemporary boom for luxury natural products that has transformed the *farmacia* from local icon into internationally coveted brand with branches in London, New York and Tokyo. The original lavender-smelling salts, 'anti-hysteria' Acqua di Santa Maria Novella, 14th-century Acqua di Rose and powder produced from the ground rhizomes of irises are practically unchanged formulas. Other renowned items include orange-blossom water and pomegranate perfume. However, with globalisation comes the march of modernity: you can now find parabens in the rose cream and tan-prolonging shower gel alongside the medieval ladies' fave: skin-whitening powder.

The oldest record shop in the city has a vast repertoire of pop, dance, jazz and indie CD recordings, some vinyl, a variety of DVDs and a great selection of portable DVD and CD players.
Other locations Via de' Pucci 16r, San Marco (055 284346).

Data Records

Via de' Neri 15r, Santa Croce (055 287592, www.superecords.com). **Open** 10am-1pm, 3.30-7.30pm Mon-Sat. Closed 2wks Aug.
Map p335 C4.
Staff here are true music buffs with a local reputation for being able to find the unfindable. Home to over 80,000 titles, new and used, with an emphasis on psychedelia, blues, R&B, jazz and soundtracks.

Marquee Moon

Piazza Santa Maria Maggiore 7r, Duomo & Around (055 211230/2645715, www.marquee moon.it). **Open** 11am-1pm, 2.30-8pm Mon-Fri; 10am-1pm, 2.30-8pm Sat. Closed 2wks Aug.
Map p334 B3.
This old-school vinyl store is a lovely place to browse for that elusive grey vinyl Devo 12in, especially as the staff are helpful and the interior a delightful one filled with old index card cupboards and racks that look like they're on their last legs.

Ricordi

Via Brunelleschi 8r, Duomo & Around (055 214104). **Open** 9.30am-7.30pm Mon-Fri & last Sun of mth except July/Aug. **Map** p334 B3.
Ricordi has the best choice of DVDs and CDs in town, with original-language films and classical, jazz, rock and dance sections. Ricordi also sells instruments, sheet music and scores.

Twisted

Borgo San Frediano 21r, Oltrarno (055 282011). **Open** 9am-1pm, 3-7.30pm Mon-Sat.
A specialist jazz centre with rare recordings and more mainstream sounds. The stocked artists span 1950s trad jazz right through to acid and nu jazz.

Video & DVD rental

Blockbuster

Viale Belfiore 6a, Outside the City Gates (055 330542, www.blockbuster.it). Bus 17. **Open** 11am-11pm Mon-Thur, Sun; 11am-midnight Fri, Sat.
Stocks some mainstream films in English.
Other locations Via di Novoli 9-11, Outside the City Gates (055 333533).

Punto Video

Via San Antonino 7r, San Lorenzo (055 2398485, www.sigrafilm.com). **Open** 9am-1pm, 4-8pm Mon-Sat. **Map** p334 A2.
Punto has over 500 titles in English.

CONSUME

SPORTS & FITNESS

See also pp207-212.

Il Rifugio Sport

Piazza Ottaviani 3r, Santa Maria Novella (055 294736, www.rifugiosport.it). **Open** 9.30am-7.30pm Mon-Sat. **Map** p334 B2.
Sporting equipment and accessories, as well as trainers and clothing. Staff are friendly and helpful.
Other locations Piazza della Stazione 1, Santa Maria Novella (055 289328).

Universo Sport

Piazza del Duomo 6-8r, Duomo & Around (055 284412, www.universosport.it). **Open** 10am-7.30pm Mon-Sat; 11.30am-1.30pm, 3-7.30pm Sun. **Map** p335 B4.
Very central sports equipment shop, with specialist and designer sports clothing.

TICKET AGENCIES

When booking tickets for events by phone, ensure that all the arrangements for collection or delivery are clearly specified.

Box Office

Via delle Vecchie Carceri 1, Santa Croce (055 210804, www.boxol.it). **Open** 9.30am-7pm Mon-Fri; 9.30am-2pm Sat. **Map** p334 C6.
Box Office sells tickets for concerts, plays and exhibitions in Italy and abroad.

TRAVELLERS' NEEDS

For luggage, *see p162*; for phone rental, computer repairs, banks and shipping services, *see pp307-316*.

Travel agents

Biemme

Via delle Belle Donne, Santa Maria Novella (055 294329, www.biemmeviaggi.it). **Open** 2.30-6.30pm Mon-Sat. **Map** p334 B2.
The staff here are experts at finding the best deals for holidays and flights, train and boat tickets.

La Travelleria di CTS

Borgo La Croce 42r, Santa Croce (055 289570, www.cts.it). **Open** 9.30am-1pm, 2.30-6pm Mon-Sat. **Map** p335 B6.
The official student travel centre offers discounted air, coach and train tickets, some to under-25s only, some to students only and some for all. Obligatory membership is €10 for students and €11 for non-students. With the main office outside the city, this smaller central office is most convenient.
Other locations Via Maragliano 86i, Outside the City Gates (055 334164).

Arts & Entertainment

Teatro del Maggio Musicale Fiorentino. *See p196.*

Calendar

Tuscany's heritage and history are celebrated year-round.

Feast on Tuscany's art treasures, soothing landscape and culinary delights all you want, but for an insight into the finer textures of this charming land and its indomitable people, you really ought to time your visit to experience at least one of the many local festivals. Far from the skin-deep theatricality you might expect, events such as Siena's **Palio** (*see p179*) speak volumes about Tuscan character, and the subtle balance between religious and civic powers past and present. The Tuscans' wry and bold sense of humour also surfaces: take the subjects of the

floats in the **Viareggio Carnival** (*see p181*), for example, which often feature caricatures of politicians and celebrities. On the other hand, any country *sagra* (food festival) will demonstrate how life here is still geared towards the countryside and the natural rhythm of the seasons.

For **music** festivals, *see p197 and p200*; for **film**, *see p187*; for **theatre and dance**, *see p215*.

SPRING

Festa della Donna
Date 8 Mar.
For International Women's Day, women are traditionally presented with yellow mimosa flowers. In the evening, restaurants and clubs get packed with girlie gangs set on having a wild night out.

Holy Week
Date wk leading up to Easter.
Many Tuscan towns celebrate Holy Week with religious processions, often in period costume. The most impressive of them involves almost 600 performers and takes place in the evening of Good Friday at Grassina by Bagno a Ripoli, just outside Florence (055 646051, www.rievstoricagrassina.it).

Scoppio del Carro
Piazzale della Porta al Prato to piazza del Duomo, Florence. **Date** Easter Sun.
At 9.30am on Easter morning, a parade of costumed musicians, flag-throwers and dignitaries escort a wooden cart, laden with fireworks and pulled by four white oxen, from via il Prato (watch for the three-storey wooden doors on the left of the Hotel Villa Medici) to a jam-packed piazza del Duomo. Meanwhile, another parade departs from the church

of Santissimi Apostoli (*see p68*) with a holy fire kindled with the flints from the Holy Sepulchre. At 11am, during mass, a dove-shaped rocket shoots along a wire from the high altar to the *carro* outside, starting the fireworks. If all goes smoothly, it's said that the year's harvest will be good.

Mostra Mercato di Piante e Fiori
Giardino dell'Orticoltura, via Vittorio Emanuele 4, Outside the City Gates, Florence (055 2625385). Bus 4. **Date** late Apr/early May, early Oct.
Growers from all over Tuscany proudly exhibit and sell their plants and blooms at these spectacular horticultural shows, which are laid out around a grand 19th-century glasshouse.

★ Maggio Musicale Fiorentino
Teatro del Maggio Musicale Fiorentino, corso Italia 16, Santa Maria Novella, Florence (055 213535, www.maggiofiorentino.com). **Date** late Apr-early July.
Founded in 1933, Florence's 'Musical May' is universally acclaimed as one of the best festivals in Italy for opera, concerts and dance performances. It closes with two free jamborees (one ballet, one music) in piazza della Signoria.

Settimana dei Beni Culturali
Throughout Italy (055 290832). **Date** 1wk in Apr/May.
'Culture Week' means free admission to state museums and archaeological sites, including the Uffizi,

Scoppio del Carro.

Bargello, Accademia and Palatina galleries in Florence, as well as special events (concerts, talks, guided visits and exhibitions). Queues are less daunting than one might expect, possibly because dates keep shifting every year and few manage to time their visit accordingly.

Artigianato e Palazzo
Palazzo Corsini sul Prato, via della Scala 115, Florence (055 2654589, www.artigianatoe palazzo.it). **Date** wknd in mid May.
Master artisans demonstrate their skills and sell their wares at this upmarket craft show in one of Tuscany's finest Italianate gardens.

Festa del Grillo
Parco delle Cascine, Outside the City Gates, Florence. Bus 17C. **Date** 6th Sun after Easter.
On the feast of Ascension, Florentine families used to come to the Cascine park for a picnic, and part of the fun was chasing (or buying) crickets and taking them home in brightly painted little cages. Live crickets have been replaced by chirping mechanical devices, and this traditional event now has the feel of a general meeting.

Amico Museo
Throughout Tuscany (www.regione.toscana.it/ amicomuseo). **Date** 3wks in May.
Special and late openings and events to familiarise the crowds with the region's lesser-known and local museums. Pick up a brochure from any tourist office.

Genio Fiorentino
Florence & around (055 2760061, www.geniofiorentino.it). **Date** 2wks in May.

An eclectic programme of arts and music events celebrating Florence's cultural heritage. Events explore the elusive Florentine mentality, which over the centuries has fostered an endless string of 'geniuses' in science, poetry, exploration, art and politics.

Mille Miglia
Across Tuscany (030 280036, www.millemiglia.it). **Date** Sat in late May.
Almost 400 vintage cars take part in this three-day, 1,600km (1,000-mile) race. The teams wind along the Cassia road for the length of Tuscany, on their way back from Rome to Brescia, passing through Siena and entering Florence (through Porta Romana, en route to piazza della Signoria). Then it's onwards to Bologna via the Mugello. *Photo p178.*

Cantine Aperte
Throughout Italy (0577 738312, www.movimento-turismovino.it). **Date** last Sun in May.
Wine-producing estates, many of which would not normally be open to the public, show their cellars to visitors and hold tastings.

INSIDE TRACK CAFÉ CULTURE

Few festivals in Florence and Tuscany are widely publicised, so keep an eye out for posters and flyers in cafés and bars, and ask local tourist boards for information about their region's events. Although many of the websites listed here are in Italian only, photos, maps, dates and prices (where applicable) should prove helpful.

Mille Miglia. *See p177.*

SUMMER

Around the end of May, Tuscany's open-air venues emerge from hibernation. In Florence, outdoor cinemas screen movies (*see p187*), open-air bars double as music venues (*see p201*) and many clubs move dancefloors under the stars. Cloisters and squares host classical concerts, as locals take to the city's squares and gardens.

Estate Fiesolana

Fiesole (800 414240, www.estatefiesolana.it). Bus 7. **Date** mid June-early Sept.
An assorted mix of performing arts shows in scenic settings like the Roman theatre and the Maiano stone quarries. The Vivere Jazz Festival stands out for the quality of its guests. Related events are held in the town's churches and museums.

★ Estate Fiorentina

www.firenzestate.it, www.comune.fi.it.
Held in July and August, this festival is a feast of arts and cultural events, held predominantly at three terrific locations: the newly restored Ampitheatre at Le Cascine, the city's new contemporary space at Le Murate, and the Biblioteca delle Oblate. But piazza Strozzi, the courtyard of the Bargello museum, and piazza Santo Spirito have all hosted events in the past, sometimes with an element of surprise, such as a Flash Football tournament in a piazza. Concerts are mostly held at the Cascine and an outdoor cinema season at Le Murate (with headphones). Possibly because many natives leave the city in summer, the festival caters well for non-Italian speakers, with films and live events often in English or not requiring language; past events have included a projection of the 1911 silent film of Dante's *Inferno* set to live electronic and ambient soundtrack, and University of Texas drama students performing bilingual theatre. There are events for little ones as well, such as sandcastle competitions on Lungarno beach.

Giugno Pisano

Pisa (050 910393). **Date** 16, 17 & last Sun in June.
On 16 June, eve of the feast of Pisa's patron saint, 70,000 candles are lit on the façades of the palaces along the Arno for the charming Luminara di San Ranieri. The following day, at 6.30pm, the Palio di San Ranieri boat race takes place between the town's ancient quarters. To round off the 'Pisan June' events, Il Gioco del Ponte – a 16th-century 'push-of-war' (a reverse tug-of-war) – is fought on the last Sunday of the month on the ponte di Mezzo between teams from the two sides of the Arno. Processions start at 4.30pm and the competition begins two hours later. A historic regatta (Regata Storica) between the Ancient Maritime Republics of Pisa, Genoa, Venice and Amalfi also takes place in May or June every year.

Giostra del Saracino

Piazza Grande, Arezzo (0575 377462, www.giostradelsaracino.arezzo.it). **Date** penultimate Sat in June; 1st Sun in Sept.
This ancient jousting tournament was first recorded in 1535. Five centuries later, it's still plenty of fun. The procession of horses, knights and their escorts arrives in the piazza at 9.30pm in June, and at 5pm in September. Then the action begins, with four couples of riders representing the four city quarters trying to achieve the highest score by hitting a dummy of an Arab soldier (the Saracino). The days leading to the challenge are also rich in events (check the website for dates). About a week before, in a solemn ceremony, the lances and starting order are cast by lot, and the prize (the Golden Lance) is brought to the cathedral. There follow four or five nights of unofficial trial runs, followed by a pageant 'dress rehearsal' and a Giostra run by the junior jousters.

Festa Internazionale della Ceramica

Montelupo (0571 518993). **Date** 8 days in mid-late June.

The town's reputation as a prime manufacturing centre for ceramics dates from the Middle Ages. This festival celebrates the craft with exhibitions, markets, workshops and demonstrations of techniques.

★ Calcio Storico
Piazza Santa Croce, Florence (055 290832). **Map** p335 C5. **Date** June.
When the 2006 and 2007 events were cancelled due to violence, the future for Florence's rugby-football-boxing hybrid known as the *calcio storico* looked a little uncertain, but after a few refinements it's still going, pretty much as it has been since the 16th century, allowing for a couple of centuries' break when it fell out of favour. Now closer to a rugby match, it's an amazing spectacle. Two preliminary matches are normally played in early June, while the final is normally held on 24 June, a city holiday. Teams representing the city's ancient quarters (Santa Croce, Santa Maria Novella, Santo Spirito and San Giovanni) parade through the streets before settling old rivalries in a no-holds-barred 27-a-side match played by bare-chested lads in bright medieval breeches. Yes, really.

Festa di San Giovanni
Florence. **Date** 24 June.
A public holiday in Florence. A huge fireworks display takes place at 10pm from near piazzale Michelangelo to honour the city's patron saint. Best enjoyed from the *lungarni* (just follow the crowds).

★ Palio delle Contrade
Piazza del Campo, Siena (0577 280551, www.palio.comune.siena.it). **Date** 2 July & 16 Aug.
Although this bareback, breakneck race is staged primarily for the natives, it's a major attraction for visitors. The horses' safety is a controversial issue – the animals are adored but several have been fatally injured in the past – but there's little denying that this is Tuscan pageantry at its best. Trial races are run prior to the two main dates, the last at 9am on the days themselves. At 2.30pm, the horses and jockeys of the ten participating *contrade* (out of 17) are blessed in their neighbourhood's church. At 5pm the procession enters the piazza del Campo, and after some elaborate flag-throwing and maybe a couple of false starts, the race – three laps of the square – gets going around 7pm and is all over in 90 seconds. It's free to stand, but get there by 4pm and take a sun hat. Tickets for balconies overlooking the piazza are sold in the bars and cafés, but they're hard to come by and expensive. *See also p250* **Horsing Around**.

On the Road Festival
Pelago (055 8327301). **Date** early July.
A four-day (Thur-Sun) competitive showcase of street performers and buskers in a pretty country village. The action starts at 6pm.

Medieval Festival
Monteriggioni (0577 304810, www.monteriggioni medievale.com). **Date** 2 wknds in mid July.
This re-enactment, in period dress, of medieval town life and warfare features food, drink and craft stalls, plus music, dancing and other performances. A different theme is chosen each year.

Giostra dell'Orso
Pistoia (0573 21622, www.giostradellorso.it). **Date** 25 July.
Pistoia's annual festival culminates in the city's cathedral square at 9.30pm on St James's feast day after a month of concerts, markets and pageantry. The joust sees 12 riders, three for each city quarter,

Calcio Storico.

ARTS & ENTERTAINMENT

Join the Literati

There's culture in them there hills.

If the stifling heat of downtown Florence gets too much for you, head for the hills. Specifically, the hills of Fiesole, where the 15th-century **Villa il Palmerino** (via del Palmerino 12, 339 8944725, www. palmerino.it) offers not just a respite from town but an interesting cultural experience. For it's here that you'll find the Associazone Culturale il Palmerino, founded by Federica Paretti, who is continuing a centuries-old tradition of cultural activities at the villa.

One of Il Palmerino's most illustrious owners was British author Vernon Lee (pseudonym: Violet Piaget). In the 46 years she resided here, she held court with such cultural and intellectual luminaries as Bernard Berenson, Edith Wharton, Oscar Wilde, Aldous Huxley and Henry James. Lee was considered a great interpreter of Italian art and culture, and Il Palmerino thrived as a literary salon.

After Lee's death in 1935, English painter and writer Carola Costa and her husband, the Florentine artist Federigo Angeli, bought the villa, and it's their grandchildren who now run the cultural activities. Key to these is an Artists in Residence scheme under which a small group of artists is invited by a curator/administrator to collaborate on projects and initiatives, culminating in an exhibition, open to the public, and to programme artist seminars and events. They're intimate, fascinating events – and ones that really will help you to feel the spirit of artistic Tuscany.

In addition to its lectures, concerts and cultural programmes, the association offers (for a fee) afternoon visits to the property and its exquisite English gardens, during which a professional actress reads from Vernon Lee's books. Lunch or dinner is an option – both will include vegetables and wines from the villa's organic kitchen garden and vineyard. Fittingly, the recipes for the meals are from historian and Tuscan cookbook-writer Janet Ross, who was herself a frequent visitor to Il Palmerino.

Jane Fortune is a Florence-based arts writer and the author of To Florence Con Amore: 90 Ways to Love the City *and* Invisible Women, *both published by the Florentine Press (www.theflorentinepress.com).*

---

gallop in pairs and attempt to spear with a lance two 'bears' (wooden dummies in checked cloaks).

Effetto Venezia

Livorno (0586 204611, www.comune.livorno.it).
Date early Aug.
A ten-day run of shows and concerts in Livorno's 'Venetian quarter', so called because of its canals. Restaurants and street stalls stay open late serving *cacciucco* (spicy fish stew) and other tasty morsels. Don't miss a boat tour of the Fossi Medicei.

★ Calici di stelle

Throughout Tuscany (www.movimentoturismo vino.it). **Date** 10 Aug.
About 50 Tuscan 'Città del vino' participate in this 'wine under the stars' event – held on the night of San Lorenzo – by hosting a fascinating combination of wine tastings and meteor gazing from historic *piazze* and courtyards throughout Tuscany. Details of the specific events are advertised on the website listed above from July. Music and fireworks add to the convivial atmosphere.

Tuscan Sun Festival

Cortona (0575 630353, www.tuscansunfestival. com). **Date** 8 days early Aug.

Bestselling author Frances Mayes is the co-director of this cultural festival, which launched in 2003 and attracts an international line-up. The programme features concerts by high-profile musicians, alongside art and culinary events and lectures.

Volterra AD 1398

Volterra (0588 86099, www.volterra1398.it).
Date last 2 Sun in Aug.
Life as it would have been in 1398 is painstakingly recreated throughout the old city centre of Volterra, with markets, workshops, musicians, jugglers, commoners, clergymen, soldiers and nobles. Crafts and refreshments can only be bought with *grossos* – the medieval local currency.

Bravio delle botti

Montepulciano (0578 757575, www.braviodelle botti.it). **Date** last Sun in Aug.
Champions from the eight city neighbourhoods compete in an exhausting wine barrel-rolling contest up the steep and winding route to piazza Grande. The race starts at 7pm, but colourful celebrations take place over the week leading up to the event.

La Rificolona

Florence. **Date** 7 Sept.

In the past, country folk used to walk to Florence on the eve of the Nativity of the Virgin Mary, as a pilgrimage as well as for the fair that's still held in piazza SS Annunziata. They carried paper lanterns, or *rificolone*, to light their way. Today, children still parade through the city proudly swaying their colourful candlelit paper lanterns.

Ostensione della Sacra Cintola & Corteggio Storico

Prato. **Date** 8 Sept.

The Holy Girdle of the Virgin, allegedly the belt that Mary handed to St Thomas on ascending into Heaven, was brought to Prato from the Holy Land around 1141. The relic is displayed from Donatello's pulpit on the cathedral façade on four other occasions annually – Easter Sunday, 1 May, 15 August and Christmas Day – but 8 September is the grandest celebration, with parades and drum-beating.

AUTUMN

Boccaccesca

Certaldo (0571 663384, www.boccaccesca.it). **Date** 1st 2wknds in Oct.

Over two long weekends (Fri to Sun), the charming medieval setting of Certaldo hosts this much-acclaimed celebration of the finest Tuscan produce, with wine, olive oil and the unique local onions.

Sagra del Tordo

Montalcino (0577 849331). **Date** last wknd in Oct.

After all the customary blessing, dancing and parading in medieval costume for this 'feast of the thrush', two champions for each of the town's four neighbourhoods compete in an archery tournament in the grounds of a 14th-century stronghold. Later, attention turns to the succulent fowl and meat roasting on the coals, and to a glass of storied Brunello wine.

Florence Marathon

Florence (055 5522957, 055 5536823 fax, www.firenzemarathon.it). **Date** last Sun in Nov.

The race kicks off at 9am from piazzale Michelangelo and finishes in piazza Santa Croce. Anyone over 18 can enter; applications can be made online or by post up to the day before. A health certificate must also be presented.

WINTER

Nativities

Throughout Tuscany. **Date** Dec-Jan.

As Christmas approaches, the Italian tradition of Nativity scenes is embraced in various ways and places. Many churches set up cribs, the main ones in Florence being in the Duomo, at San Lorenzo, Santa Croce, Chiesa di Dante and Santa Maria de' Ricci. Some country villages also stage *presepi viventi* – live re-enactments of the Nativity.

Christmas Market

Date 1st 2wks in Dec. **Open** 10am-10pm daily.

This picturesque German-style *Weihnachtsmarkt* has become an irresistible destination for the Florentines' Christmas shopping sprees.

Christmas

Christmas in Florence is marked by the usual suspects of shopping, decorations, eating and drinking and special events throughout December. An ice-skating rink is set up at the Parterre on piazza della Libertà, while piazza della Repubblica hosts a huge Christmas tree and an information booth on ongoing events. Meanwhile, the Amici degli Uffizi puts up a free themed exhibition displaying major artworks from the Uffizi deposits, and free concerts are held daily. Some restaurants are open on Christmas Day, but you'll find more choice on 26 December.

New Year's Eve

With restaurants and clubs charging preposterous figures for dinner and dancing parties, increasing numbers of Italians spend the long festive night of San Silvestro among friends and family at home, with a gigantic meal (including the mandatory stuffed pigs' trotters and lentils) and a fair supply of firecrackers and sparklers to 'burn' the past year and welcome in the new. An inexpensive and fun option is the many street parties and free concerts put on in several Tuscan towns.

La Befana (Epiphany)

Date 6 Jan.

La Befana, a ragged old woman riding a broomstick, rewards well-behaved children with stockings full of toys and sweets, while naughty kids just get a sockful of coal. Many small towns around the region hold street parties in celebration, while in Pistoia La Befana gets stuck up the cathedral belfry due to a failure of her broom, and firemen perform a spectacular rescue. Fun for children.

★ Carnevale di Viareggio

Viareggio (0584 962568, www.ilcarnevale.com). **Date** late Jan-early Mar.

Most Tuscan towns have *carnevale* celebrations, ranging from parades of elaborate floats to simple fancy-dress parties. In Florence, children dress up and scatter confetti along lungarno Amerigo Vespucci. However, the biggest carnival in the region dates back to 1873 and is held in the seaside town of Viareggio on the three Sundays before Shrove Tuesday (at 3pm), on Mardi Gras (again at 3pm) and on the following Sunday (from 5pm, followed by the award ceremony for the best floats and a fireworks display). The parades consist of over-the-top processions of gigantic papier-mâché satirical floats that take 100 people the best part of a year to assemble. You can buy seats in one of the stands flanking the Lungomare, but, as long as you watch out for your valuables, it's more fun among the revelling crowds.

ARTS & ENTERTAINMENT

Children

Dazzling views, Pinocchio puppets, fun activities – and, yes, ice-cream.

One vital trick to make your family holiday in Tuscany a success is timing your visit outside peak tourist season, so you don't need to fret about the kids getting lost in the crowds; Florence is a fairly child-sized – and child-friendly – place, and your main concern should be making sure your kids have *fun*. Their sense of the place improves dramatically if you show them the city from above early on and pinpoint the main sights on a good, visual map: climb the stairs to the top of the **Cupola** or **Campanile** (*see p54*), or catch a bus to **piazzale Michelangelo** (*see p96*). Children take the spotlight at **La Befana** festival in January (*see p181*), **Carnevale** (*see p181*) in February and **La Rificolona** in September (*see p180*). On a sultry summer day, head for an outdoor swimming pool (*see p211*) or plan an outing to the beach or the countryside.

The good news is that under-18s can enter all state-owned museums (listed on www.polo museale.firenze.it) free of charge. Museum bookshops often stock activity books and special kids' guidebooks. The **Associazione Musei dei Ragazzi** (*see p61*) runs activities and guided visits for children and families in several galleries, including at least a dozen programmes in Palazzo Vecchio alone. For shops with children's clothes, *see p155*.

BOOKSHOPS & LIBRARIES

Most of the largest bookshops in town, including **Edison** and **Feltrinelli International** (for both, *see p154*), stock a fair selection of videos,

games and children's books. The **Paperback Exchange** (*see p154*) occasionally runs readings of children's books in English on Saturday afternoons. For **Libri Liberi**, *see p184* **Teatrino del Gallo**.

Biblioteca delle Oblate
Via dell'Oriuolo 26, Duomo & Around (055 2616512, www.bibliotecadelleoblate.it). **Open** 8.30am-6.30pm Mon-Fri; 8.30am-1.30pm Sat & 16 July-31 Aug. **Admission** free. **Map** p335 B4.
The new city library has an attractive, open-plan room on the top floor designed for children. Books in several languages can be taken directly from the shelves, while games and DVD cartoons may be requested from the desk by an adult free of charge.

BM American British Bookstore
Borgo Ognissanti 4r, Santa Maria Novella (055 294575, www.bmbookshop.com). **Open** 9am-7.30pm Mon-Sat. *Apr-June, Sept, Oct, Dec* 9am-7.30pm Mon-Sat; 10.30am-7pm Sun. **Map** p334 B1.
A tiny independent with one of the best collections of English titles in Florence, including a wide range of new and collectable children's books.

TOY SHOPS

Bartolucci
Via della Condotta 12r, Duomo & Around (055 221779, www.bartolucci.com). **Open** 9.30am-7.30pm daily. **Map** p335 C4.

THE BEST MUSEUMS FOR KIDS

For mummies galore
The expanded **Museo Archeologico**.
See p79.

For shrunken heads
Museo di Antropologia e Etnologia.
See p85.

To get stuffed
In 23 rooms of animals at the **Zoology Museum La Specola**. See right.

Individually crafted pinewood rabbit-clocks and cat-lamps, spring guns and rocking horses, as well as Vespa replicas and Pinocchio puppets, all the result of three generations' worth of Bartolucci expertise. **Other locations** Borgo de' Greci, 11a-r, Santa Croce (055 2398596).

Città del Sole

Via de' Cimatori 21r, Duomo & Around (055 219345, www.cittadelsole.com). **Open** 3.30-7.30pm Mon; 10am-7.30pm Tue-Sat. Closed 1wk Aug. **Map** p335 C4.
Educational toys, board games and puzzles.

Dreoni Giocattoli

Via Cavour 31-33r, San Marco (055 216611, www.dreoni.it). **Open** 3.30-7.30pm Mon; 9am-1pm, 3.30-7.30pm Tue-Sat. Closed Mon morning in winter, Sat afternoon in summer. **Map** p335 A4.
A model car collector's heaven, this gallery is also great for Carnevale and Halloween costumes.

Natura e...

Via dello Studio 30r, Duomo & Around (055 2657624, www.natura-e.com). **Open** *Summer* 10am-2pm, 3-7.30pm Mon-Fri; 10am-2pm Sat. *Winter* 10am-2pm, 3-7.30pm Mon-Sat. **Map** p335 B4.
Nature-lovers of all ages will find anything from scientific toys to outdoor trekking gear.

EATING OUT

Bustling family *trattorie* and *pizzerie* that make dishes to order are the best choices for children. Just ask for *pasta al pomodoro* (with tomato sauce), or a half portion (*mezza porzione*) of what you're ordering. For lunch, instead of heading for the ubiquitous fast-food options, try buying picnic goodies at a market (*see p164* **Market Forces**) and head for a park (*see right*). For the best ice-cream parlours, *see p151*.

Il Cucciolo

Via del Corso 25r, Duomo & Around (055 287727). **Open** 7.30am-8.30pm Mon-Sat. Closed 3wks Aug. **No credit cards**. **Map** p335 B4.
This bar is popular with Florentine children due to the *bomboloni* (doughnuts), made on the upper floor then dropped down a tube and served hot.

Mr Jimmy's American Bakery

Piazza Pitti 6, Oltrarno (055 2480999, www.mr-jimmy.com). **Open** 10am-8pm Mon-Sat. Closed Aug. **Map** p335 D5.
Bakery specialising in American-style pies, cakes and pastries as well as Neapolitan seasonal sweets.

I Tarocchi

Via de' Renai 12-14r, Oltrarno (055 2343912). **Open** 12.30-2.30pm, 7pm-1am Tue-Fri. **Average** €12. **Map** p335 D4/5.

Child-friendly pizza and pasta portions, in an informal room with long tables. High chairs available.

LEISURE ACTIVITIES
Gardens, museums & parks

Boboli Gardens

For listings, *see p90*.
The Boboli Gardens' labyrinths, grottoes, fountains, statues and hiding places make great diversions for children, while parents can enjoy magnificent views.

Museo del Calcio

Viale Palazzeschi 20, Coverciano, Outside the City Gates (055 600526, www.museodelcalcio.it). Bus 17 to the Viale Volta Terminus. **Open** 9am-1pm, 4-6pm Mon-Fri; 9am-1pm Sat. Closed Aug. **Admission** (incl audio guide) €3; €1.50 6-14s; free under-6s.
Budding champions will be enthralled by Florence's football museum, housed in a converted barn adjoining Casa Italia in Coverciano. 'Casa Italia' is the nickname for the central training grounds of the Italian national football team and technical headquarters of the Italian Football Association. Exhibits in the museum range from the actual World Cups won by Italy to a vast collection of football-related postage stamps, as well as the shirts of Italian and international footballers. The huge multimedia databank provides entertaining photos and video footage from 1898 to the present day.

Museo Fiorentino di Preistoria

For listings, *see p85*.
Would-be cave dwellers can learn to paint, weave and make pots. There's a regular programme of activities, but workshops lasting one to three hours can also be scheduled on demand (9.30am-12.30pm Mon, Sat; 1.30-4.30pm Tue, Thur) for a €40-€70 fee.

Museo Zoologico La Specola

For listings, *see p92*.
Kids will love the eerie fustiness of this museum, actually the zoology department of the natural history museum, where room after room is filled with stuffed and pickled animals. After Room 23, a

---

INSIDE TRACK
ALL PLAYED OUT

There aren't many playgrounds in
Florence, but a lovely one can be found
in piazza dell'Azeglio in Santa Croce
(just north of the Synagogue); this quiet
recreational space is a haven for parents
and kids alike.

---

macabre collection of wax sculptures in various
states of decay and disease will enthrall older kids,
but could scare younger visitors.

Parco Carraia
*Entrance off via dell'Erta Canina, San Niccolò,
Outside the City Gates. Bus 23.*
This little-known park is just a stroll up from Porta
San Miniato but feels miles away from the city.
You'll find swings, picnic facilities and green space.

Parco delle Cascine
*Entrance nr ponte della Vittoria, Outside the City
Gates. Bus 17C.*
Stretching west of the city on the right river bank,
Florence's largest park hosts regular fairs and mar-
kets. It's at its busiest on Sundays, with parties play-
ing football and families picnicking. Playgrounds
dot the park, and in-line skates can be hired.

Play centres

La Bottega dei Ragazzi
*Via dei Fibbiai 2, San Marco (055 2478386,
www.istitutodeglinnocenti.it). Open 9am-1pm,
3-7pm Mon-Sat. Closed Aug. Admission €10
for 1 entrance; €50 for 8 entrances. No credit
cards. Map p335 A5.*
Learn-through-play workshops in Italian, English,
French and Spanish, lasting 90mins and aimed at
three- to 11-year-olds (10am-noon, 5-6.30pm Mon-
Sat). Workshops do not require the presence of parents and focus either on art history and techniques
or on issues such as children's rights, multicultural-
ism and recycling. There's also a free playroom with
games and books for children accompanied by an
adult (9am-1pm, 3-6pm Mon-Sat).

Canadian Island
*Via de Gioberti 15, Outside the City Gates (055
677567, www.canadianisland.com). Bus 3, 6,
14. Open June, July, Sept 8am-5pm Mon-Fri.
Oct-May 8am-2pm, 3.30-6.30pm Mon-Fri; 9am-1pm
Sat. Closed Aug. Admission €30 afternoon.
No credit cards.*
Childcare for kids aged between three and 12 by
responsible, English- and Italian-speaking adults.
They also organise summer sleepover and day
camps in the Tuscan countryside.

Mondobimbo Inflatables
*Parterre, via Mafalda di Savoia (by piazza della
Libertà), Outside the City Gates (055 5532946).
Open June-July 10am-1pm, 4.30-11.30pm daily.
Sept-May 10am-1pm, 3.30-7.30pm daily. Closed
Aug. Admission €5 day ticket.*
Huge bouncy castles, whales, dogs and snakes for
under-tens. Children must wear socks.

St James's American Church
*Via Bernardo Rucellai 9, Santa Maria Novella
(055 294417, www.stjames.it). Open 9am-1pm
Mon-Fri (office). Activities phone to check. No
credit cards. Map p334 A1.*
Child- and family-oriented activities, as well as
English-language Sunday School and nursery care.
Also provides referrals for dependable babysitters.

Theatre

For the children's shows at **Teatro Cantiere
Florida**, *see p214.*

Teatrino del Gallo
*Via San Gallo 25-27r, San Lorenzo (055
2658324, www.teatrinodelgallo.it). Open see
website for show times. Closed 3wks Aug.
Tickets €5 children; €7 adults. Map p335 A4.*
The lemon house and garden of the Libri Liberi
bookshop host a regular afternoon programme of
puppet and theatre shows for kids aged three to 13.

OUT OF TOWN

Bambimus Museo d'Arte per Bambini
*Santa Maria della Scala, piazza del Duomo 2,
Siena (0577 46517, www.comune.siena.it/
bambimus). Open 10.30am-6.30pm daily;
school visits some mornings, phone to check.
Admission €6. No credit cards. Map p334 C2.*
This museum's activities provide an introduction to
art appreciation for children over three. In Italian,
but with English and French support.

Giardino Zoologico
*Via Pieve a Celle 160, Pistoia (0573 911219, www.
zoodipistoia.it). Open Summer 9am-6.30pm Mon-
Fri; 9am-7pm Sat, Sun. Winter 9am-5pm daily.
Last entry 1hr before closing. Admission €10.50;
€8.50 3-9s; free under-3s. No credit cards.*
Home to over 600 animals, including 65 species of
mammals, 40 species of birds and 30 of reptiles.

Parco Preistorico
*Peccioli, via Cappuccini 20, Pisa (0587 636030/
635430, www.parcopreistorico.it). Open Apr-Aug
9am-7pm daily. Admission Apr-Aug €4. Sept-
Mar €4 adults; €3 children. No credit cards.*
About 40km (25 miles) south-east of Pisa, this park
has life-size model dinosaurs, a play area and picnic
facilities. Free overnight stay for motor caravans.

Film

Film sets that are pure romance and a fine alfresco cinema scene.

Romanticised, picture-perfect scenes from *A Room with a View* have burned an image of Florence into the collective psyche of the English-speaking world and beyond. Although Merchant-Ivory's adaptation of the Edwardian classic is now over two decades old, it still strikes a chord with visitors who, like Lucy Honeychurch, come to Florence to be transfigured by Giotto's frescoes in Santa Croce. Ridley Scott's *Hannibal* represents the polar perspective, being the movie that best captures the psychopathic, dark, medieval heart of Florentine history, through its allusion to the Pazzi conspiracy. An equally suave but rather less terrifying character made an impression on Tuscany in 2007, when Daniel Craig's James Bond shot *Quantum of Solace*, the 22nd film in the 007 franchise, in Siena.

Back in Florence, a prettified version of the city at war is evoked by Franco Zeffirelli's *Tea with Mussolini*, all English stiff-upper-lip resistance to Fascist bully boys. Other celluloid visions of Florence are Jane Campion's version of Henry James's *The Portrait of a Lady*, *Up at the Villa* – a lesser-known adaptation of a Somerset Maugham story starring Sean Penn – and Anthony Minghella's multiple award-winning *The English Patient*, which captures the magic of ancient Tuscan churches, isolated villas and quaint hill towns in another wartime tale. Adaptations of two Shakepeare tales, Kenneth Branagh's *Much Ado About Nothing* and Michael Hoffman's *A Midsummer Night's Dream,* make the most of the unique Tuscan landscape as a backdrop for their comic romps. But best forgotten is the sentimental *bella Toscana* nonsense of *Under the Tuscan Sun* – a ghastly San Franciscan interloper trying to ingratiate herself with the locals in a self-serving bid for mid-life transformation.

GETTING A SEAT

Florence's cinematic circuit is not generally accessible for non-Italian-speakers, while Italians are generally loath to sit through a subtitled film. The Warner Village 11-screen multiplex **Il Magnifico** (via del Cavallacio, 055 7870000, www.warnervillage.it, bus 1), slightly out of town, has been drawing cinemagoers away from the city centre and the consequence has been predictable, if unfortunate: some of the old cinemas in the city centre can no longer maintain their customer base, so some are turning into bingo halls while others just lie idle and abandoned. Nonetheless, the very central **Odeon Cinema**, with its Original Sound programme (*see p186*), continues to show international films in their original languages (*versione originale*) three nights a week. More varied programmes, including subtitled films, are offered at film clubs (*cineclubs; see p187*).

Italians have an aversion to booking, especially for the cinema, so expect chaos on Friday and Saturday nights for new releases. You may also find yourself invaded by people looking for the best seats for the next show before your show has finished. When the *posto in piedi* light is lit, the tickets sold are standing-room only. If you speak Italian, check the cheaper matinées offered at many main cinemas on weekdays before 6.30pm or all day Wednesday, when it costs €5 instead of the standard €7.20. (The reduction doesn't usually

Odeon Original Sound.

apply to original-language screenings.) For information, check *La Maschera*, an information sheet on display at most bars that contains movie and theatre listings. The *Florentine* also has cinema listings for anglophones. For festivals and other special events, check local listings such as *Firenze Spettacolo* or in the local supplement of the national daily *La Repubblica*.

Online resources include www.mymovies.it and *La Repubblica*'s cinema-search website (www.repubblica.it/trovacinema).

CINEMAS

Astra 2

Piazza Beccaria, Santa Croce (055 2343666, www.cinehall.it). **Open** *Box office* times vary. Closed Aug. **Tickets** €5.50-€7.50. **No credit cards**. With just under 300 seats, the Astra, on the eastern outskirts of Santa Croce, offers a range of English-language screenings as part of the English Original Sound programme in a pleasant screening room, and holds regular talks and events associated with its screenings. At the time of writing, plans were under way to overhaul the cinema into a multi-purpose arts venue (*see p188*).

British Institute Cultural Programme

Lungarno Guicciardini 9, Oltrarno (055 267781, www.britishinstitute.it). *Screenings* from 8.30pm. **Tickets** €5 plus €5 membership. **No credit cards**. **Map** p334 C2. The British Institute runs a Talking Pictures programme on Wednesday evenings. A movie is sandwiched between an introduction and a discussion, all in English. It also runs courses in Italian cinema.

★ Odeon Original Sound

Piazza Strozzi 2, Duomo & Around (055 295051/ 295331, www.cinehall.it). **Open** *Box office* times vary. Closed Aug. **Tickets** €7.20. **No credit cards**. **Map** p334 B3.

Mondays, Tuesdays and Thursdays are big draws for English-speakers at this stunning art nouveau cinema. Films on current release in English are screened, sometimes with Italian subtitles. There's a discount of up to 40% with a club card for eight films from a programme of 13 (€36); alternatively, use the voucher from the previous Sunday's *La Repubblica* for 30% off. After your screening, you can socialise with other English-speakers in the new bar and bistro.

Cineclubs

Part of the attraction of Florence's film clubs is the value for money they offer, especially for students, although you normally have to buy membership first.

CineCittà

Via Pisana 576, Scandicci, Outside the City Gates (055 7324510). Bus 6. **Shows** times vary. **Tickets** €3-€5. **Membership** €1. **No credit cards**. Hollywood action pictures and festivals of obscure Italian films. Some screenings are shown in their original language or with subtitles.

Cineteca di Firenze

Via R Giuliani 374, Outside the City Gates (055 450749, www.cinetecadifirenze.it). Bus 2, 18, 28. **Shows** times vary. **Tickets** €4-€5. **Membership** €3. **No credit cards**. Cycles of films showcasing various actors, some in their original language.

Stensen Cineforum

Viale Don Minzoni 25c, Outside the City Gates (055 576551/5535858, www.stensen. org). Bus 1, 7, 12. **Shows** usually 9.15pm Thur-Sat (except in summer), but phone to check. **Tickets** prices vary. **No credit cards**. **Map** p334 B2.

The Stensen screens Italian and foreign films, but only for holders of season tickets. It also runs lectures and debates. The Korea Filmfest (www.koreafilmfest.com), usually held in March, showcases contemporary and classic South Korean cinema.

SEASONAL CINEMA

The newly tagged '50 Days of International Cinema', which runs from October to December, is essentially a rebranding of all Florence's long-standing major international film festivals. Screenings are usually in original language, and in Florence or Fiesole. In November or December the **Festival dei Popoli** (055 244778) screens dramas and documentaries – centring around a single social issue – in clubs and cinemas throughout Florence. The **Premio Fiesole ai Maestri del Cinema** (055 597107, www.comune.fiesole.fi.it), held in July/August in Fiesole's open-air Roman theatre, pays homage to the works of one director – recently Ken Loach, Bernardo Bertolucci and Spike Lee have been featured. **France Cinema** (055 214053, www.francecinema.it) is usually held in November at the French Institute (piazza Ognissanti 2, 055 2398902) and the Teatro della Compagnia (via Cavour 50r, 055 217428). The annual **River to River** Indian film festival (055 286929, www.rivertoriver.it) is held in December; films are mostly in English, or the original language with English subtitles.

Italians regard cinemagoing in the summer months as an eccentricity reserved for mad dogs and Englishmen. However, a pleasant alternative for Italian-speakers (though international films are sometimes shown in their original languages) or those wanting to sample local life are the **open-air cinemas**, which show recent films from June to September. Shows start as darkness falls – around 9pm or 9.30pm – and some cinemas run double bills, with the second film finishing around 1.30am.

Open-air screens

Arena Raggio Verde
Palacongressi Firenze, viale Strozzi, Outside the City Gates (www.ateliergroup.it). **Dates** late June-late Aug. **Tickets** vary. **No credit cards.**
This stunning amphitheatre-style cinema, overlooking a 16th-century villa, runs nightly double bills during summer.

Cinema Arena di Marte
Palazzetto dello Sport di Firenze, viale Paoli, Outside the City Gates (055 289318, www.ateliergroup.it). **Bus** 10, 20, 34. **Dates** late June-late Aug. **Open** 8pm (shows 9.30pm daily). **Tickets** €5. **No credit cards.**
One of the two screens at this major outdoor venue shows cult and non-mainstream films; the larger screen runs the previous year's major blockbuster movies. There's a good outdoor restaurant too.

Cinema Chiardiluna Arena
Via Monte Oliveto 1, Outside the City Gates (055 218682). **Bus** 12, 13. **Dates** June-Sept. **Open** 8pm (shows 9.30pm) daily. **Tickets** €5. **No credit cards.**
Surrounded by woodland, Chiardiluna is cooler than the other outdoor cinemas. The movies are generally recent commercial releases, with some double bills.

Cinema Arena di Marte.

ARTS & ENTERTAINMENT

Galleries

The city's vibrant contemporary scene shouldn't be overlooked.

Contemporary art in Florence is increasingly an outdoor affair. The early demise of Quarter – a contemporary art centre that opened to considerable fanfare – and continuing delays for a major public art forum at the former Meccanotessile factory have led to a change in emphasis. Private donations and public acquisitions are now proudly displayed in main city squares and gardens. The city's most crucial contributions to contemporary art continue to come from the restaurants, bars and hotels that show the work of local and even international artists. **Astor Caffè** (*see p204*), **Rex Café** (*see p206*) and **Gallery Hotel Art** (*see p99*) are among those putting on regular, gallery-worthy exhibitions. *See also p102* **Rooms with a View**.

Base

Via San Niccolò 18r, Oltrarno (055 2207281/ 679378, www.baseitaly.org). **Open** 5-8pm Mon-Sat. **No credit cards. Map** p335 D4.
A centre of excellence for Tuscany-based artists specialising in film, installation and digital art.

BrancoliniGrimaldi

Vicolo dell'Oro 12r, Duomo & Around (055 2396263, www.isabellabrancolini.it). **Open** 10am-7.30pm Mon-Fri. Closed Aug. **No credit cards. Map** p334 C3.
A dozen emerging artists from all over the world are chosen for their originality and outlandish styles for this gallery, part of the Ferragamo Gallery Hotel Art and Lungarno Suites complex.

★ EX3 Centro per l'Arte Contemporanea Firenze

Viale Giannotti 81/83/85, Outside the City Gates (055 6287676, www.ex3.it). **Open** 3-10pm Wed-Sun. **Admission** free.
Opened in 2011, this gallery is more exhibition hall than art centre, its 700sq m (7,500sq ft) offering the space modern artists haven't had in Florence. Located in the Gavinana neighbourhood, the aim is to show multimedia temporary exhbitions that are often site-specific, with a focus on experimental, conceptual work from international artists.

Falteri

Via della Spada 38r, Santa Maria Novella (055 217740, www.falteri.it). **Open** 10am-1pm,

4-7.30pm Tue-Sat. **No credit cards. Map** p334 A2.
A small gallery specialising in master prints and drawing from the early 1500s to the first half of the 20th century. Since the move to its current home, the gallery has also shown contemporary painters, such as Antonio Biancalani and Ana Kapor.

Fondazione Pitti Immagine Discovery

Via Faenza 111, San Lorenzo (055 36931, www.pittimmagine.com). **Open** 9am-1pm, 2-5pm Mon-Fri. **Map** p334 A2.
Pitti Immagine stages major fashion, textiles and interiors shows in Florence. It also offers exhibitions – anything from installations to displays of fashion photography – in the Pitti building on via Faenza.

Galleria Alessandro Bagnai

Via Salutati 4r, Outside the City Gates (055 6802066, www.galleriabagnai.it). **Open**

INSIDE TRACK ADD ASTRA

Plans are under way to expand the **Astra 2** cinema (*see p186*) into a multi-faceted arts space for live music, poetry readings, cultural events and more. Chief among the new features will be a top-floor gallery, accessed from the auditorium level, which will host exhibitions as well as live events and art performances.

10am-1pm, 3-7pm Mon-Sat, Sun by appointment. Closed Aug. **No credit cards**. **Map** p334 D2.
Bagnai has moved to a calm, cavernous space, with skylights creating good viewing light. The gallery is outside the centre, but worth making the trip to see Tuscan sculptor Roberto Barni's nonchalant bronze men, Paolo Grassino's proud but legless reindeer, Dormice's defiant bimbo paintings, and work from modern and contemporary art icons.

Galleria Biagiotti Arte Contemporanea

Via delle Belle Donne 39r, Santa Maria Novella (055 214757, www.artbiagiotti.com). **Open** 2-7pm Tue-Sat. Closed Aug. **No credit cards**. **Map** p334 B2.
Carole Biagiotti runs this stunning 15th-century converted atrium gallery like a fairy godmother, supporting young international artists. Installations are a favourite, and have previously featured elephants in 'un-gilded' cages and even the artists themselves in 'live' works. Pieces often sell to collectors unseen.

Galleria Il Ponte

Via di Mezzo 42b, Santa Maria Novella (055 240617). **Open** *Sept-June* 4-7.30pm Tue-Sat. *July* 4-7.30pm Mon-Fri. Closed Aug. **No credit cards**. **Map** p335 B6.
Modern and contemporary abstract painters and sculptors feature in major retrospectives at this respected gallery and art publishing house. Recent

shows have seen the gallery broaden its horizons to include younger up-and-coming artists.

Galleria del Palazzo Coveri

Lungarno Guicciardini 19 (055 281044, www.galleriadelpalazzo.com). **Open** 11am-7pm Tue-Sat. **Admission** free.
A great space opened in 2004 by former ad man Massimo Martini to show Italian artists of the 20th century, ranging from interestingly themed group shows – a recent homage to film director Luchino Visconti, for example, to up-and-coming artists. An exchange programme with Baltic and Nordic galleries also make this a great place to see emerging and contemporary art from further afield.

Galleria Pananti

Via Maggio 15, Oltrarno (055 2741011, www. pananti.com). **Open** 9.30am-1pm, 3-7pm Mon-Fri. Closed Aug. **No credit cards**. **Map** p334 C5.
One of the city's most important art hubs, this gallery and auction house hosts major contemporary shows and retrospectives of modern artists, with an emphasis on figurative photos and painting.

Galleria Paradigma

Via de' Fossi 41r, Santa Maria Novella (055 2776265, www.galleriaparadigma.it). **Open** 10.30am-12.45pm, 3.30-7pm Mon-Fri. **Map** p334 B2.
A prestigious yet understated gallery showing 20th-century art and *objets*. Highlights are Paolo

EX3 Centro per l'Arte Contemporanea Firenze.

Staccioli's Etruscan-inspired vases and iridescent female figures, and Pino Chierchi's bright, totemic glass discs.

Galleria Santo Ficara

Via Ghibellina 164r, Santa Croce (055 2340239, www.santoficara.it). **Open** 9.30am-12.30pm, 3.30-7.30pm Mon-Sat. Closed Aug. **Map** p335 C5.
The walls of this important city-centre gallery, with its tall vaulted ceilings, are hung with works by established artists with an international market, such as 1950s Gruppo Forma member Carla Accardi.

Galleria Tornabuoni

Borgo San Jacopo 53r, Oltrarno (055 284720, www.galleriatornabuoni.it). **Open** 3.30-7.30pm Mon; 9.30am-1pm, 3.30-7.30pm Tue-Sat. **Map** p334 B2.
This important gallery was forced out of via de' Tornabuoni by rising rents. It's fallen on its feet with its new home (though it's kept the old name). The gallery still works with iconic local artists such as Guiliano Tomaino and Francesco Musante.

Ken's Art Gallery

Via San Niccolò 23r, Oltrano (055 242895, www.kensartgallery.com). **Open** 10am-1pm, 3-8pm Mon-Sat. **Map** p334 C3.

Mirabili.

Walter Bellini's exciting gallery was one of the first in the city to exhibit mixed media. The contemporary pieces are all by Florence-based artists.

Mirabili

Lungarno Guicciardini 21r, Oltrarno (055 294257, www.mirabili.it). **Open** 3-7.30pm Mon; 9.30am-1pm, 3-7.30pm Tue-Sat. Closed Aug. **Map** p334 C2.
The collections of furniture, *objets* and artworks here have been exhibited in high-profile international spaces. Artists include Ettore Sottsass and Max Ernst.

Otto luogo dell'arte

Via Maggio 43r (055 288977, www.ottoluogodell arte.it). **Open** 3.30-7.30pm Mon; 10am-1pm, 3.30-7.30pm Tue-Fri; 10am-1pm, 2.30-7.30pm Sat. **Map** p334 D2.
Opened in March 2011, this gallery and shop space is the brainchild of Olivia Toscani, whose mother is an artist and father is the photographer most associated with Benetton's controversial global advertising campaigns. Initial exhibitions, curated by art director Mauro Lovi, suggest an eclectic approach to contemporary art, with a focus on Italian artists.

Poggiali e Forconi

Via della Scala 35a, Santa Maria Novella (055 287748, www.poggialieforconi.it). **Open** *June-Sept* 9.30am-1.30pm Mon-Sat. Closed 2wks Aug. *Oct-May* 9.30am-1.30pm, 3-7pm Mon-Sat. **Map** p334 B2.
This series of arched spaces showcases the works of some of Italy's best-known young artists. Shows have featured Livio Scarpella's brash nudes.

Strozzina

Fondazione Palazzo Strozzi, piazza Strozzi (055 2776461, 055 2645155 ticket office, www. strozzina.org). **Open** 10am-8pm Tue-Sun. **Admission** €5, €3 reductions; free 6-11pm Thur.
Billing itself as a 'Contemporary Art Centre For Contemporary Culture', this modern space inside Palazzo Strozzi holds great international contemporary shows with imaginative curatorial directions and works by the likes of Cindy Sherman, Bill Viola, Andreas Gursky and Gerhard Richter, but it's also strongly committed to showcasing and promoting the work of emerging artists.

Tethys Gallery

Via Maggio 58r, Oltrarno (055 2286064, www. tethysgallery.com). **Open** 9am-7pm Mon-Fri; 3-7pm Sat. **Admission** free. **Map** p334 D2.
This cool white space is a great place in which to see contemporary art and photography spanning the latter half of the 20th century; shows by famous names such as Harri Peccinotti are alternated with less well-known but equally arresting Italian artists working today, including local photographer Guido Cozzi.

Gay & Lesbian

The coast is where the action is.

Though Florence has been popular with gay writers, artists and travellers for centuries, it was only in 1970 that the city got its first proper gay disco, **Tabasco** (*see p192*); it's still going strong today. Around the same time, the **Fronte Unitario Omosessuale Rivoluzionario Italiano** (FUORI – Italian for 'out'), Tuscany's first gay and lesbian organisation, was set up. Other landmarks include the opening of the gay cultural space **Banana Moon** in borgo degli Albizi in 1977 and the founding of the regional chapter of **ArciGay/Lesbica**, the leading organisation for gay political initiatives in 1980s Italy. In the 1990s, it split into two groups: **IREOS** (www.ireos.org), a social, cultural and information centre, and more political **Azione Gay e Lesbica** (www.gayelesbica.it).

Florence has lost quite a few gay and lesbian entertainment spaces in the last few years, with the scene less active than in the golden years of the 1980s – on weekends, many people prefer to head to Bologna or Rome.

No problems should arise from holding hands in the street in Florence and Tuscany, but anything much more overt in public is less acceptable (outside the gay resorts). Men have several cruising options, though some can be dangerous. The **Parco delle Cascine**, for instance, is active from sunset till late, but local cognoscenti warn against it. Another popular area is the **Campo di Marte** (in western Florence), where most cruising takes place in cars. The park at **viale Malta** near the football stadium is active too, but subject to frequent incursions from police checking IDs.

The age of consent in Italy is 18; clubs and bars check ID. For some venues you will need an ArciGay/Lesbica membership card, which currently costs €14 per year and is available at any of the venues that require it (noted below).

FLORENCE
Bars

Bar 85
Via Guelfa 85r, San Lorenzo (055 216050, www.bar85.eu). **Open** 5pm-3am Mon-Thur; 5pm-6am Fri, Sat. **Admission** €6; membership free. **Map** p335 A4.

A relative newcomer but already a firm favourite on the Florence gay scene, with a 'leather' vibe geared to a mature crowd. Music caters to all tastes.

BK Bar – Butterfly Kiss
Via Alfieri 95, Sesto Fiorentino, Outside the City Gates (055 4218878, www.bkbar.com). Bus 2, 28. **Open** 7am-2am daily. **Admission** free. **No credit cards**.
This pub is highly popular with women, who come for the parlour games, themed performances and photography exhibitions.

THE BEST GAY-FRIENDLY EATS

Upmarket
Cantina Barbagianni *via Sant'Egidio 13r (055 248 0508, www.cantina barbagianni.it).*

Trattoria
Mastro Ciliegia *via Matteo Palmieri 30r (055 293372).*

Flirty pizzeria
Semolina *piazza Lorenzo Ghiberti 87r (055 2347584).*

Crisco
Via Sant'Egidio 43r, Santa Croce (055 2480580, www.crisco.it). **Open** 11pm-3am Mon, Wed, Thur, Sun; 10pm-6am Fri, Sat. Closed 2wks mid Feb. **Admission** free membership. **Map** p335 B5.
A well-known, long-standing bar offering videos (mostly X-rated), special events, parties and a variety of performances. The exclusively male crowd is mixed, but leathermen and bears prevail.

Piccolo Caffè
Borgo Santa Croce 23, Santa Croce (055 2001057, www.piccolofirenze.com). **Open** 6.30pm-2.30am daily. **Admission** free. **Map** p335 C5.
Attracting a very mixed crowd, the Piccolo Caffè gets especially packed on Friday and Saturday nights. Check out the frequent art exhibitions and live shows.

YAG B@R
Via de' Macci 8r, Santa Croce (055 2469022, www.yagbar.com). **Open** 8pm-3am daily. **Admission** free. **Map** p335 C6.
This spacious, futuristic dance bar draws a young crowd of both genders, often here as a first stop on the city's club-hopping route. Current tunes dominate, and internet access and video games are also to hand.

Clubs

Azione Gay e Lesbica at Auditorium FLOG
For listing, *see p199* **Auditorium FLOG**.
Once a month on a Friday, a megafest of DJs, cabaret acts and bands draws a huge and diverse crowd out to this Poggetto venue in support of Azione Gay e Lesbica (*see p193*). It's also a great place to stock up on literature and information.

Fabrik
Viale del Lavoro, 19, Calenzano (349 8906645 mobile, www.fabrikfirenze.it). **Bus** 2, 28. **Open** 10pm-4am Tue-Sun. **Admission** €12 with ArciGay membership. **No credit cards.**
About 15km (nine miles) from Florence, Fabrik constitutes two storeys of post-industrial decor, featuring a video-bar and an open-air garden. There's a cruising area with roomy cabins and a darkroom.

Tabasco Disco Gay
Piazza Santa Cecilia 3r, Duomo & Around (055 213000, www.tabascogay.it). **Open** 10pm-6am Tue-Sun. **Admission** €13 Tue-Fri; €15 Sat. **Map** p335 C5.
Founded almost 40 years ago, Tabasco was Florence's first gay club, and has stood the test of time, remaining popular among tourists and young locals of both sexes. Music is mostly techno.

Torre Adore
Sitges in Tuscany.

Italy's answer to Spain's Sitges is to be found in the Versilia Riviera – specifically at **Torre del Lago Puccini** (named in honour of composer and former resident Giacomo Puccini, but often referred to as just 'Torre del Lago'), near Viareggio. The town has become something of a gay mecca, with a host of gay-friendly and gay-owned clubs and bars and several annual events – including **Mardi Gras** in mid August, **Bears on the Beach** at the end of June and **Les Week e Miss Gaya** in mid July. The organisation Friendly Versilia (www.friendlyversilia.it) has further information.

During the daytime, **Mama Mia Beach**, in the north of the resort and about 100 metres from the club of the same name, is a very elegant bathing spot, equipped with umbrellas, cabins and bar.

Nightlife in Torre del Lago centres on the lively Europa boardwalk, which attracts thousands nightly to its clubs; the most popular include **Mama Mia**, with its waterside terrace (viale Europa 5, 389 6262642 mobile, www.mamamia.tv); trendy **Boca Chica** (viale Europa 1, 338 5951208 mobile, www.bocachica.dj); hotspot **Priscilla**, with drag queen performances (viale Europa 7, 0584 341804, www.priscillacaffe.it); chill-out space **Adagio** (viale Europa 11, 392 923 2446 mobile, www.adagiolounge.com); and **Frau Disco** (viale Europa, 0584 342282).

If you want to start partying early, head into Viareggio for the **Voice Music Bar** (viale Margherita 63, 0584 943321); the club opens in the morning (9.30am-midnight), hosting parties and small raves into the night.

Accommodation is reasonably plentiful. Gay-friendly options include **Caffeletti** (via Pardini 34C, 347 1964685 mobile, www.caffeletti.com, €80), which is close to the beach, popular gay venues and the Torre del Lago nature reserve, while **Le Villi** (viale Puccini 178, 0584 340355, www.levilli.com, €80-€130) is a relaxing, colourful spot with a Mediterranean vibe.

Tenax

*Via Pratese 46, Peretola, Outside the City Gates
(055 308160, www.tenax.org).* Bus 29, 30. **Open**
10pm-4am Sat. Closed mid May-Sept. **Admission**
€25 women; €30 men.

Saturday nights at this trendy Peretola club go by
the name of Nobody's Perfect. But that doesn't stop
an international fashion crowd going all out to look
flawless – so make sure you dress the part.

Saunas

Florence Baths

*Via Guelfa 93r, San Lorenzo (055 216050, www.
tabascogay.it).* **Open** 2pm-2am Mon-Thur, Sun;
2pm-4am Fri, Sat. **Admission** €13 Mon-Fri; €14
Sat, Sun. **Membership** €16/yr. **Map** p334 A3.

Florence's only sauna offers excellent dry and steam
rooms, a jacuzzi (always cold), a bar, and TV and
private rooms. It's usually best to arrive in the late
afternoon or the early evening.

Services

Associazione Italiana Transessuali

*Arci Il Progresso, via Vittorio Emanuele 135,
Calenzano (347 3086110 mobile).* **Open**
4-8pm Mon.

Support association for identity disorders.

Azione Gay e Lesbica

*Via Pisana 32-34r, Oltrarno (055 220250,
www.azionegayelesbica.it).* **Open** 6-8pm Mon-Fri.
Closed 3wks Aug. **Map** p334 D2.

In addition to the Azione Gay e Lesbica parties it
runs, this organisation has a library and offers easy
HIV-testing and community information.

IREOS Queer Community Service Centre

*Via de' Serragli 3-5, Oltrarno (055 216907,
www.ireos.org).* **Open** 5-8pm Mon-Thur, Sat.
Map p334 D1.

IREOS hosts a social open house every Wednesday
evening, offering referrals for HIV testing, psychological counselling and self-help groups. The Centre
also organises hikes and other day trips, as well as
running the Florence Queer Festival (see www.flo-
rencequeerfestival.it for details) in November. The
festival showcases recent films and documentaries
on gay, lesbian and transgender issues, as well as
organising plays, literature and music events and
photography exhibitions.

Bed & breakfasts

The following are gay-friendly options. The
Relais Grand Tour *(see p111)* is also a great
option. For the centrally located, friendly B&B
Dei Mori, *see p103.*

Tabasco Disco Gay.

MartinDago

*Via de' Macci 84, Santa Croce (055 2341415, www.
martindago.com).* **Rates** €120. **Map** p335 C6.

Situated in the Santa Croce area, this recently opened
B&B has frescoed ceilings in the bedrooms.

Soggiorno Gloria

*Via Nazionale 17, San Lorenzo (055 288147, www.
soggiornogloria.eu).* **Rates** €80. **Map** p334 A3

A pleasant and comfortable hotel with big, bright
rooms and generous balconies overlooking the old
heart of Florence near the train station. Reception
staff can be rather nonchalant.

Radio

Controradio FM 93.6

055 7399970, www.controradio.it.

Every Thursday at 12.30pm, Italian-speakers should
tune into *La Casalingay.*

TUSCANY

In Pisa, **Colors** (via Mossotti 10, 050 500248,
www.colors.fm, admission free, closed Mon &
Tue) is a mixed high-tech DJ bar, while sauna,
steam, jacuzzi and private room facilities can be
found at **Sauna Siesta Club 77** (via di Porta
a Mare 25-27, 050 2200146, www.siestaclub77.
com, admission €12, €10 reductions, closed
Sept-Apr, 2wks mid July).

In Lucca, **Hub** (via di Poggio 29, Ponte San
Pietro, 389 6262642 mobile, www.hub.fm,
admission €10, closed Sun-Fri, 1st 2wks June
& 1st 2wks Sept) is a great place for a boogie.

Music

Take your pick, from heavyweight opera to chilled-out jazz.

Florence's classical musical life focuses around the **Teatro del Maggio Musicale Fiorentino** (*see p196*), one of Italy's foremost opera houses. Opera has a special place in the heart of many Italians, and if you get the chance to catch a production at the Maggio, go for it: a performance of a Puccini or Verdi by a good Italian orchestra and chorus is almost always a worthwhile experience, even though the performances here are rarely innovative.

By contrast, more modern genres of music are surprisingly lively. Overshadowed by Rome, Milan and Turin, Florence is often left off the touring itineraries of major musical acts, but – mainly thanks to the large student population – the city has a surprisingly good array of nightly gigs at the more intimate end of the scale.

ARTS & ENTERTAINMENT

Classical Music & Opera

With the odd exception, opera productions here are unlikely to be avant-garde. Conservative Florentines – like most Italians – don't take kindly to directors messing with their favourite operas, and any experimenting is likely to be met with slating critiques and boos from the audience. It wasn't always this way. Back in the 15th century, Florence was on the cutting-edge of musical culture thanks to the Florentine Camerata, intellectuals who began experimenting with the setting of words to music. Pieri and Caccini's *Euridice*, widely

considered to be the world's first opera, was performed in the Boboli Gardens in 1600 and Florence's musical importance continued into the early 17th century; after this time, the country's musical focus shifted northwards, with the Venetian school of composition becoming admired as the country's most progressive.

Nowadays, Florence plods on with a steady, if not particularly exciting, line-up. There's lots on offer in the way of symphonic and chamber concerts, with two resident symphony orchestras, a clutch of smaller groups and a world-class chamber music series. Smaller events are promoted on fly posters and in local media. From June to October there are concerts in churches, plus outdoor concerts at villas, gardens and museums, some of them free. Keep an eye open for summer performances in the Boboli Gardens; while the standard isn't always the highest, the setting is superb.

Not all these events are well advertised, but tourist offices usually have information. For events taking place outside Florence, *see p198* **Seasonal Settings**.

TICKET INFORMATION

For main ticket agencies, *see p174*. Many hotels and travel agents also book tickets for the biggest venues. Tickets for the Teatro del Maggio can be hard to come by, as many seats are taken by holders of season tickets. Advance

---

THE BEST VENUES

For star spotting
Estate Fiesolana. *See p197*.

For cult acts
Tenax. *See p200*.

For great acoustics
Saschall-Teatro di Firenze. *See p198*.

For jazz
Pinocchio Jazz. *See p200*.

Magical Classical

The Linari Festival is one of Tuscany's finest musical events.

Tuscany abounds with outdoor concerts in the summer, but one of the most magical is the Linari Classical Music Festival (www.linariclassic.com, 055 8068022), held in and around the small tenth-century hilltop town in Chianti Classico, between Florence and Siena. Begun in 2003, the festival consists of an international programme of ten concerts ranging from early Baroque to 20th-century compositions, and features young musicians who perform in orchestras from around the world. The beauty of these concerts is their locations: ancient churches, medieval castles, starlit intimate *piazze* and the frescoed salons of splendid private villas all form part of the festival. This is made all the more special by the after-concert dinners: classic Tuscan dishes are served in the venues, allowing performers and concertgoers to mingle and chat. There's even a cookbook in the works: the *Linari Dinner Cookbook* will contain photos and recipes for the meals served at previous Linari Festivals.

Airdrie Armstrong Terenghi, founder and artistic director of the festival, uses it to foster young and talented artists, who can spend their entire summer performing. It's an ideal situation – the artists have wonderfully atmospheric and unusual venues in which to perform, and the public gets to enjoy very special evenings of music, performed by accomplished artists who come to Linari to hone their skills and build their self-confidence – among them Martin Forni, Jayson Gilhan, Benjamin Hudson, Pepijn Meeuwes, Naomie Atherton, Johan Van Hersel and Giulia Nuti. It adds up to a metaphorical feast for classical music fans, a literal one for fans of Tuscan cuisine, and a grand evening out for both.

Jane Fortune is a Florence-based arts writer and the author of To Florence Con Amore: 90 Ways to Love the City *and* Invisible Women, *both published by the Florentine Press (www.theflorentinepress.com).*

bookings for the opera and concert seasons (Sept-Mar) open around mid September. Tickets for the **Maggio Musicale Fiorentino** (*see p176*) go on sale in early April. You can book online (www.maggiofiorentino.com) up to a week before the performance. Phone bookings through the theatre's ticket office can't be paid for with credit cards; those through the call centre (199 112112, only within Italy) can.

If you can't get a seat in advance, turn up on the night for the chance of a return or one of the restricted-vision seats that go on sale an hour before the start of each performance. For chamber concerts and Orchestra Regionale Toscana concerts, tickets are usually available on the door half an hour beforehand. Note that not all theatres accept card payments.

VENUES

Accademia Bartolomeo Cristofori

Via di Camaldoli 7r, Oltrarno (055 221646, www.accademiacristofori.it). **Open** by appointment.
Named after the piano's inventor, the academy houses a fine private collection of early keyboard instruments. Chamber concerts and seminars are held in a beautiful little hall next door, usually at 9pm on Tue (Jan-May; tickets €10, €5 reductions).

Chiesa Luterana

Lungarno Torrigiani 11, Oltrarno (055 2542775, 055 290832 tourist office). **Map** p335 D4.
Organ recitals and chamber music, often involving early repertoire and international artists, are held at Florence's Lutheran church every Wednesday from April to October, and are usually free.

Chiesa di Santo Stefano al Ponte

Piazza Santo Stefano 5, Duomo & Around (tourist office 055 290832). **Map** p334 C3.
Located just north of the ponte Vecchio, this large, deconsecrated church hosts regular concerts.

Scuola Musica di Fiesole

Villa La Torraccia, via delle Fontinelle 24, San Domenico, Fiesole (055 597851, www.scuolamusica.fiesole.fi.it). Bus 7, then 10min walk. **Open** 8.30am-8.30pm Mon-Sat.
One of Italy's most famous music schools occupies a 16th-century villa in beautiful grounds. Founded by the charismatic viola player of the Quartetto Italiano, Piero Farulli, it's the home of the Orchestra Giovanile Italiana, the country's number one youth orchestra. Farulli is now in his dotage, but his teaching legacy is very much alive. The annual Festa della Musica, a musical open day with concerts and workshops by pupils, is held on 24 June, while the Concerti per gli Amici series takes place in the 200-seat auditorium from September/October to June.

★ Teatro Goldoni

Via Santa Maria 15, Oltrarno (055 229651,
055 213535 Teatro Comunale). **Open** *Box office*
1hr before performance. **Map** p334 D1.
This divine little theatre in the Oltrarno dates from
the early 18th century and seats only 400 people. A
long drawn-out restoration was finally finished in
the late 1990s and the theatre is now partially under
the direction of the Teatro del Maggio (*see below*).
It's used – though not regularly enough – for chamber music, small-scale opera and ballet.

Teatro del Maggio Musicale Fiorentino

Corso Italia 16, Santa Maria Novella (055 287222
box office, 055 2779350 call centre, www.maggio
fiorentino.com). **Open** (by phone) 10am-1pm, 2.30-
4.30pm Mon-Fri. *Box office* 10am-4.30pm Mon-Fri;
10am-1pm Sat.
The Maggio Musicale Fiorentino festival (hosted by
the Teatro del Maggio) has been going almost non-
stop since 1933, and despite financial worries and gargantuan overheads (it sustains a full orchestra, chorus
and ballet company, plus armies of staff) a revamp
and modernisation have successfully revitalised it
both in terms of programming and visitors. The
charismatic Zubin Mehta hit 74 in 2011, but is showing no signs of retiring as principal conductor. When
on form, the Teatro del Maggio's resident orchestra
and chorus are on a level with La Scala in Milan, but
lack of funds means that big-name conductors and
soloists are often padded out with mediocre
unknowns who just don't get the same results.

The theatre's performing year is divided roughly
into three parts: January to March is the concert season, with performances on Fridays, Saturdays and
Sundays (the programme changes each week);

October to December is the opera and ballet season,
with about four operatic productions, a couple of bal-
lets and the odd concert; and the Maggio Musicale
Fiorentino festival runs for two months from late
April/early May. The latter offers a mix of opera,
ballet, concerts and recital programmes, and culminates in a free open-air concert and free dance
extravaganza in piazza della Signoria.

The theatre building itself, constructed in 1882
and renovated in 1957, is architecturally unexciting.
Of the 2,000-odd seats, the best acoustics are to be
had in the second gallery (they are also the cheapest),
but if you want to strut your stuff alongside the
designer outfits of *Firenze per bene*, you need to fork
out for an opening night in the stalls or one of the
palchi (boxes). *See also p214.*

★ Teatro della Pergola

Via della Pergola 18-32, San Marco (055
2264316, www.teatrodellapergola.com). **Open**
Box office 9.30am-6.45pm Mon-Sat; 10am-12.15pm
Sun. **Season** Oct-Apr. **Map** p335 B5.
Inaugurated in 1661, the exquisite, intimate Pergola
is one of Italy's oldest theatres. Richly decorated in
red and gold and with three layers of boxes, it's ideal
for chamber music and small-scale operas. The
excellent series of chamber music concerts promoted
by the Amici della Musica (*see below*) is held here,
while the Teatro del Maggio also occasionally uses
it for opera during the Maggio festival (*see p176*).

Teatro Verdi

Via Ghibellina 99, Santa Croce (055 212320,
www.teatroverdifirenze.it). **Open** *Box office*
10am-1pm, 4-9pm Mon-Sat. **Season** Sept-June.
Map p335 C5.

Teatro della Pergola.

This large theatre was extensively revamped in 2004 for its 150th anniversary. A wood floor was added in the auditorium and new splendid red velvet seats were installed. They may be by Poltrona Frau, but they are extremely uncomfortable, with less legroom than a holiday charter flight. Teatro Verdi is the home of the Orchestra della Toscana (*see below*) and is the orchestra's principal Florence venue. See also p214.

PERFORMANCE GROUPS/PROMOTERS

Amici della Musica
Via Pier Capponi 41 (055 608420/607440, www.amicimusica.fi.it).
This organisation, founded in 1906, promotes world-class chamber music concerts, mostly at the gorgeous Teatro della Pergola (*see left*), from September through to late April/early May. The annual series always features some of the world's great string quartets and recitalists such as Andras Schiff (a Florence resident), Alfred Brendel, and the Emerson and Alban Berg string quartets. Early music groups of the calibre of Fabio Biondi's Europa Galante and Jordi Savall also appear regularly. Afternoon and evening concerts are usually on Saturdays and Sundays.

L'Homme Armé
055 695000, www.hommearme.it.
Until recently, the repertoire of this small, semi-professional chamber choir ranged from medieval to Baroque, but they have introduced an interesting contemporary element. It gives about ten concerts a year in Florence and runs excellent courses on aspects of early music.

Orchestra da Camera Fiorentina
055 783374, www.orcafi.it.
This young chamber orchestra, under its principal conductor Giuseppe Lanzetta, plays a series of concerts mostly at Orsanmichele (*see p63*) between February and September. The venue means it attracts a good tourist-based audience in summer, but standards vary. Concerts are usually held on Sunday and Monday evenings.

Orchestra della Toscana
055 2340710, www.orchestradellatoscana.it.
If you're looking for something creative, try to catch a concert given by the Orchestra della Toscana. Founded in 1980 with the brief of taking classical music into Tuscany, it has a dynamic management team and artistic director, who are responsible for a wider repertoire than that of the Maggio orchestra. Emphasis is placed on rarely heard 19th-century music, early 20th-century composers and contemporary works, but there's plenty more. International names frequently appear as soloists and conductors, and during the season

INSIDE TRACK
HEAVENLY SOUNDS

Numerous churches offer concerts and opera performances throughout the year; those at St Mark's English Church (via Maggio 16-18, 340 811 9192, www.stmarksitaly.com) are usally free, although there's an admission fee for the acclaimed St Mark's Opera Company performances, while grander settings that charge a small admission include the magnificent Chiesa di Orsanmichele and the gorgeous 12th-century Chiesa di Santo Stefano al Ponte Vecchio.

(Nov/Dec-May) the orchestra gives two or three concerts a month at the Teatro Verdi (*see left*), and up to 40 in other Tuscan towns.

FESTIVALS

In addition to the festivals listed below, *see also p178* **Estate Fiorentina**, *p178* **Estate Fiesolana**, *p176* **Maggio Musicale Fiorentino** and *p180* **Effetto Venezia**. For **Estate Musicale Chigiana**, **Puccini Festival** and **Incontri in Terra di Siena**, *see p198* **Seasonal Settings**.

Christmas Concert
Teatro Verdi (055 2340710, tickets 055 212320). **Map** p335 C5. **Date** 24 Dec.
This annual concert by the Orchestra Regionale Toscana doesn't necessarily include Christmas music, but there is usually something good.

Florence Opera Festival
055 5978309, www.festivalopera.it. **Admission** €15-€75.
Held in two evocative venues – the Boboli Gardens and San Galgano Abbey, this enchanting programme of performances sticks firmly to the old favourites when it comes to opera and ballet – Swan Lake, La Traviata and Don Quixote last year – but also incorporates solo concerts by acclaimed soloists such as Ludovico Einaudi and even physical theatre such as Le Cirque Invisible.

New Year Concert
Teatro Comunale (055 597851). **Date** 1 Jan.
Put on by the Scuola di Musica di Fiesole. Call the above number for free tickets.

Settembre Musica
Teatro della Pergola & other venues (055 608420, www.amicimusica.fi.it). **Date** Sept.
Annual early music concerts, by young or up-and-coming ensembles with the odd bigger name.

Seasonal Settings

Classical treats abound, from church concerts to open-air arias.

There's something about hearing music in the setting of a beautiful church or cloister, a historic piazza, an elegant villa or a tiny, restored theatre that is compelling even for people who don't normally 'do' classical music and opera. Tuscany is a great place to indulge such urges, as seasons and festivals spring up all over the place, particularly in summer. Some of these events have a high-enough profile to be well advertised, while others often go unnoticed by anyone not in the know. So read the local press and search out the smaller, one-off performances, as well as the better-known seasons listed here.

Events worth looking out for include the **Estate Musicale Chigiana** series of concerts in Siena and at such gorgeous venues as the nearby abbey of Sant'Antimo (July-Aug, 0577 22091, www.chigiana.it); the **Tavernelle Val di Pesa** concerts at the Badia in Passignano monastery (late May, tourist office 055 8077832); the **Barga Opera Festival**, which features productions of little-known operas (July-mid Aug, 0583 723250, www.operabarga.it); the **Incontri in Terra di Siena** chamber music festival based at La Foce in the Val d'Orcia (late July, 0578 69101, www.lafoce.com); the **Festival Puccini**, during which several of the Lucca-born composer's favourite operas are performed on the lakeside in an open-air theatre near his Torre del Lago villa (0584 359322, www.puccinifestival.it); and the **Tuscan Sun Festival** (*see p180*), inaugurated in 2003 on the back of Francis Mayes' bestseller *Under the Tuscan Sun*, and featuring high-profile conductors and singers for two weeks of music in Cortona.

Concerts are held in Pisa's Duomo for the **Anima Mundi** festival of Sacred Music under the direction of Sir John Eliot Gardiner (Sept-Oct, 050 835029, www.opapisa.it).

Local tourist offices can supply further information about these and other events.

Rock, Pop & Jazz

One of the best ways to find out about events is to pick up *Firenze Spettacolo*. This monthly Italian-language magazine showcases what's hot in Florence. And don't fret if your language skills aren't up to scratch, as there's a huge event calendar in English with information on live gigs, from international musicians and rock bands to local home-grown jazz musicians and beatniks. It's also worth picking up a copy of free local English-language newspaper the *Florentine*, which has a great spread of upcoming live events and concerts; or drop into one of the city's record shops (*see p172*) to pick up flyers. For jazz events, it's also worth contacting gig-promoter **Musicus Concentus** (piazza del Carmine 19, 055 287347), which can give information on forthcoming events.

To book tickets for concerts (regardless of genre), call the venue directly or contact the Box Office ticket agency (*see p174*).

BIGGER VENUES

Obihall

Via Fabrizio de André, nr lungarno A Moro 3, Outside the City Gates (055 6504112, www. obihall.it). Bus 14. **Tickets** prices vary.

This 4,000-capacity venue hosts mainstream acts from Italy and abroad. There are upper balcony seats, but the main standing hall downstairs has better sound.

Palasport Mandela Forum

Viale Paoli 3, Outside the City Gates (055 678841, www.mandelaforum.it). Bus 3. **Tickets** prices vary. **No credit cards.**

This 7,000-capacity hall is where Florence houses major touring artists – Italian stars like Zucchero and international acts such as Michael Bublé.

Sala Vanni

Piazza del Carmine 19, Oltrarno (055 287347, www.musicusconcentus.com). **Tickets** prices vary. **No credit cards. Map** p334 C1.

Sadly underused, this warehouse-like auditorium is a great place to hear good progressive jazz and contemporary classical groups. The venue hosts a sparse but excellent series of concerts organised by Musicus Concentus in autumn and winter.

Stadio Artemio Franchi

Viale Manfredo Fanti 14, Campo di Marte, Outside the City Gates (055 667566). Bus 10, 11, 17. **Tickets** prices vary. **No credit cards.**

If not even the Palasport Mandela Forum (*see above*) is big enough to meet your musical needs, this football stadium might fit the bill: it moonlights as a music venue where you can see acts such as Italian megastars Vasco Rossi and Renato Zero.

SMALLER VENUES

Admission to the following venues is free unless otherwise stated.

Caruso Jazz Café.

Auditorium FLOG

Via M Mercati 24b, Outside the City Gates (055 487145, www.flog.it). Bus 4, 8, 14, 20, 28. **Open** 10pm-late Tue-Sat. Closed June-Aug. **Tickets** €10-€15. **No credit cards**.

At FLOG, music runs from rock to Tex-Mex rockabilly, with Fridays for reggae and ska, and a DJ after the bands. Dance parties and theatrical shows take place early in the week, and the venue hosts the Rassegna Internazionale Musica dei Popoli (*see p200*) and Azione Gay e Lesbica parties (*see p193*).

★ Be-Bop

Via de' Servi 76r (055 2396544). **Open** 8pm-2am daily. **Admission** free-€10.

With a focus on 1950s music and a delightfully retro interior to match, the sweaty, subterranean Be-Bop attracts both local and international students to its rock 'n' roll-led mix of acts, though you're just as likely to hear a Led Zeppelin cover band or a jazz funk ensemble.

Caruso Jazz Café

Via Lambertesca 14-16r, Duomo & Around (055 281940, www.carusojazzcafe.com). **Open** 9.30am-3.30pm, 6pm-midnight Mon-Sat. **Map** p334 C3.

This cavernous bar is a magnet for talented jazz musicians, including many famed Italians. Every Thursday and Friday jazz echoes around the bar's brick vaults in a buzzy atmosphere.

Dolce Vita

Piazza del Carmine 6r, Oltrarno (055 284595, www.dolcevitaflorence.com). **Open** 5pm-2am Tue-Sun. Closed 2wks Aug. **Map** p334 C1.

Dolce Vita is one of the city's swankier clubs. It's filled with beautiful people dancing to live Brazilian, jazz and contemporary music on Wednesdays and Thursdays. The drinks prices are a little steep, but the atmosphere, decor and scenery make up for it. There's no official dress code, but showing up in jeans and a T-shirt will incur plenty of unwelcome glances.

Girasol

Via del Romito 1, Outside the City Gates (055 474948, www.girasol.it). Bus 14. **Open** 7pm-2am Tue-Sun. Closed June-Aug. **No credit cards**.

One of the most colourful bars in Florence, Girasol tops the list when it comes to Latin sounds, playing live music pretty well nightly. Instructors from local dance schools occasionally give free lessons in tango and samba to get you in the mood. Drinks are on the pricey side, but the exotic mixes blend in perfectly with the colourful decor. The recent addition of a pizzeria has made it a bit more mainstream than it once was, but it's still a good bet for Latin music.

Golden View

Via de' Bardi 58r, Oltrarno (055 214502, www. goldenviewopenbar.com). **Open** 11.30am-2am daily. **Map** p335 D4.

The uninspiring decor of this restaurant and bar is more than made up for by the direct views afforded of the ponte Vecchio and the Uffizi. The jazz comes from a resident pianist, in duos and trios on a Monday, Wednesday and Sunday.

INSIDE TRACK
FREE JAZZ – NO, REALLY

Every evening from mid June until September, jazz concerts are staged at piazza della SS Annunziata (www. santissima.it), courtesy of the Comune di Firenze, Quartiere Centro Storico and Firenze Estate. The programme is wonderfully eclectic, spanning everything from heavyweight tributes to the likes of Miles Davis and Billie Holiday to Cuban-inspired tango-jazz and Afro-Brazilian pop. Chairs and tables are set out, and food is provided by the non-profit Slow Food International.

★ Jazz Club

Via Nuova de' Caccini 3, Santa Croce (055 2479700, www.jazzclubfirenze.com). **Open** 9pm-2am Tue-Fri; 9pm-3am Sat. Closed July, Aug. **Tickets** €8 membership (€5 renewals). **No credit cards. Map** p335 B5.

One of the few places in Florence where you can hear live jazz almost nightly, this hard-to-find club is worth searching out. From Tuesday to Saturday, it hosts an array of popular local jazz bands, and it has also welcomed notable international acts such as jazz musician/actor Peter Weller (probably better known for his role in the first two *Robocop* films than playing the trumpet on stage). Every Monday there's a live jam session where you can hop on stage with the house band accompanying.

★ Pinocchio Jazz

Viale Giannotti 13, Outside the City Gates (055 680362, www.pinocchiojazz.it). Bus 8, 23, 31, 32, 80. **Open** 9pm-2am Sat. Closed May-Oct. **Tickets** €10-€13; €7-€9 reductions; ARCI or UISP membership required.

Pinocchio Jazz hosts internationally recognised jazz stars such as Chris Speed, Anthony Coleman and Richard Galliano, as well as Italian artists. Later in the evening, the atmosphere becomes more mellow, with soft jazz filling the air. The Pinocchio Jazz Live Festival is held from January to March, showcasing the best of Italian jazz musicians, plus a smattering of international talent, every Saturday night.

Porto di Mare

Via Pisana 128, Outside the City Gates (055 7191160, www.portodimarelive.it). **Open** 7pm-3am daily. Closed Aug.

This club is perfect for a simple night out. Starting at the top floor of the three-tiered club is a rustic pizzeria that makes a great *penne alle Calabrese*. On the second floor is a quaint pub with a large TV screen and comfy chairs. Head down to the basement to catch a live show – local rock and folk musicians play seven days a week.

INSIDE TRACK
TERRACE CHANTS

Perhaps inspired by the still-stirring memory of that special relationship between Luciano Pavarotti and Italia '90, an opera about the local football team, ACF Fiorentina, is in the pipeline for the chamber orchestra Orchestra della Toscana (www.orchestradellatoscana.it), with a debut planned for spring 2012. The libretto will centre around the club's many genuinely dramatic moments in its recent history, and promises to be one for both fans of modern opera and football.

Stazione Leopolda

Via Fratelli Rosselli 5, Outside the City Gates (055 89875/3245485, www.stazione-leopolda. com). Bus 1, 9, 12, 16, 17, or tram T1. **Tickets** vary.

This huge disused station is beloved of street-chic designers, who host catwalk shows here, but it's also occasionally called into service by artists such as jazz pianist Stefano Bollani and Liars, a US noise-rock band. The Fabbrica Europa performing arts festival is held here (*see p215*).

Tenax

Via Pratese 46, Outside the City Gates (055 308160, www.tenax.org). Bus 29, 30. **Open** 10.30pm-4am Thur-Sat. Closed mid May-Sept. **Tickets** prices vary.

New Order played here in the 1980s, with Basement Jaxx visiting in the '90s, and Tenax's cultish line-ups are still strong in the 21st century, with acts such as Ani DiFranco and Tricky. The club has a huge raised dancefloor and antechambers stuffed with computers, pool tables and bars for post-gig entertainment. Upstairs are more bars and café-style seating areas with balconies. Great acoustics. *See also p196.*

Williams Pub

Via Antonio Magliabechi 7r (055 263 8357, www.thewilliam.it). **Open** 1pm-1am Mon-Thur, Sun; 1pm-2am Fri, Sat.

Despite temporarily losing its licence in 2010 in a crackdown on excessive drinking by Florentine teenagers, this popular drinking den does a fine line in live music on a tiny stage, where you're just as likely to see an Irish folk musician as a noisy Italian thrash metal band.

FESTIVALS

Tuscany in the summer is a great place to catch some quality music festivals: **Pistoia Blues Festival** (www.pistoiablues.com) stages a number of open-air blues concerts, with big-names like Patti Smith and Joe Cocker heading the bills, while the **Porretta Soul Festival** (www.porrettasoul.it), going for some 20 years, is always a big affair. Held in Porretta Terme, a small spa town 30 kilometres (19 miles) north of Pistoia, past performers have included Booker T. Porretta lies in the Tuscan-Emilian Apennines, a wonderful natural setting of beech, pine and chestnut woods.

Festivals are not just held in the summer, however; the most noteworthy autumn event is **Musica dei Popoli** (www.musicadeipopoli. com), held at FLOG (*see p199*). Starting the first weekend in October, this world music festival has varied artists playing their original folk sound, and is not to be missed.

Nightlife

As night falls, indulge in a different kind of culture.

Italians may be creatures of habit, but the popularity of the *aperitivo* (*see p205* **The Aperitivo Awards**) has led to a seismic shift in Florentine nightlife patterns. Instead of going home for dinner after work, then venturing out at 9pm or 10pm, it's now the done thing to go straight from work to one of the many bars serving complimentary buffets with drinks – and then move on somewhere else.

The late-night club is the loser in this new timetable, and not by chance several city-centre clubs have closed in the last couple of years, while others have morphed into bar/clubs serving early-evening *aperitivi* in the hope of roping punters in for the night. That's not to say clubbing has died a death. It's just now treated less as nightly entertainment and more as a one-off occasion, frequently taking advantage of venues such as the **Stazione Leopolda** (*see p200*) and villa parties on the hills.

Most clubs charge an admission fee that includes a drink, but some clubs still use the unpopular card system. At these venues, you're given a card that's stamped whenever you buy drinks or use the cloakroom. You then hand the card in at the till and pay before leaving. Some smaller clubs are members-only, but these will almost always give out free membership.

Note that opening times and closing days of bars and clubs are notoriously vague and erratic, and phones that are answered are the exception. Musical genres often vary with the day of the week – check flyers, English-language newspaper *The Florentine* (www.theflorentine.net) or *Firenze Spettacolo* for information.

SUMMER CLUBBING

From the end of May to the beginning of September most Florentine nightlife shifts from crowded underground clubs to outdoor venues in *piazze*, gardens and villas. Most have free admission and stay open until the small hours. Each summer brings new openings to replace previous closures, as well as the return after absence of established venues. Two of the most popular places in previous years, **Parterre** (piazza della Libertà) and **Le Rime Rampanti** (above piazza Poggi), are current no-shows but

may reappear, while **Vie di Fuga** is now a year-round restaurant.

Temporary bars, set up in streets and squares, are also a hot summer phenomenon, with **piazza Santo Spirito** usually playing host to nightly gigs and events. Other one-off events are organised in **piazza Pitti**, the **Boboli Gardens** and **Forte di Belvedere** (currently closed for refurbishment), and the **Stazione Leopolda** is increasingly used as a summer venue. Jazzy nights at the **Sant'Ambrogio Summer Festival** also run from June to July in piazza Ghiberti (www.firenzejazz.it) and the newest summer venue is the **Loggia del Pesce** in piazza dei Ciompi, which had a bar and restaurant, and music swinging from bossa nova and samba to jazz and blues. For riverside seats, head to **Teatro sull'Acqua** (lungarno Pecori Giraldi, 055 2343460), a sprawling bar-cum-club.

Bear in mind that the local council grants permission to these summer-only venues on a year-by-year basis, so the situation can change at any time. Check the local press for details.

CLUBS

★ Central Park
Via Fosso Macinante 2, nr ponte alla Vittoria, Outside the City Gates (055 359942,

www.centralfirenze.it). Bus 1, 9, 26, or tram T1.
Open *Summer* 11.30pm-4.30am Tue-Sat. *Winter*
11pm-4am Fri, Sat. **Admission** €10-€30.
The greatest of summer disco venues, Central Park
comes into its own in hot weather, when the huge
garden areas with bars and outdoor dancefloors provide the perfect environment for sun-frazzled dancing legs. The music is progressive by Florentine
standards. You might heed the siren call of trance,
techno, garage, drum 'n' bass and deep house classics, or strike lucky when the organisers have
arranged an Amnesia from Ibiza night – even
Frankie Knuckles has been known to show up. Then
again, you might stumble on mediocre live acts and
play-by-rote hits. Thursdays (some of the best drum
'n' bass in Italy) and Fridays are usually good bets.
Saturdays see an influx of out-of-towners.

Full-Up
*Via della Vigna Vecchia 23r, Santa Croce (055
293006, www.fullupclub.com).* **Open** 11pm-4am
Tue-Sat. Closed June-Sept. **Admission** free.
Map p335 C4.
With the demise of Dolce Zucchero, the winner is
old-hand Full-Up. Friendly staff from the defunct DZ
have set up residence in this long-running club,
bringing new ideas and pepping up the proceedings.
The best night to go is Thursday, when the team
from YAB (*see below*) is enlisted to re-run its legendary Monday hip hop night, Smoove. Also worth
a look-in is Friday's house night, B.fly, with live
music from international bands. Saturday is an altogether more commercial affair with sounds from resident DJs Remo e Timmy. The club's flash *VIP privé*
is unusual in that it often really does have celebrities
(albeit minor ones) quaffing bubbly at its eight
tables. Ring ahead to book if you're impressed.

Lochness Lounge
*Via de' Benci 19r, Santa Croce (055 241464,
www.lochnessfirenze.com).* **Open** 7pm-3am daily.
Admission free. **Map** p335 C4.
A late-night studenty hangout with a spit 'n' saw-
dust style. Nessy is generally filled with foreign girls
and Italians on the pull, though the hunky doormen
seem to monopolise the girls' attentions (hence the
constant crowd at the door). Out-of-luck boys can
console themselves with pool or table footie.

★ Tenax
For listings, *see p200*.
The most influential and international of the
Florentine clubs is the warehouse-style Tenax in
Peretola. Far enough outside the centre to make a
night out an adventure, but not too far to be imprac-
tical without a car, it's best known as a live venue
for hip international bands and for its DJ exchanges
(Pete Tong, Deep Dish and Ashley Beedle have all
hit the decks here). When it's closed in the summer,
Tenax also organises one-off events, often in
the Stazione Leopolda. Big-name DJ Alex Neri's

Nobody's Perfect on Saturday is the hottest night in
the city by a long shot, heaving with house, big beat,
progressive and drum 'n' bass. There's free parking
for Tenax punters in via del Palagio degli Spini.

Twice
*Via Verdi 57r, Santa Croce (055 0517374,
www.twiceclub.com).* **Open** *Bar* 7.30-11pm daily.
Club 11pm-3am daily. **Admission** free.
The main news at the latest incarnation of this long-
running venue is the division of the night into early-
evening wine bar and club, hence the name. The
gimmicks don't stop there, and while the wine bar's
a safe stop-off for an *aperitvo*, the themed club nights
become a tad tedious. Saturday is Hawaii house
night, complete with flower leis; Tuesday is Lollipop
Night (guess what's in the goody bag), with a hefty
serving of old-school music. Hip hop and R&B
Thursdays shed the tack and are worth a punt.

Viper Theatre
*Via Pistoiese, Outside the City Gates (055
318231, www.viperclub.eu). Bus 35.* **Open**
varies. **Admission** €5-€35. **No credit cards.**
One of Florence's best places to catch the latest
sounds, whether live – the likes of Black Mountain
and Marracash – or in storming DJ sets from international names.

YAB
*Via de' Sassetti 5r, Duomo & Around (055
215160, www.yab.it).* **Open** 9pm-4am Mon, Tue,
Thur-Sat. Closed June-Sept. **Admission** free (€15
drinks minimum-spend Fri, Sat). **Map** p334 B3.
Some refer to this large, trendy city-centre locale as
a disco; others, a 'glamour club'. You Are Beautiful
– popularly known as YAB – has existed since the
late 1970s, and plays up to any narcissist tendencies,
not only by its name but also its liberal use of mirrors, flattering lighting and on-tap female-focused
compliments from the stalwarts. The powerful
sound system has the mammoth dancefloor shim-
mying with dancers, while the wall-to-wall bar areas
cater to those with tired feet. Monday hip hop nights
are an institution among Americans, and Thursday
is deep house played to a young crowd letting it all
hang out; the place is packed on Saturdays.

ARTS & ENTERTAINMENT

Art Bar.

Perhaps because of its roots as a wine producer, this spin-off bar is one of the more grown-up of the central hangouts. It's packed with designer-clad model types till late, from Thursdays to Saturdays. Upstairs is the Attico, the *VIP privé*, to enter which you have to book a table, while the outside area is often booked for private parties for luxury car and fashion launches, especially during the Pitti shows. If you have no invite in your paw, no amount of blagging will get you past the impassive bouncers.

Dolce Vita
For listings, *see p199*.
Despite the influx of trendy new bars, Dolce Vita is still going strong after years of hegemony in the summer nights-out stakes. Crowds spill out on to the medieval square during warm evenings. Inside, the cold metal and glass bar leads to a cosier salon, with sofas and soft lighting from beautiful crystal lamps, usually inhabited by those too weary to move on to the clubbing scene.

Ideal Firenze
Via il Prato 4b, Santa Maria Novella (055 2654348, www.idealfirenze.it). **Open** 7am-1am Mon-Thur; 7am-2am Sat, Sun. **Admission** (tango classes and events) €8-€15.
This spacious, minimal bar to the west of Santa Maria Novella is a great place to chill over a cocktail while enjoying a fun range of live performances that might be anything from an acapella women's group to a blues duet or tango classes going on around you. It's open from morning through to late night and also holds exhibitions, making it a mini-culture centre with alcohol and copious *aperitivi*.

James Joyce
Lungarno Benvenuto Cellini 1r, Oltrarno (055 6580856). **Open** 6pm-2am Mon-Thur; 6pm-3am Fri-Sun. **No credit cards. Map** p335 D6.
The large enclosed garden with long wooden tables makes this one of the best of Florence's pubs in spring and summer. JJ has a high-spirited vibe, especially around happy hour (7.30-9.30pm). To go with the name, there's a small bookshop selling paperbacks, some of them in English.

Kikuya English Pub
Via de' Benci 43r, Santa Croce (055 2344879, www.kikuyapub.it). **Open** 6pm-2am daily. **Map** p335 C5.
Feeling homesick for something louty and lively? Here's a taste of British pub culture, with Guinness and John Bull English Ale, live footie on plasma screens and Tex-Mex cuisine. Allusions to authenticity stop there, though: Brazilian barmaids mix the drinks with panache and Kikuya's claim to fame is that it was voted one of the best pubs in Italy by *Playboy* magazine (draw your own conclusions). There's free Wi-Fi for anyone who cares to risk a

PUBS & BARS

Art Bar
Via del Moro 4r, Santa Maria Novella (055 287661). **Open** 7pm-1am Mon-Thur; 7pm-2am Fri, Sat. Closed 3wks Aug. **No credit cards. Map** p334 B2.
Battered French horns hanging from the ceiling and sepia photos of blues and jazz musicians lend a beatnik air to this perennially popular bar. The ambience is cosy but animated, with student types holed up in the brick cellar sipping their potent piña coladas. During happy hour (7-9pm), drinks cost a bargain €5; on Mondays and Wednesdays, the happy 'hour' lasts all night.

Astor Caffè
Piazza del Duomo 20r (055 284305). **Open** 9am-3am daily. **Map** p334 C3.
This huge, lively jazz bar draws an enthusiastic young crowd. The big skylight, soft red lighting and flash chrome bar are a clean backdrop for the regular art exhibitions, while internet points provide distraction from the busy socialising of the main bar.

Cabiria
For listings, *see p148*.
After a long history as the wildest and grungiest of the pre-club bars, Cabiria has grown up into a thirtysomething, along with its customers, a well-behaved, well-to-do genial crowd. The pretty candlelit terrace on piazza Santo Spirito is enjoyed on warm nights, while soft jazzy sounds emanate from the DJ sets inside.

Colle Bereto
For listings, *see p146*.

pint down their laptop – this pub packs 'em in, especially during happy hour, from 7pm to 10pm.

Mayday Lounge Café
Via Dante Alighieri 16r, Duomo & Around (055 2381290, www.maydayclub.it). **Open** 8pm-2am Mon-Sat. Closed 2wks Aug. **Admission** free, membership required (free). **Map** p335 B4.
This wacky joint with odd art installations and hundreds of old Marconi radios hanging from the ceilings has something of a cult following. Somewhere between a beatnik refuge and something from *Lost in Translation*, Mayday is dark and edgy. There's a diverse programme of events, with the only constant being a jazzy basis to the sounds. *Photo p206.*

Moyo
Via de' Benci 23r, Santa Croce (055 2479738, www.moyo.it). **Open** 6pm-2am daily. **Admission** free. **Map** p335 C5.
The cool wood decor and outdoor seating make for a welcoming year-round environment at this buzzy bar. Come *aperitivo* time, it's packed out with hip Florentines. It's on the edge of the no-drive zone, so parking is only a five-minute walk away

Negroni
Via de' Renai 17r, Oltrarno (055 243647, www.negronibar.com). **Open** 8am-2.30am Mon-Sat; 6pm-2am Sun. Closed 2wks Aug. **Map** p335 D5.

The Aperitivo Awards

We dish out the gongs for the very best of the trend.

Putting a few free snacks on the bar has always been a mark of Italian hospitality, but now almost any bar worth its salt serves up a full free buffet with its pre-dinner drinks (which generally cost between €5 and €10). This is the nationwide *aperitivo* craze, which started in Milan and has spread steadily southwards. Reminiscent of the medieval races to build the tallest towers, a keen competitive spirit has been stirred up among the main Florentine nightlife bars, all competing to provide the most exciting, gourmet, imaginative or just plain enormous feast.

For an *aperitivo* that looks almost too good to eat, walk along the riverbank to the **Fusion Bar Shozan** in the Gallery Hotel Art (*see p99*), where snacks of authentic sushi and tempura are beautifully presented on black lacquer plates lined up on the blue-backlit bar. Prize for best *aperitivo* with a view goes to another Ferragamo joint – the Sky Lounge terrace bar of the **Hotel Continentale** (*see p101*). Take the lift up to the fifth floor for a breathtaking 360º sunset panorama. Silver medal goes to the rooftop bar of the **Grand Hotel Minerva** (*see p107*), where the marinated tuna, king prawns, gazpacho and squid-ink risotto are served poolside. There's no buffet but drinks come with crudités and delicacies such as artichoke dips and truffle canapés. Most atmospheric *aperitivo* is served at **Slowly** (*see p206*), where the coloured lanterns and LED-lit floor and bar lead to a balconied room with gold-leaf luminaire and central pedestal laden with platters of hot and cold delicacies from the bar's kitchens.

Hotel Continentale.

Many bars season the evening's snacks with music or DJ sets that go on well into the night. Two of the best bets if you want to settle in for the night are **Twice** (*see p203*) and **Rex** (*see p206*). Twice does a Tuscan buffet with wine tastings from 7pm, while club nights kick off at 11pm. Rex serves up a 'Mediterranean' feast from 6pm. The night gets hotter after the chocolate fondue has been licked.

ARTS & ENTERTAINMENT

Named after Signor Negroni himself – the man who invented the eponymous cocktail (gin, red vermouth, Campari) while sitting at a bar that used to be on this site – this is one of the coolest destinations in town. The streamlined, sleek, red and black interior is a backdrop for art and photography exhibitions, while the outside seating in the garden square is crowded on hot summer nights. The music works around CD promotions run in conjunction with Alberti record shop, and showcases the latest releases from progressive lo-fi bands.

Porfirio Rubirosa

Viale Strozzi 38r, San Lorenzo (055 490965).
Open 11am-2am Tue-Sun. Closed 2wks Aug.
A hedonist's haven, this bar is named after a Dominican playboy and the locals flock here to do their best attempts at emulating the man himself. Weekend traffic restrictions in the city centre mean that the area is mobbed on Fridays and Saturdays – the outside bar could easily be mistaken for a flash car showroom, so many motors pull up outside.

Rex Café

Via Fiesolana 25r, Santa Croce (055 2480331).
Open 6pm-2.30am daily. Closed June-Aug.
Map p335 B5.
With more of a club than a bar vibe, Rex is king of the east of the city, filling up with loyal subjects who sashay to the sounds of the session DJs playing bassy beats and jungle rhythms. Gaudi-esque mosaics decorate the central bar, wrought-iron lamps shed a soft light while a luscious red antechamber creates welcome seclusion for more intimate gatherings. Tapas are served during the *aperitivo* happy hour (5-9.30pm), and the cocktails are especially good.

Il Rifrullo

For listings, *see p150.*
It's not unknown for people to wander in here for Sunday brunch and not emerge again until Apollo has well and truly left the building. Rifrullo has something of the hospitable friend's house vibe, what with the chatty bar staff, well-worn upholstered chairs, the continuous arrival of plates of homely food at *aperitivo* time, the fire in the grate in winter and the newly extended garden area with views of the old city walls. Don't bring the knitting – things liven up plenty as the night wears on.

Sky Lounge, Bar Continentale

Vicolo dell'Oro 6r, Duomo & Around (055 27262, www.lungarnohotels.com). **Open** Mar-Oct 2.30-11.30pm daily. **Map** p334 C3.
In-the-know Florentines mix with hotel guests at sundown for aperitifs at the Hotel Continentale's swanky rooftop bar. The sides are lined with smart biscuit-coloured upholstered benches, and cocktails are served with crudités and mini-brioches. The main attraction, though, is the 360° bird's-eye view of the city. The bar is open in 'fine weather'; while officially closed in winter, it may be open or closed for a few weeks longer depending on the weather.

Slowly

Via Porta Rossa 63r, Duomo & Around (055 2645354, www.slowlycafe.com). **Open** 7pm-2am Mon-Sat. **Map** p334 C3.
The ultimate chill-out bohemian-chic bar, Slowly is softly lit by candles in mosaic lanterns, with big soft sofas in alcoves, laid-back staff and mellow Buddha Bar sounds when the DJ gets stuck in. Even the inevitable crowds of pretty young things can't break the nice and easy spell. The restaurant overlooking the bar serves imaginative global cuisine. At the time of writing owner Luciano Peruzzi was about to close for a major refurb that would turn the basement space into Chez Moi, a jazz club-style lounge bar that would act as a live music venue and club; fitting, considering Josephine Baker once sang here.

Zoe

Via de' Renai 13r, Oltrarno (055 243111, www.zoebar.it). **Open** 8am-1.30am Mon-Thur; 8am-2am Fri, Sat; 6pm-1am Sun. **Map** p335 D5.
Zoe's red neon sign lures punters in with the promise of the sexiest atmosphere of the Oltrarno's many drinking holes. The long thin bar area is a proxy catwalk and bassy beats pump out from the DJ room at the back. Zoe also has the best red cocktails in town: there's the lethal Crimson Zoe with vodka, gin and Cointreau and the Red Caipiroska with crushed strawberries. Rule of thumb: if it's red, drink it.

Mayday Lounge Café. *See p205.*

Sport & Fitness

Get pecs like David.

With health advice plastered on every TV channel, billboard and magazine, Florentines have become a lot more health- and body-conscious in recent years. Fitness enthusiasts, and those who want to work off that extra helping of *gelato*, can benefit from a huge growth in the number of gyms in the city, offering a wide variety of activities, from Pilates to step and yoga. Fresh air exercise can be had at the city's outdoor swimming pools and along its scenic jogging paths.

SPECTATOR SPORTS

Car & motorbike racing

Autodromo del Mugello
Nr Scarperia (055 8499111, www.mugello circuit.it). **Open** Mar-Nov. **Tickets** phone for details.
Top-notch racing, including Formula 3 and motorcycle world championships, are held at this circuit 30km (20 miles) north of Florence. Bikers can live out their Carl Fogarty fantasies on the track (€50 for 20 minutes), but you have to bring your own Ducati. Call Paolo Poli at 055 480553 for reservations.

Calcio Storico

See p179.

Football

★ Stadio Artemio Franchi
Campo di Marte, Outside the City Gates (055 503011, www.acffiorentina.it). Bus 11, 17. **Open** Aug-May. **Tickets** approx €20-€150; reduced prices for women and children. **No credit cards**.
ACF Fiorentina had a tumultuous opening to the 21st century, what with their financial problems in 2002, and penalisation for involvement in the Calciopoli match-fixing scandal in 2006; but by 2008 the Viola were largely back on form, re-establishing themselves in the top half of Serie A. The season runs from August to May; home matches are generally held every other Sunday, with kick-off at 3pm. You can buy tickets at the stadium, online (the website also has a list of authorised resellers) or up to three hours prior to a match at Chiosco degli Sportivi

(via Anselmi, near piazza della Repubblica, Duomo & Around, 055 292363).

Horse racing

Ippodromo Le Cascine
Via delle Cascine 3, Parco delle Cascine, Outside the City Gates (055 422591, www.ippodromi fiorentini.it). Bus 17C. **Open** Apr-May, Sept-Oct. **Admission** free. **No credit cards**.
Florence's *galoppo* (flat-racing) course. Keep an eye out for leading Tuscan jockeys such as Alessandro Muzzi and Claudio Colombi.

Ippodromo Le Mulina
Viale del Pegaso, Parco delle Cascine, Outside the City Gates (055 4226076, www.ippodromi fiorentini.it). Bus 17C. **Open** Nov-Mar, June-July. **Admission** free. **No credit cards**.
Florence's racecourse for *il trotto* (trotting), where the driver sits in a carriage behind the horse. The Premio Duomo in June is among Tuscany's biggest equine events.

ACTIVE SPORTS & FITNESS

Climbing & trekking

For books and information on trekking and mountaineering in the whole of Tuscany, visit Il Romito's **Libreria Stella Alpina** (via Corridoni 14, Outside the City Gates, 055 411688, www.stella-alpina.com).

Cave di Maiano
Via Cave di Maiano, Outside the City Gates (no phone). Bus 7.

If you're into free-climbing, the Cave di Maiano in Fiesole is the place to go – actually old mines, they make ideal climbing walls. You'll be on your own, without guides or instructors, so bring equipment.

Gruppo Escursionistico CAI (Club Alpino Italiano)

Via del Mezzetta 2, Outside the City Gates (055 6120467, www.caifirenze.it). Bus 6, 20. **Open** 4-7pm Mon-Thur; 9am-1pm, 4-7pm Fri. Closed Aug. **Rates** vary.

Guided Sunday treks through the Tuscan countryside, mostly rated easy to moderate. Prices include transport to and from the city centre, but not lunch. In May, the Prato section of CAI organises 'Piazza to Piazza', an 84km (52-mile) two-day walk, including overnight arrangements. For more information, get in touch with the Associazione Sportiva Sci CAI Prato, via Altopascio, Prato (0574 29267).

Guide Alpine

338 9313444, www.ufficioguide.it.
These mountaineering experts organise courses throughout the summer. Phone Ufficio Guide on the above numbers for details, or check online.

Cycling

See also pp48-49 **Touring Florence***.*

Florence by Bike

Via San Zanobi 120-122r, San Lorenzo (055 488992, www.florencebybike.it). **Open** *Mar-Oct* 9am-7.30pm daily. *Nov-Feb* 9am-1pm, 3.30-7.30pm daily.

Bike rental and organised bike tours. Especially recommended is the one-day tour through Chianti (35km/22 miles) costing €70 per person and including bike and helmet rental, an English-speaking guide and lunch in a restaurant. Book in advance, as the maximum number in a group is 12.

Walking Tours of Florence

Via de Sassetti 1, Duomo & Around (055 2645033, 329 6132730 mobile, www.italy. artviva.com). **Open** *Office* 8am-6.30pm Mon-Sat; 8.30am-1.30pm Sun. *Mobile* 8am-8pm daily. **Map** p334 C3.

Despite the name, this well-regarded company offers just about every kind of tour under the sun, including half-day bike tours of Tuscany. For €65, you'll get a guide, bike, helmet, equipment, snacks and wine. Tours leave from the office, tucked away on a little square off piazza Davanzati.

Football

Tennis Carraia (*see p212*) has facilities for *calcetto* – a five-a-side, extremely fast-paced local variety of football. Most of the pitches there are outdoors and can be used by anyone.

There's another, more popular football pitch behind piazzale Michelangelo, with floodlights at night, which is also open to outsiders. Whether you opt for a proper pitch or simply fancy a kickabout in a park, it is – as you'd expect – never hard to find a group of Italians eager to join in with you.

Golf

Circolo Golf Ugolino

Via Chiantigiana 3, Grassina (055 2301009, www. golfugolino.it). Bus SITA. **Open** *Winter* 8.30am-6.30pm daily. *Summer* 8.30am-7.30pm daily. Closed Jan. **Rates** €70 Mon-Fri; €85 Sat, Sun.

This 18-hole course is the nearest to the city (about 20 minutes south by bus), but it's closed to non-members during the frequent weekend tournaments. It's best to phone or email (info@golfugolino.it) for reservations, at least a week in advance.

Poggio dei Medici

Via San Gavino 27, Scarperia (055 84350, www.golfpoggiodeimedici.com). Bus SITA, then by taxi. **Open** 24hrs daily. **Rates** €52 Mon-Fri; €80 Sat, Sun; €30 club rental.

This 18-hole, par 72 course, built to USGA standards, opened in 1995 and was immediately recognised by *Il Mondo del Golf* as the best new course in Italy. Designed by Italian architect Alvise Rossi Fioravanti and professional player Baldovino Dassù, it allows for four different playing routes within its 18 holes. Carts and clubs are available for rent and private lessons are also available.

Gyms

Fonbliù

Piazzale di Porta Romana 10r, Outside the City Gates (055 2335385, www.fonbliu.com). Bus 11, 36, 37. **Open** *Winter* 8.30am-9pm Mon-Fri; 8.30am-6pm Sat. *Summer* 8.30am-8.30pm Mon-Fri; 8.30am-1.30pm Sat. **Membership** €40/day; €120/mth.

A small, high-tech spa at Porta Romana, which also has a fitness centre and indoor pool. Classes are normally limited to five people.

Klab Wellness Centers

Via de' Conti 7, Santa Maria Novella (055 7184300, www.klab.it). **Open** 8.30am-10.30pm

ARTS & ENTERTAINMENT

Mon, Wed; 8.30am-10pm Tue, Thur, Fri. Closed Aug. **Rates** €84/mth; phone for info on day passes.

One of the biggest and best-equipped gyms in Florence, with three locations. Personal trainers, huge workout areas and a large pool are joined by a bio-sauna and massage and tanning facilities.

Palestra Ricciardi

Borgo Pinti 75, Santa Croce (055 2478444, www.palestraricciardi.it). **Open** 9am-10pm Mon-Fri; 9.30am-6pm Sat; 10am-2pm Sun. Closed Aug. **Membership** €100/mth, then €20/day. **Map** p335 B5.

Staying fit in Florence generally requires exercising your wallet as much as your body, and this place proves no exception. There's a small garden outside where you can top up your tan after taking spinning, step or hip hop classes.

Tropos

Via Orcagna 20a, Outside the City Gates (055 678381, www.troposclub.it). Bus 14. **Open** 8am-10pm Mon-Fri; 8am-8pm Sat. **Membership** €30 trial visit, then various options.

A luxurious (though correspondingly pricey) setting, whether you're splashing about in the aerobics pool, clocking up laps in the main pool or steaming yourself in one of the saunas.

Virgin Active

Via Generale Alberto dalla Chiesa, Outside City Gates (800 914555, www.virginactive.it). **Open** 8am-11pm Mon-Fri; 9am-7pm Sat, Sun. **Membership** phone for details.

This complex has it all, with several pools and fitness areas, personal trainers, therapeutic services and even a babysitting facility.

Horse riding

Maneggio Marinella

Via di Macia 21, Outside the City Gates (055 8878066). Bus 28. **Open** 9am-1pm, 3-7pm daily. **Rates** €18/hr. **No credit cards.**

Phone ahead to book one of the daily rides at this stable in the northern suburbs. Lessons and special group trips are also organised on request.

Rendola Riding

Rendola, Montevarchi (055 9707045, www.rendolariding.it). **Open** 9am-1pm, 3-7pm daily. **Rates** €18/hr. **No credit cards.**

This stable – situated about 30 minutes' drive south of Florence, on the border with Chianti – offers respite from the busy city and an opportunity to enjoy the fabulous countryside. Various packages are offered, covering everything from one-hour rides through the countryside to two- to three-day trips (with lodging at a neighbouring *agriturismo*). Book at least a day in advance. There's a weight limit of

85kg (187lbs) because of the hilly tracks – which, for the same reason, are not recommended for children under ten.

Ice skating

Florence sets up a temporary ice-skating rink every winter from December to January. The venue tends to change every year, so contact the APT (055 23320) for the latest information. You pay by the session (there are three or four daily); the last ends at about 11pm.

In-line skating

Le Pavoniere

Viale della Catena 2, Parco delle Cascine, Outside the City Gates (335 5718547 mobile). Bus 17C. **Open** 5-8pm Tue-Wed; 10am-7.30pm Sat, Sun. Closed when raining. **Rates** €5/hr. **No credit cards.**

Hire in-line skates from this kiosk in the Parco delle Cascine and take advantage of miles of traffic-free paths along the banks of the Arno.

Rowing

Canottieri Comunali

Lungarno Francesco Ferrucci 2, nr ponte Verazzano, Outside the City Gates (055 6812151, www.canottiericomunalifirenze.it). **Open** 8.30am-9pm Mon-Fri; 8.30am-7pm Sat; 8am-1pm Sun. **Membership** €620/3mths. **No credit cards.**

This rowing club enjoys a delightful location among the trees along the Arno – it's perfect in sunny weather. There's also a full range of lessons and activities on offer, including white-water rafting excursions in Tuscany.

Società Canottieri Firenze

Lungarno Luisa de' Medici 8, Duomo & Around (055 282130, www.canottierifirenze.it). **Open** 8am-8.30pm Mon, Sat; 8am-9.30pm Tue-Fri; 8am-1pm Sun. **Membership** €70/mth. **No credit cards. Map** p334 C3.

Tucked away in the caverns below the Uffizi (you enter the club through a tiny green door on the *lungarno*), this fairly exclusive club has boats that go out on the Arno. There's also a gym, indoor rowing tank, sauna and showers.

Running

Most joggers hit the **Parco delle Cascine** along the river, but you can also head for the hills. Your best bet is **viale Michelangelo**, where there's a wide pavement under trees. Small roads branch off and will have you in Tuscan countryside within minutes. Be particularly careful of cars on these back lanes; there are often no pavements.

Piscina Bellariva. *See p212.*

Associazione Atletica Leggera
*Viale Manfredo Fanti 2, Outside the City Gates
(055 576616). Bus 10, 20.* **Open** 1-6pm Mon,
Wed; 9am-1pm Tue, Thur-Sat.
This is Florence's best source for running clubs and
meets. Foreigners can only participate in amateur
races – phone for further details.

Florence Marathon
Florence (055 5522957, www.firenzemarathon.it).
Normally held in late November, the increasingly
popular Florence Marathon snakes through the centre of the city and the suburbs. It's open to anyone
over the age of 18, providing they can show a certificate of health.

Skiing

For the **Abetone** ski area in the province of
Pistoia (an easy weekend or day trip from
Florence), *see p230.*

Squash

Centro Squash Firenze
*Via Empoli 16, San Quirico (055 7323055).
Bus 1.* **Open** 9.45am-9.45pm Mon-Fri; 9.30am-
6pm Sat. Closed Sat June-Aug. **Rates** €8/hr Mon-
Thur; €5/hr Fri, Sat. **No credit cards.**
If you're dying to get some squash practice in while
you're in Florence, this is the place to go. It has
a fully equipped gym and a sauna, as well as aerobics, spinning and step classes. Equipment is available for hire.

Swimming

Many swimming pools are open only in the
summer. During winter some pools require
at least a month's membership and may limit
access to a few occasions a week. In summer
most public pools get packed early, but with
more than 40, you should find one to suit you.
Most city pools are open from 10am to 6pm;
for a list of all of them, see www.uisp.it.

Costoli
*Viale Pasquale Paoli, Outside the City Gates (055
6236027). Bus 10, 17, 20.* **Open** *June-Aug* 2-6pm
Mon; 10am-6pm Tue-Sun. *Sept-May* phone for
details. **Admission** €4.10/hr; free-€4.50/hr
reductions. **No credit cards.**
This is a swimmer's dream, with Olympic-size, div-
ing and children's pools, surrounded by a lovely
green park. Perfect for families. There's also an
indoor pool for the winter. Membership required.

INSIDE TRACK
POOLING RESOURCES

When things get too hot to handle, head
for one of Florence's impressive outdoor
pools. You can get a half-day ticket at any
of the city's municipal pools (after 2pm)
for €4, and swim at the Paolo Costoli (*see
p212*) for free every Thursday in July and
August until 8pm.

FLOG

Via Mercati 24b, Outside the City Gates (055 484465/www.flog.it). Bus 4, 8, 14, 20, 28. **Open** *June, July* 10am-6.30pm Sat, Sun. *Aug* 10am-6.30pm daily. Closed Sept-May. **Admission** €6; €4 reductions.
No credit cards.
This small outdoor pool in Poggetto is a great place to hang out on a baking hot day. Part of an 'after-work club' of a metalworking factory, it has a sun terrace and refreshments stand.

★ Hidron

Via di Gramignano, area adjacent to Esselunga, Campi Bisenzio (055 892500, www.hidron.it). **Open** *Outdoor pool* 10am-8pm daily in summer. *Indoor pool* 8am-10.30pm Mon, Wed; 7.15am-10.30pm Tue, Thur; 8am-9.30pm Fri; 9am-10pm Sat, Sun. *Fitness centre* 8am-10.30pm Mon-Fri; 9am-7pm Sat, Sun. **Admission** varies.
This water park and spa a few miles north-west of the city centre is a real beauty, with a vast indoor pool complete with slide, whirlpool baths, geysers, waterfalls, a 50m saltwater outdoor pool with a whirlpool area heated to 36°, an eight-lane lap pool and a dedicated kids' pool, as well as restaurant, café and bars.

Hotel Villa Le Rondini

Via Vecchia Bolognese 224, Outside the City Gates (055 400081, www.villalerondini.com). Bus 25. **Open** 10am-7pm daily. Closed Oct-Apr. **Admission** €17 Mon-Fri; €20 Sat, Sun. **No credit cards.**
A small outdoor pool beside a chic, hillside hotel at La Ruota just outside of town, surrounded by a lovely lawn and shady trees.

NUOTO+

Giovanni Franceschi (0571 993721/335 6172453 mobile, www.giovannifranceschi.it).
Through this organisation you can book week-long swim camps in locations across Italy. They run during the summer and are open to children, adults and whole families. Instruction at all levels is combined with a relaxing holiday. Give them a call or visit the website for enquiries.

Le Pavoniere

Viale della Catena 2, San Jacopino (055 362233). **Open** *June-mid Sept* 10am-6pm, 8pm-2am daily. **Admission** €7.50; €4.50 reductions.
Located on the east side of the Cascine Park and so great for a quick dip, but it does gets very crowded in the summer, so be prepared to queue and don't expect to find a spot big enough to sunbathe in. Having said that, once you do get in, you'll find an enormous open-air swimming pool attended by lifeguards during the high season, a poolside bar, restaurant and pizzeria, and even a beach volleyball court and aquatic gym for the sports-minded. Events

are held here regularly, including art, music, fashion shows, beauty pageants and tango Tuesdays.

Piscina Paolo Costoli

Via Pasquale Paoli 9 (055 6236027). **Open** 2-5pm Mon; 10am-6pm Tue-Sun. **Admission** €6.50; €4.50 reductions; free under-7s with paying adult. Located near the Franchi stadium, the Paolo Costoli, named for the Florentine Olympic swimmer, is the largest and one of the most popular public swimming pools in the city. It gets horribly overcrowded so swimming laps can be a challenge, but kids love the noise, energy and liveliness of the place, so a good choice for kids in need of a museums break.

★ Piscina Bellariva

Lungarno Aldo Moro 6, Outside the City Gates (055 677521). Bus 14. **Open** *May-Sept* 10am-6pm Mon, Wed, Fri-Sun; 10am-6pm, 8.30-11.30pm Tue, Thur. *Oct-Apr* 8.30-11pm Tue, Thur; 9.30am-12.30pm Sat, Sun. **Admission** €6.50; €4.50 reductions. **No credit cards.**
A lovely indoor Olympic-size pool in a beautiful green park to the east of town. There's a refreshments stand and a separate pool for small children, so it's a good option for a family trip. *Photo p211.*

Tennis

ASSI

Viale Michelangelo, Outside the City Gates (055 687858). Bus 12, 13. **Open** *Summer* 8am-11pm daily. *Winter* 8am-6pm daily. **Rates** *Before 6pm* €10/hr court for 2 people; €11/hr court for 4 people. *After 6pm* €11/hr court for 2 people; €12/hr court for 4 people. **No credit cards.**
Six clay courts beautifully situated overlooking the city on the south side of the Arno. There are three full-time pros and most of the instructors speak at least a little English.

Tennis Carraia

Via dell'Erta Canina 26, Outside the City Gates (055 7327047). **Open** phone for details. **Rates** phone for details.
Set in what feels like the countryside, the Carraia courts are just a ten-minute walk from Porta San Niccolò. There are only three courts, so reservations are needed. There are programmes for children, and several friendly pros can give private lessons.

Unione Sportiva Affrico

Viale Fanti Manfredo 20, Outside the City Gates (055 600845). Bus 17, 20. **Open** 9am-10.30pm Mon-Fri; 9am-7pm Sat; 9am-1pm Sun. Closed 2wks Aug. **Rates** €11.50/hr per court. **No credit cards.**
Near the football stadium in the east, this down-to-earth tennis club has eight courts. Non-members are allowed to reserve a court up to three days in advance, though this has to be done in person.

Theatre & Dance

Despite financial woes, the performing arts scene is thriving

Tuscany is home to more than 200 active theatres, most of them running regular seasons, with more opening each year, but budget restraints are resulting in shorter seasons and cheaper stagings than in the theatre scene's heyday – a high number of monologues are shown. Theatres have learnt the hard way that their only means of escape from this long-term crisis is networking. In Florence and neighbouring towns, 16 venues have joined forces to found **Firenze dei Teatri** (055 2625903, www.firenzedeiteatri.it), giving themselves a better chance of public funding by submitting joint

projects. Together with the **Teatri Aperti** festival (*see p215*), the association's most successful scheme is **Passteatri**, a voucher booklet that allows the holder to pick six performances out of a choice of 40, put on at six different theatres. Priced at just €48, Passteatri has finally made theatregoing barely dearer than visiting the cinema – however, it mostly benefits Italian-speakers.

As a whole, the dance scene benefits from better public funding, and Tuscan dance companies have a far more solid international reputation than their theatrical counterparts. Full-length classical and contemporary productions by the **MaggioDanza** (*see p215*) are performed at the Teatro del Maggio, while modern work comes from ensembles such as the **Virgilio Sieni Dance Company**. Elsewhere in Tuscany, look out for **Company Blu** (Sesto Fiorentino), **Motus** (Siena), **Aldes** (Lucca), **Sosta Palmizi** (Cortona), **Micha Van Hoeke** (Castiglioncello), **Compagnia Xe** (San Casciano) and **Giardino Chiuso** (San Gimignano).

Theatre seasons run roughly from October to April, but the summer months offer an plenty of festivals (*see p178*) and open-air shows. As a rule, Sunday shows are matinées, and Monday is the day off. Unsold seats can be bought from the theatre's ticket office from an hour prior to the performance. Both in Florence and Tuscany, virtually all theatre productions are in Italian, but there's a fair amount of non-verbal theatre, and English-speaking companies like Festa and FITC have entered the scene (*see p215*). Details of events can be found in the local press or in the monthly brochure issued by Firenze dei Teatri.

VENUES

Cango Cantieri Goldonetta Firenze
Via Santa Maria 23-25, Oltrarno (055 2280525, www.cango.fi.it). **Box office** 10am-5pm Mon-Fri.

Seasons Sept-Dec, May-June. **No credit cards**. **Map** p334 D1.
The term *cantiere* (building site) refers to this venue's status as a project-in-progress. As well as performances by the resident Virgilio Sieni (*see p215*), there are workshops and festival dates.

Florence Dance Cultural Centre
Borgo Stella 23r, Oltrarno (055 289276, www.florencedance.org). **Box office** varies. Closed Aug. **Map** p334 C1.
Directed by former *étoile* Marga Nativo and American choreographer Keith Ferrone, this eclectic centre hosts a range of dance classes as well as a programme of visual art events called Etoile Toy.

Teatro Cantiere Florida
Via Pisana 111, Outside the City Gates (055 7131783, www.teatrocantiereflorida.it). Bus 6, 26,

27, 80. **Box office** 2-5pm Mon-Fri. **Season** late Jan-Apr. **No credit cards**.
This bare-walled 288-seat theatre aims to promote young actors, directors and playwrights, and to appeal to young audiences. Productions range from reworks of Shakespearean classics to experimental pieces. Family shows are on Sunday afternoons.

Teatro Everest
Via Volterrana 4b, Galluzzo, Outside the City Gates (055 2321754, 055 2048307 tickets, www. teatroeverest.it). Bus 36, 37. **Box office** 4-7pm Tue-Fri. **Season** Nov-May. **No credit cards**.
Launched in 2002, this refurbished 1950s parish hall belongs to Teatri Possibili, a national network of experimental theatres promoting emerging directors and actors, mixed in with a few established names.

★ Teatro Goldoni
Via Santa Maria 15, Oltrarno (call Teatro del Maggio; see below). **Box office** contact relevant organising body. **Season** varies. **No credit cards**. **Map** p334 D1.
The diminutive 19th-century Teatro Goldoni is managed by the Teatro del Maggio Musicale Fiorentino on behalf of the Florence town council and is used primarily for dance and ballet performances.

Teatro della Limonaia
Via Gramsci 426, Sesto Fiorentino, Outside the City Gates (055 440852, www.teatrodellalimonaia. it). Bus 2, 28A. **Box office** 3-6pm Mon-Fri; occasionally 4-7pm Sat. **Seasons** Feb-May, Sept-Oct. **No credit cards**.
The former lemon house of the Villa Corsi Salviati has been converted into a trendy 90-seater hosting alternative shows by up-and-coming Italian and international theatre and dance artists. Look for the Intercity Festival in Sept-Oct.

Teatro del Maggio Musicale Fiorentino
Corso Italia 16, Santa Maria Novella (055 2779350, 055 213535 tickets, www.maggio fiorentino.com). **Box office** 10am-4pm Mon-Fri; 10am-1pm Sat. **Season** Sept-July.
Home to MaggioDanza (*see p215*), this theatre features mainstream ballet year-round. In late June, the Maggio Musicale festival (*see p176*) offers a dance jamboree in piazza della Signoria. *See also p187*.

Teatro della Pergola
Via della Pergola 18-32, San Marco (055 2264316, www.teatrodellapergola.com). **Box office** 9.30am-6.45pm Tue-Sat; 10am-12.15pm Sun. **Season** Oct-Apr. **Map** p335 B5.
Shakespeare, Pirandello and Goldoni feature regularly in the programme of ancient and modern classics presented by this historic theatre, which recently celebrated 350 years of activity. Watch out for guided visits on Sunday mornings (advance booking necessary). *See also p196*.

Teatro del Maggio Musicale Fiorentino.

Teatro Puccini
Piazza Puccini, via delle Cascine 41, Outside the City Gates (055 362067, www.teatropuccini.it). Bus 17, 30, 35. **Box office** 3.30-7pm Mon-Sat; Sat also 10am-1pm. **Season** Oct-Apr. **No credit cards**.
Housed in a 1940s listed building, the Puccini focuses on comedy and satirical shows.

Teatro di Rifredi
Via Vittorio Emanuele 303, Outside the City Gates (055 4220361, www.toscanateatro.it). Bus 8, 14, 20, 28. **Box office** 4-7pm Mon-Sat. **Season** Oct-May. **No credit cards**.
A programme devoted mainly to contemporary and fringe shows with an emphasis on emerging playwrights and directors. There's also the odd classic production, plus appearances by guest companies including acclaimed visual theatre artists.

Teatro Studio di Scandicci
Via Donizetti 58, Outside the City Gates (055 751853/757348, www.scandiccicultura.org). Bus 16, 26, or tram T1. **Box office** 1hr 30mins prior to show time only. **Season** Jan-May. *Special projects* Oct-Dec. **No credit cards**.
This unusual space (formerly a school gym) is one of the best spots to see alternative theatre. Artistic director Giancarlo Cauteruccio is a respected name with a strong vision, and his Compagnia di Krypton (*see right*) is the principal resident here.

Teatro Verdi
Via Ghibellina 99, Santa Croce (055 212320, www.teatroverdifirenze.it). **Box office**

10am-1pm, 4-7pm Mon-Fri. **Season** Oct-Mar.
No credit cards. Map p335 C5.
The city's largest theatre, Teatro Verdi hosts all the
top-notch light comedies, musicals and dance shows
whose more lavish sets and elaborate choreography
would not fit in any of the smaller venues in town.
See also p196.

THEATRE COMPANIES

Compagnia Krypton
055 2345443, www.compagniakrypton.it.
This company, whose lighting, stage and sound
techniques were considered avant-garde when the
group started in 1982, is resident at the Teatro
Studio di Scandicci (*see left*). It still experiments
with projections, lasers, mics and various other
special effects.

Elsinor, Teatro Stabile d'Innovazione
055 7131783,. www.elsinor.net.
Elsinor manages the Teatro Cantiere Florida (*see
p213*) as well as theatres further afield – in Milan,
Bologna and Forlì. The company's productions
encompass a repertoire of experimental shows and
plays for children and young people.

Festa
338 918 0867 mobile, www.festatheatre.com.
The Florence English Speaking Theatrical Artists
(Festa) is a group of theatre professionals dedicated
to providing English-language theatrical and inter-
disciplinary performances for English-speakers.

FITC
055 213788, www.florencetheatre.com.
At the time of writing, the Florence International
Theatre Company (Fitc) was morphing into the
rather more grandiose Global Theatre Project
(www.theglobaltheatreproject.org/), based in the US,
but it will still work with the theatrical community
in Florence to reflect the city's international status
and develop both performances and outreach projects held in a variety of venues around town, including theatres, libraries and bookshops.

Pupi e Fresedde
055 4220361, www.toscanateatro.it.
Founded in 1976, the managing company of the
Teatro di Rifredi (*see left*) is named after Peter
Schumann's politically radical Bread & Puppet theatre. It has an eclectic repertoire of original titles
about literature, science, current social issues and
the Tuscan dialect.

Teatro delle Donne
055 8876581, www.teatrodelledonne.com.
Based at the Teatro Manzoni in Calenzano, this company promotes and performs plays by women and
organises two festivals on the subject.

DANCE COMPANIES

Compagnia Virgilio Sieni Danza
055 2280525, www.sienidanza.it.
Dancer/choreographer Virgilio Sieni directs one of
the few local avant-garde dance companies to have
achieved global recognition. Projects often involve
musicians, visual artists and even fashion designers. The company is based at the Cango (*see p213*).

MaggioDanza
055 2779350, www.maggiofiorentino.com.
The work of the official ensemble of the Maggio
Musicale Fiorentino (*see p176*) ranges from evergreens such as *Giselle* and the *Nutcracker* to contemporary works. Regrettably, financial worries and
staff changes often tell on quality standards.

Versiliadanza
055 350986, www.versiliadanza.it.
Dancer/choreographer Angela Torriani Evangelisti
founded this small company in 1993. Versiliadanza
concentrates on contemporary pieces, but also has
experience with Baroque and Renaissance dance.
The group collaborates with the German choreographer Suzanne Linke.

FESTIVALS

Fabbrica Europa
*Stazione Leopolda, viale Fratelli Rosselli 5,
Outside the City Gates (055 2480515, www.
fabbricaeuropa.net). Bus 1, 9, 16, 26, 27,
or tram T1.* **Date** May.
The large space of this former railway station by
Porta al Prato is well suited to an innovative festival
of theatre, music, dance and multimedia arts.

Florence Dance Festival
*Borgo Stella 23r, Oltrarno (055 289276, www.
florencedance.org).* **Date** June-July.
Staged in the courtyard of the Bargello Museum (*see
p84*), the festival fuses some of the greatest names
in contemporary, traditional and classical dance.

Mese Mediceo
*Florence & province (055 6120205, www.mese
mediceo.it).* **Date** May-July.
A programme of highly entertaining original plays
about the lives and flaws of members of the Medici
family. Staged in various historic locations, the
festival has become a favourite with visitors.

Teatri Aperti
*Florence & metropolitan area (055 2779362,
www.firenzedeiteatri.it).* **Date** last wknd of Sept.
Theatres in and around Florence (18 of them so
far, and growing) offer roughly 60 shows and
assorted events in this enormous festival meant to
disprove the notion of theatregoing as a stuffy, pas-
sive experience.

ARTS & ENTERTAINMENT

A world
of inspiration

Getting Started

Hill towns, olive groves, vineyards, beaches... and lots more art.

Holiday hotspots and see-before-you-die sights come and go, but Tuscany has enduring appeal. Away from the tourist hordes in Florence, the pace of life slows as the countryside opens out into panoramic vistas of vineyards, olive groves, valleys and hills, cascading gently towards a coastline with its own highlights. Nor does culture start and end in the regional capital: **Pisa**, **Siena**, **Lucca** and **Arezzo** have fabulous buildings, art and monuments, while smaller towns such as **Montepulciano**, **San Sepolcro** and **Montalcino** maintain the spirit of another age.

The only reason Florence has precedence over the destinations in the following chapters is because it emerged victorious after centuries of conflict – endless infighting that effectively ceased at the end of the 15th century, but can still be discerned in the conversation of any Tuscan. Tuscans class themselves according to their city district first, their city second and nationality third, defining themselves as 'Tuscan' only as a last resort to ensure you don't confuse them with a dastardly Pisano/Aretino/Sienese – not to mention Florentine. This visceral sense of belonging is called *campanilismo*, and epitomised by the Sienese, conscious of being frozen in their medieval glory and most likely to attach themselves to a *contrada* (city district).

Tuscans are very fond of pigeonholing their regional neighbours. Prato commands respect for its wealth-generating entrepreneurial spirit, while Pistoia elicits the same for its sense of age. Montecatini also recalls the past, with its 1890s parks and grand bathing establishments. Further west, Lucca, hermetically sealed by its chunky 16th-century walls, always managed to pay off would-be conquerors and now seems to have more friends – even in Tuscany – than enemies. Bourgeois Arezzo has also kept a high standard of living while falling under Florentine dominion, and working-class Livorno remains open-minded, with its loud-mouthed inhabitants and a pioneering spirit.

It's not all about conflict. Tuscany's geography went a long way towards ensuring its overall unity amid constant internal squabbling: more than 90 per cent of its territory is mountainous or hilly, which

leaves only small slivers of level ground along rivers and the coast to invade; the mountains to the north also prevented too many attacks from Europe. Taken in its entirety, Tuscany cradled an unmatched crop of poets, painters, scientists, explorers and architects, as well as creating a language so poetical the entire country adopted it. Its rulers also had the foresight to amass unprecedented artistic wealth: to this day, the region has the highest concentration of art in the country.

These attractions haven't escaped the notice of holiday-makers and their agents, and at times it can feel like areas of Tuscany (San Gimignano, for example) have turned into mini-theme parks. Yet, on the other hand, wandering the backstreets of a town such as Volterra (*see p242*), it's not difficult to find yourself transported from the crowds entirely.

AN OVERVIEW

Tuscany's popular image is of sun-drenched and cypress-dotted rolling hills. While this isn't untrue, particularly for the areas south and south-east of Florence, it doesn't give the whole picture. The Apuan Alps and the Apennine peaks set the region apart, providing a plethora of giddy, winding roads (ideal for hardcore cyclists), as well as ski resorts and high-altitude trekking. These self-contained, forested areas – such as the Garfagnana and Lunigiana, and the Valtiberina valley – have provided the basic ingredients for Tuscany's culinary tradition and the backdrop for many of its paintings.

In the deep south is the Maremma, a large expanse of sparsely populated and previously malarial swampland that was once the region's poorest part but now houses a coastal playground for Italy's rich and famous. Etruscan remains are scattered all around here; inland, a series of small, ancient towns, including Pitigliano, cling precariously to hillsides. Towards the northern end of the coast is the modern port of Livorno, and the Versilia, with its beach umbrellas and nightspots. Mainland Tuscany is far from ideal for a seaside holiday, however: its coast is dominated by grey-brown sand, murky water and crowds. For better beaches, head to the Argentario peninsula or one of the islands. To find out about Tuscany's underground draws (caves, mines, passageways), see www.toscanaunderground.it.

The chapters that follow don't aim to provide exhaustive information on the towns and provinces of Tuscany, so much as lead you in the direction of what we consider to be the area's very best elements.

WHERE, WHEN, HOW

The best overall advice, especially if you only have a week or two, is to concentrate on one or two provinces or parts of the region. Unless you want to dedicate your holiday to, say, wine tourism or art and architecture, Tuscany invites you to mix up your itinerary. Visit the ornate churches and galleries, but try not to saturate your days with hours spent driving around the countryside to see all the sights. Instead, spend a day walking and try to sit down once each day to a Tuscan meal. If you need to recuperate from sightseeing, spend a few hours at one of the region's many thermal spas (see p244 **Spa-spangled Manors**). Alternatively, build your holiday around a language, cookery or painting course (see p220).

In Easter and summer, many places get busy and you'll have to weigh up whether they're worth the effort. The gorgeous hill town of San Gimignano, for instance, is like honey to the tourist bees: visit in months either side of the rush, such as May or September/ October. There are few crowds in winter, but many attractions and restaurants are shut or open for limited hours, the more rural hotels and guesthouses sometimes put up their shutters off-season – and the weather won't be so good. In peak season, book rooms in advance. Prices given are for double rooms, unless otherwise stated.

TOURIST INFORMATION

The tourist information website for Tuscany is www.turismo.toscana.it. Local tourist offices are listed under the individual towns and areas. Below we list a selection of the best touring and themed holidays. All phone numbers are in the UK unless otherwise stated. At the time

of writing, the provinces of Tuscany, and their tourist boards, were undergoing a major administrative reorganisation to create fewer provinces and cut back on costs, so check websites as a starting point for all directory information.

THE BEST TUSCANY

Bathing spots
Montecatini Terme. *See p228.*
Cascaste del Gorello, Saturnia. *See p296.*
Hotel Posta Marcucci, Bagno Vignoni. *See p266.*
Elba. *See p301.*

Events
Carnevale, Viareggio (Feb). *See p181.*
Luminaria di San Ranieri/Regatta, Pisa (June). *See p178.*
Giostra del Saracino, Arezzo (June, Sept). *See p178.*
Il Palio, Siena (July, Aug). *See p179.*
Bravo delle Botti, Montepulciano (Aug). *See p180.*

Frescoes
Legend of the True Cross (Piero della Francesca), San Francesco church, Arezzo. *See p282.*
St Benedict Cycle (Giovanni Antonio Bazzi and Luca Signorelli), Monte Oliveto Maggiore abbey. *See p264.*
Old and New Testament Cycle (Ghirlandaio), San Miniato Collegiato, San Miniato. *See p241.*

Churches
Siena's Duomo. *See p251.*
Pistoia's Duomo. *See p227.*
Abbazia di Sant'Atimo, nr Montalcino. *See p265.*

Hill towns
Pitigliano, Maremma. *See p296.*
Massa Marittima, South Tuscany. *See p295.*
Anghiari, Arezzo Province. *See p290.*

Unspoilt regions
Maremma, South Tuscany. *See p294.*
Arezzo Province. *See p287.*
Mugello. *See p225.*

Worth the climb
Torre del Mangia, Siena. *See p247.*
Torre Guinigi, Lucca. *See p273.*
Campanile, Pisa. *See p234.*

TUSCANY

INSIDE TRACK
ACCESS AN ARTISAN APP

The **Arttour** iPhone app takes you on a journey through Florence and Tuscany's artisan workshops. Sponsored by Artex, which promotes arts and crafts in the region, the app enables you to easily find crafts galleries and makers' studios near you. And if you don't have an iPhone, the information is all listed on the website at www.artour.toscana.it.

SPECIALIST HOLIDAYS

Art history holidays

Prospect Art Tours *020 7486 5704, www.prospecttours.com.*
Music and art history holidays, including a five-day trip to the Puccini Opera Festival (£995 including accommodation and most meals).

Cookery schools

La Bottega Del 30 *Via Santa Caterina 7, Castelnuovo Berardenga, Siena, 0577 359226 within Italy, www.labottegadel30.it.*
Popular five-day courses focusing on Chianti cookery. Classes (for up to ten) end with lunch and wine tastings. A wine cellar, library and *videoteca* are also at students' disposal.

Italian Cookery Weeks *020 8208 0112, www.italian-cookery-weeks.co.uk.*
Excellent food and wine with daily tuition by an expert chef, accompanied by trips and excursions. Prices start at £1,599 per week, including flights.

Farming holidays

WWOOF (World-Wide Opportunities on Organic Farms) *01273 476286, www.wwoof.org.*
Working holidays on organic farms, especially during the grape and olive harvests. Food and board are usually provided in exchange for about six hours' work a day. It's wise to find out as much as you can about living and working conditions before you go. For a list of farms you need to join WWOOF.

Language schools

Italian Language Courses (www.italian-language-courses.net) and **Apple Languages** (www.applelanguages.com) are both reliable agencies with posts in Tuscany.

Cooperativa 'Il Sasso' *0578 758311 within Italy, www.ilsasso.com.*
Two- and four-week language courses based in Montepulciano for all levels, plus courses in art history. Rooms can be arranged in hotels, flats or with families. Prices start at €395 for a two-week course.

Italian Cultural Institute *020 7235 1461, www.icilondon.esteri.it.*
The Italian Cultural Institute is a good source of information about language courses in Italy.

Painting courses

See also p313.

Simply Travel *0870 166 4979, www.simplytravel.co.uk.*
Package holidays and city breaks to Florence and Tuscany, staying in private villas and hotels that are off the beaten track. A week-long holiday, including flights, transfers or car hire and accommodation in a villa, starts from £500 per person.

Verrochio Art Centre *020 8869 1035, www.verrocchio.co.uk.*
Specialist painting and sculpture courses in a hilltop village. Prices start at £779 for a two-week course (bed, breakfast and dinner, but excluding flights). The booking contact is Maureen Ruck.

Walking & cycling

Alternative Travel Group *01865 315678, www.atg-oxford.co.uk.*
Escorted walking and cycling trips (from £910, excluding flights) in small groups, plus customised unguided walking trips with rooms in family-run hotels (from £450 B&B per week, excluding flights).

Ramblers Holidays *01707 331133, www.ramblersholidays.co.uk.*
A variety of walking tours, including a week exploring the sights of Florence, from £513 half-board, including flights and accommodation.

Villa rentals & agriturismi

Many travel companies have a wide range of villas to rent across the region. Our favourites include **James Villas** (UK: 08700 556688, www.jamesvillas.co.uk), **Tuscan House** (US: 1-800 844 6939, 1-251 968 4444, www.tuscanhouse.com) and **Ville in Italia** (Italy: 055 412058, www.villeinitalia.com). Rates vary hugely according to the season and size of property, so call or browse the website.

Agriturismi – whereby farmers let out part of their property – are an increasingly common option. Check www.agriturismo.net for a wide range of properties online; for some of our favourites, *see p266* **Get a Farmer's Tan**.

Montemerano, Southern Tuscany.

Piazza del Duomo, Pistoia.

TUSCANY

Castello dei Conti Guidi, Poppi, Arezzo Province.

Florence & Prato Provinces

Homelands of Leonardo, Boccaccio, Giotto and the Medici.

Heading out in any direction from Florence you'll find a multitude of delightful towns and villages ideal for a day trip. South-west are **Vinci**, Leonardo's hometown, **Certaldo Alto**, Boccaccio's birthplace, and **Montelupo**, with its colourful ceramics. To the north, the verdant **Mugello** deserves a visit for both its natural and artistic beauties. Between Florence and Pistoia stretches the recently created Prato Province, whose underrated provincial capital boasts Tuscany's best mix of historic and contemporary attractions. Nearby, **Poggio a Caiano**, **Carmignano** and **Artimino** stand guard to prime art treasures set in some of Tuscany's finest vineyards and olive groves.

PRATO

Immediately to the west of Florence is Prato, created a province in its own right only in 1992; a short-lived achievement that's about to come to an end as the government cuts back on costs by slashing the number of provinces in the country. The town boasts Tuscany's highest per capita income, and the Pratesi joke that soon 'Prato will be Paris, and Florence its Versailles'. Prato is undeservedly considered little more than an industrial suburb of Florence, but the city council has spent squillions to upgrade Prato's attractions, and the improvements have led to a number of new restaurant, bar and club openings, and an enviable taste for contemporary art.

Prato was a thriving trading centre in the Middle Ages. The city's textile manufacturing heritage is celebrated by the **Museo del Tessuto** (via Santa Chiara 24, 0574 611503, www.museodeltessuto.it, closed Tue, admission €6). Closed at the time of writing for a complete renovation, it was due to reopen in late 2011 with a 'textiles of the future' exhibition. Prato's 13th-century **Cattedrale di Santo Stefano** (piazza del Duomo, 0574 26234, www.diocesi prato.it) is a Romanesque-Gothic brick building with a 15th-century external pulpit designed by

Michelozzo and carved with reliefs by Donatello (the originals are in the Museo dell'Opera del Duomo; *see below*). The city's religious icon, the Sacra Cintola (Holy Girdle), is shown here on festival days. Inside, the Cappella dell'Assunta has frescoes by Paolo Uccello. The choir was decorated by Filippo Lippi with beautiful frescoes. The visit is free except to the Holy Girdle and Lippi chapels (joint admission €3.50, including an audio guide; 10am-5pm Mon-Sat, 1-5pm Sun).

An €8 ticket covers three of the city's main museums: the **Museo dell'Opera del Duomo** (piazza del Duomo 49, 0574 29339, www.diocesi prato.it, closed Tue & Sun afternoon), housed in Palazzo Vescovile and exhibiting a fresco attributed to Paolo Uccello and works by both Filippo and Filippino Lippi; the **Museo di Pittura Murale** (piazza San Domenico 8, 0574 440501, closed Tue & afternoons except Fri & Sat) displaying detached frescoes, sinopias and paintings; and the 13th-century **Castello dell'Imperatore** (piazza Santa Maria delle Carceri, 0574 38207, closed Wed). A €10 ticket covers the first two of these and the Lippi frescoes. Outside the city walls, the **Centro per l'Arte Contemporanea Luigi Pecci** (viale della Repubblica 277, 0574 5317, www.centro pecci.it, closed Tue, admission €5) houses one of the country's most important collections of contemporary art. At the time of writing the permanent collection was temporarily closed, but there are numerous temporary exhibitions and events held at the centre, and its presence has drawn a small cluster of private art galleries, as well as the **Museo all'aperto di Luicciana** (0574 95681, www.comune.cantagallo.po.it, admission free). Located in the Cantagallo area north of Prato, this delightful open-air gallery is filled with sculpture and installations by avant-garde Florentine artists of the 20th century. The nearby Val di Bisenzio, a gorgeous river valley, is a delight to explore, with buildings and bridges that date back to the Middle Ages.

Where to eat

At **Enoteca Barni** (via Ferrucci 22, 0574 607845, closed Sun, average €20 lunch, €50 dinner) lunch is informal and fairly inexpensive, while dinner is more elaborate and costly. For fish and seafood the best option is **Il Pirana** (via Valentini 110, 0574 25746, www.ristorante pirana.it, closed Sun & lunch Sat, tasting menu €55). If hearty Tuscan dishes are what you fancy, **La Vecchia Cucina** (via Pomeria 23, 0574 34665, closed Sun, average €30) and **Osteria Cibbè** (piazza Mercatale 49, 0574 607509, www.cibbe.it, closed Sun, average €25) are excellent and economical choices.

Where to stay

Prato's most modern accommodation option, **Wallart** (viale della Repubblica 4-8, 0574 596600, www.wallart.it, €95-€150), is a hotel,

La Ferdinanda.

convention centre, gallery, bookshop, restaurant and bar. Nearer the Pecci museum, **Art Hotel Museo** (viale della Repubblica 289, 0574 5787, www.arthotel-museo.it, €95-€150) is another luxury choice. A cheaper option in a prime location is **Hotel Flora** (via Cairoli 31, 0574 33521, www.hotelflora.info, €60-€140), offering parking and Wi-Fi.

POGGIO A CAIANO, CARMIGNANO & ARTIMINO

Heading west from Florence on the SS66 to Pistoia you reach the village of Poggio a Caiano, home to Lorenzo il Magnifico's country retreat, the impressive **Medici Villa Ambra** (piazza de' Medici 14, 055 877012, www.polomuseale. firenze.it, closed 2nd & 3rd Mon of mth, admission free, escorted half-hourly visits). The second floor of the villa houses the **Museo della Natura Morta** (055 877012, admission free, escorted visits on the hour, reservation advised) with an impressive gallery of still lifes. The nearby **Museo Soffici** (ex Scuderie Medicee, via Lorenzo il Magnifico 5, 055 8701287, www.museoardengosoffici.it, admission €3, closed Mon May-Sept, Mon-Fri Oct-Apr) house a permanent exhibition of works by Ardengo Soffici (1879-1964), the Futurist painter, writer and poet.

At Poggio a Caiano head south through pleasant countryside to **Carmignano**, whose pride and joy is the 1530 *Visitation* by Pontormo in **San Michele e San Francesco**. Nearby estates offering wine tastings and tours daily (by appointment) include **Capezzana** (via Capezzana 100, Seano, 055 8706005, www.capezzana.it) and **Fattoria di Bacchereto** (via Fontemorana 179, 055 8717191, closed 2wks Nov or Jan).

Not far away is the delightful walled village of **Artimino**, faced with the multi-chimneyed Medici villa known as **La Ferdinanda** (viale Papa Giovanni XXIII 1, 055 87151427, www.artimino.com, visits by arrangement), built in 1596. The surrounding countryside is

TUSCANY

Museo Leonardiano

a life-size equine monument by Nina Akamu (2001) inspired by Leonardo's drawings of horses.

Where to eat

In the town centre, **Il Ristoro del Museo** (via Montalbano 9, 0571 56516, closed Fri dinner, Sat lunch & Christmas holidays, average €30) has a panoramic terrace and serves delicious traditional food. Nearby, the **Antica Cantina di Bacco** (piazza Leonardo da Vinci 3, 0571 568041, closed Mon, average €22) is a cute little wine bar that also serves food.

MONTELUPO

Montelupo has been known for its beautifully coloured glazed pottery since the Middle Ages. The main street of the town is lined with shops selling boldly patterned ceramics, and a week-long **Festa Internazionale della Ceramica** is held in late June. A joint ticket of €5.50 admits to both of Montelupo's museums: the **Museo Archeologico** (via Santa Lucia, 0571 541547, closed Mon, admission €5 with Museo della Ceramica) and the new **Museo della Ceramica** (piazza Vittorio Veneto 8-10, 0571 51372, www.museomontelupo.it, closed Mon, admission €5 with Museo Archeologico). The **San Giovanni Evangelista** church (via Baccio de Montelupo 37, 0571 51048, free) houses a beautiful Madonna and Saints painting by Botticelli and his assistants.

CERTALDO ALTO

This walled hilltop settlement's main claim to fame is that Giovanni Boccaccio (1313-75, author of the *Decameron*) was born, died and is buried here. In July the town is bathed in candlelight for the **Mercantia** festival of street arts (www.mercantiacertaldo.it), while **Boccaccesca** in October celebrates Tuscan cuisine. **Palazzo Pretorio** (piazza Vittorio Veneto 10-11, 0571 661219, closed Tue in winter) is decorated with the coats of arms of past governors. A joint ticket of €6 also admits you to **Boccaccio's House** (via Boccaccio, 0571 664208, www.casaboccaccio.it, closed Oct-mid Jan) and the **Museum of Sacred Art** (piazza SS Iacopo e Filippo, 0571 661219, closed Mon-Fri).

Where to eat & stay

Set in a former 13th-century monastery, **Osteria del Vicario** (via Rivellino 3, 0571 668228, www.osteriadelvicario.it, closed Mon, dinner Sun, 4wks Jan-Feb) has nine rooms (€90) and a celebrated restaurant (average lunch €25, dinner €50) often featuring the excellent local

rich in archaeological sites; get the gen at the Etruscan archaeology museum: **Museo Archeologico Comunale di Artimino 'Francesco Nicosia'** (055 8718124, www.parcoarcheologicocarmignano.it, closed Wed, Mon-Fri Nov-Jan, admission €4).

Where to eat & drink

In Artimino, the excellent Tuscan dishes on the menu of **Osteria Su Pe' i' Canto** (piazza San Carlo 3, 055 8712490, closed Mon & 3wks Aug, average €28) provide a perfect excuse to sample the fine wines, or try **Da Delfina** (via della Chiesa 1, 055 8718074, www.dadelfina.it, closed Sun evening, Mon and Aug, average €45), which serves seasonal food such as rabbit with pine nuts and olives.

VINCI

A constant stream of visitors flocks to this quaint hill town in search of Leonardo da Vinci's origins. The stone farmhouse where he was born (open daily, admission free) is in the hamlet of **Anchiano**, a three-kilometre (two-mile) drive or 1.5-kilometre (one-mile) walk out of Vinci. The bare rooms house educational panels with Leonardo's earliest known drawing. Back in Vinci, models of his machines and instruments are on display at the **Museo Leonardiano** (0571 933251, www.museo leonardiano.it, admission €7), split between **Palazzina Uzielli** on the evocative piazza de'Guidi, designed by the artist Mimmo Paladino, and formidable **Castello dei Conti Guidi**. The panoramic piazza Guido Masi has a wooden statue of Leonardo's *Vitruvian Man* by Mario Ceroli (1987); piazza della Libertà houses

red onions. The new town down the hill is worth a visit for **Osteria la Saletta** (via Roma 3, 0571 668188, closed Tue except Aug, average €35).

GREVE, MONTEFIORALLE & PANZANO

Greve is a centre of the Slow Food movement and makes for an exceptionally pleasant base. A sliver of hairpin bends leads up from Greve's northern side to the ancient walled village of Montefioralle, a lovely spot for a quiet lunch. Further south is the fortified village of Panzano, overlooking the Conca d'Oro valley. Keep an eye out for Tuscany's adorable *cinta senese* pigs, famed for their distinctive black belts across their bellies – and for making excellent cured pork products.

Where to eat & stay

In Greve itself, you can find delectable dishes at the tiny **Mangiando Mangiando** (piazza Matteotti 80, 055 8546372, www.mangiando

mangiando.it, closed Thur, 4wks in Jan-Feb, average set €18-€30). To stay, the best option is **Albergo Verrazzano** (piazza Matteotti 28, 055 853189, www.albergoverrazzano.it, €105), which also has a charming restaurant.

Up in Montefioralle, family-run **La Taverna del Guerrino** is a rustic gem (via Montefioralle 39, 055 853106, closed Mon, Tue & Wed lunch, average €35). In Panzano, try **Villa Sangiovese** (piazza Bucciarelli 5, 055 852461, www.villasangiovese.it, average €35, doubles €125, restaurant closed Wed, & both closed mid Dec-mid Mar).

THE MUGELLO

The hilly Sieve valley north of Florence is known as the **Mugello**, while the mountainous **Alto Mugello** extends up the Apennine passes to the border with Emilia Romagna. This beautiful area of woods and pastures offers great walks, while the man-made **Lago di Bilancino** is popular for its beaches and watersports. The Medici went back to their

Leonardo

The definition of a Renaissance man.

'In the normal course of events many men and women are born with various remarkable qualities and talents; but occasionally, in a way that transcends nature, a single person is marvellously endowed by heaven with beauty, grace and talent in such abundance that he leaves other men far behind, all his actions seem inspired, and indeed everything he does clearly comes from God rather than from human art.'

This quote from Vasari's *Lives of the Artists* refers to Leonardo da Vinci (1452-1519), an *uomo universale* who, with Michelangelo and Raphael, is considered one of the three great artists of the High Renaissance. He's best known as a painter, though few of his works were ever finished, due to his impatience and low boredom threshold, and his drawings far outnumber his paintings. He was fascinated by science and the natural world, believing that to see was to know. He practically discovered the circulation of blood and the growth of the embryo in the womb. He was a keen geologist, botanist, musician and writer. He performed numerous dissections to gain a greater insight into anatomy, and designed buildings, fortifications, canals and locks.

Leonardo was born in Vinci and apprenticed to Verrochio's studio in about 1469. He helped on Verrochio's *Baptism* (now in the Uffizi; *see p65*) – you can see his hand in the angel on the left (he attentively observed how the cloth would fall across the forms of the body) and in parts of the landscape.

Leonardo's earliest drawing, *Arno Landscape* (Uffizi), is dated 3741 – he was left-handed and often wrote right to left, perhaps as a game, but also so that his notes would not easily be copied. He soon gained a reputation and as early as 1481 received a commission from the monks of San Donato at Scopeto for the *Adoration of the Magi*. The work was never finished, though the cartoon remains in the Uffizi. It's a masterpiece, offering a wonderful insight into his working practices. The composition is geometrically mapped out; the figures and landscape are not separate but work together as a harmonious whole.

In 1482, Leonardo set off for Milan, where he produced a number of important works. Though few good examples of his original work survive in Vinci or even in Florence, it's worth visiting the Uffizi to see for yourself the great advances he made in painting and to experience a small part of his immeasurable genius.

TUSCANY

homeland to build several mansions such as **Castello di Trebbio** and **Villa Cafaggiolo**, both near San Piero a Sieve. In the mountains of the Alto Mugello, the national farmers' association Coldiretti has created a 650-hectare organic park in the Covigliaio area, between the moutain passes that connect Tuscany and Emilia Romagna, the Passo della Raticosa and the Passo della Futa. The park houses a range of habitats and a cultivated area where locals grow produce sold in a greengrocer's located in the park, and used in an *agriturismo* and B&B within its borders (www.toscana.coldiretti.it).

Borgo San Lorenzo is the bustling commercial hub of the area. Just east of Borgo, sleepy little **Vicchio** was the birthplace of Fra Angelico and Giotto. A few kilometres north-west of Borgo is **Scarperia** (*photo p218*), founded in 1306 as the northernmost military outpost of the Florentine Republic. The crenellated **Palazzo dei Vicari** (055 8468165, admission €3, closed Mon, Tue, Sun, open only Sat in winter) boasts a 1445 clock by Filippo Brunelleschi. For the Autodromo Internazionale del Mugello racetrack, *see p207*.

Where to eat & stay

For Mugello cuisine in Scarperia, try **Il Torrione** (via Roma 78-80, 055 8430263, closed Mon, average €22). Between Borgo and Vicchio, don't miss the area's best potato *tortelli* at the rustic **Trattoria da Giorgione** (via Belvedere 23, località Sagginale, 055 8490130, closed Thur and 2wks June, average €22) – where Giorgione still writes the bill in old-fashioned lira, then 'translates' it to euros with a calculator – or enjoy refined versions of local dishes in Borgo itself, at the centrally located **Ristorante degli Artisti** (località Sagginale 46, 055 8457707, www.ristorantedegliartisti.it, closed Tue, Wed, average €50). Next door, the **Locanda degli Artisti** (piazza Romagnoli 2, 055 8455359, www.locandaartisti.it, €100-€140) has pleasant art nouveau rooms. The most stylish hotel in the area is **Villa Campestri** (via di Campestri 19-22, 055 8490107, www.villacampestri.it, closed mid Nov-mid Mar, €250), a Renaissance villa set in green hills just above Sagginale.

RESOURCES

Tourist information

Carmignano *Piazza Vittorio Emanuele II 1-2 (055 8712468, www.carmignanodivino.it).* **Open** 9.30am-12.30pm, 3-5pm Tue-Sat; 9.30am-12.30pm Sun; 9.30am-12.30pm, 3-5pm 1st Sun of mth.
Certaldo *Nr Railway Station, piazza Masini (0571 656721).* **Open** *Easter-mid Oct* 9am-1pm, 3.30-7pm daily. *Mid Oct-Dec* 10am-12pm, 3.30-6pm daily. Closed Jan-Easter.

Greve *Piazza Matteotti 1, Greve (055 8546287, www.chiantislowtravel.it).* **Open** 9am-1pm, 2.30-6.30pm Mon-Sat.
Montelupo Fiorentino *Museo della Ceramica, via Baccio da Montelupo 43, Montelupo (0571 518993, www.museomontelupo.it).* **Open** 10am-6pm Tue-Sun.
The Mugello *Villa Pecori Giraldi, piazzale Lavacchini, Borgo San Lorenzo (055 845271, www.mugellotoscana.it).* **Open** 10am-1pm, 3-6pm Tue, Thur-Sun; 10am-1pm Wed.
Poggio a Caiano *Ex Scuderie Medicee, via Lorenzo il Magnifico (055 8798779, www.prolocopoggioacaiano.it).* **Open** 10am-3pm Mon-Tue & Thur-Fri; 10am-6pm Sat, Sun.
Prato *Piazza Duomo 8 (0574 24112, www.pratoturismo.it).* **Open** 9am-1pm, 3-6pm Mon-Sat; 10am-1pm Sun.
Vinci *Via della Torre 11 (0571 568012, www.terredelrinascimento.it).* **Open** *Summer* 10am-7pm daily. *Winter* 10am-3pm Mon-Fri; 10am-6pm Sat, Sun.

GETTING THERE

By bus

For Prato, Poggio a Caiano and Carmignano check **Cap** (055 214637, www.capautolinee.it) and **Copit** (0573 3630, www.copitspa.it) services. Montelupo is served by **LAZZI** (055 363041, www.lazzi.it) and **ATAF** (800 424500, www.ataf.net). **SITA** (800 373760, 055 294955, www.sitabus.it) runs bus services to Borgo San Lorenzo and Vicchio (1hr).

By car

Head west on the A11 motorway from Florence. Montelupo is just off the Florence–Pisa–Livorno (Fi–Pi–Li) *superstrada*. For Certaldo, exit at Empoli Ovest and continue south on the SS429. For Vinci, exit at Empoli and head north for Pistoia. From Florence, Poggio a Caiano, Carmignano and Artimino are best reached via the SS66 (via Pistoiese). For Borgo San Lorenzo, take either the SS65 (via Bolognese) or the more windy SS302 (via Faentina). For Scarperia, take the SS65 and pick up the SS503 at San Piero a Sieve. For Vicchio, head for Borgo then take the SS551.

By train

Frequent trains from Florence stop at Prato Centrale (main line to Bologna) or Porta al Serraglio (local line to Lucca). Montelupo is on the Florence–Empoli–Pisa line (20-30mins). For Vinci, reach Empoli by train and catch a local bus (hourly, fewer in the weekends). Certaldo is on the Siena line; a train change may be necessary at Firenze Rifredi and/or Empoli (1hr). Borgo San Lorenzo is served by two routes from Florence, one via Pontassieve and Vicchio (1hr) and one via Vaglia and San Piero a Sieve (45mins) continuing through the Alto Mugello and Faenza. For information, call 892021 or visit www.trenitalia.com.

Pistoia Province

Pistols, Pinocchio and pools for the pampered.

The province of Pistoia is deepest Tuscany, surrounded by cool, green Apennine scenery, spas and sleepy villages, as well as skiing in Abetone. The provincial capital of Pistoia is, for some incomprehensible reason, little known outside Tuscany, and remains very much off the tourist track. Perhaps this has something to do with its violent past – the city gave its name to the pistol – but it's an unadulterated gem, offering superb art to be savoured in the absence of the crushing crowds that can mar ventures in Florence and Siena. Foreign tourists in this province tend to head for the upmarket spa town of Montecatini Terme, where you can pamper yourself at one of the swish hotels.

PISTOIA

The countryside for miles around Pistoia is characterised by neat rows of dwarf trees and small shrubs. The rich soil has given rise to a lucrative line in plant nurseries, which has become a multi-million-euro industry. The quiet old town itself is one of Tuscany's most enchanting cities, with an almost perfectly intact historic centre encircled by medieval walls and few fellow tourists to spoil your enjoyment. Despite its lovely ambience today, Pistoia's history is a bloody one: it was where the Catiline conspirators were rounded up after they failed to destroy the Roman Republic in 62 BC; it fought bitter wars with Renaissance rivals Florence and Lucca; and was the birthplace of the brutal feud between Black and White Guelphs (a struggle often referred to in Dante's *Divine Comedy*, who was himself forced into exile by rival parties).

The architectural style of many of Pistoia's monuments combines Florentine and Pisan elements. The **Cattedrale di San Zeno** has an arcaded Pisan façade and a simple Romanesque interior; the fine campanile has a plain lower section and exotic tiger-striped arcades on top. It houses the famous gold and silver *Altar of St James* within the chapel of the same name (admission €2). Across the square is the octagonal 14th-century, green and white striped Baptistery. The **Museo Civico** (0573 371296, closed Mon-Wed, Sun,

admission €3.50), behind the Duomo, has fine 14th-century paintings on the ground floor and some fairly dreadful late Mannerist works two floors above. The portico of the **Ospedale del Ceppo** (founded in the 13th century and still a functioning hospital) is decorated with a splendid ceramic frieze in the style of Giovanni della Robbia (1526-29). The nearby church of **Sant'Andrea** has a magnificent hexagonal stone pulpit (1298-1301) created by Giovanni Pisano.

Local events include the **Giostra dell'Orso** (Joust of the Bear) on 25 July and the popular **Pistoia Blues music festival** (May or June); for the latter, *see also p200*.

Where to eat & drink

La Bottegaia (via del Lastrone 17, 0573 365602, www.labottegaia.it, closed lunch Sun & all Mon, average €26) is a delightful wine bar/restaurant tucked away in a little square behind the Baptistery, which serves great food. The **Trattoria dell'Abbondanza** (via dell'Abbondanza 10, 0573 368037, closed Wed, lunch Thur, average €18) is even better, serving hearty Tuscan fare such as *baccalà alla Livornese*, superb fried chicken, tripe and rabbit. For civilised coffee and cakes, try **Caffè Pasticceria Valiani** (via Cavour 55, 0573 23034, closed Tue in winter & 1st 3wks Aug). Frescoed walls were uncovered in 1864 when its foundations were being laid.

Where to stay

One rural option is the beautiful rooms of *agriturismo* **Tenuta di Pieve a Celle** (Pieve a Celle, 0573 913087, www.tenutadipieveacelle.it, €130-€160). More mainstream is the pleasant **Hotel Leon Bianco** (via Panciatichi 2, 0573 26675, www.hotelleonbianco.it, €75-€90). **Hotel Patria** (via Crispi 8/12, 0573 358800, www.patriahotel.com, €129-€250) is also central. There are over 100 farm-stays around Pistoia – call the tourist office for a brochure.

MONTECATINI TERME

At the start of the 20th century, Montecatini Terme was one of the most fashionable destinations in Europe for royalty, aristocracy and political and literary movers and shakers. The monumental thermal buildings, set around beautiful **Parco delle Terme** and constructed in a variety of OTT styles, date from this time. Today, the place still has a very civilised air of restrained if slightly faded elegance; thousands come each year to take the waters and enjoy the

Spa-di-da

Head to Montecatini Terme for the best of Tuscany's thermal springs.

Although there are thermal springs and baths all over Tuscany, nowhere is better endowed with them than the area around **Montecatini Terme**. Discovered back in 1387, the town's therapeutic waters became popular with ailing Tuscan grand dukes in the late 18th century. Now, with the new wave of interest in alternative therapies, they're hot property once more.

Thankfully, both Montecatini, with its nine *terme*, and nearby Monsummano, with its thermal caves, are more than ready for the onslaught, offering an extensive menu of potential health and beauty treatments. At the **Terme de Montecatini** (viale Verdi 61, 0572 7781, www.termemontecatini.it), you can get anything from a divine 'massage under rain' (a pummelling beneath a warm thermal shower) to seven-day anti-stress and anti-cellulite packages.

At **Monsummano Terme**, you can take your health kick even further by living in the spa at the plush Grotta Giusti Hotel (via Grotta Giusti 1411, 0572 51165, www.grottagiustispa.com, closed early Jan-early Mar). But be warned – if you do check in here, you'll be sent, for your own good, to the 'Inferno', an underground thermal cave where temperatures hover around 34°C (90°F).

Perhaps best of all, Easter 2012 sees the reopening of the **Terme Leopoldine**, an 18th-century villa remodelled in 1926 by the Florentine architect Ugo Giovannozzi; with pools and terraces, landscaped gardens and a huge range of treatments on offer, this could well be the catalyst for the rest of the spas to up their game.

For further information on Montecatini's thermal baths go to www.terme montecatini.it or phone 0572 7781 or 0572 778487.

Montecatini Terme.

TETTVCCIO

TUSCANY

town. There are around 200 hotels, but in high season these can be packed. The place all but closes between late November and Easter.

The warm saline waters at Montecatini are supposed to be particularly beneficial for digestive complaints and are taken both internally and externally. The spas are modernising but many are still housed, at least partially, in the original buildings; grandest of all is **Terme Tettuccio**. For information about spas and the treatments on offer, contact the central Terme office at viale Verdi 41 (800 132538, www.termemontecatini.it).

On a balmy evening, a lovely diversion is to ride the funicular railway (viale Alfredo Diaz, €3 single, €5 return) up to charming Montecatini Alto and its panoramic views.

Where to eat & drink

There's a wide choice of places to eat in Montecatini Terme. You can get good pizza and pasta at **Egisto** (piazza Cesare Battisti 13, 0572 78413, www.egisto.it, closed Tue, average €23). If you want to try Tuscan wines, staff at **Enoteca Il Chicco d'Uva Vineria** (viale Puccini 2d, 338 8996159 mobile, www.ilchicco duva.com, closed Mon, Sun & Feb) are laid-back experts. **Enoteca Giovanni** (via Garibaldi 25-27, 0572 71695, www.enotecagiovanni.it, closed Mon & Feb, average €50) claims to stock close to 1,000 different wines, many of them local; it serves good traditional Tuscan food too.

Where to stay

Most hotels insist on half or even full board in high season. If you want to stay near Montecatini Alto try the upmarket **Casa Albertina e Mario B&B** (via Fratelli Guermani 12, 0572 900238, €100), which has glorious views over the Nievole valley from the garden. In town, the **Grand Hotel & La Pace** (via della Torretta 1, 0572 9240, www.grandhotellapace.com, €300-€460) is set in extensive grounds with two pools and has a sumptuous belle époque atmosphere. The revamped **Metropole** (via della Torretta 13, 0572 70092, www.hotel-metropole.it, €80-€125) is situated in a turn-of-the-19th-century villa and has 40 rooms, while the spotless, family-run **Hotel Savoia & Campana** (viale Cavallotti 10, 0572 772670, www.hotelsavoiaecampana. com, €50-€82) has an old-fashioned air and 30 pleasant rooms.

COLLODI

Collodi, on the SS435 just west of Pescia, is famous for being the birthplace of Pinocchio, Italy's most cherished fairytale character (*see also right* **Inside Track**). This claim to fame

Pinocchio.

INSIDE TRACK
CARLO COLLODI

The *Adventures of Pinocchio* has been published in so many editions and languages that only the Bible and the Koran beat it. Or at least that's what the official Pinocchio fan club in Collodi would have you believe. Carlo Lorenzini, its author, took Collodi as his nom de plume after his mother's birthplace. Lorenzini himself was born in Florence in 1826. He gained fame as a journalist and writer of educational children's books who incorporated music in his writing, often inventing sing-song names for characters. Soon after witnessing the unification of Italy, he began writing for one of Italy's first children's magazines, *Il Giornale per i Bambini*. His main contributions were instalments of the story of Pinocchio, which soon had a base of young fans. Just as the final episode was published in the magazine, *The Adventures of Pinocchio* was published as a complete book and was soon translated into English for sale in Britain and the US. Lorenzini died in 1890 and is buried in San Miniato al Monte cemetery in Florence, but it was Pinocchio's incarnation in a 1940 Walt Disney cartoon that secured his immortality.

TUSCANY

brings the tourists to what is an otherwise minor, but not unattractive, town. There's no shortage of signs directing visitors to **Parco di Pinocchio** (via San Gennaro 3, 0572 429342, www.pinocchio.it, admission €10-€11, €7-€8 under-14s). Opened in 1956, it features a walk-through maze and Pinocchio statues, including one by Emilio Greco, and a colourful mosaic-lined courtyard by Venturino Venturi. Its delightful, tactile constructions are worlds away from the blizzard of distractions found at British and American theme parks. Just across the road from the park, **Giardino Garzoni** (piazza della Vittoria 1, 0572 427314, admission €8-€13, €6-€10 under-14s, combined ticket with Parco di Pinocchio €14-€20, €10-€16 under-14s) is a Baroque garden by Romano di Alessandro Garzoni. There's a feeling of faded glory to it, although an ongoing restoration programme is sprucing up the fountains and statues.

PESCIA

Pescia is the flower capital of Italy. Some three million blooms are exported from this attractive town every day in summer. Take in the kaleidoscopic colours and head-spinning perfumes between 6am and 8.30am Monday to Saturday at the vast flower market at via Salvo d'Acquisto 10-12 (0572 440502).

THE MONTAGNA PISTOIESE

The Apennine mountains to the north of Pistoia, known as the Montagna Pistoiese, make a cool escape from the heat of the plain in summer; at the top is **Abetone**, one of Tuscany's two ski destinations (the other is Monte Amiata in Grosseto Province). Beautifully situated **San Marcello Pistoiese** is a popular summer resort standing 820 metres (2,690 feet) above sea level, while a little further on is the attractive old town of **Cutigliano**, which also fills up in summer. Reached via a splendid and ancient forest, Abetone stands at nearly 1,400 metres (4,590 feet) above sea level. Just 85 kilometres (53 miles) from Florence, it's easily accessible for a weekend or even a day trip. It gets very crowded at weekends and from January to March, when parents take kids out of school for a week on the slopes; its wide runs are ideal for beginner and intermediate level skiers. On average, ski-boot hire costs €25 per day and ski passes are €29 per weekday, €35 at the weekend.

Where to stay & eat

In Cutigliano, the old-fashioned **Miramonte** (piazza Catilina 12, 0573 68012, www.hotel miramonte.it, €70 per person full board – obligatory in high season) occupies a 16th-century *palazzo* on the main square, while the rustic **L'Osteria** (via Roma 6, 0573 68272, average €25) specialises in mushrooms; you can eat them in soups, risottos, pastas or deep fried. Up in Abetone, the modest **Noemi** (via Brennero 244, località Le Regine, 0573 60168, €35-€60, closed Oct, Nov, May) has 11 en suite rooms, or there's the four-star **Bella Vista** (via Brennero 383, 0573 60028, www.abetonebella vista.it, €80-€175). The best place to eat in Montecatini Terme is **Le Prunecce** (via Montaccolle 14, 0572 67301, closed Wed, average €25), which serves up brilliant rabbit dishes and home-made pecorino. **La Vecchia Cantina** (via Risorgimento 4, località Maresca, 0573 64158, www.vecchiacantina.it, closed Tue, average €30) serves a great range of pasta dishes and excellent juicy steaks, but specialises in dishes with *porcini*.

RESOURCES

Tourist information

Abetone *Piazza Piramida 502 (0573 60231 tourist information, 0573 60001 ski information, www.abetoneapm.it).*
Montagna Pistoiese APT *Via Brennero 42a, Cutigliano (0573 68029).* **Open** 8am-2pm Mon-Sat.
Montecatini Terme APT *Viale Verdi 66 (0572 772244, www.montecatiniturismo.it).* **Open** 9am-1pm, 3-6pm daily.
Pistoia APT *Piazza del Duomo 4 (0573 21622).* **Open** 10am-1pm, 3-6pm Sun daily.
Pistoia Province *www.pistoia.turismo.toscana.it.* **Open** 9am-1pm, 3-7pm daily.

GETTING THERE

By bus

LAZZI (055 363041, www.lazzi.it) runs regular buses from Florence to Pistoia (45mins) and Montecatini Terme (1hr). **CAP** (055 214637) links Pistoia with Florence. From Pistoia, **CAO** operates a service into the mountains (San Marcello, Cutigliano, Abetone). **CLAP** (0583 587897) buses connect Lucca with Pescia (45mins) and less regularly with Collodi. **COPIT/CAP** runs daily 'ski buses' from Florence to Abetone in season, but you must change in Pistoia. For timetables call 0573 3630 or 055 214637.

By car

Pistoia, Montecatini and the Montagne Pistoiese are accessible off the A11 *autostrada*.

By train

Regular trains on the Florence–Lucca line service Pistoia (35mins), Montecatini (50mins) and Pescia (60-75mins). For the Montagna Pistoiese, take the train to Pistoia then change to a CAP bus. See www.trenitalia.it or call 892021 for details.

Pisa

There's more to Pisa than its Leaning Tower.

Writing in the 12th century, the monk Donizone wrote: 'Those who go to Pisa can see monsters coming from the sea: this town is full of pagans.' Almost 900 years later, we might rephrase this slightly to '…this town is full of tourists', a fact that's been even more pertinent since 2007, when Pisa airport received its first direct flight from the United States. The **Campo dei Miracoli** – the ultimate Catholic theme park, where you'll find the **Duomo**, the **Baptistery** and the **Leaning Tower** (for all, *see p234*) – is the focus of this touristic onslaught, with groups of visitors

herded in and around the square all through the summer. However, although it would be a travesty to completely ignore the Campo, there's a great deal more to Pisa than the sum of its most famous parts, with interesting restaurants, shops and clubs opening all the time, and providing plenty of opportunities to escape the crowds. And the great thing about the Campo is the way the area acts as a magnet, inexorably drawing all the tourists to it and, in doing so, leaving a town centre that's one of the least touristy in Tuscany.

SOME HISTORY

Pisa is located in a broad flood plain surrounding a loop in the River Arno, ten kilometres (six miles) before it flows into the Tyrrhenian Sea. In ancient times, the estuary of the Arno was further inland, creating a lagoon inlet with easy landing for boats. The settlers there soon became traders, initially under the Etruscan sphere of influence, and then, from 27 BC, as a prosperous Roman colony. The chance discovery in 1998 of 18 2,000-year-old ships that had been preserved beneath layers of silt bore tangible witness to such early clout. On lungarno Simonelli, the **Arsenali Medici** is to house them as the key exhibits in a brand-new naval museum, but for the foreseeable future they remain at the Cantiere near the San Rossore train station (www.cantierenavipisa.it) – also closed since July 2010 due to lack of funds. Occasional visits are scheduled for European Heritage Days, Italian Culture Week and the like.

During the Middle Ages, the wealth and power of Pisa increased, and by the 11th century it had established itself as a great maritime republic. The accrued wealth paid for urban expansion, including the Campo dei Miracoli, but by the 15th century the city was in decline. It didn't do well under the Medici

Grand Dukes; their successor, Pietro Leopoldo of Lorraine, found it to be 'languid and poor, with insalubrious air, swampy lands and widespread misery'. So, in the late 1700s, he set about putting things right.

He did a pretty decent job (though much of downtown Pisa was destroyed when the Allies and Germans clashed during World War II). By 1844, Pisa was linked to Florence by rail, and had begun to develop the taste for intellectual advancement that it retains to this day. As well as its eminent university and the prestigious Scuola Normale Superiore, it is home to numerous research institutes. The academic population lends the streets a purposeful atmosphere, but also provide a youthful pulse: there are a good number of bars and nightclubs here, as well as events such as June's **Metarock** (www.metamusic.it). The two main local festivals, however, are a little more historic: the **Luminara di San Ranieri** (16 & 17 June) and **Il Gioco del Ponte** (last Sunday in June); for both, *see p178* Giugno Pisano.

An alternative way to see the city is by boat. The **Il Navicello** tour company (www.ilnavicello.it) operates two Pisan boat tours, a town-based itinerary and a Sundays-only excursion to the nearby **Parco Naturale di**

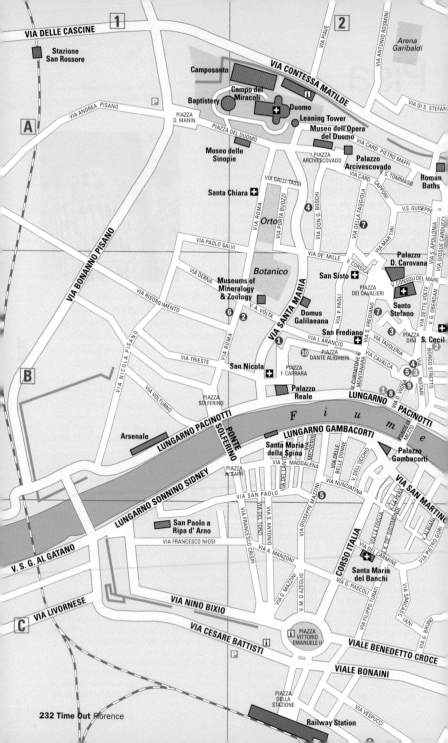

VIA DELLE CASCINE **1** **2**

Arena Garibaldi

VIA PIAVE

VIA ANTONIO ROSMINI

VIA DI S. STEFAN

■ Stazione
San Rossore

Camposanto

VIA CONTESSA MATILDE

Campo del
Miracoli

Baptistery

VIA ANDREA PISANO

P

PIAZZA
D. MANIN

PIAZZA DEL DUOMO

Duomo

Leaning Tower

Museo dell'Opera
del Duomo

VIA CARD. PIETRO MAFFI

A

Museo delle
Sinopie

PIAZZA
ARCIVESCOVADO

PIAZZA
ARCIVESCOVADO

Palazzo
Arcivescovado

VIA CARD. CAPPONI

V. S. TOMMASO

Roman
Baths

Santa Chiara ✚

VIA GALLI-TASSI

VIA ROMA

VIA PORTA BUOZZI

Orto

VIA DON G. BOSCHI

VIA DELLA FAGGIOLA

VIA MAR TIRI

4

7

V.S. GIUSEPPE

VIA S. APOLLONIA

VIA GIOSUE CARDUCCI

VIA PAOLO SALVI

Botanico

VIA DE' MILLE

Palazzo
D. Carovana

VIA DERNA

Museums of
Mineralogy
& Zoology

VIA S. MARIA

V CORSICA

San Sisto ✚

PIAZZA
DEI CAVALIERI

V. CONSOLI DEL MARE

VIA RISORGIMENTO

6

2

VIA A. VOLTA

Domus
Galilaeana

VIA P. PAOLI

Santo
Stefano

V. SETTE VOLTE

V. G. OBERDAN

VIA BONANNO PISANO

VIA ROMA

San Frediano ✚

VIA L'ARANCIO

1

VIA S. FREDIANO

VIA TAVOLERIA

3

PIAZZA
DINI

S. Cecil

BORGO STRETTO

B

VIA NICOLA PISANO

VIA TRIESTE

San Nicola ✚

PIAZZA
F. CARRARA

PIAZZA
DANTE ALIGHIERI

10

V. CURTATONE
MONTANARA

VIA CAVALCA

4

5 **3**

NOTARI

VIA VOLTURNO

PIAZZA
SOLFERINO

Palazzo
Reale

V. D. VIGNA

1 **8**

9

9

LUNGARNO   PACINOTTI

PONTE DI MEZZO

F i u m e

Arsenale

LUNGARNO PACINOTTI

PONTE
SOLFERINO

LUNGARNO GAMBACORTI

Santa Maria
della Spina

VIA DELLE
MADDALENA

V. DEL CARMINE

VIA DELLE DONNE

V. DEL L'OCCHIO

Palazzo
Gambacorti

VIA SAN MARTINO

LUNGARNO SONNINO SIDNEY

VIA SAN PAOLO

VIA DELLE
MAZZINI

VIA NUNZIATINA

5

CORSO ITALIA

VIA SANT'ALBERI

VIA DE' SISMONDO

VIA PIETRO GORI

V.S. G. AL GATANO

San Paolo a
Ripa d' Arno

VIA FRANCESCO CRISPI

VIA FRANCESCO NIOSI

VIAE TURATI

VIA S. ANTONIO

VIA A. MANZONI

VIA DEL CARMINE

VIA G. PASCOLI

Santa Maria
del Banchi

VIA FILIPPO TURATI

VIA SALICAS/IANI

C

VIA LIVORNESE

VIA NINO BIXIO

VIA CESARE BATTISTI

VIA M. D'AZEGLIO

V. M. D'AZEGLIO

VIA G. MAZZINI

i

PIAZZA
VITTORIO
EMANUELE II

V. G. BRUNO

VIALE BENEDETTO CROCE

VIALE BONAINI

P

PIAZZA
DELLA
STAZIONE

VIA VESPUCCI

Railway Station

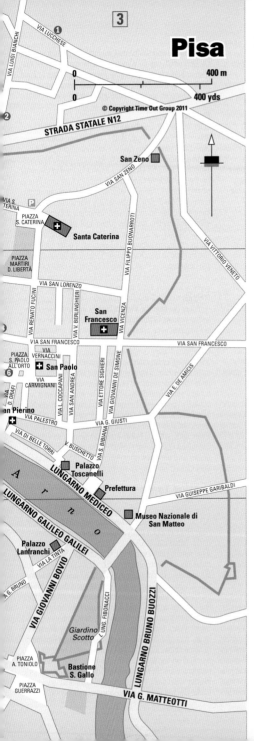

Pisa

3

400 m

400 yds

© Copyright Time Out Group 2011

1 Where to Stay pp239-240

1 Restaurants pp237-238

1 Cafés, Bars & Gelaterie pp238-239

San Rossore (050 530101, www.parco sanrossore.it), where north Italian racehorses spend their winter holidays.

SIGHTSEEING

★ Campo dei Miracoli

The scale and elegance of the layout that encompasses the Duomo, the Baptistery, the Leaning Tower and the Camposanto is undeniable. The 13th-century court astrologer Guido Bonatti argued that the spatial design was symbolic of the cosmos, and of the theme of Aries in particular. Look carefully: the Duomo and Baptistry both lean as well, though less perceptibly.

There are now ticket offices in just two sites (in the **Museo delle Sinopie**, and just north of the Tower), with the tourist office in the **Museo dell'Opera del Duomo**. There are several varieties of ticket, including one that offers admission to all the sights (except the Leaning Tower, for which *see below*) for €10. Call 050 3872210 for information, or visit www.opapisa.it.

Baptistery

050 3872210, www.opapisa.it. **Open** *Dec, Jan* 9.30am-4.30pm daily. *Mar* 8.30am-5.30pm daily. *Nov, Feb* 9am-5pm daily. *Apr-Sept* 8am-8pm daily. *Oct* 8.30am-7pm daily. **Admission** €5. **Map** p232 A1.

The marble Baptistery was designed by Diotisalvi (literally 'God-save-you') in 1152, with later decorative input by father and son Nicola and Giovanni Pisano. The magnificent pulpit by Nicola Pisano (1260) is still there to be admired in situ (compare it to his son's 1310 pulpit in the Duomo), though most of the precious artwork is now kept in the Museo dell'Opera del Duomo (*see right*). The harmonious, onion-shaped dome was a later addition, from the mid 14th century. Every half-hour, singing attendants demonstrate the building's extraordinary acoustics.

Camposanto

www.opapisa.it. **Open** *Nov-Feb* 10am-5pm daily. *Mar* 9am-6pm daily. *Apr-Sept* 8.30am-8pm daily. *Oct* 9am-7pm daily. **Admission** €5. **Map** p232 A2.

The Camposanto (Holy Field), begun in 1277 by Giovanni de Simone, is a felicitous stylistic misfit, with elements of various styles, including Gothic and Romanesque, plus more than 100 Roman sarcophagi (stone coffins). Lining the Gothic cloisters around the edge of the field are the gravestones of VIP Pisans buried in holy soil. On the west wall hang two lengths of chain that were once strung across the entrance to the Pisan port to keep out enemy ships. Pisan legend has it that the soil in the middle of the Camposanto was imported from the Holy Land. In 1944, the roof collapsed as a result of Allied bombardment, destroy-

ing frescoes and sculptures, including a fabulous cycle by Benozzo Gozzolli. However, a few survived (including, appropriately enough, *Triumph of Death*, *Last Judgement* and *Hell*), and these are being painstakingly restored as part of an ongoing project.

Duomo

050 3872210, www.opapisa.it. **Open** *Nov-Feb* 10am-12.45pm, 2-5pm daily. *Mar* 10am-6pm daily. *Apr-Sept* 10am-8pm daily. *Oct* 10am-7pm daily. **Admission** €2. **Map** p232 A2.

Begun in 1063 by Buscheto (who's buried in the wall on the left side of the façade), Pisa's cathedral is one of the finest examples of Pisan Romanesque architecture. The delicate, blindingly white marble four-tiered façade incorporates Moorish mosaics and glass within the arcades (there are more examples in the Museo dell'Opera del Duomo; *see right*). The main entrance facing the Leaning Tower is called the Portale di San Ranieri and features bronze doors by Bonanno da Pisa (1180). The brass doors (touch the lizard for good luck) by the Giambologna school were added in 1602 to replace the originals, which were destroyed in a fire in 1595.

After the fire, the Medici family immediately came to the rescue, beginning restoration work; the ornate ceiling features their coat of arms for this reason. Sadly, at the time, nothing could be done to save Giovanni Pisano's superb Gothic pulpit (1302-11), which was incinerated and lay dismembered in crates until the 1920s. Legend has it the censer suspended near the now-restored pulpit triggered Galileo's discovery of the principles of pendular motion, but it was actually cast several years later. Crane your neck to admire the Moorish dome decorated by a vibrant fresco of the Assumption by Orazio and Girolamo Riminaldi (1631). Behind the altar is a mosaic by Cimabue of St John (1302); Giuliana Vangi's 2001 pulpit and altar are noticeably more modern in style, and kicked up something of a fuss locally.

Leaning Tower

050 3872210, www.opapisa.it. **Open** *Dec, Jan* 10am-4.30pm daily. *Oct* 9am-7pm daily. *Nov, Feb* 9.30am-5.30pm daily. *Mar* 9am-5.30pm daily. *Apr, May* 8.30am-8pm daily. *June-Aug* 8.30am-11pm daily. **Map** p232 A2.

The south-east corner of the Campo holds Pisa's most popular attraction, and one of the most famous curiosities on earth. Begun in 1173 (the commemorative plaque offering 1174 as the start date is based on the old Pisan calendar) by an unknown architect, the famous tower – the campanile for the Duomo – started to lean almost as soon as it was erected, and many years before the top level, housing the seven bells, was finally added in 1350. Architect Giovanni di Simone (architect of the Camposanto; *see left*), who worked on the tower in the 13th century, attempted to correct the tilt by building floors that had one side higher than the other. However, this only served to make the tower lean in the opposite direction (which is why it's now, in fact, curved). In 1989, the year before the tower was closed to the public for 11 years of work to save it from collapse, more than a million visitors scrambled up its 294 steps. The 45cm taken off the amount of the tower's lean (*see below*) has done nothing to diminish its popularity, but a good timed ticketing system means few queues and plenty of time to get to the top of the campanile and back. It's well worth it; to experience the lean as you climb is thoroughly unnerving, and the views from the top wonderful.

Museo dell'Opera del Duomo

050 3872210, www.opapisa.it. **Open** *Dec, Jan* 9.30am-4.30pm daily. *Mar* 8.30am-5.30pm daily.

Nov, Feb 9am-5pm daily. *Apr-Sept* 8am-7.30pm daily. *Oct* 8.30am-7pm daily. **Admission** €5. **No credit cards. Map** p232 A2.

This museum contains works from the monuments of the Campo dei Miracoli. Among its more interesting exhibits is a series of sculptures from the 12th to 14th centuries, including a clutch of notable works by Giovanni Pisano. Bonanno's medieval bronze doors from the east entrance to the Duomo, fresh from recent restoration, are now on show.

★ Museo delle Sinopie

050 560547, www.opapisa.it. **Open** *Dec, Jan* 9.30am-4.30pm daily. *Mar* 8.30am-5.30pm daily. *Nov, Feb* 9am-5pm daily. *Apr-Sept* 8am-7.30pm

The Leaning Tower

Saved for the nation for another 250 years.

Pisa's emblematic campanile was an early leaner. When construction began on the bell-tower in 1173, it rapidly became clear local architect Bonnano Pisano had neglected to do his groundwork: the sand and clay beneath the new structure simply could not support it.

By the time the third storey was completed the tower was tilting markedly northwards, and in 1178 work was suspended to allow the ground to settle. It was nearly 100 years before construction resumed, during which time the tower had begun veering to the south, its present direction, using what little firm soil that existed beneath it as its fulcrum. By the second half of the 14th century, despite all attempts to correct the impression of a curve as further tiers were added, the world's most famous leaning tower was finally completed.

If the quirky tower was ever a cause of embarrassment to Pisans, its merits as a tourist attraction (and source of revenue) made up for that. But even as many of those millions of visitors made the unnerving climb of the tower's 293 steps, so the campanile continued to tilt, until in 1989, close to its maximum discrepancy from the vertical of 4.47 metres (15 feet), it was deemed in danger of collapse.

A complex rescue operation, involving enormous counterweights and suspenders and a reduction in the depth of the soil between the north and south sides of the tower, swung slowly into action. The aim was never to straighten the tower entirely (who'd visit it then?) but to correct its tilt by 40cm (18in). At one point, in around 1995, the scheme threatened to go pear-shaped as the lean increased fractionally. By 2001, however, the then Minister of Public Works, Nerio Nesi, could declare the 55 billion-lire project a triumph, with the monument now safeguarded for at least the next 250 years.

daily. *Oct* 8.30am-7pm daily. **Admission** €5.
No credit cards. **Map** p232 A2.

The 1944 bombings and subsequent restoration work uncovered the *sinopie* (preliminary sketches, made with a reddish-brown pigment composed of iron oxides) from beneath the frescoes in the Camposanto. They were meant to be hidden forever, after the artist covered the original *arriccio* (dry plaster on which the sketches were made) with a lime-rich plaster called *grassello*. The *sinopie* show what brilliant draftsmen the painters were, but also give the observer an intriguing sense of scale.

Other sights

Museo Nazionale di Palazzo Reale

Lungarno Pacinotti 46 (050 926539). **Open** 9am-2.30pm Mon, Wed-Fri; 9am-1.30pm Sat. **Admission** €5; €8 with Museo Nazionale di Matteo. **No credit cards. Map** p232 B2.

Housed in a Medici palace dating from 1583, this museum shows many Medici-related works donated by private collectors. Portraits represent members of various European dynasties; there's also traditional Gioco del Ponte gear (*see p178*).

Museo Nazionale di San Matteo

Piazza San Matteo in Soarta, lungarno Mediceo (050 541865). **Open** 8.30am-7pm Tue-Sat; 9am-1.30pm Sun. **Admission** €5; €8 with Museo Nazionale di Palazzo Reale. **No credit cards. Map** p232 C3.

Once a convent, this 12th- to 13th-century building now contains Pisan and Islamic medieval ceramics, works by Masaccio, Fra Angelico and Domenico Ghirlandaio, and a bust by Donatello.

FREE Orto Botanico

Via Luca Ghini 5 (050 2211313, www.biologia. unipi.it/ortobotanico/). **Open** 8.30am-5pm Mon-Fri; 8.30am-1pm Sat. Closed 1wk Aug, 2wks Christmas. **Admission** €2.50; €1.50 reductions; €6 family. **Map** p232 A2/B2.

The oldest university garden to be found anywhere in Europe (it was started by Luca Ghini back in 1543), the Orto Botanico was originally used to study the medicinal values of plants.

FREE Palazzo Blu

Lungarno Gambacorti 9 (050 916950, www. palazzoblu.org). **Open** 10am-7pm Tue-Fri; 10am-8pm Sat, Sun. **Admission** free.

Housed within this vibrant blue 16th-century *palazzo* on the Arno is a small collection of work by artists with Mediterranean connections, but it's the temporary exhibitions that are the real draw; since the gallery's opening in 2008 retrospectives and themed shows have included work by Picasso, Chagall and Mirò, as well as group shows on themes such as 'Women and Italy'. There's a good programme of related events too.

★ Piazza dei Cavalieri

Map p232 B2.

A focal point of Pisa, this beautiful square houses Palazzo dei Cavalieri, the seat of one of Italy's most prestigious universities, the Scuola Normale Superiore, established by Napoleon in 1810. In the 16th century, Giorgio Vasari designed most of the piazza's buildings, including the Chiesa dei Cavalieri, Palazzo della Conventuale (opposite the church, erected as home to the Cavalieri of Santo Stefano), Palazzo del Consiglio dell'Ordine and

Piazza dei Cavalieri.

INSIDE TRACK
CANDLES IN THE WIND

Each year Pisa celebrates its patron saint's day on 17 June with the Regatta di San Ranieri, a boat race between the four quarters of the town – Santa Maria, San Francesco, Sant'Antonio and San Martino – with the victor being the team whose *montatore* (climber) is the first to climb a rope and grab the correct flag at the top of a 10m pole mounted on a boat anchored at the finish line. The evening before, thousands of candles and torches are placed along the buildings lining the route, creating a truly romantic sight.

Palazzo Gherardesca. The latter occupies the site of a medieval prison where, in 1288, Count Ugolino della Gherardesca, along with three of his male heirs, was condemned to starve to death for conducting covert negotiations with the Florentines. His sons and grandsons all died relatively quickly, but Ugolino lasted nine months, after he reputedly kept himself alive by eating his own children. Although that condemned him to Hell in Dante's *Inferno*, the poet ensured that Ugolino had a measure of revenge: the count spent eternity gnawing the head of Archbishop Ruggieri, the man who had betrayed him (Canto XXXIII).

You'll see the Maltese Cross everywhere in this piazza, but nowhere else in Pisa. Cosimo wanted to hammer home the parallel between his new Cavalieri of Santo Stefano and the crusading Knights of Malta. Elsewhere, you're likely to spot the Pisan cross with two balls resting on each point.

FREE San Nicola
Via Santa Maria 2 (050 24677). **Open** 8.30am-11.30am, 5-6.30pm Mon-Sat; 9am-noon, 5.30-6.30pm Sun. **Admission** free. **Map** p232 B2.
Dating from 1150, this church is dedicated to one of Pisa's patron saints, San Nicola da Tolentino. In one chapel there's a painting showing the saint protecting Pisa from the plague in around 1400. Built on unstable ground, the campanile leans.

Santa Maria della Spina
Lungarno Gambacorti (050 3215446). **Open** 10am-1pm, 3-6pm Mon-Fri; 10am-2pm, 3-7pm Sat, Sun. **Admission** €1.50. **No credit cards**. **Map** p232 B2.
This gorgeous, tiny Gothic church on the banks of the Arno was completely dismantled and moved to higher, drier ground in 1871. Originally an oratory, it took its present form in 1323 and gets its name from the fact that it used to own what was claimed to be a thorn (*spina*) from Christ's crown, brought back by the Crusaders. *Photo p239.*

WHERE TO EAT & DRINK
Restaurants

Cèe alla Pisana (eels), one of Pisa's culinary assets for centuries, are increasingly hard to find. When they are plucked from the Arno (they're a winter delicacy), the eels are tossed in warm oil, garlic and sage, then sautéed. The best area in which to sample Tuscan *aperitivo* and sharing plates at the rising number of *enoteche* is around the Borgo Stretto, where a thriving local foodie scene is encouraging a lively mix of establishments. Il Colonnino (via Sant' Andrea 37-41, 050 3138430, www.ilcolonnino.it) is a good example.

Aphrodite I Peccati della Carne
Via Vecchia Lucchese 33a (050 830248, 347 3737307 mobile, www.ristoranteaphrodite.it). **Open** 1-3.30pm, 8pm-1am Mon-Fri; 8pm-1am Sat, Sun. **Average** €35. **Map** p233 A3 ❶
This exciting restaurant offers innovative cuisine – and interesting wines – in a cool, funky setting. Owner Emilio Traina and his chef create dishes that delight both palate and eye, with meat a particular focus. The ample garden comes into its own in summer.

Da Bruno
Via Luigi Bianchi 12 (050 560818, www. ristorante.dabruno.it). **Open** noon-3pm, 7-10.30pm Mon, Wed-Sun. **Average** €35. **Map** p233 A3 ❷
Bruno concentrates on classic, good-value Tuscan cooking. Try the *ribollita*, supposedly the best this side of the Arno, or pasta with rabbit and wild boar.

La Clessidra
Via del Castelletto 26-30 (050 540160, www. ristorantelaclessidra.net). **Open** 7.30pm-midnight Mon-Sat. **Average** €25; tasting menus €32-€35. **No credit cards**. **Map** p232 B2 ❸
Cagliostro is named after a Sicilian count who masqueraded as an alchemist in France and Italy. The extensive wine list complements the menu, which draws on recipes from all over Italy. It's hard to find – ask for the restaurant, not the street.

Drive Sushi
Piazza delle Vettovaglie 40 (050 3144006). **Open** noon-3pm, 6pm-1am daily (food served until 10.30pm). **No credit cards**. **Map** p232 B2 ❹
In the very lively piazza della Vettovaglie, where pretty porticos shelter seemingly dozens of eateries and bars, Drive stands out – partly for rarity value, but also for its good prices and friendly service. A wide range of nigiri, sashimi and temaki start from €1.50 per piece, but there's a great range of plates too – eight sashimi pieces for €8, 12 for €12, or a €6 sushi *aperitivo* with drink. Cocktails are cheap too, making this a popular spot with Pisa's thousands of students – avoid if you're after a quiet tête-à-tête.

TUSCANY

La Mescita

Via Cavalca 2 (050 957019, www.osterialamescita pisa.com). **Open** 7-11pm Tue-Sun. *Winter* 12.30-2.30pm, 7-11pm Tue-Sun. Closed 2wks Aug. **Average** €35. **Map** p232 B2 ❺

At the heart of Vettovaglie market, La Mescita is pretty and tranquil. Try the *brandade di stoccafisso* (salt cod) with tomatoes, but do also check the window for its calendar of *degustazioni* and creative cooking nights.

★ Osteria Bernardo

Piazza San Paolo all'Orto 1 (050 575216, www. osteriabernardo.it). **Open** 7.30-11pm Tue-Fri; 12.30-2.30pm, 7.30-11pm Sat, Sun. **Average** €35. **Map** p233 B3 ❻

On a quiet, pretty square in the heart of the old town, Luigi Bernardo's elegant addition to Pisa's restaurant scene is a revelation, serving modern Tuscan food that positively zings with flavour and flair. Tuscan traditionals are given inventive twists that work brilliantly in a mixed menu that is as strong on fish as it is meat; a *maccheroncelli* with fresh anchovy and courgette flowers was incredible, as was lamb in an almond, pistaccio and hazelnut crust and the weird-sounding but delicious beef carpaccio with chocolate. Luigi uses a great range of ingredients sourced as locally as possible, and obviously loves his craft. The wine list is well considered too.

Osteria dei Cavalieri

Via San Frediano 16 (050 580858, www.osteria cavalieri.pisa.it). **Open** 12.30-2pm, 7.45-10pm

Mon-Fri; 7.45-10pm Sat. Closed 1wk Jan, 4wks Aug. **Average** €35. **Map** p232 B2 ❼

One of Pisa's best eateries, especially for the money. It serves typical Tuscan dishes with flair: steak with beans and mushrooms, perhaps, or *tagliolini* with rabbit and asparagus. The wine list is noteworthy.

Osteria La Grotta

Via San Francesco 103 (050 578105, www.osteria lagrotta.com). **Open** 12.45-2.30pm, 7.30-10.30pm Mon-Sat. **Average** €25. **Map** p233 B3 ❽

Built to simulate a *grotta* or cave with rough stone walls and a cosy fire in winter, this fine spot serves hearty local soups, *maccheroncini* with sun-dried tomatoes, courgettes and pecorino, and superb *baccalà* (salt cod). The wine list is good too.

Pizzeria Il Montino

Via del Monte 1 (050 598695, www.pizzeriail montino.com). **Open** 10am-3pm, 5.30-10.30pm Mon-Sat. **Average** €15. **No credit cards.** **Map** p232 B2 ❾

Visit this small snack bar to try the unique taste of *cecina*, a bright yellow, very thin pancake made with chickpea flour from a 13th-century recipe; and *spuma*, a refreshing non-alcoholic beverage.

Re di Puglia

Via Aurelia Sud 7 (050 960157). **Open** 8-10pm Wed-Sat; 1-3pm, 8-10pm Sun. Closed 2wks Jan. **Average** €35. **No credit cards.**

Slabs of succulent meat are grilled in front of your eyes on the open fire at this rustic restaurant a few kilometres south of Pisa on the Livorno road. While meat (especially beef, lamb and rabbit) reigns supreme, the menu also includes five types of Tuscan *antipasti*. Eat outdoors in summer.

Al Vecchio Teatro

Via Collegio Ricci 3, corner of piazza Dante (050 20210). **Open** 12.30-3pm, 7.30-10pm Mon-Sat. **Average** €28; €35 tasting menu. **Map** p232 B2 ❿

Restaurant owner Giovanni displays pictures of Pisa all around the interior of his restaurant, which serves fine traditional fare such as octopus and chickpeas, and has tables facing attractive, quiet piazza Dante.

Cafés, bars & gelaterie

★ De Coltelli

Lungarno Pacinotti 23 (345 4811903 mobile, www.decoltelli.com). **Open** 1pm-1am daily. Closed Jan. **No credit cards.** **Map** p232 B2 ❶

Aside from things like vanilla (imported from Tahiti) and chocolate, all ingredients at this pretty new *gelateria* on the Arno are sourced from Italy, with a roster of flavours centred on seasonal availability, and all natural ingredients. The pine nut is incredible, the delicate flavour of the nut and creaminess of the texture creating a truly amazing ice-cream. Although the presence of some decidedly strange

---

INSIDE TRACK HARING MURAL

Unless you arrive at Pisa by train, and even then, there's a good chance you'll totally miss a key part of modern Pisan art. Head down the side street that leads from piazza Vittori Emanuele to the Domus Mazziniana, where, at the southernmost tip of town and rising up before you in his trademark technicolour, you'll find *Tuttomondo*, a Keith Haring mural that covers 180sq m of the rear wall of the convent of the Church of Sant'Antonio in 30 bright figures of fun. Tumbling, dancing, flying and running, the figures represent different aspects of peace and harmony in the world, creating a modern allegorical piece that offers food for thought in much the way medieval frescoes did. Created in June 1989, just a few months before Haring's death from AIDS-related complications in February 1990, this was his last public work and it's a fitting memorial.

Santa Maria della Spina. *See p237.*

foremost chocolate artisans and home to some beautiful and very reasonably priced tableware and tea sets (lungarno Pacinotti 5, 050 3160073, www.debondt.it), and **Scarlatti**, a lovely little mens' shop that's been here since 1896, and a great place to pick up traditional old-school gifts for men; a cut throat razor or beautiful shaving brush maybe (borgo Stretto 18, 050 573899, www.scarlatti1896.it).

NIGHTLIFE

For Pisa's best gay bar and sauna, *see p193.*

Borderline
Via Vernaccini 7 (050 580577). **Open** 9pm-2am Mon-Sat. **Admission** free-€10.50. **No credit cards. Map** p233 B3.
Good for late drinks and the occasional gig, with blues, roots and country music taking centre stage.

Teatro Verdi
Via Palestro 40 (050 941111, www.teatrodipisa. pi.it). **Open** *Box office* 4-7pm Mon, Tue, Thur, Sat; 11am-1pm, 4-7pm Wed, Fri; also 1hr before events. *Phone bookings* 2-4pm Mon-Fri. Closed 3wks Aug. **Map** p233 B3.
An enjoyable venue for dance, drama and music.

WHERE TO STAY

Accommodation in Pisa can be a bit hit or miss, with most of the latter in the budget categories. To ensure you get a decent room, reserve in advance during high season and for major festivals. The tourist information centre at the Campo dei Miracoli has a list of hotels. You'll find the nearest camping in Marina di Pisa.

Albergo Galileo
Via Santa Maria 12 (050 40621). **Rates** €60. **Map** p232 B2 ❶
Though it's illegal to employ Galileo Galilei's full name for commercial purposes in Pisa, this *pensione* manages to get away with using half of it. It's worth asking for one of the five (of nine) rooms that are decorated with 17th-century frescoes.

Amalfitana
Via Roma 44 (050 29000). **Rooms** 21. **Rates** €75-€82. **Map** p232 B2 ❷
A favourite of visiting Italians seeking central, two-star category accommodation.

Grand Hotel Duomo
Via Santa Maria 94 (050 561894, www. grandhotelduomo.it). **Rooms** 94. **Rates** €191. **Map** p232 A2 ❹
Hints of its previous opulence remain, but the Grand is now, sadly, getting somewhat frayed around the

---

varieties – like *alle vongole* (clams) – might scare off some people, rest assured that the ice-cream dished up here is tremendous.

Pasticceria Salza
Borgo Stretto 46 (050 580144, www.salza.it). **Open** 7.45am-8.30pm Tue-Sun. **Map** p232 B2 ❷
This distinguished *pasticceria*, the oldest in Pisa, is a real multitasker, with café tables in the front, a sweet shop inside and a restaurant at the back.

Pizzicheria Gastronomia Cesqui
Piazza delle Vettovaglie 38 (050 580269). **Open** 7am-1.30pm, 4-8pm Mon, Tue, Thur-Sat; 7am-1.30pm Wed. **Map** p232 B2 ❸
Stock up on cheese, pasta, wine and snacks at this deli, while bantering and gossiping with the staff.

SHOPS & SERVICES

Pisa's main shopping drag is corso Italia, but across from the ponte di Mezzo is a funkier zone, starting at the *loggia* of borgo Stretto. The **Mercatino Antiquario** takes place where the two meet, on the second weekend of every month, offering modern arts and crafts as well as antiques. The **Mercato Vettovaglie**, a fruit and vegetable market, is held every morning. Look out too for **De Bondt**, one of Italy's

TUSCANY

edges. But its location can't be faulted if you want somewhere central, especially if you land one of the fourth-floor rooms that have sweeping views over the Campo dei Miracoli from the terrace. If you arrive by car, make sure you ask for a parking permit for via Santa Maria.

★ Hotel Bologna
Via Mazzini 57 (050 502120, www.hotelbologna. pisa.it). **Rates** €99-€249. **Map** p232 B2 **⑤**
Just round the corner from the Arno and very close to downtown Pisa, this friendly hotel is a real find, with free Wi-Fi and water, a ridiculously cheap mini-bar, a shuttle service to and from the airport or station and, best of all, a very pretty and comfortable terrace and private garden. Rooms are spacious, clean and comfortable, and staff helpful.

★ Hotel Novecento
Via Roma 37 (050 500323, www.hotelnovecento. pisa.it). **Rooms** 10. **Rates** €150. **Map** p232 B2 **⑥**
Conveniently placed for both Campo dei Miracoli and downtown Pisa, this impressive modern hotel has pristine cream rooms and a pretty garden at the back. There's lots of fresh fruit for breakfast and a 12th-century well lies beneath reception.

Hotel Repubblica Marinara
Via Matteucci 81 (050 3870100, www. hotelrepubblicamarinara.it). **Rooms** 55. **Rates** €149-€199.
The rooms at this contemporary hotel come with all manner of technological bells and whistles – internet access, orthopaedic mattresses and various lighting options. Take via Matteotti, passing the Congress Palace.

Relais dell'Orologio
Via della Faggiola 12-14 (behind piazza de' Cavalieri, 050 830361, www.hotelrelaisorologio. com). **Rooms** 21. **Rates** €233-€430. **Map** p232 A2 **⑦**
Maria Louisa Bignardi's dream of turning her 13th-century house into a five-star hotel became a reality a few years back. The 21 rooms are individually decorated, so the place still has the feel of a private home. The Peli di Vaglio suite has lovely exposed frescoes.

Royal Victoria
Lungarno Pacinotti 12 (050 940111, www.royal victoria.it). **Rooms** 48. **Rates** (incl breakfast) €80-€150. Room service is charged extra. **Map** p232 B2 **⑧**
Situated on the Arno, this hotel was a popular stop back in the days of the Grand Tour and counts illustrious names, such as Charles Dickens, Theodore Roosevelt and Daryl Hannah, among its previous guests. The atmosphere still harks back to the olden times, and though the bedrooms have lumbering old furniture, they're full of character.

RESOURCES

Hospital
Santa Chiara *Via Roma 67 (050 992111, 050 992300 emergencies).*

Internet
Via La Nunziatina (no phone).

Police
Questura, via Mario Lalli 3 (050 583511).

Post office
Piazza Vittorio Emanuele II 8 (050 519514). **Open** 8.15am-7pm Mon-Fri; 8.15am-1.30pm Sat.

Tourist information
Turistica APT *Piazza Vittorio Emanuele II 16, nr train station (050 42291, www.pisaunica terra.it).* **Open** 9am-7pm Mon-Sat; 9am-4pm Sun. **Map** p232 A2.
Other locations Galileo Galilei Airport, arrivals (050 502518); piazza della Stazione 11 (050 42291).

GETTING THERE & AROUND

By air
Galileo Galilei Airport (050 849300, www. pisa-airport.com) is still Tuscany's major international airport. The airport handles flights from all around Europe and has recently started flights to and from the US. There are frequent buses and regular trains into Pisa and Lucca m here. For further information about the airport and its transport links, *see p304.*

By bus
Vaibus (piazza Sant'Antonio, 050 50550, www.vaibus.it) operates a regular service to Lucca (journey time 50mins), with onward connections to Florence (2hrs 30mins), as well as buses to Viareggio (50mins). **CPT** (piazza Sant'Antonio, 800 012773, www.cpt.pisa.it) covers the area around Pisa and runs buses to nearby areas such as Livorno and Marina di Pisa.

By taxi
You can find taxi ranks at piazza della Stazione (050 41252) and piazza del Duomo (050 561878). If you need to book a taxi in advance, call Radio Taxi on 050 541600.

By train
Pisa is on a main connecting line to Rome (journey time 3hrs on Intercity, otherwise 4hrs) as well as Genoa (2hrs). There are also frequent trains to Florence via Empoli (80mins), Lucca (25mins) and Livorno (15mins); some trains also stop at Pisa Aeroporto and San Rossore. The train station is Pisa Centrale, piazza della Stazione (information 892021, www.trenitalia.it).

Pisa & Livorno Provinces

Delve into Etruscan history – or dive into a thermal bath.

The Leaning Tower, fortunately, does not cast its shadow over the entirety of Pisa Province – or its regional neighbour, Livorno. Armed with a car and a robust road map, you can be glorying in the stunning countryside in no time – or relaxing on a beach, or having your cares steamed away in one of the many spa pools: the possibilities are many and varied.

Behind the scenes, there's a great deal of industrial activity going on; tucked-away boatyards produce some of the world's most luxurious yachts here. Meanwhile, between Bolgheri and Castagneto Carducci, a once-poor farming area produces some of Tuscany's most prestigious wines. The coast is one attraction that draws the crowds, but it's not the only reason to visit. Further inland, the northern section of the Maremma (known as the Maremma Pisana) runs between Cecina and Follonica on the coast and inland towards the Colline Metallifere.

SAN GIULIANO TERME

The healing qualities of San Giuliano's local spa waters were known to Grand Duke Stephen of Lorraine, who ordered a magnificent 18th-century residence to be constructed here, which formed the nucleus of the town. Guests at the very comfortable **Bagni di Pisa** hotel (largo Shelley 18, 050 88501, www.bagnidipisa.com; *see also p244* **Spa-spangled Manors**), the town's main building, can soak away the aches induced by too much sightseeing, before adjourning to the hotel's fine restaurant. Indeed, the town is so close to Pisa that it makes a handsome alternative base to the city.

SAN MINIATO

Snaking along the crest of a lofty hill, the town of San Miniato grew prominent on account of its strategic position above the Pisa–Florence road. It was fortified in the 12th and 13th centuries and was one of Tuscany's foremost imperial centres, but it succumbed to Florentine power in the mid

1300s. Unfortunately, the interiors of both the 13th-century Duomo and the later church of San Domenico were subjected to heavy-handed Baroque 'improvements'. The spacious *loggia* of San Domenico is used for an antiques fair on the second Sunday of each month (except July and August). The surrounding area is rich in truffles; November weekends are devoted to tasting them as part of the **Festa del Tartufo**.

Where to eat

Caffè Centrale (via IV Novembre 19, 0571 43037, closed Mon & late Aug/early Sept, average €12) serves simple pastas for lunch and has a great view, while just outside town there's **Il Convio** (via San Maiano 2, 0571 408114, www.ristoranteilconvio.com, closed Wed, average €30), with more Tuscan favourites, plus a truffle-laden vegetarian menu. An alluring spot in the old town is **Pepenero** (via IV Novembre 13, 0571 419523, www.pepenero cucina.it, closed Tue, average €40), which is liberal with white truffle. As an alternative,

INSIDE TRACK
FANGS AIN'T WHAT THEY SEEM

When Stephanie Meyer set a key scene between heroine Bella and undead lover Edward in the phenomenally successful second Twilight book *New Moon* in Volterra, the town quickly became a mecca for the vampire saga's millions of fans. In response, the tourism office has created a themed map of the city and a **New Moon walking tour** (0588 87257, www.new moonofficialtour.com, €30, 6pm Fri, reservations only), at the heart of which is the piazza dei Priori and its clock tower, home in the film to the Volturi, a coven of elite vampires. You don't have to be into the books to take a Twilight walking tour of the town; it's a wonderfully evocative, eerie and memorable way to enjoy this medieval walled town – but despite Volterra lobbying hard to get the film shot here, the five-day shoot actually took place in Montepulciano.

try **La Trattoria dell'Orcio Interrato** in nearby Montopoli Valdarno (piazza Michele da Montopoli 2, 0571 466878, closed Mon, dinner Sun in winter, 2wks Aug, 1wk Feb, average €35), which has a summer terrace and food that interprets Renaissance recipes.

CASCIANA TERME

Tucked away in the Pisan hills and less crowded than Montecatini or Saturnia, this spa town, known as Castrum ad Aquas to the Romans, was destroyed in World War II and rebuilt in the 1960s. After taking the waters at **Terme di Casciana** (piazza Garibaldi 9, 0587 64461; *see also p244* **Spa-spangled Manors**), relax out front with an espresso at the traditional café.

A kilometre east of Calci, the **Certosa di Pisa** (via Roma 79, 050 938430, closed Mon & afternoon Sun, admission €4) is a vast complex used as a monastery from 1366 until 1969, when it was abandoned by the Carthusian monks. Inside there's a 14th-century church, plus cloisters and gardens, while its former granaries, workshops and cellars now house the **Natural History Museum** (via Roma 79, 050 2212970, www.msn.unipi.it, closed Mon, admission €7), founded in 1591 by Grand Duke Ferdinando I.

Where to stay & eat

Just down the road from the thermal waters is **La Speranza** (via Cavour 24, 0587 646215, www.hotel-lasperanza.it, €100), which has an

attractive pool and gardens; not too far away is the spacious and inviting **Villa Margherita** (via Marconi 20, 0587 646113, www.margherita-hotel.it, closed 4 Nov-5 Dec & Jan-Easter, €150). Restaurant-wise, go for **Il Merlo** (piazza Minati 5, 0587 644040, average €30, closed Mon & Jan), which has a handsome wine list. A few kilometres further on from Terricciola is the stately **Villa San Marco** (via del Pino 14, Soiana–San Marco, 0587 654054, www.san marcohotels.it, €178-€520). The tourist office (c/o Agenzia di Viaggi Velathri Tour, via Roma 14, 0587 646258) can give you more accommodation information.

VOLTERRA

Volterra stands proudly on a 531-metre (1,742-foot) peak between the Cecina and Era valleys in Pisa Province. The surrounding area is rich in mineral deposits, which explains why it was settled as early as the Neolithic period. By the seventh century BC, the city known as Velathri had become one of the 12 Etruscan states, with a population of 25,000 and a prosperous trade in iron and alabaster artefacts. It put up a hearty resistance to the Romans and was the last Etruscan city to fall to the Empire. But fall it did in 260 BC, when it was renamed Volaterrae.

The town as it appears today was built in the 12th and 13th centuries; save for patches of the fortified walls, all traces of the Etruscans have been erased. Fortunately, the **Museo Etrusco Guarnacci** (via Don Minzoni 15, 0588 86347, €8) helps make up for this: among its exhibits is the celebrated 'evening shadow' statuette – a long, thin statue that was found by a local farmer and used as a fire stoker until someone recognised its importance. The ticket also admits you to Volterra's other two museums: the **Pinacoteca** (0588 87580, closed afternoons in winter, €6), located in the late 15th-century Palazzo Minucci Solaini and worth a visit purely to see the astounding use of colour in the fabulous Mannerist *Deposition* by Rosso Fiorentino, and the **Museo d'Arte Sacra** (Palazzo Vescovile, via Roma 13, 0588 86290, closed afternoons in winter), which boasts work by the same artist. Admission to the Museo d'Arte Sacra is only possible on a €10 joint ticket along with the Guarnacci and Pinacoteca.

Where to stay & eat

A convent more than five centuries ago, **Hotel San Lino** (via San Lino 26, 0588 85250, www.hotelsanlino.com, €90-€105) now has its own pool and a shady cloister. Two kilometres outside of Volterra, the 15th-century **Villa Rioddi** (0588 88053, www.hotelvillarioddi.it, €75-€110) also has a pool and a lgarden. Just outside town, **Il Vecchio Mulino** (via del Molino, località Saline, 0588 44060, www.il vecchiomulino.it, €70-€85, closed Mon) features some new guestrooms as well as a restaurant specialising in inventive Tuscan cuisine. The town's eating options are led, though, by the cosy **Trattoria del Sacco Fiorentino** (piazza XX Settembre, 0588 88537, closed Wed, Jan & Feb, average €25); located near the Museo Etrusco Guarnacci, it serves seasonal goodies, such as gnocchi with spring vegetables, and a 100-strong wine list. An elegant alternative is **Del Duca** (via di Castello 2, 0588 81510, www. enoteca-delduca-ristorante.it, closed Tue, average €40), with its ancient wine cellar and garden.

LIVORNO

By the 16th century, the Arno had silted up, leaving the maritime republic of Pisa shorn of its outlet to the sea. As a remedy, Cosimo I pounced on a tiny fishing village in 1571, with major designs for improving it. A far-sighted constitution set up in 1593 allowed foreigners to reside in the city regardless of nationality and religion, instantly endowing the place with a cosmopolitan mentality that has survived over the centuries. In fact, Livorno (bizarrely translated as Leghorn in English) has a completely different feel from other Tuscan towns. With exotic hints of Marseille (sailors, immigrants, and a busy commercial port with all that entails), it's a fun place to pass a day and is blissfully tourist-free. There are also some fabulous fish restaurants in which to sample the town's speciality, *cacciucco*, a spicy fish soup

that often has to be ordered in advance. Livorno is the hopping-off point for the islands of the Archipelago Toscano, Sardinia and Corsica.

The **Porto Mediceo**, with the red-brick bastion of the **Fortezza Vecchia**, designed by Sangallo the Younger in 1521, has long been the focus of city life. From here the charming canals of **Venezia Nuova** (or I Fossi) extend, tracing the pentagonal perimeter of Francesco I's late 16th-century plan for an ideal city. Look out for the concerts and food-fest of the **Effetto Venezia**, which takes place in late July. Sadly, bombing during World War II destroyed most of Livorno's historic monuments, and post-war reconstruction finished them off. Buontalenti's piazza Grande was cut in two; all that remains of the 16th-century Duomo is Inigo Jones's fine portico. Located near the ferry port, piazza Micheli sports Livorno's only other artistic treasure, the superb **Quattro Mori** monument by Pietro Tacca (1623), consisting of four colossal bronze slaves who sit chained to the pedestal of an earlier statue of Ferdinand I.

Where to stay, eat & drink

Osteria da Carlo (viale Caprera 43-45, 0586 897050, closed Sun & 2wks Sept, average €25) serves a decent *cacciuco*, while **La Corsara** (via Mentana 78, 0586 897208, closed Wed, average €25) is also good for fish. Other spots worth trying for local fare include **La Chiave**, across from the Fortezza Nuova (scali delle Cantine 52, 0586 888609, closed Wed & Aug, average €45) and **Il Sottomarino** (via de' Terrazzini 48, 0586 887025, closed Mon, Tue & 2wks July, average

TUSCANY

Volterra.

TUSCANY

Spa-Spangled Manors

In need of a little pampering? You're spoilt for choice in Tuscany.

Heading to Tuscany in the winter? You'd better pack your swimming costume. No Italian region is as rich in spas as Tuscany: the waters are warm, if not hot, and naturally rich with minerals that should ease your aches and uplift your spirits. You can even factor in a massage for that little bit of extra luxury. Check the websites for opening/closing times, which vary from year to year.

Just north of Pisa, in San Giuliano Terme, is the very comfortable **Bagni di Pisa** hotel (*see p241*), recently upgraded to a five-star establishment. It's found a measure of fame for its decent restaurant, but also has a small hot pool, a Turkish bath in a natural grotto and a host of good masseurs. South of Pisa, meanwhile, is **Terme di Casciana** (0587 644655, www. termedicasciana.it), which has a large, luxurious modern pool and spa facilities fronted by a more traditional café.

At Bagno Vignoni, directly south of Siena, the recently revamped **Hotel Posta Marcucci** (0577 887112, www.hotel postamarcucci.it) provides another great opportunity for aquatic indulgence. Set in pretty gardens with a magnificent view across the valley, the pool has a thundering cascade that provides a memorable hydro-massage. The water at **Bagni San Filippo** (0577 872982, www.termesanfilippo.it, €96-€120, closed Nov-1wk before Easter), a little further south, is hotter still and more sulphurous, with a scorcher of a cascade (the water is around 42°). Looking over the valley towards Monte Amiata at San Casciano dei Bagni, the **Terme di San Casciano** (0578 57241,

Tombolo Talasso Resort.

www.fonteverdespa.com, €280-€1,400) offers upmarket facilities and a pool with a powerful hydro-massage. If it's salty rubs and seawater cures you pine for, head for Marina di Castagneto Carducci on the coast, where you'll find Tuscany's only thalassotherapy escape, the **Tombolo Talasso Resort** (via del Corallo 3, Maria di Castagneto Carducci, 0565 74530, www. tombolotalasso.it, €320-€548), which has five seawater pools and a wellness centre set in pleasant gardens, just a stone's throw from the beach.

€35). Located on a hill overlooking the coast at Castellaccio, just south of the town, **Ghiné & Cambri** (via di Quercianella 263, 0586 579414, www.ghinecambri.it, closed Tue, average €25) has become something of a cult eaterie with the younger generation for its relaxed atmosphere and fine meat and vegetable dishes. For ice-cream, try **La Chiostra** (viale Italia 8, 0586 813564, closed Mon in winter).

Livorno's youth tend to head for the disco-bars on the canals. The **Barge** (scali delle Ancore 6, 0586 888320, closed Mon) has a piano bar (live music Tue, Fri & Sat), an 'English' bar and canalside tables in the summer. If you need to stay overnight, the choices in town are rather

grim, but you could try the central **Hotel Gran Duca** (piazza Micheli 16, 0586 891024, www. granduca.it, €150-€250). A more pleasant alternative is **La Vedetta di Montenero** (via della Lecceta 5, Montenero, 0586 579957, www.hotellavedetta.it, €70-€154), located on a hillside in the suburb of Montenero.

BOLGHERI, CASTAGNETO CADUCCI & SUVERETO

While **Marina di Cecina** is a pleasant enough seaside town with a popular windsurfing beach, the inland areas are more attractive. Heading south on the Aurelia (the SS1) and then inland, you'll reach **Bolgheri** via its famous approach, a straight, five-kilometre (three-mile) road lined with tall cypress trees. This beautiful little medieval town has become synonymous with **Sassicaia**, one of Italy's most prestigious (and expensive) wines. Ludovico Antonori's Ornellaia is another hallowed local label, but if your wine budget doesn't run to such elevated figures (a bottle of either of these could cost hundreds of euros), look out for the much cheaper Rosso di Bolgheri. The town boasts an inordinate number of restaurants and wine bars. One of the best is **Enoteca Tognoni** (via Lauretta 5, 0565 762001, www.enotecatognoni. it, average €50, closed Wed), which is packed with bottles and cases of wine, where you can eat a full meal or choose from a menu of snacks; wine is also sold by the bottle. Bolgheri also has a WWF nature reserve.

Further south is **Castagneto Carducci**. It's also small and charming, attracting the sort of Italian glitterati who spurn the crowded coast in the summer months. There are many good cycling routes; after a day's pedalling, put your feet up at the **Hotel Ristorante Zì Martino** just outside town at San Giusto (0565 766000, www.zimartino.com, €85, average €25, closed Mon in winter).

From here, proceed south to **Suvereto**, a lovely medieval town surrounded by wooded hillsides and dominated by an ancient *rocca* (hilltop castle). It has a splendid arcaded town hall dating from the 13th century and a set of circular walls that are almost intact. Around ten kilometres (six miles) from the coast is another medieval charmer – lively **Campiglia Marittima** has an arty subculture with great views over the Val di Cornia to the sea.

PIOMBINO & AROUND

The only reason to visit sooty **Piombino** is to catch a ferry to **Corsica**, **Elba** and the ex-prison island of **Pianosa**. Far more attractive is the stretch of coastline that runs north from here and up to the ruins of Etruscan Populonia. On the way you'll see mystifying rock formations, necropoli, beaches and clean, unspoilt waters.

Populonia, one of the most important trading ports in ancient Etruria, perches high above the golden arc of sand that fringes the **Golfo di Baratti** with its little fishing port. There's a small archaeological museum within the village, but more worthwhile is the **Parco Archaeologico di Baratti e Populonia**, which covers the lush green hillside overlooking the bay, and which incorporates Etruscan burial chambers and other remains of the once-mighty settlement. The car park and visitor centre are behind the

> ### INSIDE TRACK
> ### TRUFFLE SNUFFLE
>
> San Miniato's white truffles are rightly famed worldwide; to help you find your own white treasure, the Association of Trufflers of San Miniato has produced a handy truffling map to the area. If you're unlucky, you can ogle the best of the season throughout November at a huge weekly exhibition and market, where you can also buy truffles and truffle produce.

beach; allow several hours for a complete tour with one of the polyglot guides.

RESOURCES

Tourist information

Livorno *APT, piazza Cavour 6 (0586 204611, www.costadeglietruschi.it).* **Open** 8.30am-5pm Mon-Fri.

Piombino *Ufficio di Turismo, Torre Comunale, via del Ferruccio (0565 225639, www.turismo piombino.it).* **Open** 9am-3pm, 5-11pm Mon, Wed-Sun. Closed mid Sept-May.

San Miniato *Ufficio di Turismo, piazza del Popolo (0571 42745, www.cittadisanminiato.it).* **Open** 9am-1pm Mon; 9am-1pm, 2-6pm Tue-Sun.

Volterra *Volterratour, piazza dei Priori 19-20 (0588 87257, www.volterratur.it).* **Open** *Apr-Oct* 9am-1pm, 2-7pm daily. *Nov-Mar* 9am-1pm, 2-6pm daily.

GETTING THERE

By bus

SITA (800 373760, www.sitabus.it) runs buses from Florence to Volterra (1hr 50mins). **VAIBUS** (050 50550, www.vaibus.it) connects Livorno with Pisa, Lucca, Viareggio and Florence. Livorno is also a port, with services to Sardinia, Corsica, Capraia and Sicily.

By car

Driving is the easiest option. Livorno is just off the coastal SS1, a 20-minute drive south of Pisa along the same road. The A12 also runs past the city. The Poggibonsi exit of the Si–Fi (Siena–Florence) *autostrada* quickly gives access to Volterra.

By train

Livorno's main station (on piazza Dante) is on the Rome–Pisa train line, a 12-minute journey from Pisa. Trains also run to and from Florence (journey time 1hr 20mins) via Pisa and Empoli. National timetable information is available by calling 892021 or by logging on to www.trenitalia.it.

TUSCANY

Siena

Architectural beauty, lively nightlife and a no-holds-barred horse race.

The Sienese are fond of saying that theirs is the most perfect medieval city in the world, and it's easy to agree. Not only has Siena preserved its exquisite monuments, it has also maintained its traditions and its passion for local cuisine. Head for the centre and soak up the atmosphere of **piazza del Campo** (or just 'Il Campo'); it fans out in nine segments of herringbone paving, focusing on the grand council chambers of **Palazzo Pubblico** and the magnificent **Torre del Mangia** (for all, *see right*). Siena emerged from the Dark Ages as a robust centre of pilgrimage and trade, only for a series of events – including savage attacks of plague – to halt its development forever. What you see today is, virtually, Siena as it always has been. The historic centre of the city is divided into three sections. **Terzo di Città** was the original residential nucleus and includes the Duomo; **Terzo di San Martino** grew around the via Francigena, the pilgrim route heading south to Rome; and the **Terzo di Camollia** contains churches and basilicas to the north.

These three sections house the 17 *contrade* – city districts that largely define the citizens' perception of their own identity. During the summer, any citizen with a pulse commits their spirit to their *contrada* with a fervour unequalled anywhere else in Italy for the **Palio** (*see p250* **Horsing Around**), the world-famous horse race held in July and August, when district rivalry reaches its zenith.

While the crowded tourist corridor between the piazza and the **Duomo** has lots to offer, ambling through the quiet back alleys is the best recommendation for the idle traveller.

SOME HISTORY

The Sienese hills were inhabited in prehistoric times, and were later settled by the Etruscans, who created an important trading colony with Volterra. In 90 BC, the city became a Roman colony named Saena Julia, ruled by Emperor Augustus. However, development was slow.

What eventually put Siena on the map was the **via Francigena** (*see p262* **A Pilgrim's Progress**), the pilgrim route leading south from France and spanning the whole of Tuscany. The road was heavily trafficked throughout the Middle Ages, bringing in its wake the trade that provided Siena with commercial and political clout.

The young city had amassed enough self-confidence by 1125 to pick fights with Florence. The hatred between Tuscany's sister cities over the following century was one of history's more

malevolent rivalries. Things came to an explosive head on 4 September 1260, when Siena won the bloody Battle of Montaperti. A 15,000-strong Sienese army killed 10,000 Florentine soldiers and captured 15,000 more. The jubilant Sienese danced on the bodies of the fallen Florentines with nails in their shoes. But nine years later the two cities clashed and this time Florence came out on top. This defeat marked a profound shift in Siena's social and political identity that paradoxically forged the way for its prosperous golden age.

The Sienese then channelled their creative juices into commerce. Gradually, successful merchants and bankers gave rise to a wealthy middle class, while trade with France and England brought in cash and nourished a flourishing wool industry. The city's most important public works – much of the Duomo, the Palazzo Pubblico, the Torre del Mangia and piazza del Campo, among others – were constructed under the Council of Nine, set up in 1287 in friendship with Florence.

Siena's golden age came to an abrupt halt in 1348 with the arrival of the Black Death, which slashed the population from 100,000 to 30,000 in less than a year. Internal fighting brought down the Council of Nine in 1355; in 1399 Siena fell under the control of Gian Galeazzo Visconti, Grand Duke of Milan, who was followed by the tyrannical Pandolfo Petrucci. Spain's Charles V besieged the city in 1552, but three years later a popular insurrection against the Spanish left Siena open to Cosimo I de' Medici. Reduced to 8,000 inhabitants, the city couldn't defend itself. The end of the Sienese Republic came in 1559.

In 1859, Siena became the first major Tuscan city to join a united Italy. It soon launched a lucrative tourist trade that endures to this day.

SIGHTSEEING

★ Palazzo Pubblico
Piazza del Campo. **Map** p248 C3.
Work on this elegant example of Gothic architecture began in 1288, but the brick and stone building, which houses the town hall and the Museo Civico, wasn't completed until 1342. The *palazzo* is a symbol of medieval Siena's mercantile wealth; with its she-wolf and Medici balls, its striking façade reads like a history book of the city. Inside the *cortile* you'll find the excellent Museo Civico (*see p252*).

★ Piazza del Campo
Map p248 C3.
See p255 **Piazza del Campo**.

Piazza Salimbeni
Map p248 B2.
A beautiful square flanked by three of Siena's most glorious *palazzi*: Tantucci, Spannocchi and Salimbeni. The latter serves as the headquarters of the Monte dei Paschi di Siena, founded in 1472 by resolution of the General Council of the Sienese Republic; today with 1,900 branches, half the bank's profits are ploughed back into the community.

FREE Santuario e Casa di Santa Caterina
Costa Sant'Antonio 6 (0577 288175). **Open** 9am-12.30pm, 3-6pm daily. **Admission** free. **Map** p248 B2.
This small collection of buildings is highly revered as the house of St Catherine, Siena's patron saint.

★ Torre del Mangia
Piazza del Campo (0577 226230). **Open** *Mid Mar-Oct* 10am-7pm daily. *Nov-mid Mar* 10am-4pm daily. **Admission** €7 (from Museo Civico ticket office). **No credit cards**. **Map** p248 C3.

Torre del Mangia.

TUSCANY

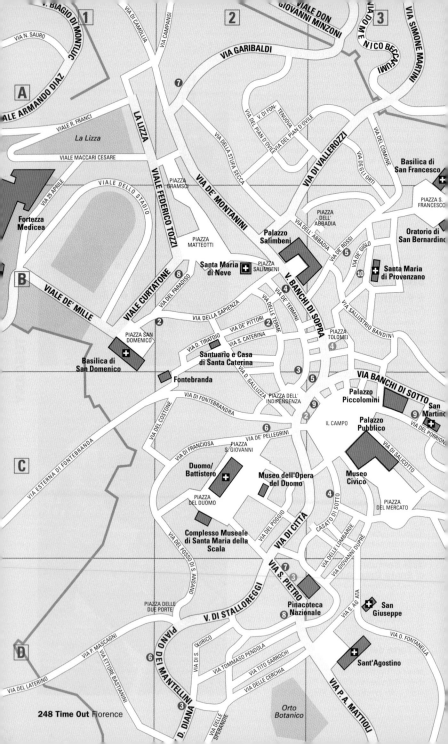

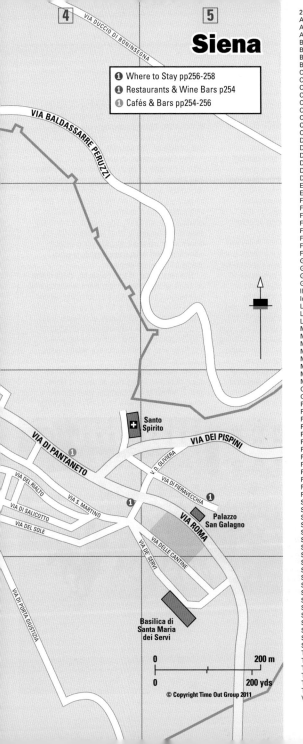

Siena

① Where to Stay pp256-258
① Restaurants & Wine Bars p254
① Cafés & Bars pp254-256

Horsing Around

The Palio is the only race in town.

Siena's Palio is the explosive culmination of centuries-long neighbourhood rivalries, and the event that defines the social, cultural and political fabric of the city each year.

There's a single objective: to win at all costs. Cheating, biting and dosing opponents' horses with laxatives have all been tried. No one seems to care very much when the hired bareback jockeys – often dismissed as mere mercenaries – fall off their horses. The horse, on the other hand, is adored, receiving special rites and banquets.

The *contrade* that contest the Palio are districts of Siena that trace their roots back to the 12th century and vaguely represent the military groups that once protected it. At the head of each was a mayor and a central governor (*podestà*), flanked by councillors. Originally, the city was divided into 42 *contrade*, but the numbers shrank to the current 17 in 1729, and of these ten are selected to participate, always including the seven who missed out last time round.

The Palio takes place in the piazza del Campo twice a year, commemorating the feast of the Virgin Mary on 2 July and the Assumption on 16 August. On the perimeter, there are balconies and stands for spectators (usually wealthy tourists) willing to shell out €300 to watch the race in comfort. Most Sienese – up to 30,000 of them – stand under the blazing sun in the centre of the square.

The Palio starts in the late afternoon with a parade of costumed drummers and flag carriers. The horses charge three times round the square; the first one over the line wins the Palio and earns a banner of the Virgin Mary as a trophy – not to mention adulation from fans. The event is normally over in a startlingly brief 90 seconds, as riders spur on their steeds (and attack enemy riders) with their *nerbo*, a whip made of dried ox penis.

The reactions of the Sienese, depending on their allegiance, range from weeping and hair-tearing to rapturous embracing; second place is considered a far worse way to lose than last place. Banquets and festivities sponsored by the winning *contrade* last into September, and animosity between the first- and second-placed teams lasts until the following year.

The actual event is preceded by three days of trials, every day at around 9am and 7.30pm in the Campo, plus dress rehearsals, banquets and horse blessing.

TUSCANY

Asked to build their tower as high as possible, architect brothers Minuccio and Francesco di Rinaldo followed their instructions to the letter: when it was completed in 1348, the Torre del Mangia, next to Palazzo Pubblico, was medieval Italy's tallest tower, checking in at 102m (335ft), with 503 steps, and affording views over Siena Province. It's named after one of its first bell-ringers: the pot-bellied *mangiaguadagni* ('eat-profits'). These days, only 15 visitors are allowed up at any one time, and tickets sell out quickly. At the foot of the tower is the Gothic Cappella di Piazza, finished in 1352 to commemorate the end of the plague.

Churches

Basilica di San Domenico
Piazza San Domenico (0577 286848, www. basilicacateriniana.com). **Open** *Mar-Oct* 7am-6.30pm daily. *Nov-Feb* 9am-6pm daily.
Admission free. **Map** p248 B1.
This soaring brick edifice was one of the earliest Dominican monasteries in Tuscany. Started in 1226, the building that remains today is mostly the result of an extensive mid 20th-century restoration. That said, a few historic features have survived intact. At the end of the nave is a *Madonna Enthroned* attributed to Pietro Lorenzetti, while halfway down on the right is the restored chapel of Siena's patron saint, St Catherine. The chapel itself is beautiful, with tromp l'œil pilasters, marble floors and works by Sodoma who also created the tabernacle. Inside it, in a container, is the relic of the saint's head.

FREE Basilica di San Francesco
Piazza San Francesco (0577 289081). **Open** 7am-1.30pm, 3.30-7pm daily. **Admission** free.
Map p248 A3.
The Franciscans built this grand, severe church of Gothic origins in 1326. Precious little of its original artwork survived a fire in 1655. However, one work that did is Pietro Lorenzetti's *Crucifixion* (1331), in the first chapel of the transept.

Battistero
Piazza San Giovanni (0577 286300, www.opera duomo.siena.it). **Open** *Mar-mid June, mid Sept-Oct* 9.30am-7.30pm daily. *Mid June-mid Sept* 9.30am-8pm daily. *Nov-Feb* 10am-5pm daily.
Admission €3. **No credit cards. Map** p248 C2.
Squeezed under the apse of the Duomo (*see right*), the Baptistery is, unusually, rectangular, rather than octagonal. The unfinished Gothic façade includes three arches adorned with human and animal busts, while inside, colourful frescoes by various artists (mainly Vecchietta) fill the room. The focal point is the central font (1417-34): designed by Jacopo della Quercia and considered one of the masterpieces of early Renaissance Tuscany, it features gilded bronze bas-reliefs by Jacopo, Donatello and Lorenzo Ghiberti. In the same complex is the restored Crypt.

Piazza del Campo.

★ Duomo
Piazza del Duomo (0577 283048, www.opera duomo.siena.it). **Open** *Mar-mid June, mid Sept-Oct* 10.30am-7.30pm Mon-Sat; 1.30-6pm Sun. *Mid June-mid Sept* 10.30am-8pm Mon-Sat; 1.30-6pm Sun. *Nov-Feb* 10.30am-6.30pm Mon-Sat; 1.30-5.30pm Sun. **Admission** €3. An all-inclusive (Duomo, Baptistery and Crypt) ticket is also available for €10. **No credit cards. Map** p248 C2.
Construction on Siena's Duomo, one of Italy's first Gothic cathedrals, started in 1150 on the site of an earlier church, but plans for a massive cathedral had to be abandoned because of the Black Death of 1348. The resulting structure is Gothic in style but Romanesque in spirit. The black and white marble façade was started in 1226; 30 years later work began on the dome, one of the oldest in Italy. The lower portion of the façade and the statues in the centre of the three arches were designed by Giovanni Pisano and built between 1284 and 1296.

Inside, the cathedral's polychrome floors are its most immediate attraction; though the intricately decorated inlaid boxes are usually covered by protective planks, they are generally visible between mid August and the end of September (a ticket then costs €6). The most impressive are those beneath the dome, by Domenico Beccafumi, who created 35 of the 56 scenes from 1517 to 1547. In the apse is a splendid carved wooden choir, built between the 14th and 16th centuries. Above it, back in place after

TUSCANY

Siena market. See p256.

a restoration-enforced absence, is a stained-glass rose window (7m/23ft across) made by Duccio di Buoninsegna in 1288 – probably the earliest Italian example of a stained-glass window. The tabernacle has Bernini's *Maddalena* and *San Girolamo* statues.

Another highlight is the pulpit, completed in 1266 by Nicola Pisano with the help of his son Giovanni and Arnolfo di Cambio. The Piccolomini altar includes four statues by a young Michelangelo (carved 1501-04). At the far end of the left aisle, a door leads to the Libreria Piccolomini (admission €3), built in 1495 to house the library of Sienese nobleman Aeneas Silvius Piccolomini, who became Pope Pius II. This vaulted chamber was constructed at the behest of his nephew (who became Pope Pius III for 28 days) and frescoed by Pinturicchio (1502-09, his last work), reportedly assisted by a young Raphael, with scenes from Pius II's life.

Oratorio di San Bernardino & Museo Diocesano d'Arte Sacra

Piazza San Francesco 10 (0577 283048, www. operaduomo.siena.it). **Open** *Mid Mar-Oct* 10.30am-1.30pm, 3-5.30pm daily. Closed Nov-mid Mar. **Admission** €3. **No credit cards.** **Map** p248 B3.

To the right of San Francesco lies this oratory, built in the 15th century on the site where St Bernard used to pray. On the first floor is a magnificent fresco cycle (1496-1518) by Beccafumi, Sodoma and their lesser contemporary, Girolamo del Pacchia.

Museums

★ Complesso Museale di Santa Maria della Scala

Piazza del Duomo 2 (0577 534511, www.santa mariadellascala.com). **Open** *Mid Oct-mid Mar* 10.30am-4.30pm daily. *Mid Mar-mid Oct* 10.30am-6.30pm daily. **Admission** €6. **No credit cards.** **Map** p248 C2.

This is the site of Siena's brilliant Museo Archeologico, which also holds various spectacular temporary exhibitions (on the upper floors, entered from the left-hand doorway). Founded in the ninth century, it was one of the earliest hospitals in Europe and one of the first to ensure disinfected medical equipment, and was still taking in patients until relatively recently: the author Italo Calvino died here in 1985. Entry to the museum is at the Pellegrinaio (Pilgrim's Hall), decorated by, among others, Domenico di Bartolo (1440-43), with elaborate frescoes depicting the history of the hospital. Underground you'll find passageways carved out of the tufa, now home to the archaeological museum in a brilliant labyrinth of corridors and chambers. Highly recommended for children.

★ Museo Civico

Palazzo Pubblico, piazza del Campo (0577 226230 council cultural office, 0577 292263 ticket office, www.comune.siena.it). **Open** *Mid Mar-Oct* 10am-7pm daily. *Nov-mid Mar*

10am-6pm daily. **Admission** €7.50. **No credit cards. Map** p248 C3.

In the Anticappella of the Museo Civico you can admire a number of frescoes by Taddeo di Bartolo (1362-1422), which reflect his fascination with Greek and Roman antiquity and mythological heroes, plus a *Madonna and Child with Saints* by Sodoma at the altar of the Cappella del Consiglio. The Sala del Mappamondo was decorated by Ambrogio Lorenzetti around 1320-30; its barely visible cosmological frescoes depicting the universe and celestial spheres. This room also houses one of Siena's most cherished jewels: the *Maestà* fresco painted by Simone Martini in 1315. Thought to be one of his earliest works, if not his very first, it's also considered one of the first examples of political art, with the devotion to the Virgin Mary depicted said to represent devotion to the Republic's princes. Finally, in the Sala della Pace, is an extraordinary fresco cycle by Lorenzetti (1338-40), the *Allegory of Good* and *Effects of Bad Government* (severely damaged). This is the largest secular fresco since Roman times and was commissioned to remind the Council of Nine of their responsibilities. The fresco's details of daily life are of exceptional interest.

Museo dell'Opera del Duomo

Piazza del Duomo 8 (0577 283048, www.opera duomo.siena.it). **Open** *Mar-mid June, mid Sept-Oct* 9.30am-7.30pm daily. *Mid June-mid Sept* 9.30am-8pm daily. *Nov-Feb* 10am-5pm daily. **Admission** €6. **No credit cards. Map** p248 C2.

Occupying the never-completed nave of the Duomo, this museum displays works taken from the cathedral. On the ground floor is a large hall divided in two by a stunning 15th-century wrought-iron gate; along the walls, you can enjoy a better view of Giovanni Pisano's 12 magnificent marble statues (1285-97) that once adorned the façade of the Duomo. In the centre of the room is the bas-relief of the *Madonna and Child with St Anthony* by Jacopo della Quercia, commissioned in 1437 and probably not quite completed when the artist died the following year. On the first floor is the *Pala della Maestà* (1308-11) by Duccio di Buoninsegna, used as the high altar of the Duomo until 1506. The front has a *Madonna with Saints*; the back depicts 26 religious scenes in dazzling colours.

★ Pinacoteca Nazionale

Palazzo Buonsignori, via San Pietro 29 (0577 286143). **Open** 9am-1pm Mon, Sun; 8.15am-7.15pm Tue-Sat. **Admission** €4. **No credit cards. Map** p248 D2.

One of Italy's foremost art collections, this lovely 15th-century *palazzo* holds more than 1,500 works of art, and is particularly renowned for its Sienese *fondi d'oro* (paintings with gilded backgrounds). The second floor is devoted to Sienese masters from the 12th to the 15th centuries, including Guido da Siena and the Lorenzettis (don't miss *A City by the Sea*). The first

floor houses works by the Sienese Mannerist school of the early 1500s, including pieces by Sodoma and Beccafumi, while the third floor holds the Spannocchi Collection, containing works by northern Italian and European artists of the 16th and 17th centuries.

Monuments, squares & gardens

Fortezza Medicea

Viale C Maccari. **Map** p248 B1.

This vast red-brick fortress just outside the city is a sore reminder of Siena's troubled past. Charles V of Spain forced the Sienese to build a fortress on this spot in 1552; as soon as his reign ended they celebrated by demolishing it, but when Cosimo I de' Medici annexed the city a few years later he demanded the fortress be rebuilt. These days, with its views over the city, it's a good place for an evening stroll or a glass of wine at the Enoteca Italiana (*see p256*), especially during the *settimana dei vini*, a week-long showcase of regional wines held here every year in early June.

FREE Orto Botanico

Via Mattioli 4 (0577 232874). **Open** 8am-12.30pm, 2.30-5.30pm Mon-Fri; 8am-noon Sat. **Admission** free. **Map** p248 D2.

The botanical gardens belong to the university and are a haven of tranquillity.

Palazzo Chigi Saracini/Accademia Musicale Chigiana

Via di Città 89 (0577 286300, www.chigiana.it). **Open** guided tours only; check website or call for schedule. **Admission** €7. **Map** p248 C2.

A must for classical music fans, this beautiful Renaissance *palazzo* has its own rococo-style concert hall, museum of instruments and library. It hosts a week of Sienese music in July, followed by a series of summer concerts until the end of August.

WHERE TO EAT & DRINK

Many recipes from the Siena region have survived since medieval times, including *pici* (thick, irregular spaghetti) and *panzanella* (dried bread soaked in water, served in a salad with basil, onion and tomato). Popular desserts include *panforte* (slabs of nuts, candied fruits and honey) and *ricciarelli* (almond biscuits).

On a summer's night, piazza del Campo turns into a great eating bowl. There are a dozen establishments from *birrerie* to *pizzerie*, most mediocre: best bets are **Al Mangia** (no.43, 0577 281121, www.almangia.it) and **L'Osteria del Bigelli** (no.60, 0577 42772, www.osteria bigelli.it), with an interesting menu. Wine bar **Liberamente Osteria** (no.27, 0577 274733, www.liberamenteosteria.it) has a short, tasty menu, and decor by artist Sandro Chia (www.sandrochia.com).

Restaurants & wine bars

Antica Trattoria Botteganova
Via Chiantigiana 29 (0577 284230). **Open** 12.30-2.30pm, 7.30-10.30pm daily. **Average** €40.
Although this *trattoria* is just out of town on the north side, it's worth the short taxi ride. The enjoyable food is complemented by a strong wine list.

Cane e Gatto
Via Pagliaresi 6 (0577 287545). **Open** 8-10.30pm daily. **Average** €45. **Map** p249 C4 ❶
The *menù degustazione* (€75) at this family-run restaurant can teach you everything you could ever wish to know about Sienese cooking. A decadent lunch is served for small groups by arrangement. Highly recommended.

Compagnia dei Vinattieri
Via delle Terme 79 (0577 236568, www.vinattieri. net). **Open** 11am-midnight daily. **Average** €30. **Map** p248 B2 ❷
Cinzia Certosini, who was previously a restaurateur in Chianti, established this excellent *enoteca* a few years ago, with an ambition to make wine more approachable. The admirable list includes a rich array of Tuscan labels, in addition to products from other regions and countries. A food menu is also served.

Enoteca I Terzi
Via de' Termini 7 (0577 44329, www.enoteca iterzi.it). **Open** 11am-1am Mon-Sat. **Average** €20. **Map** p248 C2 ❸
This wine cellar serves various light snacks, including cold cuts, cheeses and breads.

Hosteria Il Carroccio
Via del Casato di Sotto 32 (0577 41165). **Open** 12.30-2.30pm, 7.30-10pm Mon, Thur-Sun; noon-2.30pm Tue. **Average** €30. **Map** p248 C3 ❹
Run by Renata Toppi and her children, Hosteria Il Carroccio is a real find. Try the *tegamate di maiale* (pork cooked in a ceramic bowl), based on an old Sienese recipe that's virtually extinct today.

Medio Evo
Via de' Rossi 40 (0577 280315, www.medioevo siena.it). **Open** 12.30-2.30pm, 7.30-10pm Mon-Wed, Fri-Sun. **Average** €38. **Map** p248 B3 ❺
Typical Sienese cuisine served in a medieval dining hall decked out with *contrada* flags.

Da Mugolone
Via de' Pellegrini 8-12 (0577 283235). **Open** 12.30-3pm, 7.30-10pm Mon-Wed, Sat; 12.30-10pm Fri; 7.30-10pm Sun. Closed 3wks Jan. **Average** €40. **Map** p248 D2 ❻
Many residents consider this one of Siena's best eateries. It's simple yet elegant, and serves largely meat-based dishes using local ingredients, cooked and presented to unfussy perfection.

Osteria Boccon del Prete
Via San Pietro 17 (0577 280388, www.osteria boccondelprete.it). **Open** 12.30-3pm, 7.15-10pm Mon-Sat. **Average** €30. **Map** p248 D2 ❼
A lovely vaulted ceiling in this basement space makes up for the lack of natural light, and the warm red tones of the lighting and brickwork create an intimate and cosy space. A short menu ought to make selection easy but doesn't, given the adventurous nature of its contents; *cinghiale* (wild boar) with pasta, *pici pasta* with *cavolo nero* and breadcrumbs, polenta *crostini* with Tuscan sausage, salt fish crêpes and *gnocci* with sea bass, lemon and basil are just some of the selections.

Osteria Castelvecchio
Via Castelvecchio 65 (0577 49586). **Open** 12.30-2.30pm, 7.30-10pm daily. Closed Tue in winter. **Average** €30; €25 tasting menu. **Map** p248 D2 ❽
Just a few steps from the Pinacoteca Nazionale (*see p253*), in former horse stables, Castelvecchio offers vegetarian dishes at least twice a week from an inventive menu based on seasonal fare.

Osteria Le Logge
Via del Porrione 33 (0577 48013, www.osteria lelogge.it). **Open** noon-2.45pm, 7.15-10.30pm Mon-Sat. **Average** €40. **Map** p248 C3 ❾
A popular, well-established and central *osteria*, with great food and a charming setting.

★ Tre Cristi
Via Provenzano 1/7 (0577 280608, www.trecristi .com). **Open** 12.30-3pm, 7.30-2am Mon-Sat. **Average** €50. **Map** p248 B3 ❿
Three warm, wood-panelled spaces (plus a pretty and intimate private dining room) make up this 19th-century fish restaurant, located in a 15th-century *palazzo* in the *contrada* of the Giraffe. The decor is decidely fin de siècle European, with sepia photos on the walls and beautiful tiles on the floors, making it feel really special. The food too is resolutely old-school Tuscan specialities, done exceptionally well; meat is kept to a minimum but the fish selection is excellent, and beautifully presented. The service is professional and friendly, the wine list extensive.

Cafés & bars

Caffè Ortensia
Via Pantaneto 95 (0577 40039). **Open** 8am-1am Mon-Fri; 5pm-1am Sat. **No credit cards.** **Map** p249 C4 ❶
A bohemian student bar with a well-stocked bookcase, plus newspapers, magazines and games.

Fiorella
Via di Città 13 (0577 271255, www.torrefazione fiorella.it). **Open** 7am-7.30pm Mon-Sat. **No credit cards.** **Map** p248 C2 ❷

Piazza del Campo

Is this the loveliest square in Italy?

Piazza del Campo is rightly described as one of Italy's most beautiful squares. Beautiful it is, but square it isn't: the piazza is uniquely shell-shaped, and split into nine sections – said to represent both the ruling Council of Nine and the folds of the Madonna's cloak protecting the townsfolk. Eleven small streets lead down to the centre of the Campo, where the Sienese have for centuries congregated to gossip, catch up on the news, and hear the orations of St Bernardine, called by the bell 'la Martinella' placed on the top of the town hall. That air of passing the time with talk, thought and contemplation is still palpable, particularly at night, when lovers and friends come to sit and chat quietly, the shape of the piazza helping to soften the acoustics – though they do little to dampen the deafening roar of the town's 17 *contrade* as they cheer on their horse in the twice-yearly Palio (*see p250* **Horsing Around**).

Piazza del Campo first appears in documents in 1193, as the Campus Fori, although the existing piazza dates from 1293. The warm brickwork of the nine sections, separated by contrasting strips of white stone, ensures a timeless elegance to the square, which was finished in 1349, but so too do the buildings and structures that line it, beginning on the north-east side of the piazza where Jacopo della Quercia's Fonte Gaia (built 1408-19) serves as a terminus for the city's network of underground wells and aqueducts (a total of 25km/16 miles throughout the province). The existing basin in the fountain is a 19th-century copy, with Quercia's original safely housed in the archaeological museum (*see p252*). Opposite it lies the 13th-century town hall, built between 1297 and 1310 over the Customs house and Bolgano mint. Next to it, a 102-metre (335-ft) tower was added later as a symbol of the town's wealth and splendour, with crenellations designed by Lippo Memmi and a bell, called 'Sunto', that is reached via an internal staircase. At the base of the tower, a little chapel was built in 1352 and dedicated to the Virgin Mary after the plague of 1348, when two thirds of the Sienese population died. The upper part of the tower was added and adorned in the Renaissance – between

1461 and 1468 – by Antonio Federighi. To the right of the town hall lie the municipality of Siena offices, to the left the Civic Museum (*see p252*).

By law, all the other buildings around the square had to be built in the same Gothic style, and all once belonged to noble Sienese families. Standing in the square, with the fountain in front of you and the town hall behind you, the most important ones since the 18th century are: to the right, in the direction of via Rinaldini; the Palazzo Chigi Zondadari; and, next to it on its left side, the brick-red Palazzo Sansedoni, which today belongs to the oldest bank in the world – the Bank Monte dei Paschi di Siena Foundation was founded in 1472. From here, the fourth building on is the Casino dei Nobili (the old merchants' palace), and four along again brings you to Palazzo d'Elci, topped with beautiful crenellations.

Liv Inger Pompei is an authorised historical tour guide (www.norskturist guideisiena.com), covering Siena and the Province of Siena.

TUSCANY

This *caffè-bar* serves up fabulous coffee, roasted on the spot. Standing only.

Il Murello di San Pietro

Via San Pietro 48 (0577 1115883). **Open** 11am-9.30pm Mon-Sat. **Map** p248 D2 ❸
This cosy and friendly wine bar has a young clientele who like to take their glasses of wine and sit on the walls of the Pinacoteca Nazionale opposite. Inside, the warm and traditional space is a good bet for cooler evenings.

Nannini Conca D'Oro

Via Banchi di Sopra 24 (0577 236009, www.grupponannini.it). **Open** 7am-10pm daily. **Map** p248 B3 ❹
Sleek and modern, with something of a chain vibe, Nannini specialises in *panforte* and *ricciarelli*. You can sit at the back if you order a light lunch. **Other locations** via Massetana Romana 42-44.

SHOPS & SERVICES

The main shopping street in Siena is **via di Città**, which forks above the Campo: **banchi di Sotto** heads down and **banchi di Sopra** climbs up to **piazza della Posta**. Strolling along via del Terme you'll find a number of modern interiors shops. Siena's fantastic, buzzy general **market** (8am-1pm Wednesday) stretches from piazza la Lizza to the Fortezza. The third Sunday of the month also sees an antiques market at **piazza del Mercato**, behind the Campo.

9 Farmacie

Various locations around the historic centre.
Still in their original 19th-century premises, these pharmacies preserve their wonderful original architecture but prescribe modern medication.

Antica Drogheria Manganelli

Via di Città 71-73 (0577 280002). **Open** 9am-7.45pm Mon-Sat. Closed 4wks Jan-Feb. **Map** p248 C2.
Trading since 1879, this shop's antique wooden shelves and glass cabinets display a scrumptious array of traditional sweets, condiments and herbs, as well as delicious slices of *panforte* and *ricciarelli*.

Book Shop

Piano dei Mantellini 34 (0577 281757).
Open 10am-8pm Mon-Sat. **Map** p248 D2.
American-born owner Lisa Fallon runs this pleasant and relaxed English-language bookstore.

Dolci Trame

Via del Moro 4 (0577 46168, www.dolcitrameshop.com). **Open** 3.30-7.30pm Mon; 10am-1pm, 3.30-7.30pm Tue-Sat. **Map** p248 B3.
Hip women's clothing at the back of piazza Tolomei.

Enoteca Italiana

Fortezza Medicea, piazza Libertà 1 (0577 228811, www.enoteca-italiana.it).
Open noon-1am Mon-Sat.
Italy's only national wine cellar, located in the massive vaults of the fortress, stocks more than 1,000 wines from all over the country.

La Fattoria Toscana

Via di Città 51 (0577 42255). **Open** 9.30am-8pm daily. **Map** p248 D2.
La Fattoria Toscana offers an excellent selection of gastronomic goodies, including wines, oils, sweetmeats, local truffles and Val d'Orcia saffron.

Fioretta Bacci

Via San Pietro 7 (0577 282200, www.fiorettabacci.it). **Open** 10.30am-7pm Mon-Sat. **Map** p248 D2.
Beautiful hand-loomed shawls and garments, with a giant loom in the shop.

Panificio il Magnifico

Via de' Pellegrini 27 (0577 281106, www.ilmagnifico.siena.it). **Open** 7.30am-7.30pm Mon-Sat. **Map** p248 C2.
A busy bread shop and *salumeria* where you take a number and await your turn. Panini and the like are sold, as well as marvellous *panforte*, well priced and packaged in sealed foil bags.

WHERE TO STAY

Siena doesn't have enough hotels to meet the demand, so booking in advance is advisable. It's worth contacting the **Hotels Promotion Service** (0577 288084, www.hotelsiena.com).
The huge Castello di Casole estate that lies 35 kilometres (22 miles) from Siena was being restored and converted into a boutique hotel as this guide went to press; **Hotel Castello di Casole** (www.castellodicasole.com), due to open in spring 2012, will feature 41 luxury suites and a world-class spa.

Antica Torre

Via di Fieravecchia 7 (0577 222255, www.anticatorresiena.eu). **Rates** €95-€120. **Rooms** 8. **Map** p249 C5 ❶
Set in a nicely restored 16th-century tower, this eclectic and friendly hotel gets booked up well in advance: not surprising, as there are just two rooms on each floor. Those on the top two levels of the building boast views over the surrounding countryside.

Campo Regio Relais

Via della Sapienza 25 (0577 222073, www.camporegio.com). **Rates** €150-€450 (up to €600 during the Palio). **Rooms** 6. **Map** p248 B2 ❷
Just down the hill from San Domenico, this elegant little *palazzo* offers a surprising range of rooms and

a high level of comfort. Despite its tiny entrance, it has two pleasant terraces and splendid views of the valley behind. The 1500s building was the dwelling of various noble Sienese families.

Certosa di Maggiano
Strada di Certosa 82 (0577 288180, www. certosadimaggiano.com). **Rates** €370-€1,270. **Rooms** 18.
Raised from the ruins of a 13th-century monastery, Certosa di Maggiano is located just south of the city and is renowned for its stunning garden and extensive amenities, including tennis courts, swimming pools and even a heliport.

Il Chiostro del Carmine
Via della Diana 4 (0577 223885, www.chiostro delcarmine.com). **Rates** €99-€600. **Rooms** 13. **Map** p248 D2 ❸
This beautifully refurbished religious building offers business-class accommodation. All rooms have internet LAN and wireless connections, while meeting rooms, conference facilities and breakfast rooms are in the highly decorated Friars Choir and the austere, vaulted Tinaia dei Frati.

Chiusarelli
Viale Curtatone 15 (0577 280562, www. chiusarelli.com). **Rates** (incl breakfast) €97-€145. **Rooms** 48.

This three-star hotel sits on the edge of the historic centre. Rooms are unfussy but comfortable – ask for a quiet one at the back.

Grand Hotel Continental
Via Banchi di Sopra 85 (0577 56011, www. royaldemeure.com). **Rates** €540-€2,200. **Rooms** 51. **Map** p248 B2 ❹
The area's only five-star hotel is set amid the richly frescoed interiors of what was once Palazzo Gori Pannilini. If you can't afford to stay, pop in to admire the magnificently ornate first-floor reception.

Hotel Garden
Via Custoza 2 (0577 567111, www.garden hotel.it). **Rates** €109-€289. **Rooms** 122.
Set just on the northern outskirts of Siena near the Campo Sportivo, the Hotel Garden is a great choice for families, given a sizeable pool and tennis courts, large number of family rooms, and friendly, helpful staff. A lovely summer bar and terrace overlooks the city.

Palazzo Fani Mignanelli – Residenza d'Epoca
Via Banchi di Sopra 15 (0577 283566, www. residenzadepoca.it). **Map** p248 C3 ❺
A few minutes' walk from the piazza del Campo, this historic house offers charming rooms on the third

Grand Hotel Continental.

TUSCANY

floor of an old *palazzo* (with lift). The individually decorated rooms are priced according to size.

Pensione Palazzo Ravizza
Pian dei Mantellini 34 (0577 280462, www. palazzoravizza.it). **Rates** (incl breakfast) €150-€270. **Rooms** 38. **Map** p248 D1 ⑥
Owned by the same family for more than 200 years, this 17th-century *palazzo* still has its original furnishings, including lovely frescoes. Many of the 38 rooms overlook a charming, well-kept garden.

Piccolo Hotel Il Palio
Piazza del Sale 18 (0577 281131, www.piccolo hotelilpalio.it). **Rates** €65-€139. **Rooms** 26. **Map** p248 A2 ⑦
This pleasant, small hotel is housed in a former convent dating back to the 15th century. The location is convenient if you're arriving by train, and it's (unusually) accessible by car. Rooms are basic but clean.

Villa Scacciapensieri
Via di Scacciapensieri 10 (0577 41441, www.villa scacciapensieri.it). **Rates** €110-€330. **Rooms** 31.
As the name ('banish your thoughts') suggests, you can leave your worries behind as you check into this family-run hotel. It's 3km (two miles) north of the city: follow the signs up a private tree-lined drive to the crest of the hill. There's an excellent restaurant, a tennis court and a pool.

Apartments

Residence Paradiso
Via del Paradiso 16 (338 4327584 mobile, www.residenceparadiso.siena.it). **Rates** €70-€100. **Rooms** 6. **Map** p248 B2 ⑧
Accommodation in 12 furnished mini-apartments in a historic building, with the use of cooking and laundry facilities. Reductions are offered for longer stays and in winter. There are ten more apartments in via del Porrione.

Siena Soggiorno
Via di Città 15 (368 7424871 mobile, www.siena soggiorno.it). **Rates** €100-€130. **Map** p248 C3 ⑨
Three mini-apartments with kitchen and period furniture. Two apartments overlook the Campo. There's a three-night minimum stay.

RESOURCES

Hospital
Viale Bracci, north of the city (0577 586111).

Internet
Net Runner *via Pantaneto 4 (0577 44946).* **Map** p249 C4.

Police
Via del Castoro 6 (0577 201111). **Map** p248 C2.

Post office
Piazza Matteotti 37 (0577 214295). **Map** p248 B2.

Tourist information
Centro Servizi Informazioni Turistiche Siena (APT) *Piazza del Campo 56 (0577 280551, www.terresiena.it).* **Open** 9am-7pm daily. **Map** p248 C3.

GETTING THERE & AROUND
By bike & moped
For bike hire, contact **DF Bike** (via Massetana Romana 54, 0577 271905). Mopeds are rented at **Automotocicli Perozzi** (via del Romitorio 5, 0577 223157).

By bus
Siena's major bus terminal is at the edge of the historic centre at piazza Gramsci; the main ticket office (0577 204225) is underground. Most buses leave from the adjacent viale Federico Tozzi or nearby piazza San Domenico. **Tra-in**, the principal bus company serving Siena and beyond (0577 204225, www.trainspa.it), has departures every 30mins for Florence (direct service takes 75mins), as well as services to Arezzo, Grosseto and most regional towns of interest. The excellent www.comune.siena.it/train gives full timetable information on all services.

By car
The *raccordo* dual carriageway links Florence and Siena (45mins), or there's the more rural SS2. The centre of Siena is mainly traffic-free, so you'll have to park in one of nine big car parks around the city (several at the Stadio Comunale, one near the Fortezza Medicea, and the large underground Parcheggio Il Campo on via Fontanella 11); all can be busy for weekends and public holidays. To hire a car, try **Avis** (via Simone Martini 36, 0577 270305) or **Hertz** (viale Sardegna 37, 0577 45085).

By taxi
Call **Radio Taxi** (0577 49222), or go to one of the taxi ranks at piazza Stazione (0577 44504) or piazza Matteotti (0577 289350).

By train
There are some direct trains to and from Florence, but you'll normally have to change at Empoli (journey time up to 2hrs); you always have to change there for trains to Pisa. Siena's train station is at the bottom of the hill on the east side of the city (piazza Fratelli Rosselli, tickets 0577 280115, national timetable information 892021, www.trenitalia.it). A local bus makes the journey up to piazza Gramsci.

Siena Province

Breathtaking landscapes, ancient villages, food and wine in abundance.

It's no wonder that when people imagine rural Italy they conjure up thoughts of rolling hills defined by cypresses, tiny hamlets unchanged for centuries, eating alfresco or under vaulted ceilings, tables groaning with simple foods from the land and gentle, welcoming people. The province of Siena delivers the clichés with such charm and good humour that it's impossible not to feel the gentle bliss wash over you.

It's here that the 12th-century pilgrim route from France to Rome, the via Francigena, created a boom of medieval stone churches and villages, until plagues decimated the population; gradually, after a struggle, the place came under Florentine dominion.

Now promoted as the **Terre di Siena** (www.terresiena.it), the province boasts some of the most popular tourist towns in Italy, which thrive on the hordes of travellers that visit each summer. Other, smaller towns, equally beautiful, retain their odd Italian hours, falling into sleepy oblivion for the three luncheon hours. The gourmet traveller will find the area dominated by its excellent wines: Chianti to the north-east, Vernaccia di San Gimignano, Brunello di Montalcino and Vino Nobile di Montepulciano, and a sophisticated culinary culture that will satisfy any palate. For tips on visiting wineries in the region, *see p261* **Fine Vines**.

TUSCANY

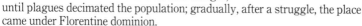

Chianti

If the words 'Chianti' and 'wine' are virtually synonymous, it's probably because good wine has been produced in the region for a very long time indeed. Renaissance, Roman, Etruscan – the story is a long one. The black cockerel logo of Chianti and the raffia-wrapped wine bottle both helped establish the wine long before the term 'wine buff' was invented.

The Chianti landscape is familiar through the art of the Renaissance – and doesn't appear to have changed much since then. Its gentle slopes are still clad with vines, olive groves abound and there's plenty of woodland, much of it inhabited by wild boar. The feeling of temporal petrification is hard to avoid.

But the region has changed, and the way people tend their land is quite unlike the methods of the past. Sunflower cultivation, for example, gives the farmland a short blast of yellow, or black when they've died off – colours that were absent from the landscape during the Renaissance. Yet changes such as these are subtle, and the area has become so desirable today there's hardly a barn that hasn't been renovated (*see p266* **Get a Farmer's Tan**).

CASTELLINA & AROUND

From Panzano, follow the SS222 to the hilltop town of **Castellina**. Originally an Etruscan settlement, its layout is essentially medieval: the imposing fortifications bear witness to the town's historic role as a bastion of Florentine dominion in its southward expansion towards Siena in the 15th and 16th centuries. The imposing **Torre** dominates the main square, piazza del Comune, and the medieval town around it. There are plenty of places to taste and buy wine; one of Chianti's top wineries, **Castello di Fonterutoli**, is nearby.

Gaiole, located on the steep eastern edge of Chianti, was a busy market town back in the Middle Ages, but it's quieter now and makes a pleasant stop on the way to the nearby castles and wineries (*see p261* **Fine Vines**). One of

Chianti.

the latter, **Badia a Coltibuono**, is an impressive spot for a meal or overnight stay.

On the western side of Gaiole, taking the SS484 will lead you to the famous **Castello di Brolio**, a 19th-century rendering of a castle wrecked by Spanish troops in 1478 and finished off by the Sienese 50 years later. Baron Bettino Ricasoli, the so-called 'Iron Baron' who was responsible for pushing Chianti's wine industry into the major league, rebuilt the castle in the 19th century. The **Ricasoli** winery below the castle remains one of the region's best, along with nearby **Felsina**. Driving south from Gaiole on the way to the next comune, Castelnuovo Berardenga, the tiny and charming San Gusmè is worth a visit.

Where to stay & eat

In Castellina, pleasant rooms are available at **Palazzo Squarcialupi** (via Ferruccio 22, 0577 741186, www.palazzosquarcialupi.com, closed Nov-mid Mar, €105-€160). For a verdant setting and a pool, head beyond **Fonterutoli** on the Siena road and stop at **Belvedere di San Leonino** (località San Leonino, 0577 740887, www.hotelsanleonino.com, closed mid Nov-Mar, €59-€189); it has its own restaurant, **Il Cortile**. **Ristorante Albergaccio** (via Fiorentina 63, 0577 741042, www.albergacciocast.com, closed Sun lunch & Wed, Thur lunch in winter & all Nov & 3wks Jan, average €50) offers two tasty fixed menus; **Antica Trattoria La Torre** (piazza del Comune 15, 0577 740236, www.antica trattorialatorre.com, closed Fri & last 2wks Feb, 1st 2wks Sept, average €35) is a classic eaterie.

In Radda, you can dine and stay at **Palazzo Leopoldo** (via Roma 33, 0577 735605, www.

palazzoleopoldo.it, €129-€376). Another dining option is the elegant **Ristorante Vignale** (via Pianigiani 9, 0577 738094, closed Dec-late Feb, average €48). Accommodation is at the beautifully restored **Relais Vignale** (via Pianigiani 8, 0577 738300, www.vignale.it, closed 2mths in winter, €230-€410). The rates at the *agriturismo* **Podere Terreno** (via della Volpaia, 0577 738312, www.podereterreno.it, €35 per person) include an excellent dinner with wine. Near Gaiole, the restaurant at **Badia a Coltibuono** (0577 749031, www.coltibuono. com, closed Mon, Nov-early Mar, average €42, tasting menu €51 incl 4 wines) specialises in game; in summer, eat at tables in the beautiful gardens; the old cloisters house some lovely guestrooms if you want to stay the night. South of Gaiole, in the hamlet of San Sano, just off SS408, the friendly **Hotel Residenza San Sano** (0577 746130, closed Nov-Mar, €130-€280) has a pool among old stone houses, and rustic boutique hotel **Relais Castellare de' Noveschi** (via Padre Chiantini 12, Gaiole in Chianti, 0577 746010, www.castellarede noveschi.com) has a good restaurant. In San Gusmè, **La Porta del Chianti** (piazza Castelli 10, 0577 358010, www.laportadel chianti.com) is a traditional Tuscan *trattoria* with great food.

Resources

Tourist information

Castellina *Ufficio Informazioni Turistiche, via Ferruccio 40 (0577 741392, www.chiantistorico. com).* **Open** 9.30am-1pm, 2-6.30pm daily.
Radda *piazza Castello 2 (0577 738494, www. chiantistorico.com).* **Open** 10am-1pm, 3-7pm Mon-Sat; 10am-1pm Sun.
Gaiole *via Ricasoli 18 (0577 749411, www.chianti storico.com).* **Open** 10am-1pm, 3-6pm daily. Closed Nov-Mar.

West of Siena

Take the Poggibonsi exit of the Si–Fi (Siena–Firenze) *autostrada* for this western section.

COLLE DI VAL D'ELSA

The historic centre of this attractive, lively town spans the hilltop (Colle Alta) and the lower-lying Colle Bassa. The two points are joined by a very modern lift. The River Elsa was channelled for power here as early as the 13th century, giving rise to flourishing industries: wool, paper and, more recently, crystalware. The **Museo del Cristallo** (via dei Fossi 8a, 0577 924135, www.cristallo.org, closed Mon, admission €3) is a beautiful underground

Fine Vines

Where to find the best of Chianti's most-famous wines.

CHIANTI CLASSICO

Castello di Fonterutoli *Fonterutoli, Castellina in Chianti (0577 73571, www. fonterutoli.it).* **Open** *9.30am-6.30pm Tue-Fri; 9.30am-12.30pm, 1.30-6.30pm Mon, Sat.* State-of-the-art cellars have been installed; you'll need to book in advance.

Felsina *SS Chiantigiana 484, nr Castelnuovo Berardenga (0577 355117, www.felsina.it).* **Open** *Mar-Oct 8.30am-6pm Mon-Fri. Nov-Feb 8.30am-12.30pm, 1.30-5.30pm Mon-Fri.* Some of Siena Province's best wines are produced here, including Fontalloro.

Further information *Consorzio Chianti Classico, via Scopeti 155, Sant'Andrea in Percussina, San Casciano (055 82285, www.chianticlassico.com).*

BRUNELLO DI MONTALCINO

Fattoria dei Barbi *Podere Novi village 170, Montalcino (0577 841111, www.fattoria deibarbi.it).* **Open** *10am-1pm, 2.30-6pm Mon-Fri; 2.30-6pm Sat, Sun.* Fine old cellars selling a variety of wines.

Fattoria del Casato *località Podere Casato 17 (0577 849421, www.cinellicolom bini.it).* **Open** *9am-1pm, 3-6pm Mon-Fri; by appointment on the weekends.* Donatella Cinelli Colombini's tour is fun and instructive, and the wines promising.

Further information *Consorzio del Vino Brunello di Montalcino, piazza Cavour 8, Montalcino (0577 848246, www.consorzio brunellodimontalcino.it).*

VINO NOBILE DI MONTEPULCIANO

Avignonesi *via Colonica 1, Valiano di Montepulciano (0578 724304, www. avignonesi.it).* **Open** *Nov-Apr 9am-6pm Mon-Fri. May-Oct 9am-6pm daily.* Approximately 23km (14 miles) outside Montepulciano, Avignonesi has tastings and tours on weekdays.

Poliziano *via Fontago 1, Montepulciano (0578 738171, www.carlettipoliziano.it).* **Open** *8.30am-12.30pm, 2.30-6pm Mon-Fri.* Closed Aug & 2wks Dec. Three different Vino Nobile are produced, two of which are single-vineyard crus.

Further information *Consorzio del Vino Nobile di Montepulciano piazza Grande 7, Montepulciano (0578 757812, www.vino nobiledimontepulciano.it).*

glass museum in the lower part of town. There are a number of crystal outlets in the upper town. The best is **La Grotta del Cristallo** (via del Muro Lungo 20, 0577 924676, www.lagrottadelcristallo.it). The **Museo Archeologico** (piazza del Duomo 42, 0577 922954, www.museisenesi.org, closed Mon, admission €3) is uncrowded and specialises in Etruscan and Roman remains from the area. Just down the road is the **Museo Civico e Diocesano d'Arte Sacra** (Palazzo dei Priori, via del Castello 31, 0577 923888, www.musei senesi.org, closed Mon, admission €3).

Where to stay & eat

In town, **Arnolfo B&B** (via F Campana 53, 0577 922020, www.arnolfobb.it, €75-€100) is handily placed. On a hillside, a stone's throw from the centre, is **Relais della Rovere** (via Piemonte 10, località La Badia, 0577 924696, www.relaisdellarovere.it, closed Nov-Easter, €128-€319), housed in a restored 11th-century abbey set in gardens with a pool.

Colle is a good place for food. **Da Arnolfo** (via XX Settembre 50, 0577 920549, www. arnolfo.com, closed Tue & Wed, average €110), carries two Michelin stars, well deserved for its superb ingredients, ingeniously combined. On the main square, **Il Frantoio** (via del Castello 40, 0577 923652, www.ristorante-ilfrantoio.com, closed Mon, average €40) serves classic Tuscan fare in historic surroundings. **Dietro le Quinte** (vicolo della Misericordia 14, 0577 920458, www.dietrolequinteristorante.it, average €40) is located on the town walls and has a lovely garden; it's hard to find, but worth the search. For an *aperitivo* (or, indeed, a handsome snack), head for the **14 in Canonica** wine bar (piazza Canonica 2, 0577 923444, closed Nov-Mar).

Resources

Tourist information

Ufficio Turistico Pro Loco *Colle di Val d'Elsa, via del Campana 43 (0577 922791).* **Open** 9.30am-1pm, 3-7pm Mon-Sat.

SAN GIMIGNANO

Of all the Tuscan towns, San Gimignano is the most easily recognisable, with its 14 towers defying the centuries, rising high above the terracotta roofs of this iconic village – whose historic centre has been a UNESCO World Heritage site since 1990. The silhouette of the town seems to draw you to it, as it may well have done to the pilgrims who passed this way from France on the via Francigena to Rome in the 12th century. They brought trade and prosperity and the families of San Gimignano flourished, commencing a peculiarly medieval practice of building ever-higher towers to assert their eminence; there were once as many as 72. But three waves of plague sent San Gimignano into an enchantment-like sleep. The best way to appreciate the heritage is to scale the 218 steps of **Torre Grossa** (54m/180ft; 9.30am-7pm Mar-Oct, 10am-5.30pm Nov-Feb), the 'big tower' of the **Palazzo Comunale**. The €5

TUSCANY

A Pilgrim's Progress

Walking in the footsteps of a British archbishop.

What is it with prime ministers holidaying in Tuscany? Obviously, it's a fabulous part of the world in which to spend any time at all, and world leaders may well be drawn to the region for its associations with power and wealth, but could its attractions also be spiritual? The Tuscan tourist board has heavily publicised a once little-known medieval pilgrimage trail, the via Francigena or via Romea, which stretches 1,600 kilometres (995 miles) from Canterbury to Rome and dates back to the eighth century.

The route became a popular pilgrim trail in 990, when Sigeric, then Archbishop of Canterbury, used it, noting in his diary all the places he passed. These 79 stages, crossing seven of Italy's regions, including Tuscany, became the basis of the pilgrims' route, and along it many *ospedale* (a sort of pilgrims' hotel) thrived. The actual route would take one of several alternatives, determined by a range of factors: not least finding a path across the Alps and Apennines – no mean feat when you're walking 20 kilometres (12.5 miles) a day with a conch (the symbol of your pilgrimage) balanced on your shoulder. Drop into the Santa Maria della Scala *ospedali* in Siena (*see p252*) for a visual record in the shape of frescoes painted by Domenico di Bartolo from 1440 to 1445.

Over the centuries the route was overtaken in popularity by that of the Way of St James Santiago de Compostela route in Spain, and largely forgotten, but in 1994 the Council of Europe designated it a cultural route, with a network of suggested trails, and it is becoming popular with tourists on foot, horseback or bikes. Maps are available from www.turismo.intotoscana.it/francigena, which also has links to guides for different parts of the trail.

In Siena Province, the main stages are:
San Gimignano The cathedral inaugurated in 1148 by Pope Eugenio III has 14th-century frescoes by Sienese painters and works by Ghirlandaio and Benedetto di Maiano.

Colle Val d'Elsa The native town of Arnolfo di Cambio, the 13th-century sculptor and architect behind Florence's Duomo. Also well known since 1331 for the production of glass.

Monteriggioni A military fortification with 14 towers, built by the Sienese in 1213-19 to control the territory and host pilgrims.

Monterroni d'Arbia The tenth-century Santa Cristina church has an *ospedale* attached to it. The magnificent Pieve di Corsano is nearby.

Buonconvento A walled fortification with towers. Considered one of the most beautiful *comuni* in Italy and the most important centre in the Val d'Arbia. The Civic Museum has paintings by such well-known Sienese painters as Pietro Lorenzetti. From here you can easily reach the abbey of Sant'Antimo.

San Quirico d'Orcia The Romanesque church dedicated to San Quirico and Giuditta dates back to the 12th and 13th centuries. The main portal is from 1080, while one of the side portals was sculpted by the school of Giovanni Pisano in the 13th century. A few kilometres away, Bagno Vignoni is famous for curative thermal springs.

Radicofani A fortress built by Pope Adriano IV from 1158 that became a stage on the route in 1191. Since 1255, citizens have been obliged by law to show pilgrims hospitality.

Liv Inger Pompei is an authorised historical tour guide (www.norskturistguideisiena. com), covering Siena and the Province of Siena.

entrance fee also includes the **Pinacoteca** (0577 990348) with its collection of 12th- to 15th-century Florentine and Sienese art.

The 11th-century **Collegiata**, or cathedral (0577 940316, closed Sun morning and late January-early Mar except services, admission €3.50) features astounding frescoes of the Old and New Testaments and a beautiful chapel dedicated to Santa Fina by Ghirlandaio. Walk down via San Matteo from the main square and you'll reach the **Museo Archeologico**, the **Spezieria di Santa Fina** and the **Galleria d'Arte Moderna e Contemporanea Raffaele De Grada**, all located in what was once the **Convent of Santa Chiara** (via Folgore 11, 0577 940348, www.comune.sangimignano.si.it, 11am-6pm daily, admission €3.50). The archaeology is largely Etruscan, found locally but influenced by the culture of nearby Volterra. The ceramics in the Spezieria were made for the convent's pharmacy.

Waves of day trippers now ply the streets but the increased human traffic has its benefits. San Gimignano has become a surprising new centre for contemporary art. **Galleria Gagliardi** (via San Giovanni 57, 0577 942196, www.galleriagagliardi.com) has a brilliant collection of contemporary sculpture, while **Galleria Continua** (via del Castello 11, 0577 943134, www.galleriacontinua.com) has a reputation for showcasing cutting-edge work.

Where to stay & eat

The classiest hotel in San Gimignano is **L'Antico Pozzo** (via San Matteo 87, 0577 942014, www.anticopozzo.com, closed 3wks Jan & 3wks Dec, €100-€180); a pleasant alternative is the family-run **Hotel Bel Soggiorno** (via San Giovanni 91, 0577 940375, www.hotelbelsoggiorno.it, closed mid Nov-Dec, €95-€170), which has a tempting restaurant. For a cheap and charming alternative, try **La Casa di Giovanna** (via San Giovanni 58, 0577 940419, www.casagiovanna.com, €55, €65 incl breakfast); this place only has three rooms, but is conveniently located on the main street.

For regional cooking with a twist, try **Osteria delle Catene** (via Mainardi 18, 0577 941966, www.osteriadellecatene.it, closed Wed, tasting menus €13-€31). One of San Gimignano's more elegant places, **Ristorante Dorandò** (vicolo dell'Oro 2, 0577 941862, www.ristorantedorando.it, closed Mon in winter, average €50) serves food based on a variety of Etruscan, medieval and Renaissance recipes. **Gelateria di Piazza** (piazza della Cisterna 4, 0577 942244, www.gelateriadipiazza.com, closed Nov-Feb) has achieved worldwide renown for its ice-cream, and has some unusual flavours on offer, like the infamous chocolate and saffron.

Colle di Val d'Elsa. *See p260.*

Resources

Tourist information
Pro Loco *piazza del Duomo 1 (0577 940008, www.sangimignano.com)*. **Open** *Summer* 9am-1pm, 3-7pm daily. *Winter* 9am-1pm, 2-6pm daily. Audio guide to the town €5.

ABBAZIA DI SAN GALGANO

Located in the Valdimerse, on the SS73, heading to the south-west of Siena, this abandoned abbey is like something out of a fairytale. Built between 1218 and 1288, it was a Cistercian powerhouse until the 14th century. Its monks devised complex irrigation systems and sold their services as doctors, lawyers and architects. But the abbey was sacked one time too many and abandoned. Its monumental, roofless ruins retain an atmosphere of eerie spirituality.

St Galgano was a noble young knight, who renounced his warlike ways to become a Cistercian hermit. When fellow knights tried to persuade him to revert to his old self in 1180, he defiantly stabbed a stone and his sword slid in. The (alleged) sword in the stone is now on display in the **Cappella di Montesiepi**, next to the abbey. This curious circular Romanesque chapel, which has fading frescoes by Ambrogio Lorenzetti, is also worth a visit.

Abbazia di San Galgano. *See p263*.

South-east of Siena

South of Siena, the landscape opens up to reveal rolling hills of open fields interspersed with solitary cypresses. Green in the spring with durum wheat that turns pale yellow in the summer, brown and beige in the autumn after ploughing, it's a simple but interesting landscape. To the south-east are the Crete Senesi or Sienese claylands. Throughout this apparently barren area there are a number of well-preserved hill towns to explore.

BUONCONVENTO

On the SS2 south, stop off in the old walled town of Buonconvento. It has two excellent museums and a pleasant enclosed ambience. The **Museo d'Arte Sacra** (via Soccini 18, 0577 807190, closed Mon, and between 1-3pm daily, admission €3.50) is housed in an art nouveau villa, works by Duccio and others illustrate the strength of Siennese early Renaissance art. The **Museo della Mezzadria** (Tinaia del Taja, piazzale Garibaldi, 0577 809075, admission €4) gives a detailed account of how hard life on the farm really was. The **tourist information office** (www.turismobuonconvento.it) is also in the foyer of the museum.

MONTE OLIVETO MAGGIORE

Up the winding road from Buonconvento, through forests of pine, oak and cypress, lies the magnificent abbey of **Monte Oliveto Maggiore**. Founded in 1313, the monastery began as a solitary hermitage in an arid area. However, due to the devotion and wealth of its founder, Bernardo Tolomei, the place soon drew a large following – the Olivetan order was

recognised by the pope in 1344 – and the place has survived the centuries with a well-preserved structure and with little deterioration to the marvellous fresco cycle in the cloister; the 36 exceptional frescoed panels, painted between 1495 and 1505 by Il Sodoma (27) and Luca Signorelli (9), portray *The Stories of St Benedict*. The library here, once one of the most famous in Europe, can now only be seen with a guide (since the theft of some volumes). The choir stalls in the church are by Giovanni di Verona and are considered among the best wood inlay work in Italy. Gregorian chant at vespers is very popular. There's also a café-cum-restaurant, and a Benedictine gift shop selling own-brewed drinks, honey and herbal medicines (0577 718567, www.monteoliveto maggiore.it, 9.15am-noon, 3.15-5pm daily; 9.15am-noon, 3.15-6pm daily in summer).

SAN GIOVANNI D'ASSO

The little Crete Sinese town of San Giovanni d'Asso has made a heady name for itself through its truffles. It holds two truffle festivals: one in the autumn, featuring the *tuber magnatum pico*, or precious white truffle, and another in March, when the less heralded but still delectable *marzuolo* variety ripens. In the town's castle there's even a multimedia **Truffle Museum** (piazza Gramsci 1, 0577 803268, www.museodel tartufo.it, Sat, Sun only, admission €3). At the rear of the castle sits the **Locanda del Castello** (piazza Vittorio Emanuele 4, 0577 802939, www.lalocandadelcastello.com, closed mid Jan-mid Mar, €120-€200), a pleasant little inn.

However, the most notable feature here is the **Bosco della Ragnaia** (www.laragnaia.com), a magical garden in a steeply sloping wood, where light flickers through foliage, trickling water provides a soothing background sound, and all formal geometries are quietly subverted. It's the creation of American painter Sheppard Craige. The garden is open daily from dawn to dusk, and admission is free.

MONTALCINO

Nearly everyone heading to Montalcino is doing so at least partly to try a glass of Brunello di Montalcino, one of Italy's most celebrated red wines. Once there, though, you'll discover a proud hill town – neither tourist hotspot nor sleepy outpost, but with a gentle Tuscan quality. Under Siena's rule in the 13th century, four families dominated the town's political identity, and are represented these days in Montalcino's four *contrade* (districts). The **Fortezza** (*see right*) was built by the Sienese in 1362, and in 1555 became the last and short-lived stronghold of the Sienese Republic.

The decline that followed didn't abate until the late 1970s, when improved cellar techniques and far-sighted marketing put Brunello di Montalcino on the wine map (*see p261* **Fine Vines**). Tourism came in its wake; and it's not just the Brunello estate that has benefited. Other estates, such as SIRO Pacenti, L'Ucceliera and Cupano, all make fine Rosso di Montalcinos.

All roads in Montalcino lead to **piazza del Popolo**, in the heart of the town. Here you'll find the shield-studded **Palazzo Comunale** (with its tall tower), modelled after Siena's Palazzo Pubblico in 1292. Around the corner, annexed to **Sant'Agostino church** (built in 1360, with superb frescoes by Bartolo di Fredi), is another admirable example of the Sistema Musei Senesi: the **Museo Civico e Diocesano** (via Ricasoli 31, 0577 846014, closed Mon, admission €4.50, €6 incl entrance to the Fortezza). Its collection includes works by Simone Martini, a brilliant altarpiece by Bartolo di Fredi and a worthy exhibit of early ceramics. Montalcino enjoys views that can extend all the way to Siena. Brace yourself for the climb up to the battlements of the **Fortezza** (0577 849211, admission free, ramparts €4). Reward yourself by sampling wines at the well-stocked *enoteca* inside the fortress walls.

Where to stay, eat & drink

On the southern edge of town, the three-star **Hotel Vecchia Oliviera** (Porta Cerbaia, corner of via Landi, www.vecchiaoliviera.com, 0577 846028, €120-€240) has a pool, a terrace and lovely views over the valley. In Montalcino itself, the **Albergo Il Giglio** (via Soccorso

Truffle Museum.

Saloni 5, www.gigliohotel.com, 0577 846577, €128-€190) is a family-run place with 12 frescoed rooms in its main building and an additional five (€75) next door. The **Castello Banfi il Borgo** (Sant'Angelo Scalo, 0577 877700, www.castellobanfiilborgo.com, €440-€1,000), 20 minutes south-west, is a huge family-owned vineyard estate quite far off the beaten track – but it's comfortably self-contained, with two restaurants, a fitness centre, a pool, cooking and wine classes and even its own museum.

Montalcino's restaurants aren't really up to the fame of its wine. The best is the **Re di Macchia** (via Soccorso Saloni 21, 0577 846116, closed Thur, tasting menu €25), which has a small, well-thought-out menu. For well-presented food and great views, head out of town towards **Torrenieri** until, on your right, you come to **Boccon di Vino** (località Colombaio Tozzi 201, 0577 848233, www.boccondivinomontalcino.it, closed Tue, average €40). People-watch over a coffee or an *aperitivo* at the **Fiaschetteria Italiana** (piazza del Popolo 6, 0577 849043, www.caffefiaschetteriaitaliana.com). **Bacchus** (via G Matteotti 15, 0577 847054, closed Mon, Tue, Thur & Sat in winter) is a decent spot for light meals.

Wine connoisseurs are well served with *enoteche* in Montalcino. The most imposing is **Enoteca Osteria Osticcio** (via G Matteotti 23, 0577 848271, closed Sun, average €20): your samplings may be pricey, but they come with a priceless view. If you want to buy a bottle or two to take away, try **Montalcino 564** (via Mazzini 25, 0577 849109, www.montalcino564.it, closed Sun in winter), where you'll also find fine glassware and table linens. For a winning location (inside the Fortezza's keep) and a vast selection, stop at **Enoteca La Fortezza** (0577 849211, www.enotecalafortezza.com); a light luncheon plate is also available.

Resources

Tourist information
Ufficio Informazioni *Costa del Municipio (0577 849331, www.prolocomontalcino.it)*. **Open** 10am-1pm, 2-5.50pm daily. Closed Mon in winter.

ABBAZIA DI SANT'ANTIMO

The lovely Benedictine abbey of Sant'Antimo lies quietly in a vale beneath the hamlet of **Castelnuovo dell'Abate**. Its founding is attributed to Charlemagne in 781, though what remains largely dates to the 12th century. The Romanesque interiors feature finely carved capitals, including one portraying Daniel in the lion's den (second column from the right of the nave). A group of French Premonstratensian

TUSCANY

Get a Farmer's Tan

The Tuscan agriturismo gets a spruce-up.

Forget the long-held, misleading concept of *agriturismi* as 'farm holidays'. While they are, technically, places that make the bulk of their profits from agriculture rather than tourism, more often than not they're swanky country-house retreats set in acres of olive groves and vineyards, where the only *agri*-related duty is the arduous task of tucking into organic produce grown on site. We list our Sienese favourites here; www.agriturismo.it and www.agriturismo.net have comprehensive lists.

FOR RUSTIC CHARM
San Giovanni (www.casagiovanni.it, €110/night per room, €440-€1,540/wk per apartment) in Cetona is an unpretentious 18th-century building set in the lush Val d'Orcia, the farmhouse apartments furnished with items handmade from wood off the farm.

FOR THE VIEW
The 13th-century shooting lodge **Fattoria di Vegi** (www.vegi.it, €100/night per person) in Castellini in Chianti is perched on a

hilltop overlooking a breathtaking sweep of olive groves, vineyards and cypresses.

FOR VINEYARD-HOPPING AND SHOPPING
At the restored 19th-century stone farmhouse **La Lodola** (www.lalodola.it, €70-€120/night, €480-€770/wk) in Asciano, you may be tempted never to leave the tear-shaped pool, but it's only a short drive to thermal springs, Siena and the wineries.

FOR BUTCH CASSIDY MOMENTS
Buonconvento's **Podere Salicotto** (www.poderesalicotto.com, €160/night, €1,080/wk) has a wonderfully relaxed atmosphere, sumptuous breakfasts and bike tours. Or enjoy a day out on the owners' fabulous six-berth boat.

FOR A RAPUNZEL MOMENT
In Gaiole in Chianti, the **Castello di Tornano** (www.castelloditornano.it, €130-€310/night), a fairytale hilltop tower dating back over 1,000 years, features a turret-top terrace and pool carved out of the rock.

monks (Cistercian branch) moved here in 1979 and salvaged it from decline. Gregorian chant (7am, 9am, 12.45pm, 1.45pm, 2.45pm, vespers 7pm, and 8.30pm, free admission) accompanies many of the day's religious functions, drawing audiences from far and wide.

SAN QUIRICO D'ORCIA & BAGNO VIGNONI

San Quirico d'Orcia is one of the lesser-known treasures of Siena Province. This perfectly preserved town, snug within its ancient walls, was a major stopping point on the via Francigena. The 12th-century Romanesque church, the **Collegiata**, with its carved stone portals of lions and dragons, has a terrific altarpiece by Sano di Pietro. Next door is the splendid 17th-century **Palazzo Chigi**. Down the main street is the main square, piazza della Libertà, with a classic **Bar Centrale** (piazza della Libertà 6, 0577 897583) where you can have a plate of the local *pici* and order its own-made *semifreddo* by the kilo. The 16th-century **Horti Leonini**, a lovely formal garden, is also accessed from the square; there's a delightful rose garden at the back. Like many towns in the area, San Quirico has its own

traditional olive press, which becomes the focal point of the annual **Festa dell'Olio** (held around 10 December). It's a convivial, bibulous opportunity for gorging on *bruschetta* soaked in the excellent, freshly pressed local produce.

Just south of San Quirico is the tiny hamlet of **Bagno Vignoni**. In summer, the place has the feel of an exotic resort, with many restaurants with outdoor seating. Piazza delle Sorgenti, the main square, has a large pool of thermal water in its centre, flanked by houses and a low Renaissance *loggia*. St Catherine and, later, Lorenzo il Magnifico came here to ease their aching limbs. Though you can't swim in the historic baths, you can soak blissfully in the thermal pool at **Hotel Posta Marcucci** (*see also p244* **Spa-spangled Manors**).

Where to stay & eat

Within San Quirico the **Palazzo del Capitano** (via Poliziano 18, 0577 899028, www.palazzodelcapitano.com, €80-€450) is a smart option serving good-quality meals and running the odd cookery course. **Hotel Osteria Val d'Orcia** (podere Osteria 15, 0577 887111, www.osteriadellorcia.com, €80-€217), on the road rising toward Castiglion d'Orcia (turn right at the first bend), is a very pleasant country inn that also has an excellent restaurant.

At Bagno Vignoni, the **Hotel Le Terme** (piazza delle Sorgenti 13, 0577 887150, www.albergoleterme.it, €150-€234), built for Pope Pius II as a summerhouse, is right beside the antique baths in the centre. There's fine food and an interesting wine list at the newly renovated **La Terrazza** restaurant. The **Locanda del Loggiato** (piazza del Moretto 30, 0577 888925, www.loggiato.it, €90-€180) has six pleasant rooms and provides light meals.

RADICOFANI & SARTEANO

Further south along the via Francigena from Bagno Vignoni, along the ancient via Cassia around Monte Amiata, lies the tiny town of **Bagni San Filippo**. Here, you can explore the forest that surrounds a natural thermal spa (*see also p244* **Spa-spangled Manors**), where hot waters run in the stream with a spectacular white moat of limestone encrustations.

Further south, **Radicofani** can be viewed from quite a distance, with its stony stronghold built from the volcanic basalt that must have erupted from Monte Amiata in its fiery prehistoric youth. To reinforce the strategic nature of this location, a **Città Fortificata** (fortress) was built on the summit of the hill to which Radicofani clings. Once home to a vagabond knight, Ghinotto di Tacco, the restored site is now a museum (0578 55905, 10.30am-7.30pm, admission €3); an excellent adjoining picnic area affords amazing views during the summer months.

Further on, you'll come to **Sarteano**, a delightful, well-preserved and relatively untouristy town. With its collection of Etruscan funerary urns shaped like heads, the tiny **Museo Civico Archeologico** (0578 269261, www.museisenesi.org, closed Mon May-Sept, open winter by appointment only, admission €4) is worth a peek; nearby is the recently opened Etruscan tomb, the Tomba della Quadriga Infernale, dating back to 330-320BC. Visits have to be booked at the museum.

Where to stay & eat

In Radicofani, **La Grotta** (piazza Santa Agata 12, 0578 55866, closed Tue, average €18) serves robust, no-frills local fare. In Sarteano, the **Residenza Santa Chiara** (piazza Santa Chiara 30, 0578 265412, www.convento santachiara.it, closed Feb, €100-€130), which was once a convent and is now a charming hotel overlooking the town, also has an excellent restaurant (average €30) and an impressive *enoteca* of its own. Down below,

opposite the museum, you can eat well at the **Osteria da Gagliano** (via Roma 5, 0578 268022, closed lunch in winter & Tue year-round, average €24). It's small, though, so book ahead.

PIENZA

Originally called Corsignano, this little town was remodelled – and consequently renamed – between 1458 and 1462 by Aeneas Silvius Piccolomini, who became Pope Pius II in 1458. If you stand in **piazza Pio II** and slowly turn around, you'll notice decorative themes and variations (the *tondo* and the garland) that lend a sense of unity to the different types of building and the materials used. It's pretty astounding to think that the whole project was accomplished in four years. The body of the Duomo is in tufa stone and, at the rear, deliberately Gothic in style, as if to fit into the existing urban context. The travertine façade, by contrast, is as Renaissance as it could be, for those days a bold declaration of modernity.

Palazzo Piccolomini (0577 286300, www.palazzopiccolominipienza.it, closed Mon mid-late Feb and mid-late Nov, admission €7), the pope's residence, was modelled after Alberti's Palazzo Rucellai in Florence (*see p70*). There's a delightful hanging garden that you can view from the gate. You need a ticket for tours of Pius II's lavish private apartments, but access to the courtyard is free.

Museo Diocesano (corso Rossellino 30, 0578 749905, closed Tue & Mon-Fri Nov-Mar, admission €4.10) holds Pienza's art collection.

Where to stay & eat

Those wanting to stay the night will enjoy the comfort and calm of **Hotel Relais Il Chiostro** (corso Rossellino 26, 0578 748400, www.relaisilchiostrodipienza.com, closed early Jan-late Mar, €100-€340), housed in a 15th-century convent. It has an inviting swimming pool and its own restaurant (closed lunch Mon, average €50). The **San Gregorio Residence** (via della Madonnina 4, 0578 748059, €75-€110) is excellent for families with small children.

For dining, **Trattoria Latte di Luna** (via San Carlo 6, 0578 748606, closed Tue & mid Feb-mid Mar & July, average €32) is a good bet. Otherwise, head down to the hamlet of Monticchiello, a few kilometres away, and eat at **La Porta** (via del Piano 1, 0578 755163, www.osterialaporta.it, closed Thur & early Jan-early Feb & late June-early July, average €30). Also in Pienza is **Enoteca di Ghino** (via delle Mura 8, 0578 748057, www.enotecadighino.it), an excellent, keenly priced wine shop with bottles from Tuscany and beyond.

TUSCANY

TUSCANY

Resources

Tourist information
Ufficio Informazioni *piazza Dante Alighieri 18
(0578 749071, www.ufficioturisticodipienza.it).*
Open 9.30am-1pm, 3-6.30pm daily.

MONTEPULCIANO

Montepulciano was an early and important
outpost for the Republic of Florence, and the
town consequently has an elegant and stately
presence in this otherwise medieval landscape.
As early as 1685, a poem entitled 'Bacco in
Toscana' declared that, 'Montepulciano of all
wine is sovereign'. Though wine (Vino Nobile
di Montepulciano) has been a mainstay of the
local economy for centuries, the town owes its
visible substance more to political nous than
viticulture. Montepulciano swore allegiance to
Florence as early as 1511, thereby defending
itself from the designs of Siena and Perugia.

The best way to see the town is by tackling
the steep via di Gracciano del Corso, which
starts near Montepulciano's northern entrance,
Porta al Prato. Along the way, note the Roman
and Etruscan marble plaques cemented into the
base of **Palazzo Bucelli**: they were gathered
by Pietro Bucelli, an 18th-century collector
whose interest in antiquities helped supply
the Museo Civico (*see below*). A bit further up,
on piazza Michelozzo, you can't help but notice
the towering **Torre di Pulcinella**, a clock
tower topped by a mechanical figure typical
of the Neapolitan *Commedia dell'Arte*.

Your efforts will eventually be rewarded
when you reach piazza Grande, the town's
highest and most beautiful point. The spacious
square paved with chunky stones is reminiscent
of Pienza's 'ideal city' layout. The **Duomo** was
never embellished with a proper façade, and
the rough brick front belies the treasures of the
interior: the fine Gothic *Assumption* by Taddeo
di Bartolo (1401) above the altar; the *Madonna
and Child* by Sano di Pietro towards the top
of the left of the nave; the marble *Ciborium*
sculpted by Vecchietta, one of the artists invited
by Pius II to embellish the Duomo in Pienza
with a painting; the delicately carved tomb
of Humanist Aragazzi (1428) by Michelozzo.

Also in the square are Sangallo's **Palazzo
Tarugi**; the 13th-century **Palazzo Comunale**
(visits to the tower €2); and **Palazzo Contucci**.
Not far away and worth a look is the **Museo
Civico** in Palazzo Neri Orselli (via Ricci 10,
0578 717300, closed Mon, admission €5).
Around 20 minutes' walk from Porta al Prato
sits the church of **San Biagio**. Designed by
Sangallo and built between 1518 and 1545,
this Bramante-influenced study in proportion
is a jewel of the High Renaissance.

Where to stay & eat

For lodgings, try the **Albergo Il Marzocco**
(piazza Savonarola 18, 0578 757262, www.
albergoilmarzocco.it, €90-€95), just inside the
Porta al Prato in a 16th-century *palazzo*. A few
of its spacious rooms have terraces. A smaller
residence, dripping in historical charm, is
Meublè Il Riccio (via di Talosa 21, 0578
757713, www.ilriccio.net, €100).

Osteria dell'Acquacheta (via del Teatro
22, 0578 717086, www.acquacheta.eu, average
€22, closed Tue) is a busy *taverna*; booking is
recommended. For drinks or snacks, don't miss
Antico Caffè Poliziano (via di Voltaia nel
Corso 27-29, 0578 758615, www.caffepoliziano.it),
an art deco institution that's a great place to
sample Vino Nobile. At San Biagio there's more
substantial food at **La Grotta** (0578 757479,
www.lagrottamontepulciano.it, closed Wed,
average €45, tasting menu €48), a former 14th-
century staging post. To dine where the stars
have dined, head to the pretty boutique hotel
La Locanda di San Francesco (piazza San
Francesco 5, 0578 758725, www.locandasan
francesco.it), where owner Cinzia Caporali closed
her wine bar so that Robert Pattinson and his
bodyguard could enjoy a private lunch while
filming *New Moon* in the town.

Resources

Tourist information
Pro Loco *piazza Don Minzoni (0578 757341,
www.prolocomontepulciano.it).* **Open** *Summer*
9.30am-12.30pm, 3-8pm Mon-Sat; 9.30am-12.30pm
Sun. *Winter* 9.30am-12.30pm, 3-6pm Mon-Sat;
9.30am-12.30pm Sun.
Strada da Vino Nobile *piazza Grande 7 (0578
717484, www.stradavinonobile.it).*
Gives tourist information and organises tastings.

Getting there

By bus
There's a regular **SITA** bus service (800 373760,
www.sitabus.it) from Florence to Greve (50mins)
and Panzano (70mins). SITA also runs buses
from Florence to San Gimignano (via Poggibonsi,
70mins) via Colle di Val d'Elsa (1hr). In addition,
Tra-in (0577 204246, www.trainspa.it) operates
a service between Siena and Montalcino (1hr),
and another service between Siena and
Montepulciano (via Pienza, 90mins).

By car
Siena Province is best experienced by car. From
the A1 Milan–Rome motorway, exit at Firenze
Certosa, Valdarno, Valdichiana or Chusi and
follow the signs to Siena; check www.autostrade.it.

Lucca

Within these walls.

A conservative bastion in left-wing, progressive
Tuscany, Lucca stands alone and slightly aloof
behind its perfectly preserved 16th-century walls.
Unlike Florence and Siena, Lucca has few must-see
sights, though in many ways it's a more attractive
proposition for the curious traveller. For Lucca's
real attraction lies in its organic wholeness,
its handsome *piazze*, its ample, tree-shaded
fortifications and its ambience: cultured, reserved
but welcoming to tourists, who rarely gather in
numbers that overwhelm Lucca's *centro storico*.
It's also one of the few cities in Europe whose

relationship to the surrounding countryside remains that of a medieval city-
state, locked in a symbiotic relationship. Its pace is gentle: much of the city is
pedestrianised and the best way to discover it is on foot. Or do as the locals do:
spend a day in the saddle.

The ornate façades of the Romanesque churches
– the wedding-cake serenity of **San Michele in
Foro**, truly one of the great sights of Tuscany;
the glistening mosaic of **San Frediano**; and
the hugely charming asymmetry of **Duomo
di San Martino** – all appear unexpectedly.
The colourful ★**piazza dell'Anfiteatro**
still retains the oval shape of an ancient
amphitheatre, while the tree-lined ramparts
and the oak-topped **Torre Guinigi** afford
splendid views of the tight cityscape. Another
good starting point for a local exploration is the
enormous **piazza Napoleone**, named after
Napoleon's sister, and home to a carousel.

Lucca's flatness and relatively simple grid
plan make everything easily accessible. One
lovely way to get your bearings is to hire a
bike (*see p279*) and cycle the four kilometres
(2.5 miles) along the top of the city walls in
the company of joggers, dog walkers and
footballing youngsters.

SOME HISTORY

Possibly the site of a Ligurian and then an
Etruscan settlement, Lucca came of age as
a Roman municipium in 89 BC and hosted
the signing of the first triumvirate between
Pompey, Julius Caesar and Crassus in 56 BC.
It was crucially positioned at the crossroads of
the Empire's communications with its northern
reaches and controlled the Appennine passes
along the Serchio valley.

Despite Rome's fall, the city continued to
maintain its supremacy in Tuscany, first as
capital of Tuscia under Lombard rule and then
as the seat of the Frankish Margravate from
774. By the turn of the first millennium, Lucca
had grown into Tuscany's largest city. Wealth
engendered commercial rivalry with its upstart
neighbours. This soon turned into open military
clashes with Pisa and a gradual loss of political
dominance to Florence.

The 14th century was a turbulent time for
Lucca. A short-lived heyday as the capital of a
mini-empire under the helm of the *condottiere*
Castruccio Castracani (1320-28) soon gave way
to a series of setbacks leading to domination
by Pisa from 1342. In 1369, Lucca was finally
granted its autonomy and independence by
Emperor Charles IV of Bohemia; this was to
last, unbroken, until 1799.

Having renounced its claims to regional
leadership, Lucca moved into relative obscurity.
An oligarchy of ruling families controlled all
public offices and private wealth and set about
enlarging the medieval urban nucleus. In 1805,
Lucca passed under the direct rule of Elisa
Baciocchi, Napoleon's sister, and then in 1817
to the Infanta Maria Luisa di Borbone of Spain.
Both did much to recast the city architecturally
and patronised a brief but highly intense period
of artistic ferment. In 1847, Lucca was ceded
to the Grand Duchy of Tuscany and thereafter
joined a united Italy in 1860. The city's almost

Duomo (Cattedrale di San Martino).

TUSCANY

uninterrupted history as a wildly opulent and free commune has left it largely unaffected by outside developments, both architecturally and in terms of the local psychology.

In so far as the timing of your own visit is concerned, some of the following dates may be worth bearing in mind: the **Santa Zita** flower show and market (four days at the end of April); a summer music festival in piazza Napoleone featuring big names in a small setting – 2011's festival featured Arcade Fire, Elton John, Burt Bacharach and Blink 182 (July, www.summer-festival.com); the **Luminara di San Paolino**, a torchlit procession celebrating Lucca's patron saint (11 July); the **Luminara di Santa Croce** procession of the *Volto Santo* (13 September); the many cultural, religious and sporting events of **Settembre Lucchese** (September, October); the popular **Lucca Comics & Games** festival (late October /early November, 0583 48522, www.luccacomicsandgames.com); and the charming **Natale Anfiteatro** Christmas market.

SIGHTS

Churches

★ Duomo (Cattedrale di San Martino)
Piazza San Martino (0583 957068,
www.museocattedralelucca.it). **Open** *Duomo*
Summer 9.30am-5.45pm daily. Winter 9.30am-
4.45pm daily. *Sacristy* Summer 9.30am-5.45pm
Mon-Fri; 9.30am-6.45pm Sat; 9-9.50am, 11.20-
1.50am, 1-5.45pm Sun. Winter 9.30am-4.45pm
Mon-Fri; 9.30am-6.45pm Sat; 11.20-11.50am,
1-4.45pm Sun. No entry during services.

Admission *Duomo* free. *Sacristy* €2; €6 incl Museo della Cattedrale & San Giovanni e Reparata. **No credit cards.**
At first glance, Lucca's Romanesque cathedral seems somewhat unbalanced. A closer look reveals why. The asymmetrical façade, with the arch and the first two series of *logge* on the right literally squeezed and flattened by the campanile. Nobody is really to blame (or commend) for this as the Lombard bell tower was erected before the rest of the church in around 1100 and completed just 200 years later. It predates the Duomo, on which work began in earnest only in the 12th century. The odd asymmetry of the façade, designed by Guidetto da Como, only adds to the overall atmosphere of wild exuberance and eccentricity.

San Martino's interior is so dimly lit that coin operated lights are on hand to illuminate paintings such as Tintoretto's *Last Supper*. Midway up the left nave is the underrated Matteo Civitali's octagonal marble *Tempietto* (1484), home to a dolorous wooden crucifix known as the *Volto Santo* (Holy Face). The effigy – what we see is a copy – was supposedly begun by Nicodemus and finished by an angel, set on a pilotless ship from the East in the eighth century and brought to Lucca on a cart drawn by steer. This miraculous arrival quickly spawned a cult following and the relic soon became an object of pilgrimage throughout Europe. Nowadays, it's draped in silk and gold garments and ornaments, and marched through Lucca's streets in highly dramatic night-time processions on 13 September.

The Duomo's Sacristy contains the other top attraction: the tomb of Ilaria del Carretto (1408), a delicate sarcophagus sculpted by Sienese master Jacopo della Quercia. It represents the young bride of Paolo Guinigi – Lucca's strongman at the time.

FREE San Francesco

Via della Quarquonia (0583 91175/338 9433388 mobile). **Open** 9-11am daily (phone in advance). **Admission** free.

Although the Franciscans left in 2002, this beautifully simple church remains open to visitors in the morning, though you must let the church custodian know so he can let you in.

★ FREE San Frediano

Piazza San Frediano (0583 493627). **Open** 8.30am-noon, 3-5pm Mon-Sat; 10.30am-5pm Sun. **Admission** free.

San Frediano's strikingly resplendent Byzantine-like mosaic façade is unique in Tuscany, rivalled only by that above the choir of San Miniato al Monte in Florence. A church was founded on this site by Fredian, an Irish monk who settled in Lucca in the sixth century and converted the ruling Lombards by allegedly diverting the River Serchio and saving the city from flooding. This miracle put the finishing touches on Christianity's hold on Lucca and earned Fredian a quick promotion to bishop, eventually leading to canonisation. A few centuries later, in the 1100s, this singular church was built for him.

Apart from its mosaic, an *Ascension* in which a monumental Jesus is lifted by two angels over the heads of his Apostles, the façade of San Frediano is in the Pisan-Romanesque style of many of Lucca's other churches and was the first to face east. Inside, immediately on the right, is a small gem: the *fonte lustrale* (or baptismal font) surrounded with scenes from the Old and New Testaments. Behind it is a glazed terracotta *Ascension* by Andrea della Robbia. In the chapel next to it is another of Lucca's revered relics, the miraculously conserved though somewhat shrivelled body of St Zita, a humble servant who was canonised in the 13th century and whose mummy is brought out for a close-up view and a touch by devotees on 27 April. Ongoing restoration projects care for San Frediano's frescoes, including those by Amico Aspertini.

San Giovanni e Reparata

Via del Duomo (0583 490530, www.museo cattedralelucca.it). **Open** Mar-Oct 10am-6pm daily. Nov-Feb 10am-5pm Sat, Sun. **Admission** *San Giovanni* €2.50; *Museo della Cattedrale & sacristy* €6. **No credit cards**.

Originally Lucca's cathedral, the 12th-century basilica of San Giovanni, now part of the Duomo, is on the site of a pagan temple. Apart from its magnificently ornate ceiling, the church's main draw is the architectural remains uncovered by excavations in the 1970s (included in the ticket price), ranging from a second-century Roman bath to a Paleo-Christian church. For the most enjoyable experience of this enigmatic attraction, ignore the baffling floor plans and just wander at will.

FREE Santa Maria Corteorlandini

Piazza Giovanni Leonardi (0583 467464). **Open** 9am-noon, 4.30-6pm daily; 8.30am-noon public hols. **Admission** free.

This overwhelming late Baroque church is Lucca's odd man out when it comes to the visual splendour

Giacomo Puccini

Lucca's most famous son.

Though in recent times Lucca has played up its link with Giacomo Puccini of *La Bohème*, *Tosca* and *Madama Butterfly* fame, the great composer was not always seen in a favourable light by his fellow citizens. Born in nearby Celle in 1858 but raised in Lucca, Puccini had a restlessness that kept him elsewhere for most of his career, and his non-conformist attitude, artistic unpredictability and unrepentant womanising made him enemies among Lucca's staid upper echelons.

A recalcitrant student, he was persuaded to study composing through spending time with his music teacher and surrogate father Carlo Angeloni, though their conversations revolved more around hunting (Puccini's other great passion). When he went to study at Milan's conservatoire in 1880 his secluded petit-bourgeois lifestyle – he was the last in a long family line of organists

and composers – quickly turned to poverty, but, following some flops, he had a big break in 1893, when he committed to music the tragedy of *Manon Lescaut*.

The success put him on his feet financially, allowing him to create a private hunting Eden at Torre del Lago on Lake Massaciuccioli, where he remained for most of the rest of his life. Creative serenity brought box-office hits flowing, but emotionally his life was a rollercoaster: he fathered a son with a married woman, Elvira Bonturi, and continued to depend upon her despite countless other escapades, including a notorious love affair with flashy German baroness Josephine von Stangel, which was consummated in the pine forests of his beloved Torre del Lago.

He wrote libretti right up until his death in Brussels in 1924, when he was still working on the unfinished *Turandot*.

TUSCANY

of interior design. Its trompe l'œil frescoed roofs, abundance of coloured marble and the gilded and ornamented tabernacle by local artist Giovanni Vambre (1673) provide a break from the stark and grey interiors of the city's other churches.

FREE Santa Maria Forisportam

Piazza Santa Maria Forisportam (0583 467769).
Open 7.30am-noon, 3-6pm daily. **Admission** free.
Set on the square known to Lucchesi as piazza della Colonna Mozza (referring to the truncated column at its centre), Santa Maria takes its name from its location just outside Lucca's older set of walls. The unfinished marble façade dates mostly from the 12th and 13th centuries, and is a toned-down version of the Pisan-Romanesque style present throughout the city.

FREE San Michele in Foro

Piazza San Michele (0583 48459). **Open** 7.40am-noon, 3-6pm daily. **Admission** free.
Set on the site of the Roman forum, San Michele's Pisan-Romanesque façade is among the finest in Tuscany, and remains Lucca's most alluring sight. Every element in the church's elaborate interior lightly plays off against the other: the oddly knotted, twisted and carved columns with their psychedelic geometric designs and the fantastical animals, and fruit and floral motifs in the capitals. The façade culminates in a winged St Michael precariously perched while vanquishing the dragon. San Michele's façade contrasts sharply with its sombre interior. On the right as you enter is a *Madonna and Child* by della Robia – a copy of the original is on the church's right-hand outside corner. Further on, you'll find Filippino Lippi's gorgeously simple and serene *Saints Jerome, Sebastian, Rocco and Helena*, arguably Lucca's greatest artistic asset.

FREE San Paolino

Via San Paolino (0583 53576). **Open** 8.15am-noon, 3.30-6pm daily. **Admission** free.
Giacomo Puccini received his baptism of fire here in 1881 with his first public performance of the *Mass for Four Voices*. San Paolino had, in fact, always been the Puccini family's second home, with five

---

INSIDE TRACK FREE MUSIC

It's often possible to get tickets to Lucca's impressive Summer Music Festival concerts (*see p270*) on the day of the gig. If you can't, or don't want to fork out the €40 or so, you can watch bands soundcheck for free in the afternoon; piazza Napoleone in which they're held isn't closed off for the concerts until around 6pm, so until then anyone can check out the likes of Arcade Fire, Elton John and Joe Cocker.

---

generations of them serving as its organists at one time or another. Built from 1522 to 1536 for Lucca's patron St Paulinus, the city's first bishop, who allegedly came over from Antioch in AD 65 and whose remains are buried in a sarcophagus behind the altar, it's Lucca's only example of late Renaissance architecture.

Museums

Casa Natale di Giacomo Puccini

Corte San Lorenzo 8 (0583 584028, www. fondazionegiacomopuccini.it). **Open** *Apr-Oct* 10am-6pm Mon, Wed-Sun. *Nov-Mar* 11am-5pm Mon, Wed-Sun. **Admission** €7; €5 reductions. **No credit cards**.
The birthplace of Lucca's most famous son, Giacomo Puccini, reopened to the public in 2011 after an extensive refurbishment that has included the restoration of original interiors and reorganisation of rooms and contents. These include memorabilia such as original librettos of his early operas, his private letters on subjects both musical and sentimental, the piano on which he composed *Turandot* and the gem-encrusted costume used in the opera's American debut in 1926. It's absorbing enough for fans of the composer, but it's the general ambience and evocation of the era that offers real insight into his life, and makes a visit here more than the sum of its parts.

Museo della Cattedrale

Piazza Antelminelli (0583 490530, www.museocattedralelucca.it). **Open** *Mar-Oct* 10am-6pm daily. *Nov-Feb* 10am-2pm Mon-Fri; 10am-5pm Sat-Sun. **Admission** €4; €6 incl San Giovanni e Reparata & Sacristy of the Duomo. **No credit cards**.
Attractively laid out over various levels, this well-curated modern museum houses many treasures transferred from the Duomo di San Martino (*see p270*) and from nearby San Giovanni (*see p271*). Displays cover everything from the cathedral's furnishings, its gold and silverware to its sculptures, including Jacopo della Quercia's *Apostle*. The free English audio guides are excellent.

Museo Nazionale di Palazzo Mansi

Via Galli Tassi 43 (0583 55570). **Open** 9am-7pm Tue-Sat; 9am-2pm Sun. **Admission** €4; free reductions; €6.50 incl Villa Guinigi. **No credit cards**.
Beyond the impressive stagecoach at the entrance to this, Lucca's single most remarkable example of Baroque exaggeration, is a 16th- to 17th-century *palazzo* home to a collection of mostly Tuscan art. While the frescoed Salone della Musica (which hosts chamber music concerts) and the neoclassical Salone degli Specchi are light on the eye, over-indulgence climaxes in the Camera della Sposa, an OTT bridal chamber with a *baldacchino* bed. The largely uninspiring art includes pieces from the Venetian school

San Michele in Foro

with lesser-known works by Tintoretto and Titian. Perhaps best is Pontormo's Manneristic portrait of his fiercesome patron, Alessandro de' Medici.

Museo Nazionale di Villa Guinigi
Via della Quarquonia (0583 496033). **Open** 9am-7pm Tue-Sat; 9am-2pm Sun. **Admission** €4; €6.50 incl Palazzo Mansi; free reductions. **No credit cards**.

This porticoed pink-brick villa (1403-20), surrounded by tranquil gardens and medieval statues, houses art from Lucca and its surrounding region. The first floor of the museum has a selection of fascinating Roman and Etruscan finds along with some 13th- and 14th-century capitals and columns. Highlights from the upstairs rooms are Matteo Civitali's *Annunciation*, some ornate altarpieces by Amico Aspertini and Fra Bartolomeo, and intarsia panels by Ambrogio and Nicolao Pucci.

Monuments

★ Ramparts
www.lemuradilucca.it

On a good day you'll see Lucchesi of all ages strolling, jogging, picnicking, cuddling and enjoying the views from *le nostre mura* ('our walls'), as the ramparts are lovingly known. Built in the 16th and 17th centuries, Italy's best-preserved and most impressive city fortifications measure 12m (39 ft) in height and 30m (98 ft) across, with a circumference of just over 4km (2.5 miles). They are punctuated by 11 sturdy bastions, designed to ward off heavily armed invaders. A proper siege never happened, though in 1812 they enabled the city to seal itself hermetically from floodwaters. Soon after, Maria Luisa di Borbone turned the walls into a public park and promenade, dotting them with plane, holm-oak, chestnut and lime trees. Today, cyclists and pedestrians are still making the most of them, not to mention the families who populate the play areas found in almost every *baluardo* (rampart) across town.

Torre Guinigi
Via Sant'Andrea 45 (0583 316846). **Open** *Nov-Feb* 9.30am-4.30pm. *Mar, Oct* 9.30am-5.30pm. *Apr-May* 9.30am-6.30pm. *June-Sept* 9.30am-7.30pm. **Admission** €3.50; €2.50 reductions. **No credit cards**.

It may be something of a slog, but it's well worth the climb to reach the tranquil and leafy summit of Torre Guinigi, with its distinctive cluster of oak trees. From the very top of this 14th-century, 44m (144ft) tower, there are spectacular views over Lucca's rooftops to the countryside beyond.

Parks & gardens

Giardino Botanico
Via del Giardino Botanico 14 (0583 583086, www.ortobotanicodilucca.it). **Open** *May, June* 10am-6pm daily. *July-Sept* 10am-7pm daily. *Oct, Mar, Apr* 10am-5pm daily. *Nov-Feb* 9.30am-12.30pm by appointment only. **Admission** €3; €2 reductions. **No credit cards**.

Nestling in the south-east corner of the city walls, the Giardino Botanico makes a relaxed spot for a

TUSCANY

romantic stroll or a quiet sit-down – as do the gardens of the Villa Bottini just a little further up via Santa Chiara. The greenhouse and arboretum are planted with a wide and impressive range of Tuscan flora, many of which are rare species.

Palazzo Pfanner

Via degli Asili 33 (0583 954029). **Open** *Apr-Oct* 10am-6pm daily. **Admission** *Palace & Garden* €5.50; free under-12s. *Palace or Garden only* €4; free under-12s. **No credit cards**.

These gardens, overlooked by the tower of San Frediano and the city walls, are a lovely place to stroll away an afternoon. The palace has been restored to its former glory, and features cabinets housing the surgical implements used by Pietra Pfanner (who rose to become mayor of the city and later Knight Commander of the Crown of Italy) beneath impressive frescoed ceilings. Film buffs might recognise the gardens as a backdrop from *The Portrait of a Lady*.

NIGHTLIFE

Bars & clubs

Don't come to Lucca for late nights and hedonism: the big nightspots are out towards the Versilia coast. There are, however, a number of decent wine bars in town. Good choices include **Rewine** (via Calderia 6, 0583 48427, closed Sun), a red and black bar that also serves decent snacks; **Vinarkia** (via Fillungo 188, 0583 495336, closed Mon), a laid-back bar with regular wine tastings and free buffet at 6pm and 10pm every night; and **La Corte dei Vini** (corte Campana 6, 0583 584460, www.lacortedeivini.it, closed Sun), notable for its cheeses and wines. The beautiful piazza Antifeatro is lined with bars at which you can spend hours over a glass of wine and *aperitivo* or a full meal – **Pane e Vino** (*see p276*) is one of the best, and up by the Porta dei Borghi, the lively and friendly **Betty Blue** (via del Gonfalone 16-18, 0583 492166, www.bettyblue lucca.it, closed Wed) is set on a sweet square and serves a great range of cocktails and snacks to a trendy local crowd.

SHOPPING

You'll find plenty of well-known designer and other high-street names on and around Lucca's main shopping artery, via Fillungo. The other main hubs are via Vittorio Veneto (leading off piazza San Michele) and via Santa Croce. Despite Lucca's staid reputation, there are several boutiques and shoe shops, in particular along via Fillungo and via Vittorio Veneto.

There are excellent food shops at each turn, stocked with everything from regional wines and olive oils to cheeses and honeys, and a .

locally produced salami made with pig's blood and raisins. Two of the best in town are **La Grotta** (via dell' Anfiteatro 2, 0583 467595, www.alimentarilagrotta.com) and **Delicatezze** (via San Giorgio 5, 0583 492633).

The town's general market is held on via de' Bacchettoni by the eastern wall on Wednesdays and Saturdays, selling clothes, food, flowers and household goods. There's an antiques market in and around piazza San Martino on the third weekend of each month, with everything from coins to jewellery, and a crafts market (*arti e mestieri*) in piazza San Giusto on the last weekend of the month.

Cacioteca

Via Fillungo 242 (0583 496346). **Open** 7am-1.30pm, 3.30-8.30pm Mon, Tue, Thur-Sat; 7am-1.30pm Wed.

An intense waft of seasoned cheese emanates from this shop. Give your taste buds a treat with the typical dairy products of the Garfagnana.

Mercato del Carmine

Off piazza del Carmine. **Open** 7am-1pm, 4-7.30pm Mon-Sat. **No credit cards**.

Between its fruit and vegetable stalls, fishmongers, butchers and delis, this superb colonnaded covered market offers the best of Lucca's regional produce: look out for the blood sausages, a local speciality. There's also a café where you can rest your weary feet and refuel along with the locals.

Pasticceria Pasquinelli

Via San Paolino 38 (339 8759297). **Open** 7am-8pm Tue-Sun. **No credit cards**.

This pretty, old-fashioned 50-year-old *pasticceria* sells gorgeous biscuits, pastries, cakes and celebration cakes (including ones decorated with Puccini opera heroines) in a setting that's a great stop for a coffee – or something stronger.

Sky Stone & Songs

Piazza Napoleone 22 (0583 491389). **Open** 9.30am-1.30pm, 3-7.30pm Mon-Sat; 9.30am-1.30pm Sun.

This record shop has a great range of vinyl and a fun series of 'Concerti in Vetrina' – concerts in the window – in which emerging bands and performers take their first steps to fame, or otherwise. It also sells tickets for the frequent music concerts held in the piazza and all the Summer Festival concerts.

Vini Liquori Vanni

Piazza San Salvatore 7 (0583 491902, www. enotecavanni.com). **Open** 4-8pm Mon; 9am-1pm, 4-8pm Tue-Sat.

This *enoteca*'s seemingly endless cellar is a treasure for those seeking out Lucca's better (and little-known) vintages. Probably also the least expensive place to get your hands on a bottle of the new range

TUSCANY

of Super Tuscan reds, as well as some of the more obscure varieties. Call ahead and book a wine lesson and *degustazione*, plus a mini-tour.

WHERE TO EAT
Restaurants

The neighbouring Garfagnana valley contributes many prime ingredients to Lucca's cuisine, including chestnut flour, river trout,

olive oil and above all *farro* (spelt grain), which pops up on every menu. The signature pudding is *buccellato* (a doughnut-shaped sweet bread flavoured with aniseed and raisins, and topped with sugar syrup).

La Buca di Sant'Antonio
Via della Cervia 3 (0583 55881, www.bucadi santantonio.it). **Open** 12.30-2pm, 7.30-10pm Tue-Sat; 12.30-3pm Sun. Closed 2wks Jan. **Average** €35-€40.

New Contemporary

The pair of new galleries making a splash out of Tuscan modern art.

With the recent opening of two new modern art galleries, Lucca is becoming something of a rival to Prato for contemporary creativity in Tuscany. First to open in 2010 was Lu.C.C.A (the Lucca Center of Contemporary Art, www.luccamuseum.com). Housed over five floors of the 16th-century Palazzo Boccella near Market Square, this excellent venue shows original mixed group exhibitions in a great, light-filled space. August 2011 saw 'Journeys of memory', an exhibition curated by artist Ezio Gribaudo, featuring works by Miró, Savinio, De Chirico and Fontana, and before that a video art exhibition imaginatively gathered together the work of international video artists. Earlier shows have included retrospectives by pop artist Ludmilla Radchenko and painter Massimo Bramandi, suggesting

an eclectic programme of shows in a space dedicated to both emerging and established artists from Italy and beyond. As such, it's a must for fans of modern art, as is the ongoing exploration of the dialogue between art, spirituality, philosophy and environment that began late in 2010 at the church of San Cristoforo (via Fillungo, 0583 957660, www.artscristoforolucca.com). In this evocative and atmospheric space, a cultural organisation dedicated to raising the profile of the city in the modern art world and bringing more culture to Lucca is developing site-specific installations and exhibitions by world-class artists such as Tony Cragg. The project is an ambitious and complex one that goes beyond providing a space for art, and certainly in the case of the Cragg exhibition, it succeeds beautifully.

Lucca Center of Contemporary Art.

TUSCANY

First stop on the tourist trail but an undeniably fine hostelry with a few outside tables amid plants and flowers, La Buca serves traditional Lucchese food – its mushroom dishes are superb – with the occasional innovative touch. You'll need to reserve in advance, but if it's fully booked, try sister restaurant Il Giglio (0583 494058) on piazza Napoleone.

Da Leo

Via Tegrimi 1 (0583 492236, www.trattoriada leo.it). **Open** noon-2.30pm, 7.30-10.30pm daily. **Average** €20. **No credit cards**.
The waiters sing and local families compete to be heard over the din of children, yet despite all this noise and bustle, Da Leo is one of Lucca's mellowest restaurants. You won't be hurried through your meal, which will inevitably be made up of hearty country dishes such as roast chicken, grilled steak, *spaghetti alle vongole* and *pappardelle broccoli e salsiccia*. Remember to bring cash, though: in true country fashion, credit cards are not accepted.

★ Gigi

Piazza del Carmine (0583 467266, www.gigi trattoria.it). **Open** 12.30-3pm Mon; 12.30-3pm, 7.30-11pm Tue-Sun. **Average** €20.
A few tables outside belie the size of the interior, where three red rooms are crammed with couples, families and friends tucking into Tuscan treats. The decor's a splendid mish-mash; a rustic look overall is punctuated with odd photos and a Stark Ghost chair here, '60s kitchen chair there, but it's the food people are here for, dishes such as vegetables fried in a delicate tempura batter, and melt-in-the-mouth *cinta senese* pork ribs with borlotti beans. People come just for dessert too; usually the chocolate flan.

★ Locanda di Bacco

Via San Giorgio 36 (0583 493136, www. ristorantelocandadibacco.com). **Open** 12.30-2.30pm, 7.30-10.30pm daily. Closed 2wks Feb & 2wks Nov. **Average** €25.
This spacious, stylish but friendly restaurant is a relative newcomer to the local restaurant scene, but already a hit with both locals and tourists. The wine list is extensive and includes a number of relatively rare northern Tuscan varieties. The starters include *crostini* with melted gorgonzola and honey; pasta dishes include *pappardelle al cinghiale* (with wild boar); and the desserts are irresistible. *Photo p268.*

Locanda Buatino

Borgo Giannotti 508, nr piazzale Martiri della Libertà (0583 343207). **Open** noon-3pm, 7.30-10.30pm Mon-Sat. Closed 2wks Aug. **Average** Lunch €10-€15. Dinner €20-€25.
Locanda Buatino is a gem in a busy street leading from the city walls. From the outside it looks little more than a bar, and the feel is low-key, with small wooden tables, strings of garlic and rustic paintings. But the food is terrific, perhaps the best in Lucca. On Mondays from October to May, it's jazz night (€25 including a meal with wine). Upstairs are basic rooms for €50 with shared bathrooms.

★ Lucca Drento

Piazza San Frediano 6 (0583 494940). **Open** 11am-12.30am daily. **Average** €20.
Billing itself as a small *osteria*, Lucca Drento is a real gem, an *enoteca* that offers a small daily changing menu of dishes such as *baccala with ceci* (salt cod with chickpeas) and *Panzanelle Lucchese*, all at around €8. Piled-high plates of cheese and *salumi* are served too, all of it for sale at the deli counter. Occasional live music makes it feel more of a bar than a restaurant, and it's tiny so gets crowded in winter, but if you're not after a huge meal, it's one of the best eats in town, particularly if you grab a seat out on piazza San Frediano on a warm summer's evening.

★ Pane e Vino

Piazza dell'Anfiteatro (340 9348448 mobile). **Open** 11am-2am daily. **Average** €25.
Apartments on the lovely piazza Anfiteatro command ridiculous prices, and it's easy to see why. The oval-shaped piazza is a delight to sit and spend time in, and Pane e Vino is one of the best places in which to do it. Bar, restaurant, cocktail bar and *enoteca*, it offers a good, cheap selection of snacks and mixed cold plates – olives and pecorino cheese, *carpaccio* of beef, *taleggio* and *radicchio* salad – through to main meals and big salads. The *aperitivo* selection is excellent too, and you could do a lot worse than sit here for the evening over some reasonably priced drinks and a good buffet.

Pizza da Felice

Via Buia 12 (0583 494986). **Open** 11am-8.30pm Mon; 10am-8.30pm Tue-Sat.
The very tiny and very popular Pizza da Felice has just a handful of seats in a shop that obviously hasn't had its decor updated since the 1960s, but the point here is to buy some incredibly good slices of pizza and *cecine* (chickpea salted cakes) and either take them to the nearest square or do as the locals do and sit on the benches outside, feasting on a meal for less than €5.

INSIDE TRACK TOONTOWN

If you're a comic fan but aren't in town for the huge **Lucca Comics & Games** (*see p270*) in autumn, you can always visit the **Museo Nazionale del Fumetto** to find out about the greatest Italian comic characters of all time. Piazza San Romano 4 (0583 56326, www.museoitalianodelfumetto.it). **Open** 10am-6pm Tue-Sun. **Admission** €3-€4. **No credit cards**.

Ristorante Puccini

Corte San Lorenzo 1-2, off piazza Cittadella (0583 316676, 338 9805927 mobile, www.ristorantepuccini.it). **Open** 12.30-2.30pm, 7.30-10.30pm daily. Closed Dec-Feb. **Average** €40.

Housed in a 15th-century *palazzo* with a quiet courtyard and secluded terrace, Puccini is widely regarded as Lucca's best fish restaurant. Prices aren't cheap – even a rocket and parmesan salad will set you back €10 – and the tasting menus (€40 for meat, €45 for fish) are the best bet. Alternatively, in summer you can order a dish at a time for €8.

Vineria I Santi

Via dell'Anfiteatro 29a (0583 496124, www. vineriaisanti.it). **Open** 11am-3pm, 7pm-1.30am Mon, Tue, Thur-Sun; 11am-3pm, 7pm-2am Sat. **Average** €25.

This superb little *vineria* oozes style – from its modern rustic furniture and delicate light fittings to the discreet wine paraphernalia dotted around its walls. Dishes are short in number but high in imagination; the likes of smoked sea bass with marinated fennel, orange and pine nuts, but simpler dishes (tomato and mozzarella lasagne) also get a look-in.

Cafés & gelaterie

Ice-cream parlours, cafés and pretty cake shops abound in Lucca. These are our favourites.

Caffè di Simo

Via Fillungo 58 (0583 496234). **Open** *Bar* 9am-7.30pm Tue-Sun. *Restaurant* 12.30-2.30pm Mon, Tue, Thur-Sun. Summer also 7-10pm Thur-Sat. **Average** €18.

Lucca's most celebrated belle époque café-*pasticceria* is surprisingly unsnobby: workmen mix amiably with upmarket tourists and civil servants. It's still mainly about pastries, ice-creams and posh chocolates, but more substantial dishes include the ubiquitous *zuppa di farro* and other regional fare. *Photo p278.*

Casali

Piazza San Michele 40 (0583 492687). **Open** *Apr-Oct* 7.30am-11.30pm daily. *Nov, Dec* 7am-8.30pm daily. *Jan-Mar* 7am-8.30pm Mon, Tue, Thur-Sun. Closed 3 wks Jan- Feb.

Casali's outside tables are the perfect spot for people-watching with an ice-cream or an aperitif in hand.

★ Gelateria Santini

Piazza Cittadella 1 (0583 55295, www.gelateria santini.it). **Open** *Winter* 9am-9pm Tue-Sun. *Summer* 9am-midnight daily.

Coming up to its 100th anniversary, the Santini is as beautiful as you'd expect a fin de siècle interior to be, its warm wooden panelling and long counter making it a welcome stop in summer or winter. Flavours are traditional and made using natural ingredients, and for Christmas and Easter the *panettone* and *colomba* filled with *semifreddo* make a great dessert.

Gelateria Venetina

Chiasso Barletti 23 (0583 55295).
Open 10am-1am daily. **No credit cards.**
Heavenly ice-creams are sold at this venerated *gelateria*. There are some good pavement tables for those who don't want to walk and lick.
Other locations Gelateria Veneta, via Vittorio Veneto 74 (0583 467037).

Girovita

Piazza Antelminelli 2 (0583 469412).
Open 8am-1am Tue-Fri, Sun; 8am-2am Sat.
Directly opposite the cathedral, the terrace of this stylish café-bar is the perfect spot for a morning coffee and pastry or, come cocktail hour, a sundowner accompanied by a great spread of free nibbles.

WHERE TO STAY

Lucca isn't known for its abundance of accommodation – and there are no signs this will change. The Lucchesi have no intention of overcrowding their civilised environs with tourists. That said, there are a number of B&Bs and a handful of decent hotels cropping up around town. It's always best to book ahead if possible, however. **Locanda Buatino** (*see p276*) also offers basic rooms.

Affittacamere San Frediano

Via degli Angeli 19 (0583 469630, www.san frediano.com). **Rates** €50-€140.
A friendly, well-located B&B with cosy rooms featuring iron bedsteads and satellite TV. The top floor, which dates back to the 16th century, was recently turned into a lounge for guests.

Alla Corte degli Angeli

Via degli Angeli 23 (0583 469204, www.allacorte degliangeli.com). **Rates** €119-€190.
This place is a few notches up from Affitacamere San Frediano just two doors down (*see above*), and is thus pricier as a result. The rooms are named after flowers and decorated to the highest quality, with bold colours, fine antiques and period furniture, and all come with their own minibars and luxurious whirlpool baths as standard.

Hotel Noblesse

Via S. Anastasio, 23 (0583 440275, www.hotel noblesse.it). **Rates** €169-€600.
On the corner of via Santa Croce, this new five-star hotel housed in a three-storey 18th-century home of an antiques dealer draws on its past to create an elegant but homey interior stuffed with antiques and rich, lush textiles and colours. Staff are unstuffy and helpful, and the 13 individually decorated rooms spacious and pretty.

TUSCANY

Caffè di Simo. *See p277.*

La Bohème

Via del Moro 2 (0583 462404, www.boheme.it).
Rates €90-€140.
A nicely decorated B&B in the heart of town, La Bohème is a stylish choice if you're thinking of stopping in town, with richly coloured walls, dark wood furniture, chandeliers and a bright, airy breakfast room. Recommended. Cash payers with this guide get a 5% discount.

La Torre

Piazza del Carmine 11 (0583 957044, www.roomslatorre.com). **Rates** €35-€80.
Staying at this small family-owned B&B is like staying in an Italian home, from the old-fashioned decor and furnishings in a rambling, slightly shabby medieval building to the spacious but basic (and clean) rooms to huge home-cooked breakfast and helpful, friendly hosts. The location is a high point, and many of the rooms offer free internet and small kitchens. If you arrive by car helpful staff will find a parking spot for you and transport you to the hotel.

Locanda L'Elisa

Via Nuova per Pisa 1952, Massa Pisana (0583 379737, www.locandalelisa.it).
Rates €190-€350.
In a league of its own, Locanda L'Elisa is an elegant four-star hotel 4km (2 miles) south of Lucca, and is one of the area's best. The villa's current appearance dates back to 1805, when Napoleon's sister and Lucca's ruler, Elisa Baciocchi, had the interiors and gardens refashioned. Highlights include a restaurant modelled after an English conservatory, 18th-century furnishings, revamped gardens and a large swimming pool.

La Luna

Corte Compagni 12, off via Fillungo (0583 493634, www.hotellaluna.com). **Closed** early January-early Feb. **Rates** €90-€190.
La Luna is well priced, given its location at the upper end of busy via Fillungo. Rooms, housed in two 17th-century *palazzi* facing each other across a courtyard, are comfortable (if plain), with the usual mod cons.

Piccolo Hotel Puccini

Via di Poggio 9 (0583 55421, www.hotelpuccini.com). **Rates** €95.
Just a baton's throw from Puccini's boyhood home, this discreet hotel is excellent value for money. The vibe is friendly and the staff speak good English.

San Luca Palace

Via San Paolino, 103 (0583 317446, www.sanlucapalace.com). **Rates** €150-€190.
A nice location near the city walls and 26 spacious, light-filled rooms make this a good four-star choice. Rooms are old-style traditional rather than modern, but they're individually decorated in warm colours, service is good and the sweet outdoor terrace and free bikes add up to make a stay here a pleasant one.

San Martino

Via della Dogana 9 (0583 469181, www.albergo sanmartino.it). **Rates** €90-€130.
This very friendly 16th-century hotel is centrally located yet far enough away from the main drag to be relaxing. Breakfast can be taken in the elegant courtyard and the two suites are perfect for families.

Universo

Piazza del Giglio 1 (0583 493678, www.universo lucca.com). **Rates** €149-€259.

Right beside the elegant piazza Napoleone, the Universo is the faded old queen of Lucca's hotels. Rooms have recently been given a facelift, but vary hugely in size and decor. The nicest (and priciest) are almost hip, with wooden beams, blonde wood, cream furnishings and rainfall showers.

RESOURCES

Hospital
Campo di Marte hospital *via dell'Ospedale (0583 9701).*

Police station
Via Cavour 120, nr train station (0583 455487).

Post office
Via Vallisneri 2, nr Duomo (0583 433555).

Tourist information
Comune di Lucca Tourist Office *piazzale Giuseppe Verdi, nr Vecchia Porta San Donato (0583 442944).* **Open** 9.30am-5.30pm daily. **Other locations** Piazza Santa Maria, viale Luporini, Porta Elisa and inside Palazzo Ducale. **APT** *Piazza Santa Maria 35 (0583 919931, www.luccatourist.it).* **Open** *Apr-Oct* 9am-7.30pm daily. *Nov-Mar* 9am-noon, 3-6pm Mon-Sat.

GETTING THERE & AROUND

By bike
Cycling is a fun way to get around the area, especially during warmer weather (but not too warm). There are several bike hire shops, with the largest concentration to be found in piazza Santa

Maria; for daily or weekly rentals, try **Cicli Bizzarri** at no.32 (0583 496031) or **Poli Antonio** at no.42 (0583 493787, www.biciclettepoli.com).

By bus
The bus station is at piazzale Giuseppe Verdi. **VAIBUS** (www.vaibus.it) operates in the Lucca area. For information on services to Lucca and the province call 0583 587897; for services to Pisa, Pistoia Montecatini, Prato and Florence, call 0583 584877.

By car
For car hire try **Europcar** (viale Castracani 110, 0583 956058), **Hertz** (via Catalani 59, 0583 505472) or **Nolo Auto Pittore** (piazza Santa Maria 34, 0583 467960). Within the city walls parking is expensive, except for hotel guests, but there's a spacious free car park just outside the walls past Porta San Donato.

By taxi
There are radio taxi ranks at piazza Napoleone (0583 492691), the train station (0583 494989), piazza Verdi (0583 581305), piazza Santa Maria (0583 494190) and the hospital (0583 950623).

By train
Lucca's train station is at piazza Ricasoli, two minutes' walk from the southern gate, Porta San Pietro. Trains from Florence to Viareggio stop at Lucca (as well as Prato and Pistoia). The trip from Florence takes about 1hr 20mins, with trains leaving almost every hour from early until 10pm. For train information call 892021 or visit www.trenitalia.com.

TUSCANY

Grand Designs

Splendid villas and beautiful gardens.

The countryside around Lucca is smattered with elegant villas and gardens that were originally the country retreats of wealthy merchants from the city. Elisa Baciocchi, Napoleon's sister, once resided at the stunning 17th-century **Villa Reale** at Marlia (0583 30108, www.parcovillareale.it, closed Mon and Dec-Feb, admission €6). Although the house is closed, you can visit the lovely statue-filled garden, which also contains a little theatre. The garden of the 16th-century **Villa Oliva Buonvisi** at San Pancrazio (0583 406462, www.villaoliva.it, admission €6) is open from March until November, as is the large English-style park and orangery of the nearby **Villa Grabau** (0583 406098, www.villagrabau.it, closed Mon Easter-Oct & Mon-Sat Nov-Easter,

admission €5 garden only, €6 villa and garden). The 17th-century **Villa Mansi** (0583 920234, www.villamansi.com, closed Mon, admission €5), over at Segromigno, is another very fine house, with frescoes of the *Myth of Apollo* by Stefano Tofanelli in the salon. The statue-filled garden was laid out by the Sicilian architect Juvarra; it's partly Italian (geometric) and partly English (not geometric) in style. There are also musical concerts in summer. The **Villa Torrigiani** (0583 928041, www.villee palazzilucchesi.it, closed Tue, admission €7 gardens only, €10 gardens and villa) and its fine park at Camigliano are open from March to November. Inside are 16th- to 18th-century paintings and an excellent collection of porcelain.

Arezzo

A working city with plenty of attractions for visitors.

Arezzo is now bearing the fruit of its hard work over the last few years, having recreated itself from a gold-oriented semi-backwater to a modern, welcoming tourist destination. Fortunately, not too many people have discovered this yet, so it's the ideal time to explore this town of art, antiques and... OK, the gold is still a big draw.

A decade or so ago, the Aretini (as the locals are known) were too busy manufacturing gold jewellery – which had turned a generation of peasants into millionaires – to devote much attention to their city. They kept to their factories in the suburbs, accruing great wealth and occasionally going out for a spin in their Ferraris. Little wonder, then, that tourists beat a retreat after admiring the frescoes. Happily, a lot has changed in a short time. Just as the city's gold and textile industries face leaner years (though they're undeniably still big businesses), a younger generation has decided to employ its own entrepreneurial acumen outside the confines of the factories. As a result, there's a real buzz about the place.

The annual local music festival, Arezzo Wave, started in 1987, was becoming a highly popular, energetic affair – but, in 2007, the organisers moved the location of the festival to Sesto Fiorentino, in Florence Province, and renamed it Italia Wave, leaving Arezzo without one of its most forward-looking events. The excellent backward-looking ones make up for this loss, however, principally the **Giostra del Saracino** (*see p178*), a heady riot of medieval pageants, straight-faced tight-wearing and jousting. Besides this explosion of excitement, Arezzo's main pleasures are to be found in the town's shopping and in its artistic heritage. It's an essential stop on any Piero della Francesca trail, housing his *Legend of the True Cross* in the church of **San Francesco** (*see p282*), and a *Mary Magdalene* in the **Duomo** (*see right*); anyone interested in Giorgio Vasari can visit the **Casa Vasari** (*see p183*) to get an insight into this prodigious artist.

SOME HISTORY

Strategically built at the intersection of four fertile valleys (the Casentino, Valdarno, Valtiberina and Valdichiana), Arezzo was a flourishing centre of Etruscan culture by the fourth century BC. It was later taken over by the Romans in their northward expansion, becoming a military stronghold and economic outpost. By 89 BC, its people were granted honorary Roman citizenship; an amphitheatre, an aqueduct and fortified walls followed. A century later, Arezzo's first industry was born: embossed pottery, traded far and wide.

Following the decline of the Roman Empire, the city was overrun by Barbarians. The darkest days came under the Lombards in the sixth century. Yet, gradually, a feudal economic system began to pull the city from its slump. The turning point arrived in 1100, when the emerging merchant class started to question its subservience to Arezzo's clerical-feudal overlords. Secular power began to shift to the budding bourgeoisie, and, in 1192, the *comune* was established. There was extensive building and Arezzo began to take on its current urban contours. However, another foreign power, this time Florence, set its sights on the city. The two clashed in the Battle of Campaldino in 1289, from which Arezzo never fully recovered. The city eventually succumbed to Florence in 1384.

Luckily, political submission didn't equal artistic or cultural paralysis: Medici patronage in Florence provided wider scope for those with talent. Foremost among the creative spirits of the time was Giorgio Vasari (1511-74), a painter, architect and historian, whose *Lives of the Artists* has enlivened our perception of the Renaissance. However, the boost to local creativity didn't last: the city had become a conservative backwater by the 17th century. And so it remained, until recently, when the parochial outlook began to be supplanted by more progressive policies. Today, a younger, better-educated generation of entrepreneurs and local administrators seems set on increasing the city's appeal. To those ends, the centre has been largely pedestrianised, and a new parking area just outside the walls on the north side, behind the church of San Domenico, makes access to the city centre far easier and more attractive.

SIGHTS

Churches

FREE Badia di Santi Fiora e Lucilla

Piazza di Badia (0575 356612). **Open** 8am-5pm Mon-Sat; 8am-12.30pm Sun. Closed during services. **Admission** free.
As well as a giant *Crucifixion* by de Segna and a marble-effect altar by Vasari, Arezzo's Badia boasts an ingenious illusory drawn dome by Andrea Pozzo.

FREE Duomo (Cattedrale di San Donato)

Piazza del Duomo (0575 23991). **Open** 7am-12.30pm, 3-7pm daily. **Admission** free.
Construction on Arezzo's Gothic Duomo began in 1277, but the finishing touches weren't made until the early 1500s, and it was a further 300 years before its campanile was erected. The overall effect of its size and the vertical thrust of its ogival vaulted ceilings are inspiring, as are the exquisite stained-glass windows (c1515-20) by Guillaume di Marcillat. But its real attractions are along the left aisle: Piero della Francesca's *Mary Magdalene* (c1465), and the Cappella della Madonna del Conforto.

★ FREE Pieve di Santa Maria

Corso Italia (0575 22629, www.santamariadella pieve.it). **Open** *Oct-Apr* 8am-noon, 3-6pm daily. *May-Sept* 8am-1pm, 3-7pm daily. **Admission** free.
A striking example of Romanesque architecture built mostly in the 12th and 13th centuries. Santa Maria's pale stone façade is harmonious, with five arcades surmounted by three increasingly busy orders of *logge*. The columns holding them up, all of which have

Piazza San Francesco. *See p282.*

an eccentric motif, reach a climax in the bell tower *delle cento buche* (of the 100 holes). As you enter, look above the doorway: the colour on the calendar-statues beneath the arch has survived from the 13th century.

FREE San Domenico
Piazza San Domenico 7 (0575 23255).
Open 8.30am-7pm daily. **Admission** free.
San Domenico was started by Dominicans in 1275, around the same time as their Franciscan brothers were getting under way with San Francesco (*see*

below). Facing a simple, open square, it has an attractive quaintness about it that's accentuated by its uneven Gothic campanile, which comes complete with two 14th-century bells. Inside you'll find a magnificent crucifix by Cimabue.

★ FREE San Francesco
Piazza San Francesco (0575 352727).
Open 8.30am-7pm daily. **Admission** free.
The interior of San Francesco, begun by Franciscan friars in the 13th century, was adorned with frescoes,

TUSCANY

Market Force

Succumb to temptation at this monthly market.

On each first Sunday of the month, splayed around Arezzo, over 500 vendors – and up to 30,000 customers – arrive from all over the country to deal in everything from ornate candlesticks to collectable junk.

The brainchild of antique-dealer Ivan Bruschi (whose house is now a museum, *see p283*), the **Fiera Antiquario di Arezzo** (www.arezzofieraantiquaria.com) was the first monthly fair of its kind in Italy and claims to be the biggest. Now well and truly established, you'll find the market buzzing in *piazze* Grande, San Francesco and della Badia on the weekend of the first Sunday of the month. In piazza Grande, the big traders are to be found selling a fascinating array of jewellery, delicate lace, traditional linen and small sculptures. The Fiera hosts furniture, plus everything from copper vessels to *palazzo* chandeliers; replacement ornaments for incomplete items can be found in corso Italia.

Some collectors scoff that the market is too expensive and offers little for the serious buyer; others will be found poking around the tables month in, month out. There's plenty to take in – but it's advisable to refrain from heedlessly rifling through that pile of old tea towels, or photographing a load of old war junk unless you want to get a frosty 'hands off' or 'no photo'.

Though a Baroque bedroom set from Puglia might stretch the luggage allowance, there are plenty of charming little things to buy. Under the Logge Vasari (piazza Grande), an enticing selection of exquisite taste is displayed by some of the region's most important antiquaries, including Bottegantica. We succumbed to temptation in the cloister of Petrarch's house (via dei Pileati) where the jewellers assemble, and on corso Italia Alessandra Tizzoni had one fewer of her fine kilims to carry home.

chapels and shrines during the 1500s, thanks to Arezzo's merchant class. By the 19th century, it was being used as a military barracks. Happily, however, *The Legend of the True Cross*, Piero della Francesca's magnum opus, survived in the Bacci Chapel, and was unveiled in an opening ceremony in 2000 after a decade-long restoration. Considered to be one of the most important fresco cycles ever produced, it was begun in 1453, the year Constantinople fell to the Ottoman Turks, and portrays the fear this induced in the Christian world. A separate ticket (€6, plus €2 booking fee, 0575 302001, www.pierodellafrancescoticketoffice.it) gains you an audio guide and access to the chapels (it's best to book in advance in high season), but note that some of the frescoes are too high to be appreciated by the naked eye: take a pair of binoculars, and be prepared for some neck-craning. *Photo p281.*

FREE Santa Maria delle Grazie

Via Santa Maria (0575 323140, www.abd.it/santa maria). **Open** 9am-7pm daily. **Admission** free.
On the site of an ancient sacred spring, the Fonte Tecta, as the religious complex built around Santa Maria delle Grazie is known, houses the Renaissance's first porticoed courtyard. Started in 1428, the religious buildings were imposed by San Bernardino of Siena on the recalcitrant Aretini, who proceeded to march from San Francesco, brandishing a wooden cross, to destroy the spring site, replacing it with a *Madonna della Misericordia* by local artist Parri di Spinello. The enlightened Antonio da Maiano, one of the Renaissance's foremost architects and the man who created the *loggia*, reconciled the church's late Gothic, essentially medieval design with the then-emergent classical style.

Museums

Casa Museo Ivan Bruschi

Corso Italia 14 (0575 354126, www.fondazione bruschi.it). **Open** *Summer* 10am-6pm Tue-Sun. *Winter* 10am-1pm, 2-6pm Tue-Sun. **Admission** €4. **No credit cards.**
Located opposite the Pieve (*see p281*), this was the home of the founder of the Arezzo antiques fair. Today, it's full of antiquarian delights, with archaeological pieces, Egyptian artefacts, musical instruments, books, stamps and more. There are tours every hour, the only way to ensure access.

Casa Vasari

Via XX Settembre 55 (0575 409040). **Open** 9am-7pm Mon, Wed-Sun; 9am-1pm Sun. **Admission** €2. **No credit cards.**
Medici favourite Giorgio Vasari bought and decorated this house in extravagant style before taking up an important post in Florence in 1564. Today, the museum houses the Archivio e Museo Vasariano and proudly exhibits a number of Vasari frescoes and other late Mannerist paintings.

Museo Archeologico Mecenate

Via Margaritone 10 (0575 20882). **Open** 8.30am-7.30pm daily. **Admission** €4. **No credit cards.**
This estimable collection of Etruscan and Roman artefacts is located just beside the Roman amphitheatre (*see below*). The Etruscan bronze votive figurines and jewellery are particularly splendid, as is the Attic bowl decorated by Euphronios (AD 500-10) and the coralline pottery.

Museo d'Arte Medioevale e Moderna

Via San Lorentino 8 (0575 409050). **Open** 8.30am-7.30pm Tue-Sun. **Admission** €4. **No credit cards.**
Once you realise that *moderna* does not mean 'contemporary', this museum reveals itself to be an interesting, if uneven, collection of sculpture and painting from the Middle Ages to the 19th century. The Baroque vestibule on the first floor is dominated by Vasari's *Wedding Feast of Ahasuerus and Esther* (1548); past it are rooms containing one of Italy's finest collections of 13th- to 17th-century glazed ceramics from the della Robbia school. Among the later works are pieces belonging to the Macchiaioli school (the name that has been given to the Tuscan Impressionists). The museum hosted a hugely successful Piero show in 2007.

Landmarks

FREE Anfiteatro Romano

Accessible from via Margaritone or via Crispi (0575 20882). **Open** 8.30am-7.30pm daily. **Admission** free.
In the second century, this amphitheatre drew crowds of up to 10,000 people, but its travertine and sandstone blocks were plundered by Cosimo I for the Fortezza Medicea (*see below*) in 1531. You can still make out its elliptical shape and stage, plus parts of what were probably the stands.

FREE Fortezza Medicea

No phone. **Open** *Summer* 7am-8pm daily. *Winter* 7.30am-6pm daily. **Admission** free.
When the Medici finally decided to turn Arezzo into a duchy in 1531, they set about improving the city's defences, and the introduction of cannons prompted them to embark on another (the eighth) stint of wall building. The perimeter is visible in sections around the city and dominated by the architecturally revolutionary Fortezza Medicea (1538-60). Its pentagonal form was designed by Antonio da Sangallo the Elder and required the razing of towers, alleys and medieval *palazzi* in the hills of San Donato.

★ FREE Piazza Grande

A bonanza of architectural irregularity, thanks to its growth from peripheral food market to political heart of the city. The jumble of styles includes the arcaded, rounded back of the Romanesque Pieve di Santa Maria at the square's lowest point, the

TUSCANY

TUSCANY

INSIDE TRACK ON YOUR BIKE

When you tire of looking at Pieros and peeking in churches, hire a bike and hop on the **Sentiero della Bonifica** (www.sentierodellabonifica.it), a new cycling and pedestrian path running along the Maestro della Chiana canal, which joins the Arezzo to Chiusi. The whole track is 66 kilometres (41 miles), but there are plenty of arresting rest stops.

Baroque Palazzo del Tribunale and, next to it, Palazzo della Fraternità dei Laici, designed mostly by Bernardo Rossellino. Vasari also had a hand in the piazza Grande: his is the typically arcaded Palazzo delle Logge, which presides over the assortment of medieval homes around the rest of the square. Arezzo holds its main biannual historic event, the Giostra del Saracino (*see p178*), in this main square.

Parks & gardens

Il Prato

Arezzo's only park – located between the Duomo and the Fortezza Medicea – has views over the town and nearby countryside. Locals flock to La Casina del Prato (*see p286*) on summer nights.

SHOPPING

As you climb corso Italia, mainstream shops give way to a proliferation of antiques vendors around piazza Grande. On Saturdays, a general market sells clothes, food, flowers and household goods, but on the first Sunday of the month (as well as the day before) the city centre is taken over by a huge and important antiques fair (*see p282* **Market Force**). The APT (*see p286*) has a handy Italian-English glossary and a map to guide you around the place.

There are more than 1,600 gold factories in Arezzo Province, so it's surprising there aren't more outlets in the town itself. Look along corso Italia.

★ Al Canto Dei Bacci

Corso Italia 65 (0575 355804).
Open 8am-1.30pm, 3.30-8pm Mon-Sat.
A sweet deli stuffed with every kind of Tuscan delicacy you can think of, including pleny of cold meats and local cheese, plus a handy *rosticceria* for takeaway dishes and a good selection of wines.

Boutique del Pane

Via Garibaldi 74 (0575 354992). **Open** 7.30am-1pm, 5.30-8pm Mon-Sat. **No credit cards**.
A wide selection of breads and baked goods.

Busatti

Corso Italia 48 (0575 355295, www.busatti.com).
Open *Winter* 3.30-7.30pm Mon; 9am-1pm, 3.30-7.30pm Tue-Sun. *Summer* 9am-1pm, 3.30-7.30pm Mon-Fri, Sun; 9am-1pm Sat.
Upholstery fabrics and household linens.

Macelleria-Gastronomia Aligi Barelli

Via della Chimera 22b (0575 357754, www. macellerialigibarelli.it). **Open** *Winter* 8am-1pm, 4-7pm Mon, Tue, Thur-Sat; 8am-1pm Wed. *Summer* 8am-1pm, 4-7pm Mon-Fri; 8am-1pm Sat. Closed 3wks Aug.
This renowned *macelleria* (butcher) has salamis from the Casentino and a range of ready-made dishes largely based around, you guessed it, meat.

Nero

Via de' Redi 7 (0575 1824461, www.nero-design.it). **Open** 10am-1pm, 4-8pm Tue-Sat, 1st Sun of mth.
Nero displays 20th-century design at its best in beautifully packaged skincare and perfumes, original jewellery, artwork, prints and elegant homeware.
▶ *Round the corner at 27 piazza San Francesco, a vintage store sells homeware from the 1950s to 1980s (0575 1822484).*

Pasticceria de' Cenci

Via de' Cenci 17 (0575 23102). **Open** 9am-1pm, 4-8pm Tue-Sat; 9am-1pm Sun. Closed 2wks Aug.
No credit cards.
Pasticceria de' Cenci is full of elegant delights like *bigné al limone* (lemon cream puff) or fluffy *budini di riso*.

Sugar

19, 43 & 45 corso Italia (0575 354631, www. sugar.it). **Open** 3.30-8pm Mon; 9am-1pm, 3.30-8pm Tue-Sat.
If you're suddenly invited to a swanky do and simply must buy some new designer gear, Sugar will sort you out. With about six stores strung like elegant pearls along the top end of corso Italia, you'll be well catered for if you're after the latest from Burberry, Prada, Balenciaga, Gucci, Lanvin or Paul Smith. No.19 is the excellent menswear store.

WHERE TO EAT & DRINK

Restaurants

Among Arezzo's favoured pasta dishes are *funghi porcini* (ceps) and *tartufo nero* (black truffle); local Chianina steak crops up on many a menu. Lunch is a serious business here – most shops and many sights shut from 1pm to 3.30pm. If you're after an *aperitivo* in the best people-watching spot in town, Vita Bella, Caffe dei Constanti or Terra di Piero on Piazza San Francesco are all good bets.

Il Cantuccio
Via Madonna del Prato 76 (0575 26830, www.il-cantuccio.it). **Open** noon-2.30pm, 7.30-10.30pm Mon, Tue, Thur-Sun. **Average** €25.
The vaulted cellar here is arguably the city's most rustic. Own-made pasta dishes include *tortelloni alla Casentinese* (with a potato filling).

Gastronomia Il Cervo
Via Cavour 38-40 (0575 20872). **Open** 7.30am-9pm Tue-Sun. Meals served 11am-3pm, 5-9pm Tue-Sun. **Average** €25-€30.
This deli prepares a whole range of goodies that you can eat at tables upstairs. Ideal for a light meal.

★ Le Chiavi d'Oro
Piazza San Francesco 7 (0575 403313, www. ristorantelechiaviodoro.it). **Open** noon-2.15pm, 7.45-10pm Mon-Sat. **Average** €30.

Pasticceria de' Cenci.

Lined with beautiful wood panelling of different hues and with a modern aesthetic that's warm and inviting, the Golden Keys looks a charmer – and it doesn't disappoint. The food is modern Tuscan, so expect the likes of rabbit, Chianina beef tartare, *baccalà*, and a small but appealing range of pastas including *paccheri* and *cappelletti*.

Miseria e Nobiltà
Via Piaggia di San Bartolomeo 2 (0575 21245, http://arezzo.miseriaenobilta.blog spot.com). **Open** 7-11.30pm Tue-Sun. **Average** €30.
A universe of culinary creativity housed in a medieval vault. The meats, pastas and fish are all highly recommended.

Ristorante La Curia
Via Pescaia 6 (0575 333007, www.ristorantela curia.it). **Open** 12.30-3pm, 7.30-11pm Mon, Tue, Thur-Sun. **Average** €25.
Grab one of the handful of tables ranged around the preposterously pretty fountain in the bottom corner of piazza Grande if you can; if you can't, the interior of this excellent restaurant is also sweet. Wherever you sit, you'll enjoy a very good meal of keenly priced modern Tuscan dishes – a three-course menu of the day with coffee is just €25.

Sbarbacipolle
Via Garibaldi 120 (0575 299154). **Open** 7.30am-8pm Mon-Sat. Closed 3wks Aug. **Average** €12. **No credit cards**.
A colourful corner deli with a good choice of *panini* and cold dishes. No surprise that it's immensely popular with the locals.

Trattoria Il Saraceno
Via Mazzini 6a (0575 27644, www.ilsaraceno. com). **Open** noon-3pm, 7-10.30pm Mon, Tue, Thur-Sun. Closed 2wks Jan. **Average** €25.
Il Saraceno does decent, reliable food, including lamb with rosemary, own-made pasta dishes and some wood-oven pizzas.

I Tre Bicchieri
Piazzetta Sopra i Ponti 3-5 (0575 26557, www.ristoranteitrebicchieri.com). **Open** 12.30-2pm, 7.45-10pm Mon, Tue, Thur-Sun. **Average** €45.
In an inner courtyard behind corso Italia, this excellent restaurant is run by two brothers who opted out of the gold business to indulge their passion for innovative cuisine. There's also a great wine list.

Bars, enoteche & gelaterie

Skip dessert and do what the locals do: work off your supper with a *passeggiata* on corso Italia, stopping for ice-cream at Gelateria de' Cenci (no.95) or, opposite it, Cremi (no.100).

TUSCANY

Canto de' Bacci
Corso Italia 65 (0575 355804). **Open** 8am-2pm,
3-8pm Mon-Sat. *Winter* also 1st Sun of mth.
A good selection of wines (some quite unusual), plus
other products of local gastronomy.

La Casina del Prato
Via Palagi 1, Il Prato park (0575 299757). **Open**
Summer 10am-1am daily. *Winter* 10am-1am Mon,
Wed-Sun. Closed Dec. **No credit cards.**
An open-air summer hotspot overflowing with a hip
crowd. Some snacks are available.

Enoteca La Torre di Gnicche
*Piaggia San Martino 8 (0575 352035, www.
latorredignicche.it).* **Open** noon-3pm, 6pm-1am
Mon, Tue, Thur-Sun. Closed 2wks Jan.
A tastefully decorated bar with a superb selection
of local wines. The hot food is also worth a try.

Fiaschetteria de' Redi
Via de' Redi 10 (0575 355012). **Open** noon-3pm,
7.30-11.30pm Tue-Sun.
A cosy bustling wine bar just off corso Italia, with
a good wine selection. *Osteria*-style food is served.

★ La Formaggeria
Via de' Redi 16 (0575 403583). **Open** Mon, Tue,
Wed morning, Thur-Sat.
This lovely *enoteca* does a fine line in Tuscan
dishes – among them *spezzato di Chianina* beef,
quail with foie gras and hearty bean stews – alongside a terrific range of cheese, *salumi* and wines. If
you eat in, you'll be doing so in a charming space
staffed by very helpful staff who, judging by Amalia
Rodriguez playing on our visit, have a good ear too.

Il Gelato
Via de' Cenci 24 (0575 300069). **Open** noon-
3pm, 7.30-10.30pm Mon-Sat, 1st Sun of mth.
An unassuming *gelateria* with great-tasting ice-
cream. Try *pinolata* (with pine nuts) or *arancello al
liquore* (liqueur orange).

WHERE TO STAY

★ La Corte del Re
*Via Borgunto 5 (0575 401603/348 6959100
mobile, www.lacortedelre.com).* **Rooms** 9
apartments. **Rates** €640-€1,000/wk.
Nine fully equipped mini-apartments just a stone's
throw from piazza Grande. The Luca Signorelli suite
has great views over the piazza.

La Foresteria
*Via Bicchieraia 32 (0575 370474, www.foresteria
sanpierpiccolo.it).* **Rooms** 12. **Rates** €55-€75.
No credit cards. Closed 2wks Dec.
A dozen simple rooms in a former 14th-century convent. Many of the rooms are frescoed and, although
simple, are stylishly furnished. A bargain.

Hotel Patio
Via Cavour 23 (0575 401962, www.hotelpatio.it).
Rooms 10. **Rates** €165-€360.
A delightful small hotel featuring comfortable rooms
designed with real flair. Original and friendly.

I Portici
*Via Roma 18 (0575 403132, www.hoteliportici.
com).* **Rooms** 8. **Rates** €155-€360.
Once a private house, I Portici is now a small upmarket hotel run by the scions of the original owners.

RESOURCES

Hospital
Ospedale San Donato *Viale Alcide de Gasperi
17 (0575 255003).*

Internet
Phone Centre *Piazza Guido Monaco 8b (0575
371245).* **Open** 9am-1pm, 3-8.30pm Mon-Fri;
9am-1pm Sat. Closed 2wks Aug.

Police
Via Filippo Lippi (0575 400602).

Tourist information
Azienda di Promozione Turistica (APT)
*Piazza della Repubblica 28 (0575 377678,
www.apt.arezzo.it).* **Open** 9am-1.30pm Mon-Fri.

GETTING THERE & AROUND

By bus
Buses from Florence are irregular. **LFI** (La Ferrovia
Italiana, 800 115605 information, www.lfi.it) has
direct buses to Siena (90mins) and Cortona (1hr).
SITA (for Sansepolcro; 0575 74361, 800 001311
information, www.sitabus.it) also covers the region.
The bus terminal is opposite the train station.
For local routes, call ATAM Point (0575 382651).

By car
Arezzo is off the A1 (Florence–Rome) *autostrada*.
Journey time from Florence is an hour. The SS73
links to Siena to the west (about 1hr) and
Sansepolcro to the north (30mins). Parking can
be difficult and expensive in Arezzo. The APT (*see
above*) has a list of free spots. The new car park on
the north side is the best. For car hire, you could
try Avis (piazza della Repubblica 1, 0575 354232)
or Hertz (via Calamandrei 97d, 0575 27577).

By taxi
Radio Taxi (0575 382626, www.taxiarezzo.net).

By train
Intercity and **InterRegionale** (892021, www.
trenitalia.it) trains link Arezzo with Florence
(50-60mins) and Rome (90mins). The train
station is located at piazza della Repubblica.

Arezzo Province

Tuscan hill towns, industry and tranquil monastic retreats.

The province of Arezzo spreads itself over several wide, fertile valleys hemmed in by the Apennines to the east. From busy tourist towns to centuries-old monastic retreats, the valleys offer diverse pleasures for the enquiring traveller. Dawdling through tranquil Tuscan hill towns, you'll chance upon opportunities to indulge in truffles, *porcini* mushrooms, local salami and the delicious feasts created from the impoverished peasant culture of times gone by; other towns give you the chance to snap up designer bargains at factory outlets or indulge in traditional linens and woollens.

Between Florence and Arezzo lies the **Valdarno**. Industry predominates, but to the north, the imposing Pratomagno Apennine range shelters early Romanesque churches that speak of quiet and reflection. By contrast, nature prevails in the **Casentino** area to the north-east of Arezzo. The steep slopes are clad with tall forests, creating the sort of isolation sought by hermits and monks, who chose this area for their sanctuaries. In the foothills, traditional wood and stonework has survived, as has the production of the thick, rough, hard-wearing Casentino cloth. The **Valtiberina**, Tuscany's easternmost fringe, should be more accessible by 2012, the scheduled completion date for the *Due Mari* ('two seas') state road. It's a lovely area, whose name derives from the Tiber, which flows down from the Apennine peaks past the town of Sansepolcro.

Finally, in the south, is the **Valdichiana**, between the Appenines and the hills of Chianti. Its name today is synonymous with Chianina beef – large, greyish, white-horned creatures, raised organically. To the west of Valdichiana are outposts such as Monte San Savino and Lucignano, while the eastern ridge is dominated by Foiano della Chiana, Castelfiorentino and the lovely sandstone town of Cortona.

Valdarno

LORO CIUFFENNA & CASTELFRANCO DI SOPRA

The ancient **Setteponti** ('seven bridges') pilgrim route along the Pratomagno foothills crosses the Arno's tributaries amid olive and chestnut groves. It's much less direct than the *autostrada*, but provides access to historic towns with artistic legacies. (If you're more intent on bagging a few designer bargains at the outlet stores around the industrial towns of Pontassieve, Incisa, San Giovanni Valdarno and Montevarchi, you'll need to take the S69, often referred to as the 'Aretino'.) From Arezzo, take the road north in the direction of Bibbiena, then take a left turn for **Quarata**, and on to **ponte a Buriano**, a 13th-century bridge – the Arno's oldest. Miraculously surviving the last war, it's said to be the bridge that's just visible over the left shoulder of Leonardo's *Mona Lisa*; a small visitor centre nearby details its history. The area is notable for its wetlands and provides excellent walking and cycling trails.

Continue through Castiglion Fibocchi to **Loro Ciuffenna**, set on the edge of a gorge over the roaring Ciuffenna torrent, once used to power flour mills. Loro grew up around an ancient *borgo* (hamlet) and has its own ponte Vecchio. Just before Loro, take a right turn to see the stark and very simple Romanesque church of **San Pietro a Gropina**, dating from the ninth century.

Here the Setteponti rises over a heavily eroded landscape known as **Le Balze**, made up of ravines and pinnacles of barren earth shaped over millions of years; the shapes and forms are said to have inspired Leonardo in his painting. Above is **Castelfranco di Sopra**, founded as a Florentine military outpost in the late 13th century. Just outside it is the **Badia di San Salvatore a Soffena**, a 12th-century abbey with a bright interior sporting an *Annunciation* and other pastel-coloured frescoes.

Where to stay & eat

Relais Villa Belpoggio (via Setteponti
Ponente 40a, Loro Ciuffenna, 055 9694411,
www.villabelpoggio.it, €130-€220) is a
pleasant country house-cum-boutique
hotel with two apartments.

Trattoria del Pescatore (ponte a Buriano
19b, near Quarata, 0575 364096) specialises in
fresh fish, while **Il Canto del Maggio** (055
9705147, www.cantodelmaggio.com, €35, closed
Mon, 1wk Mar, 1wk Sept) in the centre of the
medieval village of Penna Alta (known as 'La
Penna'), near Loro Ciuffena, is a high-quality
osteria-enoteca, with a beautiful garden and
pleasant apartments for hire.

Casentino
POPPI, BIBBIENA
& PIEVE A SOCANA

A delightful small town, **Poppi** slopes down
through arcaded streets from the 13th-century
Castello dei Conti Guidi (piazza Repubblica
1, 0575 520516, www.buonconte.com, closed
Mon-Wed Oct-Mar, admission €5) high above
the valley. The castle is worth visiting, not only
for its frescoed rooms, but also for the fabulous
view of the Casentino. Dante is said to have
stayed here, and there's a statue of him outside.

Heading out of Poppi, the road leading to
Camaldoli takes you to the small **Parco Zoo
della Fauna Europa** (via del Parco 16, 0575
504541, www.parcozoopoppi.it, admission €7),
home to European species including wolves,
lynx, deer and birds of prey; the ample
parkland has designated picnic spots, and
there's an on-site restaurant (fixed menu €16).
On the S70 heading towards Pratovecchio,
meanwhile, you'll see signs for the **Pieve
di San Pietro a Romena**, a 12th-century
baptismal church. Inside there are sculpted
stone capitals and some remarkable pieces
of art by the local priest; you can call him if
it's closed (0575 58725, 9am-noon, 3-7pm).

In the opposite direction, south of Poppi, lies
Bibbiena, a gentle walled town still largely
undiscovered by tourists and the capital of the
Casentino. In the historic centre are some fine
old *palazzi* to admire, including the elegant
Renaissance **Palazzo Dovizi**, while in
the church of **San Lorenzo** you'll find a
magnificent della Robbia glazed terracotta
Adoration of the Shepherds. A food market
takes place on Thursday mornings and every
fourth Saturday of the month.

Around 25 kilometres (18 miles) south of
Bibbiena, west of the main Bibbiena–Arezzo
road, lies **Pieve a Socana**. The town embodies

2,600 years of history and the votive aspirations
of three civilisations: Etruscan, Roman and
Christian. Excavation has brought to light a
splendid sacrificial altar and the staircase
of a temple dating back to the Etruscan period
as well as a cylindrical wall and pilaster strips
of Roman origin. The Christians subsequently
built three separate churches in addition to the
Etruscan temple.

Where to stay & eat

In Poppi, a good bet for a bed is homely
Albergo Casentino (piazza della Repubblica
6, 0575 529090, www.albergocasentino.it, €70),
which has its own little enclosed garden and
a restaurant (closed Wed, average €24).
Otherwise, in the country just beyond Bibbiena
you'll find the **Agricola Casentinese** (località
Casanova 63, 0575 594806, www.lacollinadelle
stelle.it, €90-€200), offering comfortable rooms
and an evening meal in the middle of a huge
working farm, where you can also ride and trek.

It's not hard to find decent cuisine in these
parts, but many restaurants close for the month
of November. In Poppi, head for the **Antica
Cantina** (via Lapucci 2, 0575 529844,
www.anticacantina.com, closed Mon & in
winter Tue, average €40), housed in a 12th-
century cellar, for its excellent selection of
wine. In Bibbiena, **Il Tirabusciò** (via Borghi
73, entrance on via Rosa Scoti, 0575 595474,
www.tirabuscio.it, €35 average, closed Tue
& lunch Mon) has friendly service, a range
of interesting dishes and a list of fine wines
to complement them.

CAMALDOLI & LA VERNA

In the hills north-east of Poppi lies the extremely
beautiful **Foreste Casentinesi National
Park** (www.parcoforestecasentinesi.it), a
protected area of ancient woodland, streams
and nature reserves home to deer, wild boar,
wolves and a plethora of birdlife. Hiking and
mountain bike trails weave through the park,
and it's a popular place for horse riding, or
cross-country skiing in winter. The visitor
centre at **Badia Prataglia** (via Nazionale
14a, 0575 559477, www.parks.it, closed Mon-
Fri in winter), in the midst of the park, is a
good source of information and advice.

Close to Badia Prataglia lie the monastery
and hermitage of **Camaldoli**. The latter was
founded in 1012 by St Romuald. Surrounded by
fir trees, the monks' individual cells are visible
only through a gate, though Romualdo's
original cell, with its wooden panelling and cot,
is open to visitors. Three kilometres (two miles)
downhill is the 16th-century monastery that
links the Camaldolite monks to the outside

world. Its church contains some early Vasaris, including a *Madonna and Child* and a *Nativity*. The young artist took refuge here from 1537 to 1539, following the murder of his patron, Alessandro de' Medici.

A little further south, close to the town of Chiusi, an even more important monastic complex dominates the surrounding landscape from a rocky outcrop at 1,129 metres (3,670 feet). In 1214, St Francis's vagabondage brought him to this isolated peak, where he and some followers were inspired to build cells for themselves. Ten years later, Italy's patron saint received the stigmata here and, ever since, **La Verna** has been an important stop on the Franciscan trail. The basilica contains a reliquary chapel with the saint's personal effects. The sanctuary also contains a great number of Andrea Della Robbia's glazed terracottas. This hugely impressive religious compound of interconnected chapels, churches, corridors and cloisters attracts large numbers of visitors, but on a quiet weekday the sunset over the Casentino inspires meditative silence.

Where to stay & eat

Ristorante Camaldoli (via Camaldoli, 0575 556091, www.albergoristorantecamaldoli.it, closed Tue in winter, average €30, doubles €65) has a roaring fire inside or cooling trees outside. Try *acquacotta* (soup with toasted bread) or *ravioli all'Ortica* (ricotta and nettle ravioli).

Valtiberina
SANSEPOLCRO

The Valtiberina's largest town, Sansepolcro gives meaning to the expression 'quality of life'; it's both tranquil and culturally alive, off the

beaten track yet welcoming to visitors. Sansepolcro is best known as the birthplace of the early Renaissance maestro of perspective and proportion, Piero della Francesca (*see p290*), some of whose works are prominently displayed in the town's **Museo Civico** (via Aggiunti 65, 0575 732218, www.museocivico sansepolcro.it, admission €6). Sansepolcro is the centre of the so-called 'Piero Trail' (with Arezzo, Monterchi and Urbino) where the cognoscenti can view his work in situ. Works include the important *Madonna della Misericordia* (c1445), in which Piero overturns the laws of proportion by depicting an all-encompassing, monumental Madonna dwarfing the faithful and protecting them with her mantle. The artist can't resist placing himself among the Virgin's followers, facing us from the Madonna's left. Another self-portrait appears in *The Resurrection* (c1460), where a muscular Christ steps from his tomb, awakening the somnolent soldiers at his feet. Among them, to the left, is Piero. Aldous Huxley referred to the work as 'the greatest painting in the world' – a tag that helped save Sansepolcro from bombing in World War II.

The 14th-century Romanesque **Duomo** contains on its left altar an imposing wooden crucifix known as the *Volto Santo* (Holy Face), thought to have been brought to Sansepolcro from the Orient during the crusades, and bearing a strong similarity to its better-known equivalent in Lucca's Duomo di San Martino (*see p270*).

Local events include a torch-lit procession on Good Friday and a crossbow tournament, the Palio della Balestra, on the second Sunday in September – the culmination of a festive medieval week. The place is also a food-lover's paradise: weekly food markets take place every Tuesday and Saturday, plus there's a special gourmet market held on every third Saturday of the month.

TUSCANY

La Verna.

Where to stay, eat & drink

Albergo Fiorentino (via L Pacioli 56, 0575 740350, www.albergofiorentino.com, €70) on the corner of via XX Settembre, offers a very acceptable accommodation option, while the **Ristorante da Ventura** (via Aggiunti 30, 0575 742560, www.albergodaventura.it, closed dinner Sun, all Mon, average €32) is the best of the classics. For sampling fine wine together with good food, **Enoteca Guidi** (via L Pacioli 44, 0575 741086, closed Wed, Sat, lunch Sun, average €23, €90 double) is the place. The popular **Osteria in Aboca**, past Sansepolcro, on the road to Rimini (Fraz Aboca 11, 0575 749125, www.losteriainaboca.it, closed Mon, average €25) is a good bet.

MONTERCHI

This tiny hilltop village on the road between Arezzo and Città di Castello is synonymous with Piero della Francesca's *Madonna del Parto*, the famous painting of a pregnant Madonna, and the prized possession of the eponymous **Museo Madonna del Parto** (via Reglia 1, 0575 70713, admission €3.50). Two angels lightly drawing back a canopy reveal the exquisite and melancholy young Madonna – the only one of its kind in Renaissance art.

Where to stay & eat

Driving three minutes east towards Città di Castello is restaurant and pizzeria **La Pieve Vecchia** (0575 709053, www.lapievevecchia. com, set lunch €12, evening €30). The large complex also has three en suite rooms in a newly restored barn.

ANGHIARI

Perched on a hill overlooking the Valtiberina and Sansepolcro, Anghiari's dominant position

Piero della Francesca

It's all in the detail.

It took 500 years for Piero della Francesca to receive the acclaim he deserved, but since 1992, the 500th anniversary of his death (in Sansepolcro on 12 October 1492), the swell in interest in his art has been undeniable. If it's odd to mark his death, it's possibly because it's impossible to mark his birth: born in around 1420, what little is known of the artist's early and private life is sketchy at best. He shied away from the limelight and the big city, going to Florence in 1439 for training but soon returning to his native Sansepolcro, his stylistic preference lying with more peripheral noble courts such as the Este in Ferrara and the Montefeltro in Urbino and, of course, Arezzo.

He is perhaps best known for the precision and quasi-maniacal obsession with detail in every aspect of his work. Perspective, proportion, light and shade, colour and shape: according to Piero, all needed to be portrayed following strict and unchanging mathematical and geometric laws. These in turn derived – as he would theorise in two treatises written in his later life – from a superior rational order that regulates a universal cosmic harmony. Though his approach was highly Humanist and rationalist, his subject matter remained almost exclusively sacred, with only the odd commissioned portrait of a patron. He was strongly influenced by Flemish and Northern European art, as well as by classicism in architectural design; in turn, he had a profound influence on 20th-century Cubist and metaphysical painters such as Cézanne, Seurat and De Chirico. His reclusive, low-key lifestyle was refreshing during a period crammed with exhibitionists and polemicists, and his legacy one of lasting innovation.

SEE THE WORK

Arezzo
Legend of the True Cross (1455-56), church of San Francesco; *Santa Maria Maddalena* (1460), Duomo. *See p281.*

Florence
Portraits of Battista Sforza and Federico da Montefeltro (1465-72) and Triumphs of Federico da Montefeltro and Battista Sforza (1465-75), Uffizi. *See p64.*

Monterchi
Madonna del Parto (1455-60), Museo Madonna del Parto. *See above.*

Sansepolcro
Madonna della Misericordia (1445-60) and *Resurrection* (1460), both in Museo Civico. *See p189.*

TUSCANY

and impressive walls made it a stronghold from which Florence controlled the far east of Tuscany, following victory over the Milanese Visconti family in the Battle of Anghiari in 1440. The battle is commemorated by Leonardo da Vinci in his famously unfinished and long-lost work, thought by some to be hidden behind a Vasari fresco in Florence's Palazzo Vecchio. For more information, *see p55* **Hiddens Depths**.

Today, with its maze of vaulted alleys and flower-strewn doorways, the town is a peaceful, well-preserved town, renowned for wood-based crafts and antique furniture restoration. It hosts the annual Valtiberina crafts market in late April and an antiques fair on the third Sunday of every other month. The **Museo Statale di Palazzo Taglieschi** (piazza Mameli 16, 0575 788001, closed Mon, admission €2) displays various local artefacts, a polychrome terracotta by della Robbia and a singularly striking wooden sculpture of the Madonna by Jacopo della Quercia.

Anghiari's other major traditional and commercial draw is its woven and naturally dyed textiles, exemplified by the **Busatti** store-cum-factory (via Mazzini 14, 0575 788013, www.busatti.com, closed Mon morning & Sun). Its deafening shuttle looms, some of them almost a century old, continue to produce a range of linens from natural fibres.

Where to eat

One of the great treats of the valley is **Da Alighiero** (via Garibaldi 8, 0575 788040, www.daalighiero.it, closed Tue, average €35), where regional *porcini* mushrooms often feature.

Valdichiana
MONTE SAN SAVINO

Circular and enclosed, Monte San Savino is a prominent provincial town. Its Renaissance heyday, however, was brief, coinciding with the commercial patronage and religious power exercised by the Di Monte family in the 15th and 16th centuries. The main architectural attractions, both bearing the family's imprint, face each other along corso Sangallo.

The quintessentially Renaissance Palazzo di Monte, now the **Palazzo Comunale**, contains an arcaded courtyard, through which you reach the hanging gardens and an open-air theatre overlooking a cypress-dotted landscape. Across from it is the **Loggia dei Mercanti**, attributed to architect and sculptor Andrea Sansovino, the town's most eminent son.

Monte San Savino is known for engraved pottery designed in delicate floral motifs, with examples on display at the **Museo del Cassero** (piazza Gamurrini, 0575 843098, free admission). The products at **Ceramiche Artistiche Lapucci** (corso Sangallo 8-10, 0575 844928, closed Sun, ring bell for entry) still reflect this tradition.

Where to stay & eat

For a pleasantly relaxed meal, try the *enoteca-osteria* **La Pecora Nera** (via Zanetti 4, Monte San Savino, 0575 844647, www.osterialapecora nera.it, closed Thur, average €32), nearby to the Porta San Giovanni. The medieval **Castello di Gargonza** (0575 847021, www.gargonza.it, €120-€170), six kilometres (3.5 miles) west of town, has rooms on a B&B basis as well as several mini-apartments with modern facilities.

LUCIGNANO

An urban time capsule still encased within its old walls, tiny Lucignano has managed to preserve its medieval character and its rather eccentric town planning. Walk round and up its spiral layout and you find yourself at the steps of the church of the **Collegiata di San Michele**. Behind it is the 13th-century church of **San Francesco**, barn-like in its simplicity and breathtaking in its humble beauty.

Inside the Palazzo Comunale, the **Museo Civico** (piazza del Tribunale 22, 0575 838001, closed Tue, admission €5) exhibits Lucignano's symbol, the *Albero di San Francesco*, a late Gothic reliquary representing a plant-like cross, along with panels by Signorelli and a Bartolo di Fredi triptych.

Where to eat

Lucignano has two good restaurants: **Il Goccino** (via G Matteotti 90, 0575 836707, www.ilgoccino.it, closed Mon in winter, average €25), which has a good wine list and space outdoors; and **La Rocca** (via G Matteotti 15-17, 0575 836775, www.osterialarocca.net, closed Tue, average €35), which serves an excellent *zuppa dei tarlati* (chicken soup with wild fennel and croutons). Paradise on a plate here is fried eggs topped with fresh truffle shavings.

FOIANO DELLA CHIANA

Foiano's buildings and steeples are largely distinguished by the warm, reddish tones of their *cotto* bricks. Its oval shape centres on piazza Cavour, dominated by Palazzo delle Logge, formerly a Medici hunting lodge. Today, it houses the **Fototeca Furio del Furia**, an engrossing display of early 20th-century photographs of rural life in Italy.

TUSCANY

Outside the walls is Foiano's other main draw, the neoclassical **Collegiata di San Martino**. It houses an Andrea della Robbia terracotta, the *Madonna of the Girdle*, and Signorelli's last work, *Coronation of the Virgin* (1523), influenced by Piero della Francesca.

CASTIGLION FIORENTINO

On the other side of the valley, the old town of Castiglion Fiorentino still sits behind its walls on a small hill at the very foot of the Apennines, while new developments have spilled downwards and on to the plain. It's still dominated by the impressive **Torre del Cassero** (0575 659457, admission €1.50). The Etruscan origins were reaffirmed by excavation works several years ago, while the early Christian building in the crypt of the Chiesa di Sant'Angelo al Cassero confirms continuous habitation of the site. The **Museo Civico Archeologico** (via del Tribunale 8, 0575 659457, admission €3, €5 with the Pinacoteca Comunale) displays a range of early artefacts and building materials. Above this is the **Pinacoteca Comunale** (via del Cassero, 0575 657466, closed Mon, admission €3, €5 with Museo Civico Archeologico), with paintings by Giotto's godson and follower, Taddeo Gaddi, and by 15th-century artist Bartolomeo della Gatta.

The main piazza (just keep walking up hill) has a splendid *loggia* by Vasari overlooking the Apennine valley. In the corner of the *loggia* is the bar **Café degli Ignoranti** (0575 680680).

Where to stay & eat

For a friendly, reasonably priced hotel in the country, go for **Villa Schiatti** (località Montecchio 131, 0575 651440, www.villa schiatti.it, €90-€120 double), which also serves a pleasant evening meal. It has a pool and plenty of room for children to scamper. If you've a bigger budget, Polvano's more upmarket **Relais San Pietro** (località Polvano 3, 0575 650100, www.polvano.com, €100-€300) is a rambling rustic beauty with pool, terrace and excellent meals at €20-€35. In the old town you can have a meat-eater's feast at **Da Muzzicone** (piazza San Francesco 7, 0575 658403, closed Tue, average €40).

CORTONA

Cortona is without doubt the signature Tuscan hill town. Since finding fame through *Under the Tuscan Sun* – Frances Mayes's idealised memoir on the good life in Tuscany, made into a film in 2003 – the town has rather predictably gained its fair share of tacky gift shops and

hordes of Mayes devotees. Yet even these elements cannot obliterate the beauty of the town or diminish its unique architectural and elemental charms: a jumble of irregular, angular buildings, windswept Etruscan city walls and layered urban development distinguishes it from central Italy's historic cities.

Its strategic position dominating the Valdichiana meant that Cortona grew into an important Etruscan outpost around the eighth century BC and then passed under Roman rule. The recently restored **Museo dell'Accademia Etrusca e della Città di Cortona** (0575 637235, www.cortonamaec.org, admission €10, €13 with Museo Diocesano, closed Mon Nov-Mar), in piazza Signorelli's Palazzo Casali, recounts the town's early history through imaginatively laid-out exhibits, including some truly magnificent Etruscan items.

Following depredation by the Goths, Cortona thrived as a free community from the 11th century. Sacked by Arezzo in 1258, it bounced back and was taken over and quickly sold by the King of Naples to Florence in 1411. Since then it has prospered, and today it's the quintessential provincial *città d'arte* with plenty going on: from concerts as part of the Umbria Jazz Festival in late July to the convivial Sagra della Bistecca feast in mid August (along with August's Tuscan Sun Festival; *see p180*).

To soak up the atmosphere of the place, head for the steps leading up to the crenellated clock tower of the heavy-set **Palazzo Comunale**, overlooking the small and uneven piazza della Repubblica – the elegant central square that's home to a restaurant, bar, *gelateria* and bespoke hat shop. Adjacent is the slightly larger piazza Signorelli, honouring Cortona's foremost son, High Renaissance artist Luca Signorelli (c1445-1523). The arcaded Teatro Signorelli sits neatly within the square, along with the stunning Museo dell'Accademia Etrusca (*see above*).

The nearby piazza del Duomo opens on to a picture-postcard view of the valley, while opposite the bland Duomo lies the **Museo Diocesano** (0575 62830, admission €5, closed Mon Nov-Mar), home to Fra Angelico's glorious *Annunciation* and impressive works by Signorelli and Pietro Lorenzetti. For more of Cortona's rewarding sights, climb steep via Berrettini towards the Fortezza Medicea. Here you'll find the 15th-century church of **San Niccolò**, with its delicate courtyard and Baroque-roofed interior containing a Signorelli altarpiece (you'll need to ring the doorbell to enter). Also worth the schlep is the **Chiesa di Santa Margherita**, a little further on, with its vivid ceilings; reach the fort above and you'll be rewarded with views to Lake Trasimeno, and a peaceful, tourist-free sense of tranquillity.

TUSCANY

Where to eat

The **Osteria del Teatro** (via Maffei 2, 0575 630556, www.osteria-del-teatro.it, closed Wed, 3wks Nov, average €35) serves very good food in an operatic setting. **Preludio** (via Guelfa 11, 0575 630104, www.ilpreludio.net, closed Mon & lunch Nov-May, average €28) serves highly individual pasta creations. **La Loggiata** (piazza Pescheria 3, 0575 630575, www.locanda nelloggiata.com, closed Wed, average €35) has a few tables with a balcony view over piazza della Repubblica. **Trattoria Dardano** (via Dardano 24, 0575 601944, www.trattoria dardano.com, closed Wed, average €25) is a locals' haunt that serves home cooking. **La Grotta** (piazzetta Baldelli 3, 0575 630271, www.trattorialagrotta.com, average €28, closed Tue, 4wks Jan-Feb, 1wk July) serves excellent own-made pasta.

Where to stay

Hotel Italia (via Ghibellina 7, 0575 630254, www.hotelitaliacortona.com, €95-€150) offers good quality and value for money, while **Hotel San Luca** (piazza Garibaldi 1, 0575 630460, www.sanlucacortona.com, €85-€120) is more generic and modern, but with spectacular views over the valley. If you're after something central and classy, consider the **Hotel San Michele** (via Guelfa 15, 0575 604348, www. hotelsanmichele.net, €109-€250). The spoil-yourself option comes in the form of the four-star **Hotel Villa Marsili** (via Cesare Battisti 13, 0575 605252, www.villamarsili. net, €120-€350), a beautifully restored 18th-century building.

Alternatively, three kilometres (two miles) from Cortona, **Relais Villa Baldelli** (località San Pietro a Cegliolo 420, 0575 612406, www. villabaldellicortona.com, €98-€300) offers nice rooms in an 18th-century residence. The luxurious **Il Falconiere** is about the same distance from town (località San Martino a Bocena, 0575 612679, www.ilfalconiere.com, €270-€590) and has its own Michelin-starred restaurant (average €65).

RESOURCES

Tourist information

Cortona

Piazza Signorelli 9 (0575 637223, www.turismo. provincia.arezzo.it). **Open** 9am-1pm, 3-6pm Mon-Fri; 9am-1pm Sat.

Sansepolcro

Via Matteotti 8 (0575 740536). **Open** 9am-1pm, 3.30-7pm daily.

GETTING THERE

By bus

LAZZI (055 9199922, www.lazzi.it) has regular buses linking Montevarchi, Terranuova Bracciolini and Loro Ciuffenna with Arezzo. Irregular **LFI** buses (0575 39881) serve Camaldoli and Chiusi Verna from Bibbiena station. They run more regular buses between Cortona (from piazzale Garibaldi) and Arezzo, which also stop in Castiglion Fiorentino. **SITA** (0575 74361, 800 001311 information, www.sitabus.it) runs buses between Arezzo and Sansepolcro (journey time 1hr) that also stop in Anghiari (45mins) and, sometimes, in Monterchi. The bus companies LAZZI, LFI and SITA are now pooled in the society **Etruria Mobilità** (0575 39881, www.etruriamobilita.it), which can provide information on all the provincial bus lines.

By car

There are several driving routes through the Valdarno, including the Florence–Rome *autostrada* (A1), the slower SR69, which runs through San Giovanni and Montevarchi and on to Arezzo, or the Setteponti route through the country. The region's main arteries are the SS70 and SR71. To explore the Valtiberina, take the SS73 out of Arezzo, heading north-east towards Sansepolcro. Monterchi, Citerna and Anghiari are signposted off this road, a few kilometres before Sansepolcro. The A1 *autostrada* passes right through the Valdichiana, with exits for Monte San Savino and Valdichiana (for Cortona, off the main SS75 to Perugia). From Arezzo, Castiglion Fiorentino and Cortona are reached via the SS71.

By train

Local trains on the Florence–Arezzo line stop at San Giovanni Valdarno and at Montevarchi (45mins from Florence, 25mins from Arezzo). Timetable information for this and all other routes is available by calling 892021 or by visiting www.trenitalia.it. A tiny train line run by **La Ferroviaria Italiana** (LFI) links Pratovecchio (journey time 1hr), Poppi (40mins) and Bibbiena (30mins) to Arezzo, with departures every hour during the day. Cortona has two train stations: Camucia-Cortona, 5km (3 miles) away, and Terontola-Cortona, 11km (7 miles) from town. Castiglion Fiorentino is on the same line. Trains from Arezzo take 15mins to Castiglion, 22mins to Camucia and 27mins to Terontola. Slow trains between Florence (journey time to Terontola 90mins) and Rome (Terontola 80mins) also pass through all three stations. A regular bus service links Cortona with its two stations. Sansepolcro is also linked to Città di Castello and Perugia on a local Umbrian train service (use www.trenitalia.it or www.fcu.it).

TUSCANY

Southern Tuscany

Escape the crowds in this relatively undiscovered corner of Italy.

Southern Tuscany looks towards the coast, enjoying a milder climate than the more inland reaches of the region. As the area lacks both the reputation and the popularity of other parts of Tuscany, development here has been slower; for most of the year, it's a delightfully low-key destination. However, the area can get crowded at Easter and in the height of summer, especially around the islands of Elba and Giglio. Grosseto is the provincial capital and no great attraction, but there are plenty of charming small towns to explore on the mainland too, to say nothing of good food

and wine, extraordinary wildlife reserves and rich Etruscan archaeological sites.

TUSCANY

Grosseto Province & the Maremma

The coastal and inland area south of Piombino, stretching down to the Tuscan border with Lazio, is known as the **Maremma**. The word probably derives from the Spanish *marisma*, or marsh, the linguistic legacy of 200 years of Spanish rule. Until they were definitively drained in the mid 20th century, these marshlands were poor and malarial, which explains why the area got off to a late start as a tourist destination. Farming in the area is still relatively small-scale and mixed. The resulting landscape creates a glorious patchwork of textures and colours. Here and there are patches of grazing land for the sheep, whose milk becomes pecorino cheese, and the long-horned, dark-eyed Maremma breed of cattle. For the Maremma's natural park, *see p298* **South Park**.

GROSSETO

The largest Tuscan town south of Siena, Grosseto has had to contend with a lot over the centuries. Though it gained city status in 1138, the surrounding area was so wretched that the population never thrived. The city was annexed by Siena in 1336, and became part of the Grand Duchy of Tuscany in 1559. Apart from fortifying their new outpost, the Medici clearly didn't feel that Grosseto had much scope, and by 1745 the population had dwindled to a mere 648.

Things didn't pick up until the Lorraine Grand Dukes began reclaiming the surrounding marshlands in the 18th and 19th centuries, before further agricultural improvements came under the Fascist regime in the 1920s and '30s. The strips of pinewood that stretch north and south along the coast are largely the product of this period. Planted to curb the encroaching sea, they also ensured that salt-water didn't permeate areas now devoted to fish farming.

Although Grosseto got a pasting in World War II, a central area, enclosed by high walls, was partially spared. Other attractions include the **Museo Archeologico** (piazza Baccarini 3, 0564 488750, closed Mon, admission €5, €2.50 reductions), with information on the local topography and the important Etruscan settlements in the area.

Where to stay & eat

In the pedestrianised part of town, the **Bastiani Grand Hotel** (piazza Gioberti 64, 0564 20047, www.hotelbastiani.com, €110-€275 double) is pleasant and slightly old-fashioned. Not far away is one of the town's best eating options: **Il Canto del Gallo** (via Mazzini 29, 0564 414589, closed Sun, average €35). Located in the Medici fortified walls, space is at a premium, but the food is good, and largely organic in origin. Otherwise, visit the neighbouring seaside hamlet of Castiglione della Pescaia, and stay and eat at the attractive **Locanda La Luna** (via del Podere 8, 0564 945854, www.locanda-laluna.it, €48-€100 double).

MASSA MARITTIMA

Massa dominates the high southern ranges of the Colline Metallifere, a rich source of the iron, copper and other minerals that contributed to its flourishing economy in the Middle Ages. The area's prosperity began to decline when it lost its status as an independent city-state, and it was taken over by Siena in 1337. Half a millennium of neglect followed the plague years of 1348-50, until a small-scale return to mining, along with the draining of the surrounding marshes, turned the tide in the middle of the 19th century. Today, Massa boasts one of the best-preserved and most uniform examples of 13th-century Tuscan town planning. The **Duomo** (via Giro del Duomo 6, 0566 902237) harmoniously blends Romanesque and Gothic details and its bare stone interior includes a baptistery, famous for its 13th-century bas-reliefs by Giroldo da Como.

The fountain – named **Le Fonti dell'Abbondanza** ('fountains of abundance') – was the hub of town life in the second half of the 13th century. Among the town's other diversions are the **Museo Civico Archeologico** in the 13th-century Palazzo del Podestà on piazza Garibaldi (0566 902289, closed Mon, admission €3, €1.50 reductions), which has an Etruscan collection and a marvellous 1330 *Maestà* by Ambrogio Lorenzetti, and the **Città Nuova** ('New Town', built in the 14th century) up via Moncini. There's a fine Sienese arch here: climb it for a few euros, or walk around the side (for free) to take in equally excellent views over the town and countryside.

Another draw is the **Balestro del Girifalco** festival on the fourth Sunday in May – the feast day of San Bernardino of Siena, who was born here. The *sbandieratori* (flag throwers) are faultless and the final contest, when teams attempt to shoot down a mechanical falcon with their crossbows, is fascinating. The town stages concerts in the square in August and a week-long photography festival in July (www.toscanafotofestival.it).

Where to stay & eat

If you fancy staying the night, opt for the three-star **Sole** (corso Libertà 43, 0566 901971, www. ilsolehotel.it, closed mid Jan-mid Feb, €85-€95).

Foodwise, good local dishes such as stewed wild boar with black olives can be had at **Enoteca Grassini** (via della Libertà 1, 0566 940149, closed Mon & 8 wks Jan-Mar, average €22). Even more atmospheric is **Da Tronca** (vicolo Porte 5, 0566 901991, closed lunch, all day Wed & mid Dec-mid Mar, average €30), a nearby *osteria* that serves distinctive regional fare. For more inventive cuisine, drive a couple of kilometres north to

Ghirlanda for **Bracali** (via di Perolla 2, 0566 902318, www.bracaliristorante.it, closed Mon, Tue & lunch Wed, Thur, average €140).

SCANSANO

The little town of Scansano dates back to the 12th century, but only came into its own in the early 1800s, when Grand Duke Leopoldo II decreed that all public offices should move here from pestilent Grosseto for the summer months.

Though local government no longer summers here, the air is still sweet and fresh when it's excessively hot on the coast. Don't be put off by the nondescript buildings outside the centre – this is a friendly town with a rural heart. People love to stop for a chat, especially on Friday mornings (market day).

Scansano is home to the Morellino di Scansano DOCG wine, a red with depth and structure that relies more on fresh fruit than muscle. In August and September, tasting events are held in the Dentro to showcase local wines, pecorino and cold cuts from the tasty local *cinta senese* pig.

Where to stay & eat

Outside Scansano, in the hamlet of Montorgiali, there's an attractive inn with a good restaurant: **La Tana dei Lupi** (via del Corso 10-16, 0564 580221, closed Thur, dinner only Fri-Sun, average €28). Another pleasant place to stay is **Agriturismo Casa Nova**, an organic farm located at Montepò (località Montepò 42, 0564 580317, www.agriturismocasanova.it, €115). The **Antico Casale di Scansano** (0564 507219, www.anticocasalediscansano.com, €100-€125), just out of town at Castagneta, offers board and lodging, plus opportunities for horse riding and spa facilities. In Scansano itself, try **Osteria Rifrullo** (via Marconi 3, 0564 507183, www.osteriailrifrullo.it, closed Sun, average €30) for local fare, just up from piazza Garibaldi. **La Cantina** (via della Botte 1, 0564 507605, closed Sun eve & Mon, average €40) has a fine cellar to accompany a thoughtful approach to Maremma cuisine. For creative cooking, try the more expensive **Pane e Tulipani** (via Diaz 3, 0564 507531) near the old hospital. Ten minutes outside town on the SP9 towards Montiano lies **Le Mandorlaie** (0564 507149, average €25), where Graziella provides good food using produce from the family farm.

ROCCALBEGNA & SANTA FIORA

A number of the towns on the slopes that embrace **Mount Amiata** (the highest mountain in Tuscany, at 1,738 metres/5,702 feet) are well worth a visit for the magnificent scenery, good hiking and excellent food. Relatively removed from Grosseto and the main highways because of the steep, winding roads leading up to them, these communities offer a glimpse of rural Tuscany as it was several decades ago.

Roccalbegna is a walled medieval town that seems to grow out of the chalky rock of Monte Labbro. A monolithic stony peak defends the back of the town, while limestone outcrops feature like giant statues in the olive groves below the walls, where the view opens up to embrace a glorious landscape. Walk through the atmospheric narrow streets, and take a look at the Ambrogio Lorenzetti triptych (1340) in the central church of **SS Pietro e Paolo**, a rare example of a painting of such importance still to be found in a parish church.

In the immediate vicinity of Raccalbegna are three WWF-protected nature reserves with mapped-out paths: the **Monte Labbro** reserve is north; **Pescinello** is just outside the town; while **Bosco di Rocconi** is due south.

While in the area, it's worth visiting **Santa Fiora**, which overlooks the source of the River Fiora; the hamlet reverberates with the sound of rushing water. The hillside town features some fine old houses and a certain grandeur deriving from its history as a stronghold of the powerful Aldobrandeschi family. The **Pieve delle Santa Fiora e Lucilla** church houses some fine glazed terracotta works by Andrea della Robbia. Visit in July/August to coincide with the **Santa Fiora in Musica** festival (www.santafiorainmusica.com).

Where to stay & eat

In Roccalbegna, **Antica Locanda La Pietra** (via XXIV Maggio 69b, 0564 989019, www. locandalapietra.it, €80-€90) has been run by the same family for six generations and offers old-fashioned rooms, home-made bread for breakfast and one of the best restaurants in the area. In Santa Fiora, a good meal can be had at **Il Barilotto** (via Carolina 24, 0564 977089, www.ristoranteilbarilotto.it, closed Wed in winter & 2 wks June, €20).

SATURNIA, MONTEMERANO & MANCIANO

According to legend, Saturn once sent down a thunderbolt that split open the earth, in order to punish those who thought only of war. Steamy water poured forth from the gash; earthlings found solace in it and became calm. That was a while ago; these days, the road to **Saturnia** is well worn by tourists seeking regeneration in the small, sulphurous tributary of the Albenga. The **Hotel Terme** (*see below*) offers mud treatments and massages, as well as its own mineral-rich

pool, while the **Terme di Saturnia** (0564 600111, www.termedisaturnia.it, closed 2 wks mid Jan, €360-€3,000) has a park full of different pools, and cascades to give you a good pummelling. For a cheaper choice, head down the road and bathe for free in the pretty **Cascate del Gorello** falls and pools, where the rocks are stained green. It can get crowded, but on a warm, clear and quiet night, it's magical.

Six kilometres (four miles) away sits **Montemerano**, a well-preserved hillside town with a medieval castle. Beyond is **Manciano**, the main municipality. Though its outskirts have not been enhanced by modern buildings, the old centre is pleasant and quite lively.

Where to stay & eat

Saturnia's **Hotel Terme** (0564 600111, www. termedisaturnia.it, €360) is pretty pricey, but fitted out with a gym, a golf driving range and tennis courts to go with the mineral-rich pool. Much more reasonable is the family-run **Villa Clodia** (via Italia 43, 0564 601212, www. hotelvillaclodia.com, €110-€120), in a country house two kilometres (1.2 miles) from the spa.

For lunch or dinner, Saturnia's **Bacco e Cerere** (via Mazzini 4, 0564 601235, open dinner only, average €50) is great for meat. If you've cash to splash, make for Montemerano and the renowned **Da Caino** (via Canonica 4, 0564 602817, www.dacaino.it, closed all day Wed, lunch Thur & mid Jan-mid Feb, average €150), which also has three guestrooms. Otherwise, there's **Passaparola nell'Antico Frantoio** (via delle Mura 21, 0564 602835, closed Thur, 2wks July & Feb, average €25). In Manciano, **Da Paolino** (via Marsala 41, 0564 629388, closed Mon, average €30) is a good, traditional *trattoria* with an interesting wine list and very reasonable prices.

PITIGLIANO

Perched high on a rocky outcrop, Pitigliano is an awesome sight from afar, appearing to grow from the sheer golden tuff limestone cliffs that fall away on all sides. The dramatic drop into the valley below is accentuated by an immense aqueduct, built in 1545, that connects the lower and upper parts of town. The 1527 church of **Madonna delle Grazie**, on an opposite hill as you approach, provides a vantage point over the town and countryside. During the Middle Ages, Pitigliano was one of the foremost centres of power of the Aldobrandeschi family, who were succeeded by the Orsinis in the 14th century. Both coats of arms are on display in the Orsini family's palace courtyard on piazza Orsini.

The Jewish community that was attracted here by increasing Medici tolerance in the 16th

TUSCANY

century either left or was forced out during World War II. There's a small **Museo Ebraico**, housed in the former synagogue in vicolo Marghera (0564 614230, closed Sat, admission €3, €2 reductions), once part of the ghetto. It comprises caves once used for ritual bathing and another area in which bread was baked. There's a *pasticceria* just around the corner that still makes a local Jewish pastry called *sfratti* ('the evicted'). Elsewhere, the **Museo Civico Archeologico** (piazza Orsini, 0564 614067, closed Mon, admission €4,

€2.50 reductions) has a small but well-presented collection of Etruscan artefacts.

Today, Pitigliano is home to a number of interesting craft shops: for colourful leather goods made on the spot, visit Rodolfo Cilento's **Bottega Artigiana** (via Roma 87, 0564 616218); for olive-wood kitchenware, head for **L'Albero dell'Olivo** (via Zuccarelli 90, 0564 615659); for unusual handwoven clothes and jewellery, try **Animaglia** (piazza San Gregorio VII 104, 340 8671628 mobile, www.mariateresagrilli.com).

Shingle Belles

Tuscany's best beaches and top tips for avoiding the crowds.

Cala Violina.

One glance at a map of Tuscany will reveal just how long its coastline is. Stretching from Marina di Carrara in the north to just south of Marina di Capalbio in the south, most of it is fringed with sand (and sometimes less-than-perfect water). Tuscans take full advantage of their natural holiday resource, finding any excuse to head '*al mare*' from around early May to late September and, in many cases, relocating to the beach for much of the month of August.

A beach holiday Italian style is very different from the British version; swathes of Tuscany's sand is occupied by *stabilimenti balneari*, outfits that lay out row upon row of brightly coloured umbrellas and deckchairs for which you have to pay. When all these places are filled with bronzing bodies, there's little room for manoeuvre and the noise level can be quite high.

There are alternatives, however, if you know where to go, although even the beaches listed below are crowded at weekends from June until September, and are untenable in August.

La Feniglia

Just outside Porto Ercole, Grosseto; see p294. These seven kilometres (4.3 miles) of fine pale sand are backed by a beautiful

pine forest. Avoid the umbrellas and bars near the car park and walk along the beach to find your patch. Alternatively, hire a bike and cycle through the woods; there are plenty of footpaths that lead to the sand.

Marina di Alberese

South of Grosseto.
This strip of golden sand is part of the Parco Naturale della Maremma (*see p298* **South Park**). In summer, buy a ticket for the car park (where space is limited) from the Visitor Centre at Alberese before driving the eight kilometres (five miles) to the beach.

Cala Violina

Between Follonica and Punta Ala, Grosseto.
The spectacular 'violin bay' is so called because of the sound emitted by the fine white sand (microscopic grains of white quartz) when you walk on it. The clear blue water is shallow and the beach is backed by *macchia*: Tuscan vegetation including wild juniper and myrtle.

La Sterpaia

Between Piombino and Follonica, Livorno Province/Grosseto.
Of the eight kilometres (five miles) of fine sand here, around 70 per cent is '*spiaggia libera*' (free beach). Part of a natural park, it's well organised, with parking spaces along its length. So avoid the *stabilimenti balneari* and try to ignore the power station at the northern end. The rest is gorgeous.

Golfo di Baratti

Between San Vincenzo and Piombino, Livorno Province.
This perfect half-moon of golden sand is fringed with pine trees and dominated by the ancient little town of Populonia.

TUSCANY

South Park

The stunning wilderness of the Parco Naturale della Maremma.

The beautiful, WWF-protected nature reserve of Parco Naturale della Maremma stretches from Principina Mare to Talamone, taking in the Monti dell'Uccellina. The strip – a coastal wilderness – offers miles of sandy beach, mostly unencumbered by resorts.

A train service runs from Grosseto to Marina di Alberese; from here, head for the **Visitors' Centre** at Alberese (via Bersagliere 7-9, 0564 407098, www.parco-maremma. it, 8am-8.30pm daily, Oct-May varies) for information about trails, wildlife and activities. Then, take a bus or walk (cars aren't allowed in the park) the four kilometres (2.5 miles) to the park entrance (open 9am-an hour before sunset daily, admission €5.50-€8).

Birds thrive in the reserve, including ospreys, falcons, kingfishers, herons and the rare Knight of Italy. The terrain ranges from the mudflats and umbrella pines of the estuary to the woodland of the hills.

There are two lodges, which must be booked via the **Poiana Viaggi** travel agent on 0564 412000. Otherwise, head to the charming town of Magliano in Toscana to the **Locanda delle Mura** (piazza Marconi 5, 0564 593057, www.locandadellemura.it, €79-€105), a classy B&B, or to Talamone, near the southern entrance to the park. Options around here include **Hotel Capo d'Uomo** (via Cala di Forno 5, 0564 887077, www.hotelcapoduomo.com, closed Nov-Mar, €100-€220), a three-star hotel, and **Telamonio** (piazza Garibaldi 4, 0564 887008, www.hoteliltelamonio.com, closed Oct-Mar, €90-€210), in the town. Note that camping is not allowed within the park.

Where to eat

Good food and an interesting wine list can be found at **Il Castello** (piazza della Repubblica 92, 0564 617061, €30), which marries modernity with tradition. Otherwise, try a local *trattoria* such as **Il Grillo** (via Cavour 18, 0564 615202, closed Tue & July, average €17).

SOVANA & SORANO

The Etruscans controlled the middle reaches of the Fiora river between the sixth and seventh centuries BC, thus also controlling the main communications route between the coast and the mineral rich areas of Monte Amiata. This accounts for the development of **Sovana**, which continued to grow and prosper in Roman times and during the Middle Ages.

Today, it's a charming little town, and a good place to stay when visiting the Etruscan necropolises in the immediate vicinity. There's a small museum of local history in the 13th-century **Palazzo Pretorio** (0564 614074, closed Mon-Thur in winter, admission €2.50), next door to the arched **Loggetta del Capitano**; nearby is the church of **Santa Maria** (0564 616532), with its magnificent pre-Romanesque ciborium (altar canopy).

Perched high above the Lente river as you head north-east from Sovana is the town of **Sorano**. Though less restored and touristy than Sovana, it's actually the municipal centre. It was a defence post under the Orsini empire, but at times its geology proved more dangerous

than rampaging enemies, and a series of landslides encouraged a slow but steady exodus. **Masso Leopoldino**, a giant terraced tufa cliff, peers down on the town. Sorano hosts a good crafts fair in mid August.

Where to stay & eat

Albergo Scilla (via R Siviero 1-3, 0564 616531, www.albergoscilla.com, €75-€140) has 20 nice, fairly priced rooms and a restaurant, the excellent **Ristorante dei Merli** (0564 616531, www.ristorantedeimerli.com, closed Tue & Feb, average €32). Otherwise, it's worth considering the **Sovana Hotel & Resort** (via del Duomo 66, 0564 617030, www.sovanahotel.it, €120-€250), which also owns the fine **Taverna Etrusca** (piazza del Pretorio 16, 0564 616531, www.tavernaetrusca.com, closed Wed, Jan & Feb, average €50). If you want to stay in a medieval Tuscan fortress, head to Sorano's comfortable **Della Fortezza** (piazza Cairoli 5, 0564 632010, www.fortezzahotel.it, closed Jan & Feb, €100-€160), which has amazing views. For thoughtful local cuisine try **Hostaria Terrazza Aldobrandeschi** (via del Borgo 44, 0564 638699, www.hostaria-aldobrandeschi.com, closed Mon & Wed, average €45).

MONTE ARGENTARIO & ORBETELLO

A mountain rising abruptly and dramatically from the sea, **Monte Argentario** is the Tuscan coast at its most rugged. If it looks as though it should be an island, that's because it was – until the 18th century, when the two long outer sand-spits created by the action of the tides finally reached the mainland. They created and enclose the **Orbetello** lagoon. With the smaller Lago di Burano just to the south, these shallow waters are a prime and protected birdwatching area. They are also the breeding ground for eels and grey mullet whose roe becomes *bottarga*, a local gastronomic delicacy.

Orbetello itself sits in the middle of the most central of the three isthmuses connecting Monte Argentario to the mainland. It has remnants of Spanish fortifications dating from the 16th and 17th centuries, when it was the capital of the Stato dei Presidi, a Spanish enclave on the Tuscan coast. There's a small antiquarium you can visit, with some rather uninspiring Etruscan and Roman exhibits, and the cathedral has a Gothic façade, but Orbetello is more about atmosphere than sightseeing.

Two nice beaches make up the sand-spits that join Monte Argentario to the mainland. To the north, access to **La Giannella** is from the main Talamone-Argentario road (look for any of the little pathways through the pines), while to the south, **La Feniglia** is accessible by parking at the western end. You can hire a bicycle and cycle through the protected pine woods behind La Feniglia. Both beaches have the odd paid *bagno*, but the rest is free.

On the south-east corner of Argentario lies the exclusive town of **Porto Ercole**, where Caravaggio died drunk on the beach in 1610. Easter and August holidays see this small bay packed to the gills. **Porto Santo Stefano** is another atmospheric port – you'll almost certainly find fishermen mending nets on the quay – although the vibe is more upmarket during the holidays when the yachting crowd arrives. You can catch a ferry for the **Isola del Giglio** here (*see p300*).

Where to stay & eat

In Orbetello, join the evening *struscio* (along the corso Italia promenade) before dining on a plate of eels fished from the lagoon at one of the town's simple *trattorie*. A top choice in these parts for fish is **I Pescatori** (via Leopardi 9, 0564 860611, www.ristoranteipescatori.it, closed Mon-Wed in winter & Mon-Sat lunch in winter, average €25). The best of the town's less expensive hotels is **Piccolo Parigi** (corso Italia 169, 0564 867233, www.albergopiccoloparigi.it, €60-€75).

In Porto Ercole, the best views are available at the three-star **Don Pedro** (via Panoramica 7, 0564 833914, www.hoteldonpedro.it, closed Oct-Mar, €100-€160). The charismatic two-star **Hotel Marina** (lungomare Andrea Doria 23, 0564 833055, www.bi-hotel.it, €100-€160) is

more central. There are several seafood restaurants to be found along the Porto Ercole harbour, plus a pizzeria. But the best place to eat fish in town is the **Osteria dei Nobili Santi** (via dell'Ospizio 8-10, 0564 833015, www.osterianobilisanti.eu, closed Mon & lunch Sun, average €40).

In Porto Santo Stefano, the **Hotel Vittoria** (via del Sole 65, 0564 818580/1, www.hvittoria.com, €115-€135, closed Oct-May) is a nice place to stay. Good dining can be found at **Dal Greco** (via del Molo 1-2, 0564 814885, closed Tue & Nov or Jan, average €45), a seafood restaurant with a harbour terrace, and at the slightly cheaper **Il Moletto di Amato & Figli** (via del Molo, 0564 813636, www.moletto.it, closed Wed & mid Jan-Feb, average €30), fantastically located at the end of the quay. The seafront is lined with bars, including the overwhelmingly fashionable **Il Buco** (lungomare dei Navigatori 2, 0564 818243, closed Mon, average €34).

CAPALBIO & ANSEDONIA

Close to the Lazio border, **Capalbio** is a magnet for Rome's poets, politicians and musicians, especially during August's **Grey Cat Jazz Festival**. The main attraction for tourists is **Il Giardino dei Tarocchi** (0564 895122, www.nikidesaintphalle.com, closed late Oct-mid May, admission €10.50, €6 reductions), an amazing walled garden to the south-east of the town. Founded in 1976, it contains around 20 huge sculptures (some of which house four-storey buildings) that represent characters from the tarot deck.

Due west on the coast is **Ansedonia**, on whose rocky promontory lie the ruins of Cosa, a Roman colony founded in 273 BC. Remains of walls, a gate and residential areas are still visible. The **Museo di Cosa** (via delle Ginestre 35, 0564 881421, admission €2) displays artefacts from the area.

Daily trains from Grosseto stop at Capalbio station, from where it's three kilometres (two miles) to the beach alongside the picturesque **Lago di Burano lagoon** (now a WWF reserve). The coastline stretching southwards from Ansedonia offers 18 kilometres (11 miles) of beach, but there's an industrial plant looming through the haze at the far south end, so you're better off on the beaches north of Argentario or heading straight for an island.

Where to stay & eat

La Locanda di Ansedonia (via Aurelia Sud km140.5, 0564 881317, www.lalocanda diansedonia.it, €100-€130), situated in an old farmhouse, has 12 rooms and a restaurant. Breakfast includes all sorts of home-made goodies. In Capalbio, the **Hotel Valle del Buttero** (via Silone 21, 0564 896097, www. valledelbuttero.it, €95-€115) is a large three-star structure. **Ghiaccio Bosco** (via della Sgrilla 4, 0564 896539, www.ghiacciobosco.com, €80-€160) is a lovely *agriturismo* with pool. **Trattoria La Torre da Carla** (via Vittorio Emanuele 33, 0564 896070, www.trattoria dacarla.it, closed Mon-Fri in winter & all Thur, average €40) serves a good selection of robust Tuscan cuisine.

RESOURCES
Tourist information
Grosseto *Agenzia Promozione Turismo (APT), viale Monterosa 206 (0564 462611, www.turismo inmaremma.it).* **Open** 8.30am-1.30pm, 2.30-6.30pm Mon-Fri; 8.30am-1.30pm Sat.
Massa Marittima *Consorzio A.MA.TUR. (Alta Maremma Turismo), via Todini 3 (0566 902756, www.altamaremmaturismo.it).* **Open** *Summer* 9.30am-12.30pm, 3-7pm Mon-Sat; 10am-1pm, 4-7pm Sun. *Winter* 9.30am-12.30pm, 3-6pm Mon-Sat; 10am-1pm Sun.
Pitigliano *Piazza Garibaldi 12 (0564 617111).* **Open** 10.30am-1pm, 3-7pm Tue-Sun.
Porto Santo Stefano *Piazzale Sant'Andrea (0564 814208).* **Open** 9am-1pm, 2-4pm Mon-Sat.
Saturnia *Via Mazzini 4 (0564 601280, www.laltramaremma.it).* **Open** *Summer* 10.20am-1pm, 3-7pm Mon-Sat. *Winter* 10.20am-1pm, 2-6pm Mon-Sat.

GETTING THERE & AROUND
By bus
There are about ten buses a day connecting Grosseto and Siena (journey time 90mins). Buses leave from in front of Grosseto's train station. For further information on buses serving regional towns such as Piombino and Pitigliano call **Rama** on 199 848787.

By car
The main coast road (E80/SS1) links Grosseto with Livorno to the north and the Maremma to the south. The SS223, currently being widened, is the main route down from Siena. The region's most scenic road is the SS74, which branches inland off the SS1, north of Orbetello, and winds towards Manciano and Pitigliano.

By train
Grosseto is on the main train line between Rome and Pisa (90mins from Rome, 80mins from Pisa). Trains on this line also stop at Capalbio and Orbetello (for Monte Argentario) to the south, and San Vincenzo and Cecina to the north. A local train links Grosseto with Siena (2hrs). For national train information, call 892021 or go to www.trenitalia.it.

The Islands

The islands of the Tuscan archipelago are a welcome antidote to the area's largely unremarkable coast, particularly tiny, tranquil **Isola del Giglio** west of the Argentario peninsula. Both **Elba** and **Giglio** get crowded during Easter, July and August, and their idyllic sands and scenery are best enjoyed in May, June and September. The islands and the sea in which they're set make up the **Parco Nazionale Arcipelago Toscano**, Europe's biggest protected marine park. For information, call 0565 919411 or visit www.islepark.it.

ISOLA DEL GIGLIO

A steep and winding road connects the three villages on this beautiful little island: **Giglio Porto**, where the ferry docks; **Campese**, on the other side; and **Giglio Castello**, on the ridge between the two, with its medieval walls and steep narrow lanes. The main beach is at Campese, but there are other, smaller beaches dotted around elsewhere. The two great pleasures here are exploring the virtually uninhabited south and indulging at one of the many good restaurants on the quayside in Porto. Most of the hotels on the island are in Porto; there are also rooms to let in local homes.

Where to stay & eat

Overlooking Giglio Porto, the three-star **Castello Monticello** (via Provinciale, 0564 809252, www.hotelcastellomonticello.com, closed Oct-Mar, €90-€150) occupies a crenellated folly. For a fantastic meal book at **Arcobalena** (via Vittorio Emanuele 48, 0564 806106, average €40, closed 2 wks Mar & Dec) up at the Castello. The menu depends on freshly caught fish and whatever's in the veg patch. The **B&B Airone** (contrada Santa Maria 12, 0564 806076, €40-€70) has good views. For more sun and sea, head to **Pardini's Hermitage** (Cala degli Alberi, 0564 809034, www.hermit.it, closed Nov-Mar, €125-€195 full board) in a secluded cove accessible only by foot or by boat (staff will fetch you).

While on the beach in Campese, you can have anything 'from a cappuccino to a lobster' at local stalwart **Tony's** (via della Torre 13, 0564 806453, closed Nov, average €20), on the north end of the beach below the tower.

Resources

Tourist information
Via Provinciale 9 (0564 809400, www.isola delgiglio.it). **Open** 9am-1pm, 3-7pm daily. Closed Nov-Easter.

Elba.

ELBA

Elba is Italy's third largest island, with 142 kilometres (88 miles) of coastline. Due to its wealth of mineral deposits, it was inhabited in prehistoric times, and later by the Greeks and the Etruscans. The **Museo dei Minerali Elbani** at **Rio Marina** (via Magenta 26, 0565 962088, www.parcominelba.it, closed Nov-Mar, admission €2.50) provides an alternative to the beach, where things can get a bit crowded.

Portoferraio is the island's capital and the focus of Napoleonic interest. The **Palazzo dei Mulini** (piazzale Napoleone, 0565 915846, €7, €3.50 reductions, closed Tue), Napoleon's town residence, is worth a visit. His summer retreat, the neoclassical **Villa Napoleonica di San Martino** (0565 914688, €7, €3.50 reductions, closed Mon), is roughly six kilometres (four miles) south-west of town.

Choosing between Elba's many village resorts can be tricky. Tiny **Viticcio** overlooks a pretty, secluded bay; **Biodola** has a terrific beach, but is dominated by large hotels and parasols; **Poggio** has a good portion of free beach but can get very busy; while **Marciana Marina** is an attractive port town.

Up the hill, **Marciana** itself and **Sant'Andrea** are good starting points for an ascent of **Monte Capanne**. The national park in the north-west is a walker's paradise. The tourist office has a good booklet with a list of trails.

Many of the villages on the south and south-western side of the island have good beaches; the pick of them is at **Fetovaia**.

Where to stay & eat

Affrichella, on Marciana Marina's via Santa Chiara 7 (0565 996844, closed Wed in winter, early Nov-early Dec & early Jan-early Mar, average €35), offers local fish dishes. In Poggio, head to **Publius** (piazza del Castagneto 11, 0565 99208, www.ristorantepublius.it, closed Mon in winter & Jan-Feb, average €30), which has fantastic views, the best cellar on the island and a good menu. Nearby is **Luigi** (località Lavacchio, 0565 99413, closed all Tue & Mon

mid June-Aug & Nov-Apr, average €30), offering fresh rustic dishes. As you leave Porto Azzurro heading for Portoferraio you'll find **La Botte Gaia** (viale Europa 5-7, 0565 95607, www.labottegaia.com, closed Mon & mid Jan-mid Mar, average €40), which focuses on fish and has a good wine list. Just out of Portoferraio, towards Bagnaia, is **La Carretta** (località Magazzini 92, 0565 933223, €30, closed Wed & mid Oct-mid Jan) – the owners pride themselves on their Elban cuisine.

Accommodation-wise, at Capo Sant'Andrea, **Hotel Ilio** (via Sant'Andrea 5, 0565 908018, www.hotelilio.com, €120-€180) has 20 rooms overlooking lovely gardens. Otherwise, **Casa Lupi**, on the outskirts of Marciana Marina (viale Amedeo, località Ontanelli, 0565 99143, closed Jan & Feb, €30-€51.50 per person), is one of the best one-star hotels on Elba. In Viticcio, stay at two-star **Scoglio Bianco** (0565 939036, www.scogliobianco.it, closed Oct-Easter, €42-€170 half-board). In Fetovaia, **Lo Scirocco** is smart and well located (località Fetovaia, 0565 988033, www.hotellosciroccoisoladelba.it, closed Oct-Mar, €32-€75).

Ottone is home to **Rosselba le Palme** (località Ottone, 0565 933101, www.rosselbale palme.it), one of Elba's best campsites, and **Villa Ottone** (località Ottone, 0565 933042, www.villaottone.com, €130-€650 half-board per person), a swish hotel with a restaurant open only to hotel guests. Alternatively, the **Monte Fabbrello** winery (Schiopparello, 0565 940020, www.montefabbrello.it) has rooms for €50 to €75.

Resources

Tourist information *Viale Elba 4, Portoferraio (0565 914671, www.aptelba.it).* **Open** 8am-7pm Mon-Sat; 9.30am-12.30pm, 3-6pm Sun.

Getting there

By boat Toremar (199 117733, www.toremar.it) has services from Piombino (*see p245*) to Elba and from Porto San Stefano to Giglio. **Maregiglio** (www.maregiglio.it) runs just the latter service.

TUSCANY

Directory

Getting Around

ARRIVING & LEAVING

By air

Amerigo Vespucci Airport at Peretola is by far the easiest way to reach Florence, but only CityJet from London City Airport and Meridiana from London Gatwick fly here. Pisa's **Galileo Galilei Airport** has frequent flights to and from the UK, and increasingly the US, but is a train or coach journey away. A third choice is Bologna's **Guglielmo Marconi Airport**.

Florence Airport, Peretola (Amerigo Vespucci) 055 3061300/flight information 055 3061700, www.aeroporto.firenze.it. About 5km (3 miles) west of central Florence, Amerigo Vespucci is linked to the city by the **Volainbus**, a bus shuttle service that runs half-hourly 6am-11.30pm, costs €5 and stops in the SITA station at via Santa Caterina da Siena 15 (see below). Buy tickets on the bus, at the airport bar or wherever bus tickets are sold (see right). Bus season ticket holders don't have to buy an extra ticket. A taxi to Florence costs from €20 (see right) and takes about 20 minutes. For coaches to Pisa Airport, see below.

Pisa International Airport (Galileo Galilei) 050 849111/ flight information 050 849300, www.pisa-airport.com. The direct train to Florence's Santa Maria Novella (SMN) station from Pisa Aeroporto takes just over an hour. Buy tickets (€5.50 each way) at the desk to the right of arrivals in the main airport concourse. A coach service from Pisa Airport to Florence SMN train station is run by **Terravision** (050 26080, www.terravision.eu). It leaves from outside the arrivals area and from the steps of Florence SMN train station. Tickets can be bought from the kiosk in the airport, from the Deanna/Terravision bar in the station piazza (on the corner of via Santa Caterina da Siena, from several travel agencies (see website for details), online or by phone. Tickets cost €8 each way and the journey takes 90 minutes. The coach also goes on to Florence Airport.

To get to Florence by car, take the Firenze–Pisa–Livorno road, which goes to the west of the city.

Bologna Airport (Guglielmo Marconi) 051 6479615, www.bologna-airport.it. An airport bus stops outside terminal A (arrivals) and leaves for Bologna train station every 15 minutes between the hours of 6am and 11.40pm. Tickets cost €5 from the machine in the terminal building or on board. The trip takes about 30 minutes in total. A taxi costs about €18.

From Bologna Centrale, trains to Florence are frequent and take between 50-90 minutes; prices vary. A downside of flying in to Bologna is that you may find some trains into Florence fully booked, unless you've bought a ticket in advance (which means changing your ticket if the plane is delayed).

Travelling by car, the journey to Florence takes about 90 minutes, south on the A1.

Major airlines

Alitalia 06 2222, www.alitalia.it
British Airways 199 712266, www.britishairways.com
CityJet 848 88 44 66, www.cityjet.com
Easyjet Customer service 899 234589/bookings 899 678990, www.easyjet.co.uk
Meridiana 892928/+39 0789 52692 from outside Italy, www.meridiana.it
Ryanair 899 678210, www.ryanair.com

By rail

Train tickets can be bought from the ticket desks, vending machines in the station, from www.trenitalia.com, or travel agents with the **FS** logo (Ferrovie dello Stato, state railways). Before boarding any train, stamp (convalidare) your ticket and any supplements in the yellow machines at the head of the platforms; failure to do so could mean a €50 fine.

Taxis serve Florence's main **Santa Maria Novella** station on a 24-hour basis; many city buses also stop there. It's a 5- to 10-minute walk into central Florence. Some

services go to **Campo di Marte** station to the north-east of the city. For train information call 892021 (7am-9pm daily) or visit www.trenitalia.com. Information on disabled access is available at the disabled assistance desk on platform 5 at Santa Maria Novella or on 055 2352275 or by calling the national line 199 303060. Both are open 7am-9pm daily and English is spoken.

Campo di Marte Via Mannelli, Outside the City Gates (disabled assistance 055 2352275). Florence's main station when SMN is closed at night. Many long-distance trains stop here. The ticket office is open 6.20am-9pm daily.

Santa Maria Novella Piazza della Stazione, Santa Maria Novella. **Open** 4.15am-1.30am daily. Information office 7am-9pm daily. Ticket office 5.50am-10pm daily. **Map** p334 A2.

By road

By coach, you'll probably arrive at either the **SITA** or the **LAZZI** coach stations, both near Santa Maria Novella station (see above).

Ticket Point LAZZI Piazza Adua, Santa Maria Novella (055 215155, www.lazzi.it). **Open** 9am-7pm Mon-Sat. **Map** p334 A2. Tickets for LAZZI, Eurolines coaches and Ferrovie dello Stato.

SITA Via Santa Caterina da Siena 15, Santa Maria Novella (055 4782870, www.sitabus.it). **Map** p334 A2. See also p306 Transport in Tuscany.

PUBLIC TRANSPORT

Bus services

ATAF Piazza della Stazione, opposite north-east exit of train station, Santa Maria Novella (800 424500, 199 104245 from mobiles, www.ataf.net). **Open** 7am-9pm daily. The main ATAF desk has English-speaking staff, sells a variety of bus tickets, and has a free booklet with details of major routes and fares.

DIRECTORY

Fares & tickets

It's cheaper to buy tickets before boarding buses, but you can now get tickets on board at €2 for 70mins. Tickets are available from the ATAF office in piazza della Stazione (except for season tickets), a few machines, *tabacchi*, newsstands and any bars displaying an orange ATAF sticker. When you board, stamp the ticket in one of the validation machines. Be aware that local plain-clothes inspectors regularly board buses for spot checks; anyone without a valid ticket is fined €50, payable within 30 days at the main information office or in post offices.

90min ticket (*biglietto 90 minuti*) €1.20; valid for 90mins of travel on all city area buses.
Multiple ticket (*biglietto multiplo*) €4.50; 4 tickets, each valid for 90mins.
AGILE card €10; electronic card with 10 x 70min tickets (swipe once over validating machine for each traveller).
AGILE card €20; electronic card with 21 x 90min tickets (swipe once over validating machine for each person travelling).
24-hour ticket (*biglietto ventiquattro ore*) €5; one-day pass that must be stamped at the start of the first journey.
3-day ticket (*biglietto tre giorni*) €12.
7-day ticket (*biglietto sette giorni*) €18.
Monthly pass (*abbonamento*) €34; €23 students. The ordinary pass can be bought from the ATAF office at Santa Maria Novella station, or from any outlet with an 'Abbonamenti ATAF' sign. For the student pass, go to the Ufficio Abbonamenti in piazza della Stazione (open 7am-9pm daily) with ID and two passport photos.

A special 24-hour sightseeing bus ticket, **Firenze Passepartout**, costs €22. Most ATAF routes run from 5.30am to 9pm with a frequency of 10-30 minutes. The orange and white *fermate* (bus stops) list the main stops along the route. Each of the stops has its name indicated at the top.

Disabled travellers

Most buses across Florence are now of the newer design (grey and green) and are fully wheelchair accessible via an electric platform at the rear door. The city's orange buses are sadly not.

Useful tourist routes

7 from piazza San Marco to Fiesole.
10 to and from Settignano.

12, 13 circular routes via Santa Maria Novella station, piazza della Libertà, piazzale Michelangelo and San Miniato.

ATAF also runs a network of electric buses, which covers four central routes: **C1, C2, C3 and D**. Normal bus tickets or season tickets are valid. These routes are detailed in ATAF's booklet and at www.ataf.net.

Rail services

Trenitalia

There are regular local train services from the central Santa Maria Novella station to Campo di Marte in the east and Rifredi in the west (892021, www.trenitalia.com/en/index.html). Tickets can be bought online or at the station ticket offices.

Tram services

The new **Tramvia** tram line 1, from central Florence to Scandicci, is up and running. For information, visit www.gestramvia.it.

TAXIS

Licensed cabs are white with yellow graphics, with a code name of a place plus ID number on the door; 'Londra 6', for example. If you have problems, make a note of this code. You can only get a cab at a rank or by phone. Ranks are indicated by a blue sign with TAXI written in white, but this is no guarantee that any cars will be waiting. Try piazza della Repubblica, piazza della Stazione, piazza Santa Maria Novella, piazza del Duomo, piazza San Marco, piazza Santa Croce and piazza Santa Trinità.

Fares & surcharges

Taxis in Florence are expensive. When the taxi arrives, the meter should read €3.20 during the day, €5.10 on Sundays and on public holidays, and €6.40 at night. The fare increases at a rate of €1/km. Lone women pay 10% less after 9pm, but only if they request the discount when booking. There is an overall minimum fare of €5. Taxis between the airport and anywhere in the city centre have a fixed tariff of €20 in the day, €26.40 at night.

Phone cabs

Try to book a cab at least a few hours before you need it. When your call is answered, give the

address where you want to be picked up, specifying if the street number is *nero* or *rosso* (for an explanation, *see p307*). If a cab is available, you'll be given its code and a time; for example, 'Londra 6 in tre minuti'. If not, a message or operator will tell you to call back. **Taxi numbers** 055 4390; 055 4798; 055 4242; 055 4499.

DRIVING

The centre of Florence is easily walkable and the electric bus service is a good back-up so it's usually best to leave cars at home, particularly given the permanent and expanding Traffic-Free Zones (ZTL), which include the old city centre. Only residents or permit-holders can enter from 7.30am to 7.30pm, Monday to Saturday. This is usually extended in the summer to exclude cars from the centre in the evenings from Thursday or Friday to Sunday. On top of this, the city is frequently bringing in new restrictions, so if you plan to drive check in the local press or with the municipal police (*see p312*).

Speed limits are currently 50km/h (45km/h on motorbikes and mopeds), on the *superstrada* the limit is 90km/h and on the motorway (*autostrada*) 130km/h.

Legal drink drive limits are 0.5g/litre, which as a guide are generally reached or passed with less than a quarter litre of wine or a half litre of beer.

In a traffic emergency call 055 3285 (055 328 3333 for less urgent situations). *See also p308* Emergencies. For general traffic or parking information, call 055055 (8am-8pm Mon-Sat).

Breakdown services

National motoring organisation such as the AA, RAC or AAA have reciprocal arrangements with the Automobile Club d'Italia (ACI), which will tell you what to do in case of a breakdown.

Automobile Club d'Italia (ACI)

Viale Amendola 36, Outside the City Gates (055 24861/24hr info in English 039039039/24hr emergencies 800 116800 if calling from a foreign mobile phone). Bus 8, 12, 13, 14, 31. **Open** 8.30am-1pm, 3-5.30pm Mon-Fri.
The ACI charges reasonable rates. Members of associated organisations are entitled to free basic repairs, and to other services at preferential rates.

Car hire

In Florence consider renting an electric car, a very practical option as you can drive them throughout most of the city centre. One conveniently central company with electric car hire is **Firenze by Car** (055 282825/333 1816919, www.firenzebycar.com).

Car pounds

If your car's not where you left it, chances are it's been towed. Call 055 4224142 with the car's registration number to confirm. The central car pound, Depositeria SaS (open 24hrs daily), is in via Allende, behind the Novoli fruit and veg market (bus 23 or 57). The car owner must take proof of ownership and ID to regain possession. If your car is stolen and found, it will be taken to the Ufficio Depositeria Comunale in piazza Artom 13-14 (055 3283660, fax 055 3283670, pm.depositeria@comune. fi.it). The office is open 8am-12.45pm Mon-Fri, and Thur till 6pm.

Fuel stations

All petrol stations sell unleaded fuel (*senza piombo*). Diesel fuel is *gasolio*. Many offer a discount for self-service. Attendants don't expect tips. There are stations on most main roads leading out of town. Normal hours are 7.30am-12.30pm and 3-7pm daily except Sundays. AGIP stations on via Bolognese, via Aretina, viale Europa, via Senese and via Baracca have 24-hour self-service machines.

Parking

Parking in Florence is a major problem and is severely restricted in the centre of town and cars are towed or clamped without pity (*see above* Car pounds).

Most main streets are no-parking zones. Parking is forbidden where you see *passo carrabile* (access at all times) and *sosta vietata* (no parking) signs. Blue lines denote pay-parking; there will be either meters or an attendant to issue timed tickets, which you should return to them when you get back. Disabled spaces are marked by yellow stripes and are free. *Zona rimozione* (tow-away area) signs are valid for the length of the street, while temporary tow zones are marked at each end. Signs tell you when street cleaning takes place – your car will be towed if parked on a street being cleaned.

The safest place to leave a car is in one of the underground car parks (*parcheggi*), such as **Parterre** and **Piazza Stazione**, which both have surveillance cameras.

Parcheggio Oltrarno *Piazza della Calza, Oltrarno* (055 50302209, www.firenzeparcheggi.it). **Open** 24hrs daily. **Rates** €2/hr; €20/24hrs; €55/wk.
Parcheggio Parterre *Via Madonna della Tosse 9, just off piazza della Libertà, Outside the City Gates* (055 50302209, www.firenzeparcheggi.it). Bus 8, 1, 7. **Open** 24hrs daily. **Rates** €2/hr; €20/24hrs; €65/wk.
Parcheggio Piazza Stazione *Via Alamanni 14/piazza della Stazione 12-13, Santa Maria Novella* (055 2302655). **Open** 24hrs daily. **Rates** €3/hr; 5 days €140. **Map** p334 A2.
Parcheggio S Ambrogio *Piazza Annigoni, Santa Croce* (055 244641, www.firenzeparcheggi.it). **Open** 24hrs daily. Rates €1/hr for the first hour; €2/hr for the second hour, then €3/hr.

Roads

There are three motorways in Tuscany that you have to pay a toll to use: the *autostrade* **A1** (Rome–Florence–Bologna), **A11** (the coast–Lucca–Florence) and **A12** (Livorno–Genova). *Autostrade* are indicated by green signs. As an idea of price, it costs €15-€20 to drive the 270km (168 miles) from Rome to Florence, at a rate of 5¢ or 6¢ per kilometre.

CYCLING

There are cycle lanes on the main *viali*, but that's no guarantee they'll only be used by bikes. Watch for doors being opened suddenly from cars parked on the side of the road.

Moped & bike hire

Mille e Una Bici is a council scheme to encourage the use of bikes. There are hire points all around the city including at the three main train stations, piazza Ghiberti and Parterre. Bike hire costs either €1.50/hour or €8/day and for residents and those with train or bus passes, it's 50¢ per hour, €1 a day or €15 a month. The companies below also rent out bikes. To hire a scooter or moped (*motorino*), you need a credit card, ID and cash deposit. Helmets must be worn on all mopeds. Cycle shops normally ask you to leave ID rather than a deposit.

Alinari
Via Guelfa 85r, San Lorenzo (055 280500, www.alinarirental.com). **Open** 9.30am-1pm, 3-7.30pm Mon-Sat; 10am-1pm, 3-7pm Sun. **Map** p334 A4.
Rental of a 50cc moped for use of one person only is €30/day; 125cc for one or two people is €55/day. A current driver's licence is required.
Florence by Bike
Via San Zanobi 120r, San Lorenzo (055 488992, www.florencebybike.it). **Open** 9am-7.30pm daily. Closed Nov-Feb.
Bike hire costs either €2.70/hour or €14/day. Moped hire for two is from €68 a day. Guided tours are also available, and the majority of staff speak good English.

WALKING

Walking is the quickest way to get around central Florence. Our street maps (*see p334-35*) cover most of the centre, and a good street map is available free from tourist offices. For an overview map, *see p322-33*.

TRANSPORT IN TUSCANY

Driving is the best way of getting around Tuscany. If you don't have a car, it's possible to reach many parts of Tuscany by bus, though they can be few and far between. Companies such as **Tra-in** (out of Siena) and **LAZZI** (out of Florence) operate around major towns. In most villages, buses are timed to coincide with the school day, but combining bus and rail services can make things easier.

Information

For train information, *see p305*. Major Tuscan bus companies include the following:

CAP *Largo Fratelli Alinari 9, Santa Maria Novella, Florence* (055 214637, www.capautolinee.it). **Map** p334 A2.
LAZZI *Piazza della Stazione 4, corner of piazza Adua, Santa Maria Novella, Florence* (055 351061/283878, www. lazzi.it). **Map** p334 A2.
Rama *Via Topazo 12, Grosseto* (0564 454169, www. ramamobilita.it).
SITA *Via Santa Caterina da Siena 15, Santa Maria Novella, Florence* (055 4782870, www.sitabus.it). **Map** p334 A2.
Tra-in *Piazza San Domenico, Siena* (0577 204111, www.comune.siena. it/train, www.trainspa.it).

Resources A-Z

ADDRESSES

Addresses in Florence are numbered and colour-coded. Residential addresses are 'black' numbers (*nero*), while most commercial addresses are 'red' (*rosso*). This means that on any one street, there can be two addresses with the same number but different colours and these properties can sometimes be quite far apart. Some houses are both shops and flats and could have two different numbers, one red and one black. Red numbers are followed by an 'r' when the address is written, a practice we have followed throughout this guide.

Note that the name on a business's shopfront or awning is quite often different from its official, listed name. We have used the former name wherever possible.

AGE RESTRICTIONS

In Italy, there are official age restrictions on a number of goods and activities. However, it's extremely rare for anyone to be asked to show ID in bars or elsewhere, other than in gay bars and clubs. The age of consent for heterosexual sex is 16, for gay sex 18. Beer and wine can be legally drunk in bars and pubs from the age of 16; spirits can be drunk by those 18 and over. It's an offence to sell cigarettes to children under 16. Mopeds (50cc) can be driven from the age of 14; cars from 18; only those over 21 can hire a car.

ATTITUDE & ETIQUETTE

In churches, women are expected to cover their shoulders and not wear anything skimpy. Shorts and vests are out for anyone.

Queues are a foreign concept, but in a crowded shop, customers know who is before them and who's after, and usually respect the order. In shops, say *buongiorno* or *buona sera* on entering and leaving, and bear in mind that it's generally considered rude to walk in, look around and leave without asking for what you are looking for or at least greeting the shop assistant.

When addressing anyone except children, it's important to use the appropriate title: *signora* for women, *signorina* for young women, and *signore* for men.

BUSINESS

Office services

See also p311 **Postal services**.
Emynet Lungarno Soderini
5/7/9r, Oltrarno (055 219228, emynet@emynet.com). **Open** 9.30am-1.30pm, 3-7pm Mon-Fri. **Map** p334 C1.
Full written and spoken translations in most languages.
Interpreti di Conferenza *Via Guelfa 116, San Lorenzo (055 475165, www.interpreti.net)*. **Open** 9am-1pm Mon-Fri. **Map** p334 A2.
Interpreters for business meetings.

Useful organisations

Camera di Commercio Industria, Artigianato e Agricoltura (Chamber of Commerce) *Piazza Giudici 3, Duomo & Around (055 27951, www.fi.camcom.it)*. **Open** 8am-3.30pm Mon-Fri. **Map** p335 C4.
Provides info on all elements of import/export and business in Italy, and on Italian trade fairs.
British Consulate The British Consulate in Florence closed down at the end of 2011. Its services are

being handled by the Consulate in Milan (027 23001).
Commercial Office, United States of America *Consulate Lungarno Amerigo Vespucci 38, Outside the City Gates (055 292266, http://florence.usconsulate.gov/cs.html). Bus D.* **Open** 9am-12.30pm, 2-3.30pm Mon-Fri.

CUSTOMS

EU nationals don't have to declare goods imported into or exported from Italy for their personal use, as long as they arrive from another EU country. Personal use is considered to be within the limits of 800 cigarettes (and limits on cigars), 10 litres of spirits, 90 litres of wine (and limits on other alcoholic drinks). US citizens should check their duty-free allowance on the way out. Random checks are made for drugs (*see right* Drugs). For non-EU citizens, the following import limits apply:
● 200 cigarettes or 100 small cigars or 50 cigars or 250g of tobacco
● 1 litre of spirits (over 22% alcohol) or 2 litres of fortified wine (under 22%)
● 50 grams of perfume
● 500 grams of coffee
There are no restrictions on the importation of cameras, watches or electrical goods. Visitors are also allowed to bring in up to €10,329 (or equivalent) in cash without declaring it.

DISABLED

Disabled facilities in Florence are improving. Recent laws stipulate that all new public offices, bars, restaurants and hotels must be equipped with full disabled facilities. Currently, the standard of access still varies greatly, though most museums are wheelchair-accessible, with lifts, ramps on steps and toilets for the disabled.

Pavement corners in the centre of town are now sloped to allow for wheelchair access. New buses are equipped with ramps and a wheelchair area. Trains that allow space for wheelchairs in the carriages and have disabled loos have a wheelchair logo on the outside, but there is no wheelchair access up the steep steps on the south side of the station: use the east or north entrance, or call the information office for assistance (see p306). Taxis take wheelchairs, but tell them when you book.

There are free disabled parking bays all over Florence, and disabled drivers with the sticker have access to pedestrian areas of the city. There are wheelchair-accessible toilets at Florence and Pisa airports and Santa Maria Novella station, as well as in many of Florence's main sights and at several public loos.

The Provincia di Firenze produces a booklet (also in English, available from tourist offices) with disabled-aware descriptions – how many steps on each floor, wide doorways and so on – of venues across Florence Province. For more information, call 800 437631 (some English spoken). The official council website (www.comune.fi.it) also has useful sightseeing itineraries suitable for disabled visitors.

Wheelchair hire is free of charge both from the Misericordia (055 212222) and the Fratellanza Militare (055 26021). If they don't have any available they can refer to paid hire services.

DRUGS

Drug-taking is illegal in Italy and a new law has increased the severity of sentencing and put all drugs, from cannabis to heroin, on the same level from a legal standpoint. If you're caught in possession of drugs of any type, you may have to appear before a magistrate. If you can convince him or her that your stash was for purely personal use, then you may be let off with a fine, have your passport or driving licence confiscated, have your movements restricted or be ordered to leave the country. Trafficking or dealing can land you in prison for up to 20 years. It is an offence to buy or sell drugs, or to give them away. Sniffer dogs are a fixture at most ports of entry into Italy; customs police are vigilant about

visitors entering with even the smallest quantities of any banned substances, and you could be refused entry or arrested.

ELECTRICITY

Most wiring systems work on one electrical current, 220V, compatible with British and US-bought products. A few systems in old buildings are 125V. With US 110V equipment, you'll need a current transformer: buy one before you travel as they can be hard to find. Adaptors, on the other hand, can be bought at any electrical shop (look for elettricità or ferramenta).

EMBASSIES & CONSULATES

There are no embassies in Florence. However, there are some consular offices, which offer limited services.
Australian Embassy Via Antonio Bosio 5, Rome (06 852721, www.italy.embassy.gov.au).
British Consulate The British Consulate in Florence closed down at the end of 2011. All the consular services will be handled by the Consulate in Milan, see http://uk initaly.fco.gov.uk/en/about-us/other-locations-in-italy/milan
Canadian Embassy Via Zara 30, Rome (06 854441, www.dfait-maeci.gc.ca/canada-europa/italy/menu-en.asp).
Irish Embassy Piazza Campitelli 3, Ghetto, Rome (06 6979121, www.embassyofireland.it).
New Zealand Embassy Via Clitunno 44, Rome (06 8537501/ www.nzembassy.com/italy).
South African Honorary Consulate Piazza dei Salterelli 1, Duomo & Around (055 281863, www.dfa.gov.za/foreign/sa_abroad/sai.htm#ita). **Map** p334 C3. No office. You have to call to make an appointment.
US Consulate Lungarno Amerigo Vespucci 38, Outside the City Gates (055 266951, www.florence.usconsulate.gov). Bus D. **Open** 9am-12.30pm, 2-3.30pm Mon-Fri. In case of emergency call the above phone number; a message refers you to the current emergency number.

EMERGENCIES

See also **Health: Accident & emergency, Helplines and Police**.
Emergency services & state police Polizia di Stato 113.
Police Carabinieri (English-speaking helpline) 112.

Fire service Vigili del Fuoco 115. Ambulance Ambulanza 118.
Car breakdown Automobile Club d'Italia (ACI) 116/803 116.
City traffic police Vigili Urbani 055 3285.
Pet health emergencies 800 029449.

GAY & LESBIAN

For more HIV and AIDS services, see p309.
ArciGay 199 444592. Advice line.
Azione Gay e Lesbica Circolo Finisterrae, via Pisana 22, Outside the City Gates (055 220250). **Open** 6-8pm Mon-Wed. Closed 3wks Aug. As well as organising parties, this group maintains a library and archive, facilitates HIV testing and provides general community information.
IREOS-Queer Community Service Center Via de' Serragli 3, Oltrarno (055 216907, www.ireos.org). **Open** 5-8pm Mon-Thur, Sat. **Map** p334 C1/D1.
Ireos hosts social open houses, and offers HIV testing, and referrals for psychological counselling and self-help groups. It also organises hikes and outings and has free internet access most evenings and Saturday mornings. See website for details.
LILA 055 2479013, www.lila.toscana.it. **Open** 8.30am-12.30pm, 3.30-7.30pm Mon-Fri. Not-for-profit gay health advice line.
Queer Nation Holidays Via del Moro 95r, Santa Maria Novella (055 2654587, www.qnholidays.it). **Open** 9am-7pm Mon-Fri; 9.30am-2pm Sat. **Map** p334 B2.
Queer Nation Holidays can organise individual and group travel. It can also make referrals to other gay and lesbian organisations.

HEALTH

Emergency healthcare is available for all travellers through the Italian national health system. EU citizens are entitled to most treatment for free, though many specialised medicines, examinations and tests will be charged for. To get treatment, you'll need a European Health Insurance Card. From the UK this is available by phoning 0845 606 2030 or online from www.ehic.org.uk (you need to provide name, date of birth and National Insurance number). The EHIC has replaced the E111, which is no longer valid. The card will only cover partial costs of medicines. In non-emergency situations, citizens from countries with a reciprocal agreement with Italy (eg Australia) should go to the state health centre (Azienda Sanitaria di Firenze, or ASF, www.asf.toscana.it) on the second floor of borgo Ognissanti 20 (**open** 8am-1pm Mon-Fri plus 2.30-6pm Tue). Other non-EU visitors are charged for health care.

For hospital treatment, go to one of the casualty departments listed below. If you want to see a GP, go to the ASL for the district where you are staying, taking your EHIC with you. The ASLs are listed in the phone book and they usually **open** 9am-1pm and 2-7pm Monday to Friday.

Consulates can provide lists of English-speaking doctors, dentists and clinics. *See also below* Doctors.

Non-EU citizens will need to take out private health insurance before visiting to be covered for health care.

Accident & emergency

If you need urgent medical care, it's best to go to the *pronto soccorso* (casualty) department of one of the hospitals listed below; they're open 24 hours daily. Alternatively, call 118 for an ambulance (*ambulanza*).

To find a doctor on call in your area (emergencies only), phone 118. For a night (8pm-8am) or all-day-Sunday emergency home visit, call the Guardia Medica for your area (quartiere 1: 055 2339456; Oltrarno: 055 215616).

Ospedale di Careggi *Viale Morgagni 85, Outside the City Gates (055 7949644, www.ao-careggi.toscana.it). Bus 2, 8, 14C.* The main hospital and the best place to go to for most emergencies.
Ospedale Meyer (Children) *Viale Pieraccini 24, Outside the City Gates (055 56621, www.meyer.it). Bus 14C.*
Ospedale Santa Maria Annunziata (known as Ponte a Nicchieri) *Via Antella 58, Bagno a Ripoli, Outside the City Gates (055 24961). Bus 32.*
Ospedale Nuovo San Giovanni di Dio (known as Torregalli) *Via Torregalli 3, Outside the City Gates (055 71921). Bus 6, tram T1.*
Ospedale Palagi (eye hospital) *Viale Michelangiolo 41, Outside the City Gates (055 65771). Bus 12, 13.* **Open** 8am-8pm daily. For eye emergencies; outside these opening hours go to Careggi.
Santa Maria Nuova *Piazza Santa Maria Nuova 1, Duomo & Around (055 27581).* **Map** p335 B4. The most central hospital in Florence.

There's also a 24-hour pharmacy directly outside.
If you need a translator to help out at the hospital, contact:
AVO (Association of Hospital Volunteers) *Via G Carducci 8, Outside the City Gates (24hrs 055 2344567).* **Open** *Office hours* 4-6pm Mon, Wed, Fri; 10am-noon Tue, Thur.
AVO has a group of volunteer interpreters who help out with explanations to doctors and hospital staff in 22 languages. They also give support and advice.

Contraception & abortion

Condoms and other forms of contraception are widely available in pharmacies and some supermarkets. If you need further assistance, the Consultorio Familiare (family planning clinic) at your local ASL state health centre (*see left*) provides free advice and information, though for an examination or prescription, you'll need an EHIC (*see p308*) or insurance. An alternative is to go to a private clinic like those run by AIED.

The morning-after pill is sold legally in Italy; it must be taken within 72 hours, and to obtain it, you'll need to get a prescription (*see below*). Abortion is legal in Italy and is performed only in public hospitals, but the private clinics that are listed below are able to give consultations and references.
Santa Chiara *Piazza Indipendenza 11, San Lorenzo (055 496312/ 475239).* **Open** 8am-7pm daily by appointment.
This clinic offers gynaecological examinations and general health check-ups. Phone for an appointment.

Dentists

The following dentists speak English. Always call ahead for an appointment.
Dr Marcello Luccioli *Via de' Serragli 21, Oltrarno (055 294847).* **Open** 9am-1pm, 2.45-7pm Mon-Fri. **Map** p334 C1.
Dr Sandro Cosi *Via Pellicceria 10, Duomo & Around (055 214238/ 335 332055 mobile).* **Open** 9am-1pm, 3-6pm Mon-Wed; 9am-1pm Thur, Fri. **Map** p334 C3.

Doctors

For a comprehensive list of English-speaking doctors in Florence, by specialisation, see www.ukinitaly.

fco.gov.uk/en/help-for-british-nationals/when-things-go-wrong/if-you-need-doctor/doctors-dentists-in-florence
Dr Stephen Kerr *Via Porta Rossa 1, Duomo & Around (055 288055/ 335 8361682, www.dr-kerr.com).* **Open** *Surgery* by appointment 9am-1pm Mon-Fri. *Drop-in clinic* 3-5pm Mon-Fri. **Map** p334 C3.
This friendly, knowledgeable English GP practises privately in Florence. He charges €40-€70 (standard charge €50) for a consultation in his surgery.
Medical Service *Via Lorenzo il Magnifico 59, Outside the City Gates (24hr line 055 475411, www.medicalservice.firenze.it). Bus 8, 13.* **Open** *Clinic* 11am-noon Mon-Sat; 5-6pm Mon-Fri. A private medical service that organises home visits by doctors. Catering particularly to foreigners, it promises to send an English-speaking GP or specialist out to you in the city of Florence within an hour for between €80 and €150. Clinic visit €50.

Hospitals

See left Accident & emergency.

Pharmacies

Pharmacies (*farmacia*), which are identified by a red or green cross hanging outside, function semi-officially as mini-clinics, with staff able to give informal medical advice and suggest non-prescription medicines. Normal opening hours are 8.30am-1pm and 4-8pm Mon-Fri and 8.30am-1pm Sat, but many central pharmacies are open all day. At other times, there's a duty rota system. A list by the door of all pharmacies indicates the nearest one open outside normal hours, also published in local papers. At duty pharmacies, there's a surcharge of €3 per client (not per item) when only the special duty counter is open – usually midnight-8.30am. Prescriptions are required for most medicines. If you require regular medication, make sure you know their chemical (generic) rather than brand name, as they may be available in Italy only under a different name.

STDs, HIV & AIDS

Clinica Dermatologica *Via della Pergola 64, San Marco (055 2758684).* **Open** 8am-noon Mon, Wed, Thur, Fri; 8-11am Tue, Sat. **Map** p335 A5.

DIRECTORY

Clinica Dermatologica carries out examinations, tests, treatment and counselling for all sexually transmitted diseases, including HIV and AIDS. Some services are free, while others are state-subsidised. Some staff speak English.

Ambulatorio Malattie Infettive *Ospedale di Careggi Viale Morgagni, Outside the City Gates (055 4279425/6). Bus 2, 8, 14C.* **Open** 9am-12.30pm, 3-6pm Mon-Fri; 9am-12.30pm Sat.
AIDS centre with information, advice and testing. Call ahead for an appointment. Basic English spoken.

Infoline per la Salute Omosessuale *(199 444592, 4-8pm Fri).*
Run by the ArciGay organisation, this infoline provides help about services relating to AIDS and HIV.

HELPLINES

AIDS helpline *800 861061.*
Alcoholics Anonymous *055 294417.* Regular AA and Al Anon meetings are held at St James Church (*see p313* Religion for details).
Droga che fare *800 461461.* **Open** 9am-7pm daily.
Samaritans *800 860022.* Some English-speakers.
Voce Amica *055 2478666.* **Open** 4am-6pm. The local Italian version of the Samaritans. Some English spoken.
Women and Children's Rights & Abuse 800 001122.

ID

In Italy, you're required by law to carry photo ID at all times. You'll be asked to produce it if you're stopped by traffic police (who will demand your driving licence, which you must have on you whenever you are in charge of a motor vehicle). ID will also be required when you check into a hotel.

INSURANCE

EU nationals are entitled to reciprocal medical care in Italy, provided they have in their possession a European Health Insurance Card (EHIC). *See p308* for details of how to obtain the card.

Despite this provision, short-term visitors from all countries are advised to get private travel insurance to cover a broad number of eventualities (from injury to theft). Non-EU citizens should ensure that they take out

comprehensive medical insurance with a reputable company before leaving home.

Visitors should also take out adequate property insurance before setting off for Italy. If you rent a car, motorcycle or moped, make sure that you pay the extra for full insurance and sign the collision damage waiver before taking off in the vehicle. It's also worth checking your home insurance first, as it may already cover you.

LEFT LUGGAGE

There's a left luggage point in Santa Maria Novella train station on platform 16 (055 2352190).

LIBRARIES

Biblioteca Marucelliana *Via Cavour 43-47, San Marco (055 2722200, www.maru.firenze.sbn.it).* **Open** 9am-7pm Mon-Fri; 9am-1pm Sat. **Map** p335 A4.
A diverse range of books, including some in English. ID will be needed to register.
British Institute Library & Cultural Centre *Lungarno Guicciardini 9, Oltrarno (055 26778270, www.britishinstitute.it).* **Open** 10am-6.30pm Mon-Fri. **Map** p334 C3.
The British Institute's library requires an annual membership fee (€65, students €50), but offers a reading room that overlooks the Arno, an extensive collection of art history books and Italian literature, and well-informed staff.
Kunsthistorisches Institut in Florenz *Via G Giusti 44, Santa Croce (055 249111, www.khi.fi.it/en).* **Open** 9am-8pm Mon-Fri. **Map** p335 A6.
One of the largest collections of art history books in Florence is held by the German Institute and is available to students. Books are in various languages and there's also an extensive photo library of Italian art, You'll need a letter of presentation and a summary of your research project.

MEDIA

Magazines

Many news stands in the centre of town sell *Time*, *Newsweek*, *The Economist* and other glossy English-language magazines. For Italian-speakers, Italian magazines worth checking out include *Panorama* (www.panorama.it) and *L'Espresso* (http://espresso.

repubblica.it), weekly current affairs and general interest rags, the full-frontal style covers of which do little justice to the high-level journalism and hot-issue coverage found within. There are also some useful booklets with listings of events in Florence:
Firenze Spettacolo (*www.firenzespettacolo.it*) A monthly listings and local interest magazine that has an English-language section.
Florence Concierge Information (*www.florence-concierge.it*) Found at tourist offices and most hotels, this freebie gives events, useful information, timetables and suchlike in English.
Florence & Tuscany News Available around town, this booklet is useful for concerts and temporary exhibitions in Florence and Tuscany. (It's also available as pdf from www.informacitta.net).

Newspapers

Foreign dailies
Many news-stands sell foreign papers, which usually arrive the next day (though sometimes the same evening in summer). The widest range are around piazza del Duomo, piazza della Repubblica, via de' Tornabuoni and SMN station.

Local English-language papers
The Florentine (*www.theflorentine.net*) is a free English-language newspaper distributed twice a week in restaurants, bars, hotels, language schools and the main squares. As well as news and events, it includes articles on culture, politics, travel and food.

Italian dailies
Only one Italian in ten buys a daily newspaper, so the press has little of the clout of other European countries, and the paper is generally a simple vehicle for information rather than a forum of pressure for change. Most papers publish comprehensive listings for local events. Sports coverage in the dailies is extensive, but if you're not sated, the sports papers *Corriere dello Sport* (www.corrieredello sport.it) and *La Gazzetta dello Sport* (www.gazzetta.it) offer even more detail.

Corriere della Sera
(*www.corriere.it*) Serious and relatively neutral newspaper.
Il Giornale (www.ilgiornale.it) Owned by the brother of Silvio

Berlusconi, *Il Giornale* takes the expected centre-right line. The Florence edition has a section dedicated to local news.

Libero (www.libero-news.it) Decidedly right-leaning newspaper launched in 2000, with a pull-no-punches, politically incorrect style.

La Nazione (http://qn.quotidiano.net) Selling some 160,000 copies daily, this is the most popular newspaper in Tuscany. Founded in the mid 19th century by Bettino Ricasoli, it's also one of Italy's oldest. Basically right-wing and gossipy, it consists of three sections (national, sport and local). Each province has its own edition.

La Repubblica (www.repubblica.it) Politically centre-left, with strong coverage of the Mafia and Vatican issues. The Florence edition has about 20 pages dedicated to local and provincial news.

Il Manifesto (www.ilmanifesto.it) A solidly left-wing intellectual paper.

L'Unità The media voice-piece for the far left.

Radio

BBC World Service Piggybacks live on FM on various Italian broadcasts (for a schedule see www.bbc.co.uk/cgi-bin/world service/psims/ScheduleSDT.cgi) and can also be found on shortwave (SW); details of how to listen can be found on www.britishembassy.gov.uk.

Controradio (93.6 MHz/ www.controradio.it) Dub, hip hop, progressive drum 'n' bass and indie rock feature heavily.

Nova Radio (101.5 Mhz/ www.novaradio.info) Run by volunteers and committed to social issues, Nova Radio broadcasts a very good mixture of jazz, soul, blues, reggae, world music, hip hop and rap. Best of all, there are no ads.

Radio Diffusione Firenze (102.7 MHz, www.rdf.it) This radio station plays mainstream pop, house and club music.

Radio Montebeni (108.5 MHz, www.firenzemedia.com/montebenic lassica.html) Classical music only.

Radio Montecarlo (106.6 MHz, www.radiomontecarlo.net) Best at night with Monte Carlo Nights hosted by Scottish DJ Nick the Nightfly playing smooth jazzy sounds and world music.

Virgin Radio Italia (107.2MHz/89.1MHz, www.virgin radioitaly.it) The newest

mainstream radio station with very little chat and an emphasis on British and US rock.

Television

Italy has six major networks. Of these, three are Berlusconi-owned Mediaset channels: **Italia 1** shows familiar US series, Brazilian soaps, Japanese cartoons and adventure films; **Rete 4** spews out an awful lot of cheap game shows and *Columbo* repeats but also shows decent nature documentaries; and **Canale 5** is the top dog, with the best films, quiz programmes, live shows and the most popular programme on Italian TV, the scandal-busting, satirical *Striscia la Notizia*. Programmes are riddled with ad breaks and promotions.

RAI, the state-run channels, are known for their better-quality programming but generally much less slick presenting, and there is still a relentless stream of quiz shows and high-kicking bikini-clad bimbettes. When these have bored you, there are numerous local stations featuring cleaning demos, dial-a-fortune-teller (surprisingly popular), prolonged adverts for slimming machines and trashy late-night soft porn.

Of the many satellite and cable TV subscription channels, the best is **Sky Italia**. Some packages include BBC and major US channels. The French channel **Antenne 2** is also accessible in Tuscany.

MONEY

Italy is in the euro (€) zone. There are euro banknotes for €5, €10, €20, €100, €200 and €500, and coins worth €1 and €2, plus 1¢, 2¢, 5¢, 10¢, 20¢ and 50¢ (cents). Credit cards are widely accepted, though AmEx and Diners Club slightly less so than Visa and MasterCard. Travellers' cheques can be changed at all banks and bureaux de change but are only accepted as payment (in any major currency) by larger shops, hotels and restaurants.

Banks & ATMs

Expect long queues even for simple transactions, and don't be surprised if the bank wants to photocopy your passport or driving licence as proof of ID. Many banks no longer give cash advances on credit cards, so check for the signs, or ask before queuing. Branches of most banks are found around piazza della Repubblica.

Most major banks have 24-hour cashpoint (Bancomat) machines, and the vast majority of these also accept cards with the Maestro and Cirrus symbols. To access the cashpoint lobby of some banks, you have to insert your card in the machine outside. Most machines will dispense a daily limit of €250. Your home bank will make a charge.

Bureaux de change

Changing your money in a bank usually gets you a better rate than in a private bureau de change (*cambio*) and will often be better than in your home country. However, if you need to change money out of banking hours, there's no shortage of bureaux de change (*cambi*). Commission rates vary considerably: you can pay from nothing to €5 for each transaction. Watch out for 'No Commission' signs; the exchange rate at these places will almost certainly be worse. Main post offices also have bureaux de change, where commission is €2.50 for all cash transactions (maximum €1,000). Some large hotels also offer an exchange service, but again, the rate is almost certainly worse than in a bank. Always take ID for any financial transaction.

InterChange *Lungarno Acciaiuoli 4/8r, Duomo & Around* (055 289781, www.interchange.eu). **Open** 9.30am-6pm Mon-Sat; 10am-5pm Sun. **Map** p334 C3.

One of the few exchange offices open on a Sunday. No commission for cash withdrawal via MasterCard or Visa.

Chip & PIN

The Chip and PIN system is up and running in Italy, though it's not available everywhere.

Credit cards

Italians have an enduring fondness for cash, but nearly all hotels of two stars and above, as well as most shops and restaurants (though still surprisingly few museums), now accept at least some of the major credit cards.

Lost/stolen

Most lines are freephone (800) numbers, have English-speaking staff and are open 24 hours daily.

American Express card emergencies 06 72900347.

Diners Club 800 864064.

DIRECTORY

CartaSì 800 151616.
MasterCard 800 870866.
Visa 800 819014.

Tax

Sales tax (IVA) is applied to all purchases and services at 4%, 10% and 21% in an ascending scale of luxury, but is almost always included in the price stated. At some luxury hotels, tax will be added on to the quoted rates, but prices will be clearly stated as *escluso IVA*.

By law, all non-EU residents are entitled to an IVA refund on purchases of €155 and over at shops participating in the 'Tax-free shopping' scheme, identified by a purple sticker. On presentation of your passport, they will give you a 'cheque' that can be cashed at the airport desk on your way home at the Tax Free Cash Refund desk at the airport. You'll need to show your passport and the unused goods, and there's a three-month time limit. IVA paid on hotel bills cannot be reclaimed.

OPENING HOURS

Bank opening hours are generally from 8.20am to 1.20pm and from 2.35pm to 3.35pm Monday to Friday.

All banks are closed on public holidays. Most post offices open from 8.15am to 1.30pm, closing an hour earlier on Saturdays; the main post office stays open Monday to Saturday from 8.15am to 7pm (*see also below*). Food shops generally open early morning and close for lunch from 1pm to 3.30pm (though some stay closed till 5pm), then are open again until 7.30pm. They are generally closed on Wednesday afternoons (Saturday afternoons in the summer). Other shops tend to open later in the morning and are closed on Monday mornings. Many shops now stay open all day (*orario continuato*).

POLICE

Italian police forces are divided into four colour-coded units. The *vigili urbani* and *polizia municipale* (municipal police) wear navy blue. The *vigili* deal with all traffic matters within the city, and the *polizia municipale* with petty crime. The two forces responsible for dealing with crime are the *polizia di stato* (state police), who also wear blue jackets but have pale grey trousers, and the normally

black-clad *carabinieri*, part of the army. Their roles are essentially the same. The *guardia di finanza* (financial police) wear grey and have little to do with tourists.

In an emergency, go to the tourist aid police or the nearest *carabinieri* post or police station (*questura*); we have listed central ones below, but others are found in the phone book. Staff will either speak English or be able to find someone who does. If you have had something stolen, tell them you want to report a *furto*.

A statement (*denuncia*) will be taken, which you'll need for an insurance claim. Lost or stolen passports should also be reported to your embassy or consulate. *See also p308* Emergencies.

Comando Provinciale Carabinieri
Borgo Ognissanti 48, Santa Maria Novella (055 2061). **Open** 24hrs daily. **Map** p334 B1.
A *carabinieri* post near the town centre; the best place to report the loss or theft of personal property.
Questura di Firenze Ufficio Denuncie *Via Duca D'Aosta 3, San Lorenzo (055 49771).* **Open** 24hrs daily.
To report a crime, go to the Ufficio Denuncie, where you will be asked to fill in a form.
Police *Via Pietrapiana 50r, Santa Croce (055 203911).* **Open** 8.30am-7.30pm Mon-Fri; 8.30am-1.30pm Sat. **Map** p335 B6.
Interpreters are on hand to help report thefts, lost property and any other problems.

POSTAL SERVICES

Improvements have been made to Italy's postal service, and you can now be more or less sure that the letter you sent or were sent will arrive in reasonable time.

Stamps (*francobolli*) can be bought at *tabacchi* or post offices. Most post boxes are red and have two slots, Per la Città (for Florence) and Tutte le Altre Destinazioni (everywhere else).

A letter takes about five days to reach the UK, eight to the US. There is now only one class of post (*posta prioritaria*), which generally fulfils its delivery promise of within 24 hours in Italy, three days for EU countries and four or five for the rest of the world. A small letter or postcard weighing 20 grams or less sent to addresses in Italy costs 60¢. To any EU country, it costs 75¢; to the US, it'll cost €1.60; sending mail further afield will cost €2. Special stamps can be bought at post offices and *tabacchi*.

Mail (20 grams or less) can be sent *raccomandata* (registered) for €3.30 for Italy, €4.80 for the EU and €5.60 for the US. *Assicurata* (insured) for up to €50 costs €7.80 in the EU; €8.60 to the US, from post offices only.

Heavier mail is charged according to weight. To send a parcel weighing a kilogram to the UK costs €15 (*posta prioritaria*), €25 to the US.

Italian postal charges are complicated, so be prepared for variations. For guaranteed fast delivery, use a courier or the SDA Italian post office courier service.

The Italian post call centre number is 803160 (199 100160 from mobile phones). Officially Italian only, though you may strike lucky.

Post offices

Local post offices (*ufficio postale*) in each district generally open from 8.15am to 1.30pm Monday to Friday, and from 8.15am to 12.30pm on Saturdays. The main post office (*Posta Centrale*) has longer opening hours and a range of additional services.
Posta Centrale
Via Pellicceria 3, Duomo & Around (055 2736481). **Open** 8.15am-7pm Mon-Fri; 8.15am-1.30pm Sat. **Map** p335 A4.
This is Florence's main post office.
Other post offices
Via Luigi Alamanni 14-16 (by the Train Station), Santa Maria Novella (055 2674931). **Open** 8.15am-7pm Mon-Fri; 8.15am-12.30pm Sat.
Via Pietrapiana 53, Santa Croce (055 2674231). **Open** 8.15am-7pm Mon-Fri; 8.15am-12.30pm Sat. **Map** p334 C3.
Via Barbadori 37r, Oltrarno (055 288175). **Open** 8.15am-1.30pm Mon-Fri; 8.15am-12.30pm Sat. **Map** p334 C3.

Poste restante

Poste restante (general delivery) letters (in Italian, *fermoposta*) should be sent to the main post office (*see above*), addressed to Fermoposta and the code and address of the post office you wish to pick up your mail from. You need a passport to collect mail and you may have to pay a small charge if sent from outside Italy (if sent from Italy a charge of €3 is added to the postage). Mail can also be sent to any Mail Boxes Etc branches.

RELIGION

There are Roman Catholic churches all over the city, and a few churches still sing mass. Catholic mass is held in English at Santa Maria del Fiore (the Duomo) on Saturday afternoons at 5pm and at the Chiesa dell'Ospedale San Giovanni di Dio (borgo Ognissanti 20) on Sundays and public holidays at 10am.

American Episcopal Church (St James's Church) *Via Rucellai 9, Santa Maria Novella (055 294417, www.stjames.it)*. **Services** (in English) 9am, 11am Sun. **Map** p334 A1.

Anglican *St Mark's Church, via Maggio 16, Oltrarno (055 294764/ www.stmarksitaly.com)*. **Services** 9.30am (Low Mass), 10.30am (Sung Mass) Sun; 6pm (Low Mass) Thur; 8pm (Low Mass) Fri. **Map** p334 C2.

Islamic *Associazione Islamica, via Tagliamento 3a, Outside the City Gates (055 65030331)*. Bus 23, 31.

Jewish *Comunità Ebraica, via Farini 4, Santa Croce (055 245252/www.firenzebraica.net)*. **Services** 8.30/8.45am Sat. Phone for details of Fri & Sat evening services; times vary. **Map** p335 B6.

Methodist *Chiesa Metodista, via de' Benci 9, Santa Croce (055 288143)*. **Services** 11am Sun. **Map** p335 C4.

SAFETY & SECURITY

Crime has unfortunately been on the increase in Florence though serious street crime is rare, and it remains a relatively safe city to walk in. Take care at night, when lone women in particular should stick to the main well-lit streets. For visitors to the city, the main risk comes from the numerous pickpockets and bag-snatchers. Buses, shops, bars and other crowded areas are petty criminals' hunting grounds. As you would in any major city, take common-sense precautions:

● Don't keep wallets in back pockets. This is a pickpocket's favourite swipe, especially on buses and public transport.

● Wear shoulder bags diagonally and facing away from the road to minimise the risk of *scippi* – bag-snatching from mopeds, which is still common in the city.

● Never leave bags on tables or the backs of chairs in bars.

● Keep an eye on your valuables while trying on clothes and shoes.

Also, watch out for 'baby-gangs' of children or teenagers who hang around the tourist spots and create a distraction by flapping a newspaper or card while trying to slip their hands into bags or pockets.

If you are approached, keep walking, keep calm and hang on to your valuables.

For emergency numbers, *see p308*. For information on the police, *see p312*.

SMOKING

A law banning smoking in all public places came into force in 2005 and is scrupulously respected and enforced. This includes bars, restaurants and clubs, although there is a clause that allows some venues to set aside a smoking room, as long as it is separated by double doors and adequately ventilated and filtered. Owners who allow customers to smoke are fined heavily, the smoker can also be fined. Cigarettes are on sale at *tabacchi* and *bar-tabacchi*; both are recognisable by the blue/black and white sign outside.

STUDY

With over 20 US university programmes and countless language schools and art courses, many of which have international reputations, the city's student population rivals that of its residents at some times of the year. The courses listed in this section are all generally in English. However, if you don't speak any Italian, double-check before you enrol.

To study in Florence, you will need a *permesso di soggiorno per studio*. The same requirements apply as for the *permesso di soggiorno* (*see p316*), plus a guarantee that your medical bills will be paid (an EHIC card will do for UK students), evidence that you can support yourself and a letter from the educational institution. To study alongside Florentine undergraduates, contact an Italian consulate to apply to do a *corso singolo*, or one year of study at the University of Florence. You need to register at the Centro di Cultura per Stranieri at the beginning of November. The fees for a *corso singolo* (maximum five subjects) are approximately €1,200. To complete a degree course, you must have studied to university level. For details, see www.unifi.it. There are also exchange programmes for EU students.

Several US universities, including Georgetown, Sarah Lawrence, New York, Gonzaga and Syracuse, have Florence outposts open to students from any US university for the semester and summer courses.

Università di Firenze: *Centro di Cultura per Stranieri Via Francesco Valori 9, Outside the City Gates (055 5032701/2/3, www.unifi.it/ccs)*. Bus 8, 10, 11, 17, 20. **Open** 9am-noon Mon-Fri. Offers language and cultural courses.

Art, design & restoration courses

Il Bisonte *Via San Niccolò 24, Oltrarno (055 2347215, www.ilbisonte.it)*. **Map** p335 D5. Located among the artisans' workshops in the former stables of Palazzo Serristori, Il Bisonte has specialist courses and theoretical/ practical seminars in the techniques of etching and printmaking.

Charles H Cecil Studios *Borgo San Frediano 68, Oltrarno (055 285102, www.charlescecil studios.com)*. **Map** p334 C1. The church of San Raffaello Arcangelo was converted into a studio complex in the early 19th century. It now houses one of the more charismatic of Florence's art schools, Charles H Cecil Studios, which is heavily frequented by Brits. It gives a thorough training in the classical techniques of drawing and oil painting, and runs classes for the general public.

L'Istituto per l'Arte e il Restauro *Palazzo Ridolfi, via Maggio 13, Oltrarno (055 282951, www.spinelli.it)*. **Map** p334 D2. Widely considered one of the best art restoration schools in Italy, the Institute offers a multitude of courses in the restoration of frescoes, paintings, furniture, gilt objects, ceramics, stone, paper and glass. They last between one and three years. One-month courses are held from July to September in the same disciplines.

Oro e Colore *Via Toscanella 18r, Oltrarno (055 289415, www.oroecolore.com)*. **Map** p334 D2. Month- to year-long courses in art restoration, gold leaf restoration and other techniques. No previous experience is needed; however, places on courses are limited and are taught only in Italian.

Studio Art Centers International (SACI) *Via Sant'Antonino 11, San Lorenzo (055 289948, www. saci-florence.org)*. **Map** p334 A3.

DIRECTORY

SACI offers five specific credit programmes for graduates and undergraduates. These include both academic and practical courses in the arts, ranging from museology to batik design. There is an entry requirement for certain courses.

Università Internazionale dell'Arte *Villa il Ventaglio, via delle Forbici 24-26, Outside the City Gates (055 570216, www.uiafirenze.com). Bus 7.* Based in a fabulous villa, courses cover restoration and preservation, museum and gallery management and art criticism.

Language classes

There are no end of language and culture courses in Florence, including many intensive one- or two-month courses, which should provide an adequate everyday grasp of the language. Prices refer to a standard four-week course with four hours' tuition a day.

ABC Centro di Lingua e Cultura Italiana *Via de' Rustici 7, Santa Croce (055 212001, www.abc school.com).* **Price** €640. **Map** p335 C4.
ABC offers language teaching at six levels, as well as preparatory courses for the entrance exam to the University of Florence.

British Institute Language Centre *Piazza Strozzi 2, Duomo & Around (055 26778200, www.britishinstitute.it).* **Price** €630. **Map** p334 B3.
Short courses in Italian language, history of art, drawing and cooking. For the British Institute's Library & Cultural Centre, *see p310.*

Centro Linguistico Italiano Dante Alighieri *Piazza della Repubblica 5, Duomo & Around (055 210808, www.clida.it).* **Price** €570, plus €80 enrolment fee. **Map** p335 D4.
Eleven language levels; opera and literature courses too.

Istituto Lorenzo de' Medici *Via Faenza 43, San Lorenzo (055 283142, www.lorenzodemedici.it).* **Price** €600. **Map** p334 A3.
Four different courses in Italian as well as classes in cooking, Italian cinema and art history.

Scuola Leonardo da Vinci *Via Bufalini 3, Duomo & Around (055 294420, www.scuolaleonardo.com).* **Price** €680, plus €70 enrolment. **Map** p335 B4.
Versatile language courses, plus classes in history of art, fashion, drawing, design, cooking and wine.

Scuola Machiavelli *Piazza Santo Spirito 4, Oltrarno (055 2396966,* www.centromachiavelli.it). **Price** €520, plus €40 enrolment fee. **Map** p335 D1.
This small co-op offers Italian, pottery, fresco, mosaic, trompe l'œil and book-binding classes.

Useful organisations

Council of International Education Exchange (CIEE) *300 Fore Street, Portland, Maine, ME 04101, USA (+1 207 553 4000, www.ciee.org).*
Institute of International Education *809 UN Plaza, New York, NY 10017-3580, USA (+1 212 883 8200, www.iie.org).*
Italian Cultural Institute *39 Belgrave Square, London SW1X 8NX, UK (+44 (0)20 7235 1461, www.italcultur.org.uk).*

TELEPHONES

Competition has led to price cuts for telephone customers, with Telecom Italia, the biggest and most commonly used Italian phone company, in direct competition with newer phone companies, such as Tele 2 and Infostrada. Tariffs are higher if you're calling from a public phone and usually higher still from a hotel: you're generally better off buying an international phone card, though they don't offer anything approaching the same level of discounts as in the UK or US. Calling from a phone centre costs the same as from a payphone, but it's more convenient as you pay at the end for the call.

Dialling & codes

The international code for Italy is 39. To dial in from other countries, preface it with the exit code: 00 in the UK and 011 in the US. All normal Florence numbers begin with the area code 055. The code for Siena is 0577, for Pisa 050. As with all Italian codes, these must always be used in full, even when you are calling from within the same area, and when dialling internationally. For mobile phone numbers there is no initial zero.

To make an international call from Florence, dial 00, then the country code (Australia 61; Canada 1; Irish Republic 353; New Zealand 64; United Kingdom 44; United States 1), followed by the area code (for calls to the UK, omit the initial zero) and individual number. The same pattern works to mobile phones.

All numbers beginning 800 are free lines (*numero verde*). For numbers that begin 840, you'll be charged one unit only, regardless of where you're calling from or how long the call lasts. These numbers can be called from within Italy only; some only function within one phone district. Phone numbers starting with 3 are mobile numbers; those with 199 codes are charged at local rates; 167 numbers are billed at premium rates.

Mobile phones

Pay-as-you-go mobiles can be bought from many phone shops and some post offices from around €20, including the SIM card and €5 of calls. Top-up cards are available from all *bar-tabacchi* and some newsstands; either call the number given on the card, or, if the bar has the electronic top-up facility, tap in your phone number and the amount requested will be credited automatically. One top-up has to be made at least every 11 months to keep the number active. SIM cards can also be bought without having to buy a phone; prices vary.

Italian mobile phone numbers begin with 3 (no zero).

The mobile phone shops listed below are located in central Florence.

TIM, Telecom Italia Mobile *Via de' Lamberti 12-14, Duomo & Around (055 2396066).* **Open** 9am-7pm Mon-Fri; 9am-1pm Sat. **Map** p334 C3.
Vodafone *Via de' Martelli 25-31r, Duomo & Around (055 2670121).* **Open** 9am-7pm Mon-Fri; 9am-1pm Sat. **Map** p334 A4.

Operator services

To make a reverse-charge (collect) call, dial 170 for the international operator in Italy. To be connected to the operator in the country you want to call, dial 172 followed by a country code (so 172 00 44 for the UK and 172 00 1 for the US) and you'll be connected directly to an operator in that country. The following services operate 24 hours daily (calls are charged):
Operator and directory enquiries *1254* (option 1 for Italian directory enquiries 24hrs; option 2 for international enquiries 7am-midnight).
International operator 170.
Problems on national calls 182.

Public phones

Since the popular mobile phone revolution and the opening of so many small internet point/call centres, public phones in Florence have all but disappeared, especially in less central areas. However, some bars still have payphones as do a few of the city's squares, the stations and airport. Public phones only accept phone cards with magnetic strips (*schede telefoniche*), not coins; some also accept major credit cards. *Schede telefoniche* are available from *tabacchi*, some newsstands and some bars, as are the pre-paid phone cards offering access via an 800 number to both domestic and international calls. To use a card phone, lift the receiver and wait for the tone, then insert the card (with the perforated corner torn off) and dial.

Phone centres

There are now phone centres throughout the city centre, very often combining phone services with internet services and faxes.

For a full list check in the *Yellow Pages* under '*Telecomunicazioni*'.

Telephone directories

All hotels and most restaurants and bars have phone books and *Yellow Pages* (if they're not obviously on display, ask to see the *elenco telefonico* or *pagine gialle*). Telecom Italia has a useful website (www.1254.virgilio.it) with an online directory enquiries service.

Telegrams

Telegrams can be sent from main post offices. The telegraph office at the Posta Centrale (*see p312*) is open 8.15am-7pm Mon-Fri; 8.15am-1.30pm Sat. Alternatively, dictate telegrams over the phone. Dial 186 from a private or hotel phone and a message in Italian will tell you to dial the number of the phone you're phoning from. You will then be passed to a telephonist.

TIME

Italy is one hour ahead of London, six ahead of New York and eight behind Sydney. Clocks go forward an hour in spring and back in autumn, in line with other EU countries.

TIPPING

The 10-15 per cent tip customary in many countries is considered generous in Florence. Locals sometimes leave a few coins on the counter when buying drinks at the bar and, depending on the standard of the restaurant, will drop €1-€5 for the service after a meal. That said, some larger restaurants are now starting to add a 10-15 per cent service charge on the bill automatically. Tips are not expected in small restaurants, although they are always appreciated. Taxi drivers will be surprised if you do more than add a euro or two.

TOURIST INFORMATION

To be sent an information pack in advance of your visit, get in touch with ENIT, the Italian tourist board (UK: 0800 00482542/020 7408 1254, www.enit.it; US: 212 245 4822, www.enit.it, www.italiantourism.com). Tell staff where and when you're travelling, and whether or not you have any special interests.

Florence's provincial tourist board, the Azienda Promozionale Turistica (APT; www.firenze turismo.it), and the council-run Ufficio Informazioni Turistiche have helpful, multilingual staff who do their best to supply reliable information: not easy, since museums and galleries tend to change their hours without telling them. There's no central information service for the Tuscany region; you have to contact the APT in each area. There is a head office in each provincial capital, then local offices in various towns within the province. Details of tourist offices are listed in this guide under the relevant area.

Tourist information offices

Via Cavour 1r, San Lorenzo (055 290832). **Open** 8.30am-6.30pm Mon-Sat; 8.30am-1.30pm Sun. **Map** p335 A4.
Infopoint Bigallo, piazza San Giovanni 1, Duomo & Around (055 288496). **Open** 9am-7pm Mon-Sat; 9am-2pm Sun. **Map** p334 B3.
Piazza della Stazione 4a, Santa Maria Novella (055 212245). **Open** 8.30am-7pm Mon-Sat; 8.30am-2pm Sun. **Map** p334 A2.
Run by the City of Florence, these offices provide maps and info. There are also offices in Florence and Pisa airports. Hotel bookings can be made by emailing Florence Promhotels on info@promhotels.it

(www.promhotels.it), a free hotel-booking service available by email or through the tourist office.

VISAS & IMMIGRATION

Non-EU citizens and Britons require full passports to travel to Italy. EU citizens are permitted unrestricted access to Italy to travel (*see also p316* Working in Florence); citizens of the USA, Canada, Australia and New Zealand should check about visa requirements at an Italian embassy or consulate in their own country before setting off for Italy.

WEIGHTS & MEASURES

Italy uses only the metric system; remember that all speed limits are in kilometres. One kilometre is equivalent to 0.62 mile, with 1 mile converting to 1.6 kilometres. Petrol, like other liquids, is measured in litres: one UK gallon = 4.54 litres; 1 US gallon = 3.79 litres. A kilogram is equivalent to 2.2 pounds (one pound = 0.45 kilos). Food is often sold in etti (sometimes written hg); 1 etto = 100 grams (3.52 ounces). In delicatessens, ask for multiples of etti (un etto, due etti, etc).

WHAT TO TAKE

Any prescription medicines should always be obtained before leaving. Make sure you have enough to cover the entire period of your stay, as not all US and UK medicines are available in Italy.

WHEN TO GO

Climate

The hills surrounding Florence mean that it can be cold and humid in winter and very hot and humid in the summer. Between late June and August, temperatures often soar to 40°C (104°F) and rarely fall below 30°C (86°F).

During the summer, you should be sure to take the sun seriously: every year, local doctors issue warnings about the number of visitors who are hospitalised with serious burns from spending too much time in the sun and going out in the middle of the day. (Italians stay indoors whenever they can during the hottest hours.) The short spring and autumn in Florence and Tuscany can be very warm. They're not without risk of rain, though, especially in March, April and September. Between November and February, you can't rely on

DIRECTORY

good weather: you could find anything from a week of rain to crisp, bright and sometimes even warm sunshine.

Public holidays

On public holidays (*giorni festivi*) virtually all shops, banks and businesses are shut, though most bars and restaurants stay open so you will be able to eat and drink. Public holidays are as follows:

New Year's Day (Capodanno) 1 Jan
Epiphany (La Befana) 6 Jan
Easter Day (Pasqua)
Easter Monday (Lunedì di Pasqua)
Liberation Day (Venticinque Aprile/Liberazione) 25 Apr
Labour Day (Primo Maggio) 1 May
Republic Day (Festa della Repubblica) 2 June
Florence Saint's Day (San Giovanni) 24 June
Feast of the Assumption (Ferragosto) 15 Aug
All Saints' (Tutti i Santi) 1 Nov
Immaculate Conception (Festa dell'Immacolata) 8 Dec
Christmas Day (Natale) 25 Dec
Boxing Day (Santo Stefano) 26 Dec

There is limited public transport on 1 May and Christmas afternoon. Holidays falling on a Saturday or Sunday are not celebrated the following Monday, but if a holiday falls on a Thursday or Tuesday, many locals also take the intervening day off and make a long weekend of it; such a weekend is called a *ponte* (bridge). Beware of the *rientro* or homecoming, when the roads are horrendously busy.

Many people also disappear for a large chunk of August, when *chiuso per ferie* (closed for holidays) signs appear in shops and restaurants detailing dates of closure. These closures are co-ordinated on a rota system by the city council, so there should be something open in each area at any given time. However, if you should find yourself in Florence, or many other Tuscan towns, on the Ferragosto (Feast of the Assumption; 15 August), the chances are that your only company will be other tourists wandering the baked streets in search of something to do or somewhere to eat. The Florentines desert the city, and are likely to stay away for several days either side. You'll find the exceptions to this rule are holiday resorts such as coastal towns where, although shops and public offices may close, the infrastructure doesn't

completely collapse. For a calendar of Tuscany's traditional and modern festivals throughout the year, *see p176-181*.

WOMEN

Although it's not one of the worst places for women travellers, Tuscany still has its hassles. Visiting women can feel daunted by the sheer volume of attention they receive, but most of it will be friendly; men are unlikely to become pushy or aggressive if given the brush-off. It's normally a question of all talk and no action, but be aware of who's around you: it's quite common to be followed. If things get too heavy, go into the nearest shop or bar and wait or ask for help. The notorious bum-pinching is uncommon but not unknown, especially on buses. As in Anglo-Saxon countries, it's a criminal offence, and recent prosecutions and convictions show that it's taken seriously.

Tampons (*assorbenti interni*) and sanitary towels (*assorbenti esterni*) can be bought in supermarkets, pharmacies and some *tabacchi*. For info on contraception, abortion and other health matters, *see p309*.

Artemisia *Via del Mezzetta 1/int, Outside the City Gates (055 602311, children's line 055 601375, www.artemisiacentro antiviolenza.it). Bus 10, 11, 70.* **Open** 10am-5pm Mon-Fri.
A voluntary association for women and children who have suffered from abuse. Provides legal advice, social and psychological support, group therapy and has two safe houses.

Clinica Ostetrica *Reparto Maternità, Ospedale di Careggi, viale Morgagni, Outside the City Gates (055 794111). Bus 2, 8, 14C.* **Open** 24hrs daily.
Female victims of sexual assault should go to the Clinica Ostetrica for medical attention.

International Women's Network *Villa Rossa, piazza Savonarola 15, Outside the City Gates (contact Jane Fogarty, networkfirenze@ hotmail.com). Bus 10, 11, 17.*
A professional women's organisation geared mainly towards residents whose first language is English. It aims to improve communication, exchange ideas and information among the English-speaking community. Meetings are generally on the second Wednesday of the month. Annual fees are €40, which includes newsletters and mailings.

WORKING IN FLORENCE

Finding a job in Italy is not simple. The jobs market isn't known for being mobile and unemployment is fairly high, especially for graduate positions. Most of the jobs that are available are connected to tourism in some way, although there are a few multinationals that occasionally advertise for native English-speakers. The classified ads paper *La Pulce* has job listings; it's also worth checking the local English-language press.

The bureaucracy involved is not easy but has been simplified by recent changes, at least for EU citizens. Since April 2007, EU citizens no longer need to apply for a *permesso di soggiorno* (permit to stay). For stays of over three months, EU citizens should sign up at their local *anagrafe* (Register Office) presenting proof of their work, study or training activities, or providing proof of adequate financial means to support themselves (this is judged by the number of people in the family, from just over €5,000 for single applicants, to just over €15,000 for those with four or more extra family dependents).

Citizens from outside the EU should check about visa requirements at an Italian embassy or consulate in their own country before setting off for Italy. All non-EU citizens who are planning to stay for more than three months should register with the police within eight days of arrival and then apply for their permits. More details are on the Polizia di Stato website: www.poliziadistato.it/articolo/ 10617/ (in English).

Administration & permit offices
Comune di Firenze (Florence town hall), Palazzo Vecchio & Piazza Signoria, Duomo & Around (switchboard 055 27681/800 831133, www.comune.fi.it). **Open** 8.30am-1.30pm Mon-Wed, Fri, Sat; 8.30am-6.30pm Thur. **Map** p335 C4.
For residency enquiries, ask for the Ufficio Circoscrizione. Given your address, they will then give you the number you need to call to progress further with your application.
Permits to stay
Immigration Office, via della Fortezza 17, San Lorenzo (055 4977057). **Open** 8.15-10am Mon-Thur.
To apply for your documents go here (English-speaking staff are usually available to help).

Vocabulary

Any attempt at speaking Italian will always be appreciated. Indeed, it may well be necessary: away from services such as tourist offices, hotels and restaurants popular with foreigners, the level of English is not very high. The most important thing is making the effort, not whether or not your sentences are perfectly formed with an authentic accent. The key is to take the plunge and not be shy.

It's a myth that you can get by in Italy with Spanish: true, you may well understand some Italian (both written and spoken), but try speaking it and Italians generally won't understand you (unless, of course, they speak Spanish).

Italian is a phonetic language, so most words are spelled as they're pronounced (and vice versa). Stresses usually fall on the penultimate syllable. There are three forms of the second person: the formal *lei* (used with strangers), the informal *tu*, and the plural form *voi*. Masculine nouns are usually accompanied by adjectives ending in 'o', female nouns by adjectives ending in 'a'. However, there are many nouns and adjectives that end in 'e' that can be either masculine or feminine.

PRONUNCIATION

Vowels

a – as in apple
e – like a in age (closed e), or e in sell (open e)
i – like ea in east
o – as in hotel (closed o) or in hot (open o)
u – like oo in boot

Consonants

c – before a, o or u: like the c in cat; before e or i: like the ch in check
ch – like the c in cat
g – before a, o or u: like the g in get; before e or i: like the j in jig
gh – like the g in get
gl – followed by 'i': like lli in million
gn – like ny in canyon
qu – as in quick
r – is always rolled
s – has two sounds, as in soap or rose
sc – followed by 'e' or 'i': like the sh in shame

sch – like the sc in scout
z –has two sounds, like ts and dz
Double consonants are sounded more emphatically.

USEFUL WORDS & PHRASES

hello and goodbye (informal) – *ciao*
good morning, good day – *buongiorno*
good afternoon, good evening – *buona sera*
I don't understand – *non capisco/non ho capito*
do you speak English? – *parla inglese?*
please – *per favore*
thank you – *grazie*
you're welcome – *prego*
when does it open? – *quando apre?*
where is... ? – *dov'è...?*
excuse me – *scusi (polite), scusa (informal)*
open – *aperto*
closed – *chiuso*
entrance – *entrata*
exit – *uscita*
left – *sinistra*
right – *destra*
car – *macchina*
bus – *autobus*
train – *treno*
bus stop – *fermata dell'autobus*
ticket/s – *biglietto/i*
I would like a ticket to... – *vorrei un biglietto per...*
postcard – *cartolina*
stamp – *francobollo*
glass – *bicchiere*
coffee – *caffè*
tea – *tè*
water – *acqua*
wine – *vino*
beer – *birra*
the bill – *il conto*
single/twin/double bedroom – *camera singola/a due letti/matrimoniale*
booking – *prenotazione*

DAYS OF THE WEEK

Monday – *lunedì*
Tuesday – *martedì*
Wednesday – *mercoledì*
Thursday – *giovedì*
Friday – *venerdì*
Saturday – *sabato*
Sunday – *domenica*
yesterday – *ieri*

today – *oggi*
tomorrow – *domani*
morning – *mattina*
afternoon – *pomeriggio*
evening – *sera*
night – *notte*
weekend – *fine settimana, weekend*

THE COME-ON

do you have a light? – *hai da accendere?*
what's your name? – *come ti chiami?*
would you like a drink? – *vuoi bere qualcosa?*
where are you from? – *di dove sei?*
what are you doing here? – *che fai qui?*
do you have a boyfriend/girlfriend? – *hai un ragazzo/una ragazza?*

THE BRUSH-OFF

I'm married – *sono sposato/a*
I'm tired – *sono stanco/a*
I'm going home – *vado a casa*
I have to meet a friend – *devo incontrare un amico/una amica*

NUMBERS & MONEY

0 *zero*; 1 *uno*; 2 *due*; 3 *tre*; 4 *quattro*; 5 *cinque*; 6 *sei*; 7 *sette*; 8 *otto*; 9 *nove*; 10 *dieci*; 11 *undici*; 12 *dodici*; 13 *tredici*; 14 *quattordici*; 15 *quindici*; 16 *sedici*; 17 *diciassette*; 18 *diciotto*; 19 *diciannove*; 20 *venti*; 21 *ventuno*; 22 *ventidue*; 30 *trenta*; 40 *quaranta*; 50 *cinquanta*; 60 *sessanta*; 70 *settanta*; 80 *ottanta*; 90 *novanta*; 100 *cento*; 1,000 *mille*; 2,000 *duemila*; 100,000 *centomila*; 100,000 *un milione*.
how much does it cost/is it? – *quanto costa?/quant'è?*
do you have any change? – *ha da cambiare?*
can you give me a discount? – *mi può fare uno sconto?*
do you accept credit cards? – *si accettano le carte di credito?*
can I pay in pounds/dollars/travellers' cheques? – *posso pagare in sterline/dollari/con i travellers?*
can I have a receipt? – *posso avere una ricevuta*

Glossary

Annunciation depiction of the Virgin Mary being told by the Archangel Gabriel that she will bear the son of God.

Attribute object used in art to symbolise a particular person, often saints and martyrs.

Baldacchino canopied structure; in paintings holding an enthroned Madonna and child.

Banderuola small forked flag bearing an inscription, held in Renaissance art by angels or *putti*.

Baptistery building for baptisms, usually octagonal to symbolise new beginnings, as seven is the number of completion and eight the start of a new cycle.

Baroque sumptuous art and architectural style from the 17th to mid 18th centuries.

Byzantine spiritual and religious art of the Byzantine Empire (fifth-15th centuries).

Campanile bell tower.

Cartoon full-scale sketch for painting or fresco.

Cenacolo depiction of the Last Supper.

Chiaroscuro painting or drawing technique using shades of black, grey and white to emphasise light and shade.

Classical ancient Greek and Roman art and culture.

Corbel brackets jutting from a roof.

Cupola dome-shaped structure set on a larger dome or a roof.

Deposition depiction of Christ taken down from the Cross.

Diptych painting made of two panels.

Fresco technique for wall painting where pigments bind with wet plaster.

Golden mean Renaissance art theory with division of proportions by a ratio of 8:13. Considered to create perfect harmony.

Gothic architectural and artistic style of the late Middle Ages (from the 12th century),

characterised by the integration of art forms, with pointed arches and an emphasis on line.

Grotesque ornate artistic style derived from Roman underground painted rooms (*grotte*).

Hortus conclusus garden around Madonna and child symbolising their uncontaminated world of perfection and contentment.

Iconography study of subject and symbolism of works of art. For example, in Renaissance art: a **dog** symbolises faithfulness to a master, usually the Medici; an **egg** is a symbol of perfection; a **peacock** symbolises the Resurrection; a **giglio** (lily of Florence) is often found in Annunciations to symbolise the purity of the Madonna; a **sarcophagus** (stone or marble coffin) symbolises the death of an important person; and the colour **blue** sometimes symbolises divine peace.

Illumination miniature painted as an illustration for manuscripts.

Loggia covered area with one or more sides open, with columns.

Lunette half-moon painting or semicircular architectural space for decoration or window.

Madonna of Mercy Madonna with her cloak open to give protection to those in need.

Maestà depiction of the Madonna on a throne.

Mandorla almond-shaped 'glory' surrounding depiction of holy person.

Mannerism 15th-century art movement in Italy, defined by exaggerated perspective and scale, and complex compositions and poses.

Medieval relating to the Middle Ages (from the fall of the Roman Empire in the west, in the fifth century, to the 1453 fall of Constantinople).

Modernist (Modernism) the movement away from classical and traditional forms towards architecture that applied scientific methods to its design.

Palazzo (*palazzi*) large and/or important building, not necessarily a royal palace.

Panel painting on wood.

Panneggio style of folded and pleated drapery worn by figures in 15th- and 16th-century painting and sculpture.

Pietà depiction of Christ lying across the Madonna's lap after the Deposition.

Pietra dura inlaid gem mosaics.

Polyptych painting composed of several panels.

Putto (*putti*) small angelic naked boys, often depicted as attendants of Venus.

Relief sculpted work with three-dimensional areas jutting out from a flat surface.

Renaissance 14th- to 16th-century cultural movement based on the 'rebirth' of classical ideals and methods.

Romanesque architectural style of the early Middle Ages (c500-1200), drawing on Roman Byzantine influences.

Secco the finishing-off or retouching of a fresco, done on dried plaster (*intonaco*).

Sinopia preparatory drawing for a fresco made with a red earth mix or the red paint itself.

Tempera pigment bound with egg, the main painting material from the 12th to late 15th centuries.

Tondo round painting or relief.

Triptych painting composed of three panels.

Trompe l'œil painting designed to give the illusion of a three-dimensional reality.

Vanitas objects in art symbolising mortality, such as skulls and hourglasses.

Votive offering left as a prayer for good fortune or recovery from illness, usually as a painting or a silver model of the limb/organ to be cured.

Further Reference

BOOKS

Non-fiction

Luigi Barzini *The Italians*
A dated yet hilarious portrait.
**Julia Conaway Bondanella &
Mark Musa** *Introduction to the
Major Italian Writers & Influential
Thinkers of the Renaissance*
Famous names and a few surprises.
Thomas Campanello *A Defence
of Galileo, the Mathematician
from Florence*
The life, times and influence of
Florence's most famous heretic.
Paul Ginsborg *A History of
Contemporary Italy: Society and
Politics 1943-1988*
Comprehensive modern history.
Frederick Hartt *The History of
Italian Renaissance Art*
The definitive work.
Tobias Jones
The Dark Heart of Italy
Fantastic introduction to
contemporary Italy.
Ross King *Brunelleschi's Dome:
The Story of the Great Cathedral*
A fascinating account of the building
of Florence's magnificent dome.
Mary McCarthy
The Stones of Florence
A portrait of Florence and its arts.
Caroline Moorhead *Iris Origo*
Biography of the writer who helped
protect Allies and refugee children
during the war.
Iris Origo *Images and Shadows;
The Merchant of Prato*
Autobiographical and biographical
accounts of Florence and Tuscany.
Thomas Paloscia *Accadde in
Toscana (Vol III)*
A beautifully illustrated who's who
of Tuscany's contemporary artists.
Laura Raison
Tuscany: An Anthology
A collection of writings and
illustrations, classic to contemporary.
Leon Satkowski *Giorgio Vasari:
Architect & Courtier*
A biography of the most famous
Italian art chronicler.
Dava Sobel *Galileo's Daughter*
A study of Galileo's life in the context
of his relationship with his daughter.
Matthew Spender *Within
Tuscany*
A witty account of growing up in
an unusual family in Tuscany.
Paul Strathern *The Medici:
Godfathers of the Renaissance*

An enjoyable exposition of the
remarkable influence of the Medici
in Florence and throughout Europe.

Fiction

Italo Calvino *The Florentine*
One of Calvino's 'folktales'
collections of short stories.
Jack Dann *The Memory Cathedral:
A Secret History of Leonardo da Vinci*
Mystery and intrigue in Florence.
Michael Dibdin *A Rich Full Death*
An amusing thriller with insight
into 19th-century Florence.
Sarah Dunant *The Birth of Venus*
Gender and art in Medici Florence.
EM Forster *A Room with a View;
Where Angels Fear to Tread*
Social comedy from the master.
Robert Hellenga *The 16 Pleasures*
A young American woman goes to
Florence and feels obliged to act out
16 'pleasures' from a book of erotica.
Christobel Kent *Late Season*
Past and present collide for a group
of friends and family on holiday.
Christobel Kent *A Party in San
Niccolò; A Florentine Revenge*
An eventful week leads up to the
75th birthday party of an English
expat; a tour guide becomes
involved in a gruesome murder.
W Somerset Maugham
Up at the Villa
Temptation and fate in '30s Florence.
Frances Mayes *Under the Tuscan
Sun, Bella Tuscany*
Year in Provence-style expat dreams.
Magdalen Nabb *The Monster of
Florence; Death of an Englishman*
Thriller based on a serial killer who
murdered 16 campers in the 1980s;
murder in the secretive world of
Florentine antiques dealers.
Michael Ondaatje *The English
Patient*
Booker-winning novel, partly set in
Tuscany.

Food & wine

Giancarlo and Katie Caldesi
Return to Tuscany
Recipes, lessons and culture.
Leslie Forbes *A Table in Tuscany*
A personal account of Tuscan food,
with recipes from local restaurants.
Claudia Roden *The Food of Italy*
A wonderful book of Italian recipes,
with a section on Tuscany.
Slow Food & Gambero Rosso
Italian Wines Guide

The English edition of reliable
annual guide to Italian wines.

FILM

Life is Beautiful (1997)
Roberto Benigni's bittersweet
comedy about wartime Arezzo.
Much Ado about Nothing (1993)
Kenneth Branagh's interpretation
of Shakespeare's comedy.
Portrait of a Lady (1996)
Nicole Kidman stars in this version
of Henry James's story about a New
World woman in Old World Italy.
A Room with a View (1985)
Love and loss in 19th-century
Florence.
Stealing Beauty (1995)
Bernardo Bertolucci's Tuscan-
based film brought us Liv Tyler.
Tea with Mussolini (1998)
Judy Dench and Maggie Smith form
part of an eccentric group of expats.
Up at the Villa (2000)
Sean Penn's cynical American
proves innocent in comparison to
his European companions.

MUSIC

Puccini *Gianni Schicchi*
This delightful one-act opera is set
in medieval Fucecchio, west of
Florence.
Tchaikovsky *Souvenir of Florence*
The composer wrote this string
sextet while living in via San
Leonardo in Florence.

WEBSITES

www.boxol.it
Information and online booking for
concerts and shows.
www.cultura.toscana.it
The official Regione Toscana site.
Italian only.
www.firenze.net
The best local site; has info on
cinemas, nightlife, music, art, traffic
and weather in Florence and
Tuscany, plus a booking service.
www.firenzespettacolo.it
The monthly listings mag website
has what's-on information.
www.fol.it
Plenty of links relating to health,
travel, sports, hotels and business.
www.intoscana.com
Regional updates in five languages .
www.lapulce.it
Online small ads mag. Italian only.

Content Index

INDEX

INDEX

Venue Index

INDEX

INDEX

INDEX

Advertisers' Index

Please refer to the relevant pages for contact details.

INDEX

Maps

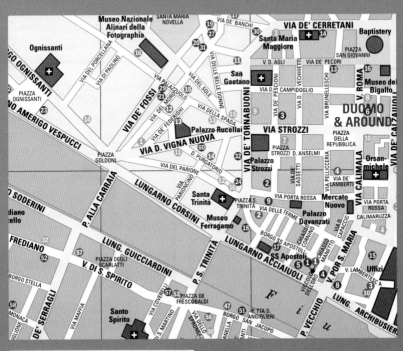

Major sight or landmark	....
Railway station	....
Park	....
Hospital/university	....
Ancient Site	....
Autostrade	....
Pedestrianised Area	....
City Wall	....
Car Park	.... P
Tourist Information	 i

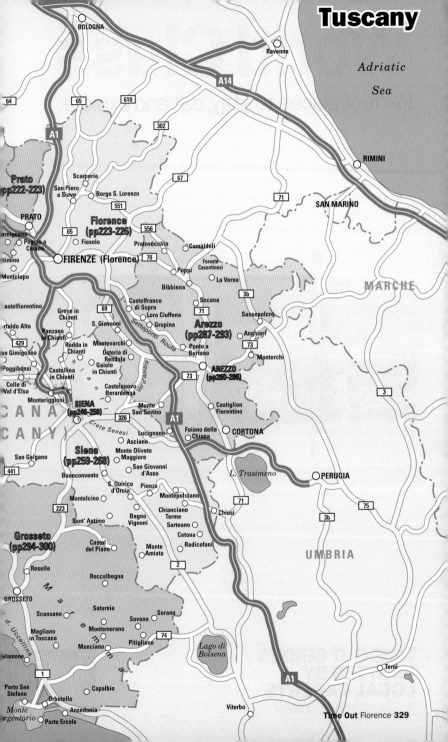

Tuscany

Adriatic Sea

64
65
610
302
A14
A1
Ravenna
BOLOGNA
RIMINI
67
71
SAN MARINO
Scarperia
Prato
(pp222-223)
San Piero a Sieve
Borgo S. Lorenzo
551
PRATO
rmignano
Florence (pp223-226)
65
556
Poggio a Caiano
Fiesole
Pratovécchio
Camàldoli
MARCHE
imino
FIRENZE (Florence)
70
Foreste Casentinesi
Montelupo
Poppi
La Verna
astelfiorentino
Bibbiena
3b
Greve in Chianti
69
Castelfranco di Sopra
Socana
71
Sansepolcro
Loro Ciuffenna
rtaldo Alto
S. Giovanni
Gropina
Arezzo (pp287-293)
Anghiari
429
Panzano in Chianti
Montevarchi
Ponte a Buriano
73
an Gimignano
Radda in Chianti
Osteria di Rendola
Monterchi
Poggibonsi
Castellina in Chianti
Gaiole in Chianti
73
AREZZO (pp280-286)
3
Colle di Val d'Elsa
Castelnuovo Berardenga
Settepónti Route
Val d'Ambra
Monteriggioni
SIENA (pp246-258)
Monte San Savino
Castiglion Fiorentino
CANA
326
A1
CANY
Crete Senesi
Lucignano
Foiano della Chiana
CORTONA
San Galgano
Siena (pp259-268)
Asciano
Monte Oliveto Maggiore
441
Buonconvento
San Giovanni d'Asso
L. Trasimeno
PERUGIA
S. Quirico d'Orcia
Pienza
Montalcino
Montepulciano
71
223
Sant' Antimo
Bagno Vignoni
Chianciano Terme
Chiusi
3b
75
Grosseto (pp294-300)
Castel del Piano
Sarteano
Cetona
Monte Amiata
Radicofani
2
UMBRIA
Roselle
Roccalbegna
M
GROSSETO
a
Scansano
r
Saturnia
Sorano
Magliano in Toscana
e
Montemerano
Sovana
74
Lago di Bolsena
amone
m
Manciano
Pitigliano
m
1
a
Terni
d' Uccellina
Porto San Stefano
Capalbio
Monte Argentario
Orbetello
Ansedonia
Viterbo
alamone
Porto Ercole

World Class

Perfect places to stay, eat and explore.

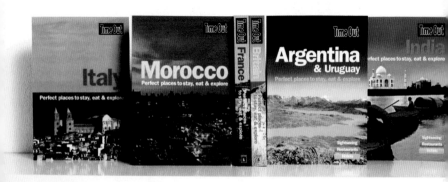

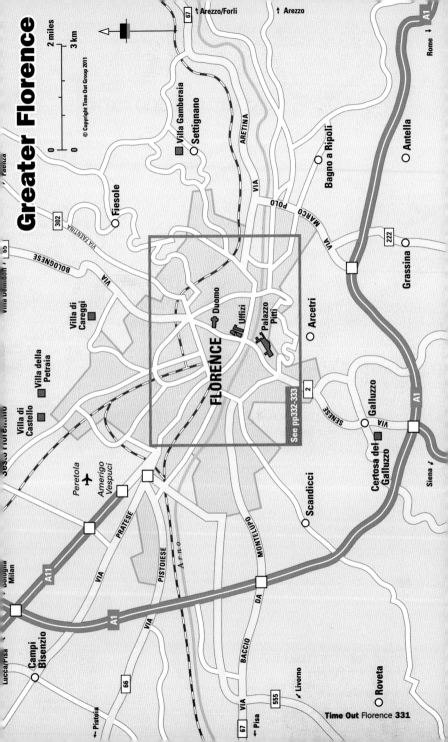

Greater Florence

2 miles

3 km

© Copyright Time Out Group 2011

↑ Arezzo/Forlì   ↑ Arezzo

FLORENCE

Duomo

Uffizi

Palazzo Pitti

See pp332-333

Villa Gamberaia • Settignano

Fiesole

VIA FAENTINA

VIA BOLOGNESE

Villa di Careggi

Villa della Petraia

Villa di Castello

Peretola

Amerigo Vespucci

PRATESE

VIA PISTOIESE

Arno

VIA PRATESE

BACCIO

VIA DA MONTELUPO

Scandicci

Arcetri

VIA ARETINA

VIA MARCO POLO

Bagno a Ripoli

Antella

Grassina

Galluzzo

VIA SENSE

Certosa del Galluzzo

Campi Bisenzio

Lucca/Pisa

Bologna Milan

Roveta

← Pistoia

← Pisa

↓ Livorno

Siena ↓

→ Rome

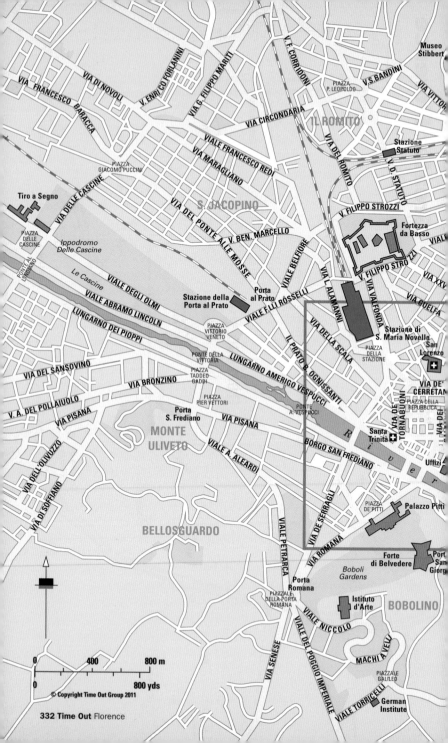

Florence Overview

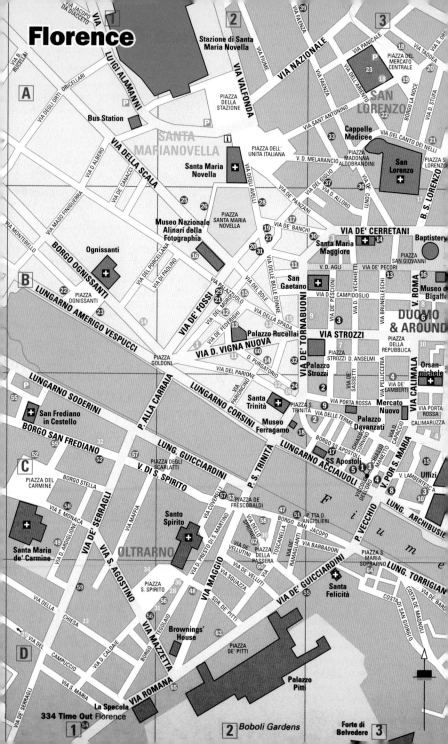

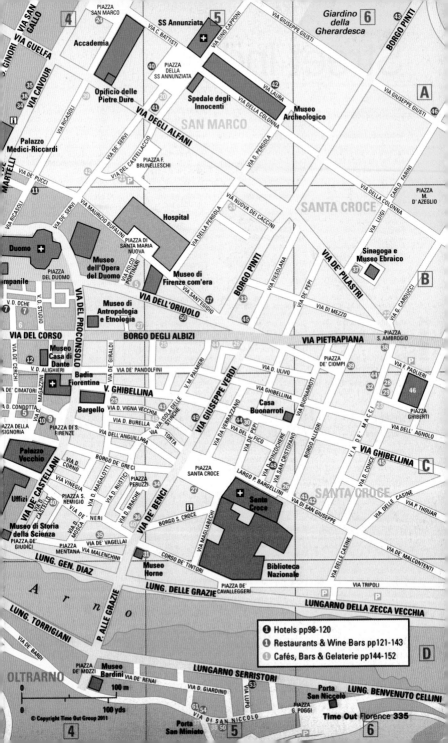

Street Index